Study Guide
ECONOMICS
second canadian edition

Åke Blomqvist
University of Western Ontario

Paul Wonnacott
University of Maryland

Ronald Wonnacott
University of Western Ontario

Peter Howitt
University of Western Ontario

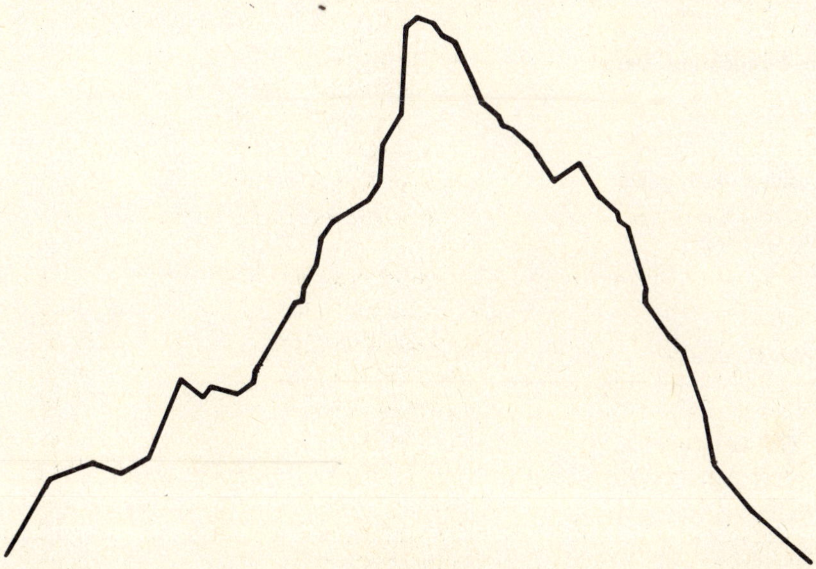

McGraw-Hill Ryerson Limited

Toronto Montreal New York Auckland Bogotá Cairo Caracas Hamburg
Lisbon London Madrid Mexico Milan New Delhi
Paris San Juan São Paulo Singapore Sydney Tokyo

Study Guide
ECONOMICS
Second Canadian Edition

ISBN: 0-07-549163-X

4 5 6 7 8 9 0 AP 6 5 4 3 2 1 0 9

Printed and bound in Canada

Canadian Cataloguing in Publication Data

Main entry under title:

Economics, second Canadian edition. Study guide

Supplement to: Blomqvist, Åke G., date—
Economics. 2nd Canadian ed.
ISBN 0-07-549163-X

1. Economics. I. Blomqvist, Åke. G., date—
Economics. 2nd Canadian ed.

HB171.5.B583 1987 330 C87-093380-9

Also available from McGraw-Hill Ryerson:

ECONOMICS
Second Canadian Edition
by Blomqvist/Wonnacott/Wonnacott
ISBN: 0-07-549159-1

AN INTRODUCTION TO MACROECONOMICS
Second Canadian Edition
by Blomqvist/Wonnacott/Wonnacott
ISBN: 0-07-549160-5

AN INTRODUCTION TO MICROECONOMICS
Second Canadian Edition
by Blomqvist/Wonnacott/Wonnacott
ISBN: 0-07-549161-3

CONTENTS

PART SIX
ECONOMIC EFFICIENCY: ISSUES OF OUR TIME

PART SEVEN
MICROECONOMICS: HOW INCOME IS DISTRIBUTED

PREFACE

This study guide is intended to help the student who is taking an introductory economics course using the second Canadian edition of *Economics* by Blomqvist, Wonnacott, and Wonnacott. It makes no attempt to be self-contained: it can be used as a supplement to , not as a substitute for, the textbook.

Each chapter is designed for you to read and work through after reading the corresponding chapter in the textbook. Each study-guide chapter contains seven sections:

1. *Major purpose.* This section sets out very briefly the basic ideas that will be developed in the chapter.

2. *Learning objectives.* This section consists of a list of tasks that you should be able to accomplish after you have studied the chapter in the textbook and in the study guide. The purpose of this section is twofold. First, it should help to give you direction and purpose while studying the rest of the chapter. Second, it should serve as a checklist to test your comprehension after reading the chapter.

3. *Highlights of the chapter.* This section contains a summary of the important points of the chapter. Its purpose is mainly to reinforce the textbook by going over these main points from a somewhat different perspective and adding illustrative examples. To a student learning a subject for the first time, everything is likely to appear equally important. This section should help sort out the more important from the less by focusing more narrowly than the text and by drawing attention to the particularly important material.

4. *Important terms:: Match the columns.* This section sets out the important concepts along with the definition of each. Your task is to match each term with its definition. One of the best ways of doing this is to write out your own definition first; this provides the most effective form of review.

5. *True-false questions.*

6. *Multiple-choice questions.*

7. *Exercise.*

These three sections are meant to help you learn by doing. Besides providing reinforcement through repetition, many of the questions and exercises are designed to guide you toward discovering ideas that will be explicitly introduced only later in the textbook. Spend a few minutes going over the true-false and multiple-choice questions as a self-test, even if you believe you understand the textbook chapter well enough to proceed without using the study guide in any other way. Answers to questions in these sections are provided at the end of each chapter.

8. *Essay questions.* This section is designed to help you apply important concepts that have been developed in the text, as well as to stimulate your imagination. No answers have been provided for this section. Thus the questions may be used as material for classroom discussion.

9. *Crossword puzzles.* These appear intermittently throughout the study guide. Our hope is that you will find them entertaining, whether or not you are a crossword puzzle enthusiast. Each puzzle, of course, draws heavily on the terms introduced in the related chapter.

This second edition of the study guide has a number of new chapters, corresponding to the new chapters of the textbook. In addition, each of the old chapters has been reworked with a view to improving the clarity of exposition, and all the old true-false and multiple-choice questions have been replaced or reworked.

As the new authors of this edition, we should like to thank Peter Howitt for his efforts in writing the original edition. Those familiar with the previous editions will clearly see the mark of his substantial contributions to this edition. At the same time we should like to point out the many contributions he has made to the textbook itself. It has been a personal and professional pleasure to be associated in this joint effort with so discerning and distinguished a colleague.

Åke Blomqvist
Paul Wonnacott
Ron Wonnacott

Part One

BASIC ECONOMIC CONCEPTS

ECONOMIC PROBLEMS AND ECONOMIC GOALS

MAJOR PURPOSE

The major purpose of this chapter is to provide a broad overview of *economic developments* and *economic objectives,* as a background for the more detailed topics of the following chapters. Five major economic objectives are discussed; *high employment,* a *stable average level of prices, efficiency, equity,* and *growth.* In this chapter you should gain some understanding of the problems that have arisen in the Canadian economy, and why it is not always easy to solve these problems. In particular, it may be difficult to deal with problems when the government has a number of goals, some of which are *in conflict*— that is, when solving one problem may make others more difficult to solve.

LEARNING OBJECTIVES

After you have studied this chapter in the textbook and study guide, you should be able to

List five major economic goals
Describe, in broad terms, how the Canadian economy has performed in terms of unemployment, inflation, growth, and the distribution of income in recent decades
Distinguish between the views of Adam Smith and J.M. Keynes with respect to the proper role of the government
Define such terms as *inflation, deflation, recession,* and *efficiency*
Distinguish between allocative efficiency and technological efficiency
Describe briefly how changes in relative prices may contribute to allocative efficiency
Explain why it is harder to identify the problems created by inflation than those created by unemployment
Explain the distinction between equity and equality
Explain how some goals may be *complementary,* while others are *in conflict*

If you have studied the appendix to Chapter 1 in the textbook, you should also be able to

Describe some of the ways in which people may be misled by graphs
Explain the advantage of using a ratio (or logarithmic) scale
Explain the difference between a nominal and a real measure

HIGHLIGHTS OF THE CHAPTER

Economics is one of the social sciences—it involves the systematic study of human behaviour. The aspect of behaviour that interests economists is how people earn a living, and the problems that may make it difficult for them to do so. In the words of Alfred Marshall, economics is the study of people "in the ordinary business of life."

The objective of *economic theory* is to discover and explain the basic principles and laws that govern economic life. Economic theory helps us to understand questions such as: Why are some prices higher than others? Why does the average level of prices rise? Why are some people richer than others? What causes large-scale unemployment?

Economic policy addresses such questions as: How can the government reduce inflation? How can it reduce the unemployment rate? What steps can individuals take to increase their incomes or reduce the risks of unemployment? How does a business increase its profits?

Economic theory and economic policy go hand-in-hand. Just as a physician needs to know how the human body works in order to heal patients, so the economic policymaker needs to understand economic theory in order to prescribe economic policies that will be successful. Scientific studies of how things work are often inspired by a policy motive—the desire to do something about problems. Thus, scientists strive to unlock the mysteries of the human cell in order to find out why cancer occurs, and ultimately to be able to cure cancer. Similarly, studies of how the economy works are often motivated by the desire to solve economic problems such as recession and large-scale unemployment.

Perhaps the most hotly contested issue in the entire field of economics is the question of how much the government should intervene in the economy. Many of those in government are motivated by the desire to promote the public welfare. After all, the policies that they promote will be their monument in history. But well-meaning policymakers do not always adopt policies that work in practice. Furthermore, the government may sometimes institute policies that benefit individuals or groups at the expense of the public as a whole.

Adam Smith attacked many governmental interventions in the economy as being contrary to the public interest. Even though tariffs benefitted the protected sectors of the economy, they inflicted higher costs on consumers, and acted as a drag on efficiency. Smith conceived of the private economy as a self-regulating mechanism. By pursuing their own interests, individuals would regularly contribute to the common good. There was no need for extensive government interference to ensure that things would come out all right.

A century and a half later, J.M. Keynes expressed his skepticism with regard to Smith's message of laissez-faire. Things were not coming out all right. The economy was in deep depression, with many people out of work. It was the responsibility of the government, said Keynes, to do something about this tragic situation. He recommended that the government make expenditures on roads and other public works in order to provide people with jobs.

Full employment is one of the major economic objectives. Four others are also described in this chapter: a *stable average level of prices, efficiency,* an *equitable distribution of income,* and economic *growth.* Other goals might be added to this list—for example, economic freedom, economic security, protection of the natural environment, and a reduction in the Canadian economy's dependence on foreign influences.

The first two goals—full employment and stable prices—come under the heading of maintaining a stable *equilibrium* in the economy. There has in fact been considerable instability in the Canadian economy. The most notable disturbance occurred during the Great Depression of the 1930s, when output and employment dropped sharply and remained at very low levels for a full decade. During World War II there was a large increase in the production of munitions and of other goods and services needed in the war effort. Unemployment ceased to be a significant problem, but prices began to rise substantially. Since the end of World War II in 1945, we have avoided disturbances as severe as those that occurred from 1929 to 1945. However, periodic recessions have taken place, with rising unemployment. Inflation was severe during the late 1940s and during the 1970s. During the decade of the 1970s, the average level of prices doubled.

Of the major economic problems, unemployment is perhaps the most obvious. When employment declines, we have less output to enjoy. We not only forego the output which might have been produced, but we also face the demoralization that comes with unemployment.

The problems posed by inflation are less obvious. When people buy goods, they obviously dislike having to pay higher and higher prices. But there are two sides to every transaction—the buyer's side and the seller's. With widespread inflation, not only do the prices of what we buy increase, but wage rates also go up. It is not clear whether individuals are net gainers or net losers.

However, certain segments of the population do, in fact, lose. Those who have pensions set in money terms lose: As prices rise, their pensions buy less. (However, some pensions, including Old Age Security and Canada Pension Plan benefits paid by the government, are increased to compensate for inflation.) Those who own government bonds or other interest-bearing securities lose. Through the years, they receive payments the value of which becomes smaller and smaller as prices rise. On the other hand, people who have borrowed can benefit: They repay their loans in money of less value.

Inflation generates a feeling that the economic system is unfair. There are arbitrary redistributions of income and wealth, such as the gains to debtors and losses to bond owners just described. Inflation can also make it more difficult to make wise and well-informed decisions. *Prices* provide an important source of information to the business executive and consumer. During periods of rapid inflation, when all prices are rising at a brisk pace, the message carried by prices may be obscured. It becomes more difficult to make good decisions.

If inflation accelerates to very high rates—such as 1,000% per year—it becomes known as *hyperinflation.* In this case, money loses its value so rapidly that people may refuse to accept it. Because money is practically useless, sellers may feel compelled to barter their products for other goods. Such barter transactions are very cumbersome and time-consuming.

Most inflations do not accelerate into hyperinflation. The majority of historical episodes of hyperinflation have occurred during wartime or early postwar periods in defeated nations. There are, however, a few exceptions, such as in present-day Bolivia, where hyperinflation is raging even though the country has not been defeated in a war.

There are two important types of efficiency. *Technological efficiency* consists of getting the most output from a given set of inputs (labour, machinery, raw materials). *Allocative efficiency* occurs when the economy is producing the best combination of outputs, using the lowest-cost combination of inputs. Allocative efficiency means producing the goods and services that the Canadian consuming public wants most, or which can be sold in foreign countries in exchange for goods that are difficult to produce here. It is possible for an economic system to produce "white elephants" in a technologically efficient manner. But since this system would not be producing what people want, it would not have achieved allocative efficiency. Similarly, if everyone were a lawyer and nobody a doctor there would be allocative inefficiency—even if everyone were a superb lawyer.

Equity means *fairness,* and that raises the question of what fairness means. There can be obvious disagreements. Those with low incomes are likely to argue that a more equal distribution of income would be fairer. Those with higher incomes often argue that their high incomes are the result of hard work and that it is therefore fair for them to be paid more.

Many people would, however, agree that the government should take some steps to help those who are poverty-stricken, for example, by taxing the rich to provide services for the needy. But the question arises as to how far this process should be taken. Clearly, if the government confiscated all income above the average and gave the revenues to low income people, it would severely interfere with the incentive to work hard. (This would also greatly increase the incentive to cheat on taxes!) Even less drastic steps to redistributee income can decrease incentives, and thus decrease the size of the national "pie." The size of the pie depends in part on how it is cut up.

Economic growth is often advocated for its own sake. In a growing economy we enjoy more goods and services. Furthermore, growth may make it easier to meet other goals, such as reducing poverty. However, we should not simply assume that the more growth, the better. Growth comes at a cost. Most obviously, if we produce more machinery and equipment to help us grow, then we will give up the current consumer goods that might have been produced instead of the machinery and equipment.

Some goals—such as a high level of employment and an elimination of poverty—are *complementary.* Progress toward the one contributes to progress toward the other. If jobs are provided, people are less likely to be poor.

Other goals are *in conflict.* If people buy more goods and services, they will help to increase the number of jobs. But they will also make it easier for sellers to raise their prices. Thus, if the government takes steps to encourage spending, it may help ease one problem (unemployment) while making another worse (inflation). In such circumstances, good policies may be particularly difficult to develop.

IMPORTANT TERMS: MATCH THE COLUMNS

Match each term in the first column with the corresponding phrase in the second column.

__J__ **1.** laissez-faire
__F__ **2.** Great Depression
__L__ **3.** labour force
__A__ **4.** population
__I__ **5.** recession
__K__ **6.** J.M. Keynes' idea
__B__ **7.** inflation
__E__ **8.** deflation
__G__ **9.** allocative efficiency
__D__ **10.** complementary goals
__H__ **11.** conflicting goals
__C__ **12.** this can help promote allocative efficiency

a. total number of people in a country
b. an increase in the average level of prices
c. change in relative prices
d. pursuing one helps in attainment of other
e. a decrease in the average level of prices
f. when large-scale unemployment existed
g. producing the best combination of outputs, using the lowest-cost combination of inputs
h. pursuing one makes other more difficult to attain
i. a broad decline in production, involving many sectors of the economy
j. leave the economy alone
k. government should spend for public works when necessary to get economy out of depression, and restore full employment
l. sum of those employed and those unemployed

TRUE-FALSE

T F 1. Canada and the United States were the only advanced countries whose rate of growth of output fell after the first great increase in oil prices in 1973-1974.

T F 2. Between 1960 and 1982, output per person in the 25 poorest countries in the world grew at an average annual rate of less than 1.5%, much slower than in most advanced countries.

T F 3. By the term "invisible hand," Adam Smith was expressing the idea that once people gain power in a government, they are generally interested in the public good.

T F 4. Since 1970, recessions have been much less severe than those of the 1950s and 1960s.

T F 5. A recession is a decline in total output, employment, and income, and is marked by a widespread contraction in *many* industries.

T F 6. Changes in the average rate of inflation make an important contribution, since they are the key to improvements in allocative efficiency.

T F 7. Most economists would agree that some degree of income inequality is desirable, as a way of providing people with an incentive to work hard.

T F 8. Not all families have the same needs. For example, a large family spends more for food than does a small one. Yet this difference has been ignored by the government in picking the income figure which represents the poverty line.

T F 9. The percentage of the population living in poverty declined during the 1960s, but increased in the early 1980s.

T F 10. Over the past three decades, there has been a consistent trend in the Canadian economy: the rich have become richer, and the poor have become poorer.

T F 11. Changes in the overall level of prices and changes in relative prices present roughly equal problems, and the government should give about equal importance to reducing changes in the average price level and changes in relative prices.

MULTIPLE CHOICE

1. Between 1929 and 1933, during the early part of the Great Depression, total output in Canada
   - **a.** declined about 30%
   - **b.** declined about 20%
   - **c.** declined about 10%
   - **d.** declined about 5%
   - **e.** remained approximately stable; the Depression represented an interruption of growth, not an actual decline in output
2. Since 1900, output per capita in Canada
   - **a.** has approximately doubled, while the length of the work week has declined
   - **b.** has approximately quintupled, while the length of the work week has declined
   - **c.** has approximately doubled, while the length of the work week has remained stable
   - **d.** has approximately quintupled, while the length of the work week has remained stable
   - **e.** has remained stable, while the length of the work week has declined sharply; all the gains have come in the form of more leisure
3. By the term "invisible hand," Adam Smith was expressing the idea that
   - **a.** there are no economic conflicts among nations
   - **b.** there would be no economic conflicts among nations if countries would eliminate tariffs
   - **c.** there are no conflicts between what is good for an individual and what is good for the government
   - **d.** by pursuing their own individual interests, people frequently promote the interests of society
   - **e.** business executives have a natural interest in keeping prices down and preventing inflation
4. The main criticism of a tariff on automobiles is that it
   - **a.** increases unemployment
   - **b.** increases government spending
   - **c.** increases government deficits
   - **d.** raises the costs of automobile companies
   - **e.** raises the price of cars bought by the public
5. In his *General Theory,* Keynes' principal concern was with the goal of
   - **a.** stable prices
   - **b.** low unemployment
   - **c.** allocative efficiency
   - **d.** technological efficiency
   - **e.** an equitable distribution of income
6. In his *General Theory,* Keynes argued that the best way to restore full employment was by
   - **a.** increases in prices, which would give employers an incentive to produce more
   - **b.** decreases in wages, which would give employers an incentive to hire more labour
   - **c.** increases in spending for public works, which would provide people with jobs
   - **d.** cuts in defence spending, which would provide incentives to produce nondefence goods
   - **e.** cuts in nondefence spending of the government,

which would provide incentives to produce goods for the private sectors of the economy

7. Which of the following is counted as being unemployed?

a. someone who has just retired at age 65
b. a full-time student not looking for a job
c. someone who has recently graduated from university and is looking for his or her first full-time job
d. convicts in prisons
e. all of the above

8. Hyperinflation is most likely to occur

a. during depressions
b. during recessions
c. when the growth of output is very rapid
d. in losing or defeated countries, during or shortly after a war
e. when allocative inefficiency exists

9. During the past two decades, the prices of computers have fallen, while the price of oil has risen. As a result, manufacturers and other businesses have used more computers, and have conserved on energy. This switch toward more computers and less energy is an illustration of

a. allocative efficiency
b. technological efficiency
c. the effects of inflation
d. a less equal distribution of income
e. a more equal distribution of income

10. Allocative efficiency occurs when

a. growth is at a maximum
b. the economy has reached its best size, and has stopped growing
c. income per capita has reached its best size, and has levelled out
d. the best combination of outputs is produced, using the lowest-cost combination of inputs
e. the best combination of outputs is produced, regardless of the cost

11. Which is the best example of *allocative* inefficiency?

a. producing too many cars, and not enough housing
b. slow growth
c. inequality of incomes
d. inflation
e. hyperinflation

12. Which is the best example of *technological* inefficiency?

a. producing too many cars, and not enough housing
b. slow growth
c. inflation
d. inequality of incomes
e. sloppy management

13. *Equity* in the distribution of income means

a. equality
b. fairness
c. more for everyone, as a result of growth
d. more for those who can't work
e. more for those who work hard

14. Which is a cost of economic growth?

a. less current output
b. less future output
c. less current consumption
d. less allocative efficiency
e. more unemployment in the future

EXERCISE

In the following passage, choose the correct word or phrase from those shown in square brackets.

Economic history is a story of both progress and problems. Some evidence of progress shows up in Figure 1-1 in the textbook. Here we see that output per person has increased by approximately [100%, 200%, 300%] since 1900, and about [25%, 75%, 150%] since 1960. If we were to look at total output of the economy—rather than at output *per person*—we would find that total output has increased by [an even greater percentage than output per person, a somewhat smaller percentage than output per person].

The right-hand panel of Figure 1-1 shows another source of gain. Not only have we produced more, but we have done so with a shorter work week. The decline in the work week was approximately [15%, 35%, 60%] between 1926 and the mid-1980s. Notice also the very sharp drop between 1925 and 1935. This decrease was [the result of a much more rapidly improving economy, which allowed more leisure, one of the unfortunate effects of the Depression, which reduced the demand for output]. We conclude that a shorter work week may be an indication of either an improvement—where people voluntarily work shorter hours because they can afford it—or an indication that work is hard to obtain.

Successes and problems also show up in Figure1-3 in the textbook. The [upward trend in output, downward trend in unemployment, both] since 1950 show(s) how things have improved. One of the problems is shown by the vertical shaded bars, which mark periods of [recession, depression, inflation, poverty]. During such periods, [the unemployment rate increases, output declines, both]. The longest period without a recession was between [1940 and 1955, 1950 and 1960, 1961 and 1969, 1975 and 1985].

Figure 1-4 shows the average level of prices. A rise in this curve is an indication of inflation. The more rapid inflation is, the steeper the curve. We see that inflation was very rapid between [1950 and 1960, 1960 and 1970, 1970 and 1980].

Finally, Figure 1-5 shows the percentage of the population living in poverty; a decline in the percentage is a sign of success. Observe that, at the beginning of the period shown, the incidence of poverty declined, from about [15%, 25%, 35%] in the mid-1960s to about [10%, 14%, 18%] when it reached its low point in 1981.

ANSWERS

Important Terms: **1** j **2** f **3** l **4** a **5** i **6** k **7** b **8** e **9** g **10** d **11** h **12** c
True-False: **1** F **2** T **3** F **4** F **5** T **6** F **7** T **8** F **9** T **10** F **11** F
Multiple Choice: **1** a **2** b **3** d **4** e **5** b **6** c **7** c **8** d **9** a **10** d **11** a **12** e **13** b **14** c
Exercise: 300%, 75%, an even greater percentage than output per person, 35%, one of the unfortunate effects of the Depression, which reduced the demand for output, upward trend in output, recession, both, 1961 and 1969, 1970 and 1980, 25%, 10%.

APPENDIX

This appendix provides additional information and practice for those who have already studied the appendix to Chapter 1 in the textbook.

Graphs

During rainy spells, sales of lawn furniture decline. A simple version of the relationship between weather and lawn furniture sales is illustrated in Figure 1-1 below.

The two measures used in this graph—furniture sales and rainfall—are examples of **variables.** A variable is something that can change, or vary, from time to time or from place to place. For example, the amount of rain can vary from April to July.

The statement that the sales of lawn furniture decline during rainy spells means that there is a relationship between the two variables in Figure 1-1. In particular, it means that when rainfall increases, then sales decrease. We want to see how this relationship is indicated by the graph.

Notice the two *axes,* marked with numbers, that meet at the point labelled 0. The *vertical axis* shows sales of lawn furniture. Every time you go up a notch it means that sales of lawn furniture go up by $1,000. The amount of rainfall is marked on the horizontal axis. Every time you go one notch to the right this indicates 1 more inch of rainfall per month. The point where the axes meet is the ***origin.*** This is the zero point on both axes—the point where there would be no rainfall and no one would sell any lawn furniture.

FIGURE 1-1

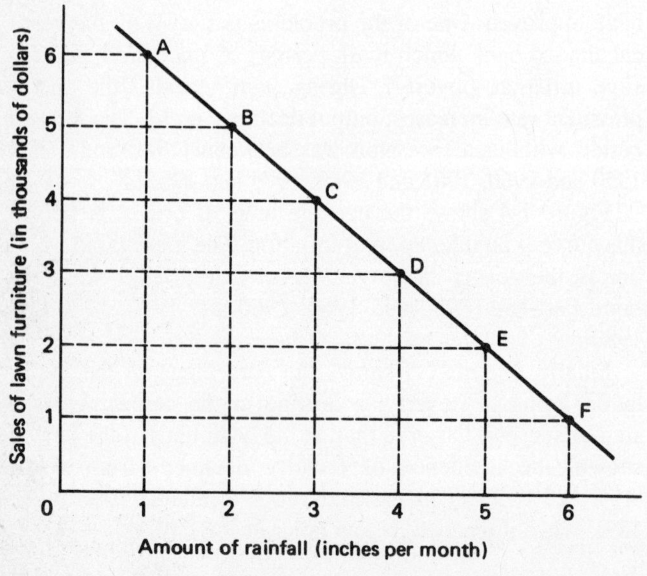

The relationship between the two variables is depicted by the line marked with the letters *A* through *F.* You "read" this line by using the axes. For example, consider point *A.* You can measure the height of this point on the vertical axis, just as you can measure a child's height on a wall. The dashed line going to the left from *A* is like a book held level on top of the child's head, showing that the height of *A* is 6. The distance that *A* lies to the right can be measured on the horizontal axis. The dashed line drawn down from *A* shows us that this distance is 1.

Here is the way to "read" point *A.* When there is only 1 inch of rainfall per month (when you go 1 notch to the right), then there is $6,000 worth of lawn furniture sold (6 notches up). Likewise, point *B* tells you that when there are 2 inches of rainfall, sales are $5,000. In this way, each time you read a point on the line you get one bit of information. These "bits" are shown in Table 1-1 below.

Table 1-1

Point	*A*	*B*	*C*	*D*	*E*	*F*
Rainfall	1	2	3	4	5	6
Sales	6	5	4	3	2	1

Thus, the rule for "reading" the graph goes as follows. Suppose you want to find out how much lawn furniture will be sold when there is some particular amount of rainfall (say, 2 inches per month). Start at the origin. Now mark off that amount of rainfall to the right, along the horizontal axis (go two notches to the right). Then the height of the line directly above that point (5) is the answer to your question. Question 1 at the end of this appendix is an exercise in reading graphs.

Slope

The statement we began with doesn't just say that rainfall and sales are related. It also says something about the *direction* of that relationship. It says that when rainfall increases, sales don't increase—they decrease. In other words, sales are ***negatively*** or ***inversely*** related to rainfall, because they change in the opposite direction.

You can tell the direction of this relationship by inspecting the line in Figure 1-1. Notice that it slopes downward to the right. This means that as you move to the right along the horizontal axis (as rainfall increases) the height of the line decreases (sales decrease). For example, compare points *A* and *B*. As rainfall increases from 1 to 2, sales decrease from 6 to 5.

A ***positive*** or ***direct*** relationship is shown in Figure 1-2. (See question 2 at the end of the appendix.) In this case, both variables change in the same direction. When snowfall increases, sales of ski equipment increase as well. You can tell this from the fact that the line slopes upward to the right. As you move to the right (as snowfall increases) the line gets higher (sales increase).

You may wonder whether a graph is needed to show the direction of a relationship. After all, the same idea of direction can be expressed in simple English by our original statement that lawn furniture sales decline during rainy spells. Why use graphs? One reason is that a graph shows more than just the *direction* of a relationship. It also shows the *strength.* For example, when rainfall increases from 1 to 2 inches per month, Figure 1-1 doesn't just show that lawn furniture sales decrease. It also shows by *how much*—they decrease by $1,000, from $6,000 to $5,000. This goes beyond our original statement, which told us that sales would decrease, but not by how much.

The *strength* of the relationship is indicated by *how steep* the line is. For example, the steep line in Figure 1-2 shows a strong relationship between snowfall and ski equipment sales. When snowfall increases by 1 (going, say, from 2 to 3), sales increase by 2 (from 1 to 3). Compare this to the much weaker relationship shown by the flatter line in Figure 1-3. In this case, when snowfall increases from 2 to 3, sales increase by only $1/2$ (from 1 to 1 $1/2$).

Thus, both of these ideas—the direction and strength of a relationship—are shown by the way the line slopes. Direction is shown by whether the curve is slanted up or down. Strength is shown by how steep the line is.

There is a mathematical term that expresses both these ideas. This term is the ***slope.*** The slope of a line is defined as *the amount by which the height of the line changes when you go one more unit to the right on the horizontal axis.* For example, the slope of the line in Figure 1-2 is 2, because when snowfall increases by 1 unit (when you go 1 unit to the right), then sales of ski equipment (given by the height of the line) change by 2 units. The slope in Figure 1–1 is –1. This is negative because when rainfall increases by 1 unit, then the change in sales (the change in the height of the line) is negative (sales decrease by 1 unit).

Thus, a positive slope indicates a line that slopes upward to the right, showing a positive relationship. A negative slope indicates a line that slopes downward to the right, showing a negative relationship.

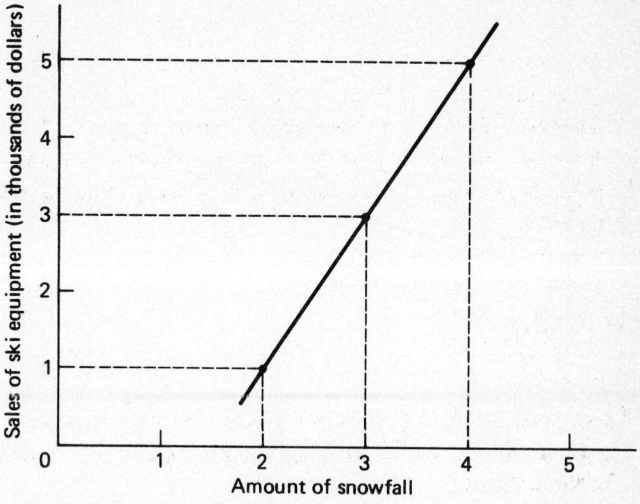

FIGURE 1-2

Likewise, a larger slope indicates a steeper line, showing a stronger relationship. For example, the slope of the line in Figure 1-3 is only $1/2$, showing that a 1-unit increase in snowfall increases sales by only $500 ($1/2$ of a unit). The slope of the steeper line in Figure 1-2 is 2, showing that the same increase in snowfall would increase sales by $2,000 (2 units). (Questions 3 and 4 at the end of the appendix are designed to familiarize you with the idea of slope.)

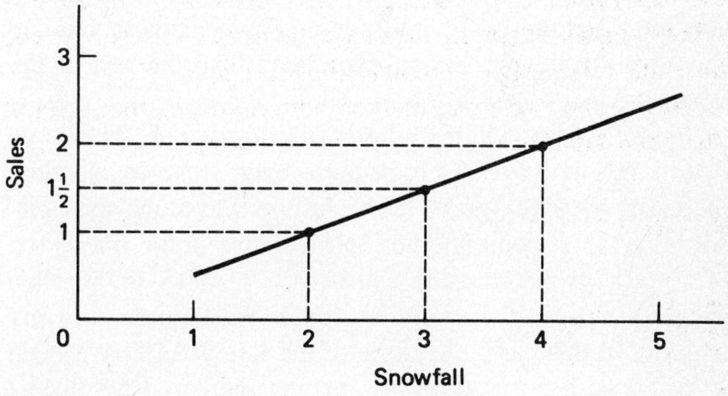

FIGURE 1-3

Linear Equations

Sometimes the relationship between two variables is shown not by a graph, but by an equation. Suppose you are told that my expenditures each month on consumer goods (*C*) depend upon my monthly income (*Y*) according to the equation:*

$$C = \$400 + 0.5Y$$

In simple English, this equation says I will spend $400 plus half my income. As my income varies from month to

* Note: To represent income, economists almost always use the letter *Y*, not *I*; *I* is reserved to denote investment.

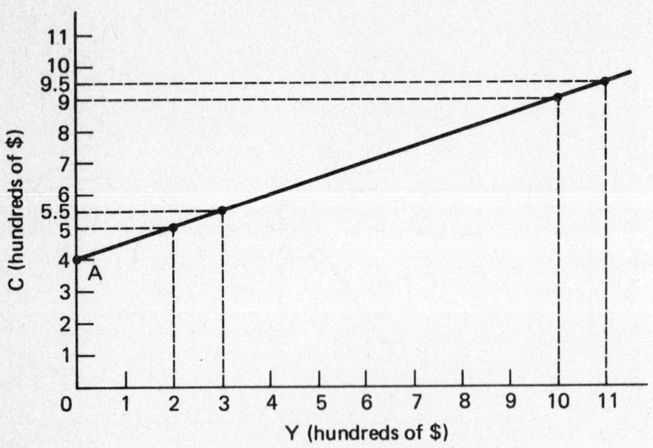

FIGURE 1-4

month, the equation tells you how my expenditures will vary. It thus describes a relationship between these two variables, Y and C. Whatever my income (Y) is, the equation tells you how much I will spend (C).

For example, choose some convenient value for my income, like $Y = 1{,}000$. Then substitute this into the equation to get $C = 400 + 0.5 \times 1{,}000 = 400 + 500 = 900$. This tells us that when my income (Y) is 1,000, my expenditures (C) will be 900. Choose any other convenient value, like $Y = 1{,}100$. Substituting this into the equation tells you that when my income is 1,100, then my expenditures will be $C = 400 + 0.5 \times 1{,}100 = 950$. Each time you choose a value of Y and make this substitution you thus get one bit of information. Two of these bits are shown in Table 1-2. As an exercise, fill in the rest of the table.

Figure 1-4 shows this relationship in a graph. The slope of this line is 0.5. This is because every time my income increases by $100 (go to the right one unit along the horizontal axis), I spend another $50 (the rise in the line is 0.5 of a unit). If the equation had been $C = 400 + 0.75Y$, then it would have said I spend $400 plus three-quarters of my income. In this case, the slope of the line would have been 0.75, because every time my income increased by $100 I would spend another $75.

In general, any equation of the sort $C = a + bY$ represents a line with a slope equal to b. Such an equation is called a *linear* equation. For example, the linear equation pictured in Figure 1-4 has $a = 400$ and $b = 0.5$.

The number b (that is, 0.5) is known as the *coefficient* of the variable Y. It indicates the slope of the line. The number a (400) shows how high the line is where it meets the vertical axis (point A). Thus, a is often called the *vertical intercept*. For example, the linear equation shown in Figure 1-4 has $a = 400$, and the line hits the vertical axis when $C = 400$.

At this point, you should try questions 5 and 6, which deal with linear equations.

Curves

So far we have drawn only straight lines. They are easy to use because they have a *constant* slope. For example, as you move down the line in Figure 1-1, from A to B, to C, and so on, every time you go 1 unit to the right the line falls by exactly 1 unit; not more or less. The slope stays constant at –1.

Not all relationships in economics can be described by straight lines. Some are described by curves, like the one in Figure 1-5. This curve shows how a student's final grade in economics depends on how many hours the student spends studying each day.

This curve does not have a constant slope. As you move to the right along the curve it gets flatter. For example, going from 0 hours to 1 hour makes the curve rise by 30—from 20 to 50. But then going from 1 hour to 2 hours makes it rise by only 20—from 50 to 70, and going from 2 to 3 hours makes it rise by only 5. Each time you go one more unit to the right on the horizontal axis, the curve rises by less than the last time.

When dealing with a curve, we can still define the *slope* the way we did before. The slope of a curve is the amount by which the height of the curve changes when you go one more unit to the right on the horizontal axis. But we must remember that this slope changes as you move along the

FIGURE 1-5

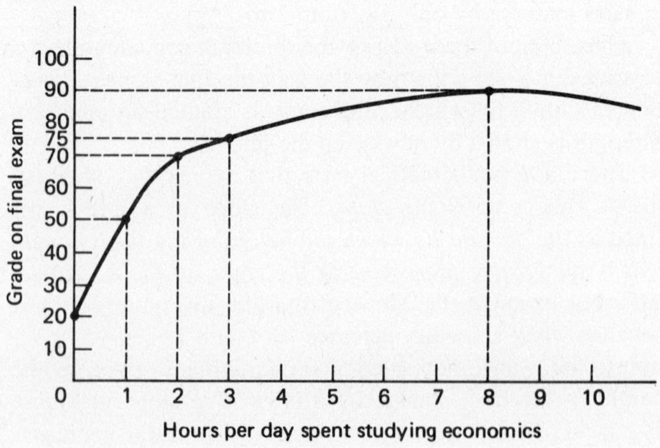

Table 1-2

Y	100	200	300	400	500	600	700	800	900	1,000	1,100
C										900	950

curve. Starting at zero hours in Figure 1-5, the slope decreases, from 30, to 20, to 5, and so on.

The decreasing slope in Figure 1-5 indicates that as you spend more and more time studying, each extra hour may raise your grade, *but not by as much as the previous hour.* The first hour raises your grade by 30 marks, the next by only 20. After 2 hours per day, you are beginning to get saturated with economics, and the next hour raises your grade only 5 marks. Thus, the strength of the relationship between hours and grades is decreasing as you spend more hours. This is an example of diminishing returns; after a certain point, the payoff (in higher grades) diminishes as you study more and more.

Notice that, according to Figure 1-5, once you get beyond 8 hours per day, the relationship not only changes in strength, it also changes in direction, from positive to negative. After 8 hours the slope becomes negative. Studying beyond this point tires you so much it does more harm than good. Each extra hour causes your grade to decrease.

Thus, a curve with a changing slope shows a relationship whose strength or direction is changing instead of remaining constant.

Other Kinds of Graphs

Sometimes we don't bother to put numbers on the axes of graphs. For example, consider the linear relationship in Figure 1-6. The variables *X* and *Y* are shown on the axes, but there are no numbers, except for the 0 at the origin. Without the numbers we can't tell exactly what the relationship is between *X* and *Y*. But the graph still tells us something. It tells us that the relationship is a positive one, because the line has a positive slope. It also tells us that the relationship is linear (with a constant direction and strength) because the line is straight (with a constant slope).

Sometimes instead of numbers we use letters, as in Figure 1-7. This still doesn't tell us the exact relationship.

FIGURE 1-6

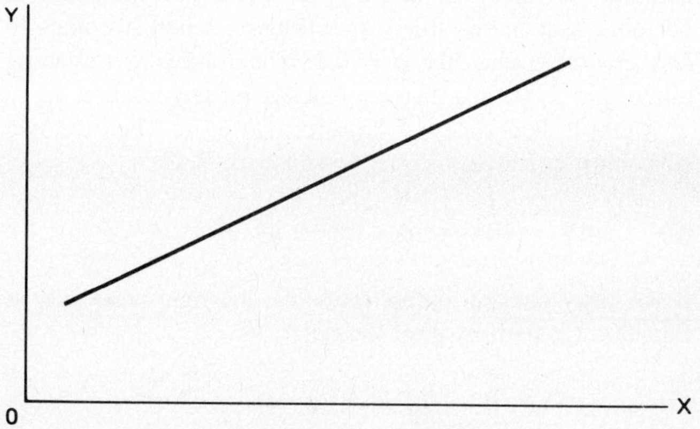

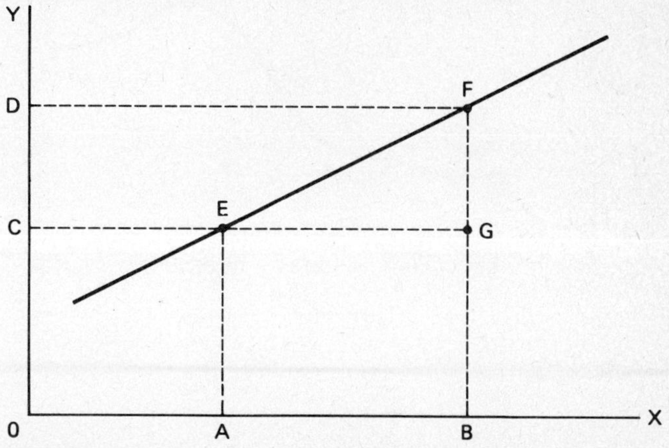

FIGURE 1-7

But the letters give us handy points of reference. For example, take point *A* on the horizontal axis. We don't know in numbers how far to the right this is. But whatever this distance is, from point *O* to point *A*, we call it the distance *OA*. Likewise, we describe the distance along the horizontal axis from point *A* to point *B* as the distance *AB*.

When describing movement from *E* to *F* along the line, it helps to look at the triangle *EFG*. The change in *X* is the difference between distance *OB* and the distance *OA;* that is, the distance *AB*. It also equals the base of this triangle, *EG*. Likewise, the change in *Y* can be read from the vertical axis as *CD,* or from the triangle as *GF*. An exercise in using this "letter code" is given in question 7.

Sometimes a graph will have numbers on it, but not starting at zero. For example, time is measured on the horizontal axis in Figure 1-8, starting at 1972. As long as each notch measures one more year, it doesn't matter that the "original" year is called 1972. A Moslem, whose time begins with Mohammed instead of Christ, would put 1392 on the origin of Figure 1-8. According to the Jewish calendar, the origin should be 5732. As long as we all know which convention is being used, the graph will have the same meaning.

The Ratio Scale

In Figure 1-8, every time you go one notch up the vertical axis, this represents the same change in the price of oil—$5. This is the way most graphs work—equal distances along an axis represent equal changes in the variable.

But there is an important exception to this rule. Look at Figure 1-9. In this graph, going up one notch on the vertical axis doesn't always mean the same change in the price level. The first notch takes you from 25 to 50—a change of 25. But when you move up to the second notch the price level goes from 50 to 100—a change this time of 50. The vertical axis measures the price level not on the usual scale, but on the ***ratio scale*** or *logarithmic scale.*

FIGURE 1-8

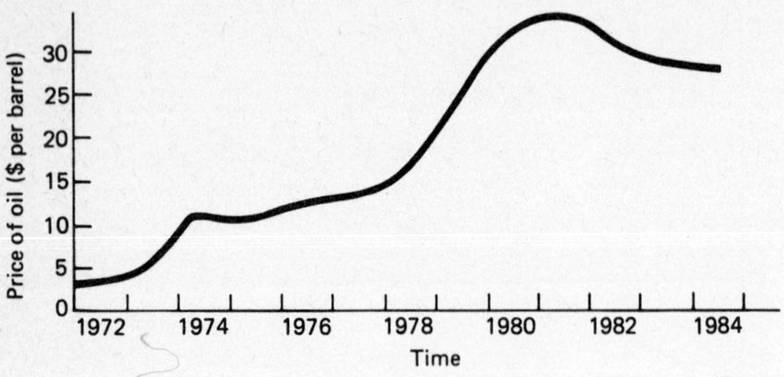

As you move up a ratio scale, equal distances represent equal *percentage* changes. Going up from 25 to the first notch, the price level goes up by 100% to 50. Going to the second notch it again goes up by 100%—this time to 100. In this case, every notch higher represents a price level that is 100% higher.

We often use a ratio scale when we're primarily interested in the *annual percentage rate* of growth in a variable. For instance, when we're looking at the price level we usually want to know the rate of inflation. Ten percent inflation means that the price level has been growing at that rate per year.

The percentage rate of growth from one year to the next can be measured in such a diagram by the slope of the line. For example, as we go from January 1984 to January 1985 the change in the height of the curve is one notch, or 100%. (This is just an illustration. In fact, the rate of inflation in Canada that year was only 4%.) Thus, the slope of the curve is 100%. This tells us that over the calendar year 1984 there was 100% inflation.

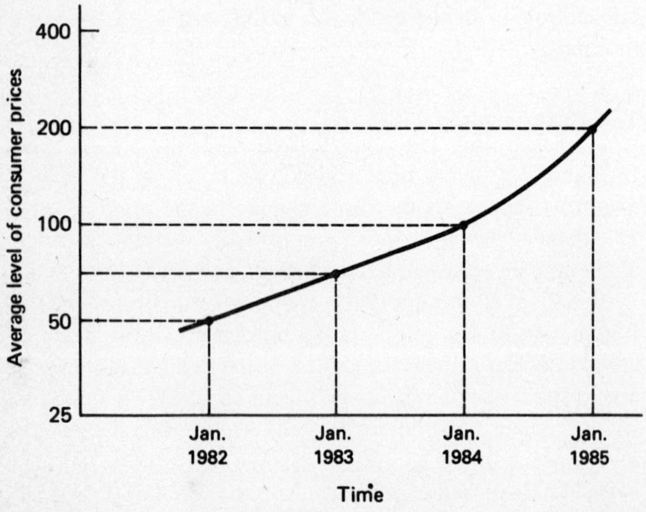

FIGURE 1-9

In this kind of graph, a straight line represents something that grows at a constant percentage. Between January 1982 and January 1984 in Figure 1-9 the curve is a straight line, showing that the rate of inflation was constant over this 2-year interval. When the slope increases, as it does starting in January 1984, it shows that the rate of inflation is rising.

Geometric Series

One important technique that comes up frequently in economics doesn't involve any graphs. Suppose that someone gave you $1 today, then 50 cents tomorrow, then 25 cents the next day, and so on, each day giving you half as much as the day before. Let us suppose that the money is infinitely divisible so that you will continue to get $12\,^1/_2$ cents, $6\,^1/_4$ cents, etc. If you stop to think how much you will be given in total, you will be faced with the problem of having to make the addition:

$$1 + {}^1/_2 + {}^1/_4 + {}^1/_8 + {}^1/_{16} + \ldots$$

There is no end to the number of terms in this series. Nevertheless, there is an answer to the addition. For as each day passes the sum grows from $1 to $1.50 to $1.75 to $\$1.87\,^1/_2$, to $\$1.93\,^3/_4$, and so forth. As you can see, the sum will approach an upper limit of $2. Every day, you are getting half of what it would take to get to $2. The shortfall keeps getting cut by half. You will never quite get there, because you will never get enough to bring you all the way up, just half that. But you will approach that sum asymptotically.

This is just one example of a problem that occurs often in economics. Suppose that a is some positive fraction, and you have to add the infinitely long series:

$$\textbf{(1)} \qquad S = 1 = a + a^2 + a^3 + a^4 + \ldots$$

This sum is called a geometric series. The previous example was obviously a special case of a geometric series, with $a = {}^1/_2$. There, I took a guess at the answer ($S = 2$), and showed how this would work. But it would be nice to be more systematic about it, especially when it comes to less obvious cases like $a = 0.8$. The following reasoning establishes a formula that can be used for any fraction a.

Multiply both sides of Equation (1) by a. Then the two sides must continue to equal one another. Thus:

$$\textbf{(2)} \qquad aS = a(1 = a + a^2 + a^3 + a^4 + \ldots)$$

If we carry out the multiplication on the right-hand side of Equation (2) term by term we get:

$$\textbf{(3)} \qquad aS = a + a^2 + a^3 + a^4 + a^5 + \ldots$$

Now suppose we subtract this equation from equation (1):

$$\begin{array}{rrcl} & S & = & 1 + a + a^2 + a^3 + \ldots \\ \text{Subtract} & aS & = & \phantom{1 +{}} a + a^2 + a^3 + \ldots \\ \hline & S - aS & = & 1 + 0 + 0 + 0 + \ldots \end{array}$$

Thus, we get the result $S(1 - a) = 1$. By dividing $(1 - a)$ into both sides of this last equation we get:

(4)
$$S = \frac{1}{1 - a}$$

Equation (4) is the solution to our problem. This formula always gives the right answer. To check it out, note that when $a = 1/2$, as in our example, then S indeed equals 2. (Now try $a = 0.8$).

QUESTIONS

1. Point *A* in Figure 1-10 has a height of ____________, and lies a distance ____________ to the right. Thus, it tells us that when there are ____________ hundred police officers, there will be ____________ hundred crimes reported. If there are 600 officers there will be ____________ hundred crimes, and with a thousand officers there will be ____________ hundred crimes.

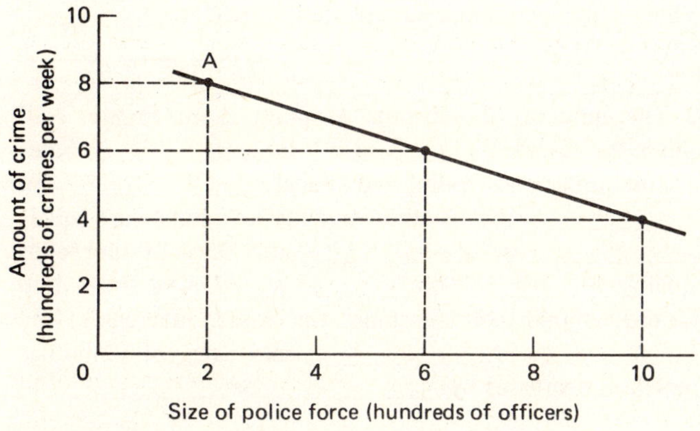

FIGURE 1-10

2. From Figure 1-2 fill in Table 1-3.

Table 1-3

Amount of snowfall	2	3	4
Sales of ski equipment			

3. Figure 1-11 contains six different lines. Fill in Table 1–4 showing the slope of each line.

Table 1-4

Line	*a*	*b*	*c*	*d*	*e*	*f*
Slope						

4. Which of the lines in Figure 1-12 show a positive relationship between the variables *X* and *Y*? ____________. When *X* increases by 1 unit, which of these lines shows the greatest increase in *Y*? ____________. When *X* increases by 1 unit, which one shows the greatest decrease in *Y*? ____________

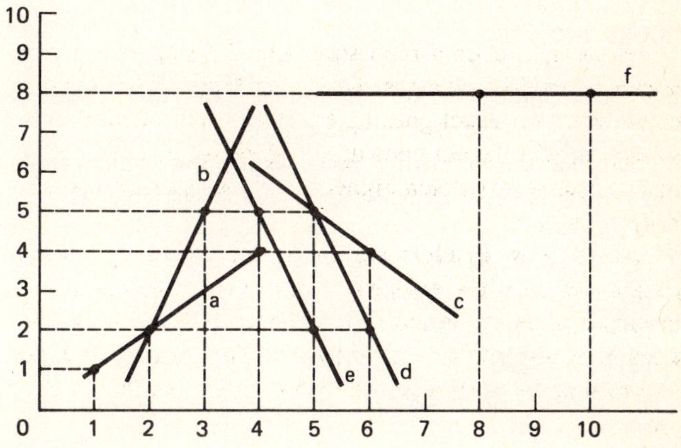

FIGURE 1-11

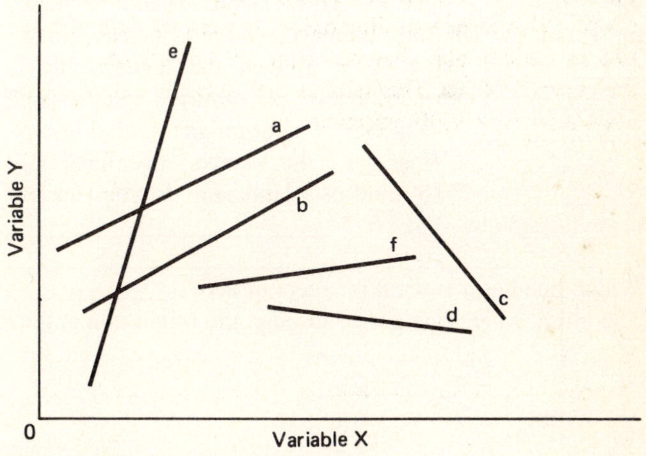

FIGURE 1-12

5. Consider any two variables, *X* and *Y*. Suppose they are related according to the linear equation $Y = 8 - 2X$. Fill in Table 1-5 according to this equation.

Table 1-5

X	0	1	2	3	4
Y					

This equation represents a straight line. Draw the straight

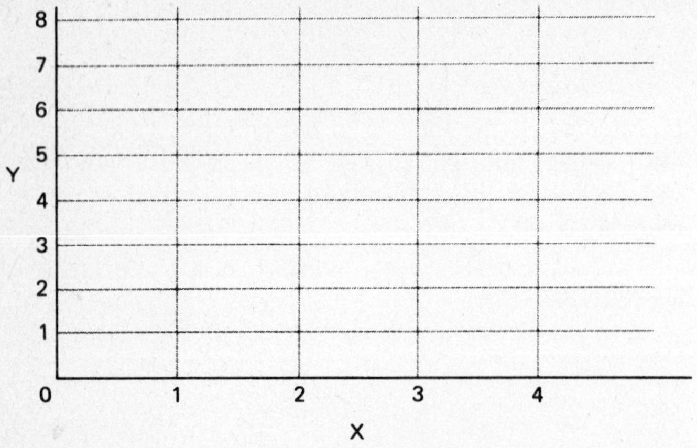

FIGURE 1-13

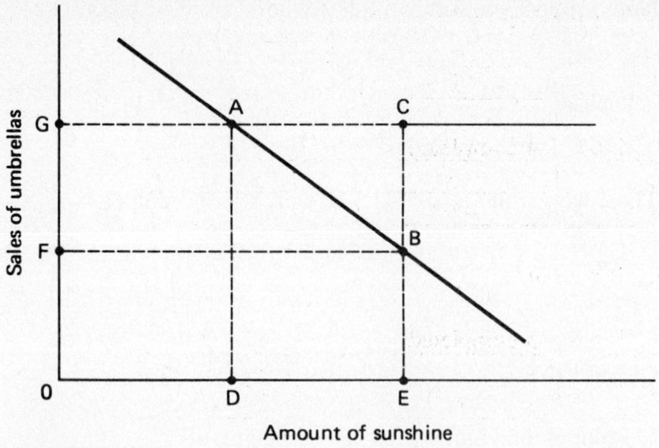

FIGURE 1-14

line in Figure 1-13. The slope of this line is __________. The vertical intercept is __________

6. Consider the following linear equations, which show how one variable, Y, depends upon another variable, X.

(a) $Y = 90 + 10X$
(b) $Y = 50 + 15X$
(c) $Y = 80 - 5X$
(d) $Y = 3X$
(e) $Y = -10 + 5X$
(f) $Y = 50$

Each of these equations describes a different line.

Line __________ has the largest vertical intercept and line __________ has the largest slope. When X increases by 1 unit, which line shows the largest increase in Y? __________. When $X = 0$, then the highest line is __________. Which show a positive relationship? __________. Which a negative relationship? __________. What is the slope of line (f)? __________. What kind of relationship do you suppose is indicated by line (f)? __________

____

Which line has a vertical intercept of zero? __________. Therefore, which line passes through the origin in a graph? __________. Which line indicates that Y is always a constant multiple of X? __________. What does this suggest is always true of lines that pass through the origin?

____

____

What is the vertical intercept in line (e)? __________
How would this show up in a graph? __________

____

7. The amount of sunshine at point A in Figure 1-14 equals the distance __________, or __________. Sales of umbrellas at point A equal __________, or __________. At B the amount of sunshine equals __________, or __________, and sales of umbrellas equal __________, or __________. Going from A to B, the amount of sunshine (increases, decreases) by __________, or __________, and sales of umbrellas (increase, decrease) by __________, or __________.

8. The sum $1 + 1/3 + 1/9 + 1/27 + \dots$ equals __________.

9. Take any positive fraction a. Then the sum $a + a^2 + a^3 + a^4 + \dots$ equals __________. [Hint: compare this with the sum (1), and use the formula (4).]

ANSWERS

Linear Equations:

Table 1-2 completed:

Y	100	200	300	400	500	600	700	800	900	1,000	1,100
C	450	500	550	600	650	700	750	800	850	900	950

Geometric Series: When $a = 0.8$, then $S = 5$.
Questions:
1. 8,2,2,8,6,4.

2. Table 1-3 completed:

2	3	4
1	3	5

3. Table 1-4 completed:

a	b	c	d	e	f
1	3	–1	–3	–3	0

4. *(a,b,e,f),e,c.*

5. Table 1-5 completed:

X	0	1	2	3	4
Y	8	6	4	2	0

–2, 8

6. *a,b,b,a,(a,b,d,e),c,*0; one in which *Y* does not vary as *X* changes; *d,d,d;* they always indicate that *Y* is a constant multiple of *X;* – 10; if you extended the vertical axis down below the horizontal axis, the line would intersect the vertical axis on this lower segment.

7. *OD* or *GA; OG* or *DA; OE* or *FB;* OF or *EB;* increases; *DE* or *AC;* decrease; *FG* or *BC*.

8. 3/2.

9. $$\frac{1}{1-a} - 1 = \frac{a}{1-a}$$

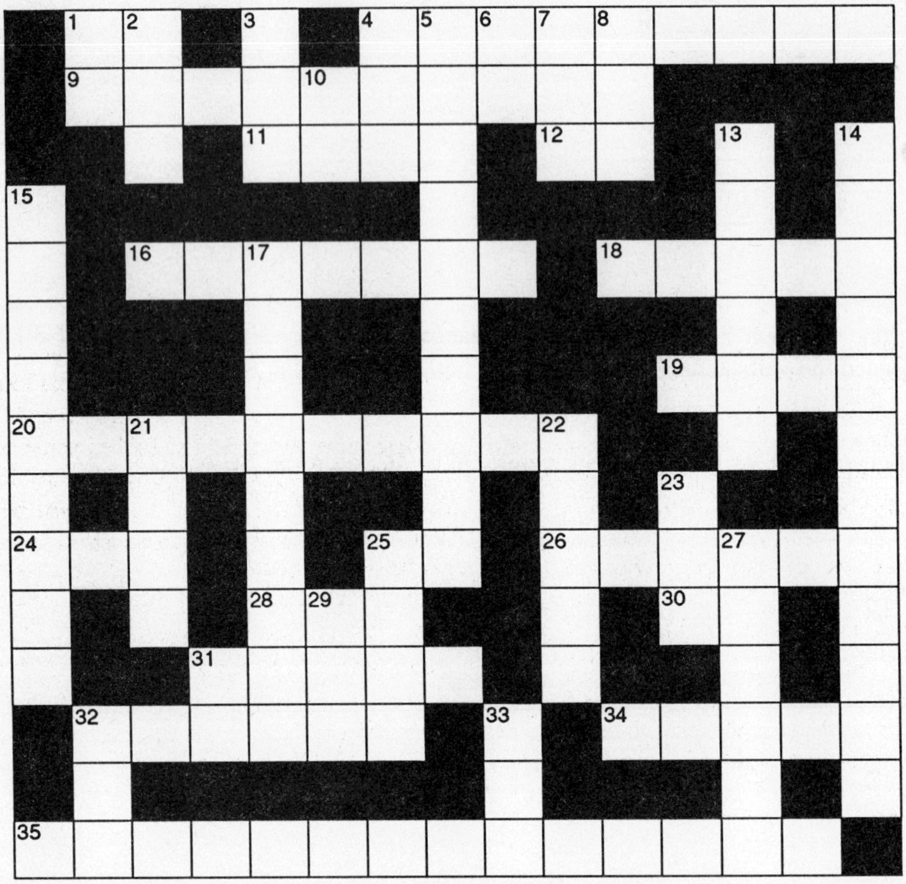

Across

1. university degree
4. His *Wealth of Nations* was an early classic (2 names).
9. getting the most from productive efforts
11. shedder of light
12. preposition
16, 18. keeping government involvement in economy to a minimum
19. assist (verb)
20. the ____________ nations, also known as the Third World
24. industrious insect
25. above
26. fairness
28. charged particle
30. ____________ garde! (French)
31. During hyperinflation, this becomes practically worthless.
32. advocated government spending to restore full employment
34. represents workers
35. Losing countries in war may suffer this.

Down

1. exist
2. toward the stern of a boat
3. be ill
4. purpose, or line up in your sights
5. the economic disease of the 1930s
6. indefinite article
7. 1101 in Roman numerals
8. artificial (abbrev.)
10. a professional business degree
13. important source of information to buyers and sellers
14. a major economic problem
15. international institution lending to developing nations (2 words)
17. rise in the average level of prices
21. document needed when looking for a job
22. large, powerful
23. owing
25. individuals
27. a deep violet-blue colour
29. number
31. first person possessive
32. under lock and ____________
33. Its price skyrocketed in the 1970s.

Chapter 2

SCARCITY AND CHOICE

MAJOR PURPOSE

The major purpose of this chapter is to introduce the concept of *scarcity*. Because of limited resources, we cannot have all the goods and services that we want. We must therefore *make choices,* picking some items and foregoing others. This idea—that we face scarcity and therefore have to make choices—is at the centre of economics. Indeed, economics is sometimes defined as "the study of the allocation of scarce resources to satisfy alternative, competing human wants."

The ideas of scarcity and choice are illustrated by the *production possibilities curve*. This illustrates the idea of *scarcity,* because we are limited to a point on (or within) the curve; we cannot go outside the curve with our present resources and technological capabilities. The curve also illustrates the need to make *choices*. When we pick a specific point on the production possibilities curve, we pass over all the other points, and forego the goods that we might have had if we had picked some other point.

Finally, this chapter provides an introduction to *economic theory*. Economic theory *must* be a *simplification* of the real world. If we strove for a complete theory which took into account all the complexities of our world, we would get bogged down in a swamp of detail. When we simplify, we should keep in mind a central question: Does our theory include the most important relationships in the economy, or *have we left out something of critical importance?*

LEARNING OBJECTIVES

After you have studied this chapter in the textbook and study guide, you should be able to

- Understand why the combination of limited resources and unlimited wants require us to make choices
- Define the three major factors of production
- Explain the difference between real capital and financial capital, and explain why economists focus on real capital when estimating the productive capacity of the economy
- Explain the concept of opportunity cost, and explain how it is related to the production possibilities curve (PPC)
- Explain why the PPC slopes downward to the right
- Explain why the PPC usually bows outward from the origin
- Explain a circumstance in which the PPC might be a straight line, instead of bowing outward
- Explain why production occurs within the PPC if there is large-scale unemployment
- Explain the difference between a high-growth and a low-growth policy, using a PPC with capital goods on one axis and consumer goods on the other (Figure 2-5 in the textbook)
- Explain the effects of an increase in the capital stock in Canada through a capital inflow from foreign countries
- Explain why it is impossible to develop a theory without simplifying

HIGHLIGHTS OF THE CHAPTER

Scarcity is one of the most important concepts in economics. Scarcity requires us to *make choices;* we cannot have everything we want. Why? The answer is that our resources are limited, while our wants are not.

When we make choices, we pick some goods and services, and forego others. If we pick a university education, for example, we may have to put off buying a car for several years. The *opportunity cost* of our education is the car, and other things that we forego to pay tuition, room, and board. Similarly, for the society as a whole, opportunity cost is an important concept. When we decide to produce more weapons, we forego the consumer goods we might have produced instead. Individuals, corporations, and governments are continuously making choices among the options open to them.

The ideas of scarcity, the need to make choices, and opportunity cost are summarized by the production possibilities curve (PPC). The PPC shows the options from which a *choice* is made. The fact that we are limited by the PPC and cannot pick a point outside it with our present resources and technology illustrates the idea of *scarcity.* The *slope* of the PPC shows how much of one good we must forego when we choose more of another. In other words, the slope shows the *opportunity cost* of choosing more of a specific good.

The PPC has two important properties. First, it slopes downward to the right. This means that, if we decide to produce more of one good, we give up some of the other. The idea that there is an opportunity cost when we produce more of one good is illustrated by the downward slope of the PPC curve.

The second feature of the typical PPC curve is that it is "bowed out"—that is, it is *concave* to the origin. This is so because resources are *specialized.* If we decide to produce more and more wheat, we will use land which is less and less suited to the production of wheat, even though it was very good for producing wool. For each additional unit of wheat, we will have to give up more wool. Thus, the outward bend in the PPC illustrates the idea of *increasing opportunity cost.*

Under certain circumstances, however, the PPC need not bow outward. It is possible that two goods might require the same set of resources in their production. For example, radios and telephones might take the same combination of resources in their production—the same combination of copper, plastic, silicon, labour, etc.—in which case the PPC would be a *straight line.* In this particular case, the *opportunity cost of radios would be constant,* in terms of the telephones foregone. (The opportunity cost of both radios and telephones might nevertheless still increase, in terms of the food or clothing foregone. In other words, the PPC would be a straight line if we put radios and telephones on the two axes, but would bow out if we put radios on one axis and food on the other.)

It is worth emphasizing that a downward slope and an outward bow are two *different* features. A PPC can slope downward without bowing outward—as in the example of radios and telephones. A downward slope means that the opportunity cost is *positive.* An outward bow means that the opportunity cost *increases* as more of a good is produced.

One of the important choices facing the society is the choice between consumer goods and capital goods. If we produce only a little capital, we will be able to enjoy a large quantity of consumer goods now. But, with little investment, we will have slow growth. In other words there is a *trade-off between a high current level of consumption and high growth.* This trade-off or choice is illustrated when we draw a PPC curve with consumer goods on one axis and capital goods on the other. For example, Figure 2-5 in the textbook illustrates the difference between a high-growth and a low-growth strategy. A high-growth strategy requires that a sizeable fraction of our resources be committed to investment in plant and equipment (capital goods). But this makes possible a rapid growth, that is, a rapid outward movement of the PPC.

When a nation is receiving a capital inflow from foreign countries, its stock of capital goods may expand rapidly even if the nation's citizens use most of their resources for present consumption. But there is an offsetting disadvantage: Part of the increased future production that is made possible by the nation's larger capital stock will have to be paid to the foreign investors or lenders who initially supplied the capital inflow, as a return to their investment.

This chapter provides a brief introduction to economic theory. When we develop economic theories, we *must* simplify. The world is too complex to be described in all its detail. The objective of theory is to strip away the nonessential complications, in order to see the important relationships within the economy. Theory should not be dismissed because it fails to account for everything, just as a road map should not be discarded as useless just because it doesn't show everything. But, because of simplifications, theory must be used carefully. Just as last week's weather map is useless for planning a trip in a car, so the theory which helped to explain one aspect of the economy may be inappropriate or useless for explaining others.

Finally, this chapter explains the distinction between *positive* and *normative* economics. Positive or descriptive economics is aimed at explaining what has been happening and why. Normative economics deals with policies; it deals with the way things *ought* to be.

IMPORTANT TERMS: MATCH THE COLUMNS

Match each term in the first column with the corresponding phrase in the second column. But before you do so, write your own definition of each term in the first column.

______	**1.** economic resources	**a.**	outward bow of PPC
______	**2.** financial capital	**b.**	choices open to society
______	**3.** real capital	**c.**	specialized resources
______	**4.** increase in real capital	**d.**	stocks and bonds
______	**5.** entrepreneur	**e.**	straight-line PPC
______	**6.** capital inflow	**f.**	organizer of production
______	**7.** PPC	**g.**	basic inputs used in the production of goods and services
______	**8.** opportunity cost	**h.**	investment
______	**9.** increasing opportunity cost	**i.**	alternative foregone
______	**10.** constant opportunity cost	**j.**	machinery, equipment, and buildings
______	**11.** cause of outward bow of PPC	**k.**	foreign-financed investment

TRUE-FALSE

T F **1.** Resources are said to be scarce because it is impossible to produce from them all the goods and services that people want; therefore, choices must be made.

T F **2.** Wants were "unlimited" during the early days of the study of economics in the eighteenth and nineteenth centuries. But they are no longer unlimited in the affluent countries of North America and Western Europe.

T F **3.** Suppose that a production possibilities curve meets the axes at 5 units of clothing, and at 20 units of food. This illustrates that the society can have a total of 5 units of clothing plus 20 units of food, but no more.

T F **4.** The production possibilities curve bends outward because resources are not uniform in quality; some are better at producing one good than the other.

T F **5.** Just as it is possible to select a combination of goods inside the PPC, so it is possible to choose a combination of goods that lies outside the PPC.

T F **6.** An increase in the quantity of labour causes the production possibilities curve to move outward from the origin.

T F **7.** Suppose that two countries, A and B, were identical in 1975. Suppose that, between 1975 and 1985, the economy of A grew at 4% per annum, while B grew at 3% per annum. Then, from that fact, we may conclude that economy A had greater allocative efficiency than B during the period 1975–1985.

T F **8.** In most less developed countries, an increase in population will make it more difficult to raise income per person. In such a country, an increase in population and in the quantity of labour will generally cause an inward movement of the production possibilities curve.

T F **9.** Less developed countries have a special problem. If they want to grow, they have to forego some consumer goods. In the affluent countries of Europe and North America, no such choice is necessary.

T F **10.** An inflow of American capital into Canada would help shift Canada's PPC outward from the origin.

T F **11.** *Positive* economics is the study of how policymakers can achieve desirable (that is, "positive") social goals

MULTIPLE CHOICE

1. Economists often speak of wants being "unlimited" because
- **a.** the cost of living has increased; it costs more to meet our basic needs now than it did 20 years ago
- **b.** more people live in the cities now than in an earlier age, and it is more expensive to live in cities than on the farm
- **c.** even though our incomes have risen, we still want "more"; we do not believe all our wants are satisfied
- **d.** resources such as oil have become scarcer because we have been using them up
- **e.** as people's incomes have risen, they have decided to take more leisure time, and work fewer hours

2. By real capital, economists mean
- **a.** real estate, particularly land
- **b.** plant and equipment
- **c.** the real value of bonds, adjusted for inflation
- **d.** the real value of common stock, adjusted for inflation
- **e.** both (c) and (d)

3. The production possibilities curve has one major purpose—to illustrate the need to
- **a.** stop inflation
- **b.** cut taxes
- **c.** cut government spending
- **d.** make choices
- **e.** stop pollution

4. The textbook has a figure showing a production possibilities curve (PPC), joining six points.
- **a.** All six points are equally desirable, since they all represent full employment.
- **b.** All six points are equally desirable, since they are all consistent with zero inflation.
- **c.** All six points are equally desirable, since they all provide for some growth.
- **d.** All six points are possible, but the PPC curve doesn't give enough information to tell which point is best.
- **e.** Only one of the six points is presently achievable; the others can be achieved only if the economy grows.

5. An *outward bow* in the production possibilities curve illustrates what concept?
- **a.** scarcity
- **b.** unlimited wants
- **c.** increasing opportunity cost
- **d.** unemployment
- **e.** inflation

6. The opportunity cost of a good is measured by
- **a.** the slope of the PPC
- **b.** how far the PPC is from the origin
- **c.** the slope of a line from the origin out to the PPC
- **d.** how far the economy is operating within the PPC
- **e.** how fast the PPC is shifting outward

7. Suppose the production possibilities curve is a straight line if goods X and Y are put on the axis. Then we know that
- **a.** X and Y are really the same good
- **b.** the problem of scarcity has been solved
- **c.** we can have all the X and Y we want without incurring an opportunity cost, even though the general problem of scarcity has not been solved
- **d.** the opportunity cost of X is zero, in terms of Y foregone
- **e.** the opportunity cost of X is constant, in terms of Y foregone

8. We speak of a production possibilities curve as a "frontier" because
- **a.** we can produce within it or on it, but not beyond it with presently available resources and technology
- **b.** it reflects the concept of scarcity, and goods were particularly scarce for settlers on the western frontier in the nineteenth century
- **c.** it is no longer relevant, now that the western frontier has been settled and we have an affluent society
- **d.** unemployment problems provide the frontier for economic research
- **e.** differences among resources provide the frontier for economic research

9. Suppose that society has only one objective, to maximize growth. Then the best choice among the five points shown in Figure 2-1 is
- **a.** *A*
- **b.** *B*
- **c.** *C*
- **d.** *D*
- **e.** *E*

FIGURE 2-1

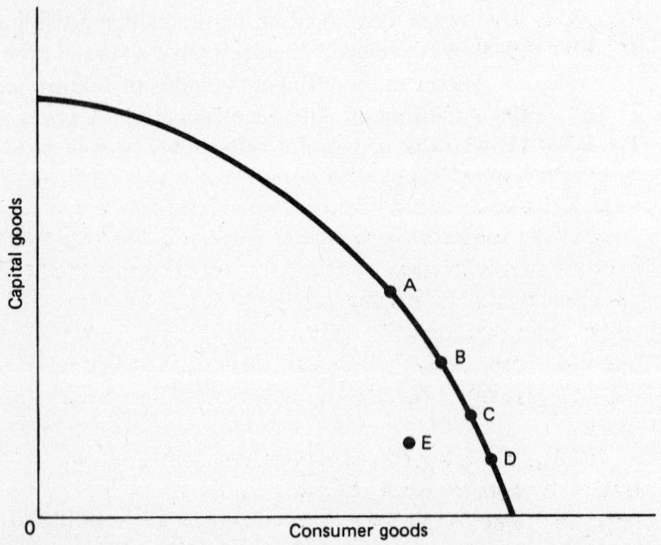

10. In Figure 2-1, a growth of the economy can be illustrated by

a. a move from point *A* to *B*
b. a move from point *B* to *A*
c. a move from point *A* to *E*
d. a move from point *D* to *E*
e. an outward shift of the production possibilities curve

11. In Figure 2 1, suppose that the economy is originally at point *E*. Then there will be

a. rapid growth
b. no capital formation
c. more capital formation than at points *A*, *B*, or *C*
d. a high rate of unemployment
e. rapid inflation

12. Which of the following is an example of a capital inflow into Canada?

a. A Canadian student spends $10,000 to study business administration at a U.S. university
b. A Japanese construction firm buys $100,000-worth of sawn timber from a mill in British Columbia
c. A Finnish sporting goods firm builds a plant in Quebec City to produce cross-country skis
d. An American couple spends $500 for hotel rooms, meals, and souvenirs during a weekend in Niagara Falls, Ontario
e. A Canadian tourist brings back a hundred dollars' worth of Mexican currency notes after a vacation in Acapulco

13. In the poorest of the less developed countries (LDCs), the growth process is more difficult than in the richer countries, because

a. an increase in population causes the PPC curve to shift outward in the developed countries, but inward in the LDCs
b. an increase in capital causes the PPC curve to shift outward in the developed countries, but inward in the LDCs
c. it may be difficult to increase investment in the poorest LDCs without depressing consumption to the subsistence level
d. when LDCs invest, they pay a penalty in terms of consumer goods foregone, but the affluent countries pay no such penalty
e. all of the above

EXERCISES

1. Consider the following production possibilities table:

Table 2-1

Options:	*A*	*B*	*C*	*D*	*E*	*F*	*G*	*H*
Consumer goods	0	1	2	3	4	5	6	7
Capital goods	23	22	20	17	13	9	5	0
Opportunity cost of consumer goods		1	2					

a. Complete the third line, showing the opportunity cost of each additional unit of consumer goods.

b. Draw the PPC in Figure 2-2.

c. What is unusual about this curve?

d. In the range between points *A* and *D*, the PPC [bows outward, bows inward, is a straight line]. This shows that opportunity cost is [increasing, decreasing, constant] in this range. However, between points *D* and *G*, the curve [bows outward, bows inward, is a straight line]. This shows that opportunity cost is [increasing, decreasing, constant] in this range.

2. Consider a hypothetical economy with a labour force of 10,000 workers, each of whom can be put to work building either houses or roads. Each worker is available for 2,000 hours per year. Thus, there are 20 million labour hours available during the year to produce houses and roads. Table 2-2 shows how many labour hours it takes to build various quantities of houses. For example, in order to build 18,000 houses, 15 million labour hours are needed. Likewise, Table 2-3 indicates how many labour hours are needed to build various amounts of roadway. In Figure 2-3, only one point, *A*, on the PPC has been plotted. It shows that if no houses are built, the 20 million labour hours can be used to produce 1,000 kilometres of road. Using the data in tables 2-2 and 2-3, plot four other points, and draw a PPC to connect them.

Table 2-2

Millions of labour hours	Thousand of of houses
20	20
15	18
10	14
5	8
0	0

Table 2-3

Millions of labour hours	Hundreds of kilometres of road
20	10
15	9
10	7
5	4
0	0

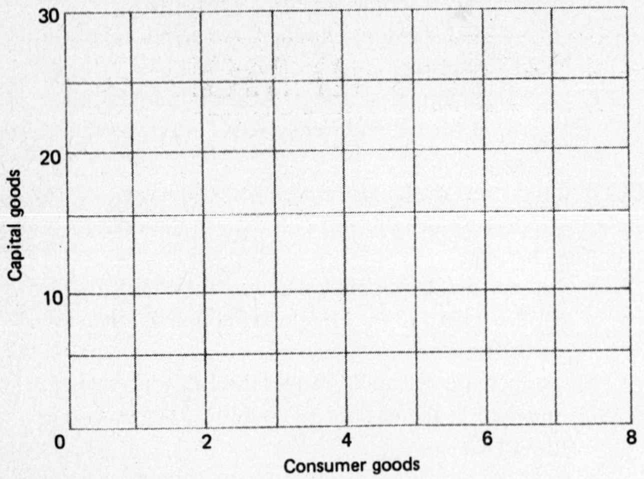

FIGURE 2-2

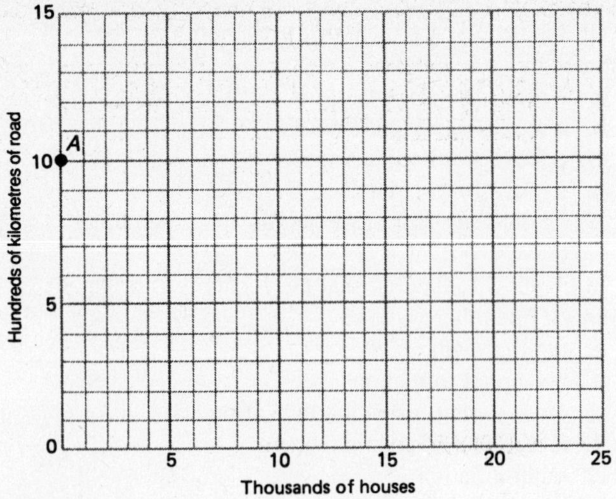

FIGURE 2-3

ANSWERS

Important Terms: **1** g **2** d **3** j **4** h **5** f **6** k **7** b **8** i **9** a **10** e **11** c
True-False: **1** T **2** F **3** F **4** T **5** F **6** T **7** F **8** F **9** F **10** T **11** F
Multiple Choice: **1** c **2** b **3** d **4** d **5** c **6** a **7** e **8** a **9** a **10** e **11** d **12** c **13** c
Exercises: **1a.** 3, 4, 4, 4, 5. **1c.** Over part of its range, it is a straight line (between D and G). **1d.** bows outward, increasing, is a straight line, constant. 2. Four other points are:

	B	*C*	*D*	*E*
Hundreds of kilometres	9	7	4	0
Thousands of houses	8	14	18	20

Chapter 3

SPECIALIZATION, EXCHANGE, AND MONEY

MAJOR PURPOSE

In this chapter, we study specialization, exchange, and money. People specialize and engage in exchange because there are *gains* from doing so: By specializing, they can achieve higher standards of living. There are *two major sources* of gain from specialization: (1) *comparative advantage,* and (2) *economies of scale*. These two phenomena are the forces that motivate specialization and exchange; that is, they are the twin *engines that drive commerce*.

Money, on the other hand, *is the oil* which makes the machinery of commerce run smoothly, with a minimum of friction. Without money, people would engage in cumbersome barter. But, if some money helps to make the system work smoothly, we should not conclude that more money would make it work even better. Just as too much oil can gum up an engine, so too much money can cause difficulty. Specifically, it causes inflation. The Bank of Canada (Canada's central bank) acts as the chief mechanic. Its task is to create the right amount of "oil" (money)—neither too much nor too little. The operations of the Bank of Canada will be considered in detail in Chapter 13.

LEARNING OBJECTIVES

After you have studied this chapter in the textbook and study guide, you should be able to:

- Explain why specialization and exchange go hand in hand
- Explain why barter is inferior to exchange with money
- Explain why people may nevertheless revert to barter in some circumstances
- Give an example of Gresham's law
- Explain the two major reasons why there can be gains from specialization and exchange
- Explain the difference between absolute advantage and comparative advantage
- Explain why a country may have an absolute advantage in a product without having a comparative advantage in that product
- Explain why a country cannot have a comparative advantage (or a comparative disadvantage) in every product

HIGHLIGHTS OF THE CHAPTER

Economic progress has occurred partly because of an increase in *specialization.* Individuals, cities, and countries are now more specialized than they were 100 years ago. When production is specialized, people engage in exchange, selling the products they produce to buy the wide variety of goods and services that they want to consume. We live in a highly interdependent economy, in which each of us depends on the specialized production of others.

Specialization and exchange would be very difficult without money. It is easy to imagine the difficulties that would arise if we tried to do without money, and engaged in barter exchange instead. Barter requires a *coincidence of wants*—two people engaging in exchange must each be able to provide a good or service that the other wants. Furthermore, for barter to work, there must be some rough equivalence in the value of the two goods or services to be exchanged. To buy toothpaste, a farmer would scarcely offer a cow in exchange. If he only wanted one tube, he would not be able to buy it because the cow could not be divided up. With money, such problems of indivisibility do not arise. The farmer may sell the cow for $1,000 and spend just a bit of the money to buy toothpaste, using the rest for a wide variety of other purchases. Money provides people with *general purchasing power;* money can be used to buy any of the wide variety of goods and services on the market. Those wishing to make exchanges no longer have to search for unlikely coincidences (such as the ill-clad farmer looking for someone who not only has clothes to exchange, but who also wants to get beef in return).

Because it is so useful for those who wish to engage in exchange, money is used even in rudimentary societies with little or no government. The prisoner-of-war camp provides a modern example of such a simple society. However, governments have become deeply involved in the monetary system. Every country uses paper money printed by a central bank.

One reason for the government to be involved in the monetary system is that the government can provide a *uniform* currency. In Canada, for example, every $1 Bank of Canada note (dollar bill) is worth the same as every other dollar bill. This uniformity of the money stock is very convenient. When selling something for $1, we only have to find out if the buyer has a $1 bill. Except for the rare cases where counterfeiting is suspected, we do not need to ask the much more complicated question of whether the dollar bill is inferior to some other dollar bill.

In passing, we might note that Canada has not always had a uniform currency. In the nineteenth century, privately owned banks issued currency. The value of this currency depended on the soundness of the bank that issued it. Thus, sellers did have to worry about the value of the dollar bills they accepted. Similar problems have arisen throughout history. For example, gold coins have often been used, whose value depended primarily on the amount of gold they contained. Before the development of modern methods of producing coins with hard edges, such coins were sometimes "clipped." That is, people chipped off bits before spending them. As a result, not every coin was worth the same as every other coin of the same denomination. People had to examine the physical condition of the coins they were accepting.

In addition to providing a uniform currency, the Bank of Canada has the responsibility of providing an appropriate quantity of money. If too many dollar bills are created, there will be "too much money chasing too few goods." Inflation will result; the dollar will decline in value. On the other hand, if the quantity of money is allowed to decline sharply, spending will decline. Sellers will have a very difficult time finding buyers. Sales will fall, unemployment will rise, and prices will be under downward pressure. The authorities do not always perform their monetary duties well. In some countries, prices are galloping ahead by more than 100% per year. This reduces the convenience of using money. If prices are rising rapidly, sellers feel under pressure to spend their money as soon as possible, before its value declines significantly.

With the proper quantity of money, the monetary system can work very smoothly, making transactions very convenient. But this is all that money does—it makes exchange convenient. It is not the reason why exchange is desirable in the first place.

There are two reasons why benefits come from specialization and exchange. The first is *comparative advantage.* The notion of comparative advantage is illustrated in the textbook by the example of the gardener and the lawyer. The lawyer has an absolute advantage in both the law and gardening; she can perform both activities more quickly than the gardener can. It follows that the gardener has an absolute disadvantage in both the law and gardening—he is slower at both. However, the gardener has a comparative advantage in gardening, while the lawyer has a comparative advantage in the law. While the lawyer is superior in both activities, her superiority is greater in the law. In other words, her opportunity cost of drawing up wills or other legal documents is lower than the opportunity cost of the gardener in performing the same activity. This provides the basis for mutually beneficial trade. Both the gardener and the lawyer can gain from specialization and exchange. (Details are provided in Box 3-3 in the textbook.)

Two points should be emphasized: (1) Absolute advantage is not necessary for gain; the gardener can gain by specializing in gardening, even though he is not the best gardener. (2) A person (or a nation) cannot have a comparative disadvantage in everything. In the simple case of two people and two activities (law and gardening), if one person has a comparative advantage in one activity, the other person *must* have the comparative advantage in the other activity.

Economies of scale provide the second major reason why there are gains from specialization and exchange. Economies of scale exist if an increase of $x\%$ in all inputs (labour, machinery, land, steel, etc.) leads to an increase of more than $x\%$ in output. Economies of scale are the major reason why large firms have an advantage in many industries, such as automobiles and mainframe computers. Economies of scale are the major reason why costs per unit of output often decline as more is produced. For example, a car company can produce 100,000 cars at a much lower cost per car than if it produces 20,000 cars. Clearly, if a person tried to put together a car in the back yard or in a small shop, it would be very expensive. There are gains when car production is left to the specialists.

Comparative advantage and economies of scale can also be used to explain international trade and specialization among countries in producing different goods. For example, land in Florida is not used to produce wood-pulp, even though Florida land can produce more wood-pulp per acre than land in northern Ontario, for instance. Instead, land in Florida is used to produce oranges, while wood-pulp is produced in northern Ontario. Even though Ontario (like the gardener in the previous example) has an absolute disadvantage in both lines of production, comparative advantage makes it efficient for northern Ontario to specialize in the production of wood-pulp and for Florida to specialize in the production of oranges. Similarly, it is to obtain economies of scale that the Canadian motor vehicle industry specializes in the production of a narrow range of models for both the domestic and the foreign markets, rather than producing all the models sold in the domestic market (Box 3-4).

IMPORTANT TERMS: MATCH THE COLUMNS

Match each term in the first column with the corresponding phrase in the second column. But before you do so, write your own definition of each term in the first column.

_______	**1.** barter	**a.** acts as a medium of exchange
_______	**2.** required by barter	**b.** bad money drives out good
_______	**3.** general purchasing power	**c.** good can be produced at lower opportunity cost
_______	**4.** function of money	**d.** exchange of one good or service for another
_______	**5.** inflation	**e.** reason costs per unit fall as more is produced
_______	**6.** Gresham's law	**f.** money
_______	**7.** absolute advantage	**g.** Adam Smith's pin factory
_______	**8.** comparative advantage	**h.** good can be produced with fewest resources
_______	**9.** economies of scale	**i.** coincidence of wants
_______	**10.** example of economies of scale	**j.** fall in value of money

TRUE-FALSE

T F **1.** One reason that barter is inconvenient is that many commodities cannot easily be divided into smaller parts.

T F **2.** Monetary systems develop only when there is a strong national government, since strong national governments are required to provide money with value.

T F **3.** Suppose that, in the prisoner-of-war camp with its "cigarette money," the value of cigarettes rises compared to the value of other items (such as beef, etc.) Such an increase is known as inflation.

T F **4.** Comparative advantage is the reason why wheat is grown in Saskatchewan and not in the city of Toronto.

T F **5.** If everyone had the same abilities, then economies of scale would not exist.

T F **6.** In the absence of a government, money is valuable only if it is useful. Therefore, cigarette money would be used exclusively in transactions between smokers in the prisoner-of-war camp.

T F **7.** Consider a world with only two countries, A and B, and only two goods, X and Y. Then, if country A has a comparative advantage in good X, country B *must* have a comparative advantage in good Y.

T F **8.** Even if everyone has the same abilities, specialization may be beneficial if there are economies of scale.

MULTIPLE CHOICE

1. One of the problems with barter is that it requires a "coincidence of wants." This means that
- **a.** everybody must want money
- **b.** everybody must want the same good
- **c.** at least two people must want the same good
- **d.** everybody must want my good before I am able to exchange it
- **e.** for an exchange to occur between individuals A and B, individual A must want what B has, while B must want what A has

2. Money is said to represent "general purchasing power" because
- **a.** it can be used to buy any of the goods and services offered for sale
- **b.** the government guarantees its value
- **c.** the government is committed to accept money in payment of taxes
- **d.** Gresham's law is no longer valid
- **e.** Gresham's law applies to other goods, but not money

3. When we draw a diagram showing the circular flow of payments between households and businesses, the two major markets we show are:
- **a.** goods and services
- **b.** capital and labour
- **c.** capital and land
- **d.** consumer goods and economic resources
- **e.** products made by private entrepreneurs, and those provided by the government

4. When the best-tasting cigarettes started to disappear from circulation in the prisoner-of-war camp, this was an example of

- **a.** economies of scale
- **b.** absolute advantage
- **c.** comparative advantage
- **d.** inflation
- **e.** Gresham's law

5. In the prisoner-of-war camp, in which cigarettes acted as money, suppose that the quantity of cigarettes coming into the camp remained constant, while the quantity of all other goods decreased. Then the most probable result would be

- **a.** a rise in the value of cigarettes, measured in terms of other items
- **b.** a fall in the prices of other goods, measured in terms of cigarettes
- **c.** inflation
- **d.** deflation
- **e.** bad money driving out good money

6. Suppose that a building supervisor can lay bricks more rapidly and better than a bricklayer. Then, considering only these two individuals, we may conclude that

- **a.** the bricklayer has an absolute advantage in bricklaying
- **b.** the supervisor has an absolute advantage in bricklaying
- **c.** the bricklayer has a comparative advantage in bricklaying
- **d.** the supervisor has a comparative advantage in bricklaying
- **e.** we can't tell which of the above is true without knowing how much bricks cost, compared to the wage for bricklayers

7. According to the theory of comparative advantage, a good should be produced in a country

- **a.** whose workers are most skillful at producing that good
- **b.** which has the greatest number of workers capable of producing that good
- **c.** which has the greatest quantity of capital capable of producing that good
- **d.** which has the lowest opportunity cost of producing that good
- **e.** where economies of scale are greatest in producing that good

8. Suppose that there are only two countries, A and B, and only two goods, food and clothing. If country A has a comparative advantage in the production of food, then we may conclude that

- **a.** country A must also have an absolute advantage in the production of food
- **b.** country B probably has an absolute advantage in the production of food
- **c.** country B probably has an absolute advantage in the production of clothing

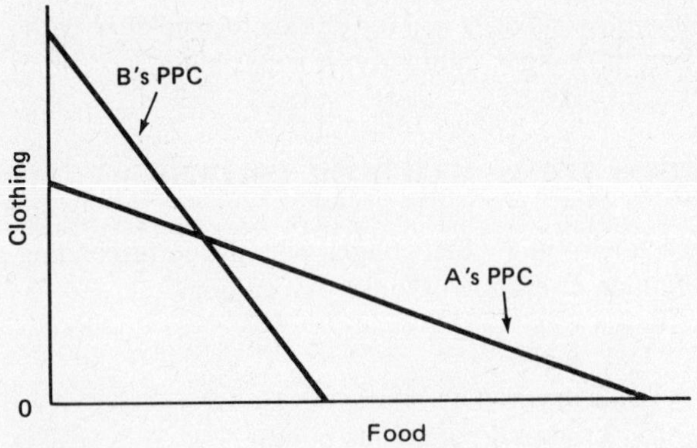

FIGURE 3-1

- **d.** country B probably has a comparative advantage in the production of clothing
- **e.** country B must have a comparative advantage in the production of clothing

9. Figure 3-1 illustrates the PPCs of countries A and B.

- **a.** Country A has a comparative advantage in the production of clothing, while country B has a comparative advantage in the production of food.
- **b.** Country A has a comparative advantage in the production of food, while country B has a comparative advantage in the production of clothing.
- **c.** Country A has a comparative advantage in the production of both goods.
- **d.** Country A has an absolute advantage in the production of both goods.
- **e.** Country B has an absolute advantage in the production of both goods.

10. Suppose that there are only two countries, A and B, and only two goods, food and clothing. We can conclude that A has a comparative advantage in the production of food if

- **a.** A's opportunity cost of producing food is less than B's opportunity cost of producing food
- **b.** A's opportunity cost of producing food is less than A's opportunity cost of producing clothing
- **c.** A's opportunity cost of producing food is less than B's opportunity cost of producing clothing
- **d.** A has more capital than B
- **e.** A has a larger population than B

11. Suppose that 120 workers with 1 machine can produce 100 TV sets in a month, while 20 workers with 2 machines can produce 250 TV sets in a month. This is an example of

- **a.** technological efficiency
- **b.** allocative efficiency
- **c.** economies of scale
- **d.** comparative advantage
- **e.** absolute advantage

12. Suppose that (1) there are economies of scale in the production of different goods, and (2) land and labour have specialized capabilities—for example, land and the climate give Brazil a comparative advantage in coffee. Then the gains from specialization will probably be

a. larger than if either (1) or (2) had existed alone
b. small, since (1) and (2) tend to offset each other
c. negative, since the combination of (1) and (2) creates confusion
d. about the same as with (1) alone, since (2) doesn't make much difference
e. about the same as with (2) alone, since (1) doesn't make much difference

EXERCISES

1. This exercise illustrates the idea of comparative advantage. Assume the following. A doctor working on home repairs can fix a leaky faucet in 10 minutes. A plumber takes 15 minutes. Then the [doctor, plumber] has an absolute advantage in plumbing. The doctor's time is worth $80 per hour in the practice of medicine. The plumber is paid $20 per hour.

Suppose the doctor's house has six leaky faucets. If he fixes them himself, it will take ____________ minutes. Thus, to fix the faucets, the doctor will use $____________ worth of his time. If the plumber is hired to fix the faucets, he will take ____________ minutes, which is [longer, shorter] than the doctor would take. The cost in this case is $ ________________, which is [more, less] by $ ____________ than if the doctor had fixed the faucets himself. The [doctor, plumber] has a comparative advantage in plumbing.

2. Table 3-1 shows how many cars can be produced in a country with various amounts of inputs. Each unit of input represents a specific quantity of labour and capital. Table 3-2 provides similar information for computers. Table 3-1 illustrates the idea of [comparative advantage, absolute advantage, economies of scale, none of these]. Table 3-2 illustrates the idea of [comparative advantage, absolute advantage, economies of scale, none of these].

Suppose that the economy has 5 units of inputs to be devoted to cars and computers. Plot the PPC for these 5 units of input in Figure 3-2. How is the shape of the PPC different from the PPCs in Chapter 2? ____________. The opportunity cost of producing cars [increases, decreases, remains constant] as more are produced.

Table 3-1
PRODUCTION OF CARS

Number of cars (millions)	Units of input
1	1
3	2
6	3
12	4
20	5

Table 3-2
PRODUCTION OF COMPUTERS

Number of computers (millions)	Units of input
20	1
40	2
60	3
80	4
100	5

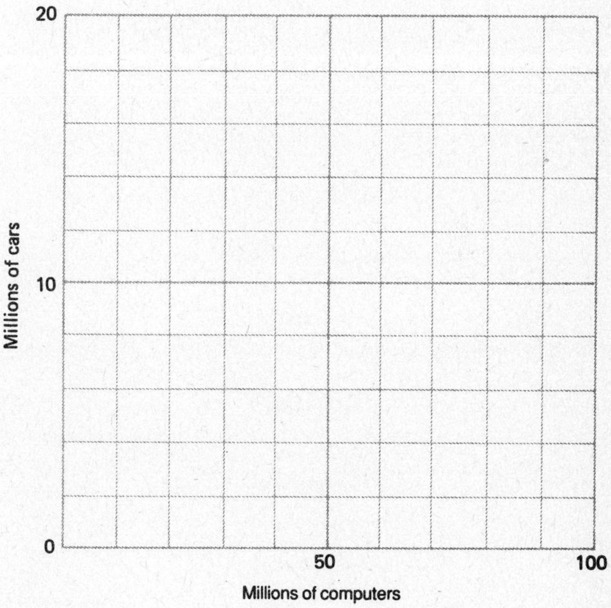

FIGURE 3-2

ESSAY QUESTIONS

1. The textbook explains why comparative advantage can mean that there are benefits from specialization and exchange. But it does not explain why specific people or nations might have a comparative advantage. How would you explain Saskatchewan's comparative advantage over Ontario in producing wheat? Why do New Brunswick and northern Ontario have a comparative advantage over most other provinces and American states in producing pulp and paper? Why does Taiwan have a comparative advantage in the production of transistor radios and TV sets?

2. Why do you think that most economists are usually in favour of reducing tariffs and other barriers to international trade? Why might anyone oppose the reduction of tariffs?

3. There are disadvantages associated with specialization, as well as advantages. What are they?

ANSWERS

Important Terms: **1** d **2** i **3** f **4** a **5** j **6** b **7** h **8** c **9** e **10** g
True-False: **1** T **2** F **3** F **4** T **5** F **6** F **7** T **8** T
Multiple Choice: **1** e, **2** a, **3** d, **4** e, **5** c, **6** b, **7** d, **8** e, **9** b, **10** a, **11** c, **12** a
Exercises: **1.** doctor, 60, $80, 90, longer, $30, less, $50, plumber
2. economies of scale, none of these, it bows inward, decreases

Chapter 4

DEMAND AND SUPPLY: THE MARKET MECHANISM

MAJOR PURPOSE

This chapter is one of the most important in the book. It introduces the concepts of *demand* and *supply,* which help us to understand what is happening in the markets for specific products. The demand curve illustrates how buyers respond to various possible prices: At lower prices, they buy more. On the other hand, sellers react negatively to low prices. They offer less for sale. This response of sellers is illustrated by the supply curve.

When drawing a demand or supply curve, we isolate the effect of *price alone* on the behaviour of buyers and sellers. Of course, many other things besides price can affect their behaviour. When we draw a demand or supply curve and look at the effect of price alone, we make the *ceteris paribus* assumption—that all these other things do not change. In cases where they do in fact change, we are no longer on a single demand or supply curve; the demand or supply curve *shifts.*

Other important concepts introduced in this chapter are the concept of *equilibrium, surplus,* and *shortage,* and *substitutes* and *complementary goods.*

LEARNING OBJECTIVES

After you have studied this chapter in the textbook and study guide, you should be able to:

- Explain why the demand curve slopes downward to the right
- Explain why the supply curve slopes upward to the right
- Explain why a price that begins away from equilibrium will move to equilibrium
- List and explain three things that can shift the demand curve, and four that can shift the supply curve
- Give one example each of a pair of goods that are (1) substitutes in use, (2) complements in use, (3) substitutes in production, and (4) complements in production. In each case, you should be able to explain why the pair fits into the category.
- Explain the distinction between product markets and markets for factors of production
- Explain how the factor markets can help answer the question For whom?
- Explain how changes in factor markets can affect what happens in a product market, and vice versa
- Explain the main strengths and main shortcomings of the market mechanism as a way of answering the questions What? How? and For whom?

HIGHLIGHTS OF THE CHAPTER

In every economy, some mechanism is needed to decide three major questions: *What* will be produced? *How* will it be produced? And *for whom* will it be produced? There are two major ways of answering these questions: (1) through the market—that is, through voluntary exchanges between buyers and sellers, and (2) through governmental decision making. (Other ways are sometimes used—for example, in a family or in a monastery. But we are not primarily interested in these alternatives.)

All nations have some reliance on markets, and some reliance on governmental decision making. However, there are substantial differences among nations. In countries such as Canada and the United States, the market is the most important mechanism, although the government does play a significant role in modifying the outcome of the market. In the U.S.S.R. government plays a much more central role, although there is some reliance on markets.

The central feature of a market is *price*. Different prices for different goods provide *incentives* for producers to make some goods rather than others, and incentives for consumers to purchase cheap goods rather than expensive ones. *Prices* also provide *signals* and *information* to buyers and sellers. For example, the willingness of buyers to pay a high price acts as a signal to producers, showing that people are eager to obtain the product.

To study how buyers respond to different prices, we use a *demand curve* or *demand schedule*. This curve or schedule shows the quantity of a specific good that buyers would be willing and able to purchase at various different prices. The demand curve slopes downward to the right, illustrating that people are more eager to buy at lower prices. A major reason is that, at a lower price, people have an incentive to *switch* away from other products, and buy the product whose price is lower instead.

On the other side of the market, the supply curve shows how much sellers would be willing to offer at various prices. It slopes upward to the right, because sellers will be increasingly eager to sell as the price rises. Again, the willingness to *switch* is an important reason for the slope. If the price of a good is higher, firms have an incentive to drop other products, and make more of this good instead.

What happens in the market depends on both demand and supply. To find the *equilibrium* price and quantity, we put the demand and supply curves together, to find where they intersect. At this price, the quantity offered by sellers is equal to the quantity that buyers want to purchase. There is no unfulfilled demand to pull prices up, nor are there any excess offers to pull prices down.

If the price were not at its equilibrium, there would be pressures on the price to change. If the price were below its equilibrium, for example, there would be eager buyers who would not be able to find the good for sale. In other words, there would be a *shortage*. Producers would notice this, and conclude that they could sell at a higher price. The price would rise to its equilibrium level. On the other hand, if the price were initially above its equilibrium, there would be a *surplus*. Eager sellers would be unable to find buyers. They would become willing to sell at a lower price. The price would fall to its equilibrium level.

When we draw a demand or supply curve, we are looking at the way in which buyers and sellers respond to price, and to price *alone*. In practice, of course, buyers and sellers are influenced by many things besides price of the good—for example, buyers generally purchase more when their incomes rise, and sellers are less willing to sell when the costs of their inputs rise. But these other things are held stable when a single demand or supply curve is drawn. This is the important assumption of *ceteris paribus*, that other things do not change. If they do change, the demand or supply curve *shifts*. For example, an increase in income generally causes a rightward shift in the whole demand curve. However, in the case of inferior goods, the demand curve shifts left; when people can afford better alternatives, they demand them.

If the demand curve shifts to the right while the supply curve remains stable, then both price and quantity will increase. On the other hand, if the supply curve shifts right while the demand curve remains stable, then quantity will increase but price will fall. In brief, *a change in demand makes price and quantity change in the same direction, whereas a change in supply makes price and quantity move in opposite directions*. In practice, of course, many things can happen at once; often the demand and supply curves both shift. In this case, it becomes more difficult to predict what will happen.

Supply and demand theory is often used to study the market for a single good. However, there are strong connections among markets. When a price changes in one market, it can change conditions in other markets. For example, an increase in the price of gasoline in the 1970s caused a decline in the demand for large cars. This is an example of *complementary goods* —large cars and gasoline are used *together*. When the price of gasoline increases, the demand for large cars shifts left.

Whereas gasoline and cars are complements, some other products—such as bus tickets and train tickets—are *substitutes*. A person wanting to travel to the next city can go either by train or by bus. The higher the train fare, the more people will use buses instead. Thus, a higher price of train tickets causes the demand curve for bus tickets to shift to the right.

Goods may also be substitutes or complements in production. Substitutes in production are goods which use the same inputs; the inputs can be used to produce either the one good or the other. For example, land can be used to produce either wheat or corn. If there is a crop failure in Russia and an increase in North American exports of wheat, the price of wheat will be bid up. Farmers will be encouraged to switch out of the production of corn, and produce additional wheat instead. The supply curve for corn will shift to the left.

On the other hand, complements are produced together. For example, wheat and straw are produced together. If the price of wheat is bid up, more wheat will be produced. In the process, more straw will be produced as a by-product. The supply curve of straw will shift to the right.

The question of *what* will be produced is decided primarily in the product market. To throw light on the other two questions—*how?* and *for whom?*—we should look first at the markets for inputs. For example, the market for labour helps to answer these two questions. If the demand for labour is high compared to its supply, then wage rates will be high. For example, wage rates are much higher in Canada than in India, because there are fewer workers for each unit of land and capital in Canada. As a result of the high wage, producers in Canada have an incentive to use only a little labour, and substitute capital instead. In an Indian factory, in contrast, many more things will be done by hand because of the low wage rate. The wage rate not only helps to determine how things are produced, but it also helps to determine who gets the product. Because Canadian wage rates are high, the Canadian worker can buy and consume many more products than the Indian worker.

Observe that high wage rates affect what the worker can buy; with high wages, workers are more likely to buy computers and homes. This means that wages—determined in the factor markets in the lower box in Figure 4-9 in the textbook—have an impact on the demand for computers, homes, and other products in the upper box. Thus, there are important connections among markets.

Finally, this chapter summarizes the strengths and weaknesses of the market as a mechanism for answering the three central questions *What? How?* and *For whom?* The strong points of the market are that (1) it encourages producers to make what consumers want, (2) it provides people with an incentive to acquire useful skills, (3) it encourages consumers to conserve scarce goods, (4) it encourages producers to conserve scarce resources, (5) it provides a high degree of economic freedom, and (6) it provides buyers and sellers with information on market conditions, including local conditions.

The market mechanism is also subject to major criticisms: (1) some people may be left in desperate poverty, (2) a market economy may be unstable, (3) monopolies and oligopolies may have the power to keep production down and keep prices up, (4) the market does not provide a strong incentive for producers to limit pollution and other negative side effects, (5) markets don't work in the case of public goods, where people benefit regardless of who pays for the good, and (6) producers may simply be satisfying a want that they have created in the first place through advertising.

To evaluate the market, it is important to compare it with the alternatives that exist in fact, not with some ideal, unattainable system. The textbook outlines a few of the problems that can arise when the government sets prices—in particular, the problem of black markets and shortages. A form of price regulation, rent control, is discussed in Box 4-1. One problem with rent control is that it may offer tenants short-run gains, and thus may be popular among the voting public, even though the results are bad in the long run.

IMPORTANT TERMS: MATCH THE COLUMNS

Match each term in the first column with the corresponding phrase in the second column. But before you do so, write your own definition of each term in the first column.

__D__	**1.** capitalism	**a.** all the producers of a single good
__H__	**2.** monopoly	**b.** if price of A rises, demand for B increases
__L__	**3.** oligopoly	**c.** surplus
__I__	**4.** perfect competition	**d.** free enterprise
__A__	**5.** industry	**e.** demand for this declines as income rises
__K__	**6.** firm	**f** nothing else changes
__C__	**7.** excess supply	**g.** goods used together
__J__	**8.** excess demand	**h.** market with only one seller
__E__	**9.** inferior good	**i** where every buyer and seller is a price taker
__G__	**10.** complementary goods	**j.** shortage
__B__	**11.** substitutes	**k.** a single business organization, such as Canadian General Electric
__F__	**12.** *ceteris paribus*	**l.** market dominated by a few sellers

TRUE-FALSE

T F 1. Perfect competition exists only when the government fixes the price, so that no single buyer or seller is able to influence the price of the good.

T F 2. Perfect competition will not exist in a market if there is only one seller, or if there is only one buyer.

T F 3. In a perfectly competitive industry, every buyer and seller takes the quantity as given, and is left with only a pricing decision.

T F 4. Even if there are many buyers, imperfect competition can exist in a market.

T F 5. Even if there are many sellers, imperfect competition can exist in a market.

T F 6. In a capitalist economy, most of the capital equipment is owned by the government.

T F 7. A surplus drives the price down; a shortage drives the price up.

T F 8. If the price of wheat increases, the supply curve of straw will probably shift to the right.

T F 9. The demand curve for Pepsi-Cola will probably shift to the right if the price of Coke rises.

T F 10. If the price of paper increases, the supply curve of books will probably shift to the right.

T F 11. If demand increases while supply decreases, the price will increase.

T F 12. If the demand curve shifts to the right, the result will be an increase in the quantity sold and an increase in the market price.

T F 13. If both the demand and supply curves for a product shift to the right, we can expect the quantity sold to increase, but we cannot be sure whether the price will rise or fall.

T F 14. One essential characteristic of a free-enterprise economy is that the government facilitates entry into business by subsidizing new businesses.

T F 15. Factor markets are different from the markets for most goods, in that goods markets are generally perfectly competitive, while the markets for factors are usually monopolized.

MULTIPLE CHOICE

1. The Canadian government uses four major ways to influence what will be produced, how, and for whom. It uses every one of the following except one. Which one does not belong in this list?
   - a. spending
   - b. taxes
   - c. regulation
   - d. comprehensive central planning
   - e. public enterprises

2. What is the most important characteristic of perfect competition?
   - a. each seller has at least one powerful competitor to worry about
   - b. there is at least one powerful, efficient producer who acts to keep prices down
   - c. every buyer can go to at least three of four sellers to see who has the lowest price
   - d. every buyer and seller is a price taker; none has any power to set price
   - e. there must be many buyers, and at least three or four sellers

3. A market with one seller and a few buyers is an example of
   - a. monopoly
   - b. oligopoly
   - c. perfect competition
   - d. technological inefficiency
   - e. a black market

4. A surplus of wheat exists when
   - a. wheat production is lower than last year
   - b. wheat production is higher than last year
   - c. wheat production exceeds the production of all other grains combined
   - d. the quantity of wheat demanded exceeds the quantity supplied
   - e. the quantity of wheat supplied exceeds the quantity demanded

5. Suppose that a surplus exists in a market. Then we may conclude that
   - a. the price is below the equilibrium
   - b. the price is above the equilibrium
   - c. the government has imposed a price ceiling
   - d. the quantity demanded has decreased
   - e. the quantity supplied has increased

6. When incomes increase, the demand curve for an individual good
   - a. usually shifts down
   - b. always shifts down
   - c. usually shifts to the right
   - d. always shifts to the right
   - e. doesn't move, since only price affects demand

7. Peanuts and tobacco can be grown on similar land. Therefore, they are
   - a. substitutes in production
   - b. joint products
   - c. inferior goods
   - d. normal goods
   - e. an oligopoly

8. Tennis rackets and tennis balls are
   a. substitutes
   b. complementary goods
   c. inferior goods
   d. unrelated goods
   e. monopolistic goods

9. Apples and textbooks are
   a. substitutes
   b. complementary goods
   c. inferior goods
   d. independent goods
   e. monopolistic goods

10. Suppose that the demand for beef increases. This is most likely to cause
   a. a rightward shift in the supply curve for beef
   b. a leftward shift in the supply curve for beef
   c. a fall in the price of beef
   d. a fall in the price of leather
   e. an upward shift in the demand for leather

11. Suppose that, between year 1 and year 2, the demand curve and the supply curve for wheat both shift to the right. From this information, we may conclude that, in year 2
   a. the quantity of wheat sold will be larger, while the price will be higher
   b. the quantity of wheat sold will be larger, while the price will be lower
   c. the quantity of wheat sold will be larger, but we do not have enough information to tell if the price will be higher or lower
   d. the quantity of wheat sold will be smaller, but we do not have enough information to tell if the price will be higher or lower

12. A black market is most likely to exist when
   a. the government controls the price of a good
   b. the supply of a good is controlled by a monopolist
   c. the supply of a good is controlled by two or three producers
   d. the government imposes an excise tax on a good
   e. the government urges producers to produce more to promote the general welfare of the public

13. The advantages of the market mechanism (as contrasted to government controls) as a way of deciding what, how, and for whom include
   a. prices provide incentives for producers to make what the public wants
   b. prices provide incentives for producers to conserve scarce resources
   c. prices provide incentives for consumers to conserve scarce goods
   d. high wages in skilled occupations act as an incentive for workers to undertake training
   e. all of the above

14. When we draw the demand curve for a product, we assume that
   a. there are many sellers
   b. there are only a few sellers
   c. all "supply shifters" are held constant
   d. all "demand shifters" are held constant
   e. both (c) and (d)

EXERCISES

1. Using the demand and supply schedules in the table below, plot the demand and supply curves in Figure 4-1. Label the axes, and mark the appropriate numbers on each axis. Then fill in the last column of the table.

a. The equilibrium quantity is ____________.

b. The equilibrium price is ____________.

c. At the equilibrium price, what is the surplus or shortage shown in the last column? ____________. Does this confirm that this price is an equilibrium?

d. Now suppose that the government sets a price of 60 cents. At this price, there will be a [surplus, shortage] of ____________.

2. Box 4-1 in the textbook describes what happens when the government sets a price below the equilibrium. In other cases, the government prevents the price from falling to its equilibrium. For example, the government has taken steps to keep the prices of agricultural commodities up.

Figure 4-2 illustrates some of the issues that arise when the government undertakes price supports.

Price of hamburgers	Quantity demanded (thousands per week)	Quantity supplied (thousands per week)	Surplus (+) or shortage (–)
$1.40	200	700	
$1.20	240	600	
$1.00	300	500	
$0.80	400	400	
$0.60	600	300	
$0.50	800	250	

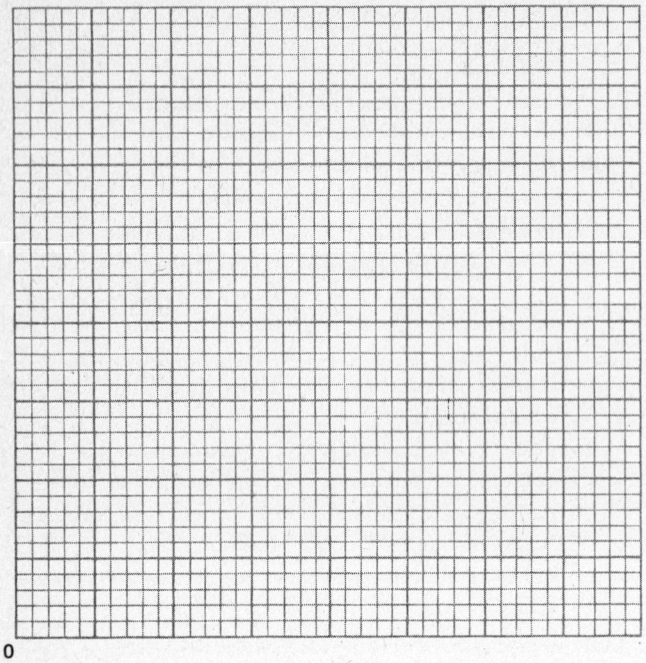

FIGURE 4-1

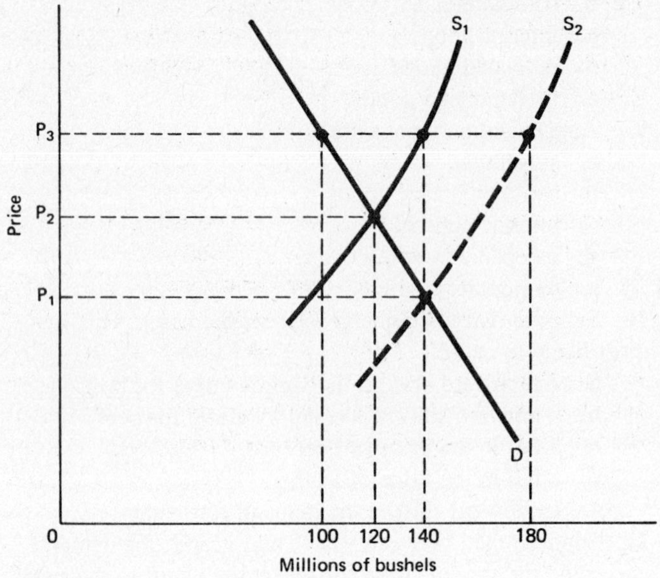

FIGURE 4-2

D shows the demand curve, and S_1 the supply curve. Initially, the equilibrium quantity is ____________ million bushels, and the price is ____________. Now suppose that the government passes a rule that says that wheat cannot be sold at a price less than P_3. The result of this law will be a [surplus, shortage] amounting to ____________ million bushels.

If all the government does is set a high price, not all wheat farmers will be better off. Those who are better off will be those who [cut back on production, sell their wheat at the high price]. On the other hand, some will be worse off, specifically those who [are unable to sell their wheat at a high price, sell their wheat at a low price]. To ensure that wheat farmers are better off, the government can [buy the surplus wheat, reduce the price to P_1].

Now suppose that the government undertakes irrigation projects to help agriculture in dry areas. This will cause an increase in supply from S_1 to S_2, and the [surplus, shortage] of wheat will [increase, decrease] to ____________ million bushels. The government will find the costs of its price support program [increasing, decreasing]. If it now eliminates the price support, the free market price will settle at ____________.

3. Suppose that supply is given by the equation

$$Q = -30 + 4P$$

This supply is plotted in Figure 4-3 in the following way. First, choose some convenient value for *P*, such as 10. Put this value into the equation to get $Q = -30 + 40 = 10$. This means that when $P = 10$, $Q = 10$, so that point *A* is on the supply "curve." Then, choose another value of *P*, say $P = 15$. Substituting this into the equation, we find that the corresponding $Q =$ ____________. This is plotted as point *B*. The supply relationship is a straight line; there are no squared terms or other reasons for supply to bend. Thus, with the two points *A* and *B*, we can draw the straight-line supply S_1.

a. Suppose that demand is also a straight line:

$$Q = 20 - P$$

Then, if $P = 15$, Q = ____________, and if $P = 5$, $Q =$ ____________. Plot demand in Figure 4-3 and label it D_1. On this figure, we see that the equilibrium price is

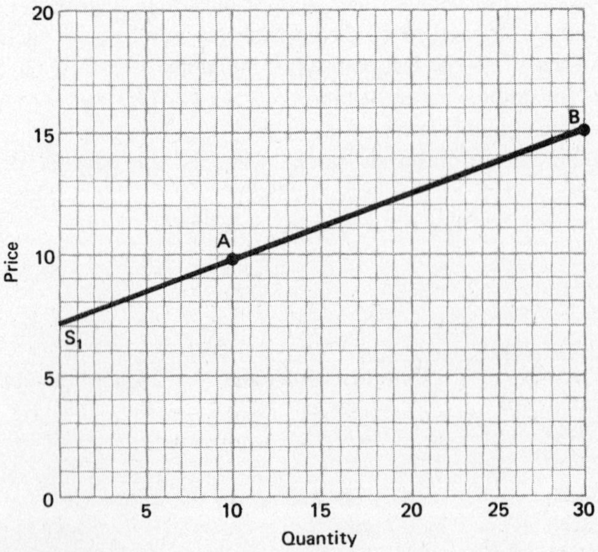

FIGURE 4-3

____________ and the equilibrium quantity ____________. Confirm these figures by solving the two equations algebraically, to find P and Q.

b. Suppose now that income increases and demand consequently increases, with 15 more units being demanded at each price. Thus, the new demand is

$$Q = 35 - P$$

To plot this new demand, we find two points. For example, if $P = 15$, $Q =$ ____________, and if $P = 5$, $Q =$ ____________. Plot the new equilibrium demand, labelling it D_2. At the new equilibrium, $P =$ ____________ and $Q =$ ____________. Again, confirm these numbers by solving the demand and supply equations. The price has [increased, decreased], and the quantity has [increased, decreased] as a result of this increase in demand.

c. Now, suppose we are back with the original demand, D_1, but that supply is now

$$Q = -10 + 2P$$

If $P = 10$, $Q =$ ____________, and if $P = 15$, $Q =$ ____________. Plot this new supply and label it S_2. With supply S_2, and demand D_1, the equilibrium price is ____________, while quantity is ____________. Again, confirm these numbers by solving the demand and supply equations.

d. Finally, suppose that demand shifts from D_1 to D_2, while supply remains at S_2. At the new equilibrium $P =$ ____________ and $Q =$ ____________. When the demand curve shifted this time, why is it that the price rose more, and the quantity less, than in part (*b*)?

Answer: ____________.

ESSAY QUESTIONS

1. A demand or supply curve applies to a specific time and a specific location. For example, the market for maple syrup in London, Ontario, is not the same thing as the market for maple syrup in Winnipeg, Manitoba. Would you expect the price of maple syrup in these two cities to be similar? Precisely the same? Explain.

2. Suppose that, as a result of an increase in the number of pancake eaters in Winnipeg, there were an increase in the demand for maple syrup in that city. If you were an all-powerful social planner, you would probably want to persuade people in London to give up some of their maple syrup in order to provide for the higher number of people in Winnipeg. What sort of rationing scheme might you devise to accomplish this goal? How would you know how much to allocate to each family? How large a staff do you think you would need?

Suppose, alternatively, that you allowed market forces to work freely. What would happen to the price of maple syrup in Winnipeg? What would happen to the quantity? How would the changing conditions in Winnipeg affect the supply curve for maple syrup in London? What would happen to the price of maple syrup in London? To the quantity? Draw demand and supply curves for Winnipeg and London to illustrate what is happening. Would your intentions as a social planner be carried out by the market instead? Which policy—rationing or the market—works more efficiently? Are there any disadvantages to the more efficient system?

3. The prices printed on a restaurant menu apply whether the restaurant is crowded or half empty on any particular evening. If you ran a restaurant

a. Would you charge higher prices on Friday and Saturday evenings when the restaurant is crowded, than on other evenings?

b. Would you charge higher prices during the evening than for an identical meal at lunch? Why or why not? (Or, under what circumstances might you?)

c. Does McDonald's behave in the way you have suggested? How do you explain that?

ANSWERS

Important Terms: **1** d **2** h **3** l **4** i **5** a **6** k **7** c **8** j **9** e **10** g **11** b **12** f

True-False: **1** F **2** T **3** F **4** T **5** T **6** F **7** T **8** T **9** T **10** F **11** T **12** T **13** T **14** F **15** F

Multiple Choice: **1** d **2** d **3** a **4** e **5** b **6** c **7** a **8** b **9** d **10** d **11** c **12** a **13** e **14** d

Exercises: **1a.** 400 **1b.** \$0.80 **1c.** zero, yes **1d.** shortage, 300 **2.** 120, P_2, surplus, 40, sell their wheat at the high price, are unable to sell their wheat at the high price, buy the surplus wheat, surplus, increase, 80, increasing, P_1 **3.** 30 **a.** 5, 15, 10, 10 **b.** 20, 30, 13, 2, increased, increased **c.** 10, 20, 10, 10 **d.** 15, 20, because S_2 is steeper than S_1

THE ECONOMIC ROLE OF GOVERNMENT

MAJOR PURPOSE

The major objective of this chapter is to explain how the government affects the economy. It does so in four ways: through spending, taxation, regulation, and the operation of public enterprises.

There are a number of reasons for government intervention in the economy. (1) The government provides *public goods*—that is, goods that everyone can enjoy, whether they actually pay for them or not. An example is police protection; we all gain the benefits of an orderly society, whether we pay taxes or not. (2) The government can control or discourage externalities, such as pollution. Free markets don't work very well in the case of polluting industries, since they provide no incentive to keep pollution down. (3) The government provides merit goods—such as education—that it considers particularly important for the society. (4) The government provides programs to help the poor.

LEARNING OBJECTIVES

After you have studied this chapter in the textbook and study guide, you should be able to

- Describe the four ways in which the government affects the economy
- Describe the major programs of the three levels of government
- Explain the difference between government spending for goods and services, and transfer payments
- Explain the difference between a progressive and a regressive tax, and give an example of each
- Explain the role and significance of Crown corporations in the Canadian economy
- Describe the five major reasons for government intervention in the economy
- Explain the objectives that should be kept in mind when designing a tax system
- Explain the difference between the *benefit principle* and the *ability to pay principle*
- Explain why the Canadian tax system is less progressive than we might guess by looking at the income tax schedule

HIGHLIGHTS OF THE CHAPTER

The government affects the economy in four major ways: (1) spending, (2) taxation, (3) regulation, and (4) public enterprises.

Spending

In nominal dollar terms, government spending has risen very rapidly in Canada, from about $4 billion in 1950 to $240 billion in 1984. However, if we look at the size of the government relative to the economy, we get a much less spectacular picture. For example, *government purchases of goods and services* have increased relatively slowly as a percentage of GNP since the mid-1940s, and the percentage remains well below what it was during World War II. Nevertheless, if transfer payments are included, government spending has risen substantially as a percentage of GNP in the past several decades, and in the mid-1980s it was as high as it had been during the war. In other words, the increase in the size of government largely reflects the increase in transfer payments such as Old Age Security, unemployment insurance benefits, and family allowances.

Taxes

The primary purpose of taxes is to raise the revenue to finance government spending. The personal income tax is the largest revenue raiser, by a large margin, for the federal and provincial governments. Other important sources of revenue are the corporate income tax, sales taxes (especially at the provincial level), and local government property taxes. At the federal level, unemployment insurance contributions and mandatory contributions to the Canada/Quebec Pension plans represent another important revenue source.

On most income—up to a maximum of $24,000 per year in 1985—a "tax" such as the worker's portion of the unemployment insurance contribution is proportional: It is calculated as a fixed percentage of income. However, no contribution is collected on incomes over the maximum, which means that, in this range, the "tax" is *regressive.* That is, it is a smaller percentage of an income of, say, $48,000, than of an income of $24,000. Nevertheless, the impact of the overall system of unemployment insurance, mandatory government pension plans, and other transfer payments is *progressive* because the net benefits to lower-income people are greater, as a percentage of their income, than the benefits to people with higher incomes.

Unlike the "tax" rates for unemployment insurance contributions, the income tax rates are *progressive*: The tax rate on high incomes is larger than the tax rate on low incomes. However, the overall tax system is less progressive than the income tax rates suggest, both because of the existence of regressive components such as unemployment insurance contributions and sales taxes, and because of "loopholes"—various tax deductions or tax credits. The term "loophole" implies that the deduction or credit is undesirable, and there is considerable debate over what is desirable and what is not. One item sometimes put on the list of loopholes—the fact that the government does not levy any tax on the implicit return on homeowners' equity—has strong political support and is rarely mentioned in the debate on tax reform. (Indeed, a 1979 proposal by the Progressive Conservatives to further favour homeowners by allowing them to deduct mortgage interest from taxable income attracted considerable political support at the time; however, it was not implemented.)

Other than raising revenues, there are a number of other objectives that should be considered in designing a tax code:

1. One objective is *equity,* or fairness. As we suggested in Chapter 1, there is some controversy over just what is fair. Nevertheless, discussions of fairness usually begin with one of two approaches to taxation:

a. *Ability to pay.* According to this idea, taxes should be imposed according to income or wealth; people with high incomes should pay more because they are better able to do so. The progressive income tax is one application of this principle. (The inheritance tax is another.)

b. *Benefit principle.* According to this idea, taxes should depend on who benefits most from government programs. Those who benefit most should pay the most.

2. *Simplicity* is an important objective in the tax system. Discussions of tax reform in recent years have often centred around the criticism that the income tax has become hopelessly complicated.

3. *Neutrality.* As a starting point, most economists believe that the tax system should be designed to disturb market forces as little as possible. It should not capriciously introduce incentives for people to change their behaviour in order to avoid taxes.

4. *Meeting social objectives.* Nevertheless, in some cases it may be desirable to encourage people to change their behaviour. For example, in order to encourage people to give to charities, the government allows people to deduct their contributions to charities from their taxable income. Taxes may also be used to discourage businesses from polluting the air or water.

Regulation

More direct means are available for encouraging some behaviour and discouraging other activities. For example, there are regulations limiting the amount of pollutants that factories are allowed to discharge into the air and water. In the early days of regulation about 100 years ago, the government took steps to discourage monopolistic behaviour by the industrial cartels ("combines") that were being organized at the time. Other regulations are aimed at protecting the safety of workers and discouraging discrimination.

Government regulations are generally aimed at reducing major problems. Nevertheless, regulation has been a source of controversy. There are two main difficulties with regulation: (1) regulatory agencies may require major reporting efforts from business, and sometimes generate expensive red tape of little value; and (2) regulatory agencies sometimes come under the control of the industry they are supposedly regulating. The government may be the means by which an industry gains oligopolistic or monopolistic power.

Public Enterprise

Another important way in which the government influences the economy is through Crown corporations, government-owned firms that derive much of their revenue from selling various goods and services to the public. In the early 1980s, Crown corporations were responsible for as much as 15% of all capital investment in Canada.

Federal and provincial governments establish Crown corporations for a variety of reasons: as an alternative to regulation in the case of a *natural monopoly*; as a way of ensuring the provision of certain services (such as transportation and communications) to communities that would not be served by private firms; to stimulate investment in risky ventures involving new technology. Sometimes Crown corporations are created when the government takes over a financially ailing firm as a way of protecting employment opportunities in particular communities.

A possible problem with Crown corporations has to do with lack of *accountability*. If the political control over the corporations' managers is weak, there may be inadequate control over costs and some corporations may end up running deficits far higher than can be justified by the special objectives they are supposed to serve. One possible way of overcoming this problem is privatization. In the mid-1980s, a number of instances of privatization occurred at both the provincial and the federal levels. However, privatization remained a controversial policy.

Reasons for Government Activity

The government becomes involved in the economy for many reasons. Here are the five most important ones:

1. Governments often provide goods and services that the private sector would otherwise fail to provide or would provide only with difficulty and at a high cost. Roads are one example. If the roads within a city were run by private entrepreneurs, motorists would have to stop frequently to pay tolls. National defence is unlikely to be organized and paid for privately. There is a problem of *free riders*—people who let others pay because they will reap the benefits even if they don't contribute. If people benefit whether they pay or not, we have an example of a *public good.*

2. The government may intervene when *side effects* prevent people from making socially desirable decisions. For example, vaccinations protect not only the individuals who are vaccinated; they also protect the public from communicable diseases. Smallpox has been eradicated by the combined action of governments and international organizations.

Benefits that go to people other than those who are vaccinated (or their doctors) are known as *external benefits.* There can also be *external costs,* such as the cost to people downwind from a polluting factory. Just as the government encourages activities with external benefits—such as vaccinations—so it may discourage those with external costs.

3. The government may provide *merit* goods or services, such as education, that it considers very desirable from a social viewpoint.

4. The government has programs to *help the poor;* for example, subsidized housing and social assistance payments.

5. The government may increase or decrease its expenditures in order to *promote economic stability.* For example, during a period of high unemployment, it may undertake public projects in order to provide jobs.

IMPORTANT TERMS: MATCH THE COLUMNS

Match each term in the first column with the corresponding phrase in the second column. But before you do so, write your own definition of each term in the first column.

F **1.** transfer payment
K **2.** progressive tax
B **3.** proportional tax
A **4.** average tax rate
M **5.** marginal tax rate
I **6.** deficit
C **7.** equalization payments
L **8.** externality
E **9.** public good
G **10.** neutral tax
H **11.** incidence of tax
D **12.** conditional transfers

a. tax paid divided by income
b. one which takes the same percentage of high and low incomes
c. transfers by the federal government to provincial governments
d. federal subsidy of provincial spending
e. people get the benefit of this, regardless of who pays
f. expenditure by government, for which government receives no good or service in return
g. tax that leaves market forces undisturbed
h. who ultimately pays tax
i. excess of expenditures over revenues
j. one which takes a higher percentage of high incomes
k. side effect of production or consumption
l. percentage of increase in income paid in tax

TRUE-FALSE

T F 1. A tax is progressive if high-income people pay a larger percentage of their income than low-income people.

T F 2. Public enterprise in Canada is about the same size (in relation to the economy as a whole) as public enterprise in the United States.

T T 3. Since 1960, transfer expenditures by the federal government have risen, both as a fraction of total federal government expenditures and as a fraction of national product.

T F 4. Suppose that a province imposes a surtax of 5% of all income. Because it "hits the poor as hard as the rich," such tax is regressive.

T F 5. According to the benefit principle of taxation, government expenditures should be undertaken if they benefit the public.

T F 6. According to the ability-to-pay principle of taxation, only those who have enough income that they are able to save should be required to pay taxes.

T F 7. The term "merit good" is used in describing a feature of the British economy. Specifically, a merit good is one which the upper class consumes more heavily than the lower classes.

T F 8. Since poor people are more likely than rich people to live in rented housing, the non-taxation of the implicit return on homeowners' equity makes the Canadian tax system less progressive.

MULTIPLE CHOICE

1. Which of the following is the best example of government expenditure for goods or services?
   - a. salaries of judges
   - b. Old Age Security benefits
   - c. social assistance payments to the poor
   - d. unemployment insurance benefits
   - e. the progressive income tax

2. Since 1980, the fastest-growing item of federal government spending has been:
   - a. defence spending
   - b. transfers to provinces
   - c. education
   - d. interest
   - e. veterans' benefits

3. Over the past three decades, transfer payments by the federal government have been rising as a percentage of GNP. From this, we may conclude that
   - a. transfer payments have become too large
   - b. transfer payments may or may not be too large now, but they were too small in 1955
   - c. transfer payments are still too small, since they are still rising
   - d. transfer payments will sooner or later bankrupt the government
   - e. we don't have enough information to come to any of the above conclusions

4. If a tax takes $1,000 from someone with an income of $10,000, and $2,000 from someone with an income of $50,000 that tax is
   - a. neutral
   - b. progressive
   - c. regressive
   - d. proportional
   - e. marginal

5. An excise tax is a tax
   - a. that has been cut out of the tax code
   - b. on goods such as gasoline or cigarettes
   - c. on corporate profits
   - d. on excess corporate profits
   - e. on incomes above $100,000

6. Prior to 1977, the federal government reimbursed half the total spending of each provincial government for health care and post-secondary education. This was an example of
   - a. government provision of public goods
   - b. equalization payments
   - c. unconditional federal-provincial transfers
   - d. the federal government's laissez-faire approach to economic policy
   - e. conditional federal-provincial transfers

7. Government subsidies of low-income housing are justified mainly in terms of
   - a. neutrality
   - b. externalities
   - c. increased property to revenue
   - d. stabilization
   - e. merit goods

8. A public good
   - a. creates no positive externalities
   - b. creates no negative externalities
   - c. cannot be produced by a private corporation
   - d. can be enjoyed by all, even those who do not pay for it
   - e. must be provided by the federal government if it is to be provided at all

9. Which of the following is the best example of a negative economic externality?
   - a. air pollution created by a steel mill
   - b. the rise in the price of steel when the government requires steel mills to reduce pollution
   - c. vaccinations
   - d. an increase in the international price of oil
   - e. an increase in the international price of grain

10. According to the "neutrality" principle of taxation,

a. taxes should be imposed only on goods about which people are neutral (that is, neither very enthusiastic nor very negative)
b. taxes should be imposed on tobacco and alcoholic beverages
c. taxes should be designed to disturb market forces as little as possible
d. income taxes should be progressive
e. the government should rely on the corporate profits tax, not the personal income tax

11. Which of the following is designed specifically to be *non*-neutral?

a. a tax on polluters
b. a proportional income tax
c. a general sales tax of 5%
d. all of the above
e. none of the above

12. The presence of externalities means that

a. a tax system that seems to be progressive will in fact be regressive
b. a tax system that seems to be regressive will in fact be progressive
c. the market system will generally not work as well as it would in the absence of externalities
d. the rich will generally get richer, and the poor poorer
e. the federal government will find it much more difficult to balance its budget

13. Which of the following is the best example of a "flat" tax?

a. a tax that collects the same number of dollars from everyone
b. a proportional income tax
c. a progressive income tax
d. a regressive income tax
e. an excise tax on beer and wine

EXERCISES

1. The table below shows two different taxes—tax A and tax B. For each of these taxes, fill in the column showing the average rate at various incomes, and the marginal tax rate. Also note on the last line whether the tax is proportional, regressive, or progressive.

2. Suppose that a family with an income of $35,000 pays $5,000 in interest on its mortgage, and is allowed to deduct that $5,000 from its taxable income. As a result, taxable income falls from $35,000 to $30,000. This would mean a reduction of $ _____ in tax payable under tax A, and a reduction of $ _____ under tax B. Thus, the higher the marginal tax rate, the [greater, less] the tax saving from a deduction.

	Tax A		Tax B	
Income	Average rate	Marginal rate	Average rate	Marginal rate
$10,000	$1,500__%		$1,500__%	
		__%		__%
$20,000	3,000__%		3,500__%	
		__%		__%
$30,000	4,500__%		6,000__%	
		__%		__%
$40,000	6,000__%		9,000__%	
Type of tax: __________				

ESSAY QUESTIONS

1. What would be the advantages and disadvantages of living in a country like Sweden, where the proportion of national output going to the government is larger than in Canada?

2. What would it be like to live in Canada if there were no federal government regulatory agencies? Describe what would happen if specific agencies, such as Environment Canada, Health and Welfare Canada, the CTC, and the CRTC were absent. What do you think the effects were when the government abolished the Foreign Investment Review Agency (FIRA) in 1986?

3. In most communities, the following services are provided by the local government: (a) police, (b) elementary education, (c) street cleaning, (d) garbage collection. Could these be provided by private enterprise? Is there any advantage to having the government provide them? Would there be any advantage to having the private sector provide them?

4. What externalities are created when individuals (a) drive on a highway, (b) mow their lawns, and (c) smoke in a theatre? In each case, do you think that the government should do anything to encourage or discourage the activity? If so, what, and why? If not, why not?

ANSWERS

Important Terms: **1** f **2** k **3** b **4** a **5** m **6** i **7** c **8** l **9** e **10** g **11** h **12** d

True-False: **1** T **2** F **3** T **4** F **5** F **6** F **7** F **8** T

Multiple Choice: **1** a **2** d **3** e **4** c **5** b **6** e **7** e **8** d **9** a **10** c **11** a **12** c **13** b

Exercises: **1.** Tax A. Average rates: 15%, 15%, 15%, 15%. Marginal rates: 15%, 15%, 15%. The tax is proportional. Tax B. Average rates: 15%, 17.5%, 20%, 22.5%. Marginal rates: 20%, 25%, 30%. The tax is progressive. **2.** $750, $1,500, greater.

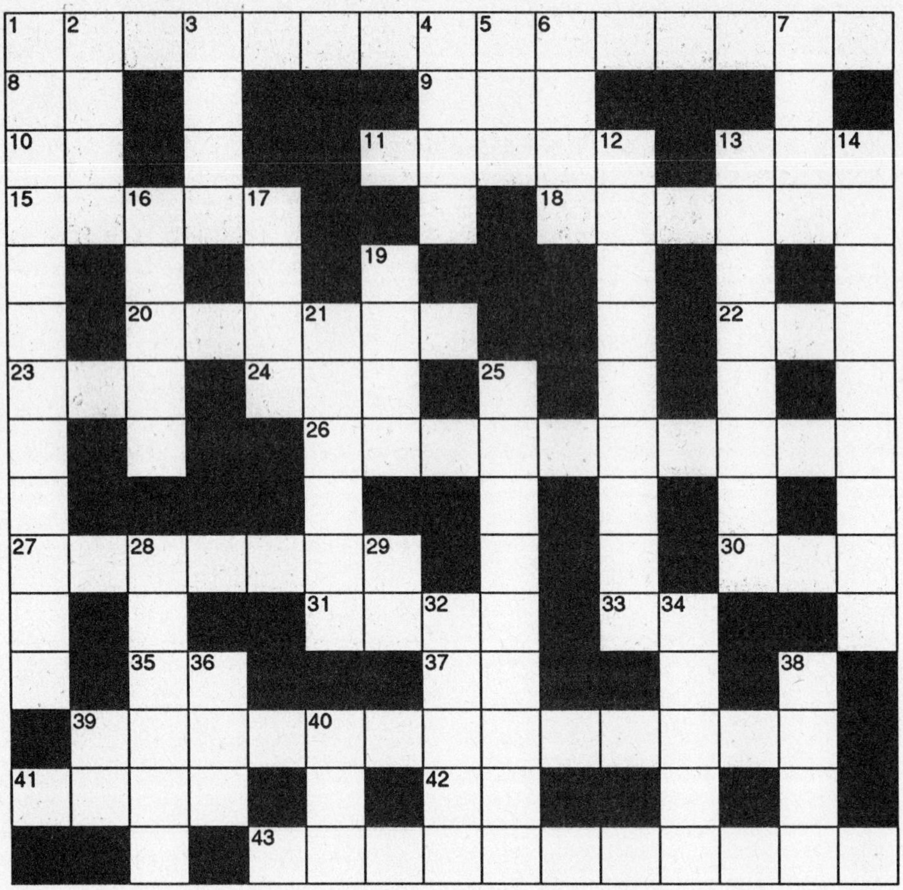

Across

1. It's important to distinguish between these two tax rates (2 words).
8. prefix meaning "two"
9. era
10. preposition
11. desirable characteristic for tax base
13. me (French)
15. what a completely flat tax would do to tax-rate schedule
18. At the end of April, you have to file your tax ___________.
20. The United States imposed restrictions on this important Canadian export in 1986.
22. here (French)
23. second person pronoun
24. long time period
26. generally considered an undesirable kind of tax
27. keeps bridges and airplanes floating
30. thus (Latin)
31. When a dog is happy, its tail does this.
33. undertake
35. preposition
37. preposition meaning "belonging to"
39. The federal government had a $30 billion one in the mid-1980s. (2 words)
41. burns you up
42. goes with "either"
43. The federal and provincial governments have this kind of arrangement in health care and post-secondary education.

Down

1. one guide in designing taxes (3 words)
2. where grapes grow
3. what marginal tax rates do as your income increases
4. His theories shook the world.
5. before this time
6. end of the line
7. love (Latin)
12. what the economy was in the 1930s
13. when the crew takes over the ship (plural)
14. tells you who really pays a tax
16. worth
17. ineffectual, or incapable of movement
19. determines what characteristics you inherit from your parents
21. what people do at a bank
25. government payments without quid pro quo
28. the great outdoors
29. can't get it (abbrev.) or it's irrelevant (abbrev.)
32. They were waiting for him in Beckett's absurdist play
34. happen
36. poem of praise
38. famous upper-class school in Britain
39. prefix meaning "two"
40. sometimes inflated when you don't know your limitations

Chapter 6

BUSINESS ORGANIZATION AND FINANCE

MAJOR PURPOSES

The major purposes of this chapter are (1) to explain the three forms of business organization, (2) to describe how businesses finance expansion, (3) to explain the differences between a balance sheet and an income statement, and (4) to describe some of the problems that arise in the financial markets.

For big business, the major legal form is the corporation. This provides owners with the protection of *limited liability*. Shareholders are not responsible for the debts of their business, and can lose only the funds they have already spent to acquire a share of the ownership. Limited liability is one othe reasons why there is such a broad market in common stock, and why it is relatively easy for corporations to raise funds by selling additional stock.

One of the major functions of the markets for financial capital—such as the stock market and the bond market—is to provide funds to new and expanding companies. People have an incentive to buy the securities of rapidly growing, profitable, and financially sound corporations. The capital markets do a fairly good job of providing resources to the most profitable and promising corporations.

LEARNING OBJECTIVES

After you have studied this chapter in the textbook and study guide, you should be able to

- Describe the three major types of business organization and explain the major advantages and disadvantages of each
- Describe the ways in which a corporation can raise funds for expansion
- Explain what a balance sheet is and how it differs from an income statement
- Explain the advantages and disadvantages to the corporation of issuing common stock rather than bonds
- Explain the advantages and disadvantages of buying common stock rather than bonds
- Explain leverage and its relation to the risks faced by corporations and bondholders
- Describe the major motives of the people who buy securities and the major motives of those who issue securities
- Describe two major problems in the financial markets

HIGHLIGHTS OF THE CHAPTER

There are three major types of business organization:

1. The *single proprietorship,* owned and operated by an individual. Many small businesses are single proprietorships.

2. The *partnership,* which is quite similar to the single proprietorship, except that there are several owners and operators. With a few exceptions, partnerships are quite small businesses.

3. The *corporation,* which is the standard organization for large businesses. The corporation provides *limited liability* to the shareholder-owners. This is a great advantage, because the shareholder-owners don't have to worry about taking responsibility for the obligations undertaken by any of the other owners. As a result, a large, well-known corporation may be able to sell shares of common stock (that is, shares of ownership) to a wide variety of people. Thus, the corporate form of organization has the advantage of making it *easier to finance growth.* A third advantage of the corporation is that it has *automatic continuity.* When one of the shareholder-owners dies, the stock goes to the heirs. The corporation continues uninterrupted. Because of the protection offered by limited liability, an heir need not be concerned about accepting the stock.

Many small corporations are not well known, and the desire to raise funds is not the reason for incorporation. For many small businesses, tax considerations are important in the decision whether to incorporate or not. The income of a proprietorship or partnership is taxed as the personal income of the owner or owners. Corporate profits are taxed differently; they are subject to a corporation income tax. For small corporations, the corporate tax rate is relatively low, and may be substantially less than the rate at which the owner's personal income is taxed. Thus, there may be an advantage in incorporating, especially if most of the corporation's profits will be reinvested rather than paid out to the owners as dividends. (Profits paid out as dividends are taxed as part of the owners' personal income, just like the profits from a proprietorship or a partnership. However, under Canadian law, shareholders who receive dividends from Canadian corporations are given credit for the corporate income tax that has already been levied on the profits from which the dividends are paid.)

The corporation can raise funds by (1) issuing additional shares of *common stock,* each representing a fraction of the ownership of the corporation; (2) *selling bonds,* which is a way of borrowing money for a long period of time from the person who buys the bond; (3) issuing shorter-term debt, such as *notes* or *commercial paper*; (4) *borrowing from a bank* or other financial institution; and (5) issuing securities that are between common stock and standard bonds—specifically, shares of *preferred stock* and *convertible bonds.* Dividends on preferred shares are somewhat more certain than dividends on common shares; the preferred dividends must be paid if any dividends at all are to be paid on the common shares. Convertible bonds can be exchanged for common shares, and thus are a way of participating in the bright future of a corporation.

All of these securities can normally be bought and sold in markets. For example, a person who owns stock or bonds of a corporation may sell them to anyone who is willing to buy. Transactions in such securities are usually facilitated by *investment dealers.* Similarly, government bonds and shorter-term securities may be sold by the present holder to someone else. Thus, if the government or corporation issues long-term bonds, it has a guaranteed use of the funds for a long period of time. But the buyer is not necessarily tying up funds for a similar long period: the bond may be sold at any time. Thus, the financial markets provide the bondholders with *liquidity.*

The prices of securities in the financial markets are determined by supply and demand; the prices of common stock, bonds, and other financial assets can fluctuate as conditions change. The major determinant of the price of common stock is the *expected profitability* of the corporation. The person who buys the share will participate in the good fortune (if any) of the corporation. Even though bonds provide a fixed contract—for, say, $12,000 in interest payments each year over 20 years—they may nevertheless fluctuate in value. In the marketplace, people have the choice of buying new bonds or old bonds. If a new bond will pay more interest—say $14,000—then the amount people will be willing to pay for the old bond (with $12,000 interest per year) will go down.

Although interest payments on bonds are set by the bond contract, the payment of interest is not guaranteed. If the issuing corporation runs into trouble, it may not have the funds to pay interest. In this case, the bondholder has the legal right to sue, and may push the corporation into the bankruptcy courts. Even then, there is no assurance that the bondholder will be paid, because the corporation may simply not have enough assets to cover its liabilities. If a corporation is in difficulty, there may be an agreement among bondholders and other creditors to give it more time to pay, and perhaps take smaller interest payments.

Because bondholders are not guaranteed payment, they must be concerned with the prospects that the issuer will in fact be able to make interest payments on schedule and repay the principal when the bond reaches maturity. If a corporation is shaky, people will avoid its bonds unless they offer an extra amount of interest to compensate for the risk—the so-called risk premium. Because of differences in risk, some bonds offer substantially higher interest rates than others.

In deciding which securities to buy, potential bond buyers weigh a number of factors: *risk, return, liquidity,* and *taxes.* Issuers of securities also have a number of factors to consider. One of their most important decisions is whether they will issue additional common stock or additional bonds. If they issue stock, they will be taking on additional part-owners. Thus, they will have to share their future profits among more people. If they issue additional bonds, they will be increasing the *leverage* of the corporation. If the business does well, the owners will only have to pay the interest; they will not have to share their profits with the bondholders. But they will be legally committed to pay the interest, whether the firm does well or not. Thus, leverage can add to the risks that the company may fail in the future.

The major function of financial markets is to allocate the saving of society to the various investment projects that can be undertaken. On the whole, the financial markets do a fairly good job in allocating funds among various projects. People who buy bonds or stock have an incentive to put their funds into the corporation with the best prospects. Nevertheless, major mistakes are made. Some mistakes are inevitable in a risky and uncertain world—the best buggy whip manufacturer in Canada became obsolete with the invention of the motor car. But some mistakes can be avoided if people have more information. This is where the provincial governments' securities commissions play an important role. They require corporations to disclose their financial condition. By enforcing a reasonable rule—that information be disclosed—government can help the private capital markets work better.

IMPORTANT TERMS: MATCH THE COLUMNS

Match each term in the first column with the corresponding phrase in the second column. But before you do so, write your own definition of each term in the first column.

_____	**1.** proprietorship	**a.** long-term debt
_____	**2.** limited liability	**b.** example of financial intermediary
_____	**3.** bond	**c.** debt divided by net worth
_____	**4.** commercial paper	**d.** way of allocating cost of capital to various years
_____	**5.** net worth	**e.** unincorporated enterprise
_____	**6.** leverage	**f.** assets minus liabilities
_____	**7.** book value	**g.** a short-term debt
_____	**8.** depreciation	**h.** chief advantage of forming a corporation
_____	**9.** trust companies	**i.** net worth divided by number of shares

TRUE-FALSE

T F **1.** Partnerships have "unlimited liability." This means that there is no limit to the amount of bonds and other liabilities they can issue.

T F **2.** Corporation profits paid out to shareholders as dividends are subject to double taxation.

T F **3.** A partnership with two partners (A and B) has its income taxed twice—once as the income of A, and once as the income of B.

T F **4.** A corporation's balance sheet shows its assets and liabilities at a *point* in time.

T F **5.** A corporation's income statement shows its sales and costs over a *period* of time.

T F **6.** A firm's net worth is the amount that shareholders originally paid into the corporation when they bought their shares.

T F **7.** A government bond is generally more liquid than a house.

T F **8.** Issuing additional common stock increases the leverage of a corporation.

T F **9.** Businesses that increase their leverage usually do so to reduce the risk of bankruptcy.

T F **10.** If a corporation buys machinery with the proceeds from newly issued bonds, the issuing of the bonds does not increase the corporation's leverage.

MULTIPLE CHOICE

1. In a standard partnership, each partner
- **a.** must pay personal income tax on all the income of the partnership
- **b.** has unlimited liability, but only for the debts which he or she undertook personally
- **c.** has unlimited liability, but only for his or her share of the debts of the corporation
- **d.** has unlimited liability for all the debts of the partnership, including those undertaken by the other partners
- **e.** can lose the amount of his or her initial investment, but no more

2. Corporations provide "limited liability." This means that
- **a.** the shareholder-owners are not personally liable for debts of the corporation
- **b.** the corporation is not legally liable for debts of more than one-half its net worth in any one year
- **c.** officers of the corporation cannot be held legally liable for any fraudulent activities of the corporation
- **d.** the corporation is legally required to make contributions to the pension fund only in the years when it is profitable

e. corporations do not have to pay dividends if they are unprofitable

3. Under Canadian law, shareholders who receive dividend income from a Canadian corporation
   a. receive a tax credit representing their share of the income tax already paid by the corporation
   b. do not have to include the dividend income in their taxable income
   c. are taxed at double the rate on income from a partnership
   d. must report their dividend income to a provincial securities commission
   e. receive a tax credit that reduces the corporation's income tax the following year

4. In the balance sheet of a corporation,
   a. net worth = assets + liabilities
   b. assets = net worth + liabilities
   c. assets = liabilities – net worth
   d. assets = liabilities + net worth
   e. profits = sales – depreciation

5. The book value of a share of common stock is equal to
   a. the value of the share when it was initially issued by the corporation
   b. today's price of a share on the books of investment dealers
   c. the market price of a share when the books were closed at the end of the most recent fiscal year
   d. retained earnings of the company divided by the number of shares outstanding
   e. net worth of the company divided by the number of shares outstanding

6. What appears on the income statement of a corporation?
   a. depreciation
   b. income before taxes
   c. income after taxes
   d. all of the above
   e. none of the above

7. If depreciation is "accelerated," this means that
   a. machines are wearing out more quickly
   b. technological change is occurring more quickly
   c. firms speed up the rate at which they depreciate capital
   d. taxes must be paid more quickly on the depreciated value of plant
   e. taxes must be paid more quickly on the depreciated value of equipment

8. Financial intermediaries
   a. offer liquidity to creditors
   b. issue only long-term securities, such as bonds
   c. hold only long-term securities, such as bonds
   d. hold mainly the warrants of other corporations
   e. require unlimited liability of their creditors

9. Those who underwrite the shares of a corporation are called
   a. investment dealers
   b. central banks
   c. savings and loan associations
   d. brokers
   e. buccaneers

10. Financial leverage is measured by
   a. the trend in net worth, measured in dollars
   b. the trend in debt, measured in dollars
   c. the trend in debt, after adjustment for inflation
   d. the ratio of debt to net worth
   e. the price-earnings ratio

11. Whenever a corporation issues bonds, rather than raising funds by issuing new common stock, it
   a. increases its leverage
   b. decreases its leverage
   c. decreases the risks faced by shareholders
   d. decreases the risks faced by bondholders
   e. increases the tax it has to pay
   d. decreases the risks faced by bondholders
   e. increases the tax it has to pay

12. Interest rates on bonds of private corporations are normally several percentage points higher than the rates on Government of Canada bonds of comparable term to maturity. The difference represents
   a. a tax premium
   b. a tax risk
   c. an inflation premium
   d. an incentive for risky businesses to borrow
   e. a sign of malfunctioning capital markets

13. A commitment by a bank to lend up to a predetermined limit to a specific customer is known as a
   a. warrant
   b. stock option
   c. commercial paper
   d. line of credit
   e. illegal overdraft

14. Interest rates on government bonds are most likely to rise during
   a. recessions
   b. depressions
   c. deflationary periods
   d. periods of rising inflation
   e. the period just prior to income tax time in April of each year

15. A major purpose of the Ontario Securities Commission is to require corporations to
   a. issue stock periodically so as to decrease leverage
   b. issue stock periodically so as to increase leverage
   c. issue bonds periodically so as to increase leverage
   d. issue bonds periodically so as to provide bondholders with a stable source of income
   e. make information available to the public

EXERCISES

1. The numbers below apply to XYZ Corporation.

a. Prepare a balance sheet for the XYZ Corporation, using Table 6-1. There are no assets or liabilities other than those listed below. However, *not* all items should be included in the balance sheet. *Use only the ones that belong.*

b. Some of the numbers not used in part (a) belong in the income statement. Use them to complete the income statement in Table 6-2. This corporation pays 30% of its income in taxes.

c. The book value of each share of stock of the XYZ Corporation is [$15, $19.50, $20, $34.50].

2. The owners of a corporation are called __________. Compared with the owners of a partnership, they have a major advantage: __________. The corporation can raise funds by issuing two types of stock, namely: __________. If it issues __________ instead, its leverage will increase. Leverage is disadvantageous, in that it increases __________.

The profits of a corporation are equal to __________ less __________. To find net profit, we also have to subtract __________.

Accounts payable	$ 800,000
Sales during year	$ 1,900,000
Accounts receivable	$ 900,000
Wages paid during year	$ 850,000
Long-term bonds of XYZ Corp. outstanding	$ 1,000,000
Plant and equipment (current value, after depreciation)	$ 2,000,000
Inventory on hand	$ 300,000
Revenue from service contracts	$ 250,000
Bank deposits and other cash items	$ 200,000
Depreciation during year	$ 300,000
Net interest paid	$ 150,000
Other cost	$ 250,000
Accrued liabilities	$ 150,000
Number of shares of common stock outstanding	$ 100,000
Holdings of notes issued by ABC Corp.	$ 50,000

Table 6-1
BALANCE SHEET (THOUSANDS OF DOLLARS)

Assets	Liabilities
	Net worth
Total assets =	Total liabilities and net worth =

Table 6-2
INCOME STATEMENT (THOUSANDS OF DOLLARS)

1. Revenues:

   Total:

2. Costs:

   Total:

3. Profit before taxes:
4. Tax:
5. Net profit:
6. Addendum: profit per share:

ESSAY QUESTIONS

1. To find net worth, what do we subtract from assets? Is it possible for the net worth of a corporation to be negative? If so, what could we say about the book value of each share of common stock of a corporation with a negative net worth? Would it ever pay to buy shares in a firm with a negative net worth? If it is not possible, explain why not. Specifically, explain what will happen as the net worth of the corporation shrinks toward zero.

2. Suppose that you are in charge of finance for a large corporation. How would you go about raising funds (a) to finance the construction of a large plant with an expected useful life of 25 years, (b) to acquire larger inventories of raw materials, and (c) to meet a temporary shortage of cash resulting from a decision by your customers to wait an extra month before paying their bills? Under what circumstances might you issue new common stock rather than borrow? Might it ever be a good idea to cut the dividend by, say, 50% to pay for any of the above? Explain why or why not. Might it ever be a good idea to cut the dividend for other reasons? Explain.

ANSWERS

Important Terms: **1** e **2** h **3** a **4** g **5** f **6** c **7** i **8** d **9** b
True-False: **1** F **2** T **3** F **4** T **5** T **6** F **7** T **8** F **9** F **10** F
Multiple Choice: **1** d **2** a **3** a **4** d **5** e **6** d **7** c **8** a **9** a **10** d **11** a **12** b **13** d **14** d **15** e
Exercises:

1a. Table 6-1 completed
BALANCE SHEET (THOUSANDS OF DOLLARS)

Assets		Liabilities	
Cash	$ 200	Accounts payable	$ 800
ABC Corp. notes	50	Accrued liabilities	150
Accounts receivable	900	XYZ Corp. bonds	1,000
Inventory	300	Total Liabilities	1,950
Plant and equip.	2,000	Net worth	1,500
Total assets =	3,450	Total liabilities and net worth =	3,450

1b. Table 6-2 completed
INCOME STATEMENT (THOUSANDS OF DOLLARS)

1. Revenues	
Sales	$1,900
Service contracts	250
Total:	$2,150
2. Costs:	
Wages	$ 850
Depreciation	300
Net interest	150
Other	250
Total:	$1,550
3. Profit before taxes	$ 600
4. Tax:	$ 180
5. Net profit:	$ 420
6. Addendum:	
Profit per share:	$ 4.20

1c. $15. **2.** shareholders, limited liability, common stock and preferred stock, bonds (or debt), risk, revenues, costs, taxes.

Part Two

HIGH EMPLOYMENT AND A STABLE PRICE LEVEL

Special note for students using the paperback
AN INTRODUCTION TO MICROECONOMICS

If you are using the microeconomics paperback, note that the study guide has corresponded with your book for the first six chapters. But now you should skip Chapters 7 through 19 in this study guide (the chapters on macroeconomics), and proceed to Chapter 20.

Chapter 7

MEASURING NATIONAL PRODUCT AND NATIONAL INCOME

MAJOR PURPOSE

Macroeconomics is about the overall magnitudes in the economy—total output and the average level of prices. The main purpose of this chapter is to provide an introduction to macroeconomics by explaining how total output and the average level of prices are measured. In calculating total output—or GNP—we want to count everything that is produced once, but only once. This means that there is an important problem to be avoided—the problem of double counting. This problem can be avoided by counting only final products such as computers, and excluding intermediate products such as the wire and chips that went into the computers.

Another important objective of the chapter is to draw a distinction between *nominal* (or current dollar) magnitudes and *real* (or constant dollar) magnitudes. Through time, GNP measured in dollar terms goes up rapidly. This rapid increase is the combined result of two things: (1) there is an increase in the quantity of goods and services that we are producing, and (2) the prices at which these goods and services are sold are going up. The first of these is desirable; the second is not. To see what is happening in real terms, national product accountants eliminate the effects of inflation. They do this by measuring the GNP of each year in the prices of a single base year, usually 1971.

LEARNING OBJECTIVES

After you have studied this chapter in the textbook and study guide, you should be able to

- Explain what GNP measures, and why the distinction between final products and intermediate products is important
- State the relationship between gross investment, net investment, depreciation, and the change in the stock of capital
- State the major differences between GNP and NNP, between NNP and national income, between national income and personal income, and between personal income and disposable personal income. (See Figure 7-3 in the textbook.)
- State the relationship between nominal GNP, real GNP, and the GNP deflator. That is, you should understand equation 7-6 in the textbook.
- Explain why the GNP deflator is not exactly the same as the consumer price index
- Explain why real GNP is a better measure of how we are doing than is nominal GNP
- Explain why real GNP is nevertheless not a very good way to measure how well we are doing
- Explain why it is so hard to calculate a more comprehensive measure of economic welfare
- Explain why the "underground economy" exists, why its size may have increased in recent years, and why this is of concern to economists

HIGHLIGHTS OF THE CHAPTER

This chapter explains how national product is measured, in both real and nominal terms. It also explains some of the limitations of GNP as a measure of economic welfare.

To calculate the total output of the nation, we must somehow add apples and oranges, steel and airplanes, haircuts and medical services. The only reasonable way to add up different goods and services is to add together the total amount of money spent on each of them. Thus, when we put together a measure of national product, we use *market prices* as a way of judging the comparative importance of each product. A car selling for $10,000 contributes as much to national product as do 20,000 bottles of Coca-Cola selling for 50 cents each.

When we measure national product, we want to measure everything produced in the economy (except for antisocial, illegal products). However, we have to be careful. If we took the value of all the cars produced in the economy, plus all the steel and all the tires, then we would be exaggerating our output. Why is that? The answer is, because much of the steel and many of the tires were used by car manufacturers to produce their cars. We didn't produce a car plus four tires, but the car into which the four tires went.

To avoid double counting of tires, steel, and other intermediate products, national product accountants concentrate on *final products*. These are placed in four main categories: (1) consumer expenditures for goods and services, (2) investment, (3) government purchases of goods and services, and (4) net exports (that is, exports minus imports).

Investment is perhaps the trickiest of these four to understand precisely. The first important point is that we are dealing with the production of capital goods—buildings, machines, etc.—and not what financial analysts mean by "investment." That is, we do not include financial investments—such as the purchase of common stock—in the investment category of GNP. The reason is straightforward. When individual A buys 100 shares of common stock from individual B, there is simply a transfer of ownership, not a direct increase in production. (Of course, the ability of firms to issue stock or bonds may help them to finance new factories, and these new factories are included in GNP.) Recall that this distinction between financial capital (such as stocks and bonds) and capital goods (such as factories) was made back in Chapter 2.

A second complication with investment is that it includes some intermediate products, such as steel, tires, or wheat. Specifically, it includes the *increases* in our inventories of such products. These inventory increases are something we have produced during the year. They are not included elsewhere—for example, they have not yet been used in the production of consumer goods. Thus, they have not yet been included when we count consumer goods. Therefore, they are counted here, in the investment category.

The final complication is that, when we count all the factories and machines produced during the year, we are in an important sense exaggerating what we have produced. The reason is that existing factories and machines have been wearing out and becoming obsolete during the year. What we should be measuring is not the total production of capital goods during the year, but only the *increase* in our capital stock. In other words, it would make sense to include only the *increase* in the stock of equipment, plant, and residential buildings, just as we include only the increase in the stocks of inventories.

This leads to the distinction between net investment and gross investment. *Gross investment* (I_g) is total output of plant, equipment, residential buildings, and increases in inventories. *Net investment* (I_n) is just the increase in our stock of plant, equipment, residential buildings, and inventories. The difference between the two is depreciation (Figure 7-2 in the textbook). GNP includes gross investment; NNP includes net investment. Accordingly, the difference between GNP and NNP is also depreciation (Figure 7-3 in the textbook).

Other important magnitudes—national income, personal income, and disposable personal income—are also shown in Figure 7-3. While you should not try to memorize the numbers on that figure, you should know the differences between the five major measures. You should also have a general idea of the magnitudes. For example, you should know that personal saving is less than 10% of disposable income; it is not 20% or 30%.

We have seen that market prices provide a feasible way to add various products. But when we use market prices, we run into difficulty. Today, a person can use $100 to buy food, clothing, or other things. The relative prices of food, clothing, or other things represent the relative amounts that people pay for the various goods; it is a way of measuring their relative value. But a person can't shop now out of the Sears catalogue of 1970. We should not conclude that a $10,000 car bought now is worth four times as much as the car that sold for $2,500 in 1965. Money has lost some of its value as a result of inflation.

This raises an important problem. We want to use GNP figures as one measure of how well the economy is performing, of how healthy the economy is now as compared to the way it was 5 or 10 years ago. If we simply used GNP measured at current prices, we would not know what to do with the comparison. Does a higher GNP today reflect success? Are we producing more? Or does it simply reflect our failure to prevent inflation? In practice, it is likely to reflect both.

In order to separate the undesirable increase in prices from the desirable increase in output, national product accountants calculate *constant-dollar GNP*. That is, they calculate what GNP would have been if prices had remained what they were in a single base year. Such constant-dollar or real GNP figures represent what has been happening to output over time.

Although real GNP is an important measure of the performance of the economy, it has major defects which mean that we should not concentrate single-mindedly on increasing real GNP. A lot of important things don't appear in GNP—the quality of the physical environment, the stability of the political system, and the degree of social harmony, to name but a few. Because of limits of GNP as a measure of welfare, some economists have considered the possibility of a broader measure, to include important features of our economic performance that are left out of GNP. Such attempts have not been very successful. The problems are apparently insoluble. In particular, it is not clear how leisure should be counted. Suppose we found that, over some period, real output per person had risen by 80%, while per capita leisure had risen by 20%. It is not clear what this would mean, in terms of an overall measure. Were we more than 80% better off, since we had 80% more goods and more leisure too? Or was the improvement only some average of the 80% and the 20%? The answer is not clear. The most promising approach is therefore not to search for some comprehensive single measure of welfare, but to look at a number of measures simultaneously—for example, not only real NNP, but also literacy, life expectancy, infant mortality, etc.

IMPORTANT TERMS: MATCH THE COLUMNS

Match each term in the first column with the corresponding phrase in the second column. But before you do so, write your own definition of each term in the first column.

____ **1.** GNP
____ **2.** NNP
____ **3.** national income
____ **4.** disposable income
____ **5.** depreciation
____ **6.** intermediate product
____ **7.** value added
____ **8.** deflate
____ **9.** underground economy

a. personal income – income taxes and other personal taxes
b. remove the effects of inflation from a time series
c. good intended for resale or further processing
d. NNP + depreciation
e. sales – cost of intermediate products bought from outside suppliers
f. NNP – sales taxes
g. unreported income
h. GNP - NNP
i. $C + G + I_n + X - M$

TRUE-FALSE

T F **1.** GNP can be determined by adding sales taxes to NNP.
T F **2.** The easiest way to calculate GNP is to add the sales of all corporations.
T F **3.** It is possible for net exports to be negative during a year.
T F **4.** Gross private domestic investment includes all the money spent on U.S. stock exchanges during the year, but it excludes money spent by Americans on foreign stock exchanges.
T F **5.** During the typical business cycle, investment fluctuates by a larger percentage than does GNP.
T F **6.** Suppose that there are no sales taxes in an economy. Then personal income will be the same as national income.
T F **7.** Gross investment is most likely to be small, as a fraction of GNP, during a depression.
T F **8.** If real GNP has gone up and the price index has gone up, then we can be sure that nominal GNP has gone up.

MULTIPLE CHOICE

1. In the GNP accounts, increases in inventories are
- **a.** excluded, since they are made up mostly of intermediate goods
- **b.** included as part of the consumption category, since they are made up mostly of consumer goods
- **c.** included as part of the government category, together with other miscellaneous items
- **d.** included as part of the investment category
- **e.** included as an item separate from *C*, *I* , and *G*

2. Suppose we know $C + I_g\ G$. Then, to get GNP, we should
- **a.** add depreciation
- **b.** subtract depreciation
- **c.** add the increase in inventories
- **d.** add sales taxes
- **e.** add exports and subtract imports

3. In the GNP accounts, which of the following is included as a final product?

a. a plane bought by the government
b. government expenditures to resurface roads
c. purchases of washing machines by households
d. purchases of washing machines by laundromats
e. all of the above

4. Last year, the XYZ Corporation issued $10 million in new common stock, and used $8 million of the proceeds to build a new factory. The other $2 billion was used to repay bank loans, and replenish XYZ's deposits at its banks. As a result, GNP went up by
a. the $8 million spent for the factory
b. the $10 million in new common stock
c. $12 million
d. $18 million
e. $20 million

5. Consider the following incorrect definition: National income equals the sum of wages and salaries, rent and interest, proprietors' income, net exports, and corporation profits. To make this statement correct, one item should be deleted. This item is
a. wages and salaries
b. rent and interest
c. proprietors' income
d. net exports
e. corporation profits

6. Some years ago, a U.S. government agency published a statistical report that, in 1932, gross private domestic investment in the United States was $1.0 billion, while depreciation was $7.6 billion. We may conclude that
a. net investment was larger than gross investment
b. net investment was negative; the capital stock was smaller at the end of the year than at the beginning
c. most investment was in the form of inventory accumulation
d. imports were larger than exports
e. there is something wrong with the statistics; maybe the government got gross investment and depreciation mixed up

7. Suppose that gross investment has been 10% of GNP, but then it falls to zero during the current year. In the current year
a. depreciation is the same size as net investment
b. depreciation is the same size as gross investment
c. depreciation is also zero
d. net investment is also zero
e. net investment is negative

8. Suppose that a firm sells its output for $40,000. It pays $22,000 in wages and salaries, $10,000 for material bought from other firms, $3,000 for interest on its bonds, and it has profits of $5,000. Then its value added is
a. $18,000
b. $22,000
c. $30,000
d. $35,000
e. $37,000

The next six questions are based on the following table, which shows national product in a simple economy with only trucks and consumer goods.

	Production of trucks	Price of trucks	Production of consumer goods	Price of consumer goods
1971	200	$100	1,000	$ 50
1986	250	$200	2,000	$150

9. In this simple economy, current-dollar GNP in 1971 was
a. $70,000
b. $125,00
c. $190,000
d. $350,00
e. $420,000

10. In this simple economy, current-dollar GNP in 1986 is
a. $70,000
b. $125,000
c. $190,000
d. $350,000
e. $420,000

11. Suppose that 1972 is the base year in this simple economy. Real GNP in 1986 is
a. $70,000
b. $125,000
c. $190,000
d. $350,000
e. $420,000

12. Suppose that 1971 is the base year in this simple economy. In this economy, the GNP deflator in 1986 is
a. 162.5
b. 250
c. 271
d. 280
e. 300

13. In this economy, how much did the average level of prices rise between 1971 and 1986?
a. 150%
b. 171%
c. 180%
d. 200%
e. 280%

14. In this economy, how much did real GNP rise between 1971 and 1986?
a. 52%
b. 79%
c. 152%
d. 179%
e. 204%

15. Suppose we divide current-dollar GNP for 1986 by constant-dollar GNP for 1986. Then the resulting figure is a measure of
a. inflation during 1986

b. real output during 1986
c. nominal output during 1986
d. the GNP price deflator for 1986
e. depreciation

16. If the price index has gone up and current-dollar GNP has also gone up, we know that
a. real GNP has gone up
b. real GNP has gone down
c. real GNP has stayed constant
d. we cannot tell from the facts cited whether (a), (b), or (c) has happened

17. Last year, Sam Brown spent each Saturday from May to November building a new wing on his family home. In last year's GNP
a. the full market value of the wing is included
b. the lumber, windows, paint, and other material he bought at the store were included, but the value of his labour was not
c. the full market value of the wing was included. plus an additional 10% if a Statistics Canada survey found that he actually enjoyed building the wing
d. the wing was not included at all, since it was not part of a market transaction
e. the wing was not included at all, since it was probably not as good as one built by a professional builder

18. In the official GNP statistics, pollution
a. has no effect on GNP
b. results in an addition to GNP, insofar as businesses buy pollution-control equipment
c. results in a subtraction from GNP, insofar as resources are diverted into the production of pollution-control equipment
d. results in a subtraction from GNP, equal to the estimated discomfort to those downstream and downwind
e. results in subtractions from GNP, equal to the estimated discomfort to those downstream and downwind and the estimated extra cost of medical care

EXERCISES

1. Suppose you have the following incomplete data:

C	$90
I_g	40
Wages and salaries	80
Interest and rent	10
Corporate profits (after taxes)	25
Personal taxes	35
Depreciation	5
G	45
Corporate income taxes	15
Canada Pension Plan contributions	0
Sales taxes	20
Transfer payments	20
Undistributed corporate profits	15
Proprietors income	40

Compute the following:

NI ____

NNP ____

GNP ____

$X - M$ ____

Personal income ____

Personal disposable income ____

I_n ____

2. Suppose that a country produces two goods: a consumption good and an investment good. The first two rows of Table 7-1 give the current-dollar value of the total production of the two goods. Fill in the next row indicating nominal GNP each year. The next two rows indicate the market prices of two goods each year. Fill in the next two rows giving the number of units of each good produced each year. Then fill in the final four rows, using 1971 as the base year.

Table 7-1

	1971	1980	1985
Current-dollar value of *C* production	200	450	600
Current-dollar value of *I* production	100	150	200
Nominal GNP			
Price of *C*	5	9	10
Price of *I*	20	25	40
Quantity of *C* production			
Quantity of *I* production			
Constant-dollar value of *C* production			
Constant-dollar value of *I* production			
Real GNP			
GNP deflator			

ESSAY QUESTIONS

1. In what ways does GNP overstate economic well-being? In what ways does it understate economic well-being?

2. Do the per capita NNP figures of two countries give a measure of their relative economic welfare? Explain the major deficiencies of NNP as a way of comparing welfare in different countries.

3. "Transfer payments to the poor and the elderly are not included in the *G* segment of national product. But the assistance to the poor and elderly make very important contributions to economic welfare. Therefore, transfer payments should be added, to get a better measure of GNP." Do you agree or not? Explain why or why not.

4. Suppose you buy a house in January and its value goes up by $10,000 by the end of the year. Would you consider this part of your income for the year? As part of your disposable income? Should the national income accountant include it as part of national income? Why or why not?

ANSWERS

Important Terms: **1** d **2** i **3** f **4** a **5** h **6** c **7** e **8** b **9** g
True-False: **1** F **2** F **3** T **4** F **5** T **6** F **7** T **8** T
Multiple Choice: **1** d **2** e **3** e **4** a **5** d **6** b **7** e **8** c **9** a **10** d **11** b **12** d **13** c **14** b **15** d **16** d **17** b **18** b
Exercises:

1.

NI	170
NNP	190
GNP	195
X – *M*	20
Personal income	160
Personal disposable income	125
I_n	35

2. Table 7-1 completed

	1971	1980	1985
Nominal GNP	300	600	800
Quantity of *C* production	40	50	60
Quantity of *I* production	5	6	5
Constant-dollar value of *C* production	200	250	300
Constant-dollar value of *I* production	100	120	100
Real GNP	300	370	400
GNP deflator	100	162	200

Chapter 8

FLUCTUATIONS IN ECONOMIC ACTIVITY: UNEMPLOYMENT AND INFLATION

MAJOR PURPOSE

This chapter describes the two major problems of macroeconomics—*unemployment* and *inflation.* These two problems are closely related to *economic fluctuations.* During recessions, when output is declining, fewer workers are needed by business, and the unemployment rate increases. During a rapid expansion, when spending by businesses and consumers is rising rapidly, inflation generally becomes more severe. Economic conditions were most unstable in Canada during the period between the two world wars. Between 1929 and 1933, output collapsed and the unemployment rate shot upward, remaining at high levels until the onset of World War II.

This chapter describes how the unemployment rate is calculated, and the various major types of unemployment. *Cyclical* unemployment is the result of fluctuations in overall economic activity. Reducing this type of unemployment is one of the major objectives of economic policy. *Frictional* unemployment results from the normal turnover of the labour force; some amount of frictional unemployment is inevitable. *Structural* unemployment arises when the labour force does not have the types of skills needed for available jobs, or if workers live a long distance from available jobs. This kind of unemployment is more severe than frictional unemployment. To escape structural unemployment, people must move or switch to different types of work.

Finally, this chapter describes some of the problems created by inflation. Specifically, inflation can cause an *arbitrary redistribution of wealth and income.* This effect is particularly strong when inflation is *unexpected.* When it is expected, people can take steps to protect themselves.

LEARNING OBJECTIVES

After you have studied this chapter in the textbook and study guide, you should be able to

- Describe the four phases of the business cycle
- Explain why people may disagree whether a downturn should be called a "recession" or not
- Describe the major features of the Great Depression of the 1930s
- Explain the major features of recent business cycles—for example, what happens to profits, investment, and the purchase of consumer durables during recessions
- Explain how the labour force and the unemployment rate are calculated
- Explain why the unemployment rate may understate the problem of unemployment during a recession
- Explain why the productivity of labour is adversely affected by recessions
- State Okun's law
- List the three major types of unemployment, and explain how they are different
- Explain potential GNP and the GNP gap
- Explain who loses from inflation, and who gains, and why
- Explain why unanticipated inflation creates greater problems than anticipated inflation

HIGHLIGHTS OF THE CHAPTER

The business cycle has four phases. During a *recession,* economic activity declines, and the unemployment rate increases. Economic activity reaches its low point at the *trough.* This is followed by the *expansion* phase, which ends at the upper turning point, or *peak.* The key to identifying a business cycle is to note when a recession has occurred.

While there is no universally accepted definition of a recession in Canada, most economists agree that the slowdown in the economy must be widespread and must last for at least two quarters before we should say that a recession has occurred; we should not classify every downward jiggle in the economy as a recession.

The most severe downturn in North American history occurred between 1929 and 1933, as the economy collapsed into the Great Depression. In this chapter, the main events of the Great Depression are summarized. Although the Depression may seem like ancient history by now, it remains a lesson in how badly things can go wrong. It thus provides a reason for studying macroeconomics. If things can go this badly when macroeconomics policy is mismanaged, it is important for us to have some idea of what macroeconomic policy is all about.

Between 1929 and 1933, the unemployment rate rose to almost 20%, real GNP fell by more than 30%, and the average level of prices declined by almost 20%. The production of capital equipment, buildings, and consumer durables fell particularly sharply. On the farm, the Depression caused a collapse of prices.

Recent recessions have been *much milder* than the downturn of 1929–33. Some have been very short and mild indeed—for example, the recession of early 1980. However, there has been no noticeable tendency for recessions to become progressively more mild over the past four decades. The most recent recession—that of 1981–82—was the worst in Canada since World War II.

The unemployment rate is calculated by Statistics Canada as a percentage of the labour force. The unemployed are people who are out of work who (1) are temporarily laid off, (2) are waiting to report to a new job, or (3) have been looking for work in the previous four weeks. If people without jobs do not meet one of these conditions, they are considered to be out of the labour force. The labour force is made up of those with jobs, plus those who are unemployed according to the above criteria.

During recessions, it becomes harder and harder to find a job. As a result, those out of work may become discouraged and stop looking for work. In this case, they drop out of the officially measured labour force and out of the ranks of those who are counted as unemployed. Consequently, the unemployment rate may understate the unemployment problem during recessions. Nevertheless, the unemployment rate is one important indicator of what is happening during recessions.

During recessions, as sales of products fall, businesses lay off some employees. However, they are often reluctant to lay off highly skilled workers, since these workers may take jobs elsewhere and be unavailable when sales recover. Hence, employment does not fall as much as output. There is a decline in output per worker—that is, in the productivity of labour.

As the unemployment rate increases during recessions, so does the number of those who have been unemployed for a long period of time. Not only are more people unemployed, but the hardship faced by the average unemployed person also becomes more severe. Not all groups are affected equally by unemployment. The unemployment rate for teenagers is much higher than for adults, and unemployment in the Maritime provinces is consistently higher than in the rest of Canada.

No matter how prosperous the economy becomes, it is not possible to eliminate unemployment altogether. *Frictional* unemployment represents those who are temporarily unemployed because they are looking for a better job, or because of adjustments associated with a dynamic, changing economy. In a changing economy, there is always some frictional unemployment.

Thus, if "full employment" is to be a meaningful goal, it cannot mean an unemployment rate of zero. There is some debate over the unemployment rate that should be considered full employment. During the 1960s, an unemployment rate of 3% was frequently looked on as representing full employment. Most economists now put the figure higher—at 6% or even 7%. Several explanations have been offered for the upward trend in unemployment; (1) changes in the labour force—for example, there has been an increase in the number of teenagers, who tend to have high unemployment rates; (2) increases in the minimum wage and in the number of people covered by the minimum wage (some low-skilled workers have been priced out of the market); (3) reduced pressures on unemployed workers to take jobs quickly.

Potential GNP is estimated as the GNP path along which the economy would move if there were no business cycles and a high level of employment were maintained continuously. The shortfall of actual GNP below the estimated potential is called the *GNP gap.* It gives a measure of the output lost because of recessions.

The costs of inflation are much more difficult to identify than the costs of unemployment. One reason is that high unemployment represents a clear net loss to society—the output foregone when people are idle. On the other hand, there are both winners and losers from inflation. Winners include those who have borrowed and who are able to repay with less valuable money. Losers include bondholders, who are repaid with money whose value has declined, and people whose money incomes are stable in the face of inflation. Between 1973–74 and 1978–79, the average weekly earnings of workers did not keep up with inflation, and their real earnings therefore declined.

There are ways in which people can be protected from inflation. The incomes of some people are *indexed*—that is, the money incomes are automatically increased in line with the rising index of prices. For example, Old Age Security payments to retirees are indexed. During the 1970s, labour unions responded to the rising rate of inflation by negotiating more cost-of-living adjustments in their contracts. This represented another form of indexation.

Owners of assets can try to protect themselves in another way. They can avoid bonds and acquire different assets instead—for example, common stock or real estate. When they do this, they will reduce the amount of funds flowing to the bond market. With fewer funds, interest rates will be bid up. If interest rates rise enough to compensate for inflation, people will be able to buy bonds without being penalized by inflation.

In protecting oneself, the *predictability* of inflation is of central importance. For example, if asset holders accurately anticipate inflation, they can refuse to buy bonds unless interest rates rise enough to compensate for the inflation. But suppose that they have already bought bonds on the expectation that inflation will be 3%, and it turns out to be 10%. They will not have protected themselves, and will lose from the unexpected inflation.

This is a very important point, to which we will return in later chapters. The effects on various groups in the economy are much greater if inflation is *unexpected* than if people expect it and take steps to protect themselves.

IMPORTANT TERMS: MATCH THE COLUMNS

Match each term in the first column with the corresponding phrase in the second column. But before you do so, write your own definition of each term in the first column.

J **1.** recession
E **2.** trough
G **3.** peak
A **4.** underemployed
K **5.** discouraged workers
D **6.** Okun's law
I **7.** frictional unemployment
B **8.** structural unemployment
F **9.** cyclical unemployment
C **10.** potential GNP
H **11.** GNP gap

a discouraged workers, plus those who are not kept busy because demand is low
b. to reduce this unemployment, people must move or acquire new skills
c. what output would be if the economy were at full employment
d. observation that unemployment rate moves less strongly than output during the business cycle
e. turning point at the end of a recession
f. unemployment caused by recessions
g. turning point as a recession is about to begin
h. potential output less actual output
i. unemployment associated with adjustments in a changing, dynamic economy
j. downward movement of the economy, usually lasting two quarters or more
k. those who have dropped out of the labour force because they were unable to find work

TRUE-FALSE

T (F) 1. Recessions in the Canadian economy have become consistently less and less severe over the past three decades.
T (F) 2. The official criterion used by Statistics Canada for declaring a recession is that current-dollar GNP has declined for at least two consecutive quarters.
T (F) 3. In percentage terms, investment fluctuates less than consumption, but more than total GNP, during the typical business cycle.
(T) F 4. In most Canadian recessions, there have been declines in both net exports and real imports.
(T) F 5. As the economy declines into recession, the number of people employed generally declines. Furthermore, the productivity of those still at work also generally declines.
(T) F 6. During the Great Depression, the prices of agricultural products fell much more than the prices of manufactured products.
T (F) 7. The Great Depression was confined to North America. Other countries experienced only mild recessions during the 1930s.

Enjoy the Silence · VIOLATOR. (DM)

T F 8. During the business cycle, consumer spending for nondurable goods fluctuates more than consumer spending for durable goods.

T F 9. People temporarily laid off, but waiting to be recalled, are included among the unemployed.

T F 10. During a recession, as workers are laid off, the remaining workers can use the best equipment. Therefore, productivity of those remaining at work generally increases rapidly during a recession.

T F 11. Inflation is more likely to lead to an arbitrary and unfair reshuffling of income and wealth when it is anticipated than when it is unanticipated.

MULTIPLE CHOICE

1. After the expansion phase of the business cycle, which comes next?
- **a.** recession
- **b.** depression
- **c.** peak
- **d.** trough
- **e.** upswing

2. Between the peak of 1929 and the trough of the Great Depression in 1933, real GNP fell by approximately
- **a.** 30%
- **b.** 15%
- **c.** 10%
- **d.** 5%
- **e.** 2%

3. Between the peak of 1929 and the trough of the Great Depression in 1933, the prices of farm commodities
- **a.** rose about 15%, in spite of the decline in the prices of most other goods
- **b.** remained stable, in spite of the decline in the prices of most other goods
- **c.** remained stable, in spite of the increase in the prices of most other goods
- **d.** fell about 10%, or slightly less than the average of other prices
- **e.** fell about 50%, or much more than the average of other prices

4. During the typical recession, profits
- **a.** fall by about as much as the decline in output
- **b.** fall by a much greater percentage than output falls
- **c.** fall, but by less than the fall in output
- **d.** remain approximately stable, as companies raise prices by whatever amount is needed to maintain their profits
- **e.** rise substantially, as companies raise prices

5. During the typical recession
- **a.** government spending falls more than consumption
- **b.** government spending falls more than investment
- **c.** consumption falls more than investment
- **d.** investment falls more than consumption
- **e.** consumption and investment generally increase, but at a slow rate

6. During recent decades, one sector of GNP has accounted for much of the downward movement during recessions. Recent recessions are therefore often referred to as
- **a.** export recessions
- **b.** tax recessions
- **c.** inventory recessions
- **d.** government recessions
- **e.** consumption recessions

7. Assume that the population is 20 million, the labour force is 10 million, and 9 million people are employed. Then the unemployment rate is
- **a.** 4.5%
- **b.** 5%
- **c.** 9%
- **d.** 10%
- **e.** 55%

8. Suppose a person quit a job in construction last month and has already lined up a job in a factory, to begin next week. This person is
- **a.** counted as still being employed in construction
- **b.** counted as being employed in the factory job
- **c.** frictionally unemployed
- **d.** structurally unemployed
- **e.** cyclically unemployed

9. A major objective of macroeconomic policy is to reduce
- **a.** cyclical unemployment
- **b.** frictional unemployment
- **c.** labour mobility
- **d.** product innovations
- **e.** all of the above

10. During the past three decades, the unemployment rate generally considered to represent "full employment"
- **a.** has been stable at 0%; at no other rate is there "full employment"
- **b.** has been stable, at about 4%
- **c.** has risen, from about 3% to 6% or 7%
- **d.** has fallen, from about 10% to about 4%, as the economy recovered from the Great Depression
- **e.** has fallen, from about 7% to about 4%

11. Suppose that the unemployment rate this month is 12%. Then we can conclude that
- **a.** the economy is still declining into a recession
- **b.** the economy is at the trough
- **c.** the economy has passed the trough, and is now in a recovery
- **d.** actual GNP is less than potential GNP
- **e.** potential GNP is less than actual GNP

12. During an unexpected inflation, who are the clearest gainers?
 a. employers
 b. workers
 c. foreigners
 d. bondholders
 e. those who have borrowed

13. Inflation is most likely to lead to an arbitrary reshuffling of wealth and income if it is
 a. erratic and unexpected
 b. erratic and expected
 c. predictable
 d. increasing slowly
 e. decreasing slowly

14. Who is most likely to gain from unexpected inflation?
 a. someone who bought a house before the inflation began, paying cash
 b. someone who bought a house before the inflation began, taking out a mortgage for most of the purchase price
 c. someone who sold a house before the inflation began, receiving cash
 d. someone who sold a house before the inflation began, taking most of the purchase price in the form of a mortgage
 e. someone who sold one house for cash, and used the proceeds to buy another

EXERCISES

1. During recessions, output declines. So does employment, [by even more than output, although less than output]. The relationship between changes in output and changes in unemployment is known as [Keynes' law, Okun's law]. This relationship is reflected in a [rapid rise in productivity, fall in productivity] during the typical recession.

When a recession becomes very severe, it is called a [depression, stagnation]. One occurred during the 1930s. At such times, prices fall, particularly those of [manufactured goods, agricultural commodities]. Output declines very sharply, especially the output of [manufactured goods, agricultural commodities]. There is a particularly sharp decline in the output of [consumer goods, capital goods]. At such times, [cyclical, frictional, structural] unemployment becomes very high.

2. Figure 8-1 shows fluctuations in real output. Recessions occurred during the time periods ____________ and ____________, and expansions during the periods ____________ and ____________. Peaks occurred at ____________ and ____________, while troughs occurred at ____________ and ____________.

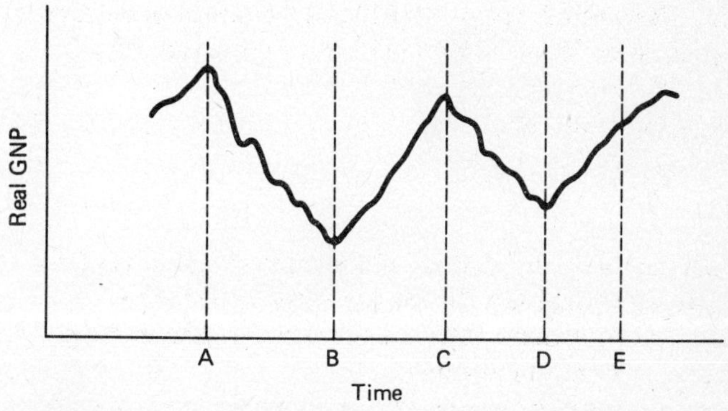

FIGURE 8-1

3. When the economy is at full employment, the unemployment rate is not zero. Rather, the full-employment rate is now generally believed to be around ____________%. The rate considered to represent full employment has [increased, decreased] in the past quarter-century. In the early 1960s, ____________% was usually identified as the full-employment rate of unemployment. Several explanations have been offered for this [increase, decrease] over the past quarter-century, specifically: (a) ____________, (b) ____________, and (c) ____________.

ESSAY QUESTIONS

1. Explain why, during a recession, (a) production of consumer durable goods decreases more than production of consumer non-durables, (b) production of capital goods decreases more than production of consumer non-durable goods, (c) output generally declines more than employment, and (d) labour productivity generally declines.

2. Explain some reasons why recessions in Canada and the United States tend to take place at about the same time.

3. Explain the conceptual difference between structural and frictional unemployment. Explain also why it may be difficult in practice to distinguish whether specific unemployed individuals are part of "structural" or "frictional" unemployment. Might it also be difficult to tell if specific individuals are part of "frictional" or "cyclical" unemployment? Why or why not?

4. Suppose that you expect inflation to rise from a present level of, say, 4%, to 10%, but nobody else does. What might you do to gain? How would you be benefitted by these actions if inflation did in fact occur? How might you lose if, contrary to your expectations, inflation declined?

5. Now suppose that you are not alone in expecting an increase in inflation, but that everybody shares your expectation. How might this affect your ability to gain from the inflation when it does occur?

ANSWERS

Important Terms: **1** j **2** e **3** g **4** a **5** k **6** d **7** i **8** b **9** f **10** c **11** h
True-False: **1** F **2** F **3** F **4** T **5** T **6** T **7** F **8** F **9** T **10** F **11** F
Multiple Choice: **1** c **2** a **3** e **4** b **5** d **6** c **7** d **8** c **9** a **10** c **11** d **12** e **13** a **14** b
Exercises: **1.** although less than output, Okun's law, fall in productivity, depression, agricultural commodities, manufactured goods, capital goods, cyclical. **2.** *AB, CD, BC, DE, A, C, B, D.* **3.** 6% or 7%, increased, 3%, increase, change in composition of labour force, increases in minimum wage and its coverage, reduced pressure on the unemployed to find jobs.

EXPLAINING UNEMPLOYMENT AND INFLATION: AGGREGATE SUPPLY AND AGGREGATE DEMAND

MAJOR PURPOSE

Chapter 8 provided an overview of macroeconomic problems—fluctuations in the overall level of production, periods of high unemployment, and the problem of inflation. The purpose of this chapter is to begin a study of *why* these macroeconomic problems arise. In explaining macroeconomic events, *aggregate supply* and *aggregate demand* are useful tools, just as supply and demand are useful in figuring out what is happening in the market for individual products such as hamburgers, shoes, or wheat.

The Great Depression of the 1930s was caused by a collapse in aggregate demand, while the milder business cycles of recent decades have been caused by more moderate fluctuations in aggregate demand. Thus, a more stable aggregate demand is the key to reducing fluctuations in output and employment.

LEARNING OBJECTIVES

After you have studied this chapter in the textbook and study guide, you should be able to

- Explain why we should not assume that aggregate demand and supply curves look like demand and supply curves for an individual product
- Draw the aggregate demand curve of classical economists, and explain why it slopes downward to the right
- Explain why classical economists drew the aggregate supply function as a vertical line
- Explain why the simple version of the Keynesian aggregate supply curve is a reversed L, and give the explanation for the horizontal section
- List the four major components of aggregate demand that Keynesians consider in detail to determine what is happening to aggregate demand as a whole
- Explain why classical economists believed that equilibrium would occur at full employment, while Keynesian economists believed that equilibrium might occur either at full employment or with large-scale unemployment
- Summarize how classical economists explained the Great Depression of the 1930s
- Summarize the three major propositions in Keynes' *General Theory,* including his major policy conclusion
- Summarize the major points of agreement between Keynesians and those in the classical tradition, and the remaining points of disagreement

HIGHLIGHTS OF THE CHAPTER

When studying the market for a specific good (such as apples or hamburgers), we use demand and supply curves. To study the overall behaviour of the economy as a whole—changes in total output and the average level of prices—we likewise use aggregate demand and aggregate supply curves.

There are major differences between demand and supply in an individual market, and aggregate demand and aggregate supply for the economy as a whole. The major difference is that when drawing a demand or supply curve for, say, hamburgers, we are looking at what happens when *only* the price of this one good changes. (Recall the *ceteris paribus* assumption—that everything else remains unchanged.) Thus, an increase in the price of hamburgers represents a change in *relative* prices; the price of hamburgers rises *relative* to the prices of other goods. Consumers and producers respond to the change in relative prices. Consumers *switch* away from hamburgers, and buy hot dogs or other products instead. Such switching is the major reason that the quantity of hamburgers is smaller when the price is higher. Similarly, producers have an *incentive to switch.* When the price of hamburgers rises, producers have an incentive to make hamburgers instead of other products. Their willingness to switch from other products, and to produce hamburgers instead, is the principal reason why the supply curve slopes upward to the right.

On the other hand, when we look at *aggregate* demand and *aggregate* supply, we are looking at the responses of buyers and sellers when the *overall* level of prices rises. In simple terms, we are looking at what happens when *all* prices rise by, say, 10%. Since all prices are rising, there is no change in *relative* prices. Thus, there is no reason for either buyers or sellers to switch as a result. Switching does *not* provide a reason for the slope of the aggregate demand or aggregate supply curve. (When foreign trade is taken into account, the possibility of switching between domestic and foreign goods *may* affect the slope of the aggregate demand curve for domestic goods. However, we disregard this complication here.)

Nevertheless, classical economists believed that the aggregate demand curve sloped downward to the right. The reason was that a fall in the average level of prices would increase the purchasing power of money. With the money in their pockets and their bank accounts, people would be able to buy more goods and services. Therefore, they would buy more.

However, classical economists did not draw the aggregate supply curve sloping upward to the right. Instead, they believed that it was vertical, at the full-employment or potential quantity of output. If, starting at full employment, all prices—including the price of raw materials and labour—were to increase by, say, 10%, then producers would have no incentive to produce more. They would get 10% more for their products, it is true, but they would have to pay 10% more for their inputs. Because they had the same incentive to produce, the total amount offered for sale would remain constant, regardless of the level of prices.

Equilibrium occurred at the intersection of aggregate demand and aggregate supply. Because they drew the aggregate supply curve as a vertical line at the full-employment output, classical economists believed that the equilibrium had to be at a position of full employment. This raised a question: How was the Depression to be explained? Classical economists believed that it was a result of disturbances that led to a temporary *disequilibrium.* The economy had moved away from its full employment equilibrium as a result of the reduction in the money stock and a fall in aggregate demand. Classical economists believed that full employment could be restored by an increase in the money stock, which would bring aggregate demand back up, or by a decrease in wages and prices, which would lead to a new equilibrium at a lower overall price level.

Keynes saw the world differently. He believed that there could be a *long-lasting equilibrium* with high unemployment. The simplest way to illustrate this is with the reversed-L aggregate supply function. In the horizontal range, prices and wages are downwardly rigid. If aggregate demand leaves the economy in this horizontal range, then an unemployment equilibrium can persist. The solution to the Depression, said Keynes, was to increase aggregate demand. The best way to get an increase would be through direct government action. The government had the responsibility, said Keynes, to increase its spending and thereby increase overall demand, leading the economy back toward full employment. (This major policy conclusion of Keynesian economics will be explained in detail in Chapter 11.)

The theoretical frameworks of both classical and Keynesian economics are still important, since they are both still used—in modified form—by present-day economists. In spite of the different approaches, there is a widespread agreement among economists on a number of central points:

1. A sharp decline in aggregate demand can cause large-scale unemployment, as it did during the Depression.

2. More moderate fluctuations in aggregate demand can cause milder business cycles and temporary periods of high unemployment.

3. If aggregate demand can be stabilized, the amplitude of business cycles can be reduced.

4. When the economy is already at full employment, any large increase in aggregate demand will cause inflation.

Nevertheless, some differences in theoretical approach and in policy conclusions remain between economists in the Keynesian tradition and those in the classical tradition. Most important are the following differences:

1. Although most economists believe that both monetary and fiscal policies are important, those in the classical tradition (monetarists) emphasize monetary policy, while those in the Keynesian tradition generally emphasize fiscal policies.

2. Keynesians believe that the government has the responsibility to *manage aggregate demand* by changing fiscal and monetary policies from time to time, in order to stabilize demand and minimize business fluctuations. Monetarists believe that active management is more likely to destabilize than to stabilize aggregate demand. They advocate a *policy rule*—the authorities should aim for a slow, steady increase in the stock of money. They believe that this will result in a slow, steady increase in aggregate demand and keep the economy at or close to full employment, without causing inflation.

IMPORTANT TERMS: MATCH THE COLUMNS

Match each term in the first column with the corresponding phrase in the second column. But before you do so, write your own definition of each term in the first column.

__D__ **1.** purchasing power of money
__G__ **2.** stickiness of prices
__K__ **3.** long run
__H__ **4.** classical aggregate supply
__B__ **5.** Keynesian aggregate supply
__J__ **6.** the classical equilibrium
__A__ **7.** cause of unemployment
__I__ **8.** monetarist
__E__ **9.** cause of inflation
__C__ **10.** Keynesian policy
__F__ **11.** monetarist policy

a. decline in aggregate demand
b. reversed L
c. active demand management
d. what a dollar will buy
e. too much aggregate demand
f. money rule
g. this accounts for the horizontal section of Keynesian aggregate supply function
h. vertical line
i. present-day classicist
j. full employment
k. in classical economics, the period when prices and wages adjust to their equilibrium levels

TRUE-FALSE

T F **1.** Even if relative prices remain stable, the aggregate demand curve can nevertheless slope downward to the right.

T F **2.** The aggregate demand curve slopes downward to the right because people switch away from services, and buy goods instead, when the average price of goods declines.

T F **3.** According to classical economists, brief recessions represented periods of disequilibrium, but the economy could be in an unemployment equilibrium during a major depression.

T F **4.** Classical economists explained the Great Depression by saying that it was the result of a fall in the money stock, plus downward stickiness of wages and prices.

T F **5.** According to classical economists, full employment could have been re-established during the 1930s if *either* of two conditions had been met: a large increase in the money stock or flexibility of wages and prices.

T F **6.** Sticky wages and prices are the reason for the horizontal section of the Keynesian aggregate supply curve.

T F **7.** Classical macroeconomists defined the long run as any period over 1 year.

T F **8.** One major shortcoming of Keynesian economics is that it assumes prices are permanently fixed. Inflation therefore cannot be explained within this theory.

T F **9.** There is general agreement among economists that very large increases in aggregate demand will lead to inflation.

T F **10.** Monetarists advocate a slow, steady increase in the money stock because they believe that the economy will work best with a slow, steady inflation.

MULTIPLE CHOICE

1. According to the classical approach, people buy more goods and services when the price level falls (*ceteris paribus*) because
- **a.** they switch among products when prices fall
- **b.** the purchasing power of their money has increased
- **c.** the purchasing power of their money has decreased
- **d.** the economy is coming out of a recession
- **e.** potential GNP has increased because of past investment

2. According to classical economists, the aggregate supply curve was
- **a.** upward sloping, like the supply curve for wheat
- **b.** downward sloping, like the supply curve for wheat
- **c.** vertical, at potential GNP
- **d.** an L
- **e.** a reversed L

3. In its simplest form, the Keynesian aggregate supply function was
- **a.** upward sloping, like the supply curve for wheat
- **b.** downward sloping, like the supply curve for wheat
- **c.** vertical, at potential GNP
- **d.** an L
- **e.** a reversed L

4. According to classical economists, when the economy was at equilibrium, then real GNP would be
- **a.** about 10% above the level in the most recent recession
- **b.** above potential GNP
- **c.** at potential GNP
- **d.** below potential GNP
- **e.** either (c) or (d), but we can't tell which without information on aggregate demand

5. According to Keynes, when the economy was at equilibrium, then real GNP would be
- **a.** about 10% above the level in the most recent recession
- **b.** above potential GNP
- **c.** at potential GNP
- **d.** below potential GNP
- **e.** either (c) or (d), but we can't tell which without information on aggregate demand

6. There is an important reason why we cannot conclude that the aggregate demand curve must slope downward to the right, just because the demand for an individual product slopes downward to the right. The reason is
- **a.** there are no "other goods" for consumers to switch from
- **b.** relative prices rather than absolute prices are on the axis
- **c.** absolute prices rather than relative prices are on the axis
- **d.** nominal prices rather than real prices are on the axis
- **e.** real prices rather than nominal prices are on the axis

7. According to classical economists, the Great Depression represented a disequilibrium caused by
- **a.** an increase in government spending, which made the economy less efficient
- **b.** a collapse in government spending
- **c.** a collapse in government spending, combined with inflation
- **d.** a fall in the quantity of money, combined with downward stickiness of prices and wages
- **e.** a collapse in government spending, combined with downward stickiness of prices and wages

8. According to classical economists, the best thing the government can do to prevent recessions and depressions is to
- **a.** cut government spending
- **b.** increase government spending
- **c.** provide a steady increase in the money stock
- **d.** promote investment
- **e.** promote imports

9. According to Keynes, the primary cause of large-scale unemployment is
- **a.** high prices
- **b.** low prices
- **c.** high exports
- **d.** low exports
- **e.** inadequate aggregate demand

10. Consider the reversed L aggregate supply function of Keynesian economics. The effects of an increase in aggregate demand will differ, depending on where the economy begins. Specifically, an increase in aggregate demand will lead to
- **a.** an increase in prices if the economy starts in the horizontal section, but an increase in output if it starts in the vertical section
- **b.** an increase in prices if the economy starts in the vertical section, but an increase in output if it starts in the horizontal section
- **c.** an increase in prices if the economy starts in the horizontal section, but a decrease in prices if it starts in the vertical section
- **d.** an increase in prices if the economy starts in the vertical section, but a decrease in prices if it starts in the horizontal section
- **e.** an increase in prices if the economy starts in the horizontal section, but a decrease in employment if it starts in the vertical section

11. According to Keynes,
- **a.** a collapse in investment demand was the primary cause of the Depression, and an increase in investment demand provided the best hope of recovery
- **b.** a collapse in government spending was the primary cause of the Depression, and an increase in government spending provided the best hope of recovery
- **c.** a collapse in investment demand was the primary cause of the Depression, but an increase in government spending provided the best hope of recovery

d. a collapse in government spending was the primary cause of the Depression, but an increase in investment demand provided the best hope of recovery

e. a collapse in government spending was the primary cause of the Depression, but an increase in saving provided the best hope of recovery

12. Shifts in aggregate demand, rather than shifts in aggregate supply, seem to be the primary reason for fluctuations in output. We come to that conclusion because declines in output are usually associated with

a. rising inflation
b. declining inflation
c. more unemployment
d. less unemployment
e. increase in government spending

13. Those in the classical and Keynesian traditions agree that

a. a decline in aggregate demand was the principal cause of the Great Depression
b. a decline in the money stock was the principal cause of the Great Depression
c. a decline in investment demand was the principal cause of the Great Depression
d. fluctuations in aggregate supply have been the major cause of fluctuations in output and employment in recent decades
e. the government now has the responsibility to manage aggregate demand actively

14. To stabilize aggregate demand and reduce the amplitude of business cycles, monetarists propose

a. active management of monetary policy
b. active management of both monetary and fiscal policies
c. active management of the government's financial accounts
d. a monetary rule, requiring the authorities to aim for a slow, steady increase in the quantity of money
e. a monetary rule, requiring the authorities to aim for a slow, steady increase in the price level

EXERCISES

1. In Figure 9-1 below, AS_1 represents the part of the aggregate supply function above point *A*. A classical economist completing this function would draw the dashed section shown as [AS_a, AS_b]. However, a Keynesian economist would be more likely to complete it with [AS_a, AS_b].

Suppose that AD_1 is the initial aggregate demand curve. Then the initial equilibrium will be at point ________, where the equilibrium quantity of output will be $0Q$________. According to [classical, Keynesian, both] economists, there will be full employment at this initial equilibrium.

Now suppose that aggregate demand collapses to AD_2. According to classical economists, the economy will move in the short run to a point such as ________. However, this point does not represent a new equilibrium, since [the economy is not at full employment, prices are below P_1]. If aggregate demand remains at AD_2, prices will [rise, fall], and the economy will move to a new equilibrium at point ________. At this new equilibrium, there will be [full employment, large-scale unemployment.]

In the face of a fall in aggregate demand from its initial AD_1 to AD_2, Keynesians see a different outcome. In the short run, the economy will move to point ________. If aggregate demand remains stable at AD_2, the long-run equilibrium will be at point ________, with output $0Q$ ________. With this output, there will be [full employment, large-scale unemployment].

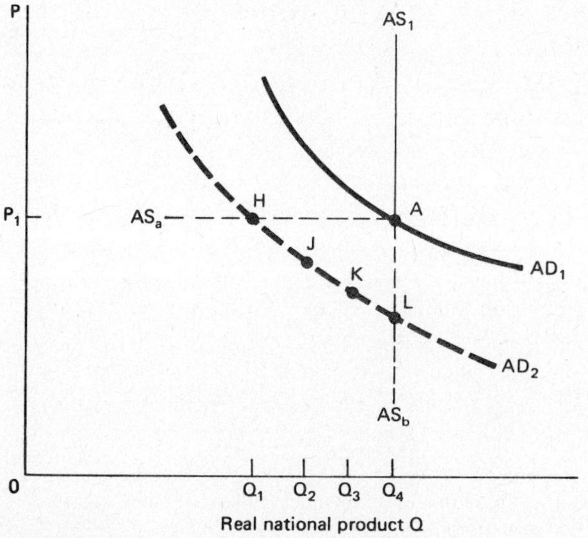

FIGURE 9-1

2. On many matters, Keynesian economists and those in the classical tradition agree. However, there are still some disagreements. Mark each of the views below with a C if it is more likely to be held by those in the classical tradition, and with a K if it is more likely to be held by Keynesians:

____ **a.** Money is by far the most important determinant of aggregate demand.

____ **b.** The government should manage aggregate demand to reduce cyclical swings in the economy.

____ **c.** Even when the unemployment rate is high, wages and prices will move down only slightly, if at all.

____ **d.** Following a rule, rather than periodically adjusting policies, is more likely to lead to a stable economy.

____ **e.** The best policy to follow is to increase the quantity of money at a slow, steady rate.

____ **f.** Large-scale unemployment represents a temporary disequilibrium.

ESSAY QUESTIONS

1. Using diagrams, explain briefly how classical economists drew the aggregate demand and aggregate supply curves. What might cause a depression? How might the economy move out of a depression and to full employment?

2. Summarize the three main points in Keynes' *General Theory*. Which points, if any, might a classical economist agree with?

ANSWERS

Important Terms: **1** d **2** g **3** k **4** h **5** b **6** j **7** a **8** i **9** e **10** c **11** f

True-False: **1** T **2** F **3** F **4** T **5** T **6** T **7** F **8** F **9** T **10** F

Multiple Choice: **1** b **2** c **3** e **4** c **5** e **6** a **7** d **8** c **9** e **10** b **11** c **12** b **13** a **14** d

Exercises: **1.** AS_b, AS_a, *A*, $0Q_4$, both, *J*, the economy is not at full employment, fall, *L*, full employment, *H*, *H*, $0Q_1$, large-scale unemployment. **2. a** C **b** K **c** K **d** C **e** C **f** C.

Across

1. Some recommend this to make the economy more stable. (2 words)
4. tree, and left over from fire
8. where you live
10. 3.14...
11. not (French)
12. builder
13. important economic objective (2 words)
17. metal
18. a fruit or a computer
19. before
20. _____ John's, Newfoundland
21. one of the three basic factors of production
22. In games of cards, it's either high or low.
23. To banks and pension funds, this is important.
25. where lawyers are called
26. He revolutionized economists' views on macroeconomics.
27. two directions (abbrev.)
28. peace (Russian)
29. long time period
31. According to Marx, capitalism would do this to the working class.
35, 38. According to classical economists, these constituted one reason why the Depression lasted so long.
39. Greek letter; used in English to refer to something very small.
40. third person singular (impersonal pronoun)
41. They pick the government.
43. what Queen Victoria did on her throne
45. the (Spanish)
46. According to Keynesians, this is the best type of policy.
48. catches the wind on a boat
49. Money has this type of power.

Down

1. encountered
2. nasty
3. major economic problem
5. the economy's performance during the Great Depression
6. Canadian character on TV
7. type of income
9. If there is too much of this, there will be inflation.
10. a football player
11. Lenin's economic program; also, Canadian government program regulating the oil and gas industry in the 1970s (abbrev.)
12. first person possessive
13. one of the two major policies for managing aggregate demand
14. big city in California (abbrev.)
15. Some advocate this for managing the economy.
16. providers of finance
22. rough or scratchy, and hard
23. exist
24. The intellectual ancestors of monetarism belonged to this school; also, type of music.
26. what the player in 10 down does
29. group of European countries (abbrev.)
30. keeps your fingers warm in winter
32. record that keeps going for a while (abbrev.)
33. ___________, ye prisoners of starvation!
34. When you look for a job, you need this.
36. helpful when you are fixing something
37. French city
42. lower part of window
44. group of people organized for play or work
47. from or of (German); also group of health care workers (abbrev.)

Chapter 10

EQUILIBRIUM WITH UNEMPLOYMENT: THE KEYNESIAN APPROACH

MAJOR PURPOSE

In Chapter 9, the main outlines of Keynesian and classical economics were presented. The purpose of this chapter is to explain the central proposition of Keynesian economics—*that the economy may reach an equilibrium with large-scale unemployment*. This happens when aggregate demand is too low to buy all the goods and services that could be produced by the economy at full employment. When aggregate demand is too low, businesses can't sell many of their products. Lacking sales, they cut back on production and lay off workers.

Aggregate demand is made up of four major components: demand by consumers, investment demand, government purchases of goods and services, and net exports. In order to present the simplest explanation, this chapter deals with an economy with only consumption and investment—that is, the government and the foreign sectors are ignored for the time being. Furthermore, investment demand is not explained here; we simply assume that investment demand exists, and see what happens when it changes. (In chapters 14 and 15, we will look at the reasons for a change in investment demand.) Thus, consumption is the only type of demand studied in detail. The main determinant of consumption is disposable income—when people have more income, they generally spend more. This has important implications for what happens when *investment* demand increases. People are put to work producing factories and machines. Their incomes rise. Therefore, they consume more. Therefore, an increase in investment demand causes—or *induces*—an increase in consumption demand, too. As a result, an increase in investment demand has a *multiplier effect*—national product goes up by a multiple of the increase in investment.

LEARNING OBJECTIVES

After you have studied this chapter in the textbook and study guide, you should be able to

- Explain the relationship between disposable income and consumer expenditures
- Explain what the MPC is, and why it is the same as the slope of the consumption function
- Explain why, when we put disposable income (or national product) on the horizontal axis, we can also measure disposable income (or national product) as the distance up to the 45° line
- Derive the saving function from the consumption function
- Explain the relationship between the MPC and the MPS
- Explain why equilibrium national product is found where the aggregate demand function cuts the 45° line
- Explain what will happen if national product is greater or less than this equilibrium quantity
- Explain why there may be large-scale unemployment at equilibrium
- Explain the difference between a leakage and an injection, and give an illustration of each
- Explain why an increase in investment has a multiplied effect on aggregate demand and national product
- Write the two equations for the multiplier in the simple economy with no taxes or international transactions
- Express the equilibrium condition for national product in three different ways, and explain why these three different statements amount to the same thing

HIGHLIGHTS OF THE CHAPTER

This chapter introduces the basic framework of Keynesian theory. Keynes' major innovation was the proposition that the economy could reach an equilibrium with large-scale unemployment. National product would not automatically move to the full-employment level; it could stay much below that level if aggregate demand were low.

As we saw in the previous chapter, there are four components of aggregate demand: consumption demand, investment demand, government expenditures for goods and services, and net exports. However, to make things simple, this chapter deals with an economy with only consumption and investment.

Consumption expenditures (C) depend on disposable income (DI). The relationship between C and DI is known as the *consumption function*. This function has three main characteristics:

1. As DI increases, so does consumption. This means that the consumption function *slopes upward*.

2. The change in $C(\Delta C)$ is less than the change in DI(ΔDI). The change in C, as a *fraction* of the change in DI (ΔDI). The change in C, as a *fraction* of the change in DI, is known as the *marginal propensity to consume* (MPC). This fraction, $\Delta C/\Delta$DI, is also the *slope* of the consumption function. Because the MPC is less than one, the slope of the consumption function is likewise less than one.

3. Below some level of DI—known as the *break-even point*—C is larger than DI. That is, people spend more than their incomes; they *dissave*. They do this by running down their assets or by borrowing.

These characteristics are illustrated by Figure 10-2 in the textbook.

In order to simplify the discussion, the consumption function is also given a fourth characteristic: it is drawn as a *straight line* in textbooks. This means that the MPC is constant. The evidence concerning consumer behaviour shown in Figure 10-1 in the textbook suggests that the MPC need not in fact be constant. Thus, we should file away in the back of our minds that we have made an assumption that is not necessarily correct.

The break-even point may be identified by drawing a 45° line on the consumption function diagram. The 45° line is equidistant from the two axes; measuring up to the 45° line gives the same number as measuring horizontally to the line. Because we measure disposable income on the horizontal axis, we may also measure disposable income in an upward direction; it is the height of the 45° line. The break-even point is the point where C = DI—that is, the point where the consumption function and the 45° line intersect.

Saving equals DI – C. (It is standard procedure to use this simple relationship, and ignore the interest paid to consumers shown in Figure 7-3 in the textbook.) Thus, a saving function can be derived directly from the consumption function. Specifically, the height of the saving function (Figure 10-3) is the vertical distance between the consumption function and the 45° line (Figure 10-2). The saving function has three main characteristics:

1. As DI increases, so does saving. This means that the saving function *slopes upward*.

2. The change in S (ΔS) is less than the change in DI(ΔDI). The change in S, as a *fraction* of the change in DI, is the *marginal propensity to save* (MPS). This fraction, $\Delta S/\Delta$DI, is also the *slope* of the saving function. Because the MPS is less than 1, the slope of the consumption function is likewise less than 1.

3. Below the *break-even point*, S is negative. That is, people *dissave*.

Because each $1 of additional disposable income is either consumed or saved, MPC + MPS = 1.

To see a simple illustration of equilibrium, we look at a simple economy in which there is no depreciation and no government. In such an economy GNP = NNP, and we can talk simply of national product, NP. Furthermore, in the absence of taxes and transfers, NP = NI = DI, and we can therefore redraw the consumption function with NP measured along the horizontal axis or up to the 45° line. To find aggregate demand (AD), we add investment demand (I*) vertically to the consumption function. Equilibrium occurs where AD = NP—that is, where the AD function cuts the 45° line. At this point, producers are able to sell what they produce. If national product were larger—say at L in Figure 10-5 in the textbook, then production would be greater than aggregate demand. Unsold goods would pile up in *undesired inventory accumulation*. In order to reduce their undesired inventories, businesses would cut back on orders from suppliers and reduce their production. Output would fall back to its equilibrium at K. At equilibrium, aggregate demand may fall below the level needed for full employment. That is, equilibrium national product K may be to the left of full-employment point F, as shown in Figure 10-5. Figure 10-5 is one of the half dozen most important diagrams in the book.

The circumstances in which there is equilibrium may be stated in three different ways, all of which amount to the same thing. Equilibrium occurs when:

1. AD = NP, as shown by the intersection of AD and the 45° NP line in Figure 10-5. At this point of intersection, there is a demand for all the goods and services produced. That is:

2. Undesired inventory accumulation equals zero, and I = I*.

3. S = I*, as shown in Figure 10-6.

If investment demand increases, the additional investment demand is added vertically to the AD function; the AD function shifts upward. As a result, national product increases. As it does so, incomes increase. People spend more. Thus, a $1 increase in investment demand leads not only to $1 more in the output of capital goods; it leads to more output of consumer goods and services, too. Overall output increases by a multiple of the $1 increase in investment. This is the important *multiplier* concept. Specifically, the multiplier is equal to $\Delta NP/\Delta I^*$. In the simple economy, this equals 1/MPS. Details on the multiplier are given in Figure 10-11 and Table 10-3 in the textbook.

IMPORTANT TERMS: MATCH THE COLUMNS

Match each term in the first column with the corresponding phrase in the second column. But before you do so, write your own definition of each term in the first column.

____ **1.** break-even point
____ **2.** marginal propensity to consume
____ **3.** marginal propensity to save
____ **4.** saving
____ **5.** equilibrium national product
____ **6.** undesired inventory accumulation
____ **7.** a leakage
____ **8.** an injection
____ **9.** multiplier

a. saving
b. NP = AD
c. 1/MPS
d. I minus I^*
e. $\Delta C/\Delta$DI
f. I^*
g. DI − C
h. C = DI
i. 1 minus MPC

TRUE-FALSE

T F **1.** The slope of the saving function = 1 − MPC.
T F **2.** At the break-even point of consumers, saving equals zero.
T F **3.** If national product is above its equilibrium, then actual investment is greater than desired investment.
T F **4.** If undesired inventory accumulation is positive, then actual national product exceeds equilibrium national product.
T F **5.** If the MPC is constant, then the MPS is equal to the MPC.
T F **6.** If the consumption function is a straight line, then the MPC is greater than 1.
T F **7.** Because all goods must be demanded if they are to be produced, the slope of the aggregate demand schedule equals 45°.
T F **8.** Businesses respond to undesired inventory accumulation by increasing their order for goods.
T F **9.** The higher the MPC, the larger the multiplier.
T F **10.** The slope of the aggregate demand function is equal to the MPS.

MULTIPLE CHOICE

1. In Keynesian theory, aggregate demand is studied as the sum of four components, including each of the items below *except one*. Which one?
- **a.** personal consumption expenditures
- **b.** personal saving
- **c.** investment demand
- **d.** government purchases of goods and services
- **e.** net exports

2. The *break-even point* in the consumption function is the point where:
- **a.** $C + I^*$ = national product
- **b.** $C + I^*$ = aggregate demand
- **c.** personal income = disposable income
- **d.** MPC = 1
- **e.** saving = 0

3. The slope of the consumption function is equal to
- **a.** the MPC
- **b.** the MPS
- **c.** the MPS + 1
- **d.** the multiplier
- **e.** 1/(the multiplier)

4. Suppose that the consumption function is a straight line. Then:
- **a.** consumption is a constant fraction of income
- **b.** saving is a constant fraction of income
- **c.** the MPC is constant
- **d.** the MPC becomes smaller as income becomes smaller
- **e.** the MPS becomes smaller as income becomes smaller

5. If the slope of the consumption function rises, then we may conclude that
- **a.** the slope of the saving function has fallen
- **b.** the marginal propensity to save has risen

c. the marginal propensity to consume has fallen
d. the multiplier has become smaller
e. undesired inventory accumulation has become larger

6. National product is at its equilibrium when
a. aggregate demand = $C + I^* + G$
b. aggregate demand = national product
c. saving = undesired inventory accumulation
d. saving = desired inventory accumulation
e. government spending = tax revenues

7. When undesired inventory accumulation equals zero
a. $S = 0$
b. $I = 0$
c. $I^* = 0$
d. government spending = tax revenues
e. national product is at its equilibrium level

8. Actual investment minus investment demand equals
a. one
b. zero
c. inventory investment
d. undesired inventory investment
e. desired inventory investment

9. Suppose that, in a simple Keynesian system, national product exceeds its equilibrium quantity. Then
a. aggregate demand exceeds national product
b. investment demand exceeds saving
c. actual investment exceeds investment demand
d. the multiplier equals 1
e. MPC = MPS − 1

10. The condition for equilibrium may be stated in three different ways—in each of the following ways *except one*. Which is the exception?
a. aggregate demand = national product
b. $I = I^*$
c. $S = I^*$
d. $S = I$

11. In the circular flow of spending
a. investment is an injection, and saving a leakage
b. saving is an injection, and investment a leakage
c. saving and investment are both leakages, and consumption is an injection
d. saving and investment are both injections, and consumption is a leakage
e. consumption and saving are both leakages, and investment is an injection

12. Consider a simple economy, with no government or international trade, and with an MPC of 0.9. According to the multiplier theory, if investment demand increases by $10 billion, equilibrium national product will rise by a multiple of the $10 billion. Specifically, equilibrium national product will rise by
a. $100 billion, made up of the original $10 billion in investment plus an additional $90 billion of investment stimulated by the initial investment
b. $100 billion, made up of the $10 billion in investment plus $90 billion in consumption as consumers move along the consumption function
c. $50 billion, made up of $10 billion in investment plus $40 billion in consumption
d. $50 billion, made up of the original $10 billion in investment plus an additional $40 billion of investment stimulated by the initial investment
e. $50 billion, made up of $10 billion in investment, $20 billion of consumption, and $20 billion of government spending for goods and services

EXERCISES

1. Figure 10-1 shows a simple economy with only two components of demand: consumption demand and investment demand. In this economy, equilibrium occurs at point ____________, with national product of ____________. At this national product, consumption is distance ____________, desired investment is distance ____________, actual investment is distance ____________, saving is distance ____________, and undesired inventory accumulation is distance ____________. Now, suppose that national product is equal to *OC*. At this national product, consumption is distance ____________, desired investment is distance ____________, actual investment is distance ____________, saving is distance ____________, and undesired inventory accumulation is distance ____________.

In this diagram, we can also tell the size of the multiplier. If, from an initial point of equilibrium, investment were to fall to zero, the equilibrium point would move to ____________. That is, when investment demand fell by distance ____________, national product would fall

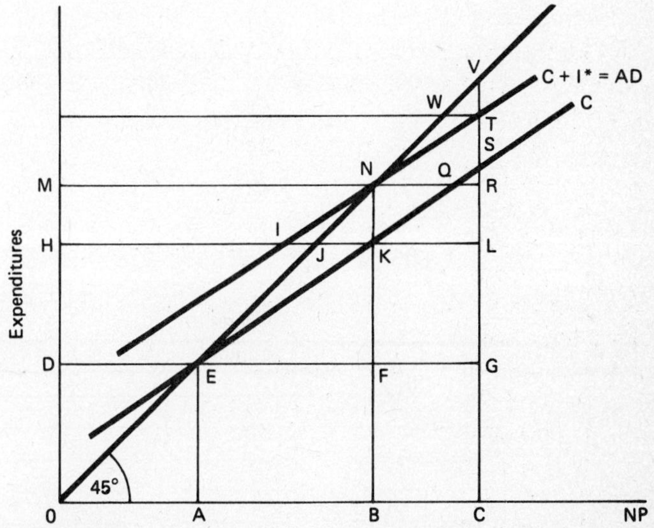

FIGURE 10-1

by distance ____________. Thus, the size of the multiplier is distance *AB* divided by distance ____________.

We can also tell the MPC in this diagram. Specifically, it is distance ____________ divided by distance *EF*.

2. Table 10-1 below represents the same sort of simple economy as the one studied in this chapter. Suppose that the MPC = 0.8. Fill in the second column, giving the level of consumption demand at each level of DI. Suppose that the demand for investment is 40. Then fill in the third column, giving the level of aggregate demand at each level of NP. Now fill in the fourth and fifth columns, giving (respectively) the amount of saving and the amount of undesired inventory investment that would occur at each level of NP. Then fill in the sixth column, giving *S* minus investment demand.

3. Suppose that the equation of the consumption function is $C = 25 + (0.75)\text{DI}$. In other words, if DI equals, say, 100, then $C = 25 + (0.75 \times 100) = 100$. Plot out the consumption function in Figure 10-2. Plot the saving function in Figure 10-3. Suppose that the demand for investment equals 25. Plot the demand for investment in Figure 10-3. Plot the aggregate demand schedule and the 45-degree line in Figure 10-2. The MPC equals ____________, the MPS equals ____________, the multiplier equals ____________, and the equilibrium level of NP equals ____________. Now, suppose that the demand for investment increases by 25; it now equals 50. Plot the new aggregate demand schedule in Figure 10-2 and the new investment demand schedule in Figure 10-3. The new equilibrium NP equals ____________. At the value of NP that used to be the equilibrium, aggregate demand is now [more, less] than NP by the amount ____________, saving is now [more, less] than the demand for investment by the amount ____________, and the level of undesired inventory investment equals ____________.

4. Suppose that the MPC equals 0.5 and that investment demand rises by 40. In the first column of Table 10-2 fill in the increase in demand at each round of spending, as in Table 10-3 in the textbook. In the second column fill in the total increase in demand (investment plus consumption) that has occurred up to and including that round. The total increase in demand in *all* the rounds (if the series is continued indefinitely) will be ____________.

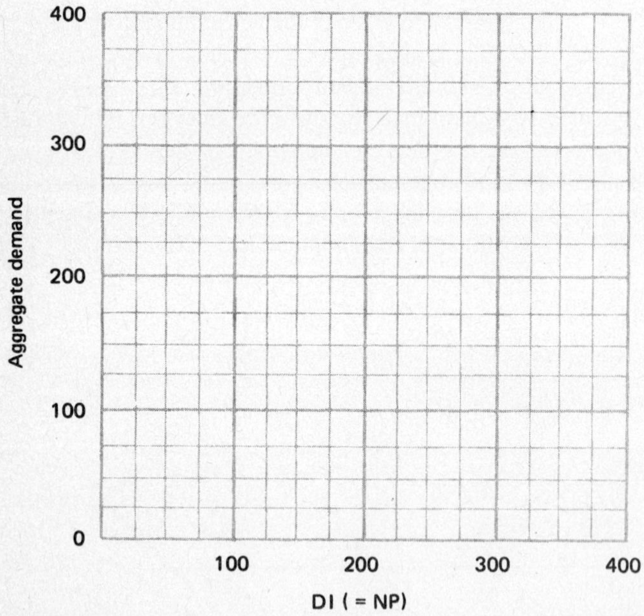

FIGURE 10-2

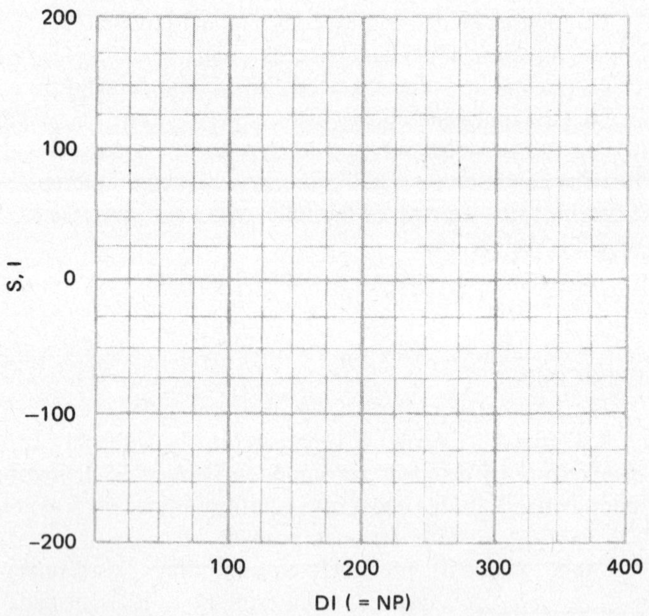

FIGURE 10-3

Table 10-1

(1) DI (= NP)	(2) *C*	(3) Aggregate demand	(4) Saving	(5) Undesired inventory investment	(6) *S* minus investment demand
0	20				
100					
200					
300					
400					
500					

Table 10-2

		(1) Change in aggregate demand	(2) Cumulative total
First round	Investment of		
Second round	Consumption of		
Third round	Consumption of		
Fourth round	Consumption of		
Fifth round	Consumption of		
Sixth round	Consumption of		
Seventh round	Consumption of		

ESSAY QUESTIONS

1. In the textbook, disposable income is the main determinant of consumption expenditures. But consumption can depend on other things, too. What other variables do you think are important, and why? (Hints: What besides disposable income determines the expenditures of a retiree in Florida? Does it make sense for a student to consume more than his or her disposable income. Why?)

2. In the textbook, the level of investment is initially assumed to be constant, and then it is assumed to change without explanation. What do you think would be the important determinants of investment? Would investment demand depend on national product? *If so,* how would this change the way in which figures 10-5 and 10-6 were drawn in the textbook? Would it make the economy more or less stable through time? *If not,* why do you think other determinants are more important than national product?

ANSWERS

Important Terms: **1** h **2** e **3** i **4** g **5** b **6** d **7** a **8** f **9** c
True-False: **1** T **2** T **3** T **4** T **5** F **6** F **7** F **8** F **9** T **10** F
Multiple Choice: **1** b **2** e **3** a **4** c **5** a **6** b **7** e **8** d **9** c **10** d **11** a **12** b
Exercises: **1** *N, OB, BK, KN, KN, KN,* zero, *CS, ST, SV, SV, TV; E, KN, AB, KN, FK.*

2. Table 10-1 completed

DI(NP)	*C*	Aggregate demand	Saving	Undesired inventory investment	*S* minus investment demand
0	20	60	– 20	– 60	– 60
100	100	140	0	– 40	– 40
200	180	220	20	– 20	– 20
300	260	300	40	0	0
400	340	380	60	20	20
500	420	460	80	40	40

3. 0.75, 0.25, 4, 200, 300, more, 25, less, 25, – 25 **4.** 800

Table 10-2 completed

	1	2
First	40	40
Second	20	60
Third	10	70
Fourth	5	75
Fifth	2.5	77.5
Sixth	1.25	78.75
Seventh	0.625	79.375

Part Three

AGGREGATE DEMAND POLICIES

Chapter 11

GOVERNMENT AND FOREIGN TRADE IN THE KEYNESIAN MODEL

MAJOR PURPOSE

The principal cause of recessions and depressions is the instability of aggregate demand. In the previous chapter, we looked at the way fluctuations in investment influence aggregate demand. In this chapter, we look at two additional influences on aggregate demand: foreign trade (exports and imports) and fiscal policy (government spending and taxes). One purpose of the chapter is to show how government spending and exports play a role analogous to investment as injections into the income stream, while taxes and imports are similar to savings in the sense that they constitute leakages from the income stream.

Since government spending and taxation are variables over which the government has direct control, they can be used by economic policymakers as tools for deliberately influencing aggregate demand so as to stabilize the economy. The second major purpose of the chapter is to explain in detail how these two fiscal policy tools can be used. Government spending for goods and services constitutes one of the components of aggregate demand, and an increase in such spending therefore increases aggregate demand directly. If, during a depression, the government builds new roads, people will be put to work building the roads and providing materials to construction companies. The initial increase in output and employment will be followed by a multiplier effect, as those engaged in roadbuilding activities find that their incomes are higher and therefore buy more consumer goods. A change in tax rates does not affect aggregate demand in the same way; taxes are not a component of demand. However, a cut in tax rates leaves the public with more disposable income, and therefore encourages consumption.

Ideally, the government should cut taxes to fight recessions and raise taxes to fight inflation, thereby stabilizing the path of demand. In practice, however, the Canadian government has had only partial success in using its fiscal policy tools.

LEARNING OBJECTIVES

After you have studied this chapter in the textbook and study guide, you should be able to

- Explain why an increase in government spending causes an increase in aggregate demand
- Explain why a cut in tax rates causes an increase in aggregate demand
- Explain why a $100 change in government spending can have a more powerful effect on aggregate demand than a $100 change in taxes
- Explain why an increase in tax rates causes the aggregate demand function to become flatter, thereby decreasing the size of the multiplier
- Explain how an increase in exports causes an increase in aggregate demand
- Explain how aggregate demand and the multiplier are influenced by the leakage into imports
- Explain and give examples of how automatic stabilizers work
- Describe how the full-employment budget is measured
- Explain why the full-employment budget (or the cyclically adjusted budget) is a better indicator of fiscal policy than the actual budget
- Explain why the government may destabilize the economy if it attempts to balance the budget every year
- Explain why a large and growing national debt can be a problem

HIGHLIGHTS OF THE CHAPTER

Government spending, like investment, is an injection into the income stream, and taxes, like saving, are a leakage. Similarly, exports of goods and services to foreign countries are an injection, and imports are a leakage. As in Chapter 10, planned injections and leakages must be equal for national product to be at its equilibrium level. In other words, G plus X plus planned I must equal I plus M plus S.

Canada's exports of goods and services, like investment spending, contribute directly to aggregate demand. Changes in exports have the same multiplied effect on national income as do changes in planned investment spending. Because foreign demand for our exports depends on economic conditions in the foreign countries, this means that economic fluctuations in other countries sometimes cause fluctuations in the Canadian economy as well, via changes in our exports. Similarly, changes in foreign countries that affect the Canadian demand for imported goods (for example, a change in the prices of foreign goods) also have an influence on our national product, because they affect the import leakage.

Like investment and exports, government spending contributes directly to aggregate demand; changes in government spending also have a multiplied effect on equilibrium national product. Changes in taxes also affect national product, but not to the same extent because they affect aggregate demand only indirectly. Any increase in taxes immediately produces a dollar-for-dollar decrease in disposable income. This, in turn, causes households to reduce consumption spending, which is one component of aggregate demand. Because the marginal propensity to consume is less than one, a one dollar increase in taxes causes the consumption function to shift down by less than one dollar. This means that if government spending and taxes are increased by equal amounts, the effects do not cancel out. Rather, national product will rise.

Because government spending and taxation are controlled by the government, they can be used deliberately to stabilize the Canadian economy; that is, the government may use *fiscal policy* as a weapon to fight unemployment and inflation.

During a depression or severe recession, aggregate demand is below full employment. If we look at the height of the aggregate demand function at the full-employment national product, we will find that it lies below the 45° line. The vertical distance between the two lines, measured at the full-employment NP, is the *recessionary gap*. This is the amount by which the aggregate demand curve should be shifted upward to get the economy to full employment. The government can eliminate a recessionary gap of, say, $10 billion by increasing its spending by that amount. If, on the other hand, aggregate demand is too high and causing inflation, an *inflationary gap* exists. Again, it can be eliminated by a change in government spending. In this case, it is appropriate for the government to cut its spending by the amount of the gap.

Government spending, like investment spending, contributes directly to aggregate demand. Furthermore, a change in government spending has the same multiplied effect on aggregate demand as do changes in investment. Once government is included in the economy, the aggregate demand function represents the vertical addition of $C + I^* + G$.

Changes in tax rates also affect national product, but not in the same direct way, because taxes are not a component of aggregate demand. However, changes in taxes affect disposable income and therefore affect consumption. For example, an increase in tax rates reduces the disposable income of the public, thereby discouraging consumption. As a result, the consumption function is lowered, and the aggregate demand function is likewise lowered. Not all changes in the amount of taxes and government spending are a result of changes in fiscal policy. For example, when national product rises, more income tax must be paid; this produces an *automatic* rise in the amount of taxes collected without any change in tax rates.

Any tax whose collections rise automatically when national income rises is an *automatic stabilizer*. Likewise, any item of government spending that falls whenever national income rises is an automatic stabilizer. Automatic stabilizers are like shock-absorbers that prevent national income from "bouncing around" too much. For example, an increase in investment demand will cause national product to increase. But the increase in taxes that automatically accompanies that increase will prevent disposable income from rising by as much as it otherwise would. This, in turn, prevents consumption expenditures from rising as much as they otherwise would, thus damping the increase in aggregate demand.

The leakage of spending into imports also tends to rise automatically when national income rises, and to fall when national income falls. The *marginal propensity to import* (MPM) is a measure of the fraction of an increase in income which leaks out as additional imports. The import leakage acts as an automatic stabilizer in the same way as do taxes. In an economy with a high tax rate and a high marginal propensity to import, the consumption function is quite flat, and this means that consumers respond weakly to a change in national product. Only a small amount of consumption is induced by a change in injections such as investment, exports, or government spending. The multiplier is small: Aggregate demand responds only weakly to changes in the level of injections.

The automatic tendency for the government deficit to rise in recessions helps stabilize the economy. However, it also introduces two important complications into fiscal policy. First, it presents a *trap* for the policymaker. If the government follows a superficially plausible strategy of trying to balance the budget every year, it will end up destabilizing the economy. As the economy swings into recession, deficits will automatically appear. If the authorities raise taxes or cut spending in an attempt to balance the budget, they will be following precisely the wrong fiscal policy; they will be depressing aggregate demand further, and adding to the depth of the recession. One of Keynes' major objectives was to warn against such blunders. He argued that it was important for fiscal policy to be aimed at *balancing the economy, not the budget.*

The second complication is the problem of *measuring* fiscal policy. Deficits *automatically* increase during a recession. Just because deficits rise during recessions, we should not conclude that the authorities are following countercyclical fiscal policies; they may be doing nothing. In order to determine what is happening to fiscal *policy,* some measure other than the actual budgetary surplus or deficit is needed. The *full-employment budget* provides such a measure. This budget gives a measure of the deficit or surplus that would occur with current tax rates and spending programs *if* the economy were at full employment. Because the full-employment budget is always measured at full employment, it does not automatically swing into deficit when the economy moves into a recession. However, the size of the deficit or surplus does change when tax rates or spending programs are changed. In brief, the full-employment budget changes when policies change; it does not change when the economy falls into recession. It therefore may be taken as a measure of fiscal policy. (A related concept, the *cyclically adjusted budget,* is sometimes also used to measure fiscal policy. It is similar to the full-employment budget in the sense that it also changes only when policy changes, not as a result of fluctuations in the economy. But it differs from the full-employment budget by measuring the deficit as it would be at the average level of cyclical unemployment, not as it would be at *full* employment.)

Keynesian economists showed how the old objectives of balancing the actual budget could lead to the wrong policies. But if the government and Parliament are not held responsible for balancing the budget, what will restrain their spending? One possibility would be to have a guideline that would require restraint, while avoiding the trap of balancing the budget every year. Suggested guidelines include: (1) balancing the full-employment budget every year; (2) balancing the full-employment budget, but only at full employment; (3) balancing the actual budget over the business cycle, with surpluses during prosperity to offset the deficits during recessions. The question of restraint has become increasingly important in recent years. Government deficits have grown rapidly, to about $30 billion per year, and large deficits will continue unless there are substantial policy changes.

When the government runs deficits, it borrows the difference between its expenditures and receipts. That is, it issues bonds or shorter-term securities. A $30 billion deficit therefore leads to a $30 billion increase in the national debt. The high deficits of recent years have made the national debt soar. A national debt is different from a personal or corporate debt, because we "owe most of it to ourselves." That is, even though we as taxpayers have to pay interest on the debt, we also receive most of the interest payments. We may not always be aware of this, because some of the interest payments are not obvious to us. For example, government bonds may be held by our pension funds, and the interest is paid into our pension funds without our necessarily being aware of the fact.

However, the national debt does raise a number of problems, particularly if it is increasing rapidly: (1) Some of the debt may *not* represent what we owe to ourselves; some government bonds may be held by foreigners. In this case, the nation is less well off. In the future, we will be taxed to make interest payments to foreign countries. (2) Even when we own our government's bonds and pay interest to ourselves, the debt is not problem-free. To pay the interest, taxes are levied. The public has an incentive to alter its behaviour to avoid the taxes. When this happens, the economy generally becomes less efficient. This decrease in efficiency is known as the *excess burden* of taxes. (3) If the national debt rises high enough, the government may find it very difficult to collect enough taxes to pay the interest. It may simply borrow more and more, to service the ever-growing debt. In other words, the debt may *grow on itself.* Again, this is an issue which has attracted much greater attention in the past few years because of the combination of rising debt and high interest rates. (4) Finally, as interest payments balloon, the government may be tempted to print money to meet these payments. If it does so to any great extent, this will add to inflationary pressures in the economy. (The government prints money through a complicated procedure. The federal government issues bonds, and the Bank of Canada prints money to buy these bonds. This is a subject that will be studied in the next few chapters.)

IMPORTANT TERMS: MATCH THE COLUMNS

Match each term in the first column with the corresponding phrase in the second column. But before you do so, write your own definition of each term in the first column.

D **1.** recessionary gap
J **2.** inflationary gap
H **3.** output gap
G **4.** injections
I **5.** leakages
L **6.** net exports
C **7.** marginal propensity to import
A **8.** deficit
E **9.** full-employment surplus
K **10.** automatic stabilizer
F **11.** policy trap
B **12.** excess burden of tax

a. the opposite of a surplus
b. the decrease in economic efficiency when people change their behaviour to reduce their taxes
c. the proportion of an increase in income that goes to buying foreign goods and services
d. vertical distance from the aggregate demand function up to the 45° line, measured at full-employment NP
e. R_{FE} - G_{FE}
f. the annually balanced budget
g. exports and government purchases of goods and services
h. full-employment NP - actual NP
i. taxes and imports
j. vertical distance from the aggregate demand function down to the 45° line, measured at full-employment NP
k. reduces the size of the multiplier and fluctuations in aggregate demand
l. the amount added to aggregate demand to account for goods and services purchased or sold by Canadian residents in foreign markets

TRUE-FALSE

T F **1.** An increase in tax rates reduces equilibrium national product.
T F **2.** An increase in government purchases of goods and services will increase aggregate demand, but an increase in transfer payments by the government will not.
T F **3.** If Americans increase their purchases of snowmobiles produced in Canada, equilibrium national product in Canada will increase by more than the increased revenue of the snowmobile producers.
T F **4.** If the marginal propensity to import increases, then the aggregate demand schedule becomes steeper and the multiplier becomes larger.
T F **5.** Lump-sum taxes constitute an automatic stabilizer.
T F **6.** An across-the-board increase in income taxes by, say, 5% has an effect similar to an increase in a lump-sum tax: It causes the consumption function to move down, but it does not change its slope.
T F **7.** An automatic stabilizer acts to stabilize the size of the government's surplus or deficit.
T F **8.** When the economy moves into a recession, the actual budget automatically moves toward deficit, but the full-employment budget does not.
T F **9.** If the government tries to balance the full-employment budget every year, it will fall into a policy trap; it will increase the severity of recessions by raising tax rates or cutting spending during recessions.
T F **10.** An increase in government spending to build roads will move both the actual budget and the full-employment budget toward deficit.
T F **11.** A decline into recession causes an increase in the deficit in the actual budget.
T F **12.** Foreign-held debt imposes no burden, because we pay foreigners with exports of goods and services, and exports make the economy stronger.

MULTIPLE CHOICE

1. To restrain aggregate demand during an inflationary boom, the appropriate fiscal policy is
- **a.** an increase in taxes and/or an increase in government spending
- **b.** an increase in taxes and/or a decrease in government spending
- **c.** a decrease in taxes and/or an increase in government spending
- **d.** a decrease in taxes and/or a decrease in government spending
- **e.** an increase in government purchases and/or an increase in transfer payments

2. The recessionary gap is
- **a.** the amount by which actual GNP falls short of equilibrium GNP
- **b.** the amount by which actual GNP falls short of full-employment GNP
- **c.** the vertical distance from the aggregate demand line to the 45° line, measured at equilibrium national product
- **d.** the vertical distance from the aggregate demand line to the 45° line, measured at full-employment national product
- **e.** the vertical distance from equilibrium national product to the aggregate demand function

3. When the economy is in equilibrium, the vertical distance between the aggregate demand function and the 45° line is equal to
- **a.** the output gap
- **b.** the recessionary gap
- **c.** investment demand
- **d.** saving
- **e.** zero

4. There is a relationship between the recessionary gap and the output gap. Specifically, the output gap is the recessionary gap
- **a.** times the multiplier
- **b.** divided by the multiplier
- **c.** times the average tax rate
- **d.** divided by the average tax rate
- **e.** minus the average tax rate

5. In a diagram with aggregate demand on the vertical axis and national product on the horizontal axis, an across-the-board cut of one-half in all income tax rates will cause the consumption function to become
- **a.** lower, with no change in slope
- **b.** lower and flatter
- **c.** lower and steeper
- **d.** higher and flatter
- **e.** higher and steeper

6. Suppose that MPC equals 0.75 and that all taxes are lump-sum taxes. If equilibrium national product is $3,000 billion and full-employment national product is $3,400 billion, then the recessionary gap is
- **a.** $100 billion
- **b.** $400 billion
- **c.** $600 billion
- **d.** $700 billion
- **e.** $1,600 billion

7. An increase in income tax rates
- **a.** makes the aggregate demand function steeper, and therefore lowers the size of the multiplier
- **b.** makes the aggregate demand function steeper, and therefore raises the size of the multiplier
- **c.** makes the aggregate demand function flatter, and therefore lowers the size of the multiplier
- **d.** makes the aggregate demand function flatter, and therefore raises the size of the multiplier
- **e.** lowers aggregate demand, but has no effect on the size of the multiplier

8. A high marginal propensity to import (MPM)
- **a.** makes the consumption function steeper than it would be with a lower MPM
- **b.** makes the multiplier larger than it would be with a lower MPM
- **c.** acts as a strong automatic stabilizer
- **d.** increases aggregate demand
- **e.** none of the above

9. Suppose that net exports are zero at the initial equilibrium national product. Suppose now that Canadian exports to foreign countries suddenly increase by $5 billion. Then
- **a.** equilibrium national product will increase by more than $5 billion
- **b.** at the new equilibrium national product, net exports will be less than $5 billion
- **c.** the aggregate demand schedule shifts upward
- **d.** at the new equilibrium, savings will be higher than before
- **e.** all of the above

10. An illustration of the term "automatic stabilizer" is provided by
- **a.** the tendency of tax collections to rise as the economy moves into a recession
- **b.** the tendency of tax collections to fall as the economy moves into a recession
- **c.** increases in tax rates as the economy moves into a recession
- **d.** decreases in tax rates as the economy moves into a recession
- **e.** public works designed to get the economy out of a depression

11. The principal purpose of the full-employment budget is to measure
- **a.** changes in fiscal policy
- **b.** the size of the deflationary gap
- **c.** the size of the inflationary gap
- **d.** the cut in taxes needed to get the economy to full employment
- **e.** the increase in taxes needed to get the economy to full employment

1-0.75= 0.25
0.25 x 400

12. The full-employment budget
- **a.** differs from the actual budget in that it does not include transfer payments
- **b.** differs from the actual budget in that it includes transfer payments, whereas the actual budget does not
- **c.** is in surplus whenever the economy falls short of full employment
- **d.** is more likely to show a surplus than is the actual budget
- **e.** is less likely to show a surplus than is the actual budget

13. A number of guidelines have been proposed as a way of exerting restraint on the government. Which of the following possible guidelines provides the greatest opportunity for an active fiscal policy aimed at reducing the amplitude of business fluctuations?
- **a.** balance the actual budget every year
- **b.** balance the full-employment budget every year
- **c.** balance the actual budget over the business cycle
- **d.** allow the government to increase spending whenever an increase in tax receipts pushes the budget into surplus
- **e.** none of the above allows an active countercyclical fiscal policy

14. In which of the following cases does the government fall into a "policy trap"?
- **a.** it cuts taxes as the economy falls into a recession, since its deficits will increase as a result
- **b.** it increases spending as the economy falls into a recession, since its deficits will increase as a result
- **c.** it increases tax rates as the economy falls into a recession, since it will depress aggregate demand
- **d.** it attempts to balance the full-employment budget every year, since this will destabilize aggregate demand
- **e.** it moves toward a full-employment deficit during recessions, since this will destabilize aggregate demand

15. The opportunity cost of government spending is
- **a.** borne entirely by future generations
- **b.** larger if the economy is at full employment than if there is large-scale unemployment
- **c.** larger if there is large-scale unemployment than if the economy is at full employment
- **d.** zero, provided that the spending is financed entirely from taxes
- **e.** always the same, regardless of the rate of unemployment and tax rates

16. The inflationary effects of deficit spending by the federal government will be greatest if the government finances the deficit by
- **a.** borrowing abroad
- **b.** borrowing from individuals
- **c.** borrowing from corporations
- **d.** borrowing from provincial governments
- **e.** printing money

EXERCISES

1. Figure 11-1 below shows a consumption function in an economy with no taxes. Its equation is $C = 200 + 0.5\text{DI}$, where units are billions of dollars and DI stands for disposable income. In the no-tax economy, DI = NP. The MPC equals ______. Now, suppose that the government imposes a *lump-sum* tax of $200 billion. When NP = $400 billion, DI = $______ billion, and *C* = $______ billion. When NP = $600 billion, DI = $______ billion, and *C* = $______ billion. Plot this consumption function in the same diagram. The new consumption function is [flatter than, steeper than, has the same slope as] the initial consumption function.

Now suppose that the lump-sum tax is eliminated, and replaced with a proportional tax: $T = (1/3)\text{DI}$. The marginal tax rate is ______. When NP = $300 billion, *T* = $______ billion, DI = $______ billion, and *C* = $______ billion. When NP = $600 billion, *T* = $______ billion, DI = $______ billion, and *C* = $______ billion. Plot this new consumption function on the same diagram. This new consumption function is [flatter than, steeper than, has the same slope as] the initial consumption function. How do you account for the different behaviour of the slope here, compared to what happened when a tax was imposed in the previous paragraph?

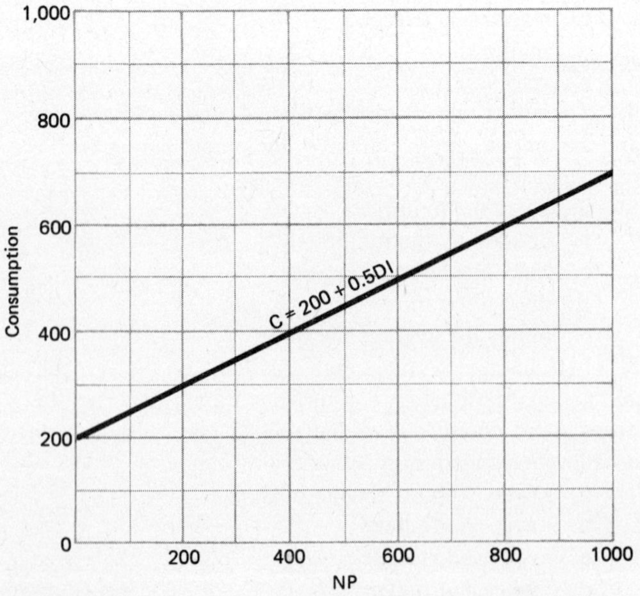

FIGURE 11-1

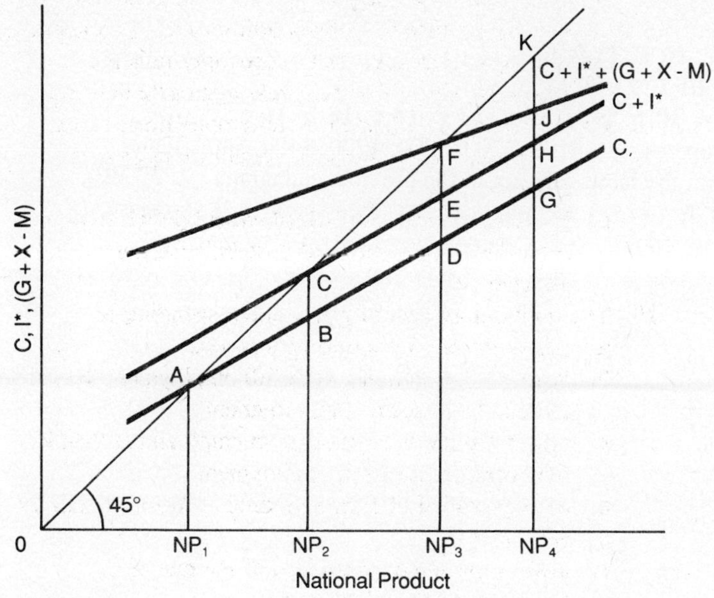

FIGURE 11-2

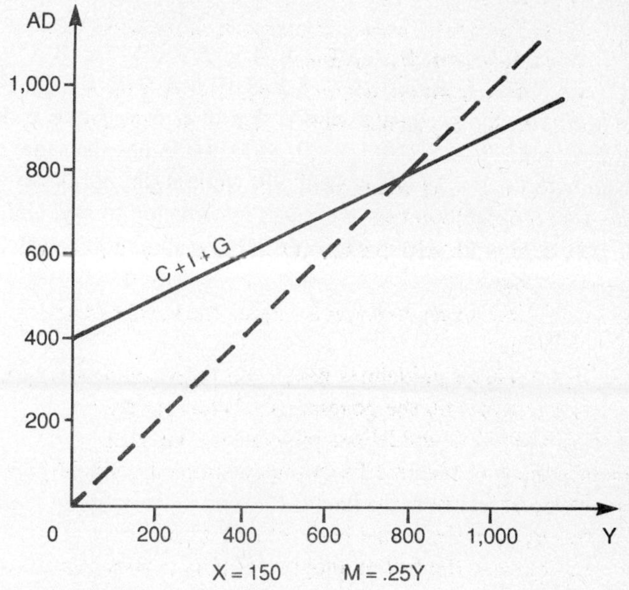

FIGURE 11-3

2. Figure 11-2 shows aggregate demand and its components. In this economy, equilibrium is at point ____________, with national product = ____________. At this equilibrium, government purchases plus net exports ($G + X - M$) amount to distance ____________, I^* = ____________, and I = ____________. *Personal saving* (S) equals [*DE*, *DF*, we don't have enough information to say].

Now, suppose that national product is at the disequilibrium amount NP_4. I^* = ____________, while I = ____________, and undesired inventory [accumulation, decumulation] = ____________.

Now, suppose that this disequilibrium quantity NP_4 represents the full-employment output. There is an [inflationary, recessionary] gap equal to distance ____________. The appropriate fiscal policy is an [increase, decrease] in government purchases of goods and services amounting to distance ____________.

3. Figure 11-3 (above) shows the aggregate demand schedule before taking into account exports and imports. You can see that if there were no exports and imports, equilibrium national product would be ____________.

Suppose now that exports are constant at 150. Imports are one-quarter of national product; that is $M = 0.25Y$. Thus the marginal propensity to import is ____________. At $Y = 0$, net exports are ____________; at $Y = 1{,}000$, net exports are ____________. Net exports are zero when national product equals ____________. Plot the aggregate demand schedule that takes net exports into account in Figure 11-3. It will cut the old aggregate demand schedule at Y = ____________. (Explain why.) From your diagram you can see that the new equilibrium national product is (approximately) ____________. At the new equilibrium, exports are [larger, smaller] than imports. Suppose full-employment national product is $Y = 1{,}000$. Then the recessionary gap is (approximately) ____________. Suppose now that government spending is increased until the recessionary gap is closed. Then net exports will become ____________. If, instead, the recessionary gap were to be eliminated by an increase in exports, exports would have to rise to ____________. At full-employment income, net exports would then be ____________.

ESSAY QUESTIONS

1. For each of the following, state whether you agree or disagree, and explain why: (a) A tax acts as an automatic stabilizer only if it makes the aggregate demand function flatter; (b) whenever the aggregate demand function becomes flatter, the multiplier is lower; and (c) automatic stabilizers reduce the size of the multiplier.

2. If the government increases transfer payments, how does this affect aggregate demand? Will a \$100 increase in transfer payments have the same effect as a \$100 million increase in government purchases of goods and services? Why or why not?

3. Critically evaluate the following statement: "Any system of unemployment insurance will be completely useless as a way of reducing business cycles. Even though the payment of benefits to the unemployed will help to raise aggregate demand during recessions, the taxes to support the system will lower aggregate demand."

ANSWERS

Important Terms: **1** d **2** j **3** h **4** g **5** i **6** l **7** c **8** a **9** e **10** k **11** f **12** b
True-False: **1** T **2** F **3** T **4** F **5** F **6** F **7** F **8** T **9** F **10** T **11** T **12** F
Multiple Choice: **1** b **2** d **3** e **4** a **5** e **6** a **7** c **8** c **9** e **10** b **11** a **12** d **13** c **14** c **15** b **16** e
Exercises: **1.** 0.5, $200, $300, $400, $400, has the same slope as, 1/3, $100, $200, $300, $200, $400, $400, flatter than, here the tax increases with NP, while it did not do so with the lump-sum tax in the previous paragraph. **2.** *F*, NP_3, *EF, DE, DE,* we don't have enough information to say, *GH, GH* + *JK,* accumulation, *JK,* recessionary, *JK,* increase, *JK.* **3.** 800, 0.25, 150, –100, 600, 600, 750, smaller, 200, –100, 350, 100

Across

4. a way to combat a depression (2 words)
7, 10. This can be a trap for fiscal policymakers.
14. type of investment
15. When government runs a deficit, the national ___________ increases.
18. no (slang)
19. what you do with disposable income that you do not spend on consumption
20. change in saving, divided by change in disposable income
23. change in equilibrium national product, divided by change in government spending for goods and services
26. precious stone
28. one of the factors of production
29. investment or government spending
32. He said an increase in real holdings of money leads to an increase in consumption. (Appendix to Chapter 10)
33. $C + I^* + G + X - M$ (2 words)
35. largest component of national product

Down

1. saving and taxes
2. huge bodies of water
3. national income + sales tax
5. He was a U.S. oil billionaire.
6. a banned insecticide
8. one (German)
9. This carries the code of life (abbrev.).
10. to ___________ or not to ___________
11. To reduce this, deficit spending may be desirable.
12. move
13. make a mistake
16. university degree
17. a popular type of entertainment (abbrev.)
21. should precede action
22. transgression
24. small picture case worn as pendant
25. remove errors from a manuscript
26. NNP + depreciation
27. Russian-made jet fighter plane
30. number (abbrev.)
31. famous student of psychology
34. Government spending can be used to fill recessionary ___________.

Chapter 12

MONEY AND THE BANKING SYSTEM

MAJOR PURPOSE

The major purpose of this chapter is to explain how the banking system creates money. The details of money creation, as set out in the various tables in this chapter, are important. A number of specific conclusions are also important: (1) Even though the banking system can create money equal to a multiple of its reserves, an individual bank cannot do so. (2) Instead, an individual bank receiving a deposit of $100 can lend only a fraction of this $100 (specifically, $100 x 0.8, if the required reserve ratio is 0.2). (3) The bank sees nothing particularly magical or peculiar about such loans, even though they result in an increase in the money stock. (4) Fractional-reserve banking developed as a natural result of the desire to make profits. (5) Fractional-reserve banks can be subject to runs. Because each bank holds reserves equal to only a fraction of its deposit liabilities, no bank can withstand an all-out run without outside help, no matter how sound the bank was originally. (6) Bank runs are not only unfortunate for the banks and individual depositors who are too late to get their funds; they also can have strong adverse effects on the economy. Because reserves are being withdrawn from the base of the monetary pyramid, bank runs cause strong downward pressures on the money stock. One of the major tasks of the monetary authorities is to prevent bank runs and instability of the monetary supply, as we shall see in Chapter 13.

LEARNING OBJECTIVES

After you have studied this chapter in the textbook and study guide, you should be able to

- Describe the three basic functions of money
- Explain the differences between M1, M1A, M2, and M3
- Explain why a bank might want to hold only fractional reserves, rather than reserves equal to 100% of its deposit liabilities
- Explain why fractional-reserve banking leads to the risk of a bank run, and why no bank can withstand a severe run without outside help
- Explain in detail (using balance sheets) how an individual bank responds to an increase in its reserves and how the overall banking system can increase money by a multiple of the increase in reserves
- State the formula for the deposit multiplier
- Give two reasons why the actual expansion of deposits is likely to be less than indicated by this formula

HIGHLIGHTS OF THE CHAPTER

This chapter introduces the basic concepts of money and banking as a background for studying monetary policy in the next chapter.

Money performs three interrelated functions:

1. It is a *medium of exchange*; that is, it is used to buy goods and services.

2. It is a *standard of value*; that is, we keep accounts, quote prices, and sign contracts in dollar terms.

3. It is a *store of value*; that is, you can hold money for future purchases rather than spending it right away.

The traditional basic definition of the money stock, M1, includes items that are used as money in everyday transactions—coins, paper currency, and demand deposits in chartered banks. More recently, the slightly broader M1A definition has been commonly used: it also includes daily interest chequable deposits and corporate notice deposits. Each of these items represents wealth to the holder; if you have $100 in your pocket, you are better off than you would be without it. In this way, money is different from a credit card, which represents a convenient way to run up debt, rather than an asset. Thus, even though credit cards (and the corresponding lines of credit) are often used to make purchases, lines of credit are not included in the money stock.

M2 includes M1A plus other notice deposits and personal term deposits in chartered banks. Although such deposits are not used directly in making purchases, they can be turned into money quickly. Thus, they can have a powerful effect on people's spending behaviour. When we are concerned about the relationship between "money" and aggregate demand, we often use the broader definition of money, M2. An even broader concept of money is M3 (which includes large term deposits and some foreign-currency deposits in the chartered banks).

Chartered banks and similar financial institutions—such as trust companies—accept deposits, using most of the proceeds to make loans. They hold reserves equal to only a fraction of their deposit liabilities. *Fractional-reserve banking* developed centuries ago, when financial institutions realized that they could cover their costs and make profits from the interest on loans. Through history, fractional-reserve banks have been plagued by the problem of runs, which have not only been dangerous for them, but have also had very disruptive effects on the economy. One conspicuous example occurred in 1932–33 when the U.S. banking system collapsed, adding to the downslide into the Depression.

Even in olden times, when there were no required reserve ratios, banks kept reserves to use as working balances and to meet unexpected withdrawals; they provided some modest protection against a run. Now, the function of reserves is not to provide protection against a run. Rather, it is to give the authorities control over the money stock. The Bank Act, which contains the legislation that governs the operations of Canada's chartered banks, requires the banks to hold reserves equivalent to specified percentages of demand and notice deposit liabilities. If the requirement specifies a ratio of say, 10%, then a $100 withdrawal from a bank deposit will reduce the required reserves by only $10. The other $90 will have to be obtained elsewhere by the bank, most likely by reducing its portfolio of loans or bonds. In other words, reserves in this case would provide only one-tenth of the funds needed to meet the withdrawal.

If there is a required reserve ratio specified by law, then the banking system as a whole can increase its deposit liabilities by as much as $1/R$ times any increase in its reserves. Tables 12-4 to 12-9 in the text explain in detail how banks do this. These tables are not repeated here, but they are of central importance in any study of the monetary system. They often appear on examinations. Students should go over them particularly carefully, together with the balance sheets in the exercises below. This idea—of the multiple expansion of bank deposits—is one of the most important and difficult in introductory economics.

The deposit multiplier, $D = 1/R$, shows the *maximum* increase in deposits that can occur when the banking system acquires additional reserves. In practice, the actual increase is likely to be much less, for two reasons. Most important is that, as people acquire more demand deposit money, they are likely to want to hold some of the additional money in the form of currency. When they make withdrawals from their banks, the reserves of banks are reduced. The second reason is that banks may hold excess reserves rather than lending all that they are permitted to lend. In recent years, excess reserves have been very small, and this second point represents only a minor complication. However, it was quite important back in the 1930s, when excess reserves were large. There were two reasons for this. Interest rates were very low, which meant that bankers didn't forego much interest when they kept excess reserves. Second, bankers were frightened to lend to businesses, since so many businesses were going bankrupt. This failure to lend was unfortunate, since more lending and more money would have promoted economic recovery. This was but one illustration of the difference between what is good for an individual or an institution, and what is good for the economy as a whole. Risky bank lending would have increased the money stock and contributed to economic recovery. But it could have meant financial suicide for any bank making risky loans. Bankers cannot be expected to commit suicide for the public good. It is up to the Bank of Canada, not up to individual banks, to see that the money stock is at the right level to keep aggregate demand close to its desired path. How the Bank of Canada does this will be studied in the next chapter.

(A second example of the conflict between what is good for the individual and what is good for the overall economy occurs during a bank run. Each individual has an incentive to be first in line. But severe bank runs can disrupt the economy.)

IMPORTANT TERMS: MATCH THE COLUMNS

Match each term in the first column with the corresponding phrase in the second column. But before you do so, write your own definition of each term in the first column.

H	**1.** currency	**a.** assets – net worth
E	**2.** M1	**b.** deposit liabilities x *R*
G	**3.** liquid assets	**c.** major reason for risk of runs
A	**4.** liabilities	**d.** actual reserves – required reserves
D	**5.** what a single bank can prudently lend	**e.** coins, paper currency, and demand deposits
B	**6.** required reserves	**f.** increase in reserves x 1/*R*
F	**7.** maximum increase in deposits	**g.** short-term government securities and savings bonds
C	**8.** fractional-reserve banking	**h.** coins and paper currency

TRUE-FALSE

T F **1.** Demand deposits held by manufacturing corporations—such as Canadian General Electric—are included in the money stock (M1).

T F **2.** Bank deposits owned by the federal government are included in the money supply, provided they are demand deposits.

T F **3.** Reserve deposits held by the Bank of Nova Scotia are included in the money stock (M1).

T F **4.** When Canadian General Electric deposits $100,000 in the Bank of Nova Scotia, the resulting deposit appears as an asset on the CGE balance sheet, and the same deposit appears as a liability on the Bank of Nova Scotia's balance sheet.

T F **5.** Fractional-reserve banking was invented by the U.S. Federal Reserve Bank.

T F **6.** In the modern Canadian banking system, most chartered bank reserves are held in the form of gold.

T F **7.** If a chartered bank receives a deposit of currency, then its actual reserves and excess reserves both increase by the same amount (specifically, by the amount of the deposit).

T F **8.** If a chartered bank receives the deposit of a cheque drawn against an account in another bank, its actual reserves and its excess reserves both increase as a consequence.

T F **9.** A bank can safely lend the amount of its excess reserves x 1/*R*.

T F **10.** Banks are more likely to hold excess reserves during a depression than during prosperity.

MULTIPLE CHOICE

1. Between 1929 and 1933, during the early part of the Great Depression,

- **a.** the quantity of money rose, but aggregate demand nonetheless collapsed
- **b.** the quantity of money fell, but prices nevertheless rose moderately
- **c.** there was hyperinflation, even though the money stock fell
- **d.** the quantity of money fell, and this contributed to the downturn
- **e.** the quantity of money increased at a slow, steady rate, as advocated by monetarists, but the Depression nevertheless occurred

2. Even though credit cards are used by many people in making purchases, they are not included in M1. A major reason is that

- **a.** credit cards are a way of going into debt, whereas the components of M1 represent assets
- **b.** credit cards had not yet been invented when money was defined
- **c.** some credit cards are issued by stores (such as Sears), whereas all money is issued by banks
- **d.** credit cards are much less liquid than M1
- **e.** credit cards don't affect consumer expenditures, whereas M1 does

3. Demand deposits are included in the money stock M1

- **a.** only if they are owned by individuals
- **b.** if they are owned by individuals or non-bank corporations (such as Bell Canada or a local car dealer)
- **c.** if they are owned by individuals, other banks, or the Bank of Canada
- **d.** if they are owned by individuals, other banks, or the federal government
- **e.** if they are owned by individuals, the Bank of Canada, or the federal government

4. Which of the following is the best example of a liquid asset?

a. real estate whose price has been rising
b. real estate whose price has been falling
c. short-term securities issued by the Government of Canada
d. long-term corporate bonds
e. shares traded on the Toronto Stock Exchange

5. The primary reason why the activities of early goldsmiths developed into "fractional-reserve banking" was the desire to

a. keep the money stock down to a fraction of its earlier level, in order to restrain inflation
b. increase the quantity of money, in order to finance the growth of trade
c. provide a more stable money system, in order to reduce the size of business fluctuations
d. provide a broader range of financial services to their customers
e. increase profits, by lending out some of the gold deposited with them

6. A bank run is most likely to occur at a time when

a. government surpluses are high
b. tax rates are high
c. many non-bank businesses are going bankrupt
d. investment by non-bank businesses is large
e. banks have reserves equal to 100% of their deposit liabilities

7. The Bank of Canada performs all the following functions *except one*. Which is the exception? The Bank of Canada

a. issues paper currency
b. conducts fiscal policy
c. controls the quantity of money in Canada
d. acts as the federal government's bank
e. acts as a bankers' bank

8. Chartered banks are required by law to hold reserves. These reserves are specified as percentages of a bank's

a. total assets
b. total liabilities
c. deposit liabilities
d. holdings of government securities
e. net worth

9. Suppose that the required reserve ratio is 20% and that a person deposits $100 in his or her bank. Then that single bank can create

a. $80 in additional money by lending $80
b. $100 in additional money by lending $100
c. $400 in additional money by lending $400
d. $500 in additional money by lending $500
e. no additional money; it takes the actions of the whole banking system to create more money, not just one bank

10. Suppose that the required reserve ratio of a chartered bank is represented by the fraction R. Suppose that this chartered bank receives a deposit of currency of $100. Then, as a result, *this single chartered bank* can make a loan of as much as

a. $100/$R$
b. $100 x R
c. $100/(1 − R)
d. $100 x (1 − R)

11. Suppose that someone in Toronto who banks at the Bank of Montreal sends a cheque for $1,000 to someone in Calgary, who deposits it in the Royal Bank. The required reserve ratio is R. In the process of cheque clearing, the reserves of the Bank of Montreal will

a. increase by $1,000, while those of the Royal Bank will decrease by $1,000
b. decrease by $1,000, while those of the Royal Bank will increase by $1,000
c. increase by $1,000 x R, while those of the Royal Bank will decrease by $1,000 x R
d. decrease by $1,000 x R, while those of the Royal Bank will increase by $1,000 x R
e. increase by $1,000 divided by R, while those of the Royal Bank will decrease by $1,000/$R$

12. An increase in the required reserve ratio on demand deposits would most likely cause

a. an increase in M1
b. a decrease in M1
c. an increase in demand deposits
d. an increase in bank profits
e. an increase in the demand deposit multiplier

13. Banks are most likely to hold significant quantities of excess reserves

a. when their profits are high, and they can afford to hold excess reserves
b. when economic activity is buoyant, and interest rates are high
c. when economic activity is buoyant, and interest rates are low
d. when economic activity is slack, and interest rates are high
e. when economic activity is slack, and interest rates are low

14. The monetary system is sometimes said to form an inverted pyramid. By this, we mean that

a. a large quantity of deposit money can be built on a small quantity of reserves
b. a large quantity of reserves can be built on a small quantity of deposit money
c. a large quantity of currency can be built on a small quantity of deposit money
d. demand deposits are the largest component of M1
e. currency is the largest component of M1

EXERCISES

1a. If I deposit $100,000 in currency into a demand deposit with bank A and the required reserve ratio is 20%, then the immediate increase in bank A's total reserve is $ ________, and the immediate increase in bank A's required reserves is ________. Thus, the immediate increase in bank A's excess reserves is ________. As a result of this transaction, the total amount of currency in the hands of the public has gone [up, down] by the amount ________, the total amount of demand deposits has gone [up, down] by the amount ________, the total amount of M1 has [increased, decreased, not changed], and the total amount of M2 has [increased, decreased, not changed].

1b. If bank A now lends its new excess reserves and the proceeds of the loan are deposited into a demand deposit in bank B, then the immediate effect is to make bank A's total reserves go [up, down] by ________, to make bank A's required reserves [increase, decrease, stay unchanged], to make bank A's excess reserves go [up, down] by ________, to make bank B's total reserves go [up, down] by ________, to make bank B's required reserves go [up, down] by ________, and to make bank B's excess reserves go [up, down] by ________. As a result of this loan and subsequent deposit, the total amount of currency in the hands of the public has [increased, decreased, stayed the same], the total amount of demand deposits has [increased by ________, decreased by ________, stayed the same], the total amount of M1 has gone [up, down] by ________, and the total amount of M2 has [increased by ________, decreased by ________, stayed the same].

1c. If the process continues in this way until all excess reserves have been eliminated, then the result of the whole process, starting from my initial deposit, will have been to make the total supply of currency in the hands of the public go [up, down] by ________, to make the total amount of demand deposits go [up, down] by ________, to make M1 go [up, down] by ________, and to make M2 [go up by ________, go down by ________, stay the same].

2. Show what happens as a direct result of each of the following transactions by filling in the appropriate number for that transaction in the balance sheet. Each balance sheet should represent the *change* in total assets and total liabilities of all banks. In each case, suppose that the required reserve ratio on demand deposits is 20%, and that the required reserve ratio on all other deposits is 10%. Each transaction should be considered separately from all the others.

a. Someone puts $25,000 of currency into a demand deposit.

b. Someone makes a cash withdrawal of $100,000 from a non-chequable notice deposit account, in order to hold the money in the form of currency.

c. Someone switches $200,000 from a demand deposit to a non-chequable notice deposit.

d. A bank lends $40,000 to someone who takes the proceeds of that loan in the form of currency.

e. A bank lends $100,000 to someone who uses that $100,000 to pay off a loan to someone who puts the $100,000 into a non-chequable notice deposit.

BALANCE SHEET A

Change in Assets		Change in Liabilities	
Loans	________		
Total reserves	25,000		
		Demand deposits	25,000
Required reserves	5,000		
		Other deposits	________
Excess reserves	________		

BALANCE SHEET B

Change in Assets		Change in Liabilities	
Loans	________		
Total reserves	________		
		Demand deposits	________
Required reserves	-10,000		
		Other deposits	-100,000
Excess reserves	10% -90,000		

BALANCE SHEET C

Change in Assets		Change in Liabilities	
Loans	________		
Total reserves	________	Demand deposits	________
Required reserves	________	Other deposits	________
Excess reserves	________		

BALANCE SHEET D

Change in Assets		Change in Liabilities	
Loans	________		
Total reserves	________	Demand deposits	________
Required reserves	________	Other deposits	________
Excess reserves	________		

BALANCE SHEET E

Change in Assets		Change in Liabilities	
Loans	________		
Total reserves	________	Demand deposits	________
Required reserves	________	Other deposits	________
Excess reserves	________		

ESSAY QUESTIONS

1. Why are bank runs most likely to occur during a depression or severe recession? Are bank runs most damaging to the economy at such times? Why or why not?

2. By his term "invisible hand," Adam Smith suggested that self-interested actions tend to benefit society. This chapter has explained two cases where pursuit of self-interest leads to undesirable results for the society as a whole. What are these two cases, and why does self-interest lead to socially undesirable outcomes? Can you think of any way to deal with these problems?

3. Individual bankers often argue, "We don't create money; we just lend money that has already been deposited with us." Is this correct? If so, explain why. If not, explain why not.

4. What would happen if Parliament abolished all reserve requirements in the Bank Act?

ANSWERS

Important Terms: **1** h **2** e **3** g **4** a **5** d **6** b **7** f **8** c

True-False: **1** T **2** F **3** F **4** T **5** F **6** F **7** F **8** T **9** F **10** T

Multiple Choice: **1** d **2** a **3** b **4** c **5** e **6** c **7** b **8** c **9** a **10** d **11** b **12** b **13** e **14** a

Exercises: **1a.** $100,000, $20,000, $80,000, down, $100,000, up, $100,000, not changed, not changed. **1b.** down, $80,000, stay unchanged, down, $80,000, up, $80,000, up, $16,000, up, $64,000, stayed the same, increased by $80,000, up, $80,000, increased by $80,000. **1c.** down, $100,000, up, $500,000, up, $400,000, go up by $400,000.

2.

BALANCE SHEET A

Change in Assets			Change in Liabilities	
Loans		0		
Total reserves		25,000	Demand deposits	25,000
Required reserves	5,000		Other deposits	0
Excess reserves	20,000			

BALANCE SHEET B

Change in Assets			Change in Liabilities	
Loans		0		
Total reserves		– 100,000	Demand deposits	0
Required reserves	– 10,000		Other deposits	– 100,000
Excess reserves	– 90,000			

BALANCE SHEET C

Change in Assets			Change in Liabilities	
Loans		0		
Total reserves		0	Demand deposits	– 200,000
Required reserves	– 20,000		Other deposits	+ 200,000
Excess reserves	+ 20,000			

BALANCE SHEET D

Change in Assets			Change in Liabilities	
Loans		+ 40,000		
Total reserves		– 40,000	Demand deposits	0
Required reserves	0		Other deposits	0
Excess reserves	– 40,000			

BALANCE SHEET E

Change in Assets			Change in Liabilities	
Loans		100,000		
Total reserves		0	Demand deposits	0
Required reserves	+ 10,000		Other deposits	100,000
Excess reserves	– 10,000			

Chapter 13

THE BANK OF CANADA AND THE TOOLS OF MONETARY POLICY

MAJOR PURPOSE

There are two major tools for controlling aggregate demand —fiscal policy and monetary policy. Fiscal policy, which involves changes in tax rates and in government spending, is in the hands of the government and Parliament. Monetary policy, which involves changes in the rate of growth of the money stock, is in the hands of the Bank of Canada. The major purpose of this chapter is to explain how the Bank of Canada can influence the money stock.

As we saw in Chapter 12, most of the money stock consists of deposits in chartered banks. The amount of money that banks can create depends on the quantity of cash reserves that they own, and on the required reserve ratio. The Bank of Canada has a number of tools with which it can influence the quantity of money in circulation:

1. It can *purchase government securities* on the open market.

2. It can *purchase foreign currencies* from Canadian chartered banks or non-bank corporations or individuals.

3. As the government's bank, the Bank of Canada can *transfer federal government deposits* to the chartered banks.

Through these three types of transactions, the Bank of Canada can directly increase the reserves of chartered banks, and therefore influence the money stock. In addition, there are several indirect methods through which the Bank can affect the money stock:

4. It can *change the Bank Rate* (and the rate it charges on loans to investment dealers). Since the reserves of chartered banks increase when they borrow from the Bank of Canada (or when the investment dealers borrow from the Bank of Canada), changes in the Bank Rate indirectly influence the quantity of reserves in the banking system, and hence the money stock.

5. Before 1967, the Bank of Canada had the power to use *changes in the required reserve ratio* as a tool for deliberately controlling the money stock; such changes influence the quantity of deposit money that can be created on any given base of cash reserves.

LEARNING OBJECTIVES

After you have studied this chapter in the textbook and study guide, you should be able to

- Describe the organization of the Bank of Canada and its relation to the federal government
- Describe how the Bank of Canada can use each of the tools at its disposal to affect the size of the money stock
- Explain how open market operations affect not only the size of the money stock but also interest rates
- Give an example that shows why the yield (interest rate) on a Treasury bill falls when its price rises
- Explain why a restrictive monetary policy does not usually involve an open market sale, but rather just a reduction in the rate of purchases on the open market
- Explain how Bank of Canada purchases and sales of foreign currencies and transfers of federal government deposits to and from chartered banks influence the size of the money stock
- Explain how Bank of Canada loans to chartered banks or to investment dealers influence the size of the money stock
- Explain why the Bank Rate is usually set high enough to be a "penalty rate"
- Explain why the Bank of Canada did not use changes in the required reserve ratio as a policy tool even when it had the legal power to do so
- Explain why government deposit insurance reduces the risk of a run on banks

HIGHLIGHTS OF THE CHAPTER

The Bank of Canada is our central bank. It is the "bankers' bank," and it is responsible for controlling the quantity of money.

The Bank of Canada is formally owned by the federal government. It is managed by a government-appointed board of Directors, which, in turn, appoints the Bank's Governor and Deputy-Governor, subject to the government's approval. While the Bank of Canada retains a considerable degree of independence in its day-to-day management of monetary policy, the present Bank Act clearly specifies that the federal government has final responsibility for the overall conduct of monetary policy: If a fundamental conflict develops between government and the Governor of the Bank of Canada, the Governor is obliged to resign.

Open market operations, sales and purchases of foreign currencies, and transfers of federal government deposits to the chartered banks are the tools most frequently used by the Bank of Canada to influence the money stock.

Consider first open market operations. When the Bank of Canada purchases securities worth, say, $10 million on the open market, it increases chartered bank reserves by the same $10 million. Because they have additional reserves, the banks are able to make loans; the money stock can increase by a multiple of the $10 million. As we saw in Chapter 12, the *maximum* increase in the money stock is the $10 million times $1/R$, where R is the required reserve ratio. (For simplicity, we disregard the complication that the Bank Act stipulates different reserve ratios for demand deposits and other deposits.) However, in practice, the actual increase is not likely to be this great. As banks make loans and the quantity of money increases, the public is likely to want not only more bank deposits, but more currency, too. People therefore withdraw some currency from their bank accounts. When they do so, the reserves of banks decline, and the amount of money they can create likewise declines.

The maximum increase in the money stock depends on the size of the open market operation ($10 million in the above example) and on the required reserve ratio. It does not depend on whether a chartered bank, a non-bank corporation, or an individual sells the securities to the Bank of Canada. However, the details of the way in which the money supply increases will vary, depending on who the seller is. If a non-bank corporation—such as Molson Breweries—or an individual is the seller, then the money stock will go up immediately as a result of the open market purchase. For example, if Molson sells the $10 million in securities that the Bank of Canada buys, Molson will deposit the proceeds from the sale in its demand deposit, and its holdings of money will therefore increase by $10 million. Molson's bank will now have larger deposit liabilities, and its required reserves will rise—by $10 million times the required reserve ratio. If this ratio is, say, 15%, the bank will have $8.5 million of excess reserves (the $10 million addition to reserves less the increase of $1.5 million in required reserves). It will safely be able to lend the $8.5 million. There will be a series of expansions: $10 million + ($10 x 0.85) million + ($10 x 0.85^2) million, and so on.

On the other hand, if a chartered bank sells the $10 million in securities, there is no initial increase in the quantity of money, since the deposits held by the public have not been affected. Required reserves likewise remain unchanged, but the banks have $10 million in excess reserves. They can therefore lend the full $10 million, again initiating an expansion of $10 million + ($10 x 0.85) million + ($10 x 0.85^2) million, and so on. Although the initial, first-round effects of the two types of transactions are different, their ultimate effects on the money stock will be the same.

Thus, when the Bank of Canada buys securities on the open market, the money stock increases. If the Bank of Canada sold securities on the open market, it would likewise cause a multiple decrease in the money stock. However, this would cause *very* tight monetary conditions. In our growing economy, the money stock can grow at a moderate rate without causing inflation. Therefore, when the Bank of Canada wants to tighten monetary conditions, it normally does not sell securities. Instead, it simply *reduces the rate of purchases* on the open market.

When it buys securities on the open market, the Bank of Canada bids their prices *up*. But this is just another way of saying that it bids interest rates *down*. As a result of the Bank of Canada's purchase, the banks have excess reserves. As they make loans or buy bonds with these reserves, the banks bid interest rates down even further.

Bank of Canada purchases of foreign currencies from Canadian residents influence the money stock in precisely the same way as purchases of government securities. Again, the ultimate effect does not depend on whether the foreign currency is bought from a chartered bank or from a non-bank corporation or individual.

Unlike open market operations or Bank of Canada transactions in foreign currencies, transfers of federal government deposits to the chartered banks do not directly influence the money stock, since federal government deposits in the chartered banks are not counted as part of the money stock. However, such deposit transfers create excess cash reserves in the chartered banks. When these excess reserves are lent out, the money stock increases, just as in the case of Bank of Canada purchases of government securities or foreign currencies.

Changes in the Bank Rate form another major tool of the Bank of Canada. By cutting the discount rate, the Bank of Canada encourages chartered banks to borrow more. When they borrow more, their reserves increase. Thus, a cut in the discount rate is an expansionary policy; increases in the rate constitute a contractionary policy. The Bank of Canada is sometimes spoken of as the "lender of last resort"; the chartered banks can go to the Bank of Canada to borrow reserves if they are temporarily short and cannot get funds elsewhere.

The Bank of Canada also makes loans to authorized investment dealers. A reduction in the rate that the Bank charges on such loans can also be used as a way of increasing chartered bank reserves: With a lower rate on loans from the Bank of Canada, investment dealers have an incentive to borrow from the Bank, using the proceeds to repay some of the loans they have taken from the chartered banks. As they do this, the reserves of chartered banks increase, and the money stock expands.

Another possible tool with which a central bank can control the money stock is a change in the required reserve ratio. As we have seen in Chapter 12, chartered bank deposits can be as much as $1/R$ times reserves where R is the required reserve ratio. By changing R, the Bank of Canada can thus change the size of the deposit multiplier.

Partly because of the fear that even relatively small changes in required cash reserve ratios might cause disruptions in the monetary system, the Bank of Canada never used this tool to control the money stock even when it had the authority to do so before 1967; since that year, the required ratios of cash reserves have been laid down in the Bank Act and cannot be varied by the Bank of Canada. The Act does allow the Bank of Canada to impose a minimum ratio of *secondary* reserves on the chartered banks, with secondary reserves being defined to include Treasury bills, loans to investment dealers, and excess cash reserves. However, while changes in the secondary reserve ratio may force chartered banks to rearrange the asset side of their balance sheets, it is unlikely to have any major effect on the stock of money.

Finally, the Bank of Canada can influence chartered bank behaviour by *moral suasion*—informal suggestions to chartered banks to take certain kinds of action and refrain from others. Moral suasion has been used by the Bank of Canada on many occasions. However, it has most often been used as a way of accomplishing special policy objectives (such as increasing bank lending to house building, or assisting financial institutions in difficulty), rather than as a device for controlling the money stock.

When the Bank of Canada purchases securities on the open market, it creates money "out of thin air." Our money is not backed by gold. Money retains its value because the Bank of Canada limits its supply; money is scarce. Bank of Canada deposits are backed not only by the assets of the banks, but also by the Canada Deposit Insurance Corporation. Insurance is important for individual depositors; it offers them protection. It is also important for the stability of the system as a whole: Deposit insurance greatly reduces the risk of a run on banks.

At times in our history, money has also been backed by gold (and silver). This system had one great advantage, in that it limited the amount of money that could be created, and thus acted as a restraint on reckless, inflationary expansions in the money stock. However, it had two great defects: (1) Increases in the quantity of gold played a function similar to open market purchases in the present system; they increased bank reserves, and permitted a multiple increase in the money stock. However, there was no assurance that the amount of gold mined or imported from abroad would provide the amount of money needed for a full-employment, non-inflationary economy. (2) The gold standard pyramid was vulnerable to runs. Whenever gold was withdrawn from the base of the pyramid, there was a powerful contractionary effect on the quantity of money. In other words, the gold standard could make financial crises and recessions worse—as it did in some countries in the early 1930s. This was the major reason for the abandonment of the gold standard.

IMPORTANT TERMS: MATCH THE COLUMNS

Match each term in the first column with the corresponding phrase in the second column. But before you do so, write your own definition of each term in the first column.

f **1.** the Bank of Canada
i **2.** open market operation
l **3.** example of restrictive policy
h **4.** example of expansive policy
k **5.** Government of Canada
c **6.** Bank Rate
j **7.** prime rate
e **8.** price of a Treasury bill
b **9.** authorized investment dealers
d **10.** legal tender
a **11.** fiat money
g **12.** secondary reserves

a. money unbacked by gold or silver; it is money because the government says so
b. may borrow from the Bank of Canada
c. interest rate on Bank of Canada's loans to chartered banks
d. creditors must accept this money in repayment of debts
e. this rises when interest rates fall
f. Canada's central bank
g. includes Treasury bills and loans to investment dealers
h. reduction of discount rate
i. purchase or sale of government securities by the Bank of Canada
j. a bank's publicly announced interest rate for short-term loans
k. this institution initially issues securities bought or sold in open market operations
l. increase in the required reserve ratio

TRUE-FALSE

T F 1. During the early years of the Great Depression, there was no central bank in Canada.
T F 2. Changes in required reserve ratios are the commonly used tools of monetary policy.
T F 3. If the required reserve ratio of chartered banks is 10%, then an open market purchase of $1 million by the Bank of Canada permits the chartered banks to increase their deposits by a maximum of $10 million.
T F 4. The appropriate strategy for the Bank of Canada during a depression is to sell government bonds, to make low-risk, sound assets available for the chartered banks to buy.
T F 5. When the Bank of Canada sells securities to the commercial banks, it increases their earning assets, and thus makes possible an increase in the money stock.
T F 6. When the Bank of Canada increases its purchases of government securities, it is engaging in an expansionary act; when it sells government securities, it is engaging in a restrictive act.
T F 7. If the interest rate doubles, then the price of a Treasury bill falls by 50%.
T F 8. Bank of Canada notes (Canada's paper currency) are backed dollar for dollar with gold held by the Bank of Canada.
T F 9. The existence of government insurance for bank depositors reduces the danger of bank runs. Indeed, one of the major purposes of such insurance is to reduce this danger.
T F 10. When the Bank of Canada buys foreign currency from Canadian residents, the money stock in Canada increases.
T F 11. Since 1980, the Bank Rate has usually been higher than the interest on Treasury bills.
T F 12. Changes in the secondary reserve ratio have a powerful effect on the money stock, and have almost never been used as a tool of monetary policy.

MULTIPLE CHOICE

1. When the Bank of Canada purchases securities on the open market, the securities it buys are generally
   a. common stock of the Canadian corporations whose stocks are included in the Toronto Stock Exchange industrial average
   b. corporate bonds
   c. securities issued by Crown corporations
   d. securities issued by the federal government
   e. any of the above; as it is a transaction on "the open market," the Bank of Canada buys whatever is offered for sale at the best price

2. During a depression, the best strategy of the Bank of Canada is to
   a. buy government securities
   b. sell government bonds, in order to make low-risk, sound assets available for commercial banks to buy
   c. sell government bonds, in order to reduce the size of the government's deficits
   d. sell government bonds, in order to increase aggregate demand
   e. exhort banks not to lend to businesses, in order to reduce their risks of loss

3. Suppose that (a) the Bank of Canada purchases a $100,000 government security on the open market, (b) the required reserve ratio is 20%, (c) CP Air sells the security, and (d) CP Air deposits the proceeds from the sale in a demand deposit account in its chartered bank. The effect of this single transaction will be to increase the money stock by
   a. $20,000
   b. $100,000
   c. $200,000
   d. $500,000
   e. zero

4. If bank deposits are $10 billion, bank reserves are $2 billion, and excess reserves are $500 million, then the required reserve ratio is
   a. 5%
   b. 10%
   c. 15%
   d. 20%
   e. 25%

5. If the price of a Treasury bill falls,
   a. all interest rates certainly fall
   b. all interest rates probably fall
   c. the interest rate on this bill certainly falls
   d. the interest rate on this bill probably rises
   e. the interest rate on this bill certainly rises

6. When the Bank of Canada purchases Treasury bills on the open market
   a. the quantity of chartered bank reserves falls
   b. the interest rate on Treasury bills rises
   c. the price of Treasury bills rises
   d. the risk premium on business loans usually rises
   e. the required reserves of banks fall

7. If the required reserve ratio is 20%, and if chartered banks borrow $100 million from the Bank of Canada, the effect on chartered bank reserves is
   a. an increase of $100 million
   b. an increase of $500 million
   c. a decrease of $100 million
   d. a decrease of $500 million

e. no change

8. The Bank of Canada would *tighten* monetary conditions by *lowering*

a. required reserve ratios
b. the prime rate
c. the Bank Rate
d. the interest rate on Treasury bills
e. the rate at which it is buying securities on the open market

9. The Bank Rate refers to

a. the penalty paid by risky bank borrowers; that is, the amount of interest they pay in excess of the prime rate
b. the rate at which banks write off bad loans
c. the rate at which assets lose their real value as a result of inflation
d. the rate at which money loses its value as a result of inflation
e. the rate of interest that the Bank of Canada charges on loans to chartered banks

10. If the Bank of Canada transfers federal government deposits from the chartered banks to the Bank of Canada, the result is

a. a decrease in chartered bank reserves and therefore a decrease in the money stock
b. a decrease in the money stock but no change in chartered bank reserves
c. a lower interest rate on government securities
d. an increase in foreign currency reserves as the Bank will use the funds to buy more foreign money
e. a decrease in the Bank Rate

11. When the Bank of Canada makes loans to authorized investment dealers, this

a. contributes to financial instability because the investment dealers often experience difficulties in repaying the loans
b. has little effect on the money stock because it does not change chartered bank reserves
c. increases the prime rate
d. tends to lower the prices of government securities because the Bank of Canada has to sell government securities to raise the funds that it lends to the investment dealers
e. affects the money stock in about the same way as Bank of Canada loans to the chartered banks would do

12. If the Bank Rate were to fall below the Treasury bill rate, chartered banks would be tempted to

a. increase their holdings of excess reserves
b. sell their Treasury bills in order to pay off their loans from the Bank of Canada
c. call in loans in order to lend to the Bank of Canada
d. borrow from the Bank of Canada to buy Treasury bills
e. increase their investments in the stock market

13. The Bank of Canada issues paper currency which acts as money in Canada. It is most accurate to say that this money is "backed" by Bank of Canada assets in the form of

a. loans to member banks
b. government securities
c. gold (or gold certificates)
d. required reserves of the chartered banks
e. the value of the Bank of Canada buildings in Ottawa

14. Suppose that you were a central banker facing the problems of the Great Depression in the early 1930s. You fear a run on the banks. To reduce this risk, the best of the following options would be to

a. increase required reserves, so that banks will have greater reserves and be better able to meet withdrawals of depositors
b. hold firm to the gold standard, in order to restore confidence
c. centralize the banking system's gold reserves in the central bank, in order to restore confidence
d. centralize the banking system's gold reserves in the central bank, in order to have more reserves available to meet any run
e. purchase securities on the open market in order to increase bank reserves

15. Economists sometimes speak of the "monetary pyramid" under the old gold standard. By this they mean that

a. the money stock was just a small fraction of the quantity of gold
b. reserve ratios automatically fell whenever the quantity of gold increased
c. required reserve ratios automatically rose whenever the quantity of gold increased
d. the quantity of money could be a multiple of the quantity of gold
e. bank reserves increased whenever the public decided to hold more money in the form of gold

16. Which of the following is an example of the Bank of Canada's use of "moral suasion"?

a. suggesting that legislation restricting chartered bank lending might be passed unless the banks voluntarily reduce their lending to foreign-owned firms
b. persuading buyers in the Treasury bill market to part with their securities at the market price
c. persuading the government that the Bank of Canada is pursuing good policies
d. raising secondary reserve requirements
e. increasing lending to authorized investment dealers

EXERCISES

1. Suppose the required reserve ratio on all deposits is 20 percent.

a. In balance sheets A, show the initial effects of an open market purchase of $10 million of securities by the Bank of Canada where the seller is a corporation that deposits the proceeds of the sale immediately with its bank, which keeps the funds in the form of a deposit with the Bank of Canada.

b. In balance sheets B, show the ultimate effects of the above transaction, assuming that the deposit expansion process continues up to its maximum limit given by the deposit multiplier. Assume that each bank in the process holds all its extra reserves in the form of deposits with the Bank of Canada.

c. In balance sheets C, show the initial effects of an open market purchase of $10 million of securities by the Bank of Canada where the seller is a chartered bank. Is the initial change in the money stock the same as in part (a)? Why or why not?

d. In balance sheets D, show the ultimate effects of the open market purchase in part (c), assuming that the deposit expansion process continues up to its maximum limit given by the deposit multiplier. Assume that each chartered bank holds all its extra reserves in the form of deposits in the Bank of Canada. Compare the results with those in part (b).

BALANCE SHEETS A

Bank of Canada				All chartered banks			
		Bank of Canada notes	___	Loans	___	Deposits	___
				Total Reserves	___		
Federal government securities	___	Deposits of chartered banks	___	Required reserves	___		
		Net Worth	___	Excess reserves	___		

BALANCE SHEETS B

Bank of Canada				All chartered banks			
		Bank of Canada notes	___	Loans	___	Deposits	___
				Total Reserves	___		
Federal government securities	___	Deposits of chartered banks	___	Required reserves	___		
		Net Worth	___	Excess reserves	___		

BALANCE SHEETS C

Bank of Canada				All chartered banks			
		Bank of Canada notes	___	Loans	___	Deposits	___
				Government securities	___		
				Total Reserves	___		
Federal government securities	___	Deposits of chartered banks	___	Required reserves	___		
		Net Worth	___	Excess reserves	___		

BALANCE SHEETS D

Bank of Canada				All chartered banks			
		Bank of Canada notes	0	Loans	50	Deposits	50
				Government securities	10		
				Total Reserves	10		
Federal government securities	10						
		Deposits of chartered banks	10	Required reserves	10		
		Net Worth	0	Excess reserves	0		

2. The Great Depression of the 1930s provided many lessons for macroeconomics; it was a painful demonstration of how badly things go wrong if poor policies are pursued.

Specifically, the Great Depression was a time of [large-scale unemployment, inflation, both]. Major mistakes were made in both monetary and fiscal policies. Specifically, the government [cut, raised] tax rates in an attempt to eliminate deficits and move the budget toward balance. This change in taxes [increased, decreased] disposable income, and thus caused an [increase, decrease] in aggregate demand. This made the problem of [unemployment, inflation, both] worse.

In the United States, the Federal Reserve allowed the money stock to [increase, decrease] by more than 25% between 1929 and 1933, thereby adding to the problem of [inflation, unemployment, both]. During this period, the Federal Reserve Board took the position that vigorous open market operations would be unsound. However, the collapse into the Depression would have been less severe if the Fed had made vigorous [purchases, sales] of government securities on the open market.

3. (This exercise is only for those who have studied Box 13-1 in the textbook.) Consider a $100 bond with an annual coupon of $10. In the table below, fill in the approximate price of the bond under the different assumptions concerning the term to maturity and the rate of interest. What general proposition is suggested by the example concerning the relationship between (a) the term to maturity of the bond and (b) the size of the effect upon the price of the bond of a change in the rate of interest?

	Term to Maturity		
Rate of Interest	**1 year**	**2 years**	**Perpetuity**
8%	______	______	______
10%	______	______	______
12%	______	______	______

ESSAY QUESTIONS

1. Open market operations constitute the most important tool with which the Bank of Canada affects the money stock. But the Bank of Canada can also change the quantity of money by changing required reserve ratios. Why should the Bank of Canada rely primarily on open market operations rather than changes in required reserve ratios?

2. In the United States, financial institutions called savings and loan associations have traditionally held most of their assets in the form of mortgages on homes, with initial terms of 20, 25, or 30 years. Suppose that many of these mortgages are made at interest rates of 8% or 9%. Then suppose that long-term interest rates increase to 12%. What happens to the value of an S&L's mortgages? Can the S&L continue to offer low interest rates in order to keep interest payments less than interest receipts? If it does so, what is likely to happen? Do you see why many S&Ls ran into difficulty when interest rates soared in the late 1970s?

3. In Canada, some trust companies with large mortgage portfolios experienced similar problems. However, the problems were not as severe as those of the S&Ls in the United States. Can you explain why?

ANSWERS

Important Terms: **1** f **2** i **3** l **4** h **5** k **6** c **7** j **8** e **9** b **10** d **11** a **12** g
True-False: **1** T **2** F **3** T **4** F **5** F **6** T **7** F **8** F **9** T **10** T **11** T **12** F
Multiple Choice: **1** d **2** a **3** b **4** c **5** e **6** c **7** a **8** e **9** e **10** a **11** e **12** d **13** b **14** e **15** d **16** a

EXERCISES

1.

BALANCE SHEETS A

Bank of Canada				**All chartered banks**			
		Bank of Canada notes	0	Loans	0	Deposits	$10 million
				Total reserves	$10 million		
Federal government securities	$10 million	Deposits of chartered banks	$10 million	Required reserves	$2 million		
		Net worth	0	Excess reserves	$8 million		

BALANCE SHEETS B

Bank of Canada				**All chartered banks**			
		Bank of Canada notes	0	Loans	$40 million	Deposits	$50 million
				Total reserves	$10 million		
Federal government securities	$10 million	Deposits of chartered banks	$10 million	Required reserves	$10 million		
		Net worth	0	Excess reserves	0		

BALANCE SHEETS C

Bank of Canada				**All chartered banks**			
		Bank of Canada notes	0	Loans	0	Deposits	0
				Government securities	– $10 million		
				Total reserves	$10 million		
Federal government securities	$10 million	Deposits of chartered banks	$10 million	Required reserves	0		
		Net worth	0	Excess reserves	$10 million		

BALANCE SHEETS D

Bank of Canada				**All chartered banks**			
		Bank of Canada notes	0	Loans	$50 million	Deposits	$50 million
				Government securities	– $10 million		
				Total reserves	$10 million		
Federal government securities	$10 million	Deposits of chartered banks	$10 million	Required reserves	$10 million		
		Net worth	0	Excess reserves	0		

2. large-scale unemployment, raised, decreased, decrease, unemployment, decrease, unemployment, purchases.

3.

	TERM TO MATURITY		
Rate of interest	**1 year**	**2 years**	**3 years**
8%	$101.85	$103.57	$125.00
10%	$100.00	$100.00	$100.00
12%	$ 98.21	$ 96.62	$ 83.33

The longer the term to maturity, the greater the change in the price of the bond for any change in the interest rate.

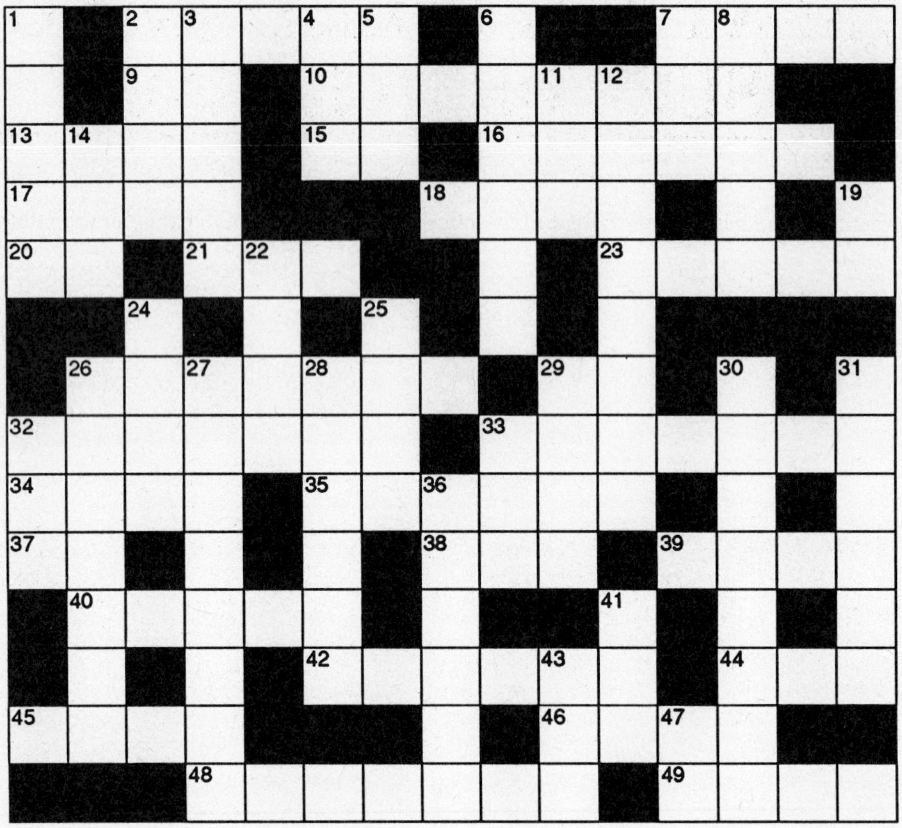

Across

2. Italian city
7. animal associated with rising stock market, or with nonsense
9. indefinite article
10. Reserves are a ____________ of deposit liabilities.
13, 15, 16. responsible for monetary policy
17. led a rebellion in western Canada in the 1800s
18. built for defence
20. interjection
21. Telepathy is an example of this (abbrev.)
23. To raise taxes in a depression would be an example of this.
26. shape, sometimes used to explain monetary instability under the gold standard
29. third person singular
32, 33. central bank of the United States
34. smallest units of paper money in Canada
35. give an account
37. Egyptian god
38. a charge for service rendered
39. currency of South Africa
40. not small
42. a stiff, boring writing style
44. former Middle East group of countries (abbrev.)
45. computer measure of information
46. not far
48. Moral ____________ is sometimes used by the Bank of Canada.
49. in Parliament, those who vote "yes"

Down

1. weapon used to fence with
2. part of a window made of glass
3. sometimes gets twisted
4. visitor from another world? (abbrev.)
5. what dogs say in cartoons
6. agreement
7. constrictor
8. beneath
11. black sticky substance
12. return on a loan
14. what we breathe
19. either… ____________ …
22. heavenly body
24. Dr. Jekyll's alter ego
25. African river
26. The Bank of Canada rate is usually a ____________ rate.
27. Chartered banks are required to hold these.
28. open ____________ operations
29. denotes present location
30. type of bill that can be counted as part of chartered banks' secondary reserves
31. In this country, Bank of Canada notes are legal ____________.
32. preposition meaning "on behalf of"
33. fish eggs
36. Persian language
41. poem of praise
43. place where a traveller can eat and sleep
47. helps those with a drinking problem (abbrev.)

Part Four

GREAT MACROECONOMIC ISSUES OF OUR TIME

Chapter 14

MONETARY POLICY AND FISCAL POLICY: WHICH IS THE KEY TO AGGREGATE DEMAND?

MAJOR PURPOSE

One of the important controversies of recent decades has centred around the relative importance of monetary and fiscal policies. If the economy is heading into an inflationary boom or into a recession, should we turn to fiscal policy to stabilize the economy? Or should we turn to monetary policy? Most economists would now say that a *combination* of monetary and fiscal policies is best. However, there has been a sharp debate between Keynesians, who have often emphasized fiscal policy, and monetarists, who have emphasized that money is the key to aggregate demand. The purpose of this chapter is to review the highlights of this debate, and explain why it is unwise to rely exclusively on either monetary or fiscal policy.

Keynes suggested that the effects of monetary policy be viewed as a three-step process: (1) the effect of a change in the quantity of money on the interest rate, (2) the effect of a change in interest rates on investment demand, and (3) the multiplier process, whereby the change in investment demand has a magnified effect on aggregate demand. Keynes believed that expansive monetary policies might be of little value during the Great Depression, because interest rates were already low, and therefore not much would happen at step 1. Until about 1960, his followers also had major doubts about the second stage. Now, however, almost all Keynesians see an important role for monetary policy. On the other side, some monetarists are quite skeptical that fiscal policy has much effect on aggregate demand. The effects of an increase in government spending can be offset if interest rates increase and cause a reduction in investment or in net exports.

LEARNING OBJECTIVES

After you have studied this chapter in the textbook and study guide, you should be able to

- Describe the three steps in the Keynesian explanation of how a change in the quantity of money can cause a change in aggregate demand
- Explain how problems at two of these three steps might mean that aggregate demand will not change much as a result of a change in the quantity of money
- Explain how, at the first step, the quantity of money and people's willingness to hold money determine the rate of interest
- Explain what the MEI curve means, and what is measured on the vertical axis
- Explain why monetary policy might be quite effective, even if the MEI curve is very steep
- Explain why monetary policy might be less effective in expanding aggregate demand than in restraining it
- Explain the key propositions of monetarists, and the major points of disagreement between monetarists and Keynesians
- Explain how deficit spending may lead to a decrease in investment and/or in net exports
- Explain the case for using monetary policy in conjunction with fiscal policy
- Explain why, in spite of the strength of the case for using both policies, Canada has nevertheless relied mostly on monetary policy as a demand-management tool in recent years

HIGHLIGHTS OF THE CHAPTER

This chapter deals with the controversy over the relative importance of monetary and fiscal policies. Although most economists take an intermediate position, two extreme views may be identified. One position—the position of strong Keynesians, particularly during the 1950s and 1960s—is that fiscal policy is very important, while monetary policy has little or no effect. The other extreme position—the strong monetarist view—is just the opposite. An earlier chapter explained the Keynesian view of how fiscal policy affects aggregate demand. This chapter rounds out the discussion by explaining (1) the reasons why strong Keynesians have dismissed monetary policy, (2) the monetarist view as to why monetary policy is important, and (3) the monetarist view as to why fiscal policy may not have much effect on aggregate demand. This chapter also explains why the historical evidence does not give unqualified support to either extreme view; we are left with a case for using both monetary and fiscal policies.

The Keynesian View of Monetary Policy

In the Keynesian view, there are three links in the chain of events whereby an open market purchase can increase aggregate demand. At the *first link*, an open market purchase can cause a *fall in the interest rates*. We have already seen in Chapter 13 why. Specifically, the initial increase in the Bank of Canada's demand for bonds and the secondary increase in bond purchases by chartered banks will both work to bid up the prices of bonds; that is, interest rates will fall. This chapter explains this first link in more detail.

To see how monetary policy affects interest rates, Keynesian economists look at the demand and supply of money. By the supply of money, they mean the quantity of money that exists in the economy. By the demand, they mean the *willingness* of people to hold money. This willingness depends in part on interest rates—the lower the interest rates, the more money people are willing to hold. This is reflected in the downward slope of the demand curve in Figure 14-2 in the textbook.

Now, suppose that the economy is initially in equilibrium, and that the Bank of Canada then increases the quantity of money. At the existing interest rate, people now have more money than they are willing to hold. They try to reduce their money balances. How do they do so? The answer is: by buying bonds. As people buy bonds, bond prices rise. That is, interest rates fall. Once the interest rate has fallen to its equilibrium, people no longer have more money than they are willing to hold; the demand for bonds levels off.

The *second link* represents the *effect that a change in interest rates has on investment*. Businesses will undertake investment projects as long as their *rate of return* is at least as great as the interest rate. The rate of return can be calculated if we know (1) the initial cost of the investment project, (2) the lifetime of the project, (3) the additional sales from the project, and (4) the costs associated with running the project. For the economy as a whole, the potential investment projects can be ranked according to their rates of return. When this is done, we have a schedule or curve that shows the amount of investment that will yield at least 15%, the amount that will yield at least 14%, the amount that will yield at least 13%, and so on.

This is the marginal efficiency of investment (MEI) curve, also known as the investment demand curve. It shows the amount that will be invested at various rates of interest. For example, if the interest rate is 12%, businesses have an incentive to undertake any project the return of which is more than 12%—that is, any project with a return high enough to meet interest payments and leave something over to be added to profits. If, then, the interest rate falls to 11% as a result of an expansionary monetary policy, more investment will be undertaken. In other words, the policy leads to an increase in investment at this second step.

At the *third step*, an increase in investment has a *multiplied effect on aggregate demand*. The theory of the multiplier was explained in detail in Chapter 10.

Keynesian economists foresee two situations in which monetary policy may not have much effect. First, Keynes himself saw a problem at the first step. He was skeptical that monetary policy could be used as a way out of the Depression of the 1930s. Interest rates were already very low, and there was not much prospect that they could be lowered significantly with monetary policy. After all, there is a downward limit on interest rates—they cannot be pushed below zero. In other words, in the special case of the Depression, when interest rates were already low, Keynes believed that the authorities could not rely on monetary policy. They would have to use fiscal policy to get the economy out of the Depression.

Some of his followers had a more general skepticism regarding monetary policy; they doubted its effectiveness even during more normal times. Specifically, they foresaw a problem at the second step. They believed that the MEI curve might be almost vertical. As a result, they were skeptical that changes in interest rates would lead to a significant change in investment. Even if monetary policy did change interest rates at step 1, there might be very little change in investment at step 2.

One rebuttal was that monetary policy might have an effect *even* if the MEI curve were almost vertical. When the Bank of Canada tightens monetary policy, it restricts chartered bank reserves. Because they must meet required reserve ratios, banks *must* limit their loans—regardless of the demand by businesses. As a consequence, investment may be limited by an *unavailability of funds*, rather than by a lack of desire by businesses to invest. Banks may *ration* their available funds among eager buyers.

For three reasons, a restrictive monetary policy may be more effective than an expansive policy:

1. The rate of interest cannot be driven below zero, but there is no limit to how high it can be driven.

2. Banks cannot increase their loans and other earning assets when they lack excess reserves; the Bank of Canada can firmly restrain their lending by limiting their reserves. But when the Bank of Canada increases chartered bank reserves, it cannot force banks to lend. They may hold large excess reserves—as many of them in fact did during the late 1930s.

3. Through credit rationing, banks can keep loans below the amounts demanded by businesses. But banks cannot force businesses to borrow more than they want.

The Monetarist View of Monetary Policy

The monetarist view can be expressed in terms of the equation of exchange: $MV = PQ$, where M is the stock of money, V is the velocity of money, P is the average level of prices, and Q is the quantity of output (that is, "real national product"). This equation is not a "theory," because it is simply true *by definition.* Specifically, V is defined as PQ/M. However, on this equation a theory has been built. This theory—the *quantity theory*—is the proposition that V is stable. If this is so, then a change in M will cause an approximately proportional change in PQ. In other words, monetary policy has a strong and predictable effect on nominal GNP.

The following are five key propositions of monetarism:

1. The money supply M is the most important determinant of aggregate demand and nominal national product PQ.

2. In the *long run,* real GNP tends toward its full employment level. Consequently, the only long-run effect of M is on P, not on Q.

3. However, in the short run, an increase (decrease) in M can cause *both* P and Q to increase (decrease).

4. If M is increased at a slow, stable rate, then aggregate demand will also increase at a slow, stable rate.

5. Such a slow, stable increase in aggregate demand is the best way to reduce the magnitude of business cycles and keep inflation down. Therefore, the central bank should follow a monetary *rule*, aiming for a slow, steady increase in M.

The Monetarist View of Fiscal Policy

Monetarists doubt that fiscal policy has a strong and predictable effect on aggregate demand. This is largely because of "crowding out." Suppose that the government spends more, and finances the resulting deficit by borrowing from the public. Interest rates will rise. As a result, businesses will move upward to the left along the MEI curve; investment demand will decline. Thus, the government spending will *crowd out* investment; the net effect on aggregate demand will be smaller than foreseen in the simple discussion of Chapter 11. The strength of this crowding-out effect will depend on the slope of the MEI curve. The flatter it is, the more investment will fall for any increase in the interest rate. Monetarists generally believe that the MEI curve is quite flat (in contrast to the almost vertical curve of early Keynesians). As a result, they foresee a strong crowding-out effect, with little or no net effect of fiscal policy on aggregate demand.

This crowding-out argument is based on the assumption that the government sells bonds *to the public.* In this case, there will be no effect on the money stock; this will be a *pure* fiscal policy. If, on the other hand, the Bank of Canada buys the additional government bonds, interest rates may be kept down and investment demand and aggregate demand will increase. But the money stock will rise, and a monetarist will consider money, not government spending, to be the cause of the increase in aggregate demand. Thus, if we want to distinguish between the Keynesian and monetarist viewpoints, we should look at a *pure* fiscal policy—a change in G or in tax rates with no change in M—and compare it with what we might call a *pure* monetary policy: an open market operation and a change in M with no change in fiscal policy. If an expansive fiscal policy is accompanied by an increase in M, there is no disagreement: aggregate demand will increase. Keynesians will generally attribute the increase to fiscal policy, and monetarists to a change in M.

A second reason that deficit spending may have a weak effect on aggregate demand has attracted considerable attention in recent years. An increase in deficit spending by the government can cause an increase in interest rates, encouraging foreigners to buy Canadian bonds and bidding up the price of the Canadian dollar in terms of foreign currencies. Canadian exports are discouraged, and imports stimulated. In other words, a budgetary deficit can cause a deficit in international trade, with the trade deficit offsetting the stimulative effects of the government's deficit spending.

Statistical evidence does not give unqualified support to either the strong monetarist or the strong Keynesian view. There is still some uncertainty about the relative effectiveness of monetary and fiscal policies. Because we do not know exactly how the economy operates, it makes sense to diversify—to use some of each policy, rather than putting all our eggs in one basket. But, while the importance of diversification is widely recognized, we have in fact placed almost exclusive reliance on monetary policy as a demand-management tool in recent years. The reason is that fiscal policy is caught in a political impasse. Many people believe that smaller deficits would be desirable, but there is little agreement on how to achieve that goal.

IMPORTANT TERMS: MATCH THE COLUMNS

Match each term in the first column with the corresponding phrase in the second column. But before you do so, write your own definition of each term in the first column.

d 1. MEI curve
f 2. credit rationing
a 3. credit crunch
g 4. quantity theory
b 5. equation of exchange
h 6. velocity
e 7. crowding out
c 8. pure fiscal policy

a. severe credit rationing
b. $MV = PQ$
c. change in G with no change in rate of growth of M
d. relationship between interest rate and I^*
e. G leads to higher i, which leads to less I^*
f. funds are unavailable, even for credit-worthy borrowers
g. proposition that V is stable
h. PQ/M

TRUE-FALSE

T F 1. According to Keynes, interest rates might be low during a depression. He argued that in this case, expansive monetary policy would not be an effective tool for promoting recovery.
T F 2. The flatter the marginal efficiency of investment curve, the more effective is monetary policy as a way of controlling aggregate demand.
T F 3. The flatter the marginal efficiency of investment curve, the more effective is fiscal policy as a way of controlling aggregate demand.
T F 4. Most Keynesians argue that the equation of exchange is incorrect; specifically, they argue that V does not equal PQ/M.
T F 5. According to the quantity theory of money, V tends to be stable through time, and PQ therefore tends to change by about the same percentage as M.
T F 6. According to quantity theorists, a change in M will have little or no effect on P in the long run.
T F 7. According to quantity theorists, a change in M will have a greater effect on P in the long run than in the short run.
T F 8. According to monetarists, fiscal policy can have a powerful effect on aggregate demand, provided that changes in government spending are financed by borrowing from the central bank.
T F 9. The stronger the crowding-out effect, the more powerful will be the effect of fiscal policy on aggregate demand.
T F 10. The steeper the aggregate supply curve, the more powerful is fiscal policy as a way of changing output and employment.

MULTIPLE CHOICE

1. Which of the following is most likely to *decrease* when the quantity of money *increases*?
- **a.** P
- **b.** Q
- **c.** $P \times Q$
- **d.** the interest rate
- **e.** the quantity of money demanded

2. In the Keynesian approach to monetary policy, if the quantity of money exceeds the quantity demanded, the most likely result is a
- **a.** fall in the interest rate
- **b.** rise in the interest rate
- **c.** fall in investment
- **d.** fall in national product
- **e.** fall in the size of the multiplier

3. Suppose that the amount of money people have exceeds the quantity that they want to hold. Then, Keynesian theory emphasizes that they will try to get rid of excess money balances by
- **a.** saving more
- **b.** buying bonds
- **c.** buying goods
- **d.** switching from currency to bank deposits
- **e.** switching from bank deposits to currency

4. Suppose that the amount of money people have exceeds the quantity that they want to hold. Monetarists emphasize that they will try to get rid of excess money balances by
- **a.** saving more
- **b.** buying bonds
- **c.** buying goods
- **d.** switching from currency to bank deposits
- **e.** switching from bank deposits to currency

5. Suppose that a company is going to buy a machine costing $100,000, which is expected to last one year, after which it will have no scrap value. With this machine, the company can produce $250,000 worth of additional goods, while spending $100,000 for additional raw materials, supplies, and labour. The expected rate of return on that machine is

- **a.** –100%
- **b.** 0
- **c.** 10%
- **d.** 50%
- **e.** 150%

6. If the marginal efficiency of investment curve is quite flat, we would expect the effects on aggregate demand of

- **a.** monetary policy to be strong while the effects of fiscal policy will be weak
- **b.** fiscal policy to be strong while the effects of monetary policy will be weak
- **c.** both monetary and fiscal policies to be strong
- **d.** both monetary and fiscal policies to be weak

7. If credit rationing occurs,

- **a.** the interest rate will be above its equilibrium level
- **b.** bond prices will rise
- **c.** funds will flow from the corporate sector into housing
- **d.** investment will be at a point to the left of the MEI curve
- **e.** saving will be greater than investment

8. The quantity theory of money is best described as the proposition that

- **a.** Q is stable
- **b.** P is stable
- **c.** V is stable
- **d.** $MV = PQ$
- **e.** $MQ = PV$

9. Keynesians and monetarists are most likely to agree that

- **a.** monetary policy is more effective than fiscal policy
- **b.** fiscal policy is more effective than monetary policy
- **c.** neither fiscal nor monetary policy can affect Q; the only effect will be on P
- **d.** the MEI curve is generally steep
- **e.** $V = PQ/M$

10. Which of the following views is most likely to be held by a monetarist?

- **a.** A decrease in the rate of growth of the money stock will cause the level of national product to stay below the full-employment level permanently.
- **b.** The money stock should be increased at a steady, constant rate.
- **c.** Investment demand is quite unresponsive to changes in the rate of interest.
- **d.** The quantity of money demanded responds strongly to changes in the rate of interest
- **e.** Monetary policy is like trying to control aggregate demand with a string.

11. According to monetarists, an increase in M will have a strong effect in the long run on

- **a.** V
- **b.** Q
- **c.** real national product
- **d.** current-dollar national product
- **e.** none of the above

12. The "crowding-out" effect of fiscal policy applies to which of the following ideas?

- **a.** An increase in G leads to an increase in interest rates, which leads to an increase in I^*.
- **b.** An increase in G leads to a decrease in interest rate, which leads to an increase in I^*.
- **c.** An increase in G leads to an increase in interest rates, which leads to a decline in I^*.
- **d.** An increase in G leads to an increase in I^*, which leads to an increase in interest rates.
- **e.** An increase in G leads to an increase in I^*, which leads to a decrease in interest rates.

13. By "pure" fiscal policies, economists mean

- **a.** fiscal policies uninfluenced by special interests
- **b.** fiscal policies where all changes take place in the nondefence sectors of the government's budget
- **c.** fiscal policies concentrated in the defence sectors of the government's budget, because these have little effect on the productive capacity of the economy
- **d.** changes in government spending or tax rates unaccompanied by changes in the rate of growth of the money stock
- **e.** changes in government spending or tax rates while interest rates are held constant.

14. Some economists believe that expansions will be *lopsided* if large government deficits persist. By this, they mean that during expansions, production of

- **a.** exports will be too high, and production of capital goods too low
- **b.** capital goods will be too low, and exports will also be too low
- **c.** capital goods will be too high, and exports will also be too high
- **d.** capital goods will be too high, and exports too low
- **e.** consumption goods will be too low, and capital goods too high

15. If the aggregate supply curve is quite steep

- **a.** an expansive monetary policy will have a powerful effect on aggregate demand, but an expansive fiscal policy will not
- **b.** an expansive fiscal policy will have a powerful effect on aggregate demand, but an expansive monetary policy will not
- **c.** an expansive monetary policy will have a powerful effect on real output, but an expansive fiscal policy will not
- **d.** an expansive fiscal policy will have a powerful effect on real output, but an expansive monetary policy will not
- **e.** neither an expansive fiscal nor an expansive monetary policy will have a powerful effect on real output

EXERCISES

1. According to Keynesians, money can affect aggregate demand as a result of a three-step process. Specifically, an increase in the quantity of money will lead to (a) ____________, which in turn will cause (b) ____________, which in turn will lead to (c) ____________.

Keynesians foresee no problem at the third step. However, problems might occur at each of the first two steps. Specifically, there might be a problem at the first step, particularly if [interest rates were already very low, interest rates were already high, the rate of inflation were high]. There could also be a major problem at the second step, if [the demand for money, the MEI curve, the consumption function] were steep.

In Keynesian theory, if the amount of money people have exceeds the quantity that they want to hold, they will [buy bonds, buy goods, save more]. As a result, [prices will rise, interest rates will fall]. Monetarists foresee a somewhat different response. If the amount of money people have exceeds the quantity that they want to hold, they will [buy bonds, buy goods, save more]. As a result, [aggregate demand will increase, interest rates will fall]. In the short run, monetarists believe that this will lead to [higher *P*, higher *Q*, both]; in the long run, it will cause [higher *P*, higher *Q*, both]. Monetarism is based on the quantity theory of money. That is, it is based on the view that [*M*, *V*, *P*, *Q*, all of them] is/are stable.

2. Suppose that the MEI curve is very steep. This suggests that monetary policy will be [effective, weak]. Specifically, suppose the Bank of Canada engages in a very restrictive policy, selling Treasury bills on the open market. As a result, the prices of bills will [fall, rise], and their interest rates or yields will [fall, rise]. This will lead to a(n) [increase, decrease] in I^*, with the size of this effect being very [large, small] because of the steepness of the MEI curve.

Some economists suggest that monetary policy can be quite [effective, ineffective] even if the MEI curve is steep, because of what happens to the availability of funds. Specifically, the open market sale will lead to an [increase, decrease] in chartered bank reserves. As a result, banks will be *forced* to [increase, decrease] their portfolio of loans and other earning assets. Businesses will find that bank loans are [easier to get, rationed]. This will means that I^* is [greater, less] than we would have expected by looking simply at the MEI curve and interest rates.

3. In Figure 14-1, above, the curves labelled *A* and *B* are two alternative ways in which the MEI curve may be drawn. Of the two, curve [*A*, *B*] is the one in which I^* is the more responsive to changes in the rate of interest. According to curve *A*, when the rate of interest is 10%, I^* will be ____________; when the rate of interest is 5%, I^* will be ____________. According to curve *B*, when the rate of interest is 10%, I^* will be ____________; when the

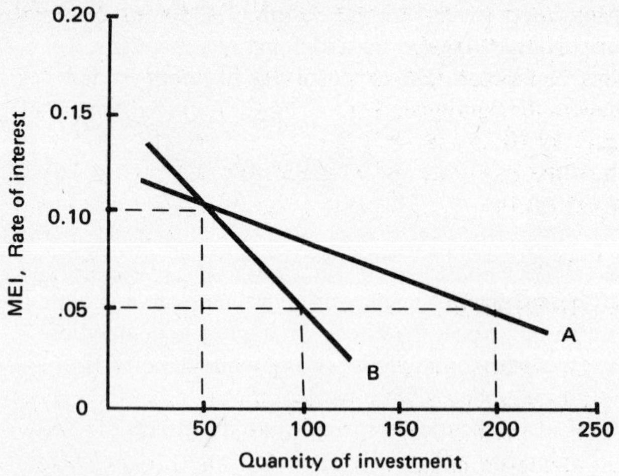

FIGURE 14-1

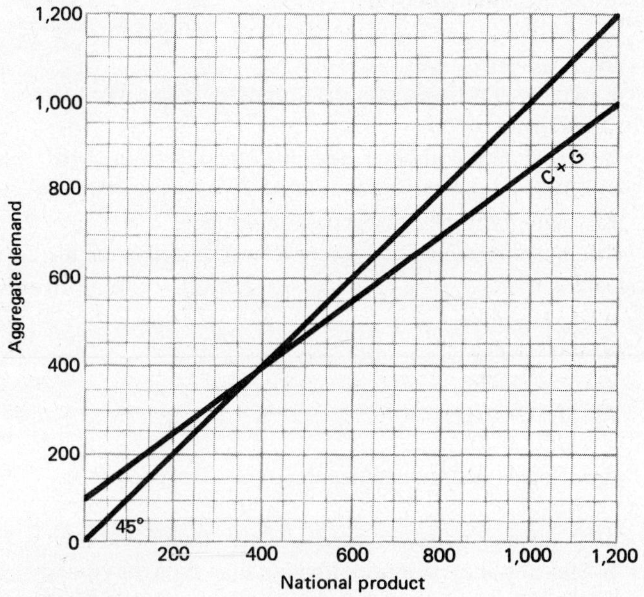

FIGURE 14-2

rate of interest is 5%, I^* will be ____________. If the two economies are identical except for the MEI, then monetary policy will be more powerful in economy [A, B], and fiscal policy will be more powerful in economy [A, B].

Figure 14-2 shows the 45° line and the line indicating consumption demand plus government demand for goods and services in either economy A *or* B. The slope of this line is equal to ____________. This means that the multiplier is equal to ____________. (If you have trouble with this point, refer back to Chapter 10.) Suppose that the interest rate in economy A is 10%. Draw the aggregate demand line ($C + I^* + G$) for economy A. The equilibrium is at a national product of ____________. Now suppose that the interest rate decreases to 5%. I^* will [increase, decrease] from ____________ to ____________ in economy A. Draw in a new aggregate demand line. The new equilibrium national product is ____________. From your last two answers, confirm the size of the multiplier shown earlier in the paragraph.

Now go through the same exercise for economy B. That is, draw in the aggregate demand line when the interest rate is equal to 10%, and then when it is equal to 5%. As a result of the fall in the interest rate, investment [increases, decreases] from ________ to ________, and equilibrium national product [increases, decreases] from ________ to ________. By comparing answers, we see that the multiplier is [higher than in A, lower than in A, the same as in A]. (Do you see why this is so?) A fall in interest rates from 10% to 5% has [a more powerful, a less powerful, the same] effect on national product in economy B, than/as it has on economy A.

ESSAY QUESTIONS

1. One reason for using monetary and fiscal policies together is that diversification spreads the benefit or pain. For each of the following policies, explain who the major gainers and losers are, and why; (a) expansive monetary policy, (b) expansive fiscal policy, (c) restrictive monetary policy, and (d) restrictive fiscal policy.

2. Suppose one economist told you that the MEI curve was quite steep, and another told you it was quite flat. Which is more likely to be a monetarist, and which a Keynesian? Explain.

3. "The equation of exchange, $MV = PQ$, is a tautology. Therefore it is useless in helping us understand how the economy works." Evaluate this statement. Also evaluate the following: "The basic Keynesian equation, aggregate demand = $C + I^* + G + X_n$, is also a tautology. Therefore it is also useless in helping us understand how the economy works."

ANSWERS

Important Terms: **1** d **2** f **3** a **4** g **5** b **6** h **7** e **8** c
True-False: **1** T **2** T **3** F **4** F **5** T **6** F **7** T **8** T **9** F **10** F
Multiple Choice: **1** d **2** a **3** b **4** c **5** d **6** a **7** d **8** c **9** e **10** b **11** d **12** c **13** d **14** b **15** e
Exercises: **1a.** a fall in the interest rate **1b.** a rise in investment demand **1c.** a multiplied increase in aggregate demand, interest rates were already very low, the MEI curve, buy bonds, interest rates will fall, buy goods, aggregate demand will increase, both, higher *P*, *V*. **2.** weak, fall, rise, decrease, small, effective, decrease, decrease, rationed, less. **3.** *A*, 50, 200, 50, 100, A, B, 0.75, 4, 600, increase, 50, 200, 1,200, increases, 50, 100, increases, 600, 800, the same as in A (because the multiplier depends on the slope of the aggregate demand function, which is the same in the two countries), less powerful.

Figure 14-2 completed:

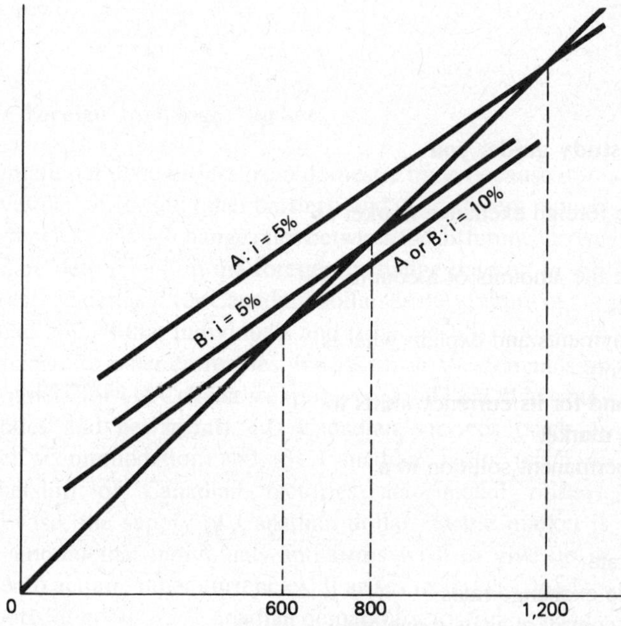

payments surplus (when total credits exceed the remaining debits so that there is an increase in official reserves) or a deficit (when debits exceed credits so that official reserves are decreasing).

World Experience with Fixed (or Pegged) Exchange Rates

During the nineteenth century and the early twentieth century (before the First World War), exchange rates between the world's major currencies were kept fixed through the gold standard. Under the gold standard, governments undertook to redeem their currencies for a specific amount of gold. As long as each country maintained the value of its currency in terms of gold, exchange rates between currencies also remained fixed.

While several countries tried to re-establish the gold standard after the First World War, these attempts were not successful, and the gold standard was finally abandoned in the late 1920s and early 1930s. However, at the Bretton Woods Conference, shortly after the Second World War, a system of *pegged but adjustable* exchange rates was once again established.

The adjustable peg system remained in force in most countries of the world between 1945 and 1971. However, Canada maintained pegged rates for only part of this period: The Canadian dollar was allowed to float between 1950 and 1962. In 1970, the Canadian government again allowed the dollar to float, and since 1973 most other countries have allowed their currencies to float as well.

Advantages of Fixed Exchange Rates

Economists who favour fixed exchange rates point to several advantages of a fixed-rate system over a system of flowing or flexible exchange rates:

1. When exchange rates remain fixed, the risk of exchange rate fluctuations is eliminated in international transactions; as a result, international trade and capital flows are encouraged and the world economy becomes more efficient.

2. When a government is committed to maintaining fixed exchange rates, it will be forced to avoid inflationary policies, since a high rate of domestic price inflation will make it possible to maintain fixed rates.

3. Exchange rate fluctuations under flexible rates may aggravate domestic problems. For example, when the exchange rate depreciates under a floating rate system, this adds to domestic inflation.

Advantages of Flexible Exchange Rates

Advocates of flexible exchange rates list several advantages of floating rates and disadvantages of fixed rates:

1. The government's commitment to maintaining a fixed exchange rate may sometimes force it to pursue tight monetary and fiscal policies even when such policies are not appropriate (such as the beginning of the Great Depression).

2. In practice, fixed exchange rates must sometimes be adjusted through devaluations or revaluations of currencies. But once we recognize that such adjustments may occur, it is no longer true that a system of fixed (pegged) exchange rates eliminates the exchange risk in international transactions.

3. This kind of instability in a pegged-rate system may be made worse by currency speculation.

4. A country on fixed exchange rates may lose control over its monetary policy, as Canada discovered in 1950. If the central bank tightens monetary policy, the domestic interest rate rises. But this results in a capital inflow and the balance of payments moves toward surplus. To maintain the fixed exchange rate, the central bank is forced to buy foreign exchange; this causes the money supply to rise, counteracting the initial tight policy.

Monetary and Fiscal Policies under Fixed and Flexible Exchange Rates

The relative effectiveness of monetary and fiscal policies as tools for stabilizing a country's economy (first discussed in Chapter 14) depends on whether the country is on fixed or flexible exchange rates. As already noted, fixed exchange rates may make a country lose control over its monetary policy: Monetary policy cannot be effectively used to stabilize the domestic economy if the central bank must react passively to the balance of payments. But if capital is highly mobile internationally, fixed exchange rates may *add* to the effectiveness of *fiscal* policy. As we saw in Chapter 14, the effectiveness of an expansionary fiscal policy, say, may be diminished if the increased need for government borrowing drives up interest rates and thus reduces private investment (the "crowding-out" problem). With fixed exchange rates and internationally mobile capital, however, the tendency for interest rates to rise will be counteracted by an inflow of foreign capital and (as the central bank buys foreign currencies) an increase in the domestic money supply; this will reduce both the tendency for interest rates to rise and the extent of crowding out.

With flexible exchange rates, on the other hand, *monetary* policy tends to be much more effective. For example, an expansionary monetary policy will reduce interest rates and therefore stimulate private investment, as outlined in Chapter 14. But the lower domestic interest rate will tend to cause a capital outflow. This will lead to a depreciation in the value of the country's currency, which, in turn, stimulates exports and makes the domestic goods more competitive with imports. The increased demand for exports and import-competing goods reinforces the effectiveness of monetary policy in stimulating aggregate demand. (The effectiveness of fiscal policy, by contrast, tends to be weakened by flexible exchange rates if capital is highly mobile. For example, as an expansionary fiscal policy puts upward pressure on domestic interest rates, a capital *inflow* results. But this tends to make the domestic currency *appreciate*, which reduces the demand for the country's exports and import-competing goods. Thus, the initial stimulative effect of an expansionary fiscal policy is diluted.)

Highlights of Appendix

By 1971, the IMF system of pegged but adjustable exchange rates was beginning to break down. Apart from the disadvantages posed by fixed exchange rates mentioned above, two other kinds of problems were becoming increasingly apparent:

1. "Surplus" countries were reluctant to revalue or to take expansionary measures that might cause inflation. As a consequence, "deficit" countries believed that they had to bear an unfair share of the adjustment burden.

2. The position of the U.S. dollar was somewhat precarious. If the U.S. government maintained a strong payments position (with a surplus or a small deficit), then other countries found it difficult to acquire foreign exchange reserves (most of which were held in the form of U.S. dollars). But if it ran large deficits (thereby providing the other countries with dollars), the holders of the U.S. dollars might fear that the United States would be unable to maintain the convertibility of dollars into gold. This could induce them to sell their dollars for gold, which would deplete the U.S. government's gold reserves, making it even more difficult for the U.S. to maintain the dollar's convertibility. Thus a "run" on the U.S. gold reserves could start, similar in nature to the banking panics of the nineteenth and early twentieth centuries.

When signs of such a run did develop in 1971, the United States decided to suspend convertibility of the U.S. dollar into gold. In spite of some attempts to patch up the system during the next two years, more and more countries opted for flexible exchange rates, and by 1974, the adjustable peg system had essentially disappeared.

IMPORTANT TERMS: MATCH THE COLUMNS

Match each term in the first column with the corresponding phrase in the second column. But before you do so, write your own definition of each term in the first column.

e **1.** foreign exchange
g **2.** exchange rate
l **3.** current account
j **4.** capital flows
i **5.** deficit in the balance of payments
f **6.** par value
h **7.** foreign exchange reserves
a **8.** devaluation
k **9.** depreciation
b **10.** sterilization
c **11.** speculate
d **12.** dirty float

a. reduction in the par value of a currency
b. operations to offset the impact of balance-of-payments deficit on the domestic money stock
c. buy something in anticipation of a price rise
d. occurs when governments intervene to influence price of currency
e. money of another country
f. officially chosen exchange rate
g. price of one currency in terms of another
h. government's holdings of foreign currency
i. exists when foreign expenditures exceed foreign receipts
j. international transactions involving ownership of assets
k. fall in the market price of a currency
l. record of international transactions in goods and services

TRUE-FALSE

T F **1.** When the Japanese buy Saudi Arabian oil, this creates a supply of yen in the exchange market.

T F **2.** If Canada cuts its tariffs, this will lead to an increase in imports and an increase in the supply of Canadian dollars in the exchange market.

T F **3.** A restrictive monetary policy in a country will shift the supply curve for the country's currency to the right in the foreign exchange market.

T F **4.** Payments of interest and dividends by Canadian residents to foreign owners of stock and bonds issued by Canadian firms are included in the capital account in the balance of payments.

T F **5.** A country's overall balance-of-payments accounts can show a deficit or a surplus only if there was a change in the country's foreign exchange reserves.

T F 6. A foreign takeover of a previously Canadian-owned firm is recorded as a long-term capital inflow in Canada's balance-of-payments accounts.

T F 7. An expansionary fiscal policy usually tends to cause deficits in both the current account and the capital account.

T F 8. A fixed exchange rate usually increases the effectiveness of fiscal policy because it reduces the tendency for government spending to crowd out private investment.

T F 9. The reason why an expansionary monetary policy tends to be highly effective under flexible exchange rates is that it usually causes an appreciation of the domestic currency, making imported goods cheaper.

MULTIPLE CHOICE

1. Which of the following is a source of demand for the Canadian dollar on the foreign exchange markets?

- **a.** purchases of foreign currencies by the Bank of Canada
- **b.** Canadian demand for foreign goods
- **c.** Canadian demand for foreign services
- **d.** Canadian investment in foreign countries
- **e.** foreign demand for Canadian exports

2. Which of the following leads to a decline in the demand for British pounds on the foreign exchange markets?

- **a.** a decrease in British purchases of German chemicals
- **b.** an increase in the number of U.S. tourists in Britain
- **c.** a switch by Canadian consumers from British to Japanese cars
- **d.** an increase in Canadian purchases of British cars
- **e.** an increase in British sales of textiles to the United States

3. Suppose that, on the foreign exchanges, $1 = 3 DM, while $1 = 12 francs. The exchange rate between the DM and the franc will then be

- **a.** 1 DM = 36 francs
- **b.** 1 DM = 4 francs
- **c.** 1 DM = 1 franc
- **d.** 1 franc = 4 DM
- **e.** 1 franc = 36 DM

4. Suppose that a British machine costs £400,000 while the exchange rate is £1 = $2. Then the price of that machine, in dollars is

- **a.** $800,000
- **b.** $600,000
- **c.** $400,000
- **d.** $200,000
- **e.** $100,000

5. Which of the following transactions is *not* recorded in the capital accounts of Canada's balance-of-payments statistics?

- **a.** a deposit by a Canadian executive of $1,500 in an account with a New York bank
- **b.** purchases by the Bank of Canada of $10-million-worth of German marks from a Canadian chartered bank
- **c.** payment by an American firm of a debt to a Canadian supplier
- **d.** contributions by an American resident to a Canadian foundation for the protection of Arctic wildlife
- **e.** an American takeover of a Canadian auto parts firm

6. Under the IMF system of adjustable pegs, one problem was that of "self-fulfilling expectations." This meant that

- **a.** when countries expected to have surpluses, they in fact had them
- **b.** when countries expected to have deficits, they in fact had them
- **c.** when officials expected to avoid a devaluation, they usually succeeded, because of the power of positive thinking
- **d.** when speculators thought that a currency might be devalued, they sold it, increasing the probability that it would in fact have to be devalued
- **e.** when speculators thought that a currency might be devalued, they bought it, increasing the probability that it would in fact have to be devalued

7. A "dirty float" is called "dirty" because

- **a.** it is unfair to foreign countries
- **b.** it is unfair to exporters
- **c.** it is unfair to importers
- **d.** it is not "clean"; that is, the central bank intervenes in exchange markets to influence exchange rates
- **e.** it is not "clean"; that is, the central bank departs from the rule of aiming for a steady growth in the money stock

8. Which of the following is *not* a common criticism of a system of fixed or pegged exchange rates?

- **a.** It may make a country lose control of its monetary policy.
- **b.** It tempts governments to follow more inflationary policies than their neighbours.
- **c.** It may lead to a great deal of uncertainty if speculators begin to anticipate a devaluation.
- **d.** It tends to make a country with a small population (such as Canada) highly sensitive to business fluctuations in other countries (such as the United States).
- **e.** It may force a country with high unemployment to follow contractionary policies.

9. With fixed exchange rates, an increase in the U.S. inflation rate tends to increase Canada's inflation rate because

a. it increases the demand for Canadian exports
b. it tends to raise the prices of goods imported into Canada
c. it tends to cause an increase in the stock of money in Canada
d. it tends to increase aggregate demand in Canada
e. all of the above

10. An expansionary monetary policy
a. tends to move both the current account and the capital account toward a deficit
b. has little effect on the domestic economy if exchange rates are flexible
c. tends to move the capital account toward a surplus but may cause either a surplus or a deficit in the current account
d. will work under flexible exchange rates only if the Bank of Canada is prepared to sterilize the effects of the balance-of-payments deficit on the Canadian money stock
e. tends to expand the thickness of your wallet

11. Under flexible exchange rates, the restrictive effect of a contractionary fiscal policy tends to be
a. partially offset by an increase in investment but reinforced by a decrease in net exports
b. partially offset by an increase in net exports but reinforced by a decrease in investment
c. stronger than it would be under fixed exchange rates
d. partially offset by reductions in both investment and net exports
e. strengthened by an increase in Canada's foreign exchange reserves

12. Under a flexible exchange rate system, which of the following would be a "vicious circle" for Canada?
a. Canadian inflation causes an appreciation of the dollar on the exchange markets, which causes higher Canadian inflation, which causes more appreciation of the dollar
b. Canadian inflation causes a depreciation of the dollar on the exchange markets, which causes higher Canadian inflation, which causes more depreciation of the dollar
c. higher Canadian interest rates lead to a depreciation of the Canadian dollar, which causes even higher interest rates
d. lower Canadian interest rates lead to an appreciation of the dollar, which causes even lower interest rates
e. lower Canadian interest rates lead to an appreciation of the dollar, which causes Canadian interest rates to rebound sharply

13. Suppose that the price of the Canadian dollar rises on the foreign exchange markets. This will
a. encourage Canadian exports, and slow down inflation in Canada
b. discourage Canadian exports, and make inflation worse in Canada
c. discourage Canadian exports, and slow down inflation in Canada
d. encourage Canadian exports, and make inflation worse in Canada
e. encourage Canadian exports, and ease the Canadian problem of unemployment

14. Which of the following discourage exports of Canadian goods and encourage imports of foreign goods into Canada?
a. Canadian inflation and depreciation of the dollar
b. foreign inflation and a depreciation of the dollar
c. Canadian inflation and an appreciation of the dollar
d. foreign inflation and an appreciation of the dollar
e. a depreciation of the dollar, and an appreciation of foreign currencies

EXERCISES

1. The data in Table 15-1 describe the demand and supply of pounds in the foreign exchange market. Plot the demand and supply curves in Figure 15-1, and label the demand curve D_1.

a. The equilibrium exchange rate is $________ per pound, or £________ per dollar. The equilibrium quantity of pounds sold is £________ million, in exchange for $________ million.

Table 15-1

Exchange rate ($ per £)	Amount demanded (millions of £)	Amount supplied (millions of £)
1.25	100	40
1.50	90	50
1.75	80	60
2.00	70	70
2.25	60	80
2.50	50	90
2.75	40	100

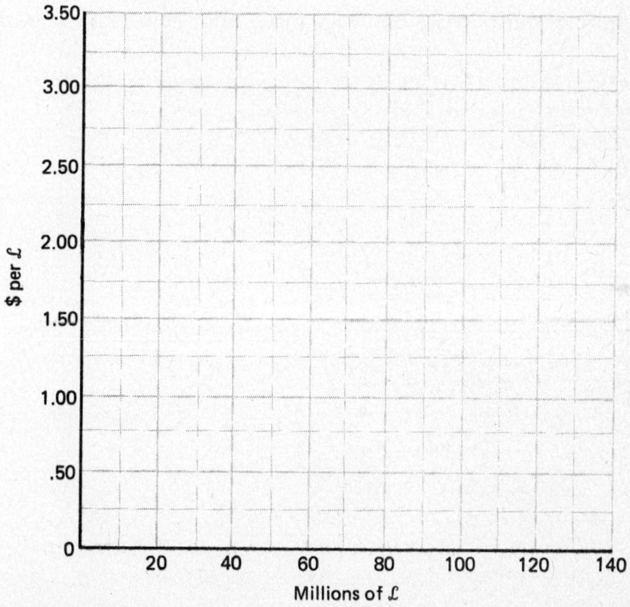

FIGURE 15-1

b. Suppose now that the demand for pounds decreases by £20 million at each exchange rate. Plot the new demand curve, and label it D_2. The new equilibrium exchange rate is $ ____________ per pound. The equilibrium quantity of pounds sold is now £ ____________ million, in exchange for $ ____________ million. If the exchange rate were held fixed by the British government at its *previous* equilibrium (in part (a)) Britain would now have a balance of payments [surplus, deficit] of £ ____________ million; that is, $____________ million.

2. Suppose the Bank of Canada sells government securities in the open market. This [increases, decreases] the reserves of chartered banks, [increases, decreases] the stock of money in Canada, and [raises, lowers] Canadian interest rates. As a result, Canada will experience an increased capital [inflow, outflow] and there will be tendency toward a balance-of-payments [deficit, surplus].

If exchange rates are [fixed, flexible], this tendency will force the Bank of Canada to intervene in the foreign exchange market, [selling, buying] Canadian dollars in exchange for foreign currencies. As a result, there will now be a tendency for chartered bank reserves to [increase, decrease], and this will [counteract, reinforce] the effect of the original sale of government securities.

If exchange rates are [fixed, flexible], the change in Canadian interest rates resulting from the Bank of Canada sale of government securities will tend to make the Canadian dollar [appreciate, depreciate]. As a result, net exports will [increase, decrease]. The effect of the original open market sale is to make domestic investment [increase, decrease]. The change in net exports therefore [reinforces, counteracts] the effect of the change in investment on aggregate demand. This exercise therefore shows that monetary policy is most likely to be a powerful economic policy tool under a system of [fixed, flexible] exchange rates.

ESSAY QUESTIONS

1. Suppose that, under the adjustable peg, the British government announced that it was going to devalue the pound by 10% in 1 week. How would this affect the demand and/or supply of pounds today? What would happen to the British government's holdings of dollar reserves? Would there be much risk in speculating today in the market for pounds? Why or why not? Would the government in fact be able to wait for a week before devaluing? Why or why not?

2. In early 1969, there was a public controversy between the German central bank (which wanted to raise the par value of the DM) and the German government (which didn't). What effect do you think this had on exchange markets? Why do you think the central bank took the position that it did? Why do you think the government took the position that it did?

3. How does the gold standard impose a "discipline" upon central banks and governments? What are the advantages of such discipline? the disadvantages? Is there a similar discipline with a pegged-but-adjustable rate? Why or why not? Is there discipline with a floating rate? Why or why not?

4. Explain how a country might fall into a "vicious circle." Now suppose that the world has only two countries, and they are approximately the same size. If one country is in a "vicious circle," will the other country also be in a "vicious circle" or will it be in a "virtuous circle"? Why?

5. Many U.S. economists believe that there is a relationship between the two large American deficits of the early 1980s—the large deficit in the budget of the American federal government, and the U.S. deficit in international trade. How might one cause the other?

ANSWERS

Important Terms: **1** e **2** g **3** l **4** j **5** i **6** f **7** h **8** a **9** k **10** b **11** c **12** d
True-False: **1** T **2** T **3** F **4** F **5** T **6** T **7** F **8** T **9** F
Multiple Choice: **1** e **2** c **3** b **4** a **5** d **6** d **7** d **8** b **9** e **10** a **11** d **12** b **13** c **14** c
Exercises: **1a.** $2, £0.50, £70 m, $140 m. **1b.** $1.75, £60 m, $105 m, deficit, £20 m, $40 m.

Figure 15-1 completed:

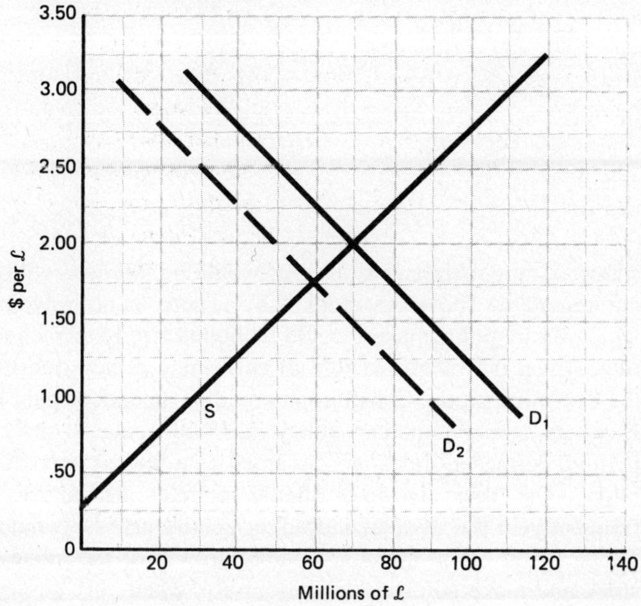

2. decreases, decreases, raises, inflow, surplus, fixed, selling, increase, counteract, flexible, appreciate, decrease, decrease, reinforces, flexible.

Chapter 16

FINE TUNING OR STABLE POLICY SETTINGS?

MAJOR PURPOSE

This chapter deals with one of the major, continuing controversies in macroeconomics: Should aggregate demand policies be adjusted as conditions change, or should the Bank of Canada follow a monetary policy rule? On the one side are those in the Keynesian tradition, who argue that aggregate demand should be *actively managed* in pursuit of the goals of high employment and stable prices. On the other side are the monetarists, who favour this rule: The Bank of Canada should aim for a *slow, steady increase in the money stock.* No matter how well intentioned the authorities, they do now know enough to stabilize the economy. Discretionary policies do not work in practice. So say the monetarists.

This debate has been dominated by strong advocates of rules, on the one hand, and strong opponents of rules, on the other. One of the major conclusions of this chapter is that the question before us is not really whether we should choose a rigid, permanent rule that would be followed without regard to "how the chips fall." There is no way in which future policymakers could be bound firmly to such a rule. (Even if it were feasible to enshrine a policy rule in the Constitution, the Constitution could be amended again.) However, a *very* important policy issue still remains—even if rigid, permanent rules are discarded as a logical impossibility. The issue is this: Should policies be adjusted frequently in the light of unfolding conditions? Or would we be better off to aim for a stable growth of the money stock and make adjustments only rarely, when very strong evidence for a change accumulates? Unfortunately, the experience of the past quarter-century does not provide a clear answer. Sometimes discretionary policies have worked quite well; sometimes they have not. The ambiguous lesson of history is, of course, one of the reasons why the controversy continues.

LEARNING OBJECTIVES

After you have studied this chapter in the textbook and study guide, you should be able to

- Describe the various steps in the active Keynesian approach to aggregate demand management
- Explain why lags make it difficult to stabilize aggregate demand through active management
- Explain the important role of potential GNP in the active approach
- Explain how problems in estimating potential were a major source of difficulty during the 1970s
- Explain the case for and the case against a discretionary policy

If you have studied the appendix, you should also be able to

- Explain why investment is much more volatile than consumption during the business cycle
- Explain why a moderate expansion may be more likely to last than a very rapid expansion

HIGHLIGHTS OF THE CHAPTER

Keynes and his followers argued that the government has the responsibility to maintain full employment and reasonably stable prices. Particularly in the early years between 1935 and 1965, Keynesians believed that an untended market economy would suffer from two major problems: Aggregate demand would be (1) often inadequate and (2) unstable. Authorities should actively intervene to bring aggregate demand up to the full employment level, and then manage it on a continuing basis to offset forces of instability.

This idea was particularly influential during the 1960s, a decade that has sometimes been called the "age of Keynes," Figure 16-1 in the textbook illustrates the general Keynesian demand-management strategy; Figure 16-2 presents the same idea applied to the situation in the early 1960s. There were several major steps in bringing aggregate demand up to the full-employment level: (1) First, the path of potential GNP was estimated. (2) Next, forecasts were made of where actual GNP would go in the absence of policy changes; in other words, the size of the prospective GNP gap was estimated. (3) Finally, fiscal and monetary policies were adjusted with the objective of closing the gap in a reasonably brief period. Until about 1966, this strategy was very successful. The estimated GNP gap closed, and prices remained reasonably stable. However, by the late 1960s, inflation began to accelerate, and during the first half of the 1970s, attempts to keep the economy on target seemed to result only in even more inflation, without bringing down the unemployment rate. In the years following the 1974–75 recession, the unemployment rate remained high by earlier standards, indicating that the economy was below potential. But at the same time, inflation also remained high. With the economy's performance giving conflicting signals, it was difficult to tell what was an appropriate policy at any given time, and even more difficult to say when there should be a policy change. The experience of the 1970s gave much less grounds for optimism regarding the possibilities of Keynesian demand management than did the experience of the 1960s.

Critics of active management make four major arguments:

1. *Lags* in the operation of policies mean that the government, like the panicky helmsman, may overreact to current events. Because of lags, policies developed today must be designed to deal with problems several months in the future. But economists are *only moderately successful in their ability to forecast* either the probable course of the economy in the absence of policy changes, or the effects of policy changes themselves.

2. Activists may *overestimate potential GNP*. As a result, they may strive to achieve an unattainable goal, creating strong inflationary pressures in the process. Figure 16-4 in the textbook illustrates this argument in general terms; Figure 16-5 applies it to the 1970s.

3. *Prices respond even more slowly* than real output when monetary and fiscal policies are changed. As a consequence, there may be an *inflationary bias* to discretionary policies. Decision makers may choose expansionary policies for the short-run benefits of higher output, and worry later about the inflationary consequences.

4. The active management of aggregate demand involves additional government meddling in the economy; rules are more consistent with a free-enterprise economy than are discretionary policies.

Advocates of rules recognize, of course, that it is important to pick the correct rule—one that is consistent with economic stability. It won't do to pick any old rule. There are some seemingly plausible rules that it would be a mistake to choose. For example, the gold standard rule made the banking system vulnerable to runs; it added to the North American banking chaos of 1931–33. However, proponents of rules believe that if the money stock were increased at a slow, steady rate, the economy would be more stable than it has been in the past, when proponents of active demand management were in charge. The proposal for a slow, steady increase in the money stock is based directly on the quantity theory of money—that is, on the view that velocity V is stable. If V is in fact stable, then a stable increase in M will mean a stable increase in nominal, income PQ.

Opponents of a monetary rule emphasize four points:

1. The government would be foolish to adopt rigid rules that may become outdated as circumstances change in unforeseen ways. Indeed, a truly rigid rule is a *logical impossibility*. Future decision makers cannot be bound inflexibly by the present. The *real issue is one of degree*: Will policies be adjusted in the light of a moderate amount of new information, or will policy changes be postponed until the evidence becomes overwhelming? While advocates of policy rules are correct in pointing out that lags create difficulties for discretionary policies, their proposals would increase lags in a major way. The government would be so committed to a course of action that it would not change policy until conditions became very bad indeed.

2. The rule advocated by monetarists—a slow, steady growth in the money stock—may lead to aggregate demand that is too low to buy the increasing volume of goods and services that the economy is capable of producing. In other words, the adoption of a rule aimed at slow growth of demand and stable prices may result in high unemployment and slow growth of real output.

3. There is no guarantee that stable monetary growth will lead to a stable increase in aggregate demand. In the period since 1975, the velocity of MI (which was the money supply concept used by the Bank of Canada during the years 1975–81 when it used a "gradualist policy") was highly unstable. Thus, a steady growth of MI did not lead to a stable increase in aggregate demand.

4. When strong evidence does accumulate that something is wrong, the government may then make abrupt changes in policy. In other words, the desire to follow a stable policy rule may paradoxically lead to *abrupt changes in practice*. An example was provided by the Bank of Canada's monetary policy during 1980–82. As the Bank made the switch from its earlier policy of making MI grow within a specified target range, to a policy of defending the external value of the Canadian dollar by making sure Canadian interest rates stayed close to U.S. interest rates, it produced an extreme and sudden monetary contraction, especially in 1981. According to the critics, this policy switch was a major contributor to the depth of the 1981–82 recession.

Note the contrast between point number 3 in the list of criticisms of fine tuning and point number 2 in the list of criticisms of a monetary rule. There is a significant difference in the approach of the two groups to the problems of unemployment. Advocates of discretionary policies consider monetarists heartless in their willingness to accept unemployment; monetarists consider some Keynesians to be crude inflationists.

As noted earlier, forecasting is required for the implementation of discretionary policies. Some forecasting, either formal or informal, is also needed by businesses that are planning their investment programs. Economic forecasters often use *econometric models*, modified by the results from surveys and the judgement of the forecaster. The record of forecasters is fair. It is much better than would come from a very simple approach, such as projecting the trends of the previous year or so. However, forecasters have not done a very good job in anticipating what will happen during recessions. In particular, they substantially underestimated the depth of the severe recession of 1981–82. This is worrisome to the advocates of active demand management. It is particularly important to anticipate recessions in order to be able to shift to more expansive policies in a timely manner.

IMPORTANT TERMS: MATCH THE COLUMNS

Match each term in the first column with the corresponding phrase in the second column. But before you do so, write your own definition of each term in the first column.

f 1. potential GNP
d 2. GNP gap
e 3. *V*
b 4. policy rule
g 5. recognition lag
a 6. action lag
c 7. impact lag

a. time that passes between recognition of weakness and change of policies
b. keep money growth low and stable
c. time that passes between a change of policy and the point at which aggregate demand responds
d. aggregate demand policies are aimed at eliminating this
e. if this isn't stable, money rule won't work
f. target path for those who manage aggregate demand
g. time that passes between the point at which a weakness begins and the point at which it is recognized

TRUE FALSE

T F 1. Monetarists advocate that the money stock be adjusted to keep interest rates stable.
T F 2. "Fine tuner" is a term applied to someone who wants to adjust policy frequently to stabilize demand.
T F 3. The "recognition lag" is the interval between the time when a problem is recognized and the time when corrective action is taken.
T F 4. The "action lag" is the interval between the time when action is taken, and when the action has its effect on aggregate demand.
T F 5. The case for active, discretionary monetary and fiscal policies would be stronger if economists could forecast better.
T F 6. If the potential GNP path is overestimated, active demand managers are likely as a consequence to follow overly stimulative demand management policies.
T F 7. If the rate of increase in productivity unexpectedly falls, potential GNP is likely to be overestimated as a result.
T F 8. Because of the errors in estimating potential GNP during the 1970s, almost all economists now believe in a monetary policy rule.
T F 9. Those who advocate a monetary "rule" argue that a rule is more conducive to freedom than is discretion by policymakers.
T F 10. The inflation rate is a leading indicator.

MULTIPLE CHOICE

1. An economist is most likely to favour discretionary aggregate demand policies, rather than a policy rule if he or she is in which economic tradition?
- **a.** Keynesian
- **b.** classical
- **c.** monetarist
- **d.** marginalist
- **e.** libertarian

2. Economists who argue for a policy rule aimed at stabilizing aggregate demand are most likely to favour which rule?
- **a.** the gold standard
- **b.** a balanced actual budget
- **c.** a balanced full-employment budget
- **d.** a steady growth in the money stock
- **e.** all the above rules are equally good; the thing that matters is to have *some* rule

3. A monetarist is most likely to advocate which of the following policy rules?
- **a.** increase the money stock, measured in dollars, by 4% every year
- **b.** increase the money stock by 4% in real terms; that is, increase the money stock by 4% plus the amount of inflation
- **c.** increase the money stock, measured in dollars, by 4% plus a fraction of the output gap
- **d.** increase the real money stock by 4% plus a fraction of the output gap
- **e.** increase the real money stock by 4% plus a fraction of the inflationary gap

4. The discretionary policies of the 1960s involved each of the following steps *except one* . Which is the exception?
- **a.** estimate potential GNP
- **b.** forecast the probable course of GNP in the absence of policy changes
- **c.** forecast the effects of various changes in aggregate demand policies
- **d.** select the policies aimed at closing the GNP gap in a reasonably brief time
- **e.** revise the potential GNP path upward, since an even better performance now becomes possible

5. Suppose that economic forecasters predict a GNP gap of $20 billion for the coming year if no change is made in policies. Then an advocate of
- **a.** rules would prescribe a faster growth in the quantity of money
- **b.** rules would prescribe a faster growth in government spending
- **c.** active management would prescribe an increase in tax rates, to balance the budget
- **d.** active management would prescribe an increase in government spending
- **e.** active management would prescribe an increase in government spending to increase real output, plus a decrease in the money stock to reduce inflation

6. The recognition lag is the lag between the time when
- **a.** a problem is recognized and the time when corrective action is taken
- **b.** a problem is recognized and the time when it is corrected
- **c.** a recession begins and the time when the authorities recognize it has begun
- **d.** aggregate demand increases and the time when producers realize that they can raise their prices
- **e.** aggregate demand increases and producers recognize that they should produce more

7. The "helmsman's dilemma" illustrates the difficulty of making policy in the presence of
- **a.** inflation
- **b.** deflation
- **c.** unemployment
- **d.** low growth
- **e.** lags

8. Those who advocate policy rules rather than active management argue that active managers tend to
- **a.** overestimate potential, and therefore follow inflationary policies
- **b.** underestimate potential, and therefore follow deflationary policies
- **c.** underestimate growth, and therefore follow inflationary policies
- **d.** underestimate the effects of government spending, and therefore rely too much on monetary policy
- **e.** underestimate the effects of tax changes, and therefore rely too much on monetary policy

9. At times during the business cycle, "everything seems to be going right"—that is, output is rising, unemployment falling, and the rate of inflation falling. This is most likely to occur
- **a.** at the peak of the expansion
- **b.** early in the expansion
- **c.** late in the expansion, about 3 or 4 months before the peak
- **d.** late in the recession, when people are beginning to become more optimistic
- **e.** at the trough, when people are beginning to become more optimistic

10. The monetarist case is based on each of the following propositions *except one* . Which is the exception?
- **a.** The desirable path of aggregate demand is one of steady, moderate growth.
- **b.** The desirable trend of prices is a gradual upward movement, by about 4% per year.
- **c.** The best way to get a steady, moderate increase in aggregate demand is by a steady, moderate increase in the money stock.
- **d.** Following a monetary rule increases economic freedom, and probably political freedom, too.

11. Suppose that you were looking for a set of policy rules to keep aggregate demand reasonably stable. Which set of rules would hold the most promise?

a. keep interest rates fixed, and balance the actual budget each year
b. keep interest rates fixed, and balance the full-employment budget each year
c. increase the quantity of money at a steady rate, and balance the actual budget each year
d. increase the quantity of money at a steady rate, and balance the full-employment budget every year
e. re-establish the gold standard

12. Those who advocate active demand management oppose policy rules on a number of grounds, including the argument that
a. proposed rules are likely to result in excessive unemployment
b. proposed rules are likely to result in ever-increasing inflation
c. rules won't work unless "you can fool some of the people all the time, or all the people some of the time"
d. rules require an estimate of potential GNP, and we are able to estimate potential GNP only imperfectly
e. rules will result in too much saving and investment

13. Opponents of a monetary rule argue that there cannot in fact be a rigid rule because
a. it would be unconstitutional
b. the Bank of Canada in fact has almost no control over the money stock
c. money does not affect aggregate demand
d. money does not affect interest rates
e. future governments cannot be committed to a rule regardless of the consequences

14. Suppose that C = 0.5 GNP; $I^*_g = 50$; $G = 70$; X = 30; and imports are 10% of GNP. Then equilibrium NP equals
a. 250
b. 300
c. 375
d. 395
e. 520

EXERCISES

1. There are three lags before monetary and fiscal policies affect aggregate demand. First is the ____________ lag, next the ____________ lag, and then the ____________ lag. In addition there is another lag that occurs after aggregate demand changes. Specifically, the effects on demand on [output, prices] generally lags behind its effect on [output, prices]. Critics of active demand management argue that the first three lags mean that policies may destabilize the economy. The fourth lag means that discretionary policies can have an [inflationary, deflationary] bias.

Lags are, however, not only the problem facing the managers of aggregate demand. They also have the difficult task of estimating [the path of potential GNP, the effects of monetary policy on demand, the effects of fiscal policy on demand, all of these]. Suppose they overestimate the potential path. This means that, starting from a recession, they are likely to [keep expansive policies too long, abandon expansive policies too soon].The reason is that [the economy will remain below the potential path, they will soon give up trying]. As a result, the problem of [inflation, low growth] may become worse.

2. In this exercise you must choose a fiscal policy. See if you can learn from this what kind of problems beset policymakers.

a. Suppose your advisors tell you that potential GNP is now $198 billion and that it will grow by $12 billion per year for each of the next four years. (All figures are in constant dollars.) Last year (year zero) and the year before, actual GNP was $162 billion and *G* (the level of government spending on goods and services) was $50 billion. Next, suppose that your advisors tell you that the government spending multiplier is 3, that they do not foresee any lags in the economic system, and that aggregate demand will not change unless *G* changes. In Table 16-1, chart the behaviour of potential GNP and of actual GNP and the GNP gap under different assumptions about *G*. In this example, policy [A, B, C] is the neutral policy of keeping the same level of government spending, policy [A, B, C] is the activist policy of trying to eliminate the GNP gap immediately, and policy [A, B. C] is the "gradualist" policy of eliminating the GNP gap in stages over 4 years.

Table 16-1

	Year 1	Year 2	Year 3	Year 4
Potential GNP	198			
G	50	50	50	50
A. Actual GNP	162	162	162	162
GNP gap	36			
G	62	66	70	74
B. Actual GNP				
GNP gap				
G	56	62	68	74
C. Actual GNP				
GNP gap				

b. Now suppose that your advisors were mistaken. Instead of no lag, the multiplier operates with a 1-year lag, so that any change by one unit in *G* this year would cause a 3-unit change in GNP *next* year, but no change in GNP *this* year. Then show the results of the three policies in Table 16-2.

Table 16-2

G	Year 1	Year 2	Year 3	Year 4
A. Actual GNP	162	162	162	162
GNP gap	36			
B. Actual GNP	162			
GNP gap				
C. Actual GNP				
GNP gap				

c. Next, suppose that as well as the lag there are shifts in aggregate demand that were unforeseen by your advisors. Suppose that the changes in investment from one year to the next were as indicated in Table 16-3, and that these changes, just like changes in *G*, affected GNP with a multiplier of 3 and with a 1-year delay. Show in Table 16-4 the outcomes of the three policies. Table 16-4 shows a potential hazard of activist policies. The activist policy, B, instead of just closing the GNP gap in 2, 3, and 4, would result in a sizeable [recessionary, inflationary] gap. The less active, "gradualist" policy, C, would result in a [smaller, larger] gap. And the best policy in terms of producing the smallest average gap over the years 2 through 4, would be the [neutral, activist, gradualist] policy.

Table 16-3

	Year 0	Year 1	Year 2	Year 3
Change in investment over previous year	0	+ 10	+ 8	+ 4

Table 16-4

	Year 1	Year 2	Year 3	Year 4
A. Actual GNP				
GNP gap				
B. Actual GNP				
GNP gap				
C. Actual GNP				
GNP gap				

ESSAY QUESTIONS

1. Why can't the government always eliminate the GNP gap by continuing to increase its spending as long as the gap exists?

2. Suppose that a 4% monetary rule were adopted. Then suppose that the introduction of an electronic transfer system for making payments caused a large increase in the velocity of money. What would happen to the price level? Could this have been avoided if the rule hadn't been adopted? Can you think of a rule that would allow for such contingencies?

3. Elected governments have objectives in addition to their economic goals—for example, regional development and getting re-elected. How do these other goals strengthen or weaken the case for discretionary policies, rather than a monetary rule?

4. A passage in the chapter highlights section reads as follows: "Advocates of discretionary policies consider monetarists heartless in their willingness to accept unemployment; monetarists consider some Keynesians to be crude inflationists." Explain why these criticisms are made. In the first case, what defence might a monetarist have? (Hint: Does it depend on the aggregate supply function?) In the second case, what defence might a Keynesian have?

ANSWERS

Important Terms: **1** f **2** d **3** e **4** b **5** g **6** a **7** c
True-False: **1** F **2** T **3** F **4** F **5** T **6** T **7** T **8** F **9** T **10** F
Multiple Choice: **1** a **2** d **3** a **4** e **5** d **6** c **7** e **8** a **9** b **10** b **11** d **12** a **13** e **14** a
Exercises: **1.** recognition, action, impact, prices, output, inflationary, all of these, keep expansive policies too long, the economy will remain below the potential path, inflation

2a. Table 16-1 completed

Year 1	Year 2	Year 3	Year 4
198	210	222	234
36	48	60	72
198	210	222	234
0	0	0	0
180	198	216	234
18	12	6	0

A, B, C

2b. Table 16-2 completed

Year 1	Year 2	Year 3	Year 4
162	162	162	162
36	48	60	72
162	198	210	222
36	12	12	12
162	180	198	216
36	30	24	18

2c. Table 16-4 completed

Year 1	Year 2	Year 3	Year 4
162	192	216	228
36	18	6	6
162	228	264	288
36	– 18	– 42	– 54
162	210	256	282
36	0	– 30	– 48

inflationary, smaller, neutral

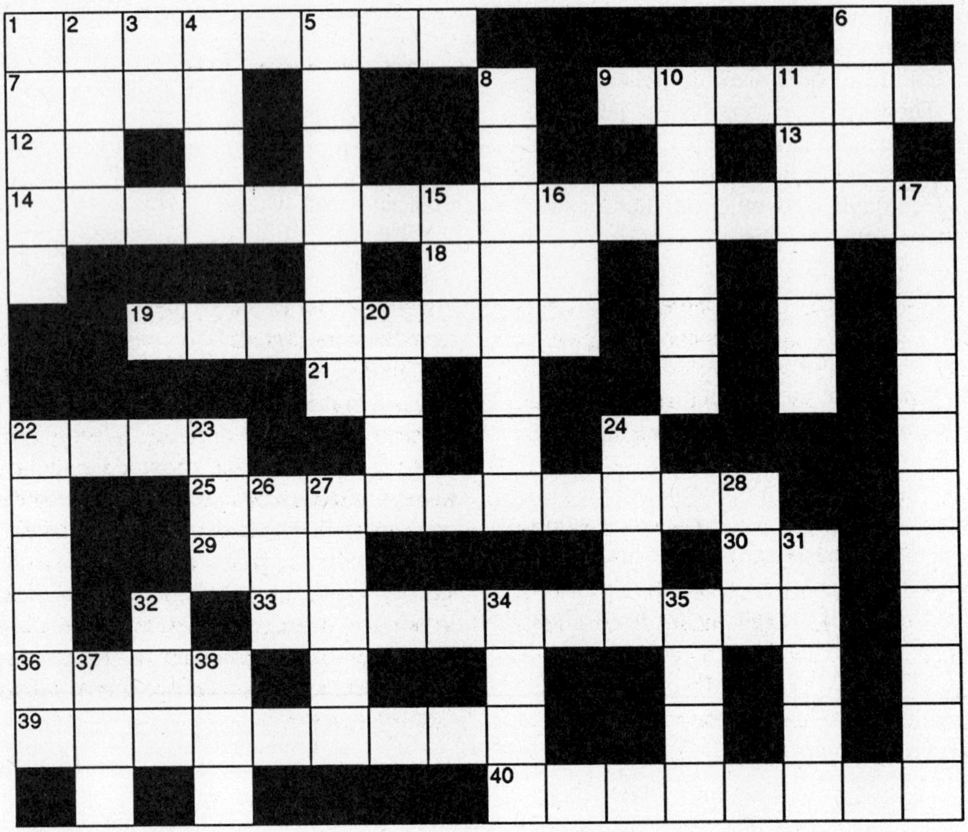

Across

1. someone to whom money is owed
7. holiday season
9. type of lag
12. a chemical element (abbrev.)
13. on Swiss car licence plate
14. This is watched by forecasters. (2 words)
18. society of Canadian economists (abbrev.)
19. ____________ of money is the key, say proponents of rules.
21. proceed
22. a healthy economy will do this
25. Policymakers want to keep this high.
29. sound of disapproval
30. first person plural
33. Should we use this, or follow rules?
36. old
39. This level of GNP is sometimes used as a target.
40. Classical macroeconomics is built on the ____________ of exchange.

Down

1. The business ____________ is a major macroeconomic problem.
2. alternative to active management
3. Keynesian aggregate supply schedule reverses this.
4. our condition in the long run, noted Keynes
5, 27. peak or trough
6. sound repeated faintly
8, 34. what monetarists want
10. famous mouse
11. type of lag
15. here (French)
16. fraction of a week
17. type of lag
20. hard work
22. Eliminating this may be a policy objective. (2 "words")
23. spider's home
24. encounter (verb)
26. stylish (slang)
28. pair
31. French word, used in English to denote boredom
32. group; in tennis, lasts several games
35. Researchers get paid for this, even if not every one is good.
37. His Muslim name is Allah.
38. bear's home

Chapter 17

AGGREGATE SUPPLY: HOW CAN INFLATION AND UNEMPLOYMENT COEXIST?

MAJOR PURPOSE

For several decades following the Great Depression, macroeconomists concentrated on the management of aggregate demand. When the economy was declining into a recession, they advocated expansive demand policies to keep output and employment at high levels. When inflationary pressures were strong, they advocated tighter policies to restrain demand and keep inflation down.

However, during the past two decades, the economy has from time to time given conflicting signals. There have been bouts of *stagflation*—that is, periods when high unemployment was combined with rapid inflation. The high unemployment suggested that demand should be expanded; the rapid inflation indicated the opposite. To understand this complex economy, we must look not only at aggregate demand, but also at aggregate supply. Our purpose in Chapter 17 is to study aggregate supply, and, in doing so, to explore stagflation.

The simplest way to approach aggregate supply is the one presented earlier, in a diagram with real national product on the horizontal axis and the average level of prices on the vertical. However, this is not the approach most commonly used. Instead, economists generally begin with a diagram in which the two macroeconomic problems—unemployment and inflation—appear on the axes. The smooth curve traced out by historical data during some periods, such as the 1960s, is known as a *Phillips curve*. However, the Phillips curve has not been stable in recent decades. One of the major purposes of this chapter is to try to explain why the Phillips curve shifts.

LEARNING OBJECTIVES

After you have studied this chapter in the textbook and study guide, you should be able to

- Summarize Canada's experience with inflation and unemployment since 1960
- Explain why demand-management authorities sometimes feel that they face a policy dilemma
- State the two major reasons why the (short-run) Phillips curve can shift upward
- Explain the difference between cost-push inflation and demand-pull inflation, and explain why cost-push inflation can lead to higher prices *and* higher unemployment
- Explain why demand-management authorities face a very difficult problem when there is a large upward shift in the Phillips curve (such as in 1973–74 and 1979–80)
- Explain why inflation can accelerate to higher and higher rates if the authorities try to keep unemployment below the natural rate
- Explain why many economists believe that the long-run Phillips curve is vertical
- Explain why Milton Friedman argues that "there is *always* a temporary trade-off between inflation and unemployment; there is *no permanent trade-off*"
- Explain why some economists argue that there is no trade-off—even in the short run (if you have studied Box 17-2)
- Explain why the process of reducing inflation can be painful, in terms of high unemployment
- Explain why a stable path of aggregate demand results in a lower average rate of unemployment than a fluctuating path
- Describe Canada's experience with wage and price controls during the 1970s, and explain the pros and cons of using such controls or other incomes policies

HIGHLIGHTS OF THE CHAPTER

When the demand for a specific commodity—such as wheat—changes, there is a movement *along* the supply curve (as illustrated in Figure 4-8 in the textbook). Similarly, when aggregate demand changes, the economy moves along the aggregate supply curve. Thus, when we study aggregate supply in this chapter, we are studying how the economy responds to a change in aggregate demand. This is an important and puzzling topic. From time to time, the economy has suffered from *stagflation*—a combination of high unemployment and high inflation. In such circumstances it is not clear what the authorities should do. If they take steps to increase aggregate demand in an attempt to increase output and employment, they may get more inflation instead. If they restrain demand in an attempt to reduce inflation, they may get more unemployment. Making sense of the aggregate supply puzzle is an important topic; it is the main purpose of this chapter.

To study aggregate supply, it is possible to use the aggregate supply curve introduced in Chapter 9, with real national product (*Q*) on the horizontal axis and the average level of prices (*P*) on the horizontal axis. However, this is not the approach most commonly used. Instead, economists generally begin with a diagram in which the two macroeconomic problems—unemployment and inflation— appear on the axes.

When historical data are plotted on such a diagram in Figure 17-3 in the text, two main conclusions stand out:

1. For most of the 1960s, the points trace out a smooth curve, sloping upward to the left. This is known as a *Phillips* curve.

2. Since 1970, the observations have been above and to the right of that Phillips curve. We have experienced more unemployment *and* more inflation. Strong movements upward and to the right occurred during the 1971–75 period and also in 1977–78.

During the 1960s, when most economists believed that the Phillips curve being traced out by the data represented a stable relationship, authorities felt trapped on the horns of a *dilemma*. If they expanded aggregate demand briskly, they would get more output and employment. But inflation would rise. On the other hand, if they restrained demand in order to keep inflation down, the unemployment rate would remain high. They hoped to escape from this dilemma by using expansive aggregate demand policies to reduce unemployment, and incomes policies to directly restrain inflation. They were not entirely successful. Inflation did, in fact, increase as output expanded and unemployment declined. The economy did, in fact, move upward as it moved to the left in Figure 17-3 in the text.

Shifts in the Phillips Curve

Even worse problems were to come in the 1970s however, as both inflation and unemployment increased. Part of the strong movements upward and to the right in Figure 17-3 took place during a period of spiralling oil prices on international markets. This suggests one explanation for the stagflation since 1970: Rising oil prices shifted the Phillips curve upward, and meant more inflation combined with more unemployment. Inflation was caused by the *upward push of costs*.

Oil prices certainly do not provide the whole explanation, however., The first major movement to the northeast, between 1967 and 1969, and again between 1971 and 1972, occurred while international oil prices were stable at a low level.

To explain these early episodes of stagflation, we must look elsewhere. The *accelerationist theory* provides the most generally accepted explanation.

The Accelerationist Theory

The accelerationist theory, put forward in the late 1960s by Edmund Phelps and Milton Friedman, has one core idea. The Phillips curve—such as that observed in the 1960s—is fundamentally *unstable*. If the authorities attempt to reduce the unemployment rate to a very low level, they will succeed, but *only temporarily*. In particular, they will succeed only during the interval between the time when demand is expanded and the time when contracts are renegotiated to take the resulting inflation into account. When people renegotiate contracts, they will demand compensation for inflation; wages and other contractual prices will be adjusted upward. Inflation will accelerate; a *wage-price spiral* will gain momentum. This is illustrated by points *H*, *J* and *K* in Figure 17-7 of the text. At each of these points, actual inflation is higher than people expected when they negotiated contracts. For example, at *H*, people expect zero inflation (as illustrated by the Phillips curve), but get 2% instead. They then renegotiate contracts on the expectation of 2% inflation. But, with higher costs, businesses raise prices; the economy moves to *J*. People expect 2% inflation; they get 4% instead.

How, then, can we return to macroeconomic equilibrium, once the wage-price spiral has begun? Equilibrium occurs only when *people get the amount of inflation they expected*. It is easiest for this to happen when the rate of inflation levels out. For inflation to level out, the authorities must depart from their single-minded attempt to keep unemployment low; they must introduce a degree of restraint in aggregate demand policies. As restraint occurs, businesses will find it hard to raise prices more and more rapidly; inflation will indeed level off. However, as it becomes hard to sell goods, output will increase more slowly and the unemployment rate will rise.

Once people get the amount of inflation they expect, the unemployment rate will move back to its *natural*, or *equilibrium* rate, illustrated by point *N* in Figure 17-8 of the text. A central proposition of the accelerationist theory is that this equilibrium rate of unemployment *doesn't depend on the rate of inflation*; once people adjust completely to inflation, the inflation rate doesn't affect their behaviour. They are neither more nor less willing to work, and businesses are neither more nor less willing to hire them. Because the equilibrium rate of unemployment isn't affected by inflation—once people have become used to it—*the long-run Phillips curve is vertical.* In the short run, the central bank can lower the rate of unemployment by an inflationary policy. But in the long run, their willingness to accept an inflation rate of, say, 6% will not result in any gain in output and employment. There is a *short-run trade-off* between the goals of low inflation and low unemployment, but there is *no long-run trade-off*.

Just as low unemployment is associated with an acceleration of inflation, so high unemployment is associated with a deceleration of inflation. If aggregate demand is too low to buy the goods and services being offered at the current rate of inflation, output will fall and businesses will settle for smaller increases in price. This is illustrated by point *V* in Figure 17-11 of the text. *V* is not a good place to be; the unemployed are being used as cannon fodder in the war against inflation. In order to avoid painful periods at point like *V*, it is important to stop the inflationary spiral from gathering momentum in the first place. To those who asked in the 1970s how we might get out of stagflation, there was only one easy—although unsatisfactory—answer: Go back to 1965 and do it right this time. Stop inflation from accelerating in the first place. But of course we could not go back to 1965 again. The economy was, in fact, dragged through the severe recession of 1982 before the inflation rate was brought down to 4%—a rate that was still much higher than that of the period from 1955 to 1965.

Incomes Policies

Incomes policies have often been used in both Europe and North America in efforts to break inflationary spirals without having to go through extended periods of high unemployment. In Canada, the most serious attempt at using incomes policies was the wage and price control program administered by the Anti-Inflation Board during the years 1975–78. This program specified maximum percentage increases in wages and salaries, and set targets for the maximum rate of price inflation as well.

Incomes policies are controversial. Proponents say that they are the only compassionate way to deal with the inflationary problem—the only alternative is to let unemployment soar. Opponents say that incomes policies may do more harm than good. For example, by suppressing inflationary pressures temporarily, they may provide the illusion of success, with the authorities unwittingly continuing expansive policies as underlying inflationary pressures build up. The result can be an explosion of inflation, and a worse situation than would be faced if the inflation had not been temporarily suppressed. The Canadian experience with the 1975–78 anti-inflation program was not encouraging. Even though the rate of price inflation came down somewhat following 1975, there was no subsequent reduction in unemployment, and by 1979–80, just after the program had ended, both unemployment and inflation were again as high as they had been in 1975 at the beginning of the program.

IMPORTANT TERMS: MATCH THE COLUMNS

Match each term in the first column with the corresponding phrase in the second column. But before you do so, write you own definition of each term in the first column.

e ____ **1.** Phillips curve
i ____ **2.** trade-off
f ____ **3.** stagflation
j ____ **4.** cost-push inflation
c ____ **5.** natural rate of unemployment
k ____ **6.** accelerationist theory
b ____ **7.** incomes policy
d ____ **8.** wage-price controls
a ____ **9.** AIB
g ____ **10.** TIP
h ____ **11.** import price increases

a. government agency charged with overseeing program of wage-price controls
b. this is aimed at easing the inflation-unemployment dilemma
c. equilibrium rate of unemployment
d. used as part of an incomes policy to bring down inflation
e. relationship between inflation and unemployment
f. high unemployment combined with high inflation
g. an incomes policy backed with tax incentives
h. create difficulties for Canadian incomes policy
i. choice between conflicting goals
j. the rise in the international price of oil is an example
k. view that there is trade-off in the short-run, but not in the long run

TRUE-FALSE

T F 1. According to the aggregate supply function of simple Keynesian theory, large-scale unemployment *or* rapid inflation can exist, but not both simultaneously.

T F 2. Suppose that money wages were constant through time. Then it would be possible to have a continuous downward trend in prices, if productivity rises.

T F 3. Those who emphasize cost-push inflation are more likely to believe that market power is important than are advocates of the accelerationist theory.

T F 4. According to the accelerationist theory, the economy can be in equilibrium only when inflation rate is zero; any positive rate of inflation will tend to accelerate.

T F 5. Even when the unemployment rate is at its natural level, there is still frictional unemployment.

T F 6. Even when the unemployment rate is at its natural level, there is still structural unemployment.

T F 7. The short-run Phillips curve has shifted down since 1960; it is now lower than it was in 1960.

T F 8. If the long-run Phillips curve is vertical, then the average rate of unemployment over the long run is independent of both the trend and stability of aggregate demand; aggregate demand is irrelevant in determining the average unemployment rate.

T F 9. Although the actual rate of unemployment has been on an upward trend during the past two decades, the evidence indicates that the natural rate has declined.

T F 10. The TIP proposal is supposed to work by stimulating aggregate demand.

MULTIPLE CHOICE

1. If we compare the Canadian experience since 1970 with that of the 1960s, we find that, on average
- **a.** the rate of unemployment and the rate of inflation have both been lower since 1970 than during the 1960s
- **b.** the rate of unemployment has been lower since 1970 than during the 1960s, but the rate of inflation has been higher
- **c.** the rate of inflation has been lower since 1970 than during the 1960s, but the rate of unemployment has been higher
- **d.** the rate of unemployment and the rate of inflation have both been higher since 1970 than during the 1960s

2. The Phillips curve traced out by the Canadian data of the 1960s suggested that there was a policy "trade-off." Specifically, there seemed to be a conflict between achieving the goal of high employment and the goal of
- **a.** an equitable distribution of income
- **b.** allocative efficiency
- **c.** technological efficiency
- **d.** high growth
- **e.** low inflation

3. Economists are most likely to conclude that "cost-push" inflation is occurring when a rise in the rate of inflation is accompanied by an increase in
- **a.** output
- **b.** the rate of growth of output
- **c.** the unemployment rate
- **d.** government deficits
- **e.** the money stock

4. Which of the following is an assumption of the accelerationist theory?
- **a.** there is downward rigidity in nominal wages
- **b.** inflation is caused mainly by unions
- **c.** inflation is caused mainly by OPEC
- **d.** inflation is caused mainly by an acceleration in investment
- **e.** people's expectations of inflation have an important effect on the contracts they negotiate

5. Suppose we draw a diagram with both a short-run Phillips curve and a long-run Phillips curve. At the point where they intersect
- **a.** the inflation rate is zero
- **b.** the unemployment rate is zero
- **c.** actual inflation is the same as expected inflation
- **d.** inflation is accelerating
- **e.** the rate of unemployment is rising

6. According to the accelerationist theory, the unemployment rate will be greater than the natural rate when inflation is
- **a.** greater than people expected
- **b.** less than people expected
- **c.** low and steady
- **d.** high and steady
- **e.** zero

The next three questions are based on Figure 17-1.

7. In Figure 17-1, the natural rate of unemployment is 6%. Which of the points represent an equilibrium?
- **a.** *A*
- **b.** *B*
- **c.** *C*
- **d.** *D*
- **e.** *E*

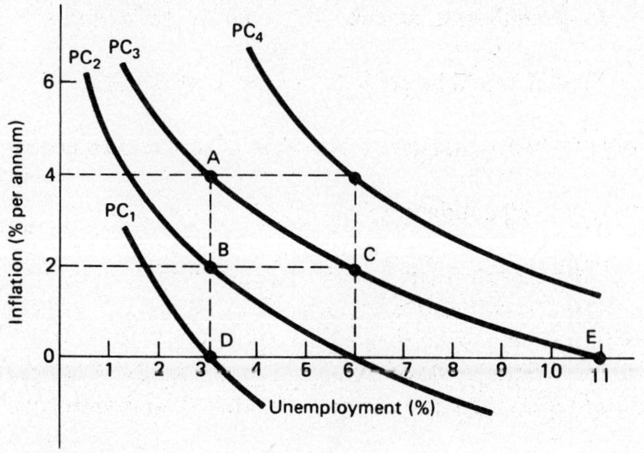

FIGURE 17-1

8. In Figure 17-1, the natural rate of unemployment is 6%. When the economy is at point *A* on Phillips curve PC_3, the expected rate of inflation is

- **a.** zero
- **b.** 2%
- **c.** 3%
- **d.** 4%
- **e.** 6%

9. In Figure 17-1, the natural rate of unemployment is 6%. Last year, the economy was at point *A* on short-run Phillips curve PC_3. If contracts are now renegotiated, which of the short-run Phillips curve is most likely to result?

- **a.** PC_1
- **b.** PC_2
- **c.** PC_3
- **d.** PC_4
- **e.** either PC_1 or PC_2, but we can't be sure which

10. According to the accelerationist theory, equilibrium can exist only when

- **a.** the unemployment rate is at its natural rate
- **b.** the inflation rate is zero, since any non-zero rate of inflation will tend to accelerate
- **c.** the expected inflation rate is zero, since inflation will accelerate otherwise
- **d.** the growth of the money stock is zero, since inflation will accelerate otherwise
- **e.** all of the above conditions are met

11. Which of the following is likely to cause the highest average rate of unemployment in the long run?

- **a.** a highly variable rate of growth of aggregate demand
- **b.** a steady rate of growth of aggregate demand at about 5% per annum
- **c.** a steady rate of growth of aggregate demand at about 10% per annum
- **d.** a reduction in the minimum wage
- **e.** a reduction in the fraction of teenagers in the labour force

12. Which of the following is likely to reduce the natural rate of unemployment?

- **a.** a rise in the minimum wage
- **b.** a fall in the proportion of teenagers in the labour force
- **c.** more emphasis on fiscal policy, and less on monetary policy
- **d.** more generous unemployment insurance benefits
- **e.** all of the above

13. During the period of wage-price controls in Canada during the mid-1970s, the government

- **a.** increased tariffs to keep out expensive foreign products
- **b.** specified that wages and prices had to rise at the same percentage rates
- **c.** maintained a fixed exchange rate in order to prevent import prices from rising
- **d.** reduced unemployment insurance benefits in order to decrease the natural rate of unemployment
- **e.** specified maximum allowable wage increases, but did not specify maximum rates of price increases

14. Which of the following is *not* a common criticism of wage and price controls in Canada?

- **a.** they are complicated to administer
- **b.** experience from the Second World War and from the early 1960s demonstrates that controls will not work in Canada
- **c.** because labour unions believe that wages are easier to control than prices, unions usually oppose controls
- **d.** in a country like Canada where imports are large, it is difficult to enforce controls effectively because it is difficult to control the prices of imported goods
- **e.** the wage-price controls in the 1970s did not seem to improve the inflation–unemployment trade-off

15. The major case for wage-price guidelines or controls is that

- **a.** they are the only way to stop inflation
- **b.** they are the only way to keep profits from falling when labour unions bargain aggressively for higher wages
- **c.** they are essential if income is to be distributed in a more equitable way
- **d.** if we rely solely on the restraint of aggregate demand, the fight against inflation will have a high cost in terms of unemployment
- **e.** they help to shift the long-run Phillips curve to the right

16. Price controls sometimes create shortages. Shortages are most likely in the market for

- **a.** luxuries, since their prices are likely to be controlled most tightly
- **b.** necessities, since their prices are likely to be controlled most tightly

c. luxuries, since producers will realize that they're not very important socially, and cut back on their production
d. necessities, since there is a tendency for the demand for necessities to increase at the most rapid rate
e. services, since their prices are harder to control than goods

EXERCISES

1. Figure 17-2 represents the Phillips curve for year 1, when the expected rate of inflation is zero. The natural rate of unemployment is ___________%. If unemployment is at the natural rate, the rate of inflation will be ___________ in year 1. If, alternatively, the unemployment rate is 3%, the actual rate of inflation will be [more, less] than the expected rate by ___________%.

Suppose now that the expected rate of inflation is 2% in year 2. Draw the Phillips curve for year 2 in Figure 17-2. If the rate of unemployment is still 3% in year 2, the rate of inflation will be ___________%.

If, on the other hand, inflation is 3% in year 2, the rate of unemployment will be slightly more than ___________%. Now suppose that the rate of inflation is kept at 3% indefinitely, into years 3, 4, 5...The expected rate of inflation will move to ___________%. Alternatively, if aggregate demand policies are aimed at keeping the unemployment rate at 3%, the rate of inflation will ___________.

2a. Suppose the economy is initially at point *A* on Phillips curve 1 in Figure 17-3. Now the curve shifts to Phillips curve 2. If policymakers pursue restrictive monetary and fiscal policies that keep inflation from increasing, then unemployment will [increase, decrease] by the amount ___________. If, on the other hand, they keep the rate of unemployment constant by following more expansionary policies, then inflation will [increase, decrease] by the amount ___________.

2b. Suppose this shift in the Phillips curve was caused by workers observing a rate of inflation higher than they had expected. Then, according to the accelerationist theory, the rate of unemployment at *A* must have been [higher than, lower than, equal to] the natural rate. Therefore, the attempt by policymakers to go to point *C* this year will cause the Phillips curve to ___________next year.

3. In Figure 17-4, the curve labelled PC_1 is a short-run Phillips curve of the usual shape, based on an expected rate of inflation of 5%. According to this curve, if inflation equals 5% every year, then the rate of unemployment will equal ___________% every year. The natural rate of unemployment is ___________%. Suppose that the rate of expected inflation remains constant at 5%. Then, if the actual rate of inflation is increased temporarily to 6%, the rate of unemployment will [increase, decrease] to ___________%, and if the actual rate of inflation is decreased to 4%, the rate of unemployment will [increase, decrease] to ___________%. Therefore, if actual inflation is 6% half the time and 4% the other half of the time, the average rate of inflation will be [higher, lower, no different] than if the rate of inflation was 5% all the time, but the average rate of unemployment will be [more, less] by an amount equal to ___________%.

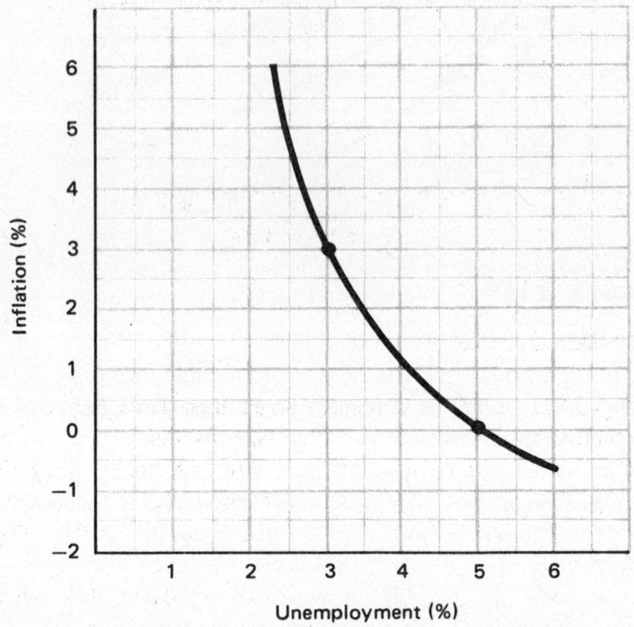

FIGURE 17-2

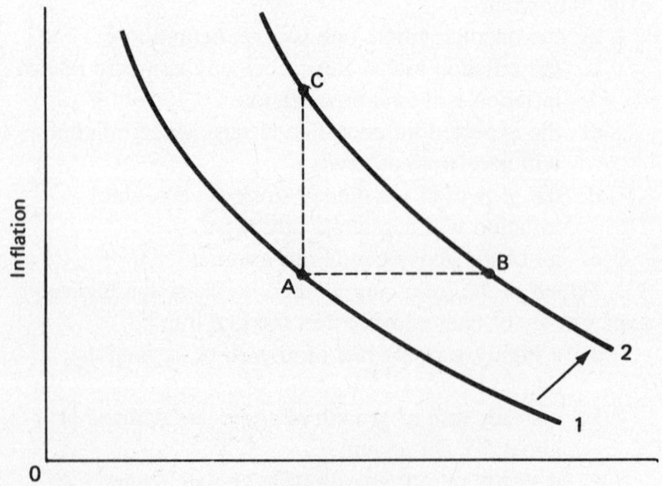

FIGURE 17-3

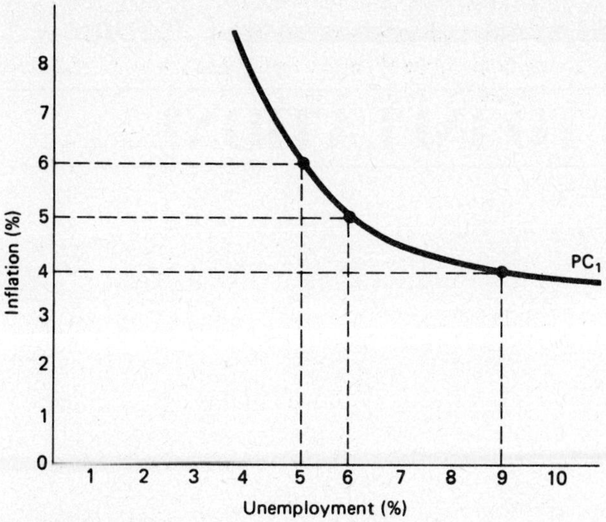

FIGURE 17-4

ESSAY QUESTIONS

1. According to the accelerationist theory, the rate of unemployment cannot be kept permanently below the natural rate by an expansive aggregate demand policy. Explain why. Can the rate be kept permanently above the natural rate by a restrictive aggregate demand policy? Explain why or why not.

2. The short-run Phillips curve indicates that when unemployment rises, inflation should fall. But in some years, both inflation *and* unemployment rise. How would an accelerationist explain this? Is there any other explanation?

3. Critics argue that the use of wage-price controls is like trying to cure a sick person by using a thermometer that won't register higher than 37°C. Why? How can wage-price controls lead to a "sicker" economic patient? How would the defenders of wage-price controls respond?

ANSWERS

Important Terms: **1** e **2** i **3** f **4** j **5** c **6** k **7** b **8** d **9** a **10** g **11** h
True-False: **1** T **2** T **3** T **4** F **5** T **6** T **7** F **8** F **9** F **10** F
Multiple Choice: **1** d **2** e **3** c **4** e **5** c **6** b **7** c **8** b **9** d **10** a **11** a **12** b **13** e **14** b **15** d **16** b
Exercises: **1.** 5, 0, more, 3, 5, 4, 3, become more and more rapid.
Figure 17-2 completed:

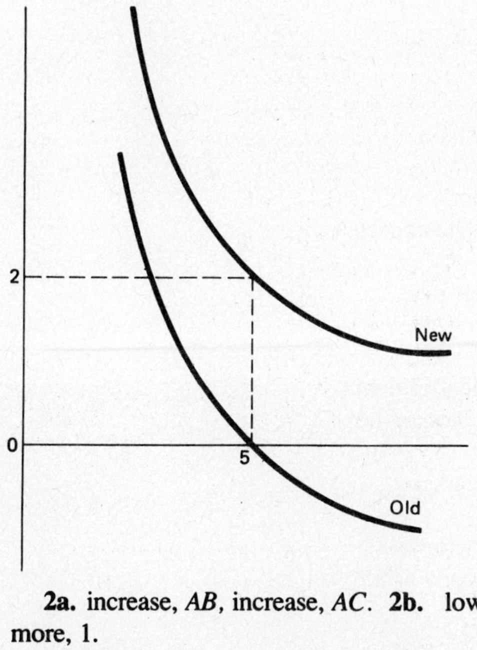

2a. increase, *AB*, increase, *AC*. **2b.** lower than, shift further up. **3.** 6, 6, decrease, 5, increase, 9, no different, more, 1.

Chapter 18

HOW DO WE ADJUST TO INFLATION?

MAJOR PURPOSE

In the previous chapter, we saw how wage contracts can be adjusted to take inflation into account. The theory of the vertical Phillips curve is based on the view that inflation won't have any effect on the unemployment rate, once people get used to the inflation and adjust to it. This chapter deals with the way in which individuals, businesses, and the government adjust to inflationary environment. By adjusting, they reduce the effects of inflation on real magnitudes, such as real output and real wages. However, even after two decades of rather rapid inflation, the economy has not adjusted fully to inflation; inflation has significant real consequences. The purpose of this chapter is to study the ways in which the economy does and does not adjust to inflation.

One important set of adjustments is in the market for bonds and other debt instruments. Unanticipated inflation hurts bondholders; they are repaid in less valuable dollars. If they anticipate inflation, however, they can adjust for it. They can withdraw from the bond market until interest rates rise to compensate for inflation. However, even if this happens, with real interest rates remaining constant, inflation can still have important consequences for borrowers and lenders. In particular, the combination of high inflation and high nominal rates of interest means that debt is front-loaded—payments in the early years are high, in real terms. As a result, young people often have difficulty buying their first homes.

Another important issue is the effect of inflation on the tax system. Some of the effects of inflation can be offset by *indexation* of tax brackets, deductions, etc. Such indexation has existed in Canada since 1974, and was introduced in the United States in 1985. However, there are other important effects, such as those arising from the taxation of nominal interest, that are not so easily dealt with. Inflation continues to cause quirks and distortions in the tax system.

LEARNING OBJECTIVES

After you have studied this chapter in the textbook and study guide, you should be able to

- Explain why unanticipated inflation has much stronger effects on the economy than anticipated inflation
- Give examples of those who lose from unanticipated inflation, and those who gain
- Explain how the real rate of interest is related to the nominal rate of interest and the expected rate of inflation (equation 18-1)
- Explain how the behaviour of borrowers and lenders tends to stabilize real interest rates
- Explain how borrowers—and particularly purchasers of first homes—can be adversely affected by inflation, even if the real rate of interest remains constant
- Explain how a graduated payment mortgage can deal with the problem of front-loaded debt
- Give an example of how the after-tax real rate of interest may be negative, even though the pretax real rate has remained constant in the face of higher inflation
- Explain why a high, uncertain rate of inflation can cause problems in the bond market
- Explain the advantages and disadvantages of indexed wages
- Explain the problems that can arise if the government uses the real government deficit as a measure of fiscal policy, or if the Bank of Canada uses the real quantity of money as a measure of monetary policy

HIGHLIGHTS OF THE CHAPTER

In Chapter 17, we began to see how the economy can adjust to inflation. As inflation continues, people come to expect it and change their behaviour accordingly. For example, labour unions bargain for higher nominal wages to compensate for the increase they have come to expect in the cost of living. If people's expectations are accurate, then the inflation need not affect real wages; it will be taken into account by both workers (who will demand higher money wages) and employers (who will be willing to pay higher money wages). In addition, the rate of unemployment may be unaffected; this was the idea behind the vertical long-run Phillips curve of Chapter 17.

The Real Rate of Interest

Adjustments like this can occur not only in the labour market, but also in other markets. Among the most important are the markets for corporate bonds, government bonds, mortgages, and other debt instruments. If owners of bonds fail to adjust to inflation, they can be severely hurt; they will be repaid in dollars with smaller value. If they anticipate inflation, they will take steps to protect themselves. They can switch out of bonds and into other assets, such as common stock or real estate. When they do so, bond prices fall; that is, interest rates rise. The rise in interest rates is reinforced by the eagerness of borrowers. Because they will be able to repay in less valuable dollars, they have an incentive to borrow more as inflation increases.

The *real rate of interest* is the rate of interest after inflation is taken into account. It is (approximately) the nominal rate of interest less the expected rate of inflation. For example, if the nominal interest rate is 10%, someone lending $100 today will be repaid $110 in one year's time. If the rate of inflation is 10% during that year, the $110 will buy no more than $100 would have bought originally. In real terms, the lender has no gain. The nominal interest rate of 10% is no more than enough to compensate for the 10% inflation; the real interest rate is zero (10% – 10%). This is not very good from the lender's viewpoint. Lenders are therefore likely to be reluctant to make loans, causing a further rise in the interest rate. When this happens, the real interest rate becomes positive. Many observers of financial markets believe that the behaviour of lenders and borrowers will act to stabilize the real interest rate. This is a difficult hypothesis to test, because the *expected* rate of inflation provides the motive for borrowers and lenders, and expected inflation is not directly observable. Until the early 1970s, evidence suggested that the real interest rate was quite stable. In the early 1980s, however, there was evidence that the real interest rate was high by historical standards.

Even if the real interest rate is constant and inflation is perfectly anticipated, a combination of high inflation and high nominal interest rates can have an important effect on borrowers and lenders. There are two main reasons for this. The first has to do with front loading; the second has to do with the tax system.

The Duration of Debt: Front Loading

Bonds, mortgages, and other types of debt usually specify a constant *nominal* rate of interest. In a world of zero inflation, a nominal interest rate of 3% represents a real rate of 3%. Someone who has issued a bond with a face value of $100,000 will pay $3,000 in interest each year.

Suppose now that inflation accelerates to 10%, with the nominal rate of interest keeping step at 13%. Someone issuing a $100,000 bond will now have to pay $13,000 in interest per year. This $13,000 includes $10,000 to compensate for the loss of value by the $100,000 principal over the year. The remaining $3,000 represents a real interest payment. In a sense, $10,000 of the $13,000 may be looked on as a partial repayment of principal. In real terms, the borrower is not only paying interest, but is also repaying part of the principal each year. Payments in early years are very high in real terms—the $13,000 represents a lot in the first year. The debt is *front-loaded.*

During periods of rapid inflation and high nominal interest rates, mortgages are similarly front-loaded. As a result, it is very difficult for first-time buyers to afford homes. If they take out a mortgage now, they may face a crushing burden in the early years. This problem would be solved if mortgage payments were fully graduated—that is, if nominal payments rose through the years to keep real payments stable. Such fully graduated mortgages are not available, nor are they likely to become available. The major reason is that they would lead to a rise in the burden of mortgage payments through time if inflation unexpectedly slowed down.

Taxation and Inflation

Taxation is another reason that inflation can have lasting real consequences, even if it is perfectly anticipated. Some taxes, like sales taxes, are a constant percentage of expenditures. If all incomes and prices rise by 10%, so will the number of dollars spent on sales taxes. In real terms, there will be no change in the taxes paid.

Income taxes are different, however. The income tax schedule is progressive; tax rates rise as incomes rise. Thus, in the 1960s and early 1970s, there was a problem of tax-bracket "creep." When prices doubled and income doubled in money terms, people were pushed into higher tax brackets. The percentage of their incomes paid in taxes rose. In order to correct the unlegislated increase in taxes that resulted from inflation, the income tax was *indexed*, beginning in 1974. With indexing, tax brackets, exemptions, etc., rise in proportion to prices. If all prices and incomes increase at the same rate, so do tax payments.

However, inflation still has peculiar effects on taxes. Most notably, people pay taxes on their *nominal* interest. In the earlier example, with $13,000 interest on a $100,000 bond, the taxpayer in the 50% bracket would pay half of the $13,000 in taxes, leaving only $6,500, or 6.5% after taxes. But this would not be enough to compensate for the 10% inflation. The after-tax real rate of interest would be negative.

Similarly, a corporation facing a 50% corporate income tax might end up paying a negative real after-tax rate of interest on the money it has borrowed, since it can deduct the entire nominal interest payments when computing taxable income.

Inflation and Uncertainty

Another complication that prevents perfect adjustment to inflation is uncertainty. Periods of *rapid* inflation also tend to be periods of *erratic* inflation. This means that bond buyers are taking a risk. High nominal interest rates may compensate for the inflation they expected when they bought the bond. But suppose that inflation speeds up unexpectedly. The bondholder will lose. Similarly, there are risks for the borrower: If inflation unexpectedly slows down, the real burden of interest payments increases. Because erratic inflation poses risks for both borrowers and lenders, a high, erratic inflation may cause the long-term bond market to dry up.

One way to deal with the problem of uncertainty is to issue mortgages that have to be renegotiated every few years, or to issue variable-rate mortgages with an interest rate that is tied to a short-term market rate of interest (such as the chartered bank prime rate). Renegotiable or variable-rate mortgages fill a useful function, because they ensure that mortgage money is available to home-buyers even during periods when there is uncertainty about the future inflation rate. But they do not solve the front-loading problem associated with *high* rates of inflation and interest. Fully graduated mortgages are unavailable.

Indexed Wages

Indexed wages—with adjustments for changes in the cost of living during the contract period—are another way of responding to erratic inflation. Wage indexation became much more common during the 1970s, when inflation was becoming both higher and more erratic.

Indexation is a natural response of labour negotiators to the uncertainties they face. The question arises as to whether indexation makes the economic system work better or not. The answer is that it may. In particular, indexation may make it easier to unwind inflation without long periods of unemployment. But, on the other hand, indexed wages can speed up a wage-price spiral. Indexation—which represents a way in which labour tries to protect itself from erratic inflation—tends to make inflation even more erratic.

Real Magnitudes and Fiscal and Monetary Policies

Finally, this chapter considers how the government itself might respond to an inflationary situation. One question is how we should measure fiscal policy. Some argue that we should look at the changes in the real deficit of the government. When inflation is rapid say, at 10%—then the first 10% in interest doesn't really represent interest; it represents a partial repayment of the real value of the debt. Thus, a government with a $300 billion debt and a $30 billion deficit is not running a deficit at all. In real terms, its budget is balanced; the real value of its debt is constant.

This is a rather interesting idea, but it presents a problem. Indeed, it represents a trap that can be added to the earlier list of traps—such as an annually balanced budget or a monetary policy aimed at a stable nominal rate of interest. Specifically, if inflation increases, the real value of the debt declines. This causes a swing toward surplus in the real budget. If we take the real budget as our guide, we may respond by increasing government spending or cutting taxes. But these steps will increase aggregate demand and make inflation worse.

Similarly, it would be a trap for the Bank of Canada to focus on the real quantity of money. During periods of inflation, the real value of the outstanding money stock declines. If the central bank responds by increasing the amount of money in order to restore the real quantity, it will make inflation worse.

Nevertheless, the real debt and the real quantity of money are important. For example, the real quantity of money is an important determinant of how much people will buy. The problem is that real measures must be used *very* cautiously by policymakers. One of the problems with inflation is that it introduces an element of confusion and chaos into the debate over aggregate demand policies.

IMPORTANT TERMS: MATCH THE COLUMNS

Match each term in the first column with the corresponding phrase in the second column. But before you do so, write your own definition of each term in the first column.

_____ **1.** anticipated inflation
_____ **2.** unanticipated inflation
_____ **3.** the real rate of interest
_____ **4.** front loading
_____ **5.** graduated-payment mortgage
_____ **6.** variable–rate mortgage
_____ **7.** tax-bracket "creep"
_____ **8.** indexation
_____ **9.** cap

a. a limit on indexation
b. a way of dealing with the problem of front loading
c. the effect of inflation in making people pay higher tax rates in an unindexed tax system
d. this type of inflation has relatively small real effects
e. automatic adjustment for inflation, as in wages or a tax system
f. this type of inflation has large real effects
g. an effect of inflation, even if real interest rates are constant
h. a way of dealing with the problem of erratic inflation
i. the nominal rate, less the expected rate of inflation

TRUE-FALSE

T F **1.** People who have borrowed large sums of money usually gain from unanticipated inflation.
T F **2.** Inflation makes lenders more eager to lend, and borrowers less eager to borrow.
T F **3.** When nominal interest rates rise, a new mortgage is "front-loaded" as a result, even if monthly payments on that mortgage are constant in dollar terms throughout the life of the mortgage.
T F **4.** A variable-rate mortgage eliminates the "front-loading" of mortgages.
T F **5.** Once tax brackets, deductions, and exemptions are indexed, inflation has no further effect on the real taxes paid by individuals or corporations.
T F **6.** Inflation provides one incentive for corporations to borrow. The tax system provides another.
T F **7.** If replacement-cost depreciation were introduced in Canada, businesses would face heavier tax burdens.
T F **8.** Wage indexation reduces uncertainty about real wage rates, but increases uncertainty about nominal wage rates.
T F **9.** A COLA clause in an indexed wage contract provides a fixed amount to cover an increase in the cost of living, no matter what the rate of inflation.
T F **10.** Wage indexation generally leads to a more stable, predictable rate of inflation.

MULTIPLE CHOICE

1. Unanticipated inflation
- **a.** inflicts losses on bond owners
- **b.** inflicts losses on people who have borrowed
- **c.** provides gains to bond owners, while leaving borrowers unaffected
- **d.** inflicts losses on borrowers, while leaving bond owners unaffected
- **e.** has no effect on real magnitudes because people adjust to it

2. Someone who has taken out a mortgage to buy a house will probably
- **a.** lose from inflation, especially if it was unexpected when the house was bought
- **b.** lose from inflation, especially if it was expected when the house was bought
- **c.** gain from inflation, especially if it was unexpected when the house was bought
- **d.** gain from inflation, especially if it was expected when the house was bought
- **e.** lose from inflation, but only if there is no mortgage on the house

3. If the nominal rate of interest is 12% and the real rate of interest is 3%, then the expected rate of inflation is
- **a.** 18%
- **b.** 15%
- **c.** 12%
- **d.** 9%
- **e.** 3%

4. Market forces can work to keep real interest rates stable. Specifically, in the event of an accelerating inflation
- **a.** lenders become more eager, and borrowers less eager, causing a rise in the nominal rate of interest
- **b.** borrowers become more eager, and lenders less eager, causing a rise in the nominal rate of interest
- **c.** lenders become more eager, and borrowers less eager, causing a fall in the nominal rate of interest
- **d.** borrowers become more eager, and lenders less eager, causing a fall in the nominal rate of interest

5. A mortgage is most likely to be front-loaded if
- **a.** nominal interest rates are high, reflecting a high rate of inflation
- **b.** real interest rates are high
- **c.** real interest rates are low
- **d.** inflation decelerates after the house is bought
- **e.** taxes rise after the house is bought

6. If you have a "fully graduated" mortgage
- **a.** real payments would rise when prices rose
- **b.** real payments would rise when your real income rose
- **c.** real payments would rise when the value of the home rose
- **d.** nominal payments would rise when prices rose, keeping real payments constant
- **e.** nominal payments would rise when your nominal income rose, keeping payments at a constant fraction of your income

7. If the tax code is fully indexed and your money income exactly kept up with inflation, then your
- **a.** nominal income tax would stay the same
- **b.** real income tax would fall
- **c.** nominal income tax would rise by the same percent as prices, keeping your real tax constant
- **d.** real income tax would rise by the same percent as prices, keeping your nominal tax constant
- **e.** real income tax would rise, but by less than the rate of inflation

8. Consider someone in the 25% tax bracket, holding a bank account paying 8% interest. The rate of inflation is 6%. Then the after-tax return to that individual is
- **a.** – 2%
- **b.** 0
- **c.** 2%
- **d.** 4%
- **e.** 6%

9. Since 1980, real interest rates have been very high, as normally calculated (the nominal interest rate less the current rate of inflation). The most plausible explanation for the high real rates has been
- **a.** the acceleration of inflation since 1980
- **b.** high unemployment
- **c.** a collapsing stock market
- **d.** rising tax rates
- **e.** large government deficits in the United States and Canada

10. Variable–rate mortgages are aimed primarily at dealing with the problem created by
- **a.** the tendency of homes to depreciate
- **b.** high inflation
- **c.** erratic inflation
- **d.** the combined effects of inflation and taxation
- **e.** the tendency for real rates of interest to vary with the business cycle

11. During periods of rapid inflation, the real value of trading on the long-term bond market generally
- **a.** is high, because after-tax real interest rates are high
- **b.** is high, because nominal interest rates are high
- **c.** is low, because the real return on bonds is unpredictable
- d. is low, because the real return on bonds is low relative to the real return on short-term securities
- **e.** increases while inflation is accelerating, but then decreases when inflation levels out

12. Which of the following is the strongest argument against the indexation of wages? Wage indexation
- **a.** makes the rate of inflation more volatile
- **b.** is not compatible with the indexation of the tax code, and tax indexation is more important
- **c.** is not possible without the indexation of the tax code, and tax indexation is undesirable
- **d.** increases the costs, in terms of unemployment, of an anti-inflationary policy
- **e.** keeps the unemployment rate permanently above the natural rate

13. The rule of thumb most likely to stabilize real economic activity and prices is
- **a.** a slow, steady increase in the real quantity of money
- **b.** a slow, steady increase in the nominal quantity of money
- **c.** a slow, steady increase in the real value of the government's debt
- **d.** a balanced budget every year
- **e.** a stable nominal rate of interest

EXERCISES

Suppose that you put $200 into a savings account and keep it there for 1 year, at which time it has grown to $220. Then the nominal rate of interest is ____________%. If you expected inflation to be 4% during the year, you anticipated a real rate of interest of ____________%. Suppose that inflation turned out to be 6% instead. Then, after the year, you would find that your real return was only ____________%.

1b. If you are in a 40% tax bracket, you will pay $____________ in taxes. Your after-tax nominal rate of interest will be ____________%, and your after-tax real return will be ____________%.

2. Figure 18-1 shows the demand and supply for loanable funds in a non-inflationary situation. The equilibrium interest rate is ____________%. In the same diagram, draw the supply and demand curves that would exist if everyone expected 2% inflation and the economy had adjusted completely to this rate of inflation. The equilibrium nominal rate of interest is now ____________%, and the equilibrium real rate ____________%. The equilibrium

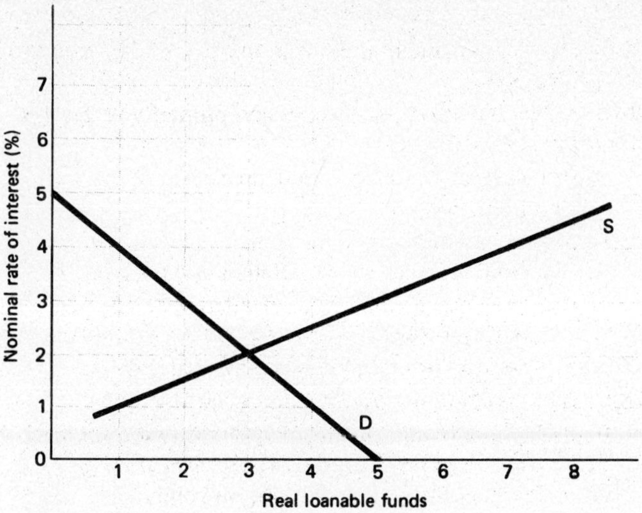

FIGURE 18-1

quantity of funds, in real terms is now [more than, less than, the same as] in the initial situation.

3. Table 18-1 illustrates a simple progressive income tax.

a. Suppose you have an income of $20,000 initially. Your income tax is $___________, or ___________% of your income. You are left with an after-tax income of $___________.

b. Now, suppose that one year later, prices are 25% higher than in the initial year. Your pretax income has also increased by 25%, to $25,000. Thus, your real pretax income has [increased, decreased, remained unchanged]. Your tax is now $___________, or ___________% of your income. In real terms—that is, measured in dollars of the first year—your tax is $___________. Thus, your real tax burden has [increased, decreased, remained unchanged]. Measured in current dollars, your after-tax income is $___________. Measured in dollars of the first year, this is equal to $ ___________. Thus, in real terms, your after-tax income has [increased, decreased, remained unchanged].

c. In Table 18-2, show what the income-tax schedule would be in the second year if the tax system were fully indexed.

d. If taxes were in fact fully indexed as shown in Table 18-2, you would pay $ ___________ in taxes in the second year, leaving $___________ in after-tax income. Measured at prices of the first year, you would pay $___________ in taxes in the second year, leaving $___________ in after-tax income. Thus, between the 2 years, when your real before-tax income was [increasing, decreasing, remaining constant], your real tax burden would [increase, decrease, remain constant].

Table 18-1

Income before tax	Tax
Less than $10,000	0
$10,000 to $20,000	10% of income over $10,000
Over $20,000	$1,000 + 20% of income over $20,000

Table 18-2

Income before tax	Tax
Less than $_____	0
$_____ to $_____	10% of income over $ _____
Over $_____	$_____ + 20% of income over $_____

ANSWERS

Important Terms: **1** d **2** f **3** i **4** g **5** b **6** h **7** c **8** e **9** a
True-False: **1** T **2** F **3** T **4** F **5** F **6** T **7** F **8** T **9** F **10** F
Multiple Choice: **1** a **2** c **3** d **4** b **5** a **6** d **7** c **8** b **9** e **10** c **11** c **12** a **13** b
Exercises: **1a.** 10%, 6%, 4%, **1b.** $8, 6%, 0% **2.** 2%, 4%, 2%,the same as.

Figure 18-1 completed:

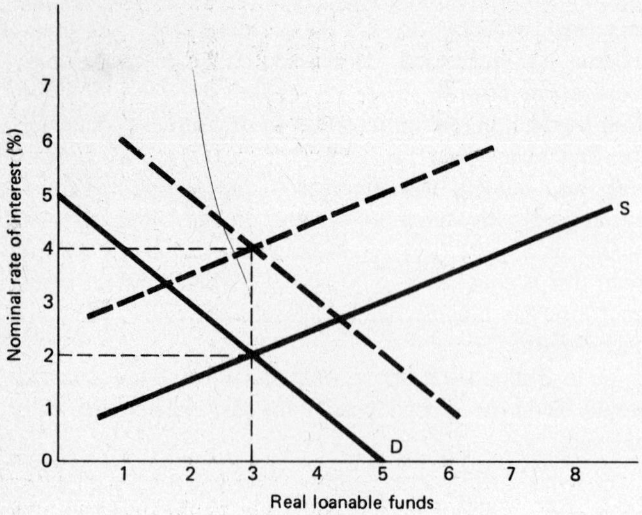

3a. $1,000, 5%, $19,000. **3b.** remained unchanged, $2,000 (that is, $1,000 + 20% of $5,000), 2/25 = 8%, $2,000 x 100/125 = $1,600, increased, $25,000 – $2,000 = $23,000, $23,000 x 100/125 = $18,400 (also equal to $20,000 in real income less $1,600 in real taxes), decreased

3c. Table 18-2 completed:

Income before tax	Tax
Less than $12,500	0
$12,500 to $25,000	10% of income over $12,500
Over $25,000	$1,250 + 20% of income over $25,000

3d. $1,250, $23,750, $1,250 x 100/125 = $1,000, $23,750 x 100/125 = $19,000, remaining constant, remain constant.

Chapter 19

PRODUCTIVITY AND GROWTH: WHY HAVE THEY BEEN DISAPPOINTING?

MAJOR PURPOSE

The major purpose of this chapter is to look at the sources of growth—why output increases. The major reasons are the increase in population, and, even more important, the increase in *productivity*. Economists have been able to identify some of the reasons for changes in productivity—the increase in the *capital stock*, the improved *education* of the labour force, and greater *economies of scale*. But economists do not have a good explanation why productivity slowed down so much during the 1970s. In the 1980s, productivity performance has shown signs of improvement. However, it is difficult to tell if the productivity problems of the 1970s are behind us. One reason is that productivity is *strongly affected by business cycles*. We cannot be sure how much of the recent improvement in productivity in 1983–85 was due to the recovery from the deep recession, and how much was due to a stronger underlying growth trend.

LEARNING OBJECTIVES

After you have studied this chapter in the textbook and study guide, you should be able to

- Explain the relationship between total output, total number of hours worked, and productivity
- Summarize Kendrick's main conclusions regarding (1) the reasons for increases in output per person in the period 1960–73 and (2) the reasons for the slowdown of the period 1973–78
- State what the "unexplained residual" may include
- Explain why we cannot be sure whether the strong productivity performance of 1983–84 is the beginning of a strong new growth trend
- Describe the relative productivity performances of the major industrial countries, and explain some of the reasons for the differences
- Explain how the objective of growth may conflict with other important objectives
- Explain the "supply-side" strategy, and how supply-side economists hope we might achieve lower inflation and lower unemployment at the same time
- Draw a Laffer curve, and explain why it has the shape you have drawn
- Using the Laffer curve, explain why an increase in taxes may sometimes lead to an increase in tax revenues, and sometimes lead to a decrease
- Explain why a cut in taxes may stimulate investment in some ways, but discourage it in others
- Explain the general idea of an "industrial policy," and why some economists are skeptical of such a policy

HIGHLIGHTS OF THE CHAPTER

The average productivity of labour is equal to total output (*Q*) divided by the number of labour hours worked (*L*). To understand the growth of output, we must look at the increases in labour hours and productivity.

Figure 19-1 in the textbook shows these changes since 1926. In the decades before World War II, output grew relatively slowly on average, reflecting in part the slump in production during the Great Depression in the 1930s. Between 1940 and 1975, however, growth was relatively fast, with output increasing at an average rate of nearly 5% per year. The rate of increase in labour hours was less than 2% per year, while labour productivity grew at more than 3% per year on average. Figure 19-1 also shows the substantial decline in productivity growth that took place in the period between 1975 and the early 1980s. Following the recovery from the deep 1982 recession, however, there have been signs of an improvement in productivity growth.

Observe in Figure 19-1 that productivity has generally improved very rapidly when labour hours were growing slowly, and vice versa. With more workers on the job, each works with less capital than would be the case with a lower growth in the labour force. As a result, there is a drag on output per labour hour. When the labour force increases, there are two important effects: (1) *total* output increases, since there is an increase in the labour input; and (2) output *per labour hour* decreases, since the amount of capital per worker is kept down.

In a careful study, which includes several industrial countries, J.W. Kendrick has estimated the reasons for the increase in Canadian productivity for two subperiods since 1960. The first column of Table 19-1 in the text lists his estimates for the period 1960–73. The most important conclusion is that *no single* item accounted for most of the increase. There were a number of sources, each contributing small amounts to the overall increase in productivity.

The third column in Table 19-1 attempts to show the reasons for the slower productivity growth during 1973–78. The most important conclusion here is that the factors that Kendrick considered explicitly account for only part of the slowdown. Over half the decrease (1.4% at the bottom of the third column) is attributed to the unexplained residual. The reasons for the poor performance during this period remain something of a mystery. One suggestion that has sometimes been made is that a substantial part of the deterioration was due to the increase in the world price of oil. Although a study by the Economic Council of Canada concluded that the oil price increase played only a minor part, the fact that productivity growth fell in most industrialized countries in the 1970s suggests that it may have been a relatively important explanation.

In the early 1980s, productivity increased more rapidly than during the period from 1973 to 1978. This raises the question of whether we have begun a new period of rapidly increasing productivity. At present, there is not enough information for a firm conclusion. Although productivity increased rapidly in 1983–84, this was at least partly due to the effects of the business cycle, and may not represent an improvement in the underlying trend.

During the 1960s and 1970s, productivity increases in Canada were substantially faster than in the United States, and similar to those in the United Kingdom. However, Canadian productivity growth fell well short of the rates in such countries as France, Japan, and West Germany. One reason for the more rapid growth abroad is that investment in these other countries has generally been a larger share of GNP. Other countries also have the advantage of copying North American technology. However, the North American technological lead is not so great as it once was, and therefore borrowed technology should give foreign countries a smaller advantage in the future than in the past.

One significant trend in recent years has been the increase in spending on R&D by countries such as West Germany and Japan. In the 1980s, these countries have been spending about as great a percentage of their GNP on R&D as the United States, which traditionally devoted a larger percentage of GNP to R&D than did other major industrialized countries.

Spending on R&D in Canada is considerably lower (as a percentage of GNP) than in the United States, West Germany, or Japan. However, technological advances originating in the United States quickly find their way into Canada because of the close economic ties between the two countries. One suggested explanation for the lagging productivity performance in the United States during the 1970s has been the observed slowdown in R&D spending in that country during the early part of the decade. This slowdown may indirectly have contributed to the reduced rate of productivity growth in Canada, since it may have meant a reduction in the inflow of new U.S. technology in Canadian industry.

Variations in productivity and growth in recent decades have drawn attention to a fundamental question: Why grow? There are obvious advantages to growth—it makes possible a higher standard of living in the future. But growth also has costs: (1) lower present consumption, as productive resources are diverted away from consumer goods and toward capital formation; (2) leisure foregone (rather than growing so fast, we could take more leisure); and (3) damage to the environment. The faster we grow, the more rapidly we create waste products, and the more rapidly we use our natural resources. However, as we will explain in Chapter 28, the relationship between pollution and economic growth is not necessarily close. It is possible to produce more goods, while at the same time paying more attention to the control of pollution.

Attitudes toward growth have been changing in recent decades. During the 1950s and early 1960s, North American governments actively sought to promote growth as a way to raise the general living standards, reduce poverty, and keep ahead of the Soviet Union. In the 1970s, the growth objective attracted less support, as people became more concerned about the speed with which we were using our natural resources.

Since 1980, the growth objective has once more moved closer to centre stage, particularly in the United States. The growth policy of the Reagan administration is sometimes known as "supply side economics." While public opinion in Canada has not swung as sharply in the direction of more emphasis on growth as in the United States, many of the ideas in the Reagan government's supply side policy have had considerable impact on the Canadian economic policy debate. An essential component of the supply side strategy is to increase aggregate supply and thus ease the inflation-unemployment dilemma discussed in Chapter 17. One way of increasing supply is to sharpen incentives by reducing taxes, and the Conservative government that came to power in 1984 has stated reduction in personal income tax rates as one of its goals; the trend in the mid-1980s toward deregulation in the transport sector and toward privatization of government business can also be taken as consistent with the supply side strategy.

One of the theoretical supports for tax cuts was the Laffer Curve. Arthur Laffer argued that tax cuts would lead to increases, not decreases, in government revenues. Thus, a tax cut would be costless: It would benefit the public, without costing the government any revenues. The ballooning of government deficits in recent years suggests that this view is too optimistic.

Some economists argue that it is desirable for the government to have an industrial policy—to direct investment into important industries and help them in other ways. One problem with such proposals is that they often encompass two quite different ideas, namely that the government should help (1) new, high-technology industries with the high profits and good growth prospects; and (2) declining industries with low profits and poor prospects.

IMPORTANT TERMS: MATCH THE COLUMNS

Match each term in the first column with the corresponding phrase in the second column. But before you do so, write your own definition of each term in the first column.

_____ **1.** average productivity of labour
_____ **2.** technological improvement
_____ **3.** economies of scale
_____ **4.** a cost of investment and growth
_____ **5.** supply-side economics
_____ **6.** Laffer curve
_____ **7.** industrial policy
_____ **8.** lemon socialism
_____ **9.** crowding out

a. this emphasizes tax cuts as a way of encouraging saving, investment, and growth
b. the negative effects on investment, resulting from high interest rates caused by government deficits
c. the direction of investment into specific sectors, and the assistance of these sectors in other ways
d. government ownership and support of declining industries
e. what exists if an increase of all inputs by 100% leads to an increase of more than 100% in output
f. inventions and better methods of production
g. foregone current consumption
h. this shows relationship between tax rates and tax revenues
i. Q/L

TRUE-FALSE

T F **1.** If the labour force grows at a rapid rate, this will act as a drag on productivity.
T F **2.** If the labour force grows at a rapid rate, this will act as a drag on the growth of output.
T F **3.** In the 1960s and 1970s, there was an increase in the average number of hours worked per person employed, and this contributed to economic growth in Canada.
T F **4.** Between 1973 and 1978, productivity in Canada grew more slowly than it had previously, but the factors considered by Kendrick explained only less than half of the slowdown.
T F **5.** As the economy moves into a recession, output declines, and so does the rate of increase of productivity.
T F **6.** The reduction in U.S. spending on R&D may have been one of the factors contributing to slower Canadian productivity growth during the 1970s.
T F **7.** The goal of economic growth was strongly emphasized by North American governments during the 1950s and early 1960s.
T F **8.** According to Laffer, higher tax rates would cause a reduction in the government's tax revenues.
T F **9.** As we would predict from the Laffer curve, when tax rates were sharply cut in the United States in 1981, tax revenues rose and the U.S. federal budget quickly swung from a deficit to a surplus.
T F **10.** Advocates of a new industrial policy usually recommend an across-the-board cut in tariffs.

MULTIPLE CHOICE

1. When the number of labour hours increases very rapidly, the most likely effect is
- **a.** a slow increase in productivity
- **b.** a very rapid increase in productivity
- **c.** a very slow increase in total output
- **d.** no change in output, since workers have less capital
- **e.** a decline in output, since workers have less capital

2. During the 1970s, the total number of hours worked in Canada
- **a.** grew at a rate faster than the average since 1926, but slower than the rate of growth of total output
- **b.** grew at a rate faster than the average since 1926, and faster than the rate of growth of total output
- **c.** grew, but at a rate slower than the average since 1926
- **d.** stayed roughly constant
- **e.** decreased sharply

3. One of the factors considered in Kendrick's analysis of Canadian productivity growth during 1973–78 was changes in the quality of the labour force as measured by education. His figures show that the education of the Canadian labour force has
- **a.** improved, and this improvement contributed as much to productivity as the increase in machinery and other physical change
- **b.** improved, although this improvement contributed less to productivity than the increase in machinery and other physical capital
- **c.** deteriorated, since examination scores have fallen
- **d.** deteriorated, since there are more young people working than there were 25 years ago
- **e.** deteriorated, at least during the 1970s, since labour productivity deteriorated during that decade

4. National output fluctuates during the business cycle, and so does labour productivity. Specifically, when compared to the long-run average increase, labour productivity during a recession increases
- **a.** more slowly, since the average worker has less capital to work with
- **b.** more slowly, since employers are reluctant to lay off skilled workers, and they accordingly keep underemployed workers on the job
- **c.** more rapidly, since the average worker has more capital to work with when other employees are laid off
- **d.** more rapidly, since the threat of layoff encourages workers to work harder
- **e.** more rapidly, since competitive pressures intensify

5. If we compare Canadian performance during the 1960s and 1970s with that of the United States, West Germany, and Japan, we find that Canadian productivity grew
- **a.** more slowly than in the other countries
- **b.** faster than in the United States, even though Canada invested a smaller percentage of its GNP than the United States did
- **c.** more slowly than in Japan but faster than in West Germany
- **d.** at about the same rate as in the United States
- **e.** more slowly than in Japan, while Canadian investment was also a smaller percentage of GNP than in Japan

6. Consider an economy in which output *per capita* grows at 2% per year, while population grows at 1.5% per year. Then growth in real GNP is approximately what percent per year?
- **a.** 2/1.5 = 1.33
- **b.** 1.5
- **c.** 2
- **d.** 1.5 x 2 = 3
- **e.** 1.5 + 2 = 3.5

7. The tax reductions enacted in 1981 are sometimes spoken of as "supply-side" cuts because
- **a.** only the taxpayers who increased their supply of goods were allowed to benefit
- **b.** an important motive was to stimulate investment and growth
- **c.** they were designed to stimulate the supply of leisure
- **d.** they were designed to stimulate the growth of the government sector and, hence, overall growth
- **e.** they were designed to stimulate the growth of the government sector and, hence, to stimulate saving

8. If a "supply-side" tax cut is successful in shifting the aggregate supply curve to the right, it will
- **a.** result in more inflation, more output, and more unemployment
- **b.** result in more inflation, more output, and less unemployment
- **c.** result in more inflation, less output, and more unemployment
- **d.** result in more inflation, less output, and less unemployment
- **e.** make it easier to suppress inflation without causing unemployment

9. The Laffer curve was intended to show that it might be possible to
- **a.** increase net exports without causing inflation
- **b.** increase net exports and growth at the same time
- **c.** cut taxes without causing unemployment
- **d.** cut taxes without causing a reduction in government revenues
- **e.** cut taxes without causing a reduction in government spending

10. Supply-side economists differ from Keynesian economists in what major way? Supply-side economists are likely to
- **a.** emphasize *fiscal* policies, whereas Keynesian economists emphasize *monetary* policy
- **b.** favour *cuts* in tax rates to stimulate the economy,

whereas Keynesian economists favour tax *increases* to stimulate the economy

c. favour *increases* in government spending to stimulate the economy, whereas Keynesian economists favour *cuts* in government spending to stimulate the economy

d. believe that cuts in tax rates will *increase* tax revenues, whereas Keynesian economists believe that lower tax rates lead to *lower* revenues

e. believe that a rightward shift in the aggregate supply curve will *reduce* inflationary pressures, whereas Keynesian economists believe that it will *increase* inflation

11. Critics of supply-side economics argue that a decrease in tax rates may cause a *decrease*, rather than an increase, in investment and growth because it will lead to

a. an increase in saving, and this will cause a recession because of the "paradox of thrift"

b. bigger government deficits and higher interest rates, which will discourage investment

c. bigger government deficits, which will lead to a recession

d. lower government deficits, which will lead to a recession

e. lemon socialism

12. Proponents of an industrial policy suggest that the government

a. encourage investment in "winning" industries, thus promoting growth

b. discourage investment in "losing" industries, such as steel, since there is no future in such industries

c. encourage investment in grain farming, in order to restore America's ability to feed the world

d. avoid "lemon socialism" by discouraging investment in the citrus industry

e. all of the above

EXERCISES

1a. Kendrick found that, during the period from 1960–73, the increase in output per hour could be attributed to the following five sources (in addition to the unexplained residual, due in part, to technological improvement): (1) ___________, (2) ___________, (3) ___________, (4) ___________, and (5) ___________.

1b. Over this period, a drag on productivity was attributable to ___________.

1c. The factors considered by Kendrick explain less than half of the slowdown in 1973–78. An important factor not considered may have been ___________.

2. A more rapid rate of increase in population leads to a [more, less] rapid rate of growth output. It generally acts as a [stimulus to, drag on] productivity, because the average worker has less ___________ to work with. However, this effect may be offset, or more than offset, by economies of ___________, which act to [increase, decrease] productivity as the size of the economy grows.

3. In Figure 19-1, curves L_1 and L_2 are two alternative Laffer curves. The tax rate in 1980 is illustrated as t_1. According to Laffer, we were at point ___________ on curve ___________ in 1980, where a cut in the tax rate would cause [an increase, a decrease] in tax revenues. According to Laffer's critics, we were at point ___________ on curve ___________ in 1980, where a cut in the tax rate would cause [an increase, a decrease] in tax revenues.

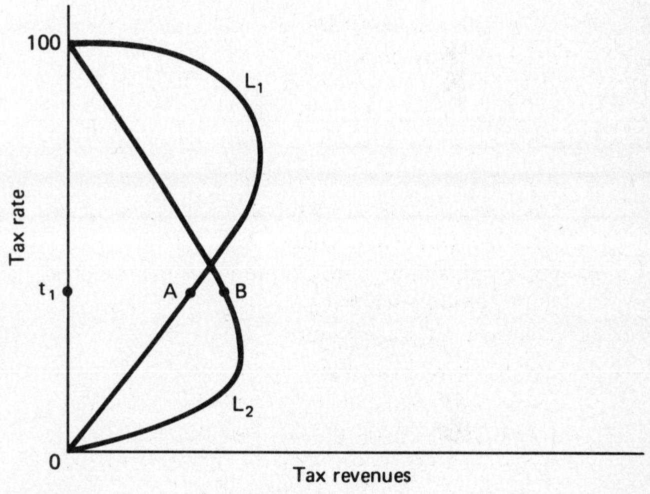

FIGURE 19-1

ESSAY QUESTIONS

1. Since 1960, labour hours (L) increased at a much faster rate than earlier. (Figure 19-1 in the textbook). How do you explain this rapid increase? Would you expect a rapid increase in the next decade? What do you think explains the *inverse* relationship between the growth in labour input and the increase in labour productivity? On the basis of these answers, do you have any predictions about what will happen to labour productivity in the next decade? How about the rate of growth of output? Are you confident regarding your last two answers? Why or why not?

2. Recall the "measure of economic welfare" (MEW) introduced in Chapter 7. If this, rather than GNP, were used to measure economic growth and productivity, how would the historical record in Figure 19-1 in the text book be affected? How would the costs of economic growth be affected? How do your answers depend on how leisure is treated in MEW?

3. (For those who have studied Box 19-10.) What is the simplest concept of an "optimal" population? Do you agree that such a population would be optimal? Why or why not? Do you think that the Canadian government should adopt policies to achieve this population size? Why or why not?

What about China? India?

4. Suppose that you were made the head of a government planning organization, to assist industries as part of a national industrial policy. Would you favour assisting new, high-tech industries, or declining industries, or both? Or perhaps neither of these, but some other group of industries? (If so, explain how you would choose your favoured industries.) Explain what problems you might encounter in picking industries for assistance, and the problems that might result from your policies.

ANSWERS

Important Terms: **1** i **2** f **3** e **4** g **5** a **6** h **7** c **8** d **9** b
True-False: **1** T **2** F **3** F **4** T **5** T **6** T **7** T **8** T **9** F **10** F
Multiple Choice: **1** a **2** a **3** b **4** b **5** e **6** e **7** b **8** e **9** d **10** d **11** b **12** a
Exercises: **1a.** better-educated labour force, increase in physical capital, economies of scale, improved allocation of resources, more capacity utilization **1b.** changed age-set composition of labour force. **1c.** higher oil prices. **2.** more, drag on, capital, scale, increase. **3.** B, L_2, increases, A, L_1, decrease.

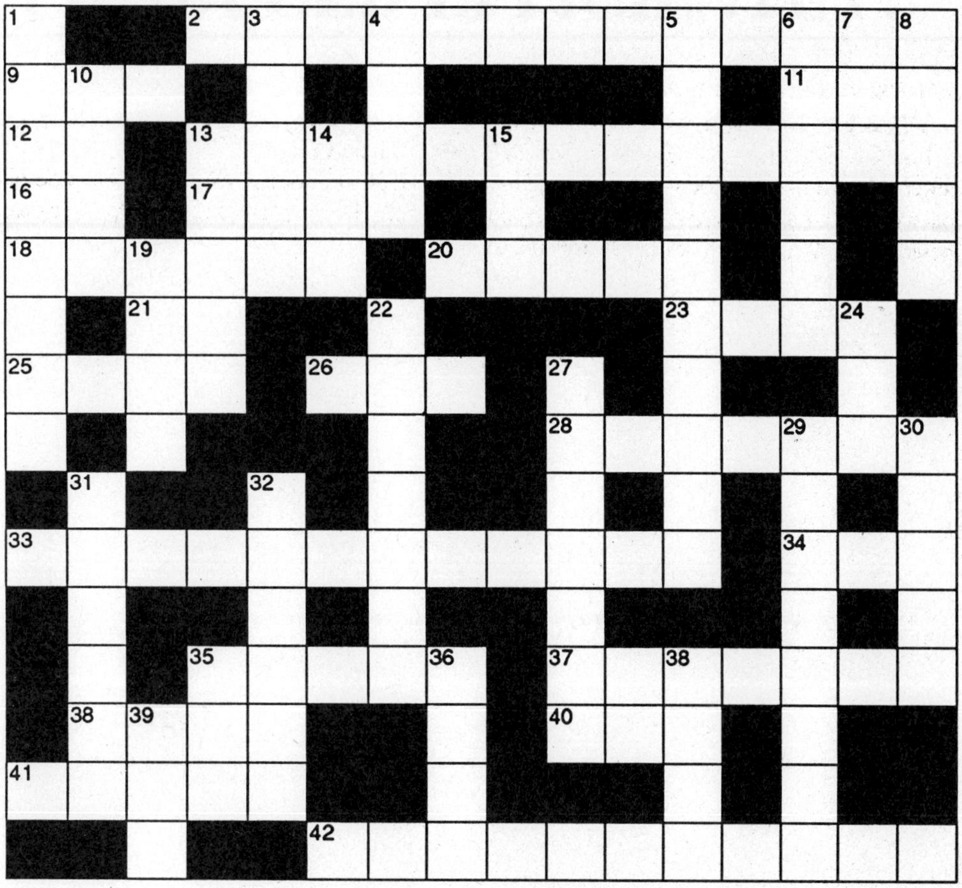

Across

2. This occurs when depreciation exceeds gross investment.
9. consume
11. respectful form of address
12. yes (Spanish)
13. fluctuations in economic activity (2 words)
16. interjection
17. untruths
18. observant, perceptive, smart
20. country with rapid economic growth
21. world organization (abbrev.)
23. warning sign for the superstitious
25. should always be put *after* the horse
26. what the politician did for office
28. study of the environment
33. Q/L
34. hint; gratuity
35. Witches sometimes cast one.
37. makes it difficult to see through
38. form of capital
40. zero
41. Rudolf's nose
42. describes relation between tax rates and tax revenues (2 words)

Down

1. where bright ideas pay off
3. one group of Canadian Native peoples
4. part of the eye
5. important contributor to growth
6. get away
7. nothing
8. present, favour
10. gives vent to; tunes
13. not sharp
14. visualize
15. long period of time
19. inhabitant of Asia Minor
22. helps workers to produce
24. to keep on asking
27. pioneering student of productivity and growth
29. not part of the in-group
30. a 25-year-old upwardly mobile lawyer might be one (slang)
31. slowed in the 1970s
32. Laffer's side
35. male offspring
36. take it easy; unit of bread
38. ____________ Guinness, a famous British actor
39. became very expensive in the 1970s

Chapter 20

DEMAND AND SUPPLY: THE CONCEPT OF ELASTICITY

MAJOR PURPOSE

In this chapter, we begin the detailed study of microeconomics by picking up from the discussion of the supply and demand curves in Chapter 4. In that earlier analysis, we saw how a demand curve describes how buyers increase their purchases of a product if its price falls. For some products, this response by buyers will be very strong; for others, it may be weak. To illustrate, visualize two demand curves with different slopes that pass through the same point. The flatter one describes buyers who are sensitive to price; they buy much more when price falls. On the other hand, the steeper demand curve describes buyers who are less responsive to price; the amount they buy changes relatively little as price falls. In this chapter we develop a measure—called the *elasticity of demand*—to describe this responsiveness of buyers to price.

A similar concept—*supply elasticity*—is developed to measure the responsiveness of sellers to price. An important question is then addressed: Why are demand and supply highly elastic in some cases, but inelastic in others? Finally, this chapter includes illustrations of how important elasticity may be in answering policy questions such as, Who bears the burden of a tax on a product—the buyers or sellers? Why do the prices of some farm products fluctuate so much? and Why has the number of Canadian farmers decreased so much since the beginning of the century?

LEARNING OBJECTIVES

After you have studied this chapter in the textbook and the study guide, you should be able to

- Define elasticity of demand and elasticity of supply
- Compare the elasticity of two demand curves that pass through the same point, showing why the flatter one is more elastic, and explain why slope and elasticity are not exactly the same when curves do not pass through the same point
- Describe how a move to a lower point on a demand curve may increase or decrease the total revenue received by sellers from buyers, depending on the elasticity of demand
- List four factors that increase the elasticity of demand for a good
- List three factors that increase the elasticity of supply for a good
- Explain how a commodity tax will affect buyers and sellers of a good, and why the group that is most sensitive to price (most elastic in its response to a price change) will be able to push the burden of the tax onto the other group
- Describe the special problems of agriculture, and show how the concept of elasticity can throw light on these problems
- Explain how increases in agricultural productivity have affected farm price
- Describe the role income elasticity plays in determining the long-run price of agricultural goods

HIGHLIGHTS OF THE CHAPTER

In developing demand curves in Chapter 4, it was argued that they slope downward to the right. However, little was said about how steep or flat they might be or, more precisely, about how responsive buyers might be to a change in price. Similarly, in developing supply curves, little was said about how responsive sellers might be. For many problems that can be analysed with supply and demand curves, it is important to have a simple and handy description of this sensitivity of buyers or sellers to price. Elasticity is such a measure.

Elasticity of Demand

This is defined as

$$\text{Elasticity of demand} = \frac{\%\text{ change in quantity demanded}}{\%\text{ change in price}}$$

To illustrate this formula, suppose that as a result of a shift in the supply of a good to the right, equilibrium moves downward to the right along the demand curve. With the decrease in the per unit price (the denominator above), there is an increase in the amount demanded (the numerator). If these two are equal—that is, if the price and the quantity demanded change at the same rate, then the elasticity of demand in the equation above is equal to 1. Moreover, the *total* payment buyers make to sellers does not change. To see why this is so, suppose that when the price P paid by buyers falls by 1%, the quantity Q that they purchase rises at the same rate. Then the decrease in P is offset by the increase in Q, and there is no change in P times Q, the total payment made to buyers. This is the first conclusion: When the elasticity of demand is 1, there is no change in the total payment of buyers—that is, in the total revenue received by sellers.

Now suppose buyers are *more responsive* to a price change—as in panel (*a*) of Figure 20-1 of the text, where the quantity they demand increases by 60% (from 1,000 to 1,600 units) when the price falls by 20% (from $10 to $8). In this case, demand elasticity exceeds 1 in the equation above, and there is an *increase* in PQ, the total revenue received by sellers from buyers. In this case, demand is described as "elastic."

In panel (*b*) of that same diagram, buyers are *less responsive* to a price change: The quantity demanded increases by only 10% when the price falls by 20%. This is the unresponsive, inelastic case; the elasticity ratio in the equation above is less than 1, and there is a *decrease* in the total revenue received by sellers. Before you leave Figure 20-1 in the text, it is essential that you are comfortable with the way elasticity and total revenue are related.

In that diagram, slope and elasticity seem to be closely related. The flatter curve in panel (*a*) is the more elastic. Is this generally true? The answer is yes—but *only if* the two curves being compared pass through the same point. (In Figure 20-1, the common point is E_1.) You should be sure that you can recognize cases—such as the one shown in Figure 20-3 in the text—where a flatter curve is *not* more elastic.

Elasticity of Supply

This can also be calculated, using a ratio like the one in the equation above. The only difference is the obvious one—quantity demanded must be replaced with quantity supplied.

$$\text{Elasticity of supply} = \frac{\%\text{ change in quantity supplied}}{\%\text{ change in price}}$$

Whereas elasticity of demand has an important "total revenue" interpretation, elasticity of supply does not. The reason is that a move upward and to the right on *any* supply curve—regardless of its elasticity—will increase total revenue. The one simple interpretation of elasticity of supply is this: If a straight-line supply curve passes through the origin, it has an elasticity of supply of 1.

What Determines Demand and Supply Elasticity?

Demand elasticity tends to be greater if (1) the product is a luxury rather than a necessity, (2) it is a large item in purchasers' budgets rather than a small one, (3) it is easy for buyers to replace it with substitutes in consumption, and (4) we are considering the long-run, rather than the short-run, demand. The elasticity of supply tends to be greater if (1) the commodity can be inexpensively stored— that is, if it is not perishable and has low storage costs; (2) it is easy for users to replace with substitutes in production; and (3) we are considering the long-run, rather than the short-run, supply.

One of the most important of these influences on both supply and demand is time—the short run versus the long run. The reason is simple: If people—whether they are consumers or producers—are given a longer time to adjust to a change in price, they will be able to do more adjusting than if they are given only a short time.

Using Elasticity to Analyse the Burden of a Tax

The first important application of the concept of elasticity is in analysing whether buyers or sellers bear the burden of a commodity tax. The conclusion from this analysis is important because it applies to any marketplace where two groups face each other, with buyers on the one hand and sellers on the other. The "inelastic" group that can't back away from the market but must complete the transaction almost without regard to price will bear more of the burden of a new tax or any other similar disturbance than will the more "elastic group" that is prepared to resist a price change by backing away from the market.

Using Elasticity to Analyse the Special Problems of Agriculture

For many food products there is (1) a highly inelastic demand curve; (2) a highly inelastic supply curve (at least in the short run); (3) large year-to-year fluctuations in the short-run supply curve, depending upon the state of the weather, and therefore on the harvest from one year to the next; (4) a great deal of technological change in recent decades which has produced large shifts to the right in the supply curve; and (5) relatively smaller shifts to the right in the demand curve, because as income increases over time, the public's spending on food doesn't increase as quickly. (There is a low-income elasticity of demand, defined as the percentage change in the quantity demanded divided by the percentage change in *income*.)

In combination, influences (1) and (3) above have created large fluctuations in price. You can see this by drawing a very inelastic demand curve and shifting the supply curve back and forth. Notice how any shift in the supply curve changes price dramatically because demand is inelastic. To confirm this conclusion, draw an elastic demand curve instead, and show how exactly the same shifts in supply result in less change in price.

Moreover, influences (1) and (3) generate large fluctuations not only in farm price, but also in the income (that is, the revenue) received by farmers. Inelastic demand means that as price falls, farmers' income falls; as price rises, so does farm income. The change in farm price becomes a dominant influence over farm income.

As a background to all this, influences (4) and (5) have contributed to a long-run downward trend in North American agricultural prices, because they have caused the supply curve to shift to the right by more than the demand curve. Note, however, that some observers think that influence (4) will be less important in the future; according to this view, the future will bring smaller shifts to the right in supply. Be sure you can show in a diagram how a slowdown in the rightward shift in supply could reverse the downward trend in prices.

IMPORTANT TERMS: MATCH THE COLUMNS

Match each term in the first column with the corresponding phrase in the second column. But before you do so, write your own definition of each term in the first column.

_____ **1.** total revenue
_____ **2.** elasticity of demand
_____ **3.** elasticity of supply
_____ **4.** income elasticity of demand
_____ **5.** cross-elasticity of demand
_____ **6.** unit elasticity of demand
_____ **7.** joint products

a. a measure of how strongly the quantity demanded responds to a change in income (It is defined as the percentage change in quantity demanded divided by the percentage change in income.)

b. the percentage change in quantity supplied divided by the percentage change in price, as equilibrium moves from one point to another on a supply curve

c. the amount of money received by sellers of a product (This also equals the amount of money spent by buyers of the product.)

d. a measure of the effect the price of good Y has on the demand for good X (It is defined as the percentage change in the quantity of X divided by the percentage change in the price of Y. This is positive if X and Y are substitutes, and negative if they are complements.)

e. the percentage change in quantity demanded divided by the percentage change in price, as equilibrium moves from one point to another on a demand curve

f. two products that result from one production process (To illustrate, beef and hides result from the production of beef.)

g. when the percentage change in the quantity demanded is equal to the percentage change in price

TRUE-FALSE

T F 1. A move to a new lower equilibrium on an elastic demand curve means that total revenue falls.

T F 2. A straight-line demand curve has the same elasticity at each point on the curve.

T F 3. If the elasticity is 1, then a 1% change in price will lead to a greater than 1% change in the quantity demanded.

T F 4. Arc elasticity of demand is defined as

$$\frac{\text{Change in quantity demanded/average quantity demanded}}{\text{Change in price/average price}}$$

T F 5. Elasticity of demand describes how responsive buyers are to a change in price, while elasticity of supply describes how responsive sellers are.

T F 6. If short-run demand elasticity is 1, then in the long run, demand will be inelastic.

T F 7. The main reason why the government intervenes in agriculture markets is to prevent prices from rising above a specified level.

T F 8. If the elasticity of supply of agricultural goods were 1, then an increase in demand would not affect price.

T F 9. The past downward trend in farm prices (relative to other prices) has occurred because improvements in farm technology have shifted the supply curve to the right more rapidly than the demand curve has been shifting.

T F 10. Because agricultural prices tend to be very stable in the short run, the only price problem in agriculture has been a long-term downward trend.

T F 11. When the government is stockpiling wheat, its price is higher than it would otherwise be.

MULTIPLE CHOICE

1. If people reduce their consumption of coffee by very little, even when its price skyrockets, we can conclude that
- **a.** supply is elastic
- **b.** supply is inelastic
- **c.** demand is elastic
- **d.** demand is inelastic
- **e.** demand has unit elasticity

2. If the elasticity of demand is greater than 1, then a 10% reflection in prices will result in
- **a.** no change in quantity demanded
- **b.** an increase of less than 10% in the quantity demanded
- **c.** a decrease of less than 10% in the quantity demanded
- **d.** a decrease of 10% in the quantity demanded
- **e.** an increase of more than 10% in the quantity demanded

3. The income elasticity of demand is the percentage change in
- **a.** quantity demanded divided by the percentage change in price
- **b.** income demanded divided by the percentage change in price
- **c.** price divided by the percentage change in quantity demanded
- **d.** quantity demanded divided by the percentage change in income
- **e.** income divided by the percentage change in price

4. If the elasticity of supply is 3, then a 1% increase in price will
- **a.** reduce the quantity supplied by 3%
- **b.** increase the quantity supplied by 3%
- **c.** increase the quantity supplied by 1%
- **d.** triple the quantity supplied
- **e.** reduce the quantity supplied by one-third

5. A move to a new, higher-price equilibrium on a supply curve means that total revenue
- **a.** will not change
- **b.** may rise or remain unchanged
- **c.** may fall or remain unchanged
- **d.** must fall
- **e.** must rise

6. If the price of X goes from $1.50 per dozen to $2.50 per dozen, and suppliers are willing to increase from 9,000 to 11,000 the amount they offer for sale, then the arc elasticity of supply is
- **a.** 0.10
- **b.** 0.4
- **c.** 0.8
- **d.** 2.5
- **e.** 4.0

7. In the long run, the elasticity of demand for foreign travel is high because
- **a.** it is a necessity
- **b.** it is a luxury
- **c.** airliners can easily switch from transporting goods to transporting people
- **d.** travel has no substitutes in consumption
- **e.** travel has no substitutes in production

8. A technological change that shifts the supply curve to the right will cause total revenue to
- **a.** rise if demand is elastic
- **b.** fall if demand is elastic
- **c.** rise if demand is inelastic

d. rise if the elasticity of demand is 1
e. fall if the elasticity of demand is 1

9. The burden of a commodity tax is borne entirely by buyers
a. in any case
b. if supply has unit elasticity
c. if demand has unit elasticity
d. if demand has infinite elasticity
e. if demand has zero elasticity

10. A bumper crop will lower farm income
a. regardless of demand and supply elasticity
b. if demand is elastic
c. if demand is inelastic
d. if demand and supply have equal elasticity
e. if demand elasticity is infinite

11. Improvements in agricultural productivity tend to
a. raise farm prices and income
b. lower farm prices
c. raise farm prices, but lower farm income
d. have no effect on farm prices
e. have no effect on farm income

12. The fact that wheat has straw as a joint product
a. makes its supply more elastic
b. makes its supply less elastic
c. makes its demand more elastic
d. makes its demand less elastic
e. has led to government intervention in the straw market

13. Some people believe that long-run food prices will rise because
a. farmers will stay on the land, rather than taking jobs in the city
b. the risk of drought in foreign countries will be eliminated
c. population growth will be reduced in developing countries
d. the supply curve will shift more rapidly to the right than the demand curve
e. the supply curve will shift less rapidly to the right than the demand curve

14. Relative to other prices, farm prices have been
a. stable in the short run, with a long-term upward trend
b. stable in the short run, with a long-term downward trend
c. unstable in the short run, with neither an upward nor a downward long-term trend
d. unstable in the short run, with a long-term downward trend
e. unstable in the short run, with a long-term upward trend

15. Increased productivity at IBM has led to
a. a cut in its prices and profits
b. an increase in its prices and profits
c. an increase in its prices, and a cut in its profits
d. a cut in its prices, and an increase in its profits
e. a cut in its prices, and no change in its profits

EXERCISES

1a. If equilibrium is at *A* in Figure 20-1 below, total revenue is area __________, which is $ __________. Total revenue at point *B* is area __________,that is, $__________. D_1 is [elastic, inelastic, unit elastic] because, as price falls, total revenue [increases, decreases]. To be more precise, we can calculate the elasticity of D_1 from the formula

$$\frac{\%\text{ change in\_\_\_\_\_\_}}{\%\text{ change in\_\_\_\_\_\_}} = \frac{\_\_\_\_\_\_\%}{\_\_\_\_\_\_\%} =$$

1b. D_2 is [more, less] elastic than D_1. We know this because the percentage change in price between *A* and *C* is [more than, less than, the same as] the percentage change in price between *A* and *B*, while the percentage change in quantity between *A* and *C* is [more than, less than, the same as] the percentage change in quantity between *A* and *B*.

2. Draw in a supply curve through point *A* and mark it S_1. Draw in another supply curve through point *B* and mark it S_2. Mark the point where S_2 cuts D_2 as *F*.If supply is initially at S_1, and it shifts to S_2, then the change in price

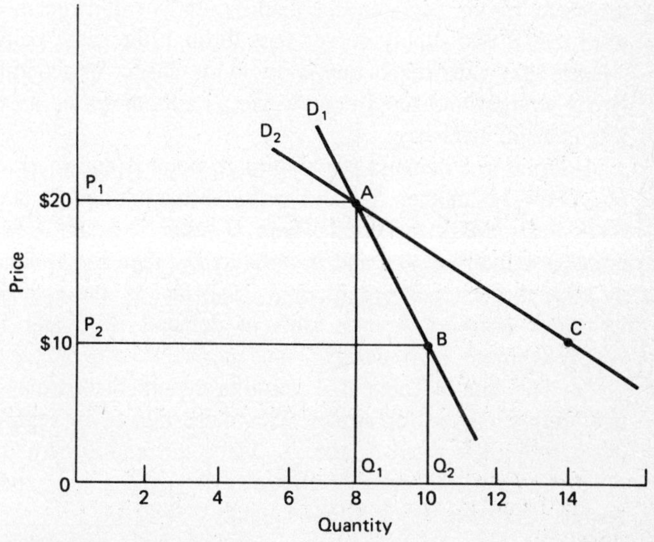

FIGURE 20-1

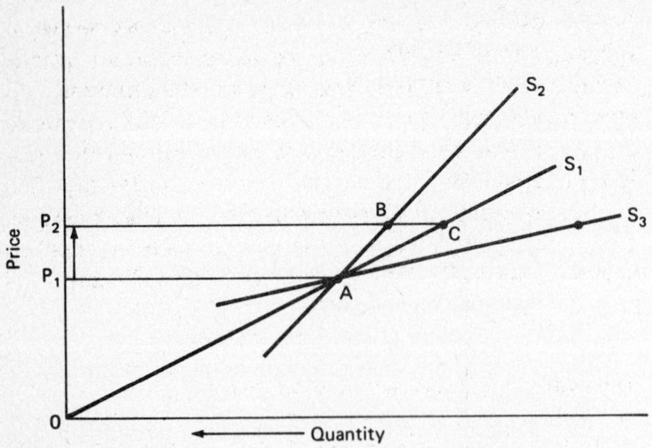

FIGURE 20-2

is greater if demand is [D_1, D_2]; that is, the change in price resulting from a shift in supply is greater if demand is [more, less] elastic.

3a. In Figure 20-2, supply curve S_1 is [elastic, inelastic, unit elastic] because it ____________. If price rises from P_1 to P_2, then the equilibrium on S_1 moves from point ____________ to point ____________. On the other hand, for supply curve S_2, this change in price would move from point ____________ to point ____________. The quantity response to this change in price is [greater, less] for S_2 than for S_1. S_2 is therefore [more, less] elastic than S_1. It is [true, not true] that if two supply curves pass through the same point—such as *A*—the flatter one is the more elastic. This conclusion is [the same as, quite different from] the one we arrived at in comparing slopes of demand curves. In general, if any straight-line supply curve such as S_2 cuts the *quantity* axis, it is [elastic, inelastic].

3b. Now consider S_3. As price rises from P_1 to P_2, the quantity response is [greater, less] than for S_1. S_3 is therefore [more, less] elastic than S_1. It is still [true, not true] that if two supply curves pass through the same point —such as *A*—the flatter one is the more elastic. In general, if any straight-line supply curve like S_3 cuts the *price* axis, it is [elastic, inelastic].

4. Draw in a demand curve through point *A* and mark it D_1. Draw in another demand curve through point *B* and mark it D_2. Mark the point where D_2 cuts S_1 as *F*. If demand is initially at D_1, and it shifts to D_2, then the change in price is greater if supply is [S_1, S_2]; that is, the change in prices resulting from a shift in demand is greater if supply is [more, less] elastic.

5a. The data in Table 20-1 describe hypothetical demand and supply curves for apples. Plot these curves in Figure 20–3 and mark them *S* and *D*. Mark the equilibrium as point *A*, where the price of apples is $ ____________ per bushel, and the equilibrium quantity is ____________ million bushels. Suppose the government sets a price floor at $19, making it illegal to sell apples at a price below this. Mark the new equilibrium in Figure 20-3 as *B*, and draw in an arrow showing the excess [demand, supply]. Mark this arrow *BC*.

Table 20-1

Price per bushel	Millions of bushels demanded	Millions of bushels supplied
$ 5	25	5
10	20	10
15	15	15
20	10	20
25	5	25

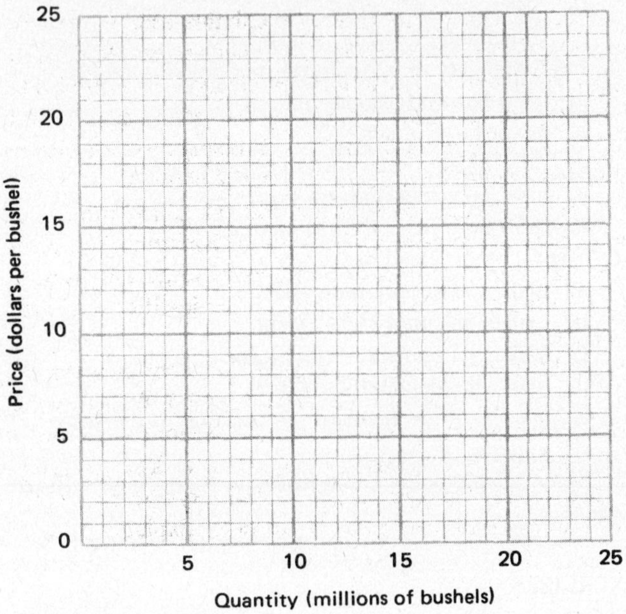

FIGURE 20-3

5b. If we compare points *A* and *C* we find that the percentage change in price is approximately ____________. The percentage change in quantity that sellers would like to supply is approximately ____________; therefore, the elasticity of supply is ____________.

6a. Suppose now that the government cancels its price floor, and instead requires the sellers of apples to pay a sales tax of $10 per bushel. When the buyers now pay $15 per bushel, the sellers can keep only $ ____________ per bushel after they pay the $10 per bushel tax. Thus, according to Table 20-1, they will supply ____________ million bushels. Fill in the rest of Table 20-2.

Table 20-2

(1) Price per bushel paid by demanders (including tax)	(2) Amount per bushel received by sellers	(3) Millions of bushels supplied
$10	$ 0	0
15	____	____
20	____	____
25	____	____

6b. Plot the new supply curve in Figure 20-3 and mark it S'. The new equilibrium price (paid by demanders) is $__________, and the new equilibrium quantity is __________. Of the $10 per bushel paid in sales tax, sellers are paying $__________, and buyers are paying $__________.

7. Draw a straight-line demand curve D' passing through point A , which is more elastic than D. If this new demand curve were to replace the old demand curve, the equilibrium price *before* the imposition of the tax would be [higher, lower, no different], and the equilibrium quantity before the tax would be [higher, lower, no different]. The equilibrium price after the tax would be [higher, lower, no different] than with the old demand curve, and the equilibrium quantity would be [less, more, no different]. With the new demand curve, the amount of tax paid by buyers would be [more, less], and the amount paid by suppliers would be [more, less] than with the old demand curve.

ESSAY QUESTIONS

1. At the end of the chapter highlights section, the following general rule is given: The smaller the elasticity of supply or demand, the larger the changes in equilibrium prices resulting from a shift in the other curve. Is it possible to state a similar rule with respect to equilibrium quantities? (Hint: See figures 20-1 and 2 above.)

2. The Canadian government will not allow a huge oil company (like Dome Petroleum) to go bankrupt, but it will allow farmers or other small businesses to go bankrupt. Is this government policy fair? Can it be justified on some other grounds?

3. Why might farmers sometimes hope for poor crops? (Hint: Refer to Box 20-2 in the textbook.) Which would result in the highest price of corn in Ontario: (a) a drought everywhere except in that province, (b) a drought everywhere except in Canada, (c) a drought everywhere except in North America, or (d) a drought nowhere. Explain.

The next two questions are more difficult.

4. If you were a monopolist (a single seller) and you discovered that the demand for your product was inelastic, would you want to raise its price or lower it? Why?

5. It has been argued that stores issue trading stamps to discriminate against people who cannot be bothered collecting, licking, and redeeming the stamps. These people end up paying a higher price for their purchases than those who use the stamps, because only the users receive a "discount" in the form of the items they get with the stamps. Suppose you were the owner of a large chain of stores and you wanted to engage in this kind of price discrimination (that is, raise the price to nonusers of stamps, and lower it to users). What would happen to your total revenue if the demand by users of stamps were elastic and the demand by nonusers were inelastic? What would happen to your total revenue if the demand by users were inelastic and the demand by nonusers were elastic?

ANSWERS

Important Terms: **1** c **2** e **3** b **4** a **5** d **6** g **7** f
True-false: **1** F **2** F **3** F **4** T **5** T **6** F **7** F **8** F **9** T **10** F **11** T
Multiple Choice: **1** d **2** e **3** d **4** b **5** e **6** b **7** b **8** a **9** e **10** c **11** b **12** b **13** e **14** d **15** d
Exercises: **1a.** P_1AQ_10, $20 x 8 = $160, P_2BQ_20, $10 x 10 = $100, inelastic, decreases.

$$\frac{\%\text{ change in quantity}}{\%\text{ change in price}} = \frac{25\%}{50\%} = 0.5$$

1b. More, the same as, more than

2. D_1, less. **3a.** unit elastic, passes through the origin 0, A, C, A, B, less, less, true, the same as, inelastic. **3b.** greater, more, true, elastic. **4.** S_2, less. **5a.** $15, 15, supply. **5b.** 27%, 27%, 1. **6a.** $5, 5 m.

Figure 20-3 completed:

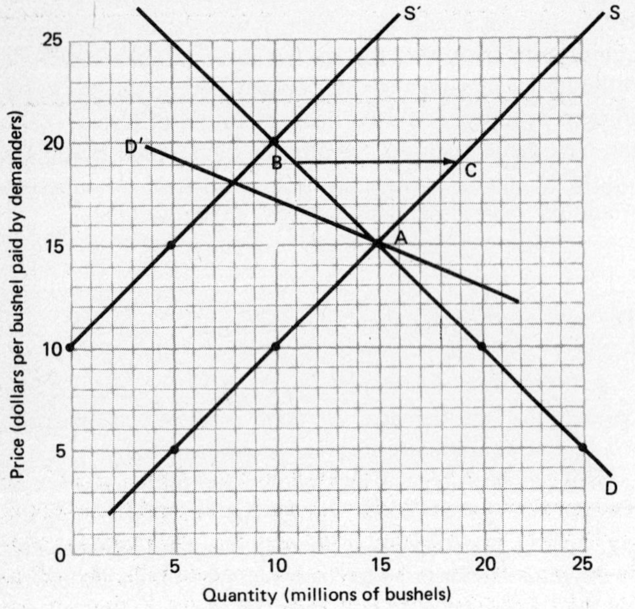

Table 20-2 completed:

(1)	(2)	(3)
10	$ 0	0
15	5	5
20	10	10
25	15	15

6b. $20, 10, $5, $5. **7.** no different, no different, lower, less, less, more.

Chapter 21

DEMAND

MAJOR PURPOSE

In the last chapter, we measured elasticity of demand and elasticity of supply, and we saw how important they are in analysing policy problems. In this chapter, we get down to the fundamentals of demand; we examine the foundations of the demand curve. (In the next two chapters, the fundamentals of supply will be similarly examined.)

Three other major objectives in this chapter are (1) to analyse how the consumer facing a given price arrives at equilibrium, (2) to examine and measure how much the consumer benefits when the price of a product falls, and (3) to consider the other costs, in addition to price, that are incurred when someone purchases a good or service.

LEARNING OBJECTIVES

After you have studied this chapter in the textbook and the study guide, you should be able to

- Show how the market demand curve is constructed by adding up the individual demand curves
- Define marginal benefit
- Explain the principle of diminishing marginal utility (diminishing marginal benefit)
- Describe the condition that must be fulfilled for a consumer to be in equilibrium
- Use Adam Smith's champagne/water paradox to explain the importance of total utility as well as marginal utility
- Use the demand curve to measure how consumers lose when price rises, citing two reasons for this loss
- Explain how this measure of damage to the consumer can be used, along with the concept of elasticity from the previous chapter, to analyse the effect, for example, of a Florida freeze. How are all parties—citrus growers, consumers, and the nation as a whole—affected?
- Show why purchasers must take into account not only price, but also transactions costs, including search (information) costs
- Explain why search costs include not only out-of-pocket costs, but also time costs, and why time costs are also important in using a product

HIGHLIGHTS OF THE CHAPTER

The first fundamental characteristic of the demand curve that must be recognized is an obvious one: A market demand curve is simply the sum of all the individual demand curves. This is illustrated in Figure 21-1 in the textbook. In turning to the other characteristics of demand, we begin by examining the demand curve of one individual consumer.

Interpreting a Demand Curve

Underlying each individual demand curve are the two basic concepts introduced in Chapter 2—scarcity and choice. Thus the consumer can be viewed as choosing between two scarce goods, such as apples and cherries. This choice is described in Box 21-1 in the textbook and in the appendix to this chapter. Another view is that the consumer chooses between apples and *all* other goods—that is, between apples and money, since money is the means of acquiring all other goods. This is the choice that is described by the demand curve for apples, which tells us how much money the consumer is willing to give up to buy one box of apples, how much more to buy a second box, and so on.

Notice that here we are taking a different approach to the demand curve. In previous chapters, we have viewed the demand curve as telling us, *at each given price*, how many boxes of apples the buyer would purchase. The answer is given by each of the *horizontal* arrows in Figure 21-2 (*a*) of the textbook. Now, we are viewing the demand curve as telling us, *at each given quantity*, how much money the consumer is willing to pay per box for that quantity of apples—as shown by the *vertical* arrows in panel (*b*) of that diagram.

Willingness to pay is typically a good indicator of how highly the consumer values each additional box of apples—that is, willingness to pay measures the *marginal benefit (marginal utility)* of apples. The more a consumer buys, the less marginal utility is derived from another box. In other words, the further to the right the consumer goes in making more and more purchases in Figure 21-2(*b*), the shorter these vertical arrows of marginal utility become. This is why the demand curve for apples slopes downward to the right. In simplest terms, the more apples you eat, the less interested you become in eating any more. Formally stated, this is the *law of diminishing marginal utility*, which states that as more and more of any product is acquired, *eventually* the utility (or benefit) provided by one more unit must fall.

Consumer Equilibrium

With this background, the equilibrium of the consumer is now easily described. Because the marginal benefits of the first box of apples—as shown by the first arrow in Figure 21-3 of the textbook—is higher than the market price of $6, the consumer buys that box. For the same reason, the consumer buys a second box, a third, and so on. Purchases cease when the marginal benefit of another box falls to the level of price. (Beyond that, where marginal benefit has fallen below price, further purchases are obviously not justified.) This, then, provides an important conclusion: In equilibrium, the consumer purchases up to the point where the marginal benefit of a product equals its price.

How the Consumer Is Affected by a Change in Price

Figure 21-3 in the text also shows the concept of consumer surplus. In purchasing the first box of apples, the consumer enjoys a $4 surplus; the individual is willing to pay $10 for that box of apples, but it costs only $6. Similarly, there is a $3 surplus on the next box, and so on. The consumer purchasing five boxes acquires a surplus equal to all these arrows above the $6 price line, that is, the surplus is equal to the area of triangle *FEP*. Thus consumer surplus is the area of the triangle to the northwest of the point of equilibrium on the demand curve.

In Figure 21-5 of the text, these concepts are used to show how much the consumer benefits from a price reduction. At original price *P* and equilibrium at *E*, the consumer surplus is area *FEP*. When the price falls to $2 and equilibrium moves to E_2, the consumer surplus is area FE_2P_2, for an increase of PEE_2P_2—the area enclosed to the left of the demand curve between the old and new price. This is the consumer benefit if the price falls from *P* to P_2—or, of course, the consumer loss, if the price rises from P_2 to *P*.

Application of the Theory

This measure of consumer loss from a price increase is applied in Figure 21-7 in the textbook to the case of the typical Florida freeze that had made citrus scarce and has drive up its price. It is shown that the consumer loss must exceed any conceivable gain to producers and thus result in an overall loss to society as a whole. (Producers did gain from the crop loss in this case because demand was inelastic; thus, the increase in price more than compensated for their reduced sales. However, in cases of elastic demand, producers would lose.)

This example also illustrates an important fallacy of composition—that is, the fallacy of arguing that what applies to an individual also applies to all individuals taken together. An individual farmer whose own crops are damaged is worse off because of a freeze. But, taken together, all farmers may benefit.

Costs to the Consumer in Addition to Price

The price of a good is not the only cost to a buyer. In addition, the buyer may also face *transaction costs*. These may include dealer or brokerage fees in making the actual purchase, plus any *search costs* (information costs) that must be undertaken. Search costs are the costs incurred in making an intelligent purchasing decision. They may include out-of-pocket costs of buying publications that compare products, plus the "time costs" involved in studying these publications. There are also time costs in using products once they are purchased. If your new car turns out to be a lemon, you will incur a lot of time costs in taking it back and forth for repair. Thus, if your time is worth a great deal, you are more likely to buy a reliable car that minimizes this time cost. In general, it is important in any purchasing decision to consider not only price, but all of these other costs as well.

IMPORTANT TERMS: MATCH THE COLUMNS

Match each term in the first column with the corresponding phrase in the second column. But before you do so, write your own definition of each term in the first column.

_____ **1.** total benefit (total utility)
_____ **2.** marginal benefit (marginal utility)
_____ **3.** substitution effect
_____ **4.** income effect
_____ **5.** law of diminishing marginal utility
_____ **6.** consumer equilibrium
_____ **7.** consumer surplus
_____ **8.** search cost (information cost)
_____ **9.** time cost
_____ **10.** transactions costs

a. the additional satisfaction derived from one more unit of a product
b. when the price of a good falls, this is the increase in sales that occurs because the purchaser's real income has risen
c. when the price of a good falls, this is the increase in sales that occurs because this good has become less expensive relative to other goods
d. a situation in which the marginal benefit of each good just equals its cost
e. the difference between the amount that a consumer would be willing to pay for a good and the amount that actually is paid for it
f. as more and more of a good is consumed, a point is eventually reached where marginal utility begins to decline
g. the time and money spent in collecting the information necessary to make an informed purchase
h. the total satisfaction derived from a product
i. all costs (except price) associated with buying or selling anything, including search costs and other costs such as fees or commissions
j. the time spent shopping for a good and using it

TRUE-FALSE

T F **1.** If marginal benefit has fallen below the price of a good, the consumer has bought too much.
T F **2.** If a consumer's purchase of a good is less than the equilibrium amount, marginal benefit will still be greater than the price of the good.
T F **3.** The reason why a demand curve slopes down is that ultimately each consumer's marginal utility falls as the individual consumes more.
T F **4.** Consumer surplus is the difference between what people would be willing to pay for a good, and what they, in fact, do pay.
T F **5.** A Florida freeze would not result in any overall loss to the United States if the elasticity of demand were equal to 1.
T F **6.** If drought damages the wheat crop, producers gain exactly what consumers lose.
T F **7.** Time-saving devices are more prevalent in low-wage countries than in high-wage countries.

MULTIPLE CHOICE

1. The market demand for a good is the
   a. vertical sum of the individual demands
   b. average of the individual demands
   c. horizontal sum of the individual demands
   d. vertical product of the individual demands
   e. horizontal product of the individual demands
2. The market demand curve has
   a. less slope than the individual demand curves
   b. more slope than the individual demand curves
   c. more slope or less; you can't tell in general
   d. the same slope as the individual demand curves
   e. more slope, if the individual demand curves are elastic
3. According to the substitution effect, a fall in the price of apples results in
   a. an increase in the purchases of apples because other goods have become cheap relative to apples
   b. an increase in the purchases of apples because apples have become less expensive relative to other goods
   c. a decrease in the purchases of apples because apples have become less expensive relative to other goods
   d. a decrease in the purchases of apples because the buyer's real income has risen
   e. an increase in the purchases of apples because the buyer's real income has risen
4. A consumer will continue to purchase a good until its
   a. marginal benefit falls to zero
   b. marginal benefit falls to the level of its price
   c. total benefit falls to the level of its price
   d. total benefit falls to zero
   e. total benefit rises to the level of its price
5. The amount of a good that a consumer purchases should depend on
   a. marginal benefit only
   b. search cost only
   c. price only
   d. price and search cost only
   e. marginal benefit, search cost, and price
6. According to the law of diminishing marginal utility
   a. the utility from another unit can never rise
   b. marginal utility must always fall
   c. marginal utility must always be negative
   d. marginal utility must rise at first, but eventually it may fall
   e. marginal utility may rise at first, but eventually it must fall
7. If water and champagne had the same upward-sloping supply curve
   a. they would certainly sell for the same price
   b. they would be likely to sell for the same price
   c. champagne would be more expensive
   d. water would be more expensive
   e. no prediction could be made about their prices
8. If we know only the selling price of a perfectly competitive good, then we know
   a. the total benefit it provides
   b. the total cost of producing it
   c. its total cost and total benefit
   d. the marginal benefit it provides
   e. none of the above
9. If price increases, there is
   a. a gain to the consumer equal to the area to the left of the demand curve between the old price and the new price
   b. a loss to the consumer equal to the area to the left of the demand curve between the old price and the new price
   c. a loss to the consumer equal to the area to the left of the supply curve between the old price and the new price
   d. a gain to the consumer equal to the area to the left of the supply curve between the old price and the new price
   e. no effect on the consumer
10. Consumer surplus is a "triangle" two sides of which are
    a. the vertical axis and the horizontal axis
    b. the horizontal axis and the price line
    c. the horizontal axis and the demand curve
    d. the vertical axis and the price line
    e. none of the above
11. In which case do consumers enjoy the least consumer surplus? (Assume in each case that they face the same price and purchase the same quantity.)
    a. when demand elasticity is 1
    b. when demand is highly inelastic
    c. when demand is highly elastic
    d. when supply elasticity is 1
    e. when supply is highly elastic
12. If drought damages the wheat crop
    a. consumers lose, producers benefit, and the nation as a whole benefits
    b. consumers lose, producers lose, and the nation as a whole loses
    c. consumers and the nation lose; producers may benefit or lose
    d. producers and the nation lose; consumers benefit
    e. producers and the nation lose; consumers may benefit or lose
13. The more willing the public is to bear search costs
    a. the more variation there will be in price quoted by sellers
    b. the less variation there will be in price quoted by sellers
    c. the higher will be the price quoted by sellers
    d. the greater the overcharging by wholesalers and retailers
    e. the greater the overcharging by wholesalers but not retailers

14. Time costs are
  a. greater in a high-income country, which is one reason why less reliable cars are purchased there
  b. greater in a high-income country, which is one reason why more expensive and reliable cars are purchased there
  c. less in a high-income country, which is one reason why more expensive and reliable cars are purchased there
  d. less in a high-income country, which is one reason why less expensive and reliable cars are purchased there
  e. less in a high-income country, but this doesn't affect the cars that are purchased there

15. A consumer buying two goods will be in equilibrium if
  a. the ratio of the marginal utilities of these goods is greater than their price ratio
  b. the ratio of the marginal utilities of these goods is less than their price ratio
  c. the ratio of the marginal utilities of these goods is equal to 1
  d. the ratio of the marginal utilities of these goods is equal to their price ratio
  e. some other condition is met; the price ratio is irrelevant

EXERCISES

1a. If the price for the product shown in Figure 21-1 (below) is $7, then ____________ units will be purchased, because this is the quantity where marginal benefit, as given by the height of the ____________ curve, is equal to ____________. There are two interpretations of any point such as *R* on an individual's demand curve. The first is that *R* indicates the *quantity* that will be purchased at a certain price—in this case, $7. This interpretation is shown by arrow ____________. The second is that *R* indicates, at a given quantity, the maximum *price* that the buyer is willing to pay for the marginal unit—in this case, the 100th unit. This second interpretation is shown by arrow ____________. Since this arrow indicates how much the consumer will pay to acquire that 100th unit, it measures the value the consumer puts on that unit—that is, the [total value of all 100 units, marginal benefit of that 100th unit].

1b. The total benefit the consumer gets from all 100 units purchased is area ____________, which is the sum of all the [horizontal, vertical] marginal benefit arrows like ____________ enclosed beneath the ____________curve throughout the range of quantities between ____________ and ____________. However, this purchase costs the consumer area ____________, which is the quantity of ____________ units multiplied by the $ ____________ price. Therefore, the *net* benefit to the consumer of this purchase is area ____________, which is sometimes called ____________.

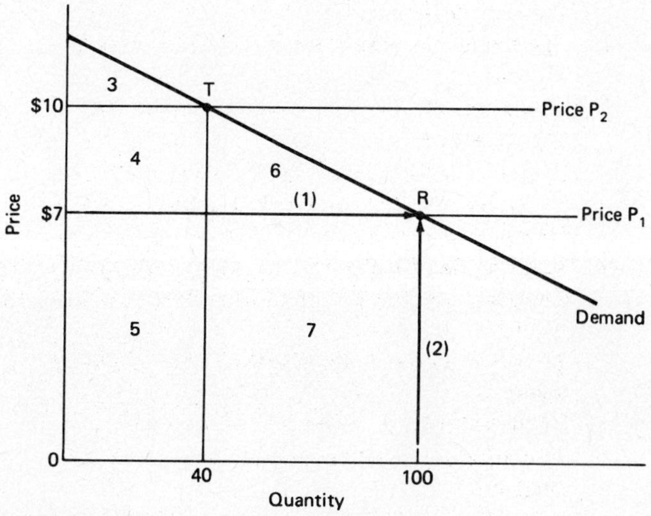

FIGURE 21-1

2. If price increases to $10, the new equilibrium is at ____________, where the quantity purchased is ____________ units. The demand curve between *R* and *T* is [elastic, inelastic] because the % change in quantity is [less, more] than the % change in price. The total benefit from this smaller purchase is area ____________. However, the cost is area ____________, which is the quantity of ____________ units times the $ ____________ price. Therefore, the *net* benefit to the purchaser when price is $10 is area ____________.

3a. Since the net benefit to the purchaser when the price was $7 was area ____________, and that benefit was reduced to area ____________ when the price rose to $10, the burden of this price increase on the consumer is area ____________, which is the area enclosed to the [left, right] of the ____________ curve between the old price and the new price.

3b. Let's look at this from another point of view. Because price has risen, the consumer is buying ____________ fewer units. The total benefit the consumer used to derive from these units—and has now lost— is area ____________. However, the consumer is no longer incurring the cost shown by area ____________, of purchasing these units, since they are no longer being bought. Therefore, the net loss of the consumer on these units that are no longer purchased is area ____________. In addition, the consumer is hurt because of the greater amount that has to be paid on the first 40 units (that *continue* to be purchased). The higher cost to the consumer on these units is area ____________, which is the $ ____________ price increase times those 40 units.

Thus, in summary, we confirm that the loss to the consumer because of the price increase is area ___________. This is made up of a loss of area ___________, because purchases are reduced, plus a loss of area ___________, because of the higher price that must be paid on purchases that continue to be made.

ESSAY QUESTIONS

1. People derive more benefit from the water in the world than they do from all the diamonds in the world. Yet diamonds cost far more than water. Would diamonds be more expensive than water if the two had the same supply curve and were thus equally scarce? Explain your answer.

2. To judge by the amount of time spent, most people seem to derive more utility from watching television than from going to movies. Yet they will pay $4 or $5 to go to a movie, when they could stay home and watch television for nothing. Can you explain this?

3. When Henry Ford invented the mass production of automobiles, what effect do you suppose this had on the typical marginal benefit schedule for horse-drawn carriages? What do you suppose it did to the price and sales of horse-drawn carriages?

4. Heroin addicts find that the more they consume, the more they want. Does this contradict or illustrate diminishing marginal utility? Can you use this heroin example to illustrate the law of diminishing marginal utility?

ANSWERS

Important Terms: **1** h **2** a **3** c **4** b **5** f **6**d **7** e **8** g **9** j **10** i

True-False: **1** T **2** T **3** T **4** T **5** F **6** F **7** F

Multiple Choice: **1** c **2** a **3** b **4** b **5** e **6** e **7** d **8** d **9** b **10** d **11** c **12** c **13** b **14** b **15** d

Exercises: **1a.** 100, demand, price, (1), (2), marginal benefit of that 100th unit. **1b.** 3 + 4 + 5 + 6 + 7, vertical, (2), demand, zero, 100, 5+ 7, 100, $7, 3 + 4 + 6, consumer surplus. **2.** *T*, 40, elastic, more, 3 + 4 + 5, 4 + 5, 40, $10, 3. **3a.** 3 + 4 + 6, 3, 4 + 6, left, demand. **3b.** 60, 6 + 7, 7, 6, 4, $3, 6 + 4, 6, 4.

Across

7. benefit of consumers in excess of what they pay
8. beef and leather are examples of ____________ ____________ (2 words)
10. laissez-____________
13. indefinite article
16. a means of travel
18. benefit from consuming one more unit (2 words)
23. When the price of one increases, the demand for the other increases.
24. where people skate
25. sound of disgust
26. first person possessive
28. unresponsive to a change in price
31. bounder
32. An important economic objective is to reduce this.
34. Price is likely to be ____________ when both demand and supply are inelastic.
37. member of one of the British Houses of Parliament
38. fundamental reason for study of economics
39. If demand is elastic, total ____________ increases when price is reduced.

Down

1. This joins all points that provide equal satisfaction (2 words).
2. oxidized iron
3. close
4. area just outside a city
5. measure of how much quantity responds to a change in price
6. a continent
8. what an unemployed person wants
9. official price of a currency under pegged exchange rate system
11. part of the eye
12. an appointment to meet made by lovers
13. in addition
14. a fruit covered with a woody shell
15. very successful movie or song
17. devoured
18. The ____________ tax rate is the tax rate on additional income.
19. central idea
20. all around
21. game without a winner
22. a small piece
27. passing fashions
29. one of the factors of production
30. one of the objectives of economic policy
32. This is used in producing many manufactured goods.
33. low business activity
35. ripped
36. The ____________ year is the year from which price changes are measured.

Chapter 22

COST AND PERFECTLY COMPETITIVE SUPPLY: THE SHORT RUN

MAJOR PURPOSE

In the last chapter we saw how a demand curve reflects the desire of buyers to acquire a good. In this chapter, our attention turns to supply. It will be shown that a supply curve reflects the marginal cost of producing a good. Specifically, just as you can visualize a whole set of marginal benefit bars enclosed below a demand curve, you can also visualize a whole set of marginal cost bars enclosed below a supply curve. To establish this important conclusion, we example the cost curves facing a firm, and analyse a profit-maximizing firm's short-run response to various market prices. At each price, the firm will supply a quantity determined by its marginal cost curve (provided its variable costs are covered). Therefore supply reflects marginal cost.

We also show how the economist's definition of a firm's cost is far broader than an accountant's. For an economist, costs include not only the out-of-pocket costs that accountants take into account, but also implicit costs, such as the opportunity costs of the owner's time and capital invested in the firm. Because the opportunity cost of capital—that is, normal profit—is included by an economist in calculating a firm's costs, any additional (excess or economic) profit is a return that can be earned in this industry above and beyond the return that can be earned elsewhere. Therefore, it is an incentive for more resources to move into the industry.

LEARNING OBJECTIVES

After you have studied this chapter in the textbook and the study guide, you should be able to

- Explain why, in the short run, some costs are fixed and some are variable, while in the long run all costs are variable
- Define total, variable, fixed, and marginal costs; also average cost, average variable cost, and average fixed cost
- Explain the law of (eventually) diminishing returns, and why this law means that marginal costs must eventually rise
- Show why the equilibrium condition "marginal revenue = marginal cost" must be satisfied by any profit-maximizing firm
- Show, as one specific case of the general theorem above, that "price = marginal cost" is the condition for profit maximization by a firm in perfect competition
- Explain, using a diagram, why a firm's average cost curve is cut, at its minimum point, by its marginal cost curve
- Demonstrate why the short-run supply curve of a perfectly competitive firm is its marginal cost curve (above its average variable cost curve)
- Explain the difference between accounting costs and economic costs, and why opportunity costs must be included in economic costs
- Explain why an economist defines costs to include normal profit, but not excess profit

HIGHLIGHTS OF THE CHAPTER

In our examination in this chapter of what underlies the cost curve—just as in our parallel examination in the last chapter of what underlies demand—we assume that rational self-interest is pursued. Specifically, in this chapter, we assume that producers supply the quantity of a good that will maximize their profit.

In this chapter, we focus on the short run—the period in which the firm cannot change the amount of plant and equipment it is using. In the next chapter, we turn to the long run, when the firm *is* able to vary the amount of capital and equipment it uses.

An important concept in this chapter is marginal cost MC—the cost of producing one more unit of output. If we graph MC, it must eventually rise, because of the law of (eventually) diminishing returns.

Given the firm's MC and other cost schedules, the question is: How much will the firm supply at any given price? The rule for *any* profit-maximizing firm is to produce until MC = marginal revenue MR, where MR is the additional revenue earned from producing one more unit of output.

This general rule—that a firm will produce until MC = MR—can be stated in an alternative way for a perfectly competitive firm. The reason is that such a firm takes the price of its output as given. Therefore, its MR is just the price that it faces. For example, if it sells apples for a price *P* = $2 a basket, then each additional basket provides $2 of extra revenue MR. Because its MR = *P* , the profit-maximizing rule for a perfectly competitive firm can be stated thus: It continues to produce until MC = *P*. Thus, at any given price, the firm will supply a quantity of output that can be read off its MC curve; in other words, the quantity supplied depends on the firm's MC curve. Be sure that you fully understand Figure 22-3 in the textbook. This is the diagram that most clearly demonstrates why the firm will produce until MC = *P*; and why, therefore, the firm's supply curve reflects its marginal costs.

In defining the firm's supply, there is one more important consideration. Prices must be above a certain minimum level, or the firm won't supply anything at all. This minimum level is the price that will generate enough revenue to cover the firm's variable costs, more specifically, price must be at least as high as the firm's "shutdown point" on its average variable cost (AVC) curve—that is, point *K* in Figure 22-5 in the textbook. As long as price is at least this high, then in the short run, the firm will supply this product. This is true, even if the price is still below the "break-even point" (*H* in the same diagram) where the firm is just barely able to cover its total cost, including both its variable costs *and* its fixed costs. Even though a firm operating between these two points is incurring a loss, it is still able to cover its variable costs and have at least something left over to cover part of its fixed costs. Therefore, it is better to continue to operate than to close down altogether. (If it closes down, it would be worse off: It would be unable to cover *any* of its fixed costs.) It should be emphasized that this analysis applies only to the short run when the firm cannot escape its fixed costs. However, in the long run it can escape these fixed costs, and it will do so. At any price below its break-even point, it will close down. Thus, our more precise conclusion is this: In the short run, the perfectly competitive firm's supply curve will be that part of its MC schedule lying above the minimum "shutdown" point on its AVC schedule. However, in the long run, the minimum price necessary to keep the firm in business will be at its break-even, rather than its shutdown, point.

The final important topic covered in this chapter is the difference between economic costs and accounting cost. While the accountant looks only at explicit, out-of-pocket costs, the economist also considers implicit costs, such as the opportunity costs of the owner of a firm. This opportunity cost includes the salary the owner could have earned in another job, and the interest income or dividends that the owner could have earned by investing his or her capital elsewhere. This alternative possible income on capital is called the firm's normal profit; it is the amount that is necessary to keep capital in that firm. Because economists thus include normal profit as a cost, when they speak of "profit" they mean excess profit—that is, additional profit above and beyond normal profit. Such above-normal or excess profit is important for the operation of the market system, because whenever it exists, it acts as a signal to attract resources into that industry.

IMPORTANT TERMS: MATCH THE COLUMNS

Match each term in the first column with the corresponding phrase in the second column. But before you do so, write your own definition of each term in the first column.

_____ **1.** short run
_____ **2.** long run
_____ **3.** short-run production function
_____ **4.** marginal product
_____ **5.** law of (eventually) diminishing returns
_____ **6.** fixed costs
_____ **7.** variable costs

a. the return an input could earn in its best alternative use
b. the sum of both fixed and variable costs
c. the increase in total revenue from the sale of one more unit (In perfect competition, this is the same as market price.)
d. the point at which the marginal cost curve intersects the average variable cost curve (If the price falls below this,

_____ **8.** total cost
_____ **9.** average cost
_____ **10.** marginal cost
_____ **11.** marginal revenue
_____ **12.** break-even point
_____ **13.** shutdown point
_____ **14.** opportunity cost
_____ **15.** economic cost
_____ **16.** normal profit
_____ **17.** economic profit
_____ **18.** long-run production function
_____ **19.** economies of scale
_____ **20.** perfect competition

the firm will cease operating even in the short run.)

e. the time period over which the firm's capital stock is variable
f. the relationship between the amount of variable factors used and the amount of output that can be produced when the amount of capital is constant
g. explicit accounting costs plus the implicit opportunity costs that are considered by economists but not by accountants
h. total revenue minus economic cost; a return in addition to normal profit
i. the income that could be earned if capital were to be invested elsewhere (Economists view this item as a cost because it is the opportunity cost of the firm's capital.)
j. the point at which the marginal cost curve intersects the average cost curve, and the firm makes a zero profit
k. total cost per unit
l. the increase in total cost when output is increased by 1 unit
m. the time period over which the firm cannot vary its capital stock
n. the relationship that shows the maximum output that can be produced with various combinations of all the different inputs
o. all costs that change with output in the short run
p. the additional output the firm can produce by hiring one more unit of a factor
q. costs that do not vary as output increases; also called *overhead* or *sunk* costs
r. description of costs if doubling all inputs more than doubles the firm's output (This typically means that the long-run average cost curve is falling.)
s. if more of a factor is employed while other factors must eventually fall
t. a market in which there is a freedom of entry and so many buyers and sellers of a standardized product that none has any influence over price

TRUE-FALSE

T F **1.** If output is zero, variable costs are zero.
T F **2.** When marginal cost is more than average cost, then average cost must be rising.
T F **3.** The law of diminishing returns states that the marginal product of any factor must eventually fall if other factors are held constant.
T F **4.** The law of diminishing returns is unrealistic because it implies that we could feed the world from our back garden.
T F **5.** Marginal revenue is total revenue less the cost that results when one more unit is produced.
T F **6.** If a competitive firm is producing slightly less than the profit-maximizing amount, then price is greater than marginal cost.
T F **7.** In the short run, the firm stops producing whenever price falls below its minimum average cost.
T F **8.** When existing firms earn economic profit, then that industry is attractive for new firms.
T F **9.** Economic profit is the profit that remains after all explicit and implicit costs, including normal profit, are taken into account.
T F **10.** If a firm is operating at capacity—that is, with a completely inelastic supply (MC) curve—then an increase in market price will result in no increase in its total revenue or output.

MULTIPLE CHOICE

1. An example of a variable cost is
   a. wage payments
   b. rental payments on a long-term lease
   c. interest payments on a mortgage
   d. depreciating costs
   e. all of the above
2. As output increases in the short run
   a. fixed costs increase, but variable costs do not
   b. fixed costs decrease, but variable costs do not
   c. fixed costs and variable costs change
   d. neither fixed costs nor variable costs change
   e. variable costs increase, but fixed costs do not
3. As output increases in the short run
   a. fixed cost fall
   b. fixed cost rises
   c. fixed cost has less and less influence on average cost
   d. fixed cost has more and more influence on average cost
   e. average fixed cost rises
4. A firm's costs are related in the following way
   a. Average cost AC cuts marginal cost MC at the minimum point of MC.
   b. Average cost AC cuts average variable cost AVC at the minimum point of AVC.
   c. MC cuts AC at the minimum point of AC.
   d. MC cuts AC where the price line intersects AC.
   e. AVC cuts AC at the minimum point of AC.
5. If total costs are rising, then marginal cost must be
   a. rising
   b. falling
   c. positive
   d. negative
   e. zero
6. The law of diminishing returns means that, as output increases in the short run
   a. fixed cost will eventually fall
   b. fixed cost will eventually rise
   c. marginal costs will eventually rise
   d. marginal costs will eventually fall
   e. marginal costs will eventually become constant
7. In the long-run decisions of a firm
   a. employment of labour is held constant, while its use of capital is allowed to increase
   b. employment of labour is held constant, while its use of capital is allowed to decrease
   c. use of capital is held constant, while its employment of labour is allowed to vary
   d. both are allowed to vary
   e. neither is allowed to vary
8. If a firm's fixed cost is $100, and its total cost is $200 to produce 1 unit and $310 to produce 2, then the marginal cost of the second unit is
   a. $100
   b. $110
   c. $200
   d. $210
   e. $310
9. If a firm's fixed cost is $100, and its total cost is $200 to produce 1 unit, and $310 to produce 2, the firm is
   a. already facing diminishing returns
   b. not yet facing diminishing returns
   c. not yet facing constant returns
   d. already facing increasing returns
   e. facing constant returns
10. The competitive firm's short-run supply curve is that part of its short-run marginal cost that lies above its
    a. average cost curve
    b. average variable cost curve
    c. average fixed cost curve
    d. total cost curve
    e. fixed cost curve
11. The shutdown point is
    a. the minimum point on the average cost curve
    b. the minimum point on the average variable cost curve
    c. the minimum point on the marginal cost curve
    d. the minimum point on the average fixed cost curve
    e. the point where marginal cost cuts the average fixed cost curve
12. If a perfectly competitive firm is producing more than the profit-maximizing amount, then price must be
    a. above marginal cost
    b. equal to marginal cost
    c. below marginal cost
    d. below average variable cost
    e. equal to average variable cost
13. In the short run, the break-even point is
    a. at the intersection of the marginal cost curve and the average fixed cost curve
    b. below the intersection of the marginal cost curve and the average fixed cost curve
    c. the same as the shutdown point
    d. above the shutdown point
    e. below the shutdown point
14. If a firm's total cost and total revenue curves (TC and TR) are plotted, the firm maximizes its profit where
    a. its TC cuts its TR from above
    b. its TC cuts it TR from below
    c. its TC is parallel to and above its TR
    d. its TC is parallel to and below its TR
    e. its TC is horizontal
15. The opportunity cost of an input is
    a. the most it could earn in the least attractive alternative use
    b. the least it could earn in its least attractive alternative use
    c. the most it could earn in its most attractive alternative use
    d. the least it could earn in its most attractive alternative use
    e. (a) or (d)

16. In defining costs
a. economists take implicit opportunity costs into account because they are an out-of-pocket cash cost
b. economists take implicit opportunity costs into account, but accountants often do not
c. accountants take implicit opportunity costs into account, but economists often do not
d. both take implicit opportunity costs into account
e. neither takes implicit opportunity costs into account

EXERCISES

1a. If the price is P_1 in Figure 22-1 (below), the quantity supplied will be ____________, total revenue will be area ____________, average cost will be ____________, and multiplying this by the number of units sold yields a total cost of area ____________. Thus, economic profit will be area ____________.

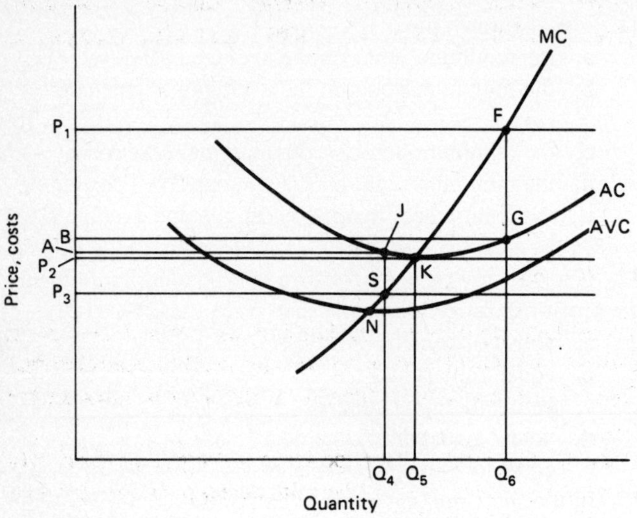

FIGURE 22-1

1b. Alternatively, we can arrive at this same profit by noting that the firm's average revenue is its price P_1, its average cost is ____________, and therefore its average profit is ____________. Multiplying this by its quantity of output yields its total profit, which is area ____________.

1c. If the price is P_2, the firm will supply quantity ____________, total revenue will be ____________, average cost will be ____________, total cost will be ____________, and economic profit will be ____________. Therefore, the [break-even, shutdown] point is ____________.

1d. If the price is P_3, the firm will supply ____________, total revenue will be ____________, average cost will be ____________, and total cost will be ____________. Therefore, total economic [profit, loss] will be ____________. If prices stay at P_3, then the firm will continue to operate in the ____________ run, but not in the ____________ run. Despite its loss, it makes this short-run decision because price P_3 is still above the firm's [shutdown, break-even] point at ____________. Another way of viewing this decision is that the firm is operating above its [MC, AC, AVC] curve. Therefore, it can more than cover its ____________ costs and thus have some left over partly to cover its ____________ costs. Shade in and mark for future reference the firm's profit when its price (in this case P_1) is above the minimum point K on its AC curve, and its loss when its price (in this case P_3) is below K.

2. Set up and fill in a table similar to Table 22-6 in the textbook, showing how an accountant and an economist would describe the costs and profit of Mark Laporte, who owns and operates a farm. His total revenue in this particular year is $180,000. His expenses include $27,000 he pays to hire farm labour, $12,000 for fertilizer and seed, $10,000 he pays to rent an adjacent farm, and $20,000 for gasoline and other supplies. Although his accountant tells him that, relative to his neighbours, he's extremely successful, he sometimes considers giving up farming to take a job managing a farm supply business nearby where he has been offered a $65,000 salary. If he did so, he would sell his farm and invest the proceeds in government bonds that would yield a $62,000 per year interest income.

What is his accounting profit and his economic profit? Assuming that he finds farming and managing the farm supply business equally attractive, what would you recommend that he do? Why?

3a. (An introduction to Chapter 23.) Table 22-1 below shows two short-run production functions for a firm that uses only two factors: labour and capital. Each production function describes the amounts of labour the firm would need to produce various amounts of output. The left panel shows the short-run production function if the firm has 20 units of capital; the right panel shows its short-run production function if it has 40 units of capital.

The cost of labour to the firm is $500 per unit, and the cost of capital is $250 per unit. Thus, producing, say, 3 units of output with 20 units of capital, costs a total of $19,000; that is, $5,000 in fixed costs (20 units of capital at $250 per unit) plus $14,000 in variable costs (28 units of labour at a $500 per unit wage rate). This $19,000 is entered in Table 22-2 above. Fill in the rest of this table.

3b. If the firm is making a long-run decision and wishes to produce 2 units of output, how much capital should it acquire—20 units or 40? Why?

3c. Answer question (3b) assuming that the firm wants to produce 5 units of output.

Table 22-1
TWO SHORT-RUN PRODUCTION FUNCTIONS

20 units of capital			40 units of capital		
Output	**Capital**	**Labour required**	**Output**	**Capital**	**Labour required**
0	20	0	0	40	0
1	20	8	1	40	7
2	20	14	2	40	12
3	20	28	3	40	20
4	20	45	4	40	30
5	20	65	5	40	46
6	20	90	6	40	66

Table 22-2
COSTS CALCULATED FROM THE TWO SHORT-RUN PRODUCTION FUNCTIONS IN TABLE 22-1, GIVEN A WAGE OF $500

Output	**Total cost**	**Fixed cost**	**Variable cost**	**Average cost**	**Average variable cost**	**Marginal cost**	**Total cost**	**Fixed cost**	**Variable cost**	**Average cost**	**Average variable cost**	**Marginal cost**
0				——	——	0						
1												
2												
3	19,000	5,000	14,000	6,333	4,667							
4												
5												
6												

ESSAY QUESTIONS

1. Draw a U-shaped average cost curve. Then draw in the corresponding MC curve and finally the AVC curve. In red, show the new curves after a cost-cutting technological innovation. What effect does this have on the firm's supply curve?

2. In Figure 22-2(*b*) in the text, the marginal product curve cuts the average product curve at the highest point on the average product curve. Explain why this must be so, using an argument similar to the one used to establish that the MC curve intersects the AC at the lowest point on the AC curve.

3. "In the short run, a perfectly competitive firm will not produce at any point where its average cost is still falling." Do you agree? Why or why not?

4. Are either normal profit or economic profit—or both—included in costs? Explain why.

ANSWERS

Important Terms: **1** m **2** e **3** f **4** p **5** s **6** q **7** o **8** b **9** k **10** l **11** c **12** j **13** d **14** a **15** g **16** i **17** h **18** n **19** r **20** t

True-False: **1** T **2** T **3** T **4** F **5** F **6** T **7** F **8** T **9** T **10** F

Multiple Choice: **1** a **2** e **3** c **4** c **5** c **6** c **7** d **8** b **9** a **10** b **11** b **12** c **13** d **14** d **15** c **16** b

Exercises: **1a.** Q_6, P_1FQ_60, B, BGQ_60, P_1FGB. **1b.** B, BP_1, P_1FGB. **1c.** Q_5, P_2KQ_50, P_2, P_2,KQ_50, zero, break-even, K. **1d.** Q_4, P_3SQ $_40$, A, AJQ_40, loss, $AJSP_3$, short, long, shutdown, N, AVC, variable, fixed. **2.** The table you derive should look like this:

Costs and profits, evaluated by:

1. An accountant		
Total revenue		$180,000
Costs:		
Labour	27,000	
Fertilizer, seed	12,000	
Rent	10,000	
Gas, etc.	20,000	
Total costs		69,000
Accounting profit		111,000

2. An economist		
Total revenue		$180,000
Costs:		
Explicit:		
Labour	27,000	
Fertilizer, seed	12,000	
Rent	10,000	
Gas, etc.	20,000	
Implicit:		
Owner's salary	65,000	
Normal profit	62,000	
Total costs		196,000
Economic (above-normal) profit		-16,000

His best course of action is to sell the farm, buy bonds with the proceeds, and take the other job, since he is now earning $16,000 less in farming than he could if he followed this alternative course of action. That is, his *economic* loss in farming is $16,000; his $111,000 of accounting income is $16,000 less than his opportunity cost of $65,000 + $62,000 = $127,000.

3a. Table 22-2 completed:

Table 22-2 completed

Output	Total cost	Fixed cost	Variable cost	Average cost	Average variable cost	Marginal cost	Total cost	Fixed cost	Variable cost	Average cost	Average variable cost	Marginal cost
0	5,000	5,000	0	—	—	0	10,000	10,000	0	—	—	0
1	9,000	5,000	4,000	9,000	4,000	4,000	13,500	10,000	3,500	13,500	3,500	3,500
2	12,000	5,000	7,000	6,000	3,500	3,000	16,000	10,000	6,000	8,000	3,000	2,500
3	19,000	5,000	14,000	6,333	4,667	7,000	20,000	10,000	10,000	6,667	3,333	4,000
4	27,500	5,000	22,500	6,875	5,625	8,500	25,000	10,000	15,000	6,250	3,750	5,000
5	37,500	5,000	32,500	7,500	6,500	10,000	33,000	10,000	23,000	6,600	4,600	8,000
6	50,000	5,000	45,000	8,333	7,500	12,500	43,000	10,000	33,000	7,167	5,500	10,000

3b. 20 units, its average cost will be $6,000, rather than $8,000. **3c.** 40 units, its average cost will be $6,000, rather than $7,500.

COST AND PERFECTLY COMPETITIVE SUPPLY: THE LONG RUN

MAJOR PURPOSES

Our major objective in this chapter is to examine costs in the long run and to show how they differ from costs in the short run. In the previous chapter, we described costs and supply in the short run. In the long run, the firm can vary not only its labour input, but also those factors of production, such as capital, that are fixed in the short run. Thus, in the long run, *all* costs become variable. The first topic in this chapter is to show how the long-run average cost curve (LAC) is related to the short-run average costs curves (SAC). There is a whole family of these SAC curves, one for each specific level of plant and equipment; and the LAC is the "envelope curve" that encloses all these SAC curves from below. With the LAC curve, we can illustrate economies of scale; these exist when the LAC has a downward slope.

With this description of long-run costs in hand, the next question is, How much will be supplied? To some degree, the answer to this question depends on the type of market; for example, a perfectly competitive firm and a monopolist will sell different quantities of output, even though these firms may have the same costs. In this chapter we continue to assume perfect competition, where there is such a large number of buyers and sellers of a standardized product that none can affect its price, and there is free entry of new producers. This last condition is important. It means that the long-run adjustment of a perfectly competitive industry includes not only an adjustment of output by *existing* firms, but also a change in the number of firms. For example, in such a market an increase in demand initially results in a short-run increase in price and profit that attracts new firms into the industry. This in turn increases supply and causes prices to fall back part or all of the way to its original level. If it falls back only part way, the resulting long-run price increase provides original producers with an increase in profit. This benefit to *producers* can be read off a *supply* curve in much the same way as the effect of a price change on *buyers* can be read off a *demand* curve.

LEARNING OBJECTIVES

After you have studied this chapter in the textbook and the study guide, you should be able to

- Show in a diagram how long-run and short-run average cost curves are related to each other by an envelope relationship
- Define economies of scale and diminishing returns, clearly distinguishing between the two, and explain why a firm may face both
- Define perfect competition, explaining each of the three important requirements
- Analyse the effect of the entry of new firms on an industry's supply
- Describe how an industry adjusts to an increase in demand, clearly distinguishing between the short-run increase in price, and the long-term drift in that price back down toward its original level as new firms enter the industry
- Distinguish between case A, where, in the long run, price falls all the way back to its original level and case B, where it falls back only part way
- Explain the underlying conditions that give rise to each of these two cases.
- Restate this analysis—for both case A and case B—to describe what happens when demand *decreases*, rather than increases

Define producer surplus, explaining why it changes as price changes
Show how the benefit to producers from a price increase can be read off a supply curve in much the same way that the loss to consumers can be read off a demand curve

HIGHLIGHTS OF THE CHAPTER

In the short run, labour is variable but capital is fixed. However, in the long run, *both* labour and capital are variable. The capital in an industry can increase because (1) existing firms decide to install more capital, and (2) new firms enter. This second issue—the entry of new firms—is discussed later in this chapter. We begin with a discussion of the first issue: In the long run, how much capital should a firm install?

Describing this decision by a firm requires knowledge of its cost curves, and Figure 23-2 in the text shows how a firm's long-run average cost curve (LAC) can be derived from its short-run average cost curves (SAC). (Each of its SAC curves applies to a specific amount of capital.) Figure 23-2 also shows that the firm's LAC curve is the envelope curve enclosing all the SAC curves from below. It shows how a firm will produce any specified level of output—say, a_5 in that figure—by selecting the lowest cost combination of labour and capital. Specifically, the firm minimizes its average cost of producing q_5 at point *S* by selecting capital stock *D*. (SAC_D, of course, is the short-run average cost curve that applies if the firm has capital stock *D*.) Alternatively, if the firm wished to produce output q_4, it would do so at minimum average cost by producing at *R* using capital stock *C*. Thus, the LAC "planning curve" tells the firm what its minimum average cost will be when, in the long run, it is free to select *any* capital stock.

This then sets the stage for comparing two important economic phenomena: economies of scale and the law of (eventually) diminishing returns. Economies of scale exist when a 10% increase in output requires less than a 10% increase in all inputs. In this situation, the cost of producing each unit of output falls as output increases (provided that input prices are stable). Thus, LAC slopes downward and to the right. An important conclusion follows: When there are economies of scale, the LAC slopes downward.

Figure 23-3 shows how a firm facing economies of scale—with a downward-sloping LAC—can also be facing diminishing returns. The reason is that diminishing returns occur when the short-run marginal cost curve SMC rises. Although economies of scale refer to falling costs (specifically, a downward sloping LAC) and diminishing returns refer to rising costs (an upward-sloping marginal cost curve) the two are not in contradiction. Diminishing returns apply to the short run, when the firm cannot change its capital stock, while economies of scale apply to the long run, when the firm *can* change its capital stock. To see this in more detail in Figure 23-2, note that in the short run, the firm *can* change its capital stock *A*. Increasing only its labour results in rising marginal cost (SMC_A)—that is, diminishing returns. However, in the long run, when the firm can vary both labour *and* capital, it operates on LAC. Because this is falling, the firm enjoys economies of scale.

In describing a firm's costs, we haven't had to specify the sort of market in which it is operating. Our description above describes equally well the costs of a firm producing in perfect competition or in any sort of a market. However, the next obvious question—What quantity of output will be supplied?—*cannot* be answered without specifying the market form. In the text, the market is assumed to be perfectly competitive, and a more complete definition of this market form is now required. So far it has been defined as a market in which there are so many buyers and sellers than none can influence price. Now we emphasize that the product must be standardized, and add another important condition: There must be no barriers to the entry of new firms.

This now sets the stage for addressing the question, 'What is the long-run supply curve of a perfectly competitive industry?' To answer that, it is necessary to consider two cases.

Case A (Figure 23-5 in the Text): Long-Run Supply Is Completely Elastic

Suppose that new firms can produce at the same cost as old firms. (For this to happen, inputs acquired by new firms would have to be as productive as those used by existing firms, and the industry would have to be small enough so that new firms can purchase inputs without bidding up their price.) In such circumstances, an increase in demand for this industry's output can, in the long run, be met entirely by new firms entering the industry and selling at the same cost and price as old firms. Since supply is increasing without any increase in price, the long-run supply is completely elastic.

It is true that when demand initially increases, price does rise *in the short run,* but before new firms can enter. It is this increase in price and, hence, profit to existing firms that provides the incentive for new firms to enter the industry. As new firms enter, supply shifts to the right. As a result, profit for new entrants is reduced. This process continues until price falls back all the way to its original level and there is no incentive left for new firms to enter.

Case B (Figure 23-7 in the Text): A Rising Long-Run Supply Curve

In this case, price does not fall all the way to its original level, because as the number of firms in the industry increases, costs rise. This may happen because new firms cannot purchase inputs without bidding up their price, or because these forms cannot acquire inputs of the same quality as those used by existing firms. (For example, new entrants into farming may find that the only available land is less productive.) Because new firms are incurring higher costs, their profits will disappear *before* price falls all the way back to its original level. With no further incentive for more firms to enter, there will be a new equilibrium at a higher price than its original level. Thus, in this case, the long-run supply curve slopes up, as does S_L in Figure 23-7.

How Producers Are Affected by a Price Change

In case B above, rising costs limit entry of new firms. But these rising costs also result in a higher price that benefits producers who are already in the industry. For example, the original farmers on the most productive land enjoy an increase in price and therefore profit. This gain for producers is measured by noting that, because this industry is producing more, its costs have increased—as shown in area 2 in Figure 23-8. However, revenue of the industry has gone up even more, by area 2 plus 3. Therefore, area 3 represents the new gain to producers from the increase in price. Note how this is the area to the left of the supply curve between the old price and new price—just as the effect on consumers of a change in price was measured in Chapter 21 as the area to the left of the *demand* curve between the old and the new price. With this description of the impact of a price change on both producers and consumers in hand, we are in a strong position to analyse how markets work in the next few chapters.

IMPORTANT TERMS: MATCH THE COLUMNS

Match each term in the first column with the corresponding phrase in the second column. But before you do so, write your own definition of each term in the first column.

_____ 1. short run
_____ 2. long run
_____ 3. short-run production function
_____ 4. law of (eventually) diminishing returns
_____ 5. long-run production function
_____ 6. economies of scale
_____ 7. perfect competition

a. a market where there are no barriers to entry, and there are so many buyers and sellers of a standardized product that none has any influence over its price
b. the time period during which the capital stock is variable
c. the table or graph showing the maximum output that can be produced with various combinations of inputs
d. if more of one factor is employed while all other factors are held constant, the marginal product of that factor must eventually fall
e. the relationship between the amount of variable factors used and the amount of output that can be produced when the amount of capital is constant
f. doubling all inputs more than doubles the firm's output, and implies a falling average cost curve (provided that input prices are stable)
g. the time period during which the firm cannot vary its capital stock

TRUE-FALSE

T F 1. Diseconomies of scale exist if a 15% increase in output requires a 16% increase in all inputs.
T F 2. It is not possible for a firm to be facing diminishing returns if its long-run average cost curve is falling.
T F 3. In the long run, there are no variable costs.
T F 4. The law of eventually diminishing returns describes a short-run situation in which labour varies but fixed factors do not.
T F 5. An increase in demand for a perfectly competitive good will result in a short-run increase in the output and profit of existing firms.
T F 6. If new entrants to an industry can obtain the same quality of inputs as existing firms and inputs are available at stable prices, then the long-run industry supply will be upward-sloping.
T F 7. The industry long-run supply curve will be horizontal if any number of new firms can enter and produce at the same cost as existing firms.

T F 8. A graph of a production function is made up of a whole set of isoquants that show how the firm's output increases as it uses more inputs.

T F 9. Whereas each indifference curve of a consumer represents a *specific number* of units of satisfaction, each isoquant in a production function represents only a "higher" or "lower" level of output.

T F *10. The short-run production function is a row from the long-run production function table.

T F *11. The long-run production function shows the minimum output that can be produced with each combination of inputs.

* Based on material from the appendices to chapters 21 and 23 in your textbook.

MULTIPLE CHOICE

1. If there are economies of scale,
   a. short-run average cost rises
   b. short-run average cost is constant
   c. short-run average cost falls
   d. long-run average cost falls
   e. long-run average cost rises
2. If there are diminishing returns,
   a. short-run marginal cost falls
   b. short-run marginal cost rises
   c. short-run marginal cost is constant
   d. long-run marginal cost falls
   e. long-run marginal cost is constant
3. Fixed costs are
   a. fixed only in the short run
   b. fixed only in the long run
   c. fixed in both the long run and the short run
   d. fixed in neither the long nor the short run
   e. variable in the short run
4. A profit-maximizing firm may be willing to produce at a loss
   a. in the short run, but not the long run
   b. in the long run, but the short run
   c. in neither the long run nor the short run
   d. in both the short run and the long run
   e. in the long run, provided there are no variable costs
5. In the long run, a firm has to decide on
   a. how much plant and equipment it uses, but not how much labour
   b. how much plant it uses, but not how much equipment and labour
   c. how much equipment and labour it uses, but not how much plant
   d. how much labour it uses, but not how much plant and equipment
   e. how much of all three it uses
6. A firm's long-run average cost curve is the envelope of its short-run
   a. marginal cost curves
   b. fixed cost curves
   c. average variable cost curves
   d. average cost curves
   e. total cost curves
7. If an industry is perfectly competitive, then
   a. there are barriers to entry that keep new competitors out and the product is standardized
   b. the product is not standardized, and there are barriers to entry
   c. the product is standardized, and there are no barriers to entry
   d. the product is not standardized, and there are no barriers to entry
   e. the government must license all firms in this industry
8. If demand decreases in a perfectly competitive industry, then
   a. price will rise in the short-run and fall in the long run
   b. price will rise in the short run and rise further in the long run
   c. price will fall in the short run and fall further in the long run
   d. price will fall in the short run and rise back toward the original price in the long run
   e. price will fall in the short run and therefore remain constant at that level
9. Suppose that demand has increased in a perfectly competitive industry and that each firm has moved to a new short-run equilibrium. Then, *in the further process of long-run adjustment,* the individual firm will face
   a. falling price and decreasing profit
   b. falling price and increasing profit
   c. falling price and constant profit
   d. increasing price and decreasing profit
   e. increasing price and increasing profit
10. If price rises and output increases, then the benefit for the producer is
    a. the increase in the firm's revenue plus the increase in its costs
    b. the increase in the firm's revenue minus the increase in its costs
    c. the increase in the firm's revenue
    d. the increase in the firm's costs minus the increase in its revenue
    e. the decrease in the firm's costs
11. If price falls, then
    a. producers benefit by the area to the left of the

supply curve between the old price and the new price

b. producers benefit by the area to the left of the demand curve between the old price and the new price

c. producers are worse off by the area to the left of the demand curve between the old price and the new price

d. producers are worse off by the area to the left of the supply curve between the old price and the new price

e. there is no effect on producers

***12.** In reading a long-run production function table, any evidence of

a. economies of scale would be found along a row, with diminishing returns along a diagonal

b. economies of scale would be found along a diagonal, with diminishing returns along a row

c. both economies of scale and diminishing returns would be found along a row

d. both economies of scale and diminishing returns would be found along a diagonal

e. economies of scale would be found along a column

***13.** Long-run equilibrium for the firm will occur where

a. an isoquant of the long-run production function is tangent to an equal-cost line

b. an isoquant of the short-run production function is tangent to an equal-cost line

c. an isoquant of the long-run production function intersects an equal-cost line

d. an isoquant of the short-run production function intersects an equal-cost line

e. an indifference curve is tangent to an equal-cost line

* Based on material from the appendices to Chapter 23 in your textbook

EXERCISES

1. Table 23-1 below presents average cost figures for four of the large number of plant sizes that a firm can select in the long run. (Note that plants B and C have costs similar to those you calculated for the two plants in Table 22-2). In Figure 23-1, graph the four average cost curves. Label them *A*, *B*, *C*, *D*, and mark the minimum point of each M_A, M_B, M_C, and M_D. Sketch in a rough long-run average cost curve (LAC) for this firm. Does it pass through all the minimum points? In particular, does it pass through M_A and M_D? Why?

Table 23-1

	Average cost, if fixed cost is:			
	$2,000	**$5,000**	**$10,000**	**$15,000**
Output	**Plant A**	**Plant B**	**Plant C**	**Plant D**
1	$ 7,100	$9,000	$13,500	$13,900
2	6,700	7,000	8,000	8,500
3	6,800	6,300	6,700	6,900
4	8,000	6,900	6,200	6,600
5	9,600	7,600	6,600	6,500
6	12,000	8,700	7,200	6,600

2. Table 23-2 describes a firm's long-run costs. In particular, column 3 shows its envelope curve LAC. Fill in the missing parts of the table. When the price of its output is $70, the firm's long-run profit maximizing output is ____________ and its profit is ____________. When the price is $85, the firm's profit-maximizing output is ____________ and its profit is ____________.

When price rises from $70 to $85, its profit [increases, decreases] by ____________.

3a. In Figure 23-2, if price is P_1, the total revenue of the perfectly competitive industry is ____________. If price falls to P_2, its total revenue is ____________, for a [decrease, increase] in revenue of ____________. However, this is partially offset by a decrease in ____________ of ____________. Therefore, the reduction in profit is ____________.

4. In Figure 23-3, when D_1 decreases to D_2 in panel (*b*), price falls from ____________ to ____________ as the short-run equilibrium of the industry shifts from ____________ to ____________. Each firm in panel (*a*) responds by moving along its supply curve from ____________ to ____________. Each firm now has a [profit, loss] of ____________. As firms therefore [enter, leave] the industry, the industry supply in panel (*b*) shifts from ____________ to ____________, and industry equilibrium moves from ____________ to ____________. The initial 30% leftward shift in demand has been offset by a ____________% shift in supply, and price [moves to, returns to] P_1. Long-run supply is constructed by joining all points such as ____________ and ____________. It is [completely elastic, unit elastic, inelastic].

FIGURE 23-1

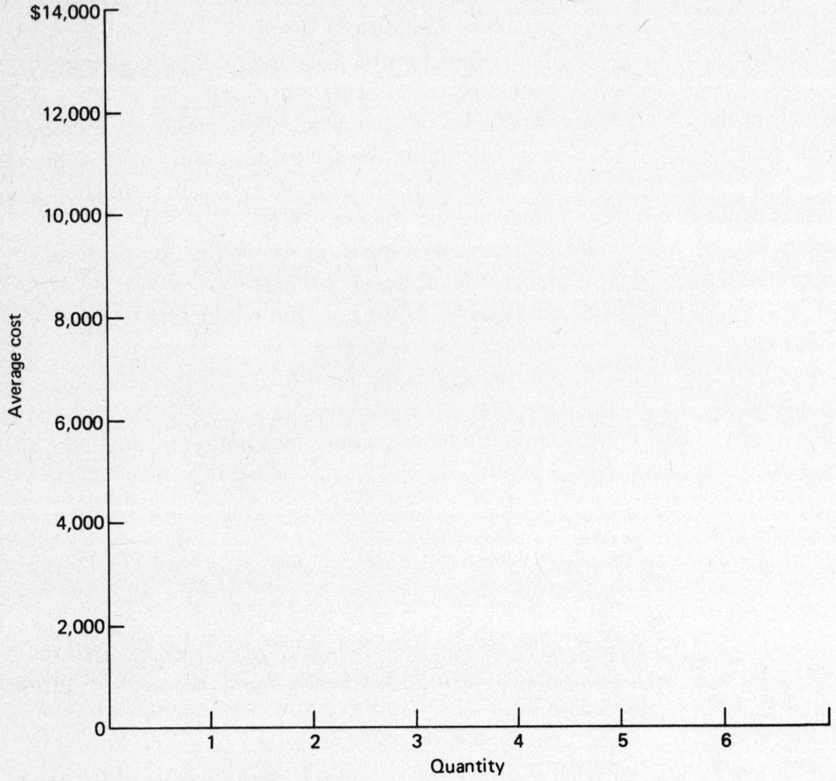

Table 23-2
A FIRM'S LONG-RUN COSTS

Output	Total cost	Average cost (LAC)	Marginal cost	Total revenue if price equals $70	Economic profit if price equals $70	Total revenue if price equals $85	Economic profit if price equals $85
1	$120		$120				
2	150						
3	200						
4	270						
5	350						
6	440						

FIGURE 23-2

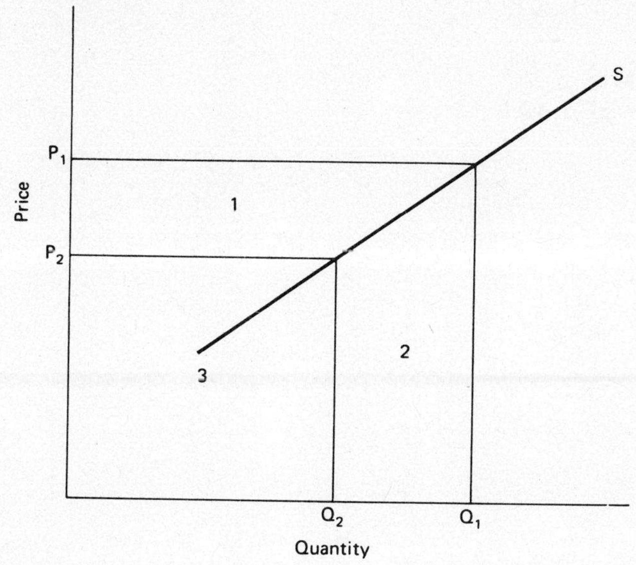

FIGURE 23-3

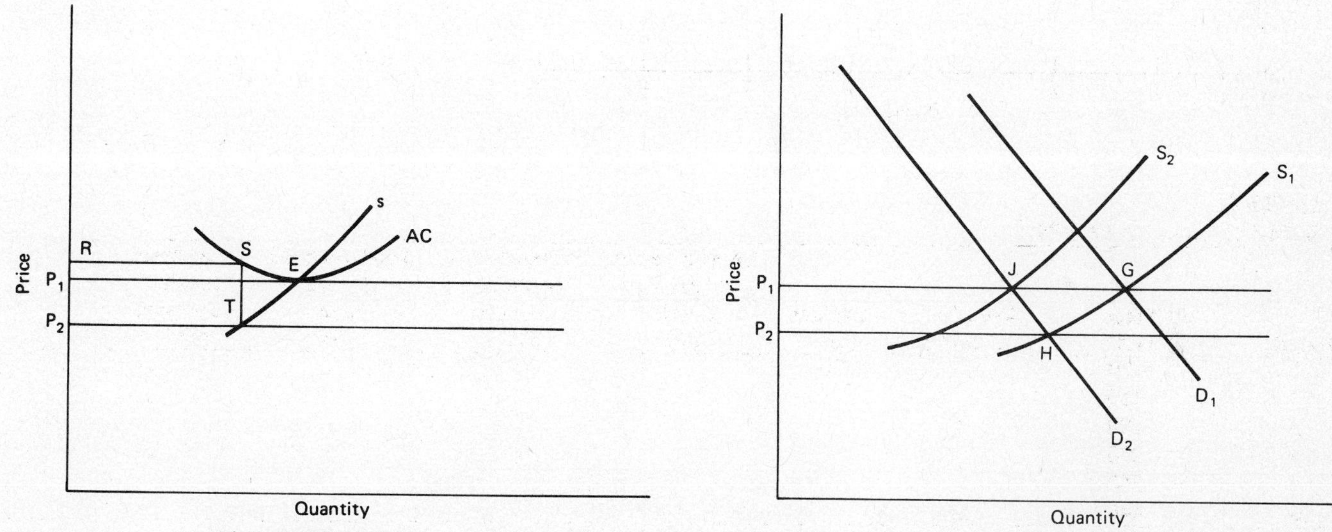

(a) An individual firm . . .

(b) . . . in a perfectly competitive industy

ESSAY QUESTIONS

1. "If a firm's overhead costs increase by, say, 20% because of an increase in its property taxes, its output will not be affected." Evaluate this statement, clearly distinguishing between the short run and the long run.

2. Do you agree with the following statement? Explain why. "If a firm producing 1000 units of output is on its long-run average cost curve, then the combination of capital and labour that it is using costs less than any alternative combination which could be used to produce 1000 units of output." Illustrate your answer with a diagram, showing two or three of the other combinations.

3. "The law of diminishing returns ensures a dismal economic future, because it tells us that as the labour force grows, it will eventually produce a lower and lower marginal product." Do you agree? Why or why not?

4. During a period in which population and income are rising rapidly, the price of good X remains constant. How would you explain this?

5. Would you expect the short run to be longer for a typing service or a steel company? Explain.

6. "If demand for a perfectly competitive product shifts downward, price must fall." Do you agree? Explain, clearly distinguishing between the long run and the short run.

ANSWERS

Important Terms: **1** g **2** b **3** e **4** d **5** c **6** f **7** a
True-False: **1** T **2** F **3** F **4** T **5** T **6** F **7** T **8** T **9** F **10** T **11** F
Multiple Choice: **1** d **2** b **3** a **4** a **5** e **6** d **7** c **8** d **9** a **10** b **11** d **12** b **13** a
Exercises: **1.** no, no, yes, because M_C is the lowest minimum value.
Figure 23-1 completed:

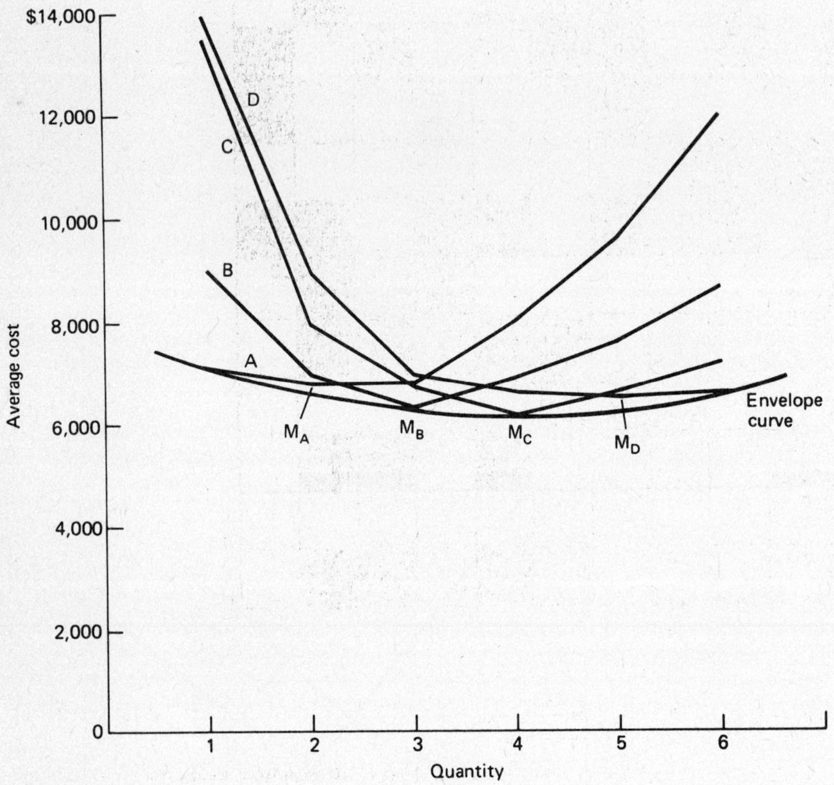

2. Table 23-2 completed:

Table 23-2

Output	Total cost	Average cost (LAC)	Marginal cost	Total revenue if P = \$70	Profit if P = \$70	Total revenue if P = \$85	Profit if P = \$85
1	\$120	\$120	\$120	\$70	\$–50	\$85	\$–35
2	150	75	30	140	–10	170	20
3	200	$66^2/_3$	50	210	10	255	55
4	270	$67^1/_2$	70	280	10	340	70
5	350	70	80	350	0	425	75
6	440	$73^1/_3$	90	420	–20	510	70

4, \$10, 5, \$75, increases, \$65. **3.** 1 + 2 + 3, 3, decrease, 1 + 2, costs, 2, 1. **4.** P_1, P_2, *G*, H, E, T, loss, $RSTP_2$, leave, S_1, S_2, *H*, *J*, 30%, returns to, *G*, *J*, completely elastic.

Across

1, 5. When you know these, you can calculate marginal costs.
7. head of a corporation (abbrev.)
9. be (first person singular)
11. in the past
13. the amount an input could earn in its best alternative use (2 words)
15. grows in damp cool places
16. The federal government has had a large deficit in its ____________ in recent years.
18. preposition
19. professional degree (abbrev.)
21, 23. the relationship of the long-run cost curve to a series of short-run cost curves
25. At this point, losses equal fixed costs.
26. sign of affection
29. third person singular (impersonal pronoun)
30. overrun and inhabit
34. the sum of fixed and variable costs (2 words)
37. This elasticity is measured between two points on a curve.
38. compulsive saver
39. more than a few
42. To maximize profits, a firm equates this with marginal cost. (2 words)
44. indefinite article preceding vowel
45. With this type of exchange rate float, governments don't accumulate foreign exchange reserves.

Down

1. forbid, prohibit
2. harvest (verb)
3. what Toronto wants to do to Montreal in football and hockey
4. a reason why there are gains from specialization (3 words)
5. expenses
6. systematic statement of principles or propositions
8. A barrier to ____________ reduces competition.
10. Things are dead around here.
12. Please don't chew this in class.
14. be (third person singular)
16. At the ____________-even point, profits are zero.
17. a number
18. Shakespeare is often called this.
19. sever
20. When night falls, so does this.
22. go to see
23. hints, signals
24. expression of choice
27. German concentration camp
28. a size of type
31. Economists consider this type of profit to be a cost.
32. main character in 1983 movie
33. Elasticity of demand and supply determines who bears the ____________ of a sales tax.
35. Your liver is one.
36. This type of cost does not affect marginal cost.
40. U.S. gun lobby (abbrev.)
41. Japanese currency
42. post-graduate degree
43. gratis (abbrev.)

Chapter 24

PERFECT COMPETITION AND ECONOMIC EFFICIENCY

MAJOR PURPOSE

The primary objective in this chapter is to demonstrate that, under certain conditions, a perfectly competitive market provides an efficient outcome. This is critical because it becomes a point of reference that allows us, in later chapters, to show clearly why many other forms of market are *not* efficient. Thus, perfect competition must be studied carefully, even though it doesn't describe a large part of the economy; most products are produced in some other type of market. Nonetheless, many agricultural markets *are* perfectly competitive, and these are used in this chapter to illustrate how the perfect competition model can be applied to analyse policy problems.

LEARNING OBJECTIVES

After you have studied this chapter in the textbook and the study guide, you should be able to

- Explain why the condition "marginal cost to society = marginal benefit to society" is necessary for allocative efficiency
- Explain why perfect competition results in allocative efficiency when there are no externalities
- Show how perfect competition tends to promote technical efficiency
- Demonstrate, in a diagram similar to Figure 24-4 in the text, that a deadweight loss to society results if either more or less than the efficient quantity of output is produced
- Explain why perfect competition tends to promote dynamic efficiency in certain ways; but why, in some other ways, other types of market may provide greater dynamic efficiency
- Show not only the great virtues of a perfectly competitive market, but also its limitations—in particular, explain why an efficient outcome is not necessarily best
- Explain why speculation sometimes benefits society, and why it sometimes damages society
- Demonstrate why government agricultural price supports increase efficiency if they *stabilize* price, but reduce efficiency if they *raise* price
- Explain how such price supports transfer income among various groups—and, in particular, identify the costs they impose on consumers and taxpayers

HIGHLIGHTS OF THE CHAPTER

You sometimes hear it said that we should learn to co-operate more with each other than compete. But the economist will say that, on the contrary, competition is often the best method of ensuring harmony. This is the message of Adam Smith's "invisible hand," as described in Chapter 1. In pursuing our own self-interest, each of us is led by market forces—as if by an invisible hand—to promote the interests of others as well. In this chapter we show how effectively this can happen through the operation of perfectly competitive markets. We also show that, despite their efficiency, these markets do have some shortcomings.

Perfect Competition and Allocative Efficiency

The core idea of this chapter is that, under certain conditions, perfectly competitive markets produce an efficient outcome. Consider first the concept of allocative efficiency, defined in Chapter 1. This requires that the marginal social cost of any activity be equal to its marginal social benefit—otherwise, a net gain can be acquired by changing the level of that activity. For example, if the marginal benefit of producing wheat is less than its marginal cost—that is, if the benefit of 1 more bushel of wheat exceeds its cost—then there is a *net* benefit from producing that bushel. The output of wheat should be increased. Moreover, it should continue to be increased until marginal benefit and cost *are* equal. Only then will the incentive for increasing output disappear; this output is efficient.

Under perfect competition, output is generally efficient because marginal social benefit (MB_S) and marginal social cost (MC_S) are equalized. The reason is that under perfect competition, supply equals demand. Supply reflects the marginal cost of producers, and demand reflects the marginal benefit to consumers. Therefore, the equality of supply and demand means that the marginal cost of producers is equal to the marginal benefit to consumers. Provided that these are the only benefits and costs—as carefully assumed in equations 24-1 and 24-2 of the text—it follows that the marginal cost to society is equal to the marginal benefit to society, and an efficient outcome results. Thus, in a perfectly competitive market, the pursuit by producers and consumers of their own *private* interest promotes the interest of society.

Figure 24-2 is particularly useful in clarifying this. In panel (*a*), consumers pursue their self-interest by responding as perfectly competitive price takers to the $10 market price. In panel (*b*), perfectly competitive producers pursue *their* self-interest by also responding as price takers to the same $10 market price; and the result in panel (*c*) is an efficient outcome for society as a whole. We emphasize that this occurs in perfect competition, because both producers and consumers are price takers who respond to the same market price.

In succeeding chapters we will examine markets that, for one reason or another, are not efficient. One possible reason is that producers are not perfectly competitive price takers. A second reason is that consumers are not perfectly competitive price takers. A third reason is that consumers are not the only ones to benefit from a good; there are benefits that go to others in society as well. (When you buy home improvements, the benefits go not only to you, but also to your neighbours.) The fourth possible reason is that producers are not the only ones who face a cost when a good is produced. (Those living downstream face a cost when a chemical producer dumps waste into a river.) Note that, in each case, inefficiency arises because of the violation of one of the key assumptions underlying the efficient, perfectly competitive model.

Perfect Competition and Other Kinds of Efficiency

Perfect competition also tends to promote technical efficiency. Technically inefficient firms that are operating above their AC curves aren't likely to survive competition with technically efficient firms that are operating *on* their AC curves.

The situation is different with respect to dynamic efficiency. Discovering innovations that generate economic growth is usually very expensive. The perfectly competitive firm is too small to be able to afford such expenditures. Nor does it have the incentive; a farmer who discovers a new strain of wheat would find that most of the benefit would go to the millions of other farmers.

Other Reservations about Perfect Competition

Efficiency isn't everything. There are problems that the perfectly competitive market doesn't solve. One is how the nation's income should be distributed. Perfect competition may not provide the best answer. The reason is that for every possible distribution of income there is a different perfectly competitive equilibrium. While each is efficient, the economist has no objective way of deciding which of these efficient outcomes is "best." This is an important point: Make sure you can explain it using Figure 24-1 and 24-6 in the textbook.

Another possible drawback of a perfectly competitive market is that it may be subject to severe fluctuations in price and quantity especially when production decisions must be based on price expectations far into the future. In the case of the hog cycle, the text shows how the expectation that future price will be the same as today's price leads to cyclical fluctuations in price and quantity. The text also describes how this problem may be reduced by private speculators or by government price-stabilization schemes. For example, if private speculators make accurate forecasts they will tend to iron out fluctuations in the market. They

10. If the price in a hog cycle is

a. low this year, then there will be decreased production, and price will be even lower next year

b. low this year, then there will be increased production, and price will be even lower next year

c. high this year, then there will be reduced production, and price will be even higher next year

d. high this year, then there will be increased production, and price will be even higher next year

e. high this year, then there will be increased production, and price will be lower next year

11. In a market with only a few sellers (where some have influence over price), which of the following efficiency conditions for perfect competition is *violated*?

a. There are costs of a product to others than producers.

b. There are benefits of a product to others than buyers.

c. Sellers equate their marginal cost and price.

d. Buyers equate their marginal benefit and price.

e. None of the above.

12. Speculation will be most effective in moderating a hog cycle if

a. speculators buy pork when it is cheap and sell it when it is dear

b. speculators sell pork when it is cheap and buy it when it is dear

c. speculators buy pork when it is cheap and buy it again when it is dear

d. speculators sell pork when it is cheap and sell it again when it is dear

e. speculators lose money on the transaction

13. Suppose speculators buy in the first year and sell in the second. Then

a. if price is higher in the second year, this speculation results in an efficiency loss for society, but a profit for speculators

b. if price is higher in the second year, this speculation results in an efficiency gain for society, but a loss for speculators

c. if price is lower in the second year, this speculation results in an efficiency loss for society, and a loss for speculators

d. if price is lower in the second year, this speculation results in an efficiency loss for society, but a profit for speculators

e. if price is lower in the second year, this speculation results in an efficiency gain for society, but a loss for speculators

14. Speculation that stabilizes price and quantity

a. is beneficial to society because goods are moved from a year of glut to a year of scarcity when they are valued more highly

b. is beneficial to society because goods are moved from a year of scarcity to a year of glut when they are valued more highly

c. is damaging to society because foods are moved from a year of glut to a year of scarcity when they are valued more highly

d. is damaging to society for other reasons; supplies are *not* moved from one year to another

e. has no effect on society

15. When the government supports farm price above its free-market level

a. there is an efficiency gain and a transfer from farmers to taxpayers

b. there is an efficiency gain and a transfer from taxpayers to farmers

c. there is an efficiency gain and no transfer

d. there is an efficiency loss and a transfer from taxpayers to farmers

e. there is an efficiency loss and a transfer from farmers to taxpayers

***16.** Marketing board quota systems

a. are used primarily in deficiency payment programs

b. are used primarily in price-support programs to ensure that there is enough production to meet export demand

c. are used primarily in price-support programs to avoid costly surplus disposal

d. require minimum production levels from each participating farmer

e. are used to ensure that each province gets an equal share of total farm exports.

* Based on material from Appendix 24-B in Chapter 24 in your textbook.

EXERCISES

1. Figure 24-1 shows the supply and demand for a particular grade of apples in a particular year in a perfectly competitive market in Toronto.

a. The equilibrium price is ____________, and the equilibrium quantity is ____________. Now suppose that the government, instead of allowing the market to operate freely, buys all the apples directly from the farmers, offering them a guaranteed price of P_2. The amount that will then be supplied will be ____________. As a result of this government intervention, producers realize a [gain, loss] of area ____________. Shade in this area in the diagram.

b. Suppose that the government, after buying these apples, now sells them all on the market for whatever price they will fetch. This price will be ____________. As a result of this government intervention, consumers realize a [gain, loss] of area ____________. Shade in this area in the diagram.

c. If we just consider these effects on consumers and producers (the two shaded areas), we would conclude

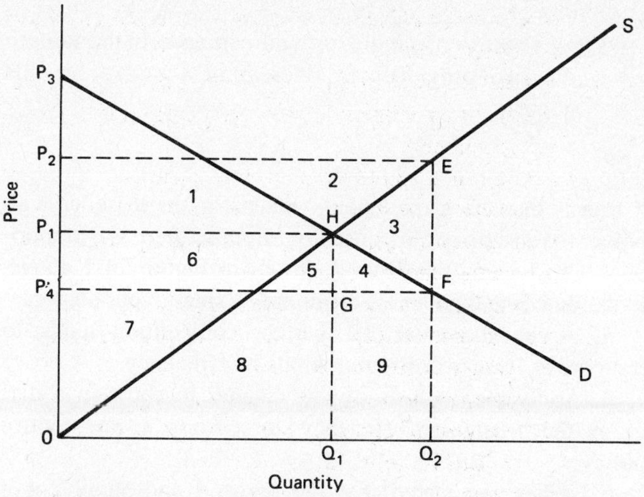

FIGURE 24-1

that there is a net [gain, loss] to the economy as a result of the government's intervention. However, the government has made a [gain, loss] on these dealings which the taxpayers must pay for. The total amount that the government paid for the apples is ____________ and the total revenue that the government received for selling the apples is ____________. Therefore the loss to the government (i.e. the taxpayers) is ____________. If this is taken into account, we conclude that the government's action results in a net [gain, loss] to the economy of area ____________.

d. Alternatively, we could have arrived at this conclusion even more easily by noting that the government's action raised output from the perfectly competitive amount ____________ to the amount ____________, thus resulting in an efficiency loss measured by the triangle ____________.

2. The purpose of this exercise is to demonstrate the social benefit that can be produced by the existence of markets. Figures 24-2 and 24-3 represent the markets for a manufactured good in Quebec and New Brunswick.

a. Suppose that initially there was no trade between the two provinces; that is, no market in which people from one province could trade with people from the other. Then the equilibrium price in Quebec would be ____________, and the equilibrium price in New Brunswick would be ____________.

b. Next, suppose that a group of traders organized a market in which people from Quebec could trade with people from New Brunswick. Suppose that there were no transportation costs or any other kind of cost to separate the market of the two provinces. Then there would in fact be only one market that included both provinces. A single equilibrium price would be established such that the total amount supplied in the two provinces was just equal to the

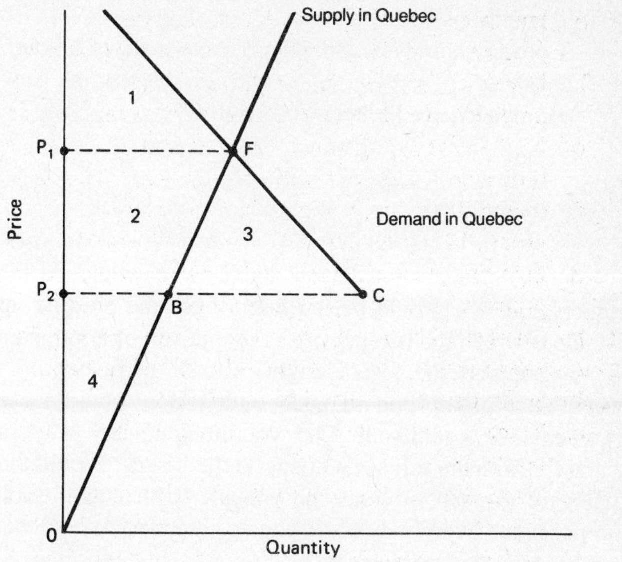

FIGURE 24-2

amount demanded in the two provinces. (Suppose that no other provinces are involved.) Therefore, the excess of supply over demand in one province must equal the shortfall in the other. In figures 24-2 and 24-3 the equilibrium price is ____________. At that price Quebec has an excess [demand, supply] of ____________. This is an equilibrium price because the excess [supply, demand] of New Brunswick is ____________, which is equal to the excess [supply, demand] of Quebec.

c. As a result of trade between the two provinces, consumers in Quebec have realized a [gain, loss] of ____________, and producers in Quebec are [worse,

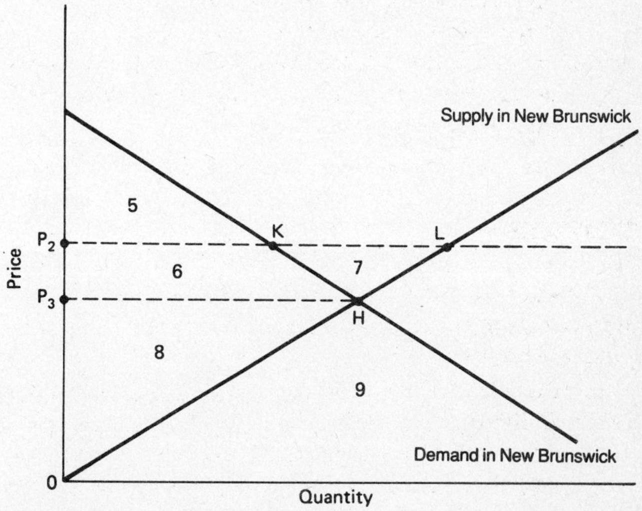

FIGURE 24-3

better] off by ____________; therefore, the net [benefit, loss] to Quebec is ____________.

d. Consumers in New Brunswick have realized a [gain, loss] of ____________, and producers in New Brunswick are [better, worse] off by ____________. Therefore, the overall [gain, loss] to New Brunswick is ____________.

These two triangles provide estimates of the gains to the two provinces from creating a market in this good.

ESSAY QUESTIONS

1. In exercise 2 immediately above, who would be the winners and who would be the losers from the opening up of trade between the two provinces? What sort of arguments do you suppose the losers might propose in favour of a government prohibition of such trade? How could these arguments be countered? Can you imagine any way in which the winners might compensate the losers? Would the total gain in each province be enough so that after such compensation everybody could end up a winner? Would this then be a Pareto improvement?

2. According to the economist's theory of how markets work, butchers provide the public with meat in an economically efficient manner, not because they hate to see people go hungry, but because they are interested in their own incomes. In this chapter we have seen that butchers produce the efficient quantity in perfect competition where there are so many buyers and sellers that none can affect price. But is it true if there is a monopoly—that is, a single seller with power to raise price? Specifically, suppose there is a monopolist who raises price from P_1 to P_2 in Figure 24-1 above. Is the outcome then an efficient one? Explain your answer.

3. Argue the case that perfect competition tends to promote at least two different kinds of efficiency.

4. Apply the analysis of this chapter to show in a diagram the triangular efficiency loss from a rent-control policy.

5. Earlier, we stated that the demand and supply of a product are defined in terms of a certain time and certain place. What is the "place," that is, the geographical extent of the market for the firms supplying the following items? (a) pastries, (b) haircuts, and (c) copper.

6. The text gave reasons why a perfectly competitive firm would not engage in much R&D expenditure. Is the same true of advertising expenditure? Explain why. Do you think it might make sense for all perfect competitors in an industry to form an association to advertise their product?

ANSWERS

Important Terms: **1** g **2** e **3** a **4** c **5** d **6** f **7** b

True-False: **1** F **2** T **3** T **4** T **5** F **6** T **7** T **8** F **9** T **10** T

Multiple Choice: **1** b **2** e **3** b **4** b **5** c **6** a **7** b **8** c **9** b **10** e **11** c **12** a **13** c **14** a **15** d **16** c

Exercises: **1a.** P_1, Q_1, Q_2, gain, 1 + 2. **1b.** P_4, gain, 4 + 5 + 6. **1c.** gain, loss, 1 + 2 + 3 + 4 + 5 + 6 + 7 + 8 + 9, 7 + 8 + 9, 1 + 2 + 3 + 4 + 5 + 6, loss, 3. **1d.** Q_1, Q_2, 3. **2a.** P_1, P_3. **2b.** P_2, demand, *BC*, supply, *KL*, demand. **2c.** gain, 2 + 3, worse, 2, benefit, 3. **2d.** loss, 6, better, 6 + 7, gain, 7.

MONOPOLY

MAJOR PURPOSE

We have now completed our analysis of one extreme of the market spectrum—perfect competition, where there is free entry and so many buyers and sellers that none can influence price. Our focus now turns to the other extreme: monopoly, where a single seller not only can influence price, but can actually *determine* it, subject only to demand conditions. The following questions will be addressed: Under what conditions does monopoly arise? How does the monopolist's price and quantity compare with the perfect competitor? How efficient is monopoly? What are the government's methods of controlling monopoly? Are there conditions in which a monopoly should be free not just to set its price, but also to go beyond this step to set several prices that discriminate among buyers?

LEARNING OBJECTIVES

After you have studied this chapter in the textbook and the study guide, you should be able to

- Explain four reasons why monopolies exist
- Describe the cost conditions that lead to a natural monopoly, and explain how, in these circumstances, competition will eliminate all firms but one
- Show why a monopolist's demand and marginal revenue are quite different from a perfect competitor's
- Explain why a monopoly can select its profit-maximizing output by equating its marginal cost and marginal revenue
- Demonstrate the alternative method of selecting this output by maximizing the rectangle defined between the firm's average cost and demand curves
- Show why a monopoly produces too low a level of output to achieve allocative efficiency
- Explain why the appropriate government policy toward collusive monopoly is to break it up or prevent it from being formed in the first place
- Demonstrate why marginal cost pricing is the appropriate government policy toward natural monopoly, provided it is feasible; and why, if it is not feasible, average cost pricing or government ownership are possible alternative policies
- Show why, in very special circumstances, price discrimination by a monopolist may benefit all concerned—both the producer and the consumers of the product

HIGHLIGHTS OF THE CHAPTER

The key questions are discussed below.

Why Does Monopoly Exist?

Monopolies exist for any or all of the following reasons: (1) the monopoly may possess something valuable that is not available to a potential competitor (for example, some talent, property, or patent); (2) government may have created the monopoly by making competition illegal, as in the case of certain kinds of agricultural marketing boards; (3) there may be a natural monopoly; or (4) the existing sellers may have colluded—that is, agreed to act in cooperation rather than competition.

The case of natural monopoly is perhaps the most important. It exists whenever there are economies of scale through a wide range—that is, whenever a firm has an average cost curve that continues to fall until its output becomes about large enough to satisfy the entire industry demand. (See panel (*b*) in Figure 25-1 in the textbook.)

How Does a Monopoly Maximize Its Profits, and How Do Its Price and Output Compare with a Perfect Competitor's?

A monopoly, just like a perfectly competitive firm, maximizes profit by choosing the level of output where its marginal revenue (MR) equals its marginal cost (MC). But whereas the perfect competitor's MR equals the market price, the monopoly's MR is less than the market price; that is, its MR curve lies below its demand curve. This is because the perfect competitor faces a horizontal demand curve. When the firm sells one more unit the price stays the same; thus, the firm's extra revenue MR is just the market price. Compare this to a monopoly, which faces a demand curve that slopes downward to the right. When this firm sells one more unit, the price *doesn't* stay the same. It falls. Thus the monopoly's extra revenue (MR) is the price that it receives from selling the extra unit, *minus* the loss it incurs because selling this extra unit lowers the price it receives for all the *other* units.

Since the monopoly's MR curve lies below its demand curve, it intersects the MC curve at a smaller output, as you can see in Figure 25-6(*b*) in the textbook; under perfect competition, output is 170,000, but under monopoly it is only 100,000 units. Thus, the monopoly exploits its advantage by reducing its output. By making the product scarce, it is able to raise price—from P_1 to P_2 in that diagram.

Like the perfectly competitive firm, the monopoly produces where MR = MC only if it is able to cover its costs. This requires that the demand curve overlap the AC curve; that is, the demand curve must not always be below the AC curve.

Is Monopoly Efficient?

The efficient output is the one under perfect competition, where supply (MC) equals demand (the marginal benefit of this good). When competitors collude to form a monopoly, output is reduced because the new monopoly is equating MC, not with demand, but instead with MR, which is *below* demand. Because this reduces output below the efficient, perfectly competitive level, monopoly is inefficient. This is the main disadvantage of monopoly. But a complete verdict on any particular monopoly is not possible without also taking into account other factors such as the technical inefficiency that may exist because there is no competition to force the monopoly to fight rising costs. It is also necessary to take into account the transfer of income from consumers to the monopoly that results from the monopoly's higher price. Strictly speaking, we can't be sure whether this transfer is desirable or undesirable, because there is no objective way of comparing one person's gain with another's loss. However, it is often reasonable to assume that these transfer effects cancel; that is, each dollar transferred is valued as highly by the person losing it as by the person receiving it. If this assumption is reasonable, then the efficiency losses of monopoly imply a welfare loss.

What Should Government Policy Be toward Monopoly?

To answer this question, it is first necessary to specify what sort of monopoly is being considered. If it is a *collusive monopoly* of firms that would otherwise be highly competitive, then the solution is to break up the monopoly—or better still, prevent it from being formed in the first place. This is a problem of competition policy that is discussed in Chapter 27. On the other hand, if it is a *natural monopoly* because of extended economies of scale, then breaking it up is no longer a simple solution. The reason is that this policy would create smaller-volume firms and thus raise costs of production, and this would impose an unnecessary cost on society. The preferred approach in this case is to leave the firm as a monopoly and continue to benefit from its relatively low costs of production; at the same time impose a government policy that forces the monopoly to act as though it were a price-taking perfect competitor. That is, take away its market power to raise its prices by imposing a ceiling on that price.

The question is, At what level should that price be set? The simple answer is the *marginal cost pricing* shown in Figure 25-7 in the text: Set the price at the efficient level where the marginal cost of producing this good (MC) equals the marginal benefit it provides—that is, the market demand.

Unfortunately, in many instances this policy is not feasible, because forcing the price down this much would turn the monopoly into a money-loser, and drive it out of business in the long run. This is the case that is examined in Box 25-2, where the government would have to supplement marginal cost pricing with whatever subsidy would be necessary to keep the firm in business; or equivalently, put the firm under government ownership and subsidize its operations in this way. A final alternative that is often used is *average cost pricing*: Instead of driving the price all the way down to the level required by marginal cost pricing, drive it down only partway—specifically, to the level where demand intersects *average* cost rather than marginal cost. Because price equals average cost, the firm breaks even. It is *not* turned into a money-loser, and the problem of going out of business does not arise.

However, since price is reduced only partway, monopoly inefficiency is only reduced partway; it is not eliminated. There is also a problem that applies not only to average cost pricing, but also to marginal cost pricing—and indeed to any government policy to control natural monopoly. Firms lack adequate incentive to keep costs down: If their costs rise, they know that the government-administered price will rise, because price is tied in some way to (marginal or average) costs.

Price Discrimination

So far we have assumed that the monopoly charges a single price to all consumers. But the firm will usually find it more profitable if it can charge a higher price to customers who are willing and able to pay. If the monopoly is profitable in any case, then there is no reason to allow the firm to do this. However, such a pricing policy by a monopoly may be beneficial if the firm would not otherwise exist. In that case, allowing the firm to discriminate might not only allow the firm to cover its costs, but also provide a benefit to consumers who would not otherwise be able to buy this product.

IMPORTANT TERMS: MATCH THE COLUMNS

Match each term in the first column with the corresponding phrase in the second column. But before you do so, write your own definition of each term in the first column.

_____ **1.** natural monopoly
_____ **2.** market power
_____ **3.** marginal revenue
_____ **4.** price discrimination
_____ **5.** marginal cost pricing
_____ **6.** theory of the second best
_____ **7.** average cost pricing
_____ **8.** marketing association

a. an agency set up by firms to raise the price of their product
b. the theory of what constitutes an efficient level of output in one industry when, due to monopoly or for other reasons, the level of output in other industries is not efficient
c. the policy of regulating a monopoly's price by setting it at the level where the firm's average cost curve intersects the market demand curve
d. the ability of a seller or buyer to influence price
e. the practice of charging different prices to different customers for the same good (This is one method a monopoly may use to increase its profits.)
f. a situation in which there are economies of scale (falling average costs) over such an extended range of output that one firm can produce the total quantity sold at a lower average cost than could two or more firms
g. the policy of regulating a monopoly's price by setting it at the level where the firm's marginal cost curve intersects the market demand curve
h. the additional revenue from selling one more unit of output

TRUE-FALSE

T F 1. Monopoly exists when there is only one buyer even if there are many sellers.

T F 2. Very heavy overhead costs tend to make average costs fall further as output increases.

T F 3. An unregulated, profit-maximizing monopoly will set a price where marginal cost intersects the demand curve.

T F 4. Oligopoly—a market dominated by a few sellers—is very rare compared to monopoly.

T F 5. A profit-maximizing monopolist will set a price above marginal cost.

T F 6. One cannot be certain that monopoly, with its efficiency loss, is damaging to society without taking into account the monopoly transfer of income.

T F 7. A likely disadvantage of breaking up a natural monopoly is that it will raise costs of production.

T F 8. One problem with government ownership or price regulation of a monopoly is this: Once the firm knows that the government will ensure that its costs are covered, the firm will have a reduced incentive to keep its costs down.

T F 9. If marginal cost pricing is feasible, it will eliminate the efficiency loss from a monopoly.

MULTIPLE CHOICE

1. An example of a monopoly is
- **a.** the auto industry, while an example of an oligopoly is the steel industry
- **b.** the auto industry, while an example of an oligopoly is the local natural gas supplier
- **c.** the steel industry, while an example of an oligopoly is the local natural gas supplier
- **d.** the local natural gas supplier, while an example of oligopoly is wheat production
- **e.** the local natural gas supplier, while an example of an oligopoly is the auto industry

2. A firm's minimum cost is $30, achievable at 1,000 units of output. This firm will be a natural monopoly if the quantity demanded at a $30 price is about
- **a.** 1 million units
- **b.** 100,000 units
- **c.** 10,000 units
- **d.** 2,000 units
- **e.** 1,000 units

3. Economists define market power as
- **a.** the ability of a firm to influence federal antipollution legislation
- **b.** the ability of a firm to influence tax legislation in its home province
- **c.** the ability of consumers to purchase imports rather than domestically produced goods
- **d.** the ability of a firm to influence Supreme Court decisions
- **e.** none of the above

4. A monopoly's marginal revenue is
- **a.** always positive
- **b.** always above average cost
- **c.** equal to the height of its demand curve
- **d.** less than the height of its demand curve
- **e.** greater than the height of its demand curve

5. Which of the following faces a completely elastic demand?
- **a.** IBM
- **b.** an individual corn farmer
- **c.** CP Air
- **d.** Air Canada
- **e.** an urban transit company that is not subject to government price regulation

6. The demand facing a monopoly is
- **a.** the same as the total market demand
- **b.** to the right of the total market demand
- **c.** to the left of the total market demand
- **d.** completely elastic
- **e.** more elastic than the total market demand

7. market power is the ability of a firm to
- **a.** shift its demand curve to the left
- **b.** shift its demand curve to the right
- **c.** adjust to a given market price
- **d.** influence market price
- **e.** shift its cost curves

8. An unregulated monopoly is inefficient because it equates
- **a.** marginal cost with demand, rather than with marginal revenue
- **b.** marginal revenue with demand, rather than with marginal cost
- **c.** marginal revenue with average cost, rather than with marginal cost
- **d.** average cost with demand, rather than with marginal revenue
- **e.** marginal cost with marginal revenue, rather than with demand

9. If the monopolist is producing more than the profit-maximizing amount, then
- **a.** marginal revenue will exceed price
- **b.** marginal cost will exceed price
- **c.** marginal cost will exceed marginal revenue
- **d.** average cost will exceed price
- **e.** marginal revenue will exceed average cost

10. If a perfectly competitive industry is monopolized, the result is

a. higher output and lower price
b. higher output and the same price
c. higher output and higher price
d. lower output and higher price
e. lower output and lower price

11. Monopoly typically results in
a. allocative efficiency
b. technical inefficiency
c. allocative inefficiency
d. (a) and (b)
e. (b) and (c)

12. When a regulatory agency controls a monopoly by marginal cost pricing, the monopoly's
a. price is reduced
b. output is reduced
c. profit is eliminated
d. level of efficiency remains the same
e. all of the above

13. The theory of the second best tells us that monopolizing one industry in an economy where monopoly exists elsewhere will
a. reduce efficiency
b. increase efficiency
c. have no effect on efficiency
d. have an uncertain effect on efficiency
e. have an uncertain effect on price in that industry

14. A government setting a price equal to a monopolist's MC is trying to induce the firm to
a. act like a perfect competitor by reducing output
b. act like a perfect competitor by taking price as given
c. produce to the point where above-normal profit finally disappears
d. produce to the point where normal profit disappears
e. reduce price while holding its output constant

15. A product is not being provided because the potential producer is a monopolist whose demand lies below its average cost curve AC. This problem may be solved by permitting the firm to discriminate and thus
a. at least cover its costs
b. shift its demand above its marginal cost curve
c. shift its demand above its average variable cost curve
d. shift its AC curve down so it overlaps demand
e. shift its demand above its AC curve

16. Economists use the assumption that firms seek to maximize profit because
a. it describes how many business decisions are made
b. alternative plausible assumptions may not be specific enough to support a theory
c. alternative assumptions will generally not do a better overall job of describing business decision making
d. all of the above
e. none of the above

*17. An agricultural marketing board organized by the government will
a. typically set quotas to ensure that producers will increase their sales
b. typically set quotas to ensure that producers will reduce their sales
c. typically set quotas to ensure that producers will maintain their previous sales levels
d. not set quotas, but will encourage producers to sell more
e. encourage the entry of new firms

* Based on material from Appendix 25-A in your textbook.

EXERCISES

1a. If the monopoly shown in Figure 25-1 is unregulated, it will maximize profits by selecting output ____________ where ____________ equals ____________. The price it will quote is ____________, the highest price at which this output can be sold. Its profits will be ____________ for each of the ____________ units it sells, that is, a total profit of area ____________. An alternative view of its decision is that it selects the point ____________ on the ____________ curve that maximizes this profit rectangle. The efficiency loss is ____________.

1b. A government regulatory agency that uses marginal cost pricing will set price equal to ____________. The firm will respond in the short run by producing output ____________ because this is where its ____________ curve cuts this price line ____________. However, in the *long run,* the firm would produce an output of ____________ because at equilibrium *T* it is operating at a

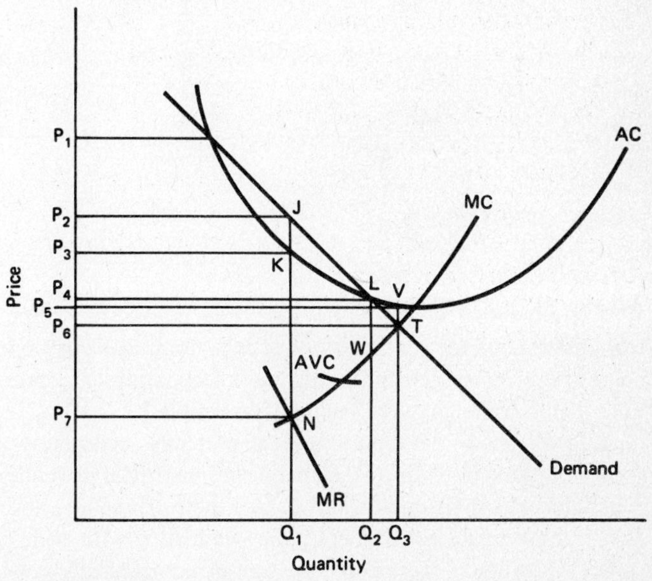

FIGURE 25-1

[profit, loss] of ____________. To keep it in business the government would have to [provide a subsidy, impose a tax] of ____________. This policy would [reduce, increase, eliminate] the previous efficiency loss of ____________; that is, it would improve efficiency by ____________.

1c. If the agency were instead to use average cost pricing, it would set price at ____________. The monopolist would produce output ____________ and earn a profit of ____________. The subsidy now necessary to keep this firm in business would be ____________. This policy would reduce the efficiency loss from the original JTN to ____________; that is, it would improve efficiency by ____________. Compared to marginal cost pricing, this average cost pricing policy improves efficiency [more, less]; but it avoids the government problem of having to [subsidize, tax] this firm.

1d. With either form of regulation, the monopoly is forced to act like [a perfect competitor, an oligopolist, a natural monopolist] facing a fixed price.

2. A monopoly has the demand and total cost figures shown in Table 25-1. Fill in this table, ignoring for now the last three columns.

a. The monopoly's fixed cost is ____________. It will choose to produce a level of output equal to ____________ and charge a price equal to ____________. Its maximum attainable profit is ____________.

b. Suppose that, in an attempt to capture some of this monopoly's profits for the taxpayer's benefit, the government imposes a lump-sum tax of $5. This tax may be regarded by the monopoly as a fixed cost, because it must be paid no matter how much output is produced. After the imposition of this tax, the monopoly's fixed cost is ____________. Fill in the third-to-last column (1) indicating the monopoly's after-tax profit. After imposition of the tax, the monopoly will choose to produce an amount of ouput equal to ____________ and to charge a price equal to ____________. Its maximum attainable after-tax profit will be ____________.

c. Suppose that instead of the lump-sum tax, the government decides to impose a 50% excise tax on the monopoly. In other words, the monopoly must now pay the government 50% of its total revenue. In this case, the monopoly's fixed cost is ____________. Fill in the second-to-last column (2), showing the monopoly's after-tax total revenue, and the last column (3), showing its after-tax profit. In this case, the monopoly will choose to produce an amount of output equal to ____________ and to charge a price equal to ____________. Its maximum attainable after-tax profit will be ____________. The amount of excise tax collected from this monopoly will be ____________.

d. From the point of view of economic efficiency the [lump-sum, excise] tax is preferable. From the point of view of maximizing the amount of tax revenue collected from the monopoly, the [lump-sum, excise] tax is preferable.

Table 25-1

P	Quantity demanded	Total revenue	Marginal revenue	Total cost	Average cost	Marginal cost	Profit	(1) Net profit with lump-sum tax	(2) Net total revenue with excise tax	(3) Net profit with excise tax
$10	0	$ 0	$ 0	$ 2	$____	$ 0	$	$	$	$
8	1	8		3						
6	2			6						
4	3			11						
2	4			18						

ESSAY QUESTIONS

1. Are economies of scale a barrier to entry? Explain. Is IBM a monopoly in the North American market for office machines? a perfect competitor? or in a dominant position somewhere in between? Do you think economies of scale give it an advantage over potential competitors?

2. Compare a monopoly and a perfectly competitive firm in terms of their (a) demand and marginal revenue schedules, (b) their market power, (c) their efficiency, and (d) the appropriate government policy in dealing with each.

3. "Allowing a monopolist to charge some of his customers more than others is not appropriate because it is unfair to those who have to pay the higher price." Evaluate this statement. Are there any circumstances in which those who pay the higher price could actually benefit?

4. Suppose that the only two firms in an industry are considering a merger that would result in a reduction in costs of production through the elimination of wasteful duplication. Is it possible to argue that this action could increase efficiency? If so, how? Might it *decrease* efficiency? If so, how?

5. It has been argued by U.S. economists that the American Medical Association is a collusive monopoly, because it restricts the output of medical services by controlling the licensing of and enrollment in medical schools. (In Canada, medical school enrollment is primarily determined by provincial governments.) How does this restriction affect the income of U.S. doctors and therefore the cost of medical services? What unfavourable consequences might there be if the government were to try to reduce this cost by allowing completely free entry into the medical profession—that is, allowing anyone, with or without training, to practise medicine? In view of this, (a) defend the position that the medical profession's collusive monopoly has been beneficial to the American economy, and (b) defend the position that the monopoly has been harmful.

6. A perfectly competitive firm can sell all it wants at the existing price. Can a monopoly do that? If it tried to, what would happen? Does that mean that a monopoly is more constrained in its decision making than a perfect competitor?

7. Recall our discussion of the elasticity of demand from Chapter 20. If a monopoly's demand function is elastic, then what happens to its total revenue as its output increases? In this case, what can be said about the monopoly's marginal revenue? If the market demand is inelastic, what can be said about the monopolist's marginal revenue? In view of this, explain why a monopoly that has discovered that its demand curve is inelastic would want to change its output.

ANSWERS

Important Terms: **1** f **2** d **3** h **4** e **5** g **6** b **7** c **8** a

True-False: **1** F **2** T **3** F **4** F **5** T **6** T **7** T **8** T **9** T

Multiple Choice: **1** e **2** e **3** e **4** d **5** b **6** a **7** d **8** e **9** c **10** d **11** e **12** a **13** d **14** b **15** a **16** d **17** b

Exercises: **1a.** Q_1, MC, MR, P_2, *JK* (or P_2 P_3), Q_1, P_2 JKP_3, *J*, demand, *JNT*. **1b.** P_6, Q_3, MC, P_6, zero, loss, P_5VTP_6, provide a subsidy, P_5VTP_6, eliminate, *JNT*, *JNT*. **1c.** P_4, Q_2, zero, zero, *LWT*, *JLWN*, less, subsidize. **1d.** a perfect competitor.

2. Table 25-1 completed:

Table 25-1 completed

P	Quantity demanded	Total revenue	Marginal revenue	Total cost	Average cost	Marginal cost	Profit	(1)	(2)	(3)
$10	0	$ 0	$ 0	$ 2	$—	$ 0	$ -2	$ -7	$ 0	$ -2
8	1	8	8	3	3	1	5	0	4	1
6	2	12	4	6	3	3	6	1	6	0
4	3	12	0	11	3²/₃	5	1	-4	6	-5
2	4	8	-4	18	4¹/₂	7	-10	-15	4	-14

2a. $2, 2, $6, $6. **2b.** $7, 2, $6, $1. **2c.** $2, 1, $8, $1, $4. **2d.** lump-sum, lump-sum.

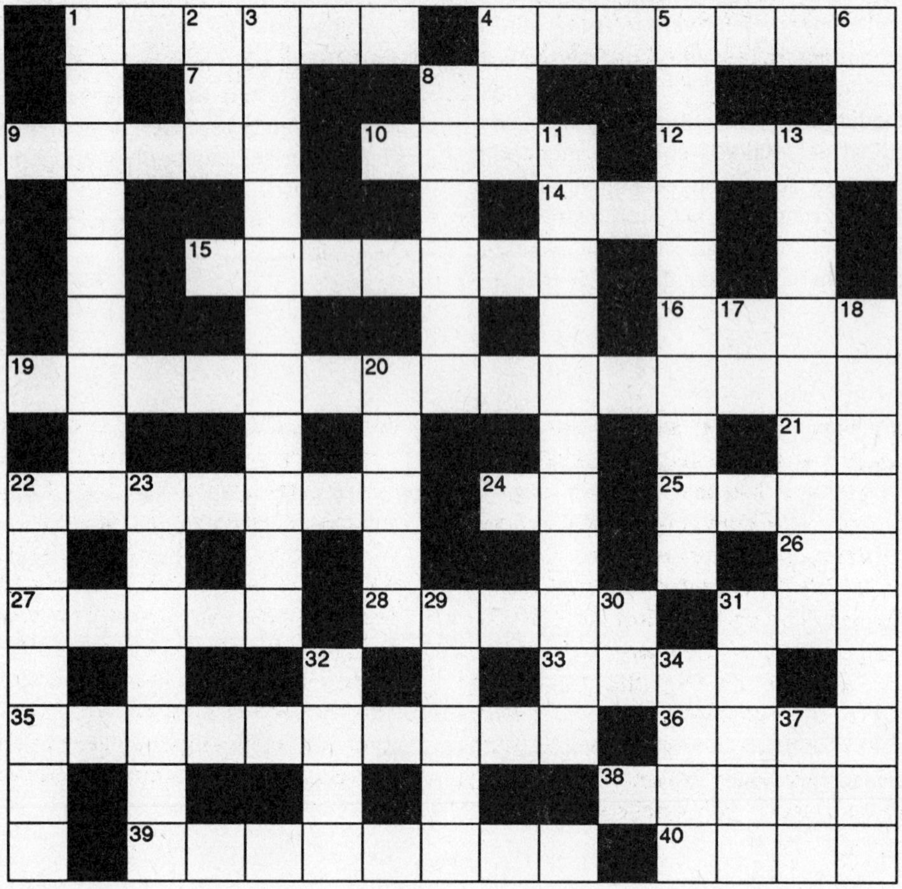

Across

1, 4. If perfect competition is to be efficient, this must equal the benefit to consumers.
7. indefinite article preceding vowel
8. _____ what?
9. major department store chain
10. business owned by a group of consumers or producers (abbrev.)
12. something that is true
14. king (French)
15. A dry ___________ consists mostly of gin.
19. To maximize profits, a firm equalizes this and marginal cost. (2 words)
21. southern American state (abbrev.)
22. fate
24. university degree
25. muse of history
26. preposition
27. poor
28. really great!
31. conjunction
33. not just apparent
35. industries with only one seller
36. to keep flowers in
38. written reminders
39, 40. the increase in variable cost when one more unit is produced

Down

1. buy or sell in the hope of profiting from a change in price
2. automobile
3. Monetary and fiscal policy should be used to avoid this in our economy.
4. sound of disapproval
5. This exists when we get the most out of our resources.
6. explosive substance (abbrev.)
8. Marginal private benefit is not always the same as marginal ___________ benefit.
11. With perfect competition, this is what all buyers and sellers are. (2 words)
13. when sellers get together to fix price
17. natural logarithm (abbrev.)
18. the best we can do when there are immutable imperfections in the market (2 words)
20. a very deep hole
22. a type of efficiency
23. breastbone
29. association of workers
30. thing (Latin)
31. A famous battle took place here during the Mexican-American War.
32. last name of famous Swedish tennis player
34. with (French)
37. signal for help (abbrev.)

Chapter 26

MARKETS BETWEEN MONOPOLY AND PERFECT COMPETITION

MAJOR PURPOSE

The last two chapters have described the two extremes in the spectrum of markets: perfect competition, where there are so many sellers that none has any influence on price; and monopoly, where the single firm is free to set any price it chooses, since it has no competitors to worry about. (A monopoly is restrained only by consumer demand and the possibility of government intervention.) Most North American industries do not conform to either of these two extremes, but lie somewhere between the two, where individual firms have *some* influence over price. The objective in this chapter is to analyse two of the market forms that lie within this intermediate range. The first is *oligopoly*, a market dominated by a few sellers, in which in the absence of government intervention, there is a strong incentive for forms to collude in order to act like a monopolist and raise price. The most prominent example of such collusive behaviour is described in this chapter: the Organization of Petroleum Exporting Countries (OPEC), which raised oil price by more than 10 times in less than a decade. The second market form analysed in this chapter is *monopolistic competition* in which—as in perfect competition—there are a large number of sellers and free entry into the market. However, it differs from perfect competition in that each firm produces a differentiated product, and this gives each firm some small degree of influence over price.

LEARNING OBJECTIVES

After you have studied this chapter in the textbook and the study guide, you should be able to

- Clearly distinguish between monopoly, oligopoly, monopolistic competition, and perfect competition
- Give two reasons why oligopoly may arise
- Explain why oligopolists have an incentive to collude and describe the effect such collusion will have on efficiency
- Explain why OPEC members were able to collude to raise the price of oil during the 1970s without effective production quotas and why they had to try to enforce production quotas in the 1980s
- Describe the kinked demand curve with a diagram
- Explain why the kinked demand curve would discourage an oligopolist from changing price frequently
- Explain the concept of price leadership, how it relates to the analysis of kinked demand, and why it is often viewed as "tacit collusion"
- Give three examples of non-price competition
- Describe why economies of scale and advertising create barriers to entry
- Summarize the arguments for and against advertising
- Explain why the run-of-the-mill firm earns no above-normal profits in the long run in monopolistic competition and why this market form is not necessarily inefficient, even though fewer firms could produce the same output at lower costs

HIGHLIGHTS OF THE CHAPTER

In discussing oligopoly and monopolistic competition—two of the "imperfectly competitive" market forms that lie between monopoly and perfect competition—our focus will be on the principles that govern business decision making in each case, and whether or not the outcome is efficient.

Oligopoly

How many sellers is "a few"? The smaller the number of sellers, the greater the market power (the influence over price) that can be exercised by each firm. Thus, our first task is to define the degree of concentration of each industry. This is traditionally measured by the proportion of the industry's output made by the four largest firms. (An alternative measure, called the *Herfindahl index*, is described in Box 26-1 in the textbook. While it is slightly more complicated, it has the desirable feature of taking into account the output of all the firms in the industry—not just the four largest.)

An oligopoly can arise because an industry is a "natural oligopoly," in which market demand would be satisfied at the lowest cost with a small number of firms. Alternatively, firms may combine or grow large, not because of cost conditions, but instead because they seek to acquire market power.

Because there are few clear-cut principles governing the behaviour of oligopolists, the theoretical analysis is not as straightforward for oligopoly as it is for other market forms. But the following points are important:

1. There is a tendency for oligopolists to collude—that is, to act like a monopolist and raise price so as to maximize the total profits of the industry. To maintain the high price, each colluding firm must restrict its output to a certain quota level. This reduction in output leads to the same sort of efficiency loss as in the case of monopoly. However, it is precisely this reduction in the output of each firm that creates a tendency for collusive arrangements to break down; each firm is asked to reduce its output when it has an incentive to produce more. The reason the individual firm in an oligopoly would like to produce more is that, at its restricted level of output, the firm's marginal cost is still below its price. Therefore, it has an incentive to increase its output if it can get away with such cheating. But if firms do cheat by producing more than their quota of output, the high price cannot be maintained, and the collusive arrangement comes apart.

2. When the oligopolistic firm chooses its price and output, it must take into account the possible reaction of its rivals—something that need not even be considered by the monopolist (with no rivals) or the perfectly competitive firm (whose rivals don't even notice what it's doing). This sort of complicated decision making is what makes the theory of oligopoly so interesting and difficult.

3. Oligopolistic firms sometimes face a *kinked demand curve*. If one firm raises its price, its rivals won't. Instead they'll hope to capture some of its sales. But if the firm lowers its price, its rivals will follow suit to avoid being undersold. In such circumstances, the firm is facing the kinked demand shown in Figure 26-6 in the textbook, and it will not want to change its price from the kinked level unless underlying cost conditions change substantially. While this theory is controversial as an explanation of how firms behave, it is very useful in making clear the issues that firms must deal with in making their decisions. For example, the kinked demand analysis in Figure 26-6 can be modified slightly to explain the Nash equilibrium in Box 26-3 in the textbook or to explain price leadership.

4. In an industry with price leadership, one firm takes on the role of being the leader in announcing a price change, on the understanding that other firms will follow. This sort of "gentlemen's agreement" has often been criticized as a collusive arrangement, with the price leader setting the price at about the level that a monopolist would select. However, it is only "tacit collusion" because there is no communication between the firms, and it is therefore very difficult or impossible to prove that collusion has taken place. (Selling at the same price is not proof of collusion because, after all, that is what perfectly competitive firms do.)

5. Oligopolists who wish to avoid potentially destructive price competition have other options, in addition to tacit collusion, in the form of price leadership. They can attempt to increase their market share by various forms of non-price competition, such as product differentiation or advertising. Advertising in particular is controversial. On the one hand, it may involve wasteful competition, distort people's values, and mislead consumers. On the other hand, it may make consumers better informed and help to promote product quality by making firms fearful of losing the goodwill that they achieve through advertising. Moreover, it provides financial support for the media.

6. Oligopolists often succeed in erecting barriers to entry against new competitors. One such barrier is advertising which creates a favourable image of an existing firm that is difficult for new firms to overcome. But the most important barrier to entry may be economies of scale that leave room for only a few low-cost firms in the industry.

OPEC: An Example of Oligopoly Collusion

In many ways, the most interesting and far-reaching example of a collusive oligopoly has been the Organization of Petroleum Exporting Countries (OPEC). This collusive arrangement succeeded in quadrupling oil prices in 1973–74, and then doubling them in 1979–80. This was even more remarkable because during the 1970s OPEC did not have effective quotas on output that are typically required to keep price up and ensure that the collusive arrangement won't come apart. There were several reasons for this, some of which are detailed in Box 26-2 in the textbook. However, the most important was that the Saudi Arabians were the dominant producers of world-traded oil, and for many years they could keep the price up by restricting just their *own* very large output.

Why were the Saudis willing to do this? One reason was that, unlike some other OPEC members, such as Nigeria or Indonesia, they did not have a large population to support. Therefore, they could afford to keep their "black gold" in the ground. Moreover, because of their extremely large reserves, they were prepared to make short-term sacrifices in order to provide more assurance of a stable and healthy oil market in the long run. However, their power to keep price up was limited: By the early 1980s, the Saudis' production had been so far reduced in the attempt to maintain price, that they could no longer bear the lion's share of the burden. Their requirement that other OPEC producers would have to share this burden more equally led to the attempts to enforce production quotas on all OPEC members. By the mid-1980s, the cartel showed signs of coming apart. OPEC members had great difficulty agreeing on quotas, and some were not abiding by their quotas. World oil demand was increasingly being satisfied by countries such as Mexico and the U.K., which were not even members of OPEC. And the Saudis had pretty well exhausted their ability to support price by making further production cuts. The weakness of the cartel was dramatically demonstrated in the spring of 1986, when the world oil price fell from more than $25 a barrel to $10 a barrel in a few weeks.

Monopolistic Competition

Whereas oligopoly, if unrestrained, often leads to a collusive outcome close to that of monopoly, the outcome in the case of monopolistic competition is closer to the other extreme of perfect competition. In monopolistic competition, as in perfect competition, a large number of firms is involved. There is also free entry of firms into the industry, which means that any short-run excess profit for the run-of-the-mill firm will be eliminated in the long run. The important difference between the two market forms is this: Under monopolistic competition, a firm produces a differentiated product and therefore faces a downward-sloping demand curve. Under perfect competition, the firm produces a standardized product and faces a completely horizontal demand curve. Because the sloping demand curve gives a firm in monopolistic competition some influence over price, the firm quotes a higher price, and therefore produces a smaller output than a perfectly competitive firm that cannot raise its price. This restricted output suggests that monopolistic competition is inefficient, but this is not necessarily the case. Lower output by each firm means more firms are satisfying total market demand. Thus, the consumer can choose from a wider range of differentiated products. This wider choice may more than make up for the disadvantage of lower output by each firm.

IMPORTANT TERMS: MATCH THE COLUMNS

Match each term in the first column with the corresponding phrase in the second column. But before you do so, write your own definition of each term in the first column.

_____ **1.** oligopoly
_____ **2.** concentration ratio
_____ **3.** natural oligopoly
_____ **4.** product differentiation
_____ **5.** cartel
_____ **6.** OPEC
_____ **7.** kinked demand curve
_____ **8.** price leadership
_____ **9.** barrier to entry
_____ **10.** monopolistic competition

a. the practice in some oligopolistic industries of having one firm announce its price change first, on the unspoken understanding that other firms will follow suit
b. the ability of each firm to distinguish its product from those of its rivals (Such distinctions may be real or imagined.)
c. a market dominated by only a few sellers
d. a market in which there are (1) a large number of firms, (2) free entry of new ones, and (3) differentiated products (The demand curve facing each seller is quite elastic, but not completely so.)
e. the proportion of an industry's output produced by the four largest firms (or, using an alternative measure, by the eight largest firms)
f. anything that makes it difficult for new firms to enter an industry to compete against existing firms
g. a formal agreement among firms to collude in order to set prices and/or determine market shares
h. an industry in which total market demand can be satisfied at lowest cost by a few firms
i. the demand curve that will face an oligopolist when its rivals follow it after its has cut its price, but will not follow it after it has increased its price
j. the Organization of Petroleum Exporting Countries

TRUE-FALSE

T F 1. The concentration ratio is relatively low in the Canadian auto industry.

T F 2. Colluding firms in a cartel typically have an incentive to cheat by producing less than their quotas.

T F 3. All cartels, regardless of where they may exist, are illegal.

T F 4. A large firm acting as s price leader may decide not to retaliate against a small firm that has cut price, for fear that this may initiate a price war with other large firms.

T F 5. Price leadership may be a disguised method of collusion.

T F 6. The kinked demand curve arises mainly in monopolistic competition.

T F 7. The theory of the kinked demand curve doesn't predict the price where the kink will occur.

T F 8. All barriers to entry take the form of economies of scale.

T F 9. Monopolistic competition is similar in many respects to perfect competition; but one important difference is that the product is differentiated.

T F 10. Because consumers like variety, we cannot conclude that monopolistic competition is inefficient.

MULTIPLE CHOICE

1. A firm's minimum cost is $10, achievable at 20,000 units of output. The industry will be perfectly competitive if the total quantity of this product that is demanded at a $10 price is
- **a.** 1 million units
- **b.** 100,000 units
- **c.** 40,000 units
- **d.** 20,000 units
- **e.** 10,000 units

2. If oligopolistic firms collude to raise price,
- **a.** each benefits, while there is an overall loss to the economy as a whole
- **b.** the price leader benefits, while the other firms and the economy as a whole lose
- **c.** each firm and the economy as a whole benefit
- **d.** each firm benefits, while the economy as a whole is not affected
- **e.** each firm and the economy as a whole lose

3. General Motors of Canada is a
- **a.** monopolist
- **b.** duopolist
- **c.** oligopolist
- **d.** monopolistic competitor
- **e.** perfect competitor

4. A high concentration ratio in an industry typically indicates that
- **a.** the dominant firms in the industry have a great deal of market power
- **b.** no firms in the industry have much market power
- **c.** no firms in the industry have any market power
- **d.** the industry is monopolistically competitive
- **e.** the industry is perfectly competitive

5. Between 1975 and 1985, Canadian industry became
- **a.** less competitive, because of the decline in international trade
- **b.** more competitive, because of the decline in international trade
- **c.** less competitive, because of the growth in international trade
- **d.** more competitive, because of the growth in international trade
- **e.** more competitive, despite the decline in international trade

6. The biggest surprise about OPEC is that it
- **a.** survived for many years without effective production quotas
- **b.** did not increase the price of oil when it had an opportunity to do so in 1973–74
- **c.** has made no further price increases since its spectacular success in 1973–74
- **d.** has been able to prevent any price reduction since 1973
- **e.** includes only countries from the Middle East

7. The success of the OPEC cartel in the 1970s and early 1980s was in substantial part due to
- **a.** strong cultural ties among the member countries
- **b.** the strong sense of political unity among the member countries
- **c.** close social ties among the member countries
- **d.** all of the above
- **e.** the willingness of the Saudis to cut back their production

8. If all firms sell at the same price,
- **a.** there must be price leadership
- **b.** there must be some other form of collusion
- **c.** the industry must be perfectly competitive
- **d.** the industry must be an oligopoly
- **e.** none of the above

9. The growing importance of international trade has
- **a.** made Canadian firms more competitive
- **b.** made Canadian firms less competitive
- **c.** not affected the competitiveness of Canadian firms
- **d.** made domestic concentration ratios more meaningful
- **e.** (b) and (d)

10. The kinked demand curve
- **a.** helps to explain why oligopoly price has some degree of stability

b. leaves unanswered the question of how price is established in the first place
c. is based on the assumption that if a firm lowers its price, its competitors will follow
d. is based on the assumption that if a firm raises its price, its competitors won't follow
e. all of the above

11. Which of the following is *not* true about advertising?
a. It may involve waste.
b. It may mislead consumers.
c. It provides financial support for the media.
d. It may help to promote product quality by making firms fearful of losing goodwill.
e. It is sometimes undertaken by single firms in a perfectly competitive market.

12. In a monopolistic competition
a. there is a standardized product, just as in perfect competition
b. there is a standardized product, unlike the differentiated product in perfect competition
c. entry of new firms is restricted, unlike the free entry that exists in perfect competition
d. entry of new firms is restricted, just as in perfect competition
e. there is a large number of sellers, just as in perfect competition

13. In monopolistic competition
a. there are very few sellers
b. it is impossible for new firms to enter the market
c. each firms sells a differentiated product
d. all of the above
e. none of the above

14. In a contestable market,
a. there is a single firm which can act as a monopolist
b. there is no free entry
c. the potential entry of new firms increases the market power of the existing firm
d. the potential entry of new firms has no effect on the market power of the existing firm
e. if there is a single firm, it cannot act as though it is a monopolist

EXERCISES

1a. In Figure 26-1 below, *D* represents the total market demand for an industry, with MR_I being the marginal revenue curve that corresponds to *D*. (For *any* demand curve, there exists a marginal revenue curve.) MC_A and AC_A are the cost curves for firm A, one of the five identical firms in this industry. Draw in the marginal cost curve *for the industry*, and label it MC_I. Label point *R*, where MC_I and *D* intersect, and point *S*, where MC_I and *D* intersect, and point *S*, where MC_I and MR_I intersect. Label *Q* the point directly above *S* on the demand curve.

If these firms act like perfect competitors and take price as given, then MC_I becomes the industry [demand, supply] curve, and the industry equilibrium is at point ____________ ____________ units are sold at price ____________, with each firm earning a profit of ____________.

1b. Now suppose that these firms collude to maximize their collective profit, which they will do by equating MC_I and ____________, at an output of ____________ units. That is, the industry will select its profit-maximizing point ____________ on the demand curve *D*. Since industry output has been reduced by one-third (from 1,500 to 1,000 units), the output of each individual firm, such as A, must be reduced by the same proportion, from 300 units to ____________. Draw in point *T*, which is the equilibrium for firm A, where this firm is now selling 200 units at a price P_2. Label as *V* the point on AC_A directly below *T*. Shade in the new profit area ____________ of firm A.

By colluding these five firms have each [increased, decreased] their profit from ____________ to

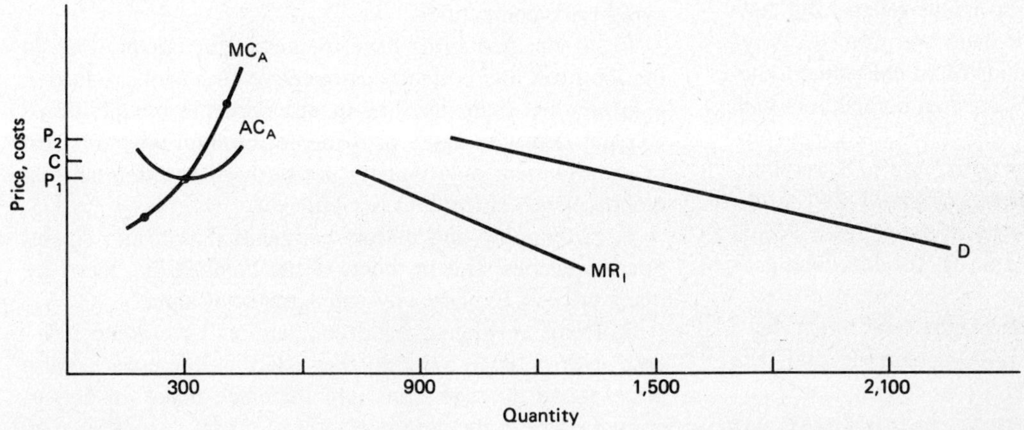

FIGURE 26-1

____________. At the same time the nation as a whole has [lost, gained] because of the efficiency [loss, gain] of area ____________ that results because output has been [reduced, increased] to the [efficient, inefficient] level of ____________ units from the [efficient, inefficient] level of ____________ units, where the marginal benefit to society shown by curve ____________ equals the marginal cost to society shown by curve ____________.

2. Figure 26-2 shows an oligopoly which—along with its rivals—is currently charging price *P* and producing quantity *Q*. This firm faces the kinked demand curve that consists of the segment of D_A *above* the existing price *P* and the segment of D_B *below* the price *P*. The respective marginal revenue curves are MR_A and MR_B.

a. If the firm increases its output to more than *Q*, it faces demand curve ____________, and its MR curve is therefore [MR_A, MR_B]. But if it decreases its output to less than *Q*, it faces demand curve ____________, and its MR curve is therefore [MR_A, MR_B]. Therefore, its complete MR curve is [MR_A, MR_B, *WXYZ*].

b. If its MC is MC_1, then it will charge a price that is [more than, less than, the same as] *P*, and it will choose a quantity that is [more than, less than, the same as] *Q*.

c. If its MC is MC_2, then it will charge a price that is [more than, less than, the same as] *P*, and it will choose a quantity that is [more than, less than, the same as] *Q*.

d. If its MC is MC_3, then it will charge a price that is [more than, less than, the same as] *P*, and it will choose a quantity that is [more than, less than, the same as] *Q*.

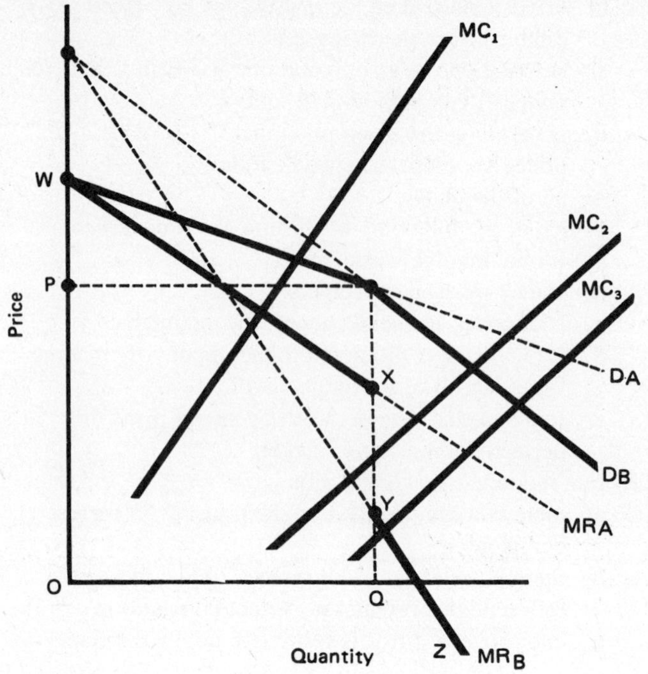

FIGURE 26-2

e. If its MC is MC_2, we now see a different point of view why the kinked demand curve results in a stable price. If MC_2 shifts up, but still intersects the horizontal segment *XY*, then the firm will [raise, lower, leave unchanged] the price. Alternatively, if MC_2 shifts down, still intersecting *XY*, the firm will [raise, lower, leave unchanged] the price. In other words, marginal cost can shift up or down within the range ____________, without affecting price at all.

ESSAY QUESTIONS

1. Will firms in an industry with a high concentration ratio be more or less likely to engage in collusive activity than those in an industry with a low concentration ratio? Why?

2. Oligopoly is a market with a few sellers. But how many is a few? Does it matter if there are 4 or 14? Why? To be specific, compare the situation of an individual Canadian firm if (a) it has only three Canadian competitors with (b) a situation in which it has the same three Canadian competitors, plus two Japanese competitors, four U.S. competitors, and two other foreign competitors. Would the Canadian firm have the same market power in either case? Would the Canadian firms be equally able to collude, tacitly or explicitly?

3. Explain why a group of oligopolists might have trouble establishing a collusive price agreement, and then have trouble keeping the agreement from coming apart.

4. It is often argued that advertising increases sales, and this permits lower prices to consumers. Explain the circumstances in which this could occur. Also explain the circumstances in which advertising would *increase* prices to consumers.

5. What industry characteristics distinguish oligopoly from monopoly? from perfect competition?

6. Explain some of the techniques oligopolists use to avoid price competition.

7. "If the two firms have identical cost curves, then in the long run, the perfectly competitive firm will produce at a lower cost than the firm in monopolistic competition." Explain why you agree or disagree. Explain why this sort of an argument may or may not be used to establish that monopolistic competition is inefficient.

8. "Monopoly and perfect competition are both single-price industries. But in monopolistic competition, there are many prices." Explain why you agree or disagree.

9. Firms in monopolistic competition have some influence over price. Why don't they use this influence to raise price above average costs and therefore make an above-normal profit in the long run?

ANSWERS

Important Terms: **1** c **2** e **3** h **4** b **5** g **6** j **7** i **8** a **9** f **10** d
True-False: **1** F **2** F **3** F **4** T **5** T **6** F **7** T **8** F **9** T **10** T
Multiple Choice: **1** a **2** a **3** c **4** a **5** d **6** a **7** e **8** e **9** a **10** e **11** e **12** e **13** c **14** e

Exercises: **1a.** supply, *R*, 1,500, P_1, zero. **1b.** MR_I, 1,000, P_2, *Q*, 200, P_2TVC, increased, zero, the shaded area, lost, loss, *QSR*, reduced, inefficient, 1,000, efficient, 1,500, *D*, MC_I.

Figure 26-1 completed:

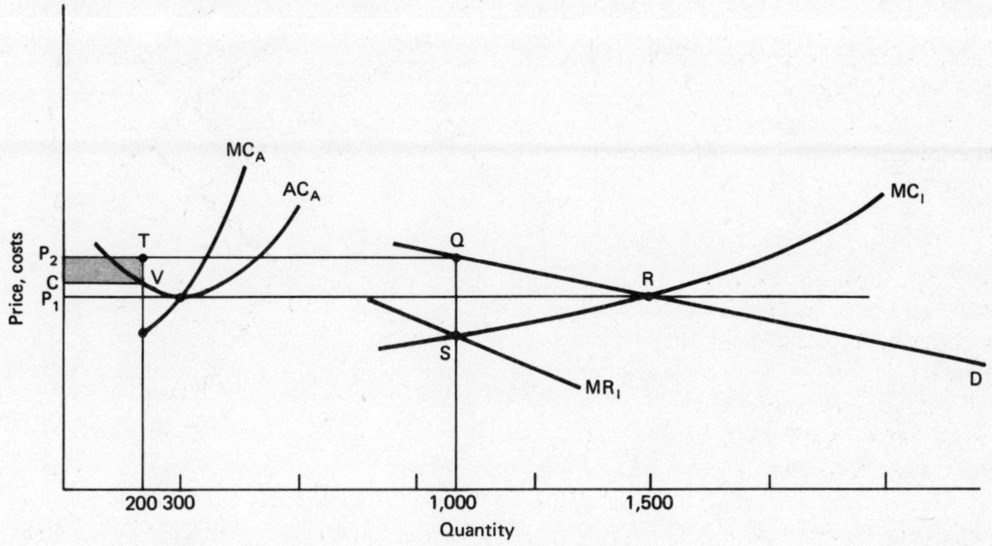

2a. D_B, MR_B, D_A, MR_A, *WXYZ*. **2b.** more than, less than. **2c.** the same as, the same as. **2d.** less than, more than. **2e.** leave unchanged, leave unchanged, *XY*.

Part Six

ECONOMIC EFFICIENCY: ISSUES OF OUR TIME

Chapter 27

GOVERNMENT REGULATION OF BUSINESS: HOW MUCH IS ENOUGH?

MAJOR PURPOSE

This chapter begins Part 6, in which a number of markets are examined to see how well they work. When they don't work well, what sort of government intervention is appropriate? For example, Chapter 27 describes the Combines Investigation Act (and the new Competition Act) under which the government intervenes when there is a threat by firms to collude in order to restrain trade or monopolize an industry. Chapter 27, and more particularly Chapter 28, demonstrates how a free market may do an inadequate job of protecting health, safety, and the environment, and how the government is justified in intervening to provide such protection. Government intervention is also sometimes justified to prevent the too rapid depletion of our resources (Chapter 29) and to provide public goods that free markets fail to provide (Chapter 30). Finally, the last two chapters in Part 6 (chapters 31 and 32) deal with the great debate: What are the gains from international trade, and should the government intervene to restrict that trade? Although there are some situations in which such intervention is justified, the broad conclusion is that, with some exceptions, international markets work reasonably well, and that a restrictive policy toward international trade is generally not in Canada's best interest. Chapter 32 also discusses the pros and cons of a free-trade agreement with the United States.

Chapter 27, to which we now turn, deals with government regulation of business: Such regulation can be divided into three categories:

1. Anti-combines laws that prevent collusion and other restraints on trade. While such laws are necessary, their application will be critically evaluated by posing such questions as, Should firms be broken up without regard to the possible effect on costs of production?

2. Regulation of a naturally competitive industry, such as trucking and the airlines, where government regulation in the past has not removed restraints on trade, but instead has created them. Government intervention of this form has often been hard to justify and in the mid-1980s, proposals to deregulate these industries were being considered by the government.

3. Quality-of-life intervention by the government to protect our health, safety, and the environment. This chapter and the next will demonstrate why such government intervention is justified, but why such intervention often takes an unnecessarily costly form.

LEARNING OBJECTIVES

After you have studied this chapter in the textbook and the study guide, you should be able to

- Identify and briefly describe the main provisions in the legislative act that forms the cornerstone of Canadian competition policy
- Explain why it may be advantageous to have large-size firms, and why a policy of preventing the emergence of large firms involves costs as well as benefits
- Show how economic efficiency may be promoted if the government on the one hand allows *natural* monopolies to exist (subject to price regulation), while on the other hand it uses anti-combines policy to break up collusive monopolies
- Explain why competition from foreign sellers reduces the ability of large Canadian firms to exercise market power in the markets for Canadian-produced goods
- Give several reasons why "market structure" regulation tends to be in the interest of the firms being regulated, rather than in the interest of consumers or the nation as a whole

Explain the two important reasons why it is feasible for a government agency to cartelize an industry, but why it is not possible for a private group of producers to do so

Explain how provincial trucking regulations affect the interest of (1) established trucking firms, (2) the nation as a whole, (3) shippers on trunk routes with high traffic volume, and (4) shippers in small communities with low traffic volume. In explaining (3) and (4), use the concept of cross-subsidization

Demonstrate the extent to which benefit-cost analysis can be used to evaluate quality-of-life regulations on health, safety, and the environment

Explain why benefit-cost analysis involves many problems; for example, this approach often requires us to attach a value to a human life

Demonstrate why government policy becomes inconsistent, with too few lives saved, if a value is *not* placed on a human life

HIGHLIGHTS OF THE CHAPTER

This chapter focuses on several ways in which the government regulates business.

Anti-combines Legislation

The first category of regulation consists of legislation designed to prevent business practices that reduce competition. This legislation is contained in the Combines Investigation Act, which has its roots in laws going back as far as 1889. The main provisions in the Act relate to

1. The prohibition of *collusive agreements* among firms to fix prices or limit production. One problem with the wording of this section of the Act is that it prohibits these activities only when they "unduly" lessen competition and limit production.

2. Making it illegal for a firm to create a monopoly position for itself by cut-throat competition to drive its competitors out of the market, or by buying out competing firms. A problem with this section (the *monopoly and merger* section of the Act) is that it prohibits these practices only if they result in a monopoly which operates "to the detriment or against the interests of the public."

3. The prohibition of *price discrimination*; that is, making it illegal for a seller to charge different prices to buyers who buy goods of like quality and in the same quantity.

4. Prohibiting *resale price maintenance*; that is, making it illegal for a manufacturer to force retailers to charge a minimum price for the manufacturer's product.

5. Outlawing *misleading advertising* and prohibiting certain forms of tied selling.

The primary objective of provisions (1) and (2) is to reduce restraint on trade and the abuse of market power by monopoly and oligopoly firms. The main tactic is to prevent a single firm or group of firms from attaining a dominant position in the market. However, a policy of preventing any one firm from becoming large enough to dominate the market may carry a cost, because size has advantages:

1. Large firms can *better afford* the expenditures on research and development (R&D) that generate growth and technological improvements. Large firms also have more incentive to undertake R&D expenditures, because their large market share allows them to capture a large share of the benefits from any new technique or product they may develop. For example, if Northern Telecom develops a superior office telephone system, it will acquire millions of dollars of benefits from this in its huge sales of telephone equipment, so it can justify this sort of R&D. However, a Manitoba farmer can't justify a similar R&D expenditure to develop a better strain of wheat; the benefits to him would be limited to a few thousand dollars, while the millions of dollars of additional benefit would be spread among thousands of wheat farmers.

2. Because of economies of scale, large firms may enjoy lower costs per unit than smaller firms; this point was demonstrated in the case of natural monopoly in Chapter 25.

In a country with relatively small domestic markets, these advantages of large firm size effectively compel the government to allow firms to have a relatively large share of many markets. However, there are some ways in which the government may lessen the ability of such firms to exploit their potential market power.

First, for goods that can be transported long distances relatively easily, the government may make sure that domestic firms are subject to competition from foreign firms by not restricting imports of foreign goods into Canada. For goods and services that cannot be transported as easily, the small size of the market may mean that the industry comes close to being a natural monopoly. In such industries, the government's best policy *may* be to let a single firm monopolize the market. The problem with this second solution, of course, is that despite its cost advantage, a natural monopoly left unregulated will produce the efficiency loss that we studied in Chapter 25. Consequently, the policy needs to be supplemented by price regulation (or by government ownership) of natural monopolies. As we have seen, this sort of regulation is imperfect, and government ownership may have problems of its own. Thus, in practice, it might sometimes even make sense to prevent the formation of a natural monopoly, despite its economies of scale, as a way of eliminating all these problems of regulation.

The enforcement of anti-combines legislation is a very difficult task, in part because it is difficult to distinguish anti-competitive practices from the normal efforts of business firms to compete in the marketplace. Consider, for example, cut-throat competition—when firms set a price below costs in order to drive competitors out of business. A problem in showing that a firm is engaged in cut-throat competition is that it is never clear whether prices are below costs because the firm is trying to starve out its competitors or because it is just trying to make the best out of a weak market. (Remember that even under perfect competition a firm might continue to operate with a price less than average cost as long as it is covering average variable cost.) Another example is the problem of showing that firms are colluding to "cartelize" an otherwise competitive industry. The fact that all firms in an industry are charging the same price is hardly enough to establish that there has been a conspiracy to fix prices. After all, this uniformity of prices is just what you would expect to see even if the market were perfectly competitive.

The Canadian courts' interpretation of the restrictive wording in the collusive agreements and monopoly and merger sections of the Combines Investigation Act, coupled with the fact that in anti-combines cases the burden of proof is on the prosecution, have also made it hard for the government to get convictions in the past. However, under the terms of the proposed new Competition Act that was introduced in Parliament in 1985, enforcement would become easier because it would put anti-combines legislation under the rules of civil law rather than criminal law.

Market-Structure Regulation

The textbook discusses this kind of regulation mainly in terms of the example of Canada's trucking industry, which has been regulated since the 1930s, even though it certainly is not an industry with a natural monopoly. (Why not?)

The regulation of trucking had its origin in the increasing competition that trucking firms were offering the (already regulated) railroads, as more efficient trucks and better roads were being built in the 1920s and 1930s. The government authorities who were regulating rail transport had required the railroad companies to maintain rail service to small, remote communities even though it was unprofitable for the railroads. In return, the authorities had allowed the railroads to charge high freight rates and earn high profits on short-haul, high-volume freight. (This illustrates the use of *cross-subsidization* as a regulatory technique; the authorities were forcing the railroads to use the high profits from the high-volume routes to subsidize the service they were forced to maintain on the low-volume service to small communities. But the high rail freight rates on the high volume routes made it easier for trucking firms to take business away from the railroads on those routes by offering lower rates. For this reason, the railroad companies were campaigning vigorously for regulation of trucking. The trucking firms themselves also wanted regulation of their own industry, since they were now competing not just with the railroads but also with other trucking firms.

Today, all provinces except Alberta have extensive legislation regulating things like entry of new trucking firms, the routes that each firm may serve, the allowable frequency of service to various communities, and types of freight that firms are allowed to carry; some provinces also regulate the rates that trucking firms are allowed to charge. Studies undertaken for the Economic Council have shown that this complicated network of regulations is very costly. In addition to the costs of administering the system (which are borne by the provincial taxpayers), the licensing system sometimes forces the firms to operate in inefficient ways, which leads to high freight rates to consumers and lower profits for the firms.

Price and entry regulation in industries that by themselves would be relatively competitive is not confined to trucking. Other examples include air transport (which continues to be regulated in Canada, even though it has been deregulated in the United States), the radio and television industry, and the taxi industry. Another area where regulation has become very extensive is that of government licensing and certification requirements for specific occupations; government regulation of pricing and production in agricultural markets has also grown rapidly in recent years.

By the mid-1980s, many types of regulation were coming under increasing criticism in both Canada and the United States. A major study by the Economic Council of Canada recommended substantial reductions in the extent of market structure regulation, and in a 1985 discussion paper, the federal government came out in favour of deregulating airlines and railroads.

Quality-of-Life Regulation

This differs from market-structure regulation in two major ways. First, whereas a market-structure agency (such as the Canadian Radio-television and Telecommunications Commission) imposes regulations on only one industry, quality-of-life regulatory agencies—such as a provincial Ministry of the Environment—impose regulations across *all* industries. *Second*, quality-of-life regulations are not imposed in the interest of the firms being regulated, as is often the case with market-structure regulation. Instead, complying with such regulation often imposes a substantial cost on business.

In this section of the chapter, one of the most important issues for you to study is how benefit-cost analysis may be used to evaluate quality-of-life regulations. Regulations to make air cleaner, jobs safer, and cars more reliable obviously have significant benefits, in terms of improving health and safety of the population and saving lives. But quality-of-life regulations may also have significant costs. One of the most important principles to be learned in a first course in economics is that any policy with a very large benefit is not *necessarily* worth undertaking; its benefit must exceed its cost. The purpose of benefit-cost analysis is to perform just such a test.

One might expect that whenever policymakers are considering a new regulation, they would perform such a benefit-cost analysis. Unfortunately, this is not always the case.

If we take a benefit-cost approach to analyse a proposed new quality-of-life regulation, costs must first be estimated. This is not an easy task, because costs of regulation fall into three categories: (1) the salaries and other operating costs of the agencies that administer the regulations; (2) the costs incurred by the firms in complying with the regulations, and (3) the efficiency costs of the regulation. The last category includes such items as the time delays because producers have to comply with regulations before selling new products; and the costs because some business ventures are not undertaken due to the regulatory paperwork that would be involved.

While it is difficult to estimate these *costs*, even greater problems are encountered in estimating the *benefits* of quality-of-life regulation. For example, one of the benefits of such regulation is the saving of lives—and no one wants to put a value on a human life. It is far easier to say that the value of a life is infinite, and leave it at that. But that's not how we value our lives. We all take some small risk with our lives whenever we take a trip in a plane—or, for that matter, an even bigger risk when we travel by car. We don't sit at home and avoid the risk, as we would if we truly believed our lives had an infinite value. But while it's easy to argue that the value of a life is less than infinite, it's very difficult to be more specific. For attempts to do so, see Box 27-5 in the textbook.

Finally, cost-benefit analysis raises broader problems. For example, one would expect that imposing a requirement that regulations pass a benefit-cost test would be a major step forward in getting a more appropriate evaluation of government policies. Not so, say critics, who charge that this is just a way of blocking desirable regulations where full information on benefits and costs is not yet available.

IMPORTANT TERMS: MATCH THE COLUMNS

Match each term in the first column with the corresponding phrase in the second column. But before you do so, write your own definition of each term in the first column.

_____ **1.** cut-throat competition
_____ **2.** price leadership
_____ **3.** tying contract
_____ **4.** resale price maintenance
_____ **5.** horizontal merger
_____ **6.** vertical merger
_____ **7.** conglomerate merger
_____ **8.** natural monopoly regulation
_____ **9.** market-structure regulation
_____ **10.** quality-of-life regulation
_____ **11.** cross-subsidization
_____ **12.** benefit-cost analysis
_____ **13.** benefit-cost test

a. charging one group of customers more in order to finance a service (which would not otherwise be available) to another group of customers
b. the union of firms in the same competing activity
c. a manufacturer's fixing of the price that retail stores can charge for its product
d. the requirement that the benefits of a program be at least as great as its costs
e. the practice in some oligopolistic industries of having one firm announce its price changes first, on the understanding that other firms will follow suit (Such a practice is sometimes suspected of being a form of "tacit," or silent collusion, in which the initial firm sets approximately the same price that a cartel would set.)
f. the union of firms in unrelated activities (This almost happened when American Express, a credit card firm, tried to take over McGraw-Hill, the company that publishes this textbook.)
g. a contract that requires purchasers to buy other items in a seller's line in order to get the items they really want (sometimes called *full-line forcing*)
h. regulation of health, safety, working conditions, and the environment
i. regulation of the price and entry conditions in a naturally more competitive industry, such as the nation's trucking firms

j. estimating and comparing benefits and costs of a program
k. pricing below costs in order to drive competitors out of business
l. the union of a firm and its supplier
m. setting the price that can be charged by a natural monopoly such as an electric power company or a telephone company

TRUE-FALSE

T F **1.** Canada's present anti-combines laws are a part of our criminal law, not our civil law.
T F **2.** If anti-combines law is used to prevent the formation of a natural monopoly, average cost of production in the industry is kept lower than it would otherwise be.
T F **3.** Tied selling is the requirement that purchasers buy a whole line of items in order to get the one they really want. The Combines Investigation Act prohibits certain forms of tied selling.
T F **4.** The freight rates charged by trucking firms in Alberta (where there is no trucking regulation) are substantially higher than in other provinces.
T F **5.** Free access of Canadian buyers to imported substitutes for domestically produced goods reduces the market power of large Canadian firms that have a large share of the domestic market.
T F **6.** Quality-of-life regulation usually favours the interests of the regulated firms over the interests of the consumers.
T F **7.** Under cross-subsidization, the price to one group is raised so that better service or reduced price can be provided to another group.
T F **8.** Benefit-cost analysis is designed to ensure that the total benefits of a policy will at least equal its total costs.
T F **9.** Costs cannot exceed benefits for any environmental or safety regulation.
T F **10.** Environment Canada has not been able to impose regulations unless they have been able to pass a benefit-cost test.
T F **11.** The time delays before the government approves the introduction of new, potentially life-saving drugs constitute one of the efficiency costs of quality-of-life regulation.

MULTIPLE CHOICE

1. In recent years, the market power of large Canadian corporations has
- **a.** decreased because of the growth of foreign competition
- **b.** decreased because of the decline of foreign competition
- **c.** increased because of the growth of foreign competition
- **d.** increased because of the decline of foreign competition
- **e.** been unaffected by changes in foreign competition

2. Which of the following is *not* dealt with in the Combines Investigation Act?
- **a.** collusive agreements
- **b.** misleading advertising
- **c.** cross-subsidization
- **d.** resale price maintenance
- **e.** price discrimination

3. The increasing strength of foreign competition makes anti-combines action against large Canadian firms
- **a.** illegal
- **b.** more necessary
- **c.** less necessary
- **d.** neither more nor less necessary
- **e.** more necessary in some respects, but less in others

4. The practice of price leadership
- **a.** makes tacit collusion difficult to detect
- **b.** is practised by monopolies
- **c.** is practised only under perfect competition
- **d.** is used primarily in cut-throat competition
- **e.** is prohibited in the Combines Investigation Act

5. The main purpose of using anti-combines law to discourage a single firm from becoming the only seller in a market is to
- **a.** allow economies of scale
- **b.** maintain safety standards
- **c.** prevent prices from falling too low
- **d.** avoid the welfare loss from reduced competition
- **e.** improve the ability of Canadian industry to compete in foreign markets

6. A merger of a firm and its supplier is called
- **a.** a vertical merger

b. a horizontal merger
c. a conglomerate merger
d. a direct merger
e. an indirect merger

7. Even though anti-combines law prohibits firms in most industries from making agreements to limit production and fix prices, provincial egg marketing organizations are allowed to limit the amount that individual egg farmers may produce and to fix the price at which eggs are sold to retailers. This is legal because

a. anti-combines law does not apply to a regulated industry
b. egg marketing boards have a natural monopoly in the egg production industry
c. if egg production were not limited, the quality of rural life would suffer because of the overpowering smell of chicken manure
d. Canadian courts have ruled that the egg marketing arrangements do not "unduly" limit competition
e. the price fixing applies only to egg exports, not to eggs sold in the domestic market

8. A cartel organized by a regulatory agency is easier to operate than a cartel in an unregulated industry because in the regulated industry

a. the quotas are imposed by law and the firms are immune from prosecution
b. the firms are free to engage in non-price competition
c. the interests of the public are being served when the industry is regulated
d. regulated firms are not forced to cross-subsidize the consumers of unprofitable lines
e. entry of new firms is encouraged

9. Which of the following is an example of an industry or profession with price and entry regulation in most places in Canada?

a. the market for legal services
b. radio and television broadcasting
c. the taxi business
d. milk production
e. all of the above

10. Regulation of trucking in most Canadian provinces tends to benefit

a. the established trucking firm and the nation as a whole
b. the nation, but not the established trucking firm
c. the established trucking firm, but not the nation
d. neither the established trucking firm nor the nation
e. potential new trucking firms and the economy as a whole

11. Regulation of radio and television broadcasting by the Canadian Radio-television and Telecommunications Commission

a. encourages competition by restricting the entry of new firms
b. encourages competition by allowing the entry of new firms
c. discourages competition by allowing the entry of new firms
d. discourages competition by restricting the entry of new firms
e. has no effect on competition because it prevents new firms from entering cities that are already served by a radio or television station

12. In controlling the release of new drugs

a. there is a cost of delay for further testing, but no benefit of delay
b. there is a benefit from delay, but no cost
c. there is neither a benefit nor a cost from delay, because health is a non-economic issue
d. there is a cost and benefit of delay; the cost is that lives may be lost because a lifesaving drug can't be used yet
e. there is a cost and benefit of delay, but neither can be specified

13. According to recent studies, the most common complaint by business firms about quality-of-life regulation is

a. the technical impossibility of complying with the very strict health, safety, and environmental impact standards set by government agencies
b. that the public is not sufficiently concerned with the environmental impact of industrial production
c. that government officials are overly concerned with benefit-cost analysis when they decide on quality-of-life regulation
d. that quality-of-life regulation causes unions to demand higher wages
e. that the regulatory process is very time-consuming and complicated, partly because each regulation may involve several government agencies

14. With the growth of regulation in the 1960s and 1970s, economic decision making shifted

a. toward the market and away from the courts
b. away from the courts
c. away from the regulatory agencies
d. away from the market and toward the courts and regulatory agencies
e. away from the market, the courts, and the regulatory agencies

15. In their daily decisions, most people implicitly value their own lives as worth

a. an infinite amount
b. zero
c. about half their current year's income
d. some value between (a) and (b)
e. some value between (b) and (c)

***16.** In any takeover bid by firm A for firm B

a. the management and shareholders of B are almost certain to welcome the bid
b. the management and shareholders of B are almost certain to oppose the bid
c. the managers may oppose it, while the shareholders welcome it
d. the managers of firm A typically employ their

golden parachutes

e. firm A usually regards firm B as a black knight

***17.** Greenmail is

a. the premium paid by a target firm to buy its own stock from a shark

b. the premium paid by a shark to buy its own stock from a target company

c. the price reduction a private firm enjoys when it buys its own stock from a shark

d. the price reduction a shark has to accept when it sells the target firm's stock

e. none of the above

* Based on material in the appendix to Chapter 27 in your textbook.

EXERCISES

1a. Suppose that the total cost for a firm producing widgets equals the fixed cost of $2 million plus a variable cost equal to $4 for every widget produced. Thus, the marginal cost of producing widgets is always [constant, increasing, decreasing], and average cost is always [constant, increasing, decreasing]. The widget industry is a ____________.

1b. Suppose this firm is being regulated using marginal cost pricing. Then its price would be $____________. Suppose the firm sells 2 million units at this price. Its cost per unit would be $____________, and its loss per unit would be $____________. Therefore, the taxpayer would have to pay a total subsidy of $____________ to keep the firm in operation.

1c. If the industry were broken up into two separate firms, each with the same cost structure as before, and each firm were to produce half of this quantity, then the cost per unit would be ____________, which is [more than, less than, the same as] before. The loss per unit would be $ ____________, which is [higher, lower, no different] than before. Therefore, the total subsidy required to keep the industry alive would be [higher, lower, no different] than before. Specifically, the total subsidy paid to both firms would be $____________.

1d. After this monopoly is broken up and all necessary subsidies are paid, the firms would [gain, lose, be unaffected], the consumers would [gain, lose, be unaffected], and the taxpayers would [gain, lose, be unaffected]. What important principle is illustrated by this hypothetical example? ____

____

____

____

2. The Apex Company employs 2,000 individuals working on high-steel construction. The firm has to pay its labour force a $1,000 per person wage premium each year in order to attract workers who are willing to risk their lives. The risks on this job raise the mortality rate by 2/1000; that is, the chance that a worker will be killed during a year is 2/1000 higher than in other jobs. The question is, Should the government introduce a safety regulation that will reduce the risk by 1/1000, if this regulation costs $1.5 million (including both government administration costs and the compliance cost by the firm)?

To answer this, we need to know the value of a human life. Because each worker is willing to take a 2/1000 chance of losing his life if he is paid $1,000 more, this means that he values his life at [$5 million, $500,000, $1,000, $500], which is his $____________ wage premium divided by the ____________ increase in risk.

Although this can't be predicted precisely in advance, the expectation is that this regulation would be expected to save ____________ lives, which is the ____________ risk reduction from this regulation times the 2,000 workers employed. Since each worker values his life at $____________, the *benefit* of this regulation is $____________. This is [greater than, less than, the same as] the $1.5 million *cost* of the regulation. Thus, this regulation [passes, fails] this benefit-cost test, and it would be [introduced, rejected].

If the cost were $500,000, then it would [pass, fail] the benefit-cost test, and it should be [introduced, rejected].

ESSAY QUESTIONS

1. Discuss the benefits and costs of breaking up a natural monopoly. Do you think these benefits and costs were also present in the U.S. government's attempt to break up IBM?

2. "Giant companies such as IBM and General Motors still dominate the production of many goods. Thus our anti-combines laws cannot have been effective." To what extent do you agree with this statement? Explain your position.

3. "Natural monopoly is one of the simplest areas of government decision making. Just set up an agency that will impose marginal cost pricing on the company." Do you agree? Explain.

4. "In restricting GM's use of its market power in the North American auto market, the competition from Japanese auto companies has been far more effective than U.S. antitrust laws or Canadian anti-combines laws. Do you agree? Explain your position.

5. Why do you suppose the unions representing truck drivers are likely to be strongly opposed to deregulation of the Canadian trucking industry?

6. Show why the value of human life may have to be taken into account in calculating the costs of regulation of the drug industry by Health and Welfare Canada, as well as in calculating the benefits of this regulation.

ANSWERS

Important Terms: **1** k **2** e **3** g **4** c **5** b **6** l **7** f **8** m **9** i **10** h **11** a **12** j **13** d
True-False: **1** T **2** F **3** T **4** F **5** T **6** F **7** T **8** T **9** F **10** F **11** T
Multiple Choice: **1** a **2** c **3** c **4** a **5** d **6** a **7** a **8** a **9** c **10** c **11** d **12** d **13** e **14** d **15** d **16** c **17** a
Exercises: **1a.** constant, decreasing, natural monopoly.. **1b.** $4, $5, $1, $2 million. **1c.** $6, more than, $2, higher, higher, $4 million. **1d.** be unaffected, be unaffected, lose, lose. From the point of view of efficiency, natural monopolies should be regulated rather than broken up. **2.** $500,000, $1000, 2/1,000, 2, 1/1000, $500,000, $1 million, less than, fails, rejected, pass, introduced.

Chapter 28

PROTECTING THE ENVIRONMENT IN A GROWING ECONOMY: HOW SHOULD POLLUTION BE LIMITED?

MAJOR PURPOSE

Many people think that environmental pollution is simply a bad thing that should be prevented. They believe that it has nothing to do with economics, and such economic considerations as cost are irrelevant. Pollution, they contend, should be cleaned up, regardless of cost. The objective in this chapter is to show that pollution *is*, in fact, an economic problem—one that involves many of the principles that have already been developed in this book. Moreover, if economic considerations are ignored, pollution will be much more costly to control. Society will waste valuable resources in the clean-up effort. Or, to put the same point another way: Our limited available funds will give us far less improvement in the environment if we ignore costs.

The specific questions we will address in this chapter are

1. What is pollution?

2. Why is it a problem that even a perfectly competitive market cannot deal with pollution efficiently?

3. What principles should guide our antipollution policy?

4. What policies have actually been used in Canada, and how successful have they been?

5. What problems are caused when pollution spills over provincial and international boundaries?

LEARNING OBJECTIVES

After you have studied this chapter in the textbook and the study guide, you should be able to

- Explain why pollution is an externality
- Explain why perfect competition does not lead to efficiency when there is pollution or any other kind of external cost (such as congestion, analysed in the appendix to this chapter)
- Measure the efficiency loss from pollution, in a diagram similar to Figure 28-2 in the textbook
- Show why we cannot and should not attempt to eliminate pollution completely
- Explain why the policy of imposing a physical limit on pollution can be a far more costly way of reducing it than imposing a tax on emissions
- Show why a third option—imposing physical limits on pollution, but allowing the rights to be bought and sold—is as efficient as imposing a tax, and compare these two preferred policies in terms of their political feasibility and equity
- Critically evaluate the policy of subsidizing pollution-control equipment
- Explain how the responsibility for protecting the environment is divided between the federal and provincial governments in Canada
- Describe some of the problems with the methods currently used by Canadian governments to control pollution
- Explain some of the problems that arise when pollution spills over provincial or international boundaries
- Explain how recycling reduces the pollution problem, and, as a favourable side effect, also reduces the problem of resource depletion, which we will be studying in the next chapter

HIGHLIGHTS OF THE CHAPTER

Each of the five key questions listed above will be considered.

1. What Is Pollution?

Pollution is an external cost. It is a cost to society resulting from our economic activities of production and consumption. But this cost is external, because it isn't paid for by those responsible for it. For example, when smoke from a factory soils someone's clothes, the factory owner doesn't have to pay the cleaning bill.

2. A Failure of the Invisible Hand: Why Does a Perfectly Competitive Market Fail to Deal with the Pollution Problem?

When there is an externality like pollution, the "invisible hand" of a perfectly competitive, free market provides an inefficient outcome. The reason is that there is a violation of one of the conditions in Chapter 24 that allowed perfect competition to deliver an economically efficient outcome. The condition that is violated is that the marginal cost to producers (MC) must be the same as the marginal cost to society (MC_S). This condition does not hold when there is an external cost such as pollution, because MC_5 is *more* than MC. The difference between the two is the marginal external cost MC_E, as illustrated in Figure 28-1 in the textbook.

Efficiency requires that the marginal benefit to society (shown by the demand curve) be equal to the marginal cost to society MC_S. In Figure 28-2 of the textbook we see that this efficient outcome is at E_2. However, this is *not* the equilibrium in a perfectly competitive free market. The reason is that, as always in such a market, supply reflects the cost facing producers. But this is only their private cost MC. The *external* cost of their actions is a cost they *don't* have to face. Because supply reflects private cost MC only, the perfectly competitive equality of demand and supply is at equilibrium E_1 rather than the efficient E_2. Thus, perfect competition is inefficient; too much output of this polluting good is produced (Q_1 rather than the efficient output Q_2). The efficiency loss is measured by the red triangle in this figure. Be sure you can explain this triangle: For each of the units of "excess" output between Q_2 and Q_1, social cost MC_S exceeds benefit D. There is therefore a net cost involved in producing each of these units—with the sum of all these costs being the red triangle.

3. What Principles Should Guide Our Antipollution Policy?

The above analysis suggests a simple way that the government can make a perfectly competitive market efficient: Impose a tax on polluting producers equal to the external cost they are creating; that is, impose tax r in Figure 28-2 in the text. This tax now becomes one of the costs producers have to face. In other words, the "external cost is now internalized," because it has now become one of the costs that producers have to pay. Since supply reflects the costs producers have to face, it now reflects both internal and external costs—that is, supply is now S_2. Now the perfectly competitive equilibrium of demand and supply is at the efficient point E_2. Thus, with this simple imposition of a tax, the perfectly competitive market does yield an efficient outcome after all. Adam Smith's "invisible hand" does work, because, with this tax, the government is applying the appropriate pressure on the market.

Figure 28-2 in the text illustrates another important principle: Polluting output can be cut back "too much." Limiting it to Q_3 is even worse than a "hands-off" policy that would allow output to continue unrestricted at Q_1. (At Q_3, the efficiency loss FE_2G is even greater than the red efficiency loss at Q_1.)

4. Antipollution Policies: The Canadian Experience

Canadian governments have not used the method of taxing polluters as a way of controlling pollution; instead they have imposed limits on the allowable amounts of pollution that individual firms may emit. The federal government has taken the lead in setting standards for the quality of air and water; however, the constitutional authority for setting and enforcing limits on allowable pollution rests with the provincial governments. Another method has also been used: subsidizing the purchase of pollution-control equipment. On the whole, these programs have resulted in a substantial reduction in pollution, but most economists believe that they could have been designed to be more efficient. They make the following criticisms:

1. Because governments have not tried to conduct systematic benefit-cost analyses of different types of pollution control, there has been little consistency in the limits set on allowable pollution: Some limits have probably been too restrictive, while others have not been restrictive enough.

2. Even if the total physical limit were to be set correctly (for example, at Q_3 in Figure 28-3 of the text), allocating individual limits for individual polluters is a much more costly way of reducing pollution than is the imposition of a pollution tax. Under a pollution tax the firms that can cut back pollution at least expense would automatically cut back more; thus, there would be a lower cost of reducing pollution. You should be able to demonstrate this in Figure 28-3. The least expensive way of cutting back pollution to Q_3 is to have the firms to the right of Q_3 cut out their pollution at a cost shown by, for example, the short red bar. But when physical limits are imposed, some of the reduction in pollution must be undertaken by firms to the left of Q_3 at the relatively high cost shown by, for example, the tall red bar. There is the same reduction in pollution, but it is achieved at an unnecessarily high cost. (For a detailed example, see exercise 5 below.)

Be sure you can demonstrate in Figure 28-3 in the textbook not only why a physical limit on pollution is less efficient than a tax, but also why a physical limit becomes as efficient as a tax, *if* the government modifies this to a "tradeable permit" policy—that is, if the government issues a certain number of permits to pollute, and allows these permits to be freely bought and sold.

3. The simple policy of just imposing physical limits on polluting firms has encouraged many of them to engage the government in costly legal actions to try to gain exemption from the limits.

4. In some cases, the government has been forced to back down from its standards when firms claimed to be unable to meet them, and threatened widespread layoffs of their labour force.

5. Governments have made few efforts to ensure that the pollution-control equipment they have subsidized is used effectively.

6. This pollution-control equipment has, at best, provided an "end-of-pipe" solution that is often more costly than other solutions such as using "cleaner" inputs. Again, either a pollution tax or a system of tradeable permits would be a lower cost policy because it would give firms not only the incentive to cure pollution but also the incentive to find the *least expensive* cure. (See exercise 6.)

Political Problems Plaguing Pollution Prevention

Even though Canadian and American governments have had remarkable success in slowing down and even reversing the deterioration of the environment during the 1970s, there are signs that further progress will be difficult. One reason for this is political. The lobbying efforts mounted by the firms opposing specific antipollution policies are likely to be more intensive than the lobbying by representatives for the beneficiaries. For a particular firm, preventing tighter antipollution rules may be a matter of life and death, while for those who benefit from antipollution policies, the effects of the rules applied to any single firm is of negligible importance. Furthermore, the pollution issue is sometimes complicated by the fact that pollution spills over boundaries. For example, some of the air pollution generated in Ontario spills over into Quebec; and pollution of the Great Lakes by industrial firms on the American side is of concern to Canadians as well as American fishermen and swimmers, as are emissions of sulphur dioxide by U.S. power plants. The problem here is this: How does one ensure that the government that has jurisdiction over the polluting firms takes into account the benefits accruing to residents in other jurisdictions when they decide how tightly to control their polluters?

As a postscript we emphasize one more important idea in this chapter. Recycling can play a role in reducing the amount of pollution by using up polluting wastes (such as empty beer cans). Such a policy would also mean that we will need to extract fewer natural resources from our environment. If we produce new beer cans out of old ones, we won't need to mine as much bauxite (aluminum ore).

IMPORTANT TERMS: MATCH THE COLUMNS

Match each term in the first column with the corresponding phrase in the second column. But before you do so, write your own definition of each term in the first column.

_____ **1.** internal cost
_____ **2.** external cost
_____ **3.** social cost
_____ **4.** international externality
_____ **5.** the marginal cost of reducing pollution (MCR)
_____ **6.** marginal cost of having pollution (MCP)
_____ **7.** "end-of-pipe" treatment
_____ **8.** recycling

a. a cost imposed on one nation by the actions of another
b. the cost that is paid by the producer (also called *private cost*)
c. the cost of having one more unit of pollution
d. the cost paid not by the producer (or consumer) of a good, but by someone else (also called *neighbourhood cost* or *cost spillover*) (Examples include costs of pollution and traffic congestion.)
e. the policy of removing pollutants just before they enter the environment (Sometimes this is a more costly method of reducing pollution than the alternative of using cleaner fuels or different production processes that produce less pollution in the first place.)
f. the total cost to society, that is, the sum of internal and external costs
g. using materials again rather than throwing them away, which can reduce pollution and preserve natural resources
h. the cost of reducing pollution by one more unit

TRUE-FALSE

T F 1. Restricting industrial growth is one of the best measures for controlling pollution.

T F 2. Inefficiency occurs if producers do not take external pollution costs into account.

T F 3. Marginal external cost equals marginal social cost minus marginal private cost.

T F 4. The main effort of Environment Canada has been to collect the taxes that the government has imposed to discourage pollution.

T F 5. A pollution tax "internalizes an externality" because the producer is forced to face not only production costs, but also the external costs imposed on society.

T F 6. Without government intervention, the marginal cost of having pollution would be zero.

T F 7. Setting an arbitrary physical limit on pollution will always be better than doing nothing at all.

T F 8. The problem with pollution is that, in the absence of government intervention, firms view it as an internal cost.

T F 9. We should continue to build more roads until all congestion is eliminated; that is, until the external costs of taking any trip become zero.

T F 10. The most important similarity that economists recognize between pollution and congestion is that both are caused by automobiles.

T F 11. If both the U.S. and Canadian governments agree to take into account the benefits to the citizens of the other country as well as to their own citizens when setting water quality standards for the Great Lakes, the lakes are likely to be cleaner than they would be if each country considers only the benefits to its own citizens.

MULTIPLE CHOICE

1. An example of an externality being internalized occurs if

- **a.** an export firm is required to raise the price of a good it is also selling in the home market
- **b.** an export firm is required to export less and sell more goods on the home market instead
- **c.** a producer is forced to pay a tax equal to the external cost his or her product imposes on society
- **d.** a producer is forced to pay a tax equal to the external cost his or her product imposes on society
- **e.** a tax is imposed on the producer equal to the marginal social cost of the good

2. In a perfectly competitive market, the marginal benefit of a polluting good will equal its marginal social costs if

- **a.** a tax is imposed on the good equal to its marginal external cost
- **b.** a tax is imposed on the good equal to its marginal internal cost
- **c.** a subsidy is provided equal to the marginal internal cost
- **d.** a subsidy is provided equal to the marginal external cost
- **e.** the government does not intervene with either a tax or a subsidy

3. In a perfectly competitive market for a polluting good where the government is following a "hands-off policy,"

- **a.** price will be higher than the efficient level
- **b.** price will be equal to the efficient level
- **c.** less than the efficient amount will be produced
- **d.** more than the efficient amount will be produced
- **e.** the efficient amount will be produced

4. In the face of external costs, efficiency can be achieved in a perfectly competitive market by setting a tax that is equal to

- **a.** the marginal social cost of producing the good
- **b.** the marginal internal cost of producing the good
- **c.** the marginal external cost of producing the good
- **d.** the total social cost of producing the good
- **e.** the total internal cost of producing the good

5. Airplanes flying low over houses near airports cause "noise pollution." The most efficient policy to deal with this would be to

- **a.** rely on the "invisible hand" to take care of the problem
- **b.** provide a subsidy to each airline depending on the total amount of noise it creates in the affected neighbourhoods
- **c.** impose a tax on each airline depending on the total amount of noise it creates in the affected neighbourhoods
- **d.** impose limits on the number of flights of each airline
- **e.** subsidize airlines that install noise-abatement devices

6. As time passes, pollution becomes a more difficult problem to deal with because the marginal cost of reducing pollution (MCR)

- **a.** shifts to the left, while the marginal cost of pollution (MCP) is rising
- **b.** shifts to the right, while MCP is rising
- **c.** shifts to the right, while MCP is falling
- **d.** shifts to the left, while MCP is falling
- **e.** remains stable, while MCP is rising

7. An effluent fee is

a. any tax imposed on the wealthy
b. a special tax on the wealthy who pollute
c. a tax on each unit of pollution
d. a subsidy provided to polluters to encourage them to use cleaner fuels
e. a subsidy provided to polluters who install pollution-abatement equipment

8. If a physical limit is set on the amount of pollutants each firm can emit
a. there will be no change in the total nationwide amount of pollution
b. there will be an increase in the total nationwide amount of pollution
c. pollution will be cut back, but at a higher cost than necessary
d. pollution will be cut back at the minimum possible cost
e. nothing can be said about the pollution that will result

9. The least-cost way of reducing pollution by an industry is to
a. encourage all firms to cut back their pollution by the same percentage
b. force all firms to cut back their pollution by the same percentage
c. let the firms with the highest profits cut back the most
d. force the firms with the lowest profits to go out of business
e. provide an incentive for the firms with the lowest cost of reducing pollution to make relatively large cutbacks

10. During the 1970s, the provincial government agencies responsible for environmental protection concentrated on
a. setting limits on the amount of output that could be produced by polluting firms
b. setting limits on the amount of pollution that could be caused by a firm or its products
c. imposing taxes on the output of polluting firms
d. imposing taxes on a firm depending on the amount of pollution that it caused or that its products caused
e. establishing rules for the sale and purchase of pollution permits

11. The government's policy of subsidizing the purchase of pollution-control equipment can be criticized because it
a. places too great an emphasis on "end-of-pipe" treatment
b. places too little emphasis on "end-of-pipe" treatment
c. has led to an overemphasis by the government on how efficiently this machinery will subsequently be operated
d. has been supported by inadequate short-term financing during its construction
e. none of the above

12. A sag point is
a. a location where pollution does the least damage
b. a location where pollution is particularly harmful
c. a location where pollution is heavy but not very damaging
d. the period before an election when unpopular pollution-control legislation cannot be passed
e. the period before an election when members of Parliament are so exhausted that they will pass unpopular pollution-control legislation

13. Which of the following is *not* a good example of an international externality?
a. congestion of Canadian highways by American tourists
b. leakage of chemicals from a plant on the Canadian side of the Niagara River
c. smoke from a U.S. power-plant that causes acid rain in Canada
d. cutting down trees in Canada to produce newsprint for U.S. newspapers
e. radioactive fallout in Sweden from a nuclear accident in the Soviet Union

14. In the face of highway congestion, efficiency requires a
a. subsidy to drivers equal to the external cost of a trip
b. subsidy to drivers equal to the internal cost of a trip
c. toll or tax on drivers equal to the external cost of a trip
d. toll or tax on drivers that will eliminate congestion entirely
e. subsidy to drivers that will eliminate congestion entirely

EXERCISES

1. Figure 28-1 on the next page represents the market for a good that causes pollution.
a. If the market is perfectly competitive, output will be ___________, market price will be ___________, marginal social cost will be ___________, and the marginal external cost will be ___________.
b. If the commodity produces no external benefits, then the *optimal* output is ___________. This output would be attained under perfect competition if the producers were faced with a tax of ___________ per unit. This would result in a market price of ___________. Without this tax, the efficiency loss will be area ___________.
c. Suppose that these firms were able to collude to form a monopoly. Then the level of output (with no tax) would be ___________, the market price would be ___________, and the efficiency loss would be ___________.

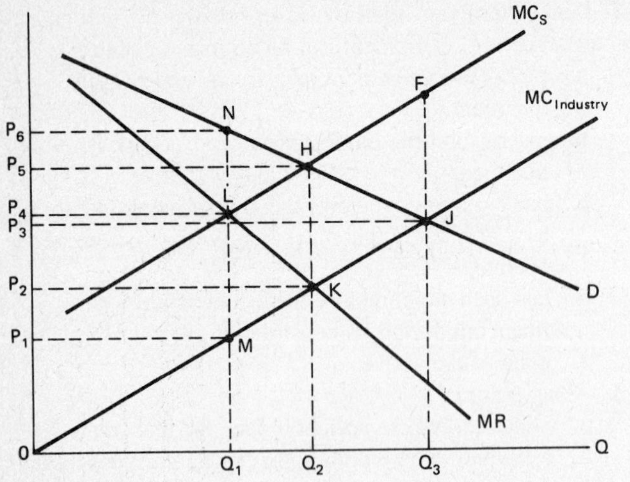

FIGURE 28-1

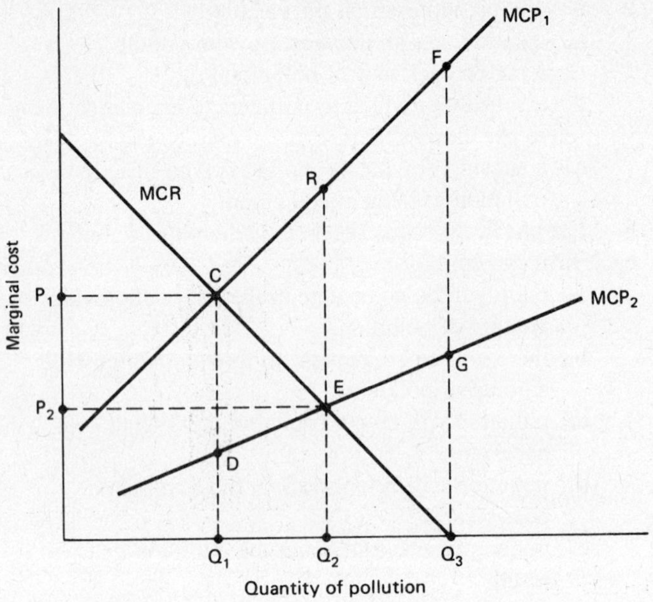

FIGURE 28-3

d. Assume that the marginal external cost is a constant—i.e., that the lines MC_S and $MC_{industry}$ are parallel, with $LM = HK = FJ$. Now suppose that the government imposes the same tax on the monopolist that it earlier charged to the perfect competitors. In this case, the monopolist will produce an output of ____________, it will charge price ____________, and the efficiency [gain, loss] will be area ____________. Thus, a per unit tax on a polluting monopolist [will, will not] necessarily lead to greater efficiency.

2. If pollution is left uncontrolled in Figure 28-2 below, the amount of pollution will be ____________. If the government imposes a tax T to reduce pollution, it will be cut back to ____________. Those firms to the [right, left] of Q_1 will stop polluting, while those firms to the [right, left] of Q_1 will continue to pollute.

3. This problem refers to Box 28-3 in the textbook.

a. If MCP_1 in Figure 28-3 is the marginal cost of having pollution and MCR is the marginal cost of reducing pollution, then, in the absence of any pollution tax, the quantity of pollution will be ____________, MCR will be ____________, and MCP will be ____________. The economically efficient reduction in pollution is to quantity ____________. This will result if firms are charged a tax of ____________ per unit of pollution.

b. Now suppose that the marginal cost of having pollution is MCP_2 instead of MCP_1. Then the economically efficient amount of pollution is ____________. This will result if firms are charged a tax of ____________ per unit of pollution. The efficient amount of pollution in this case is [more, less] because pollution is [more, less] damaging.

4. Now suppose that the marginal cost of having pollution is *really* MCP_1 but that the government makes a mistake and estimates it to be MCP_2. The government erroneously uses MCP_2 and sets the tax on pollution at ____________. The resulting quantity of pollution is ____________, which is [more, less] than the economically efficient amount. At this level of pollution, MCR is ____________, and the true MCP is ____________. There will be an efficiency [gain, loss] from the government's estimating error equal to area ____________. Thus, we [may, may not] conclude that, if the government underestimates the problem, it will take inadequate action to counter it; that is, the government will set too low a pollution tax.

5a. The two lines in Figure 28-4 show the marginal cost of reducing pollution MCR for two smoke-polluting firms (which are otherwise identical). Bars are added for detail. Reducing smoke pollution is less costly for firm [A, B]. Suppose that each firm is presently required by law to limit its output of smoke to 10 units, as shown by the dark

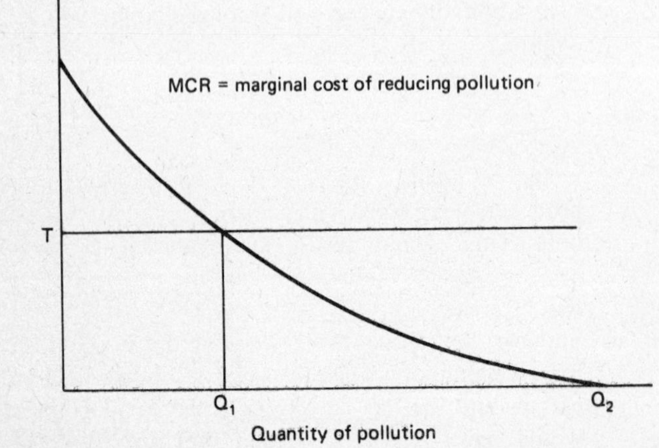

FIGURE 28-2

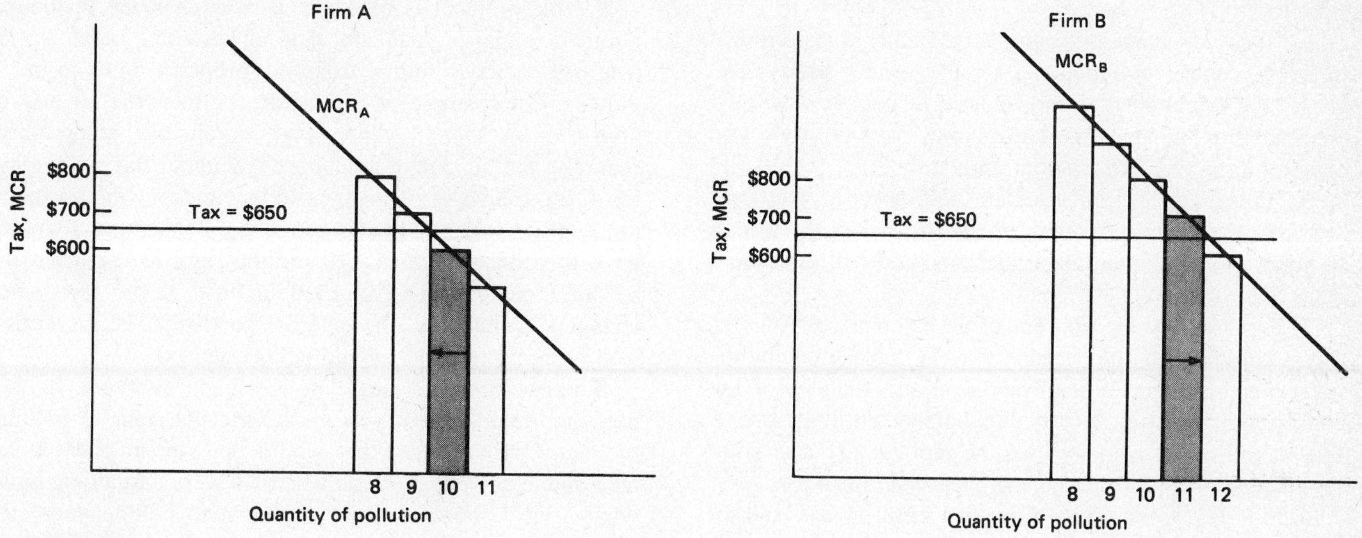

FIGURE 28-4

vertical line. Both firms together generate 20 units of pollution. Now suppose that a government official decides, after reading this study guide, to impose a pollution tax instead of limiting each firm's smoke. If he sets the tax at $650 for each unit of smoke emitted, then firm A will [cut back, expand] its emissions to ____________ units of smoke, and B will [cut back, expand] its emissions to ____________ units. Both firms together generate [more, less, the same] pollution as before. The firm with the higher MCR has [increased, decreased] its pollution, and the one with the lower MCR has [increased, decreased] its pollution.

5b. Firm A's pollution-reduction costs have [increased, decreased] by ____________, while firm B's pollution-reduction costs have [increased, decreased] by ____________. Thus, the total pollution reduction costs of the two firms have [increased, decreased, stayed the same], while the total amount of pollution by the two firms has [increased, decreased, stayed the same]. Therefore, the tax is [more, less] efficient in keeping down costs than the previous limits on pollution.

6a. Suppose that a company can produce either a car that runs on gasoline or one that runs on a newly invented fuel which sells for the same price but which reduces the emission of pollutants by 50%. Unfortunately, the car using the new gasoline costs $200 more to construct. Suppose that, in all other respects, both cars perform equally well, so that consumers do not care which fuel a car uses; if given the choice, they will buy the car with the lower purchase price. Therefore, with no regulations, the car producer will build the car using [gasoline, new fuel].

Suppose that it is also possible to install an "end-of-pipe" pollution control device on all its cars, which also reduces emissions by 50% but costs $500. Again, suppose that consumers do not care whether or not a car has this device. Then the auto producer will build the car using [gasoline, new fuel], and [with, without] the device. The cars [will, will not] pollute the atmosphere; but the car companies don't take this into account because this is an [external, internal] cost.

6b. Now suppose that a government agency wants to cut back auto emissions by 50%, so it requires the company to install the pollution-control device. The company will now build cars using [gasoline, new fuel], and with the device. The cost to society of this end-of-pipe reduction in pollution is $ ____________ per car.

Now suppose instead that the government just requires the auto producer to cut back the emission from its cars by 50%, leaving it up to the company to decide how to do this. Then the cost to the company of complying with this requirements would be $ ____________ per car if it installed the device or $ ____________ per car if it switched to the new fuel. Therefore, it would choose the [device, new fuel]. In this case the cost to society of the reduction in pollution would be $ ____________ per car.

6c. In this example, the policy of telling the company *how* to reduce pollution is $ ____________ [more, less] costly per car than the policy of just telling them to do it and leaving all details to them. If, instead, the agency had told the company to do it by making cars that use the new fuel, the cost to society would have been [more than, less than, the same as] the cost of just telling them to do it. What general rule does this suggest about the relative cost of telling companies to comply compared with telling them exactly how to comply?

____

____

____

ESSAY QUESTIONS

1. "One advantage of using taxes rather than physical limits to control pollution is that the former policy harnesses the forces of the market place to help find an efficient solution, whereas the latter policy does not." Do you agree or disagree? Explain your answer.

2. Explain why, in selecting the specific least-cost method of reducing pollution, private firms will do at least as good a job as government agencies, and will often do a better job.

3. Explain how the concept of an external cost (this is, a cost not borne by the decision maker) is illustrated by the following example. When Napoleon, the founder of the conscription system, was told that a planned military operation would cost too many men, he replied: "That is nothing. The women produce more of them than I can use."

4. In recent years a large Canadian distillery has paid for the tickets to enable people to travel free of charge on the Toronto subway system on New Year's Eve. Explain how this self-imposed tax has helped to promote economic efficiency by internalizing an external cost.

5. This problem is based on Box 28-2 in the textbook. Some economists maintain that all external costs are a result of society's failure to assign property rights to individuals. For example, if my factory pollutes the air above your house, then I am using a valuable commodity (namely, the air above your house) without having to pay for it. If our laws were changed so that anyone who owned a house also owned all the air above that house, then I would have to persuade you to sell me the right to use your air before I could pollute it. Explain how, if the law were changed in this way, the external cost—that is, the emission from my factory—would be internalized.

Suppose that I managed to persuade everyone in the neighbourhood except you to sell me the right to pollute their air. Explain how that would put you in position to take undue advantage of me when we were bargaining over what price I should pay for the right to pollute your air. Can you think of any other problems that might arise if this "property right" solution to the problem of pollution were to be attempted?

ANSWERS

Important Terms: **1** b **2** d **3** f **4** a **5** h **6** c **7** e **8** g

True-False: **1** F **2** T **3** T **4** F **5** T **6** F **7** F **8** F **9** F **10** F **11** T

Multiple Choice: **1** c **2** a **3** d **4** c **5** c **6** b **7** c **8** c **9** e **10** b **11** a **12** b **13** d **14** c

Exercises: **1a.** Q_3, P_3, Q_3F, JF. **1b.** Q_2, HK, P_5, HFJ. **1c.** Q_2, P_5, zero. **1d.** Q_1, P_6, loss, NLH, will not. **2.** Q_2, Q_1, right, left. **3a.** Q_3, essentially zero, Q_3F, Q_1, P_1. **3b.** Q_2, P_2, more, less. **4.** P_2, Q_2, more, Q_2R, loss, CRE, may. **5a.** A, cut back, 9, expand, 11, the same, increased, decreased. **5b.** increased, $600, decreased, $700, decreased, stayed the same, more. **6a.** gasoline, gasoline, without, will, external. **6b.** gasoline, $500, $500, $200, new fuel, $200. **6c.** $300, more, the same, Telling them exactly how to comply will cost more unless the government happens to pick the least-cost method—in which case it doesn't matter.

Chapter 29

NATURAL RESOURCES: ARE WE USING THEM AT THE RIGHT RATE?

MAJOR PURPOSE

In the last chapter, we saw that there was an external cost —in terms of damage to those living downstream—if chemicals are produced by a factory that dumps wastes into a river. The objective in this chapter is to use much of this same analysis to examine the external cost that is associated with resource extraction—namely, the cost to future generations because less of the resources will be available then. In this analysis, the question of who owns the resource is a critical one. If it is privately owned, then the owner will tend to take this future cost into account (since it's the owner's own resource that is being depleted) and decisions will therefore tend to be efficient. However, if the resource is common property (publicly owned), then those extracting the resource have no reason to take the future into account. Because they tend to ignore the external cost to future generations, there is an inadequate conservation effort; an inefficiently large quantity of the resource is extracted.

In this chapter, we also return to the case study of oil, one of our most important natural resources. Earlier, in Chapter 26, we examined the attempt by OPEC to keep the world price of oil high; in this chapter, we examine the difficulties and inefficiencies introduced in the 1970s and early 1980s when the Canadian government kept the domestic price of oil low. Why did the government do this, and what was the effect of this policy on oil use? Finally, we examine alternative forms of energy, since these will determine how painful any shortage of oil may be to future generations.

LEARNING OBJECTIVES

After you have studied this chapter in the textbook and the study guide, you should be able to

- Describe the internal and external costs of extracting a common-property resource, and explain why both of these are internal costs if the resource is privately owned
- Explain why a perfectly competitive market in a natural resource may be efficient if the resource is privately owned, but not if it is common property
- Describe the maximum sustainable yield (Box 29-1 in the textbook) and explain why harvests involve no future costs if the population of a species is greater than this; and why problems arise if the population is harvested down to a level below this
- Explain why simple projections of the use and availability of resources yield misleading predictions
- Give three reasons why population growth continues to be rapid in less developed countries despite the scarcity of resources
- Present the case in favour of economic growth, and the case against it
- Describe how the domestic price of oil was controlled in the 1970s and early 1980s and describe some of the practical problems that were encountered
- Explain the efficiency and transfer effects of decontrol—that is, of allowing the domestic price of oil to rise to the world price
- Explain how such a price rise affected the amounts produced, consumed, and imported
- Present an argument for raising the domestic price of oil above the world price
- Explain the advantages and disadvantages of each of the three major alternative sources of energy—natural gas, coal, and nuclear power

HIGHLIGHTS OF THE CHAPTER

Since no one owns the fish in the sea, they are a common-property resource, and provide a good illustration of one of the central issues in this chapter: Common-property resources are inadequately conserved in a free, perfectly competitive market. The reason is that fishing involves two costs: (1) the internal costs incurred by those who fish, such as the boats, nets, and labour, and (2) the external cost that falls on future generations because there is less of this resource available to them. If the resource is a common property, fishing firms don't pay any attention to this second cost. Like the polluting firm that ignores its external cost—such as the damage its pollutants do to those living downstream or downwind—the fishing firm that ignores the external cost it is imposing on future generations will produce more than the efficient amount. (Its output decision is influenced by its internal costs, but not by the external cost it creates.)

Policies to Reduce Inefficiency in Resource Extraction

There are three possible ways to reduce inefficiency:

1. Set a physical limit on the catch. The problem with this approach is that it does not use the market mechanism. The government restricts the catch (perhaps by putting a limit on the size of nets or size of boats); and, as in the case of pollution discussed in the previous chapter, too severe a physical restriction may be worse than no restriction at all. The two alternative ways to increase efficiency *do* use the market mechanism.

2. Impose a tax or fishing fee on fishermen according to the number of fish they catch—specifically, impose a tax on them equal to the external costs they generate, just like the tax on polluting firms analysed in the last chapter.

3. Create property rights; let the fish be privately owned. While this is not possible in the oceans or Great Lakes, it might be in inland lakes or ponds. (And it certainly is feasible for many other resources—such as timber—that are already privately owned.) Once the schools of fish are privately owned, the owners will take into account both the harvesting costs *and* the cost of having a reduced catch in the future. (It is *their own* future catch that will be reduced.) Thus, this future external cost is internalized once the resource is privately owned. Since the private owners will take all costs into account, the result is an efficient one. But it won't be equitable unless the new owners are charged in some way for the asset (the fish) that they now own.

Special Problems of Non-renewable Resources

Since schools of fish can eventually reproduce themselves, they are a *renewable* resource. On the other hand, there are other resources, such as coal, oil, or base metals, that are not renewable. The key questions with such resources are. Will we run out, and if so, when? And what can we do to prevent this? Simple projections of present trends point to an eventual doomsday when rising population overtakes our limited resources. But such projections are oversimplified, because they do not allow for the adjustments that will take place as resources become scarce. One of the most important kinds of adjustment is this: As a resource becomes more scarce, it becomes more expensive; this, in turn, leads to (1) a substitution in production for the scarce resource by other factors that are more plentiful, (2) a substitution in consumption by goods that require less of the scarce resource, (3) induced innovation that economizes on these resources, and (4) a reduction in the rate of growth of population because raising children becomes costly as the price of resources rise. Some have criticized this last point by noting that in the less developed countries, population growth has continued even though most parents can't afford to have children. However, the experience of these countries can be explained by three special factors: (1) Poverty is so severe that people have children to provide them with support in their old age, (2) there are religious and social objections in these countries to birth control, and (3) their recent population growth is not just a reflection of birth rates, but also of falling *death* rates, due to dramatic advances in medical services; however, falling death rates cannot continue to have the impact on population that they have had in the past.

In addition to the question of whether our future growth will be severely restricted by resource scarcity (as the doomsday models predict) or whether growth can continue because adjustment mechanisms work well, there is another overriding question: Do we really want substantial economic growth? The traditional argument in favour of growth is that it helps to relieve unemployment, reduce poverty, and raise our incomes and those of our children. However, a number of arguments have recently been put forward *against* continued growth. For example, it has been pointed out that growth contributes to pollution and depletes our natural resources. The main difficulty with such anti-growth arguments is that restricting growth is not the best way to attack these problems. Much more progress is possible if we design policies—such as taxes on polluters or on those firms extracting resources—that deal directly and specifically with each of these problems. In the case of resources, it is important to ensure that they are being priced high enough to provide adequate conservation.

Oil

Recently, this resource has been priced well above the requirements of conservation. Under the influence of OPEC—and in particular, the Saudi Arabians—the world price of oil rose over tenfold between 1973 and 1982. To provide some relief to oil users, the government instituted a policy of holding the domestic Canadian price down below the rapidly escalating world price. Full detail on the effects of this price ceiling—and the problems it raised—cannot be provided without a diagram, and you should be sure you have mastered Figure 29-6 in the text before proceeding. However, two of the broad effects of such a price ceiling can be sketched out:

1. There were winners and losers. The winners were oil users—from Sunday drivers to power-generating companies and their customers—who benefited because the price of oil was kept down. However, this lower price hurt oil producers in Canada, as well as the governments in the producing provinces whose royalty revenues were reduced.

2. There were two efficiency losses, shown by the two shaded triangles in Figure 29-6 in the textbook. The first arose because the low price encouraged oil consumption, while the second arose because the low price discouraged domestic oil production.

To reduce the negative effects on production, the government added a twist to this policy and thus created a "blended price system." Under this system, the price of "new" currently produced oil was not kept down. It was allowed to rise to the world price. Thus, domestic production of oil would not, it was hoped, be discouraged after all. On the other hand, the price of "old" oil (that was already being produced, and would continue to be produced almost regardless of price) was still kept low. Finally, the price that oil buyers paid was a "blended" average of these various prices (including, in addition, the high world price of imported oil). Because Canadian oil users were paying the average of what these various kinds of oil cost, it was not necessary for the government to provide any subsidy of the kind typically required by a price-control policy.

Unfortunately, however, it was an imperfect solution. Because it did not allow the domestic price paid by oil users to rise to the world price, Canadian consumption and, hence, imports of oil continued at a relatively high level. Furthermore, the system with different producer prices for new and old oil was difficult to administer because new and old oil cannot be physically distinguished.

In the mid-1980s, the control system was gradually dismantled, and following the decline in world oil prices in 1986, the gap between the world price and the domestic Canadian price essentially disappeared.

IMPORTANT TERMS: MATCH THE COLUMNS

Match each term in the first column with the corresponding phrase in the second column. But before you do so, write your own definition of each term in the first column.

_____ **1.** reservation price
_____ **2.** sustainable yield curve
_____ **3.** maximum sustainable yield
_____ **4.** induced innovation
_____ **5.** renewable resource
_____ **6.** OPEC
_____ **7.** blended price

a. the average of the low price of old oil and the higher price of imported and new oil

b. the curve relating the annual increase in a renewable resource (such as fish) to its population size (For any given population, this curve indicates the amount that can be extracted and still leave the population size constant.)

c. the international cartel formed in 1965 that raised the world price of oil by more than 10 times between 1973 and 1982

d. the largest value on the sustainable yield curve (This is the largest amount of a renewable resource that can be extracted each year without reducing the population size.)

e. the marginal cost of providing a resource. (It includes (1) the cost of harvesting or extraction and (2) the amount necessary to compensate for the reduction in the resources available in the future.)

f. the result when people turn their minds to finding substitutes for increasingly expensive resources

g. a resource that reproduces itself naturally (such as fish) or that reproduces itself with human assistance (such as timber)

TRUE-FALSE

T F 1. Under perfect competition, the rate of extraction of a privately owned resource is generally greater than the efficient rate.

T F 2. Those harvesting a common-property resource take into account only the harvesting cost—not the cost to society of having less of this resource available in the future.

T F 3. For a common-property resource, supply is determined by the marginal extraction cost only.

T F 4. A competitive equilibrium in the market for a privately owned natural resource is generally inefficient.

T F 5. If it were possible to tax those who fish for each fish caught, then in theory it would be possible to eliminate the efficiency loss that results because the oceans are not privately owned.

T F 6. An open border to fishermen from foreign countries would make the harvesting of fish more efficient, just as a border open to imports of foreign goods makes production within a country more efficient.

T F 7. Allowing the domestic price of oil to rise to the world price makes us more dependent on foreign supplies.

T F 8. A case can be made for keeping the Canadian domestic oil price at or below the world price, but no case can be made for keeping it higher.

MULTIPLE CHOICE

1. In a perfectly competitive market, the last unit of privately owned resource will be sold for
- **a.** more than its reservation price
- **b.** less than its reservation price
- **c.** its reservation price
- **d.** more than its conservation price
- **e.** less than its conservation price

2. The height of the supply curve for a common-property resource reflects
- **a.** the extraction cost
- **b.** compensation for the reduced amount available in the future
- **c.** the extraction cost less compensation for the reduced amount available in the future
- **d.** the extraction cost plus compensation for the reduced amount available in the future
- **e.** the extraction cost or compensation for the reduced amount available in the future, whichever is larger

3. Which of the following is a common-property resource?
- **a.** fish
- **b.** timber on privately owned land
- **c.** an oil company's reserves
- **d.** coal
- **e.** copper

4. In analysing resource use, the term "reservation price" means
- **a.** the lowest bid a buyer will make in an auction
- **b.** the highest bid a buyer will pay in an auction
- **c.** the cost of harvesting or extracting a resource today
- **d.** the amount necessary to compensate for the reduced availability of the resource in the future
- **e.** (c) plus (d)

5. The reservation price of a resource will decrease if
- **a.** the expected future cost of extracting the resource rises
- **b.** the expected future price of the resource rises
- **c.** the expected future price of the resource remains constant
- **d.** auction prices have remained constant
- **e.** auction prices have been rising

6. The creation of private property rights over what was previously a common-property resource
- **a.** is not legal for the government to do
- **b.** would increase the efficiency of the extraction of the resource
- **c.** would decrease the efficiency of the extraction of the resource
- **d.** would have no effect on the extraction of the resource
- **e.** would freeze in the previous level of inefficiency in the extraction of the resource

7. The problem with doomsday models (that is, models that predict disaster because a growing population runs out of resources) is that typically
- **a.** they are based on the assumption that current trends will continue long into the future
- **b.** they do not account adequately for the adjustments that will occur as resources become scarcer
- **c.** they do not account adequately for changing patterns of population growth as the population becomes larger
- **d.** all of the above
- **e.** none of the above

8. Which of the following is an argument commonly used in favour of economic growth?
- **a.** Unemployment is likely to be less severe in a rapidly growing economy.
- **b.** Faster economic growth helps to economize on scarce natural resources.
- **c.** Growth reduces pollution.
- **d.** Growth is necessary; otherwise our children will run out of natural resources.
- **e.** Growth reduces congestion.

9. Which of the following is most important in explaining the increase in population in most less developed countries?

a. the increase in the stock of natural resources relative to the labour force
b. constant wages
c. a change in the resource/capital ratio
d. increasing wealth
e. advances in medicine that have reduced the death rate

10. Between 1973 and 1982, the world price of oil rose from
a. less than $3 a barrel to $13 a barrel
b. less than $3 a barrel to $23 a barrel
c. less than $3 a barrel to over $30 a barrel
d. $13 a barrel to $23 a barrel
e. $13 a barrel to over $30 a barrel

11. The rapid increase in the price of oil in the 1970s
a. could be fully justified as a conservation measure
b. could be partly justified as a conservation measure, but also reflected the exercise of monopoly power
c. could not be justified, even in part, as a conservation measure
d. represented a transfer from OPEC countries to oil importing countries
e. discouraged conservation efforts

12. Which of the following measures adopted during the 1970s did *not* encourage the conservation of oil?
a. Pollution-control standards on cars sold in Canada
b. improved gas mileage requirements on North American manufactured cars
c. subsidization of home insulation
d. reduced speed limits on highways
e. lower consumer prices for natural gas

13. Keeping the domestic price of oil below the world price
a. encouraged production and consumption
b. discouraged production and consumption
c. discouraged consumption and encouraged production
d. encouraged consumption and discouraged production
e. encouraged consumption, but had no effect on production

14. Under the "blended oil price" policy of the 1970s and early 1980s, which was highest?
a. the price received by sellers of old oil
b. the price received by sellers of new oil
c. the price paid by buyers of new oil
d. none of the above because these prices were all the same
e. the policy was so confused that there was no way of telling

15. The impact of the large increase in world energy prices in the 1970s on Canada as a whole
a. was harmful because it reduced worldwide energy consumption, and Canada is a net energy exporter
b. was less harmful because many oil producing firms in Canada are foreign-owned
c. was negligible because the government decided to keep the domestic oil price lower than the world price
d. was negligible because it only affected oil from the Middle East and most of Canada's oil imports come from Mexico and Venezuela
e. was most likely a small net gain

16. Before the mid-1980s, controls kept the domestic price very low on
a. new oil
b. old oil
c. both new and old oil
d. neither new nor old oil
e. oil whose age could not be determined

17. Which of the following contributed to the slowdown of the nuclear power industry in the 1970s?
a. concern over how to dispose of radioactive wastes
b. concern over the possible proliferation of nuclear weapons
c. the fear of accidents, such as the one at Three Mile Island
d. higher-than-expected plant costs
e. all of the above

EXERCISES

1a. Figure 29-1 depicts a perfectly competitive market for a natural resource. The demand curve is *D*, the marginal cost of extraction is the height of the curve labelled *S*, and the reservation price is the height of the curve labelled *S'*. The socially efficient quantity (assuming no external benefits) is ____________, and this quantity will be demanded if the price is ____________. If the resource is privately owned, the price will be ____________, the quantity extracted will be ____________, and the size of the efficiency loss will be ____________.

1b. If the resource is not privately owned, the price will be ____________, the quantity extracted will be ____________, and the size of the efficiency loss will be ____________. The efficiency loss could be eliminated by a [tax, subsidy] on extraction equal to ____________ per unit.

2a. In Figure 29-2, D represents the demand curve for a common-property resource sold in a perfectly competitive market. The internal cost of extracting this resource is the height of S, while the external cost is the vertical distance between *S* and *S'*. The equilibrium price is ____________, and quantity extracted is ____________. The efficiency loss is ____________, because the efficiency equilibrium is at point ____________, where price is ____________ and the quantity extracted is ____________.

2b. Now suppose that the resource is given to a monopoly. Its marginal revenue will be the line ____________; it will extract a quantity equal to ____________, and set a price equal to ____________. The size of the efficiency loss will be ____________. Since

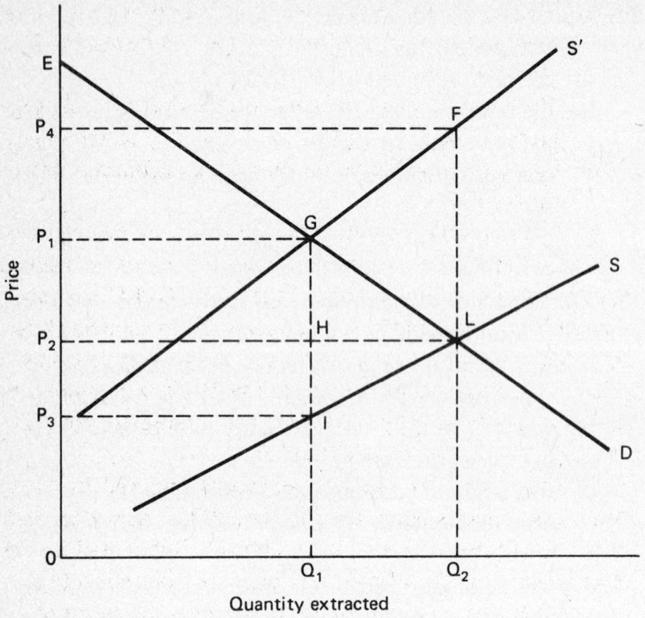

FIGURE 29-1

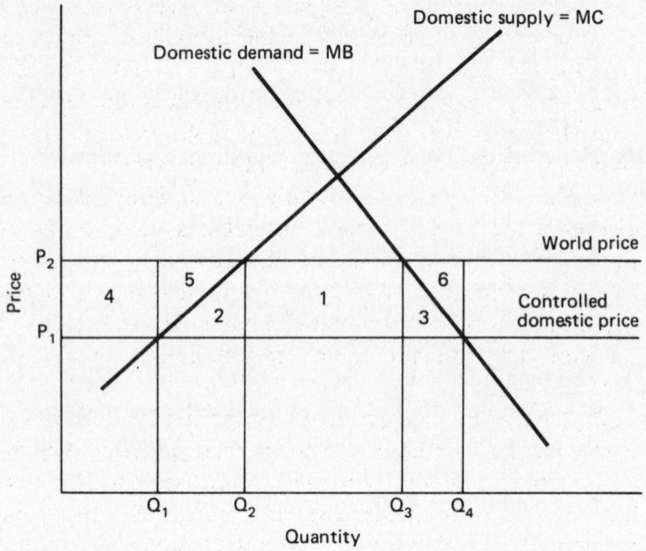

FIGURE 29-3

this efficiency loss is [greater than, less than] the original efficiency loss ____________, it means that monopolizing this industry has [increased, reduced] efficiency. The reason is that the efficiency loss from monopoly is, in this case, more than offset by the efficiency gain that results from changing the sources from [public to private, private to public] ownership.

This is one example of a "conserving monopolist" who increases efficiency. However, a conserving monopolist may *reduce* efficiency. To illustrate, redraw this diagram so that the efficiency loss under the monopoly is greater than the original efficiency loss. (Hint: Make the demand curve less elastic. Also draw S' closer to S; this reduces the advantage of private ownership.)

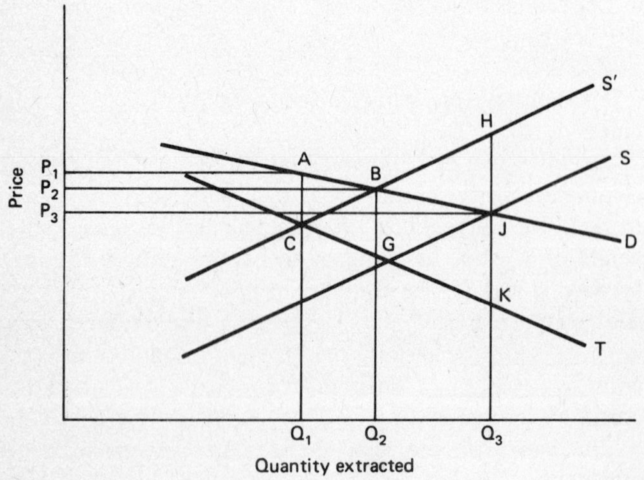

FIGURE 29-2

3a. In Figure 29-3, a controlled price of P_1 is imposed on the domestic oil market. Domestic production is ____________, consumption is ____________, and [exports, imports] are ____________. Because importers have to buy oil at the high world price P_2 and sell it domestically for only P_1, the government must compensate them by paying them a subsidy of ____________ per barrel, times the ____________ barrels they are importing, for a total government subsidy payment of area ____________.

3b. When this price control is removed, price becomes ____________, domestic production [increases, decreases] to ____________, and domestic consumption [increases, decreases] to ____________. [Imports, Exports] consequently [increase, decrease] to ____________. Consumers [gain, lose] area ____________, while producers [gain, lose] area ____________, and the government [gains, loses] area ____________, the [subsidy, tax] it no longer has to [pay, impose].

3c. When all these gains and losses are taken into account, the *net* [gain, loss] from decontrolling price is ____________. This can be broken down into its two components: (1) The efficiency gain of area ____________, because consumers are no longer buying oil they value at less than its true cost (the world price), and (2) the efficiency gain of area ____________, because domestic firms are now producing oil for less than it previously cost to import. At the same time, there has been a transfer from consumers to ____________ and ____________.

ESSAY QUESTIONS

1. Explain how the problem of an excessive use of a common-property resource is similar to the problem of environmental pollution. To deal with each of these problems, the government sometimes considers quantity restraints. Explain why you think these policies are effective or ineffective in dealing with each of these problems.

2. How does private ownership help to eliminate the inefficiency that exists when a resource is publicly owned (common property)? Would inefficiency be eliminated just as well if ownership were given to a single owner who then had a monopoly? What new problems might be created by allowing the resource to be monopolized? (Hint: See exercise 2 above.)

3. "One of the shortcomings of the market mechanism is that private business interests are concerned, not with the future, but instead with how much profit they can earn right now. We need the government to regulate the rate of extraction of natural resources to protect future generations from being deprived of their rightful share of resources." Do you agree or disagree? Why?

4. (This problem is based on Box 29-1 in the textbook.) "If the population of a species is initially greater than the point of maximum sustainable yield and if firms are now harvesting at a rate just large enough to maintain a constant size of population, then by increasing the rate of extraction they can harvest more now and more in the future." Explain this statement, using a diagram similar to Figure 29-2 in the textbook. If the cost of extraction is zero, what is the opportunity cost of raising the rate of extraction in this situation? Is this a case of being able to get something for nothing?

5. Suppose that scientists working on nuclear fusion make a major breakthrough which means that the economic break-even point in fusion energy will be reached by 1990.

a. What would you expect the effects (if any) to be on the world price of oil (1) now and (2) in 1990?

b. What would you expect the effect (if any) to be on the Canadian price of natural gas (1) now and (2) in 1990?

c. How would your answers to question (a) change if the discoveries will lead in 1990 only to the energy break-even point, rather than to the economic break-even point?

6. "It is not fair for the oil companies to make excess profits on the oil they produce and sell to us in Canada simply because halfway around the globe OPEC has raised the world price. Companies producing oil in Canada should be forced to sell us the oil we need at a more reasonable price." Which Canadian policy in the 1970s was guided by this sort of philosophy? Does it make sense to you? Did this policy create problems? Explain.

7. The strict auto emission standards imposed by North American governments during the 1970s achieved their primary purpose of reducing pollution. But it had an unfavourable side effect because it increased our consumption of gasoline and this damaged our attempts to conserve oil. Could the benefits of reduced pollution have been achieved without damaging the conservation effort if a policy of a higher oil price had been implemented instead? Explain.

8. "The reason for keeping the domestic price of oil below the world price in the 1970s was to avoid certain adverse transfer effects. However, the low-price policy gave rise to a complicated set of adverse efficiency effects that proved difficult to deal with. A better policy would have been to let the domestic price rise, and then deal directly with the transfer effects through other policies." Discuss this statement, with particular reference to what these other policies could have been, and how they would have affected federal-provincial relations.

9. Explain some of the external costs of producing and using oil. In your view, how do these costs compare with those arising from the production and use of natural gas? of coal? of nuclear fission?

ANSWERS

Important Terms: **1** e **2** b **3** d **4** f **5** g **6** c **7** a

True-False: **1** F **2** T **3** T **4** F **5** T **6** F **7** F **8** F

Multiple Choice: **1** c **2** a **3** a **4** e **5** a **6** b **7** d **8** a **9** e **10** c **11** b **12** a **13** d **14** b **15** e **16** b **17** e

Exercises: **1a.** Q_1, P_1, P_1, Q_1, zero. **1b.** P_2, Q_2, *GIL*, tax, P_1P_3. **2a.** P_3, Q_3, *HBJ*, *B*, P_2, Q_2. **2b.** *T*, Q_1, P_1, *ABC*, less than, *HBJ*, increased, public to private. **3a.** Q_1, Q_4, imports, Q_1Q_4, P_1P_2, Q_1Q_4, 5 + 2 + 1 + 3 + 6. **3b.** P_2, increases, Q_2, decreases, Q_3, imports, decrease, Q_2Q_3, lose, 4 + 5 + 2 + 1 + 3, gain, 4 + 5, gains, 5 + 2 + 1 + 3 + 6, subsidy, pay. **3c.** gain, 5 + 6, 6, 5, producers, the government

Across

1, 4. If a pasture or fishing area is owned in this manner, it may be overused.
8. partway open
10. Roman emperor who sometimes played music.
11. a common type of harmful externality
12. An emission fee is one way to protect our __________.
13. may be hard to get out of if you get into one
15. animal doctor (abbrev.)
16. The __________ yield is the amount of a renewable resource that can be harvested while still leaving the population constant.
18. One way to reduce pollution is to __________ waste.
20. exist
22. thing (Latin)
24. pig's home
26. famous Canadian hockey player
27. The efficient output occurs where the __________ social cost and social benefit are the same.
28. illegal organization in the United Kingdom (abbrev.)
30. When you pick it up, you pay.
31. what a doctor, lawyer, or teacher provides
35. is honked to give warning
36. leave out
38. rub out
41. what we will have to find if a natural resource runs out
43. be annoyed about
44. Blomqvist, Wonnacott, and Wonnacott, *Economics*

Down

1. High prices encourage people to __________ scarce raw materials.
2. If people suffer from this, they may use up scarce resources too quickly.
3. to constantly complain and criticize
4. The creation of __________ __________ is one way to discourage the overuse of a scarce resource.
5. what Petro-Canada hopes for when it drills in the Beaufort Sea
6. Overfishing today creates an __________ cost, which will be faced by future fishermen.
7. tasty fish
9. major chain of food stores (abbrev.)
14. Resources such as fish or timber, but not oil, are __________.
16. Private cost plus external cost equals __________ __________. (2 words)
17. in games of cards, may be high or low
19. Trial and __________ is often a hard way to learn.
21. At work you get your orders from this person.
24. Our __________ is sometimes called "spaceship earth."
25. substance used as an ingredient in fertilizer
29. sun god in ancient Egypt
32. one of the Great Lakes
33. see (Latin)
34. Australian bird
37. leading company in the computer business
39. We told you in 13 across not to get into one!
40. One is sometimes called fair.
42. opposite of out

Chapter 30

PUBLIC GOODS: WHAT SHOULD THE GOVERNMENT PROVIDE?

MAJOR PURPOSE

The last chapter dealt with external costs. In this chapter we use a parallel approach to analyse external benefits—that is, the benefits of a product that are enjoyed by others, above and beyond the internal benefits enjoyed by those who buy it. When external benefits exist, a free perfectly competitive market does not produce an efficient outcome. There is too little free-market production of such a good, just as there was too much production of a good with an external cost in the last chapter. The solution is to subsidize the good with the external benefits, just as the good with external costs was taxed in the last chapter.

A further objective of this chapter is to extend this analysis of external benefits to describe the concept of a public good. A flood-control dam is an example of a public good, because *no one* can be excluded from enjoying its benefits, regardless of who pays for it. Typically, with such a broad distribution of benefits, there are no specific individuals who play a significant enough role as users to be prepared to buy the good. So if it is to be provided at all, the government must purchase it. In this chapter, we describe the difficulties a government faces in trying to decide whether or not such a purchase is justified; and we also describe the more general problems that arise whenever the government provides the public with any good or service. Even when the private market fails, and a good must be provided by the government (if it is to be supplied at all), problems remain.

LEARNING OBJECTIVES

After you have studied this chapter in the textbook and the study guide, you should be able to

- Demonstrate why a free, perfectly competitive market provides less than the efficient amount of a good with external benefits
- Measure, in a diagram like Figure 30-1 in the textbook, the efficiency loss resulting from the private provision of a good with external benefits
- Show why efficiency requires a good to be subsidized by an amount equal to the marginal external benefit it provides (assuming that there are not high costs of administering the subsidy)
- Define and explain the concept of a public good
- Construct the marginal social benefit curve (1) for a public good and (2) for a private good, making clear the difference between the two
- Explain why the "free-rider" problem makes it difficult for the government to estimate the benefits of a public good simply by asking people how highly they value it
- Give the reasons for believing that when the government provides a good or service—whether or not this is in response to a failure by the free-market—major problems remain, such as the problems of bureaucracy; efficiency is still not guaranteed
- Show why it may be necessary to view as a public good any wildlife species that is becoming extinct
- Explain the concept of "option demand" and demonstrate its significance in dealing with such a wildlife species

HIGHLIGHTS OF THE CHAPTER

Why is there too little production of a good with an external benefit?

The Inefficiency of a Private Market When There Are External Benefits

A free, perfectly competitive market fails to produce enough of a product with an external benefit because the marginal cost of the product is equated to its marginal *private* benefit, rather than to its marginal *social* benefit. The reason is that, in deciding on their demand for the product, buyers look only at the *private* benefit it will provide them, and ignore the *external* benefit it will provide to others. With some of the benefit of the product thus being ignored, it is no surprise that too little is produced, as Figure 30-1 demonstrates. The appropriate government policy is to subsidize this product by the amount of the external benefit it provides (assuming there are not substantial costs in administering the subsidy). Such a subsidy will increase the demand for the product and thus increase its output to the efficient amount.

Public Goods

In the case of the products with an external benefit that we have been describing so far—such as gardening—you will receive an external benefit if your neighbour pays $100 for gardening services. But, of course, you will get an even larger benefit if you pay the $100 to have the gardening done on your lawn rather than on your neighbour's. Thus, the benefits you get depend on who pays. A public good can be viewed as the extreme case of a good with an external benefit—where the amount of benefit that an individual gets is just as great if someone else buys it as it is if he or she were to buy it. In other words, the individual cannot be excluded in any way from enjoying it. For example, you get the same benefit from cleaner air, whether or not you help to pay for antipollution measures. That is not true of a private good. You can't enjoy a movie or a restaurant meal unless you pay for it. This is the reason why the benefits of a private good are *horizontally* summed in Figure 30-2 in the textbook, while the benefits of a public good are *vertically* summed in Figure 30-3.

The Free-Rider Problem

If you will get the same benefit whether or not you help pay for a good, why not be a "free rider" and not pay at all (or pay as small a share as you can get away with)? The incentive for people to ride free raises problems for an entrepreneur who believes (let's suppose correctly) that the benefits people would get from a public good—such as a flood-control dam—exceed its costs and it therefore should be built. How can it be financed when everyone the entrepreneur asks to contribute to it tries to minimize that contribution understating the benefits the dam would provide? In short, each individual has an incentive to be a free rider, enjoying the benefits of the dam without contributing to it. Since all individuals have this incentive to understate the benefits of the dam, it appears not to be justified, and does not get built.

Suppose the government, rather than a private entrepreneur, tries to evaluate the dam by asking people how highly they would value it. If they think they will be taxed according to their answer, they will understate. On the other hand, if they think their taxes won't be affected by the project, they will tend to *overstate* their benefit—as a means of slightly increasing the chances that the project will be undertaken. In this case, they have nothing to lose, since the cost *they* incur is not affected by their overevaluation.

An Alternative Approach by the Government

In view of the difficulties in trying to get people to answer accurately, the authorities generally reject the approach of asking people for their evaluation of a project. Instead they often use a "benefit-cost analysis based on a completely different kind of information. To use the example in the text, they may estimate the benefit of a dam by examining how frequently floods have occurred without it, and the average crop loss. This approach may be superior, but it still involves major problems. For example, those who are running this analysis may have a vested interest in having the dam pass the benefit-cost test because they may hope to be employed in its construction. Or they may simply be trying to please their employer—a government that has promised this dam in the last election. They may therefore add benefits—perhaps at an inflated value—until these benefits exceed the costs, and the project is justified. Such an inflation of benefits may be easy, especially if one of the benefits of a flood-control project is to save lives. It is very difficult indeed to attach a dollar value to a human life. (Recall our discussion in Box 27-5 in the textbook.)

Other Problems with Government Expenditure Decisions

More generally, when decision making shifts from the private marketplace to the government—as indeed it must in the case of a public good which the private market fails to deliver—then a new set of special problems arises:

1. Typically, private firms stop producing goods if they are no longer profitable—or if they fail outright from the start—because these firms would lose money otherwise. On the other hand, government projects that are no longer justified are much more difficult to terminate for two reasons: (a) No politician wants to admit that a project may have been a mistake, for fear of losing the next election as a result and (b) there is no natural check, like the bankruptcy of a private firm, to force termination of a government project.

2. Political votes are not as specific and frequent as the economic votes that people cast every day when they are deciding what to buy with their money. Thus, private auto companies get a clear message of the models the public wants and does not want. Not so with public goods. It may be as long as five years before the next election when the public can vote on how it likes or dislikes the dam and the other goods and services the government is providing. And even if people do approve of what the government is doing —and vote for it in the next election—it's hard to know whether the election victory is due to the dam the government has built or to its health care policy or to some other completely different issue. (Public opinion polls make this problem less severe, but don't remove it.)

3. Special interest groups can exert an inordinate influence on government decision making. If you have no particular interest in a dam in northern Quebec, it probably doesn't pay you to oppose it, since it may add only a trivial 10 cents to your tax bill. But those directly affected in the area have a strong incentive to support it and lobby for its construction. Thus, a few large benefits concentrated in one area may *politically* outweigh many small, widely dispersed costs, even if the sum of all these small costs exceeds the benefits *economically*.

4. Politicians are mainly interested in projects with benefits that are obvious to the public and immediate. (If they don't have a payoff before the next election, it may be too late.) Thus politicians often do not take a long-term point of view; there is a tendency for much government effort to be centred on short-term decision making.

5. The job of implementing—and sometimes initiating —government policies is performed by a bureaucracy. There is a constant tendency for bureaus and their budgets to expand, in part because of the incentives for bureau chiefs to expand their personnel. Accordingly, bureaus tend to grow beyond the efficient size. This tendency is not checked by the threat of economic loss or bankruptcy that faces a private firm that overexpands.

IMPORTANT TERMS: MATCH THE COLUMNS

Match each term in the first column with the corresponding phrase in the second column. But before you do so, write your own definition of each term in the first column.

_____ **1.** external (spillover) benefit
_____ **2.** public good
_____ **3.** internal private benefits
_____ **4.** benefit-cost analysis
_____ **5.** option demand
_____ **6.** free riders
_____ **7.** internalizing an externality

a. a good whose benefits are available to everyone, regardless of who pays for it

b. forcing firms or individuals to face the external costs or benefits they are creating

c. the estimation of the dollar value of the costs and benefits that are likely to result from a particular government policy

d. those who cannot be excluded from the benefits of a public good, even though they do not pay their share of its costs

e. the benefit derived from a good by those who do not buy it

f. the desire to have something, not because we want to enjoy it today, but because we may want to enjoy it in the future (This appears to be the nature of the demand for some public goods, such as the preservation of a particular wildlife species.)

g. the benefits from a good derived by the purchaser (These are usually the only benefits that are considered by households and firms in making their purchasing decisions.)

TRUE-FALSE

T F 1. Internalizing externalities means that producers are forced to face any external costs of their actions; and buyers are allowed to enjoy any external benefits generated by their purchases.

T F 2. One benefit of having the government provide public goods such as flood control dams is that these decisions are easily reversible.

T F 3. The reason why private firms can't be relied on to produce a public good is that they would externalize the internal benefits.

T F 4. The marginal social benefit curve of a public good can be contructed by vertically summing the individual demand curves.

T F 5. You cannot be excluded from enjoying the benefits of a public good even if someone else pays for it.

T F 6. It is generally more difficult to cut out an expenditure program in the private than in the public sector.

T F 7. The public can be more specific in expressing its preferences for goods by voting in elections than by making purchases in the marketplace.

T F 8. It may make sense to vote for a party that has promised to make a certain government expenditure, even though you don't want this expenditure at all.

T F 9. Politicians prefer policies with costs that are obvious and benefits that are obscure.

T F 10. Government policy should ensure that no damage whatsoever occurs to the environment.

MULTIPLE CHOICE

1. In producing two goods (one with an external benefit, the other with an external cost) a free, perfectly competitive market will generate
- **a.** too much output of the good with the external benefit and too little of the good with the external cost
- **b.** too little output of the good with the external benefit and too much of the good with the external cost
- **c.** too little output of the good with the external benefit and just the right amount of the good with the external cost
- **d.** too little of both
- **e.** too much of both

2. Which of the following comes closest to being a private good with no external benefits?
- **a.** national defence
- **b.** painting the outside of your house
- **c.** painting the inside of your house
- **d.** hiring a gardener
- **e.** the police force

3. If the government follows a "hands-off" policy, then the production of a perfectly competitive good with an external benefit will result in
- **a.** marginal external benefit being greater than marginal social benefit
- **b.** marginal external benefit being equal to marginal social benefit
- **c.** marginal social cost being equal to marginal social benefit
- **d.** marginal social cost being greater than marginal social benefit
- **e.** marginal social cost being less than marginal social benefit

4. If a good has an external benefit, the government can ensure an efficient outcome by imposing a
- **a.** tax equal to the external benefit
- **b.** tax greater than the external benefit
- **c.** subsidy equal to the external benefit
- **d.** subsidy less than the external benefit
- **e.** subsidy greater than the external benefit

5. If there are substantial administrative costs in subsidizing a good with an external benefit, the government should
- **a.** tax it instead, to provide the same result
- **b.** subsidize the good regardless
- **c.** cancel the subsidy regardless
- **d.** cancel the subsidy if the efficiency gain it would produce is less than the administrative costs
- **e.** cancel the subsidy if the efficiency gain it would produce is greater than the administrative costs

6. The internal benefit of a good is the
- **a.** benefit enjoyed by those who haven't purchased it
- **b.** benefit enjoyed by the individual who has purchased it
- **c.** benefit enjoyed by free riders
- **d.** benefit enjoyed by the government, even though the public has purchased it
- **e.** benefit enjoyed by the public, even though the government has purchased it

7. An example of internalizing an externality occurs when
- **a.** a firm building a ski lift buys a restaurant at the bottom of the hill
- **b.** a firm buys from a domestic supplier a good that it used to buy from a foreign supplier
- **c.** a city government subsidizes exterior home improvements
- **d.** (a) and (c)

e. (b) and (c)

8. In defining the marginal benefit to society of a public good

a. the demand curves by individuals are horizontally summed

b. the demand curves by individuals are vertically summed

c. the demand curves by individuals are horizontally summed and then vertically summed

d. we use the same technique that was used to derive the market demand curve for a private good from the individual demand curves

e. we take the demand curve of the individual who is most eager and able to buy the good

9. With a public good,

a. anyone can participate in the benefits except the actual purchaser

b. everyone can participate in the benefits including the actual purchaser

c. no one participates in the benefits except the purchaser

d. only free riders participate in the benefits

e. free riders are prevented from participating in the benefits

10. Estimates the government collects from individuals on how highly they value public projects tend to be unreliable because

a. if people feel they will be taxed according to the value they state, they will tend to understate

b. if people feel they will be taxed according to the value they state, they will tend to overstate

c. if people feel they will not be taxed according to the value they state, they will tend to overstate

d. if people feel they will not be taxed according to the value they state, they will tend to understate

e. (a) and (c)

11. A free-rider is someone

a. who cannot be excluded from enjoying the benefits of a project even though this individual has paid nothing to cover its costs

b. who is trying to encourage the government to continue its transportation subsidies

c. who can be excluded from enjoying the benefits of a project

d. who is trying to discourage the government from continuing its transportation subsidies

e. who has paid more than a fair share of the costs

12. Benefit-cost analysis often involves the following problem:

a. questionable projects that have been promised in an election campaign may be justified by exaggerating benefits

b. questionable projects that have been promised in an election campaign may be justified by underestimating costs

c. it is very difficult to place a value on a human life

d. projects may be evaluated by those with a conflict of interest—for example, engineers who may eventually be employed in building the projects

e. all of the above

13. Typically, a government bureau that is a monopoly will produce

a. too much output, while a private monopoly will produce too little

b. too little output, just like a private monopoly

c. too much output, just like a private monopoly

d. the right amount of output, while a private monopoly will produce too little

e. too little output, just like a private oligopoly

14. A species of wildlife in the wilderness

a. cannot die out unless it is adversely affected by human action

b. will die out if it is left unprotected

c. may die out if it is left unprotected

d. will be prevented from dying out by free-market forces

e. should not be protected by the government because of option demand

EXERCISES

1. Figure 30-1 shows the supply curve *S* and demand curve *D* for a perfectly competitive good that provides external benefits. Assume for now that there are no external costs of producing this good, and ignore MC_S.

a. In an unregulated market, the quantity that is produced is ___________, and the market price is ___________. If the marginal social benefit curve is MB_S, then the economically efficient quantity is ___________, and the marginal external benefit is ___________.

b. The efficiency loss from relying upon the private market for the provision of this good is ___________. The government could eliminate this efficiency loss by ordering a per unit [subsidy, tax] of ___________ to the producers of this good.

c. Now suppose that the good involves external costs as well as external benefits. Let the curve labelled MC_S represent the marginal social cost of producing the good. Then the efficient amount of production of the good is ___________. At that level of production, the marginal external cost would be ___________, and the marginal external benefit would be ___________. With no tax or subsidy, the private market would produce [more, less] than the economically efficient amount, and the efficiency loss would be ___________. This efficiency loss could be eliminated if the government were to [tax, subsidize] the production of the good by

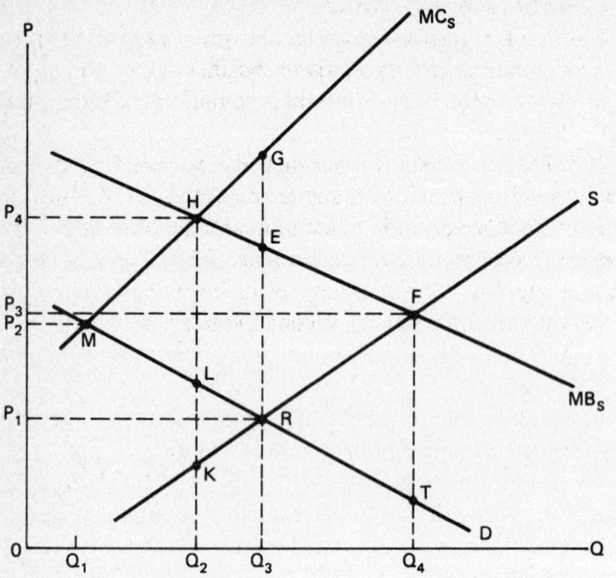

FIGURE 30-1

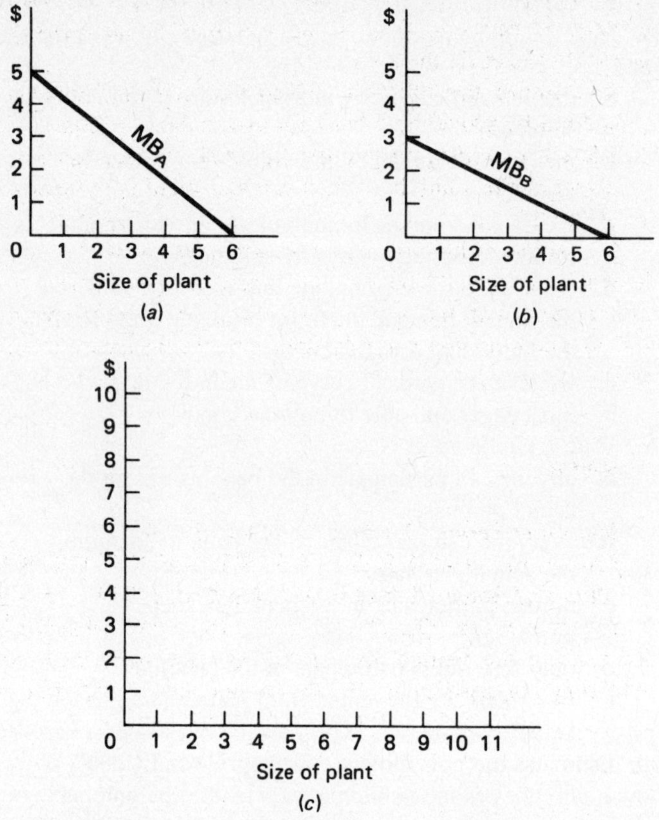

FIGURE 30-2

___________ per unit.

2. Figure 30-2 shows the marginal private benefit MB_A and MB_B that individuals A and B receive from a public good (a waste treatment plant). In Figure 30-2(*c*) show the marginal social benefit, assuming that A and B are the only members of the society affected by the project.

3a. Suppose that there are 1,000 farmers affected by a proposed dam. Each of them would receive a benefit of $1,000. The social benefit of the dam is $___________. If the dam costs $500,000 it [is, is not] worth building.

3b. Suppose you are one of the farmers. The government tells you that it intends to tax farmers according to how much each says the dam will be worth to him or her. If you tell the truth, it will cost you $___________. If you say $2,000 it will cost you $___________. If you say no benefit it will cost you $___________. You will have an incentive to [understate, overstate, reveal accurately] how much it is worth to you. Other farmers [will, will not] have the same incentive to provide this sort of answer, so the dam [will certainly, may not] be built—an [efficient, inefficient] outcome.

3c. As another example, suppose that the same 1,000 farmers would get the same true benefits from the dam, but now suppose that the cost of building the dam is $1.5 million. In this case the dam should, should not] be built. But suppose that now the government says that if it goes ahead with the dam it will tax the millions of inhabitants of your province a few cents each to finance it. Your taxes will scarcely be affected. The only question the government has is, Should it go ahead or not? That depends on how highly farmers value it. If the government goes ahead, you will have a net gain (value to you of the dam minus your new taxes) of ___________. You will maximize your chances of getting this gain if you [understate, overstate, reveal accurately] your benefit, and thus [increase, decrease] the chance that the dam will be built. Other farmers [will, will not] have the same incentive to give the same sort of answer, so the dam [may, will certainly not] be built—an [efficient, inefficient] outcome.

ESSAY QUESTIONS

1. Explain carefully whether or not each of the following might be considered to be a good with an external benefit: (a) Canada's Olympic team, (b) your telephone, (c) driver safety lessons, and (d) television programs.

2. If you ask people to reveal how much they would benefit from a public good, will they be unlikely to tell the truth? If you ask them to reveal how much they are being damaged by a good with an external cost, will they tell you the truth? Why or why not? How will their answer be affected if you tell them that the government is thinking of providing them with protection from this external cost, with this protection to be financed out of the government's general tax revenues?

3. Many industries pay law firms and consultants ("lobbyists") to influence regulatory agencies, legislative committees, and other government agencies and officials in Ottawa and the provincial capitals. These lobbyists spend a lot of time promoting the idea that their industry is a source of external benefits. Why would the firms in an industry pay lobbyists to do this?

4. Criticize the following statement: "The government should not be providing money for vaccination programs. If people are unwilling to pay the full cost without subsidy, then vaccinations fail the market test and should not be provided at all."

5. Explain why you agree or disagree with the following statement: "You can rely upon the government to provide you with the goods you want at a reasonable price just as much as you can rely upon private business firms. The reason is that the party in power wants you to be pleased with what it provides so that you will vote for it in the next election, just as a private business firm wants you to be pleased with what it provides so that you will buy the product again."

6. It has been argued that when the government spends more money, it provides many benefits to a small number of people and a very small cost to a large number of people (namely taxpayers). Give an example. Why does a government judge that such a policy is in its interests? Will it necessarily be in the nation's economic interest?

ANSWERS

Important Terms: **1** e **2** a **3** g **4** c **5** f **6** d **7** b
True-False: **1** T **2** F **3** F **4** T **5** T **6** F **7** F **8** T **9** F **10** F
Multiple Choice: **1** b **2** c **3** e **4** c **5** d **6** b **7** d **8** b **9** b **10** e **11** a **12** e **13** a **14** c
Exercises: **1a.** Q_3, P_1, Q_4, *TF*. **1b.** *EFR*, subsidy, *TF*. **1c.** Q_2, *KH*, *LH*, more, *HGE*, tax, *LK*. **2.** a straight line intersecting the vertical axis at $8, and the horizontal axis at 6. **3a.** $1 million, is. **3b.** $1,000, $2,000, 0, understate, will, may not, inefficient. **3c.** should not, almost $1,000, overstate, increase, will, may, inefficient.

Chapter 31

WHAT ARE THE GAINS FROM INTERNATIONAL TRADE?

MAJOR PURPOSE

Canadians in British Columbia gain from *domestic* trade with other Canadians in Alberta and Quebec. Similarly, Canadians gain from *international* trade with the Japanese and Americans. The reasons are the same in either case. Our purpose in this chapter is to examine the gains from trade from three broad sources: (1) increased competition, (2) economies of scale, and (3) comparative advantage. This chapter analyses these three sources of gain in detail. It also identifies the winners and losers from trade. While winners outnumber losers and the nation as a whole benefits from trade, some people are hurt. Their ability to organize themselves and apply political pressure is one of the big reasons why countries maintain restrictions on trade—restrictions that will be examined in the next chapter.

LEARNING OBJECTIVES

After you have studied this chapter in the textbook and the study guide, you should be able to

- Identify the three main sources of gain from international trade
- Explain why trade increases competition in the Canadian domestic market and reduces the market power of Canadian producers, thus generating an efficiency gain
- Explain why trade makes possible cost reductions because it provides opportunities to exploit economies of scale, with the result that income is increased and a wider variety of new products is available
- Explain the difference between comparative advantage and absolute advantage
- Explain why countries export those commodities in which they have a comparative advantage, and how comparative advantage is determined by opportunity costs
- Explain the two respects in which international trade and technological change are similar, and the respects in which they are different
- Measure diagrammatically the gains from international trade using a production possibilities curve as in Figure 31-4 in the textbook, or alternatively, using the supply and demand diagrams shown in figures 31-6 and 31-7
- Show the gain from trade in a supply-demand diagram by comparing the effect of trade on consumers with its effect on producers
- Identify the winners and losers from international trade

HIGHLIGHTS OF THE CHAPTER

The two broad questions addressed in this chapter are, Why are there gains from trade? and Who are the winners and losers? First, consider why we gain from trade.

The Sources of Gain

Increased competition. For domestic producers, there are two dramatic changes when trade is opened up. First, they face a much larger market; they can now sell to people anywhere in the world. Second, they now face many more competitors. Canadian General Electric (CGE) no longer competes against Electrohome and other Canadian producers; it now also competes with an additional group of producers from Japan, the United States, and elsewhere. Because of increased competition, oligopolists such as CGE and Electrohome lose much of their market power—their ability to influence price. Thus, they move closer to perfect competition, with the increase in efficiency that this implies. Similarly, a Canadian monopolist may, as a result of trade, find itself an oligopolist, with several foreign competitors; this industry also moves closer to perfect competition.

Economies of scale. Without international trade, each country must be self-sufficient; it must therefore produce a wide variety of products in the small quantity necessary just to satisfy its own needs. With international trade, each country can specialize, producing only a few items in large volume and trading to get the rest. Often large volume means reduced cost ; that is, there are economies of scale. And reduced cost means that we can produce and therefore consume more. In other words, our real income rises. It also rises because other countries are specializing and reducing their costs. Thus, the products we trade for, as well as the goods we produce ourselves, fall in cost.

Not only are costs reduced; in addition, variety may be increased. For example, because of international trade, someone buying a car in the tiny European country of Liechtenstein can choose among Fords, Volkswagens, Datsuns, and many others that are produced elsewhere. Without international trade, consumers wouldn't have this choice. They would have to buy cars produced in Liechenstein. But the market there is so small (the population is less than 30,000), that they would be lucky to have even one auto firm producing one model. There would be little or no variety.

Comparative advantage. To understand comparative advantage, you must first understand absolute advantage. Table 31-3 in the textbook can be used to clarify the difference between the two. In the right-hand column of this table, we see that Canada has an absolute advantage in food because a Canadian worker can produce 3 units of food, whereas a worker in Britain can produce only 1. In other words, it only takes a third as many workers to produce food in Canada as in Britain. The *input requirement*—that is, the labour requirement—to produce food in Canada is lower than in Britain. (This is the definition of absolute advantage: a country has an absolute advantage in a good if the input requirement in that country is lower than that in other countries.)

Canada also has an absolute advantage in clothing. (A Canadian worker outproduces a British worker in clothing by 6 to 4, as shown in the first column of Table 31-3, just as a Canadian worker outproduces a British worker by 3 to 1 in food production.) Because Canada has an absolute advantage in producing both goods, absolute advantage cannot be the key to explaining which country will produce what. If it were the key, then Canada would produce both goods, and Britain neither—and that is inconsistent with the two-way trade we observe.

What, then, does determine the pattern of production and trade? The answer is: comparative advantage. But in which product does Canada have a comparative advantage? The answer is: food, because this is where Canada's absolute advantage is greater; a Canadian worker can outproduce a worker in Britain by 3 to 1 in food, but by only 6 to 4—that is, 3 to 2—in clothing. Because Canada has a comparative advantage in food, Britain has a comparative advantage in clothing; that's where Britain's absolute *dis*advantage is *least*.

Using a more formal definition, we say that Canada has a comparative advantage in food if is has a *lower opportunity cost* of producing food than Britain. This is indeed the case. In the second row of Table 31-3, we see the high opportunity cost of producing food in Britain. Since a worker who is now producing 1 unit of food could instead be producing 4 units of clothing, the opportunity cost (the alternative foregone) of producing that 1 unit of food is 4 units of clothing. Compare this to the lower opportunity cost of food in Canada, derived from the top row in this table: Since a Canadian worker who is now producing 3 units of food could instead be producing 6 units of clothing, the opportunity cost in Canada of each unit of food is 6/3 = 2 units of clothing. Because it has a lower opportunity cost of food than Britain, Canada has a comparative advantage in food, and will specialize in this. Similar calculations for clothing will show that Britain has a comparative advantage here. With specialization in their products of comparative advantage, Canada and Britain can enjoy an overall gain, as is demonstrated in the calculations at the bottom of this table.

To sum up: Both absolute and comparative advantage refer to the cost of production. The difference is in how this cost is measured. For absolute advantage, cost is measured in terms of *inputs required*. For comparative advantage, cost is measured in terms of *outputs foregone*, that is, opportunity cost.

Here's an intuitive approach that may help you to understand better the gains from trade. Trade is the way a country can inexpensively acquire the goods in which it does *not* have a comparative advantage. Why produce these goods at home—where the opportunity cost is high—when they can be purchased from another country, where their opportunity cost is low?

This gain from trade is further illustrated using the production possibilities curve shown in Figure 31-4 in the textbook. The gain comes when a country uses trade to move from point *B* to point *D*. But you should be able to break down this move into its two components: (1) the move from *B* to *C*, as the country *specializes in food*, and (2) the move from *C* to *D*, when the country then *trades food for clothing*.

This production possibilities curve is also useful in comparing international trade and technological change, as shown in Figure 31-5 in the textbook. Both allow a country to consume a combination of goods lying beyond its *current* production possibilities curve, and both can be the source of unemployment that may have to be endured in the short run in order to realize income gains in the long run.

Finally, the textbook also illustrates the gains from trade using familiar supply and demand diagrams. You should be able to understand clearly why the nation gains from unrestricted exports, as shown in Figure 31-6, and unrestricted imports, as shown in Figure 31-7. We gain on the export side because we sell goods abroad for more than it costs us to produce them (or more than we lose when we switch these goods away from domestic consumption). At the same time, we gain on the import side because we can buy imports for less than it would cost us to produce them efficiently at home; and imports also allow us to increase our consumption of bargain-priced goods from abroad. For both exports and imports there is a triangular efficiency gain which you should be able to confirm by comparing the effects of trade on consumers and producers. This technique then allows you to fill in the details on the second key question in this chapter:

Who Are the Winners and Losers?

Since opening our borders to an import lowers the domestic price of this good, consumers win and domestic producers are damaged. On the export side, there is also a conflict between these two groups—although the roles are reversed: Producers win and consumers lose. Whenever trade policy is made for a specific industry, this conflict between consumers and producers arises. This must be understood before turning to the often-contentious issues on trade policy discussed in the next chapter.

IMPORTANT TERMS: MATCH THE COLUMNS

Match each term in the first column with the corresponding phrase in the second column. But before you do so, write your own definition of each term in the first column.

_____ **1.** economies of scale
_____ **2.** comparative advantage
_____ **3.** opportunity cost
_____ **4.** absolute advantage
_____ **5.** international specialization

a. Country A has this in good X if the opportunity cost of producing X is lower in country A than in any other country.
b. Each country concentrating on one product, or a small number of products, and acquiring the others through international trade.
c. Country B has this in good Y if Y can be produced with fewer inputs in country B that in any other country.
d. Falling average cost as output increases. This is one source of gain from international trade.
e. The quantity of good B that must be sacrificed in order to produce another unit of good A.

TRUE-FALSE

T F **1.** No country can have a comparative advantage in everything.
T F **2.** Comparative advantage ensures that Canadian exports of any good will equal Canadian imports of that same good.
T F **3.** International trade tends to transform a natural oligopoly into a natural monopoly.
T F **4.** Although each member country in the European Economic Community imposes tariffs in its trade with other member countries, it may trade freely with the rest of the world.
T F **5.** If Canada has an absolute advantage in a good, then it will necessarily specialize in that good.
T F **6.** If Canada has a lower opportunity cost of producing good X than any other country, then it has a comparative advantage in X.

T F 7. While improved technology allows a country to consume more by moving to a higher production possibilities curve, international trade allows a country to consume more without moving its production off its existing production possibilities curve.

T F 8. Large Canadian exports of grains following droughts abroad in the early 1970s benefitted Canadian farmers, hurt Canadian consumers, and resulted in an overall efficiency loss.

T F 9. If a country exports oranges, then consumers of oranges in that country probably lose from international trade in oranges.

T F 10. If a county imports oranges, then producers of oranges in that country probably gain from international trade in oranges.

MULTIPLE CHOICE

1. Manufactured goods are
   - **a.** imported, but not exported by Canada
   - **b.** exported, but not imported by Canada
   - **c.** exported by Canada to Europe only
   - **d.** imported and exported by Canada
   - **e.** neither imported nor exported by Canada
2. Comparative advantage provides gains in
   - **a.** domestic trade only
   - **b.** foreign trade only
   - **c.** domestic and foreign trade
   - **d.** neither domestic nor foreign trade
   - **e.** foreign trade, so long as countries do not have an absolute advantage
3. Which of the following is a possible result of international trade?
   - **a.** A natural monopoly in the domestic market may be transformed into a natural oligopoly in the world market.
   - **b.** A perfectly competitive industry may be turned into a natural oligopoly.
   - **c.** A natural oligopoly may be turned into a natural monopoly.
   - **d.** A perfectly competitive industry may be turned into a natural monopoly.
   - **e.** Large firms are able to exercise more market power because the size of the market is increased.
4. International trade increases domestic competition in terms of
   - **a.** price
   - **b.** quality
   - **c.** design
   - **d.** the introduction of new products
   - **e.** all of the above
5. In the table below, Canada has
   - **a.** an absolute advantage in machinery
   - **b.** a comparative advantage in machinery
   - **c.** an absolute advantage in newsprint
   - **d.** a comparative advantage in newsprint
   - **e.** a comparative advantage in neither

	Newsprint	Machinery
Output per U.S. worker	10	5
Output per Canadian worker	4	4

6. Under international trade we export those goods for which we have a relatively low
   - **a.** materials cost
   - **b.** implicit cost
   - **c.** accounting cost
   - **d.** opportunity cost
   - **e.** overhead cost
7. The idea of comparative advantage was developed by
   - **a.** Adam Smith
   - **b.** Karl Marx
   - **c.** David Ricardo
   - **d.** Alfred Marshall
   - **e.** John Maynard Keynes
8. If Canada has an absolute advantage in a good, then it
   - **a.** may or may not export that good
   - **b.** will necessarily export that good
   - **c.** will necessarily avoid exporting that good
   - **d.** will necessarily import that good
   - **e.** will necessarily avoid importing that good

The next five questions are based on the table below. In this simple example, the only goods that exist are the two goods shown, and labour is the only factor of production.

	Clothing	Food
Output per Canadian worker	6	3
Output per European worker	4	1

9. In the table above, international trade would induce Canada to import
   - **a.** food
   - **b.** clothing
   - **c.** both
   - **d.** neither
   - **e.** one or the other, we can't say which
10. In the table above, Canada has an absolute advantage in
    - **a.** both goods, and a comparative advantage in food
    - **b.** both goods, and a comparative advantage in clothing
    - **c.** both goods, and a comparative advantage in neither
    - **d.** neither good, but a comparative advantage in food
    - **e.** neither good, but a comparative advantage in clothing

11. In the table above, Europe has an absolute advantage in
- **a.** both goods, and a comparative advantage in food
- **b.** both goods, and a comparative advantage in clothing
- **c.** both goods, and a comparative advantage in neither
- **d.** neither good, but a comparative advantage in food
- **e.** neither good, but a comparative advantage in clothing

12. In the table above, Europe's opportunity cost of producing food is
- **a.** 3 units of clothing
- **b.** 6/3 = 2 units of clothing
- **c.** 6/4 = $1\frac{1}{2}$ units of clothing
- **d.** 4 units of clothing
- **e.** 3 units of food

13. If the lower right-hand number in the table above is changed from 1 to 2, then Canada has an absolute advantage in
- **a.** both goods, and a comparative advantage in food
- **b.** both goods, and a comparative advantage in clothing
- **c.** both goods, and a comparative advantage in neither
- **d.** neither good, but a comparative advantage in food
- **e.** neither good, and a comparative advantage in neither

14. A nation's real income can be increased by
- **a.** international trade, but not by improved technology
- **b.** improved technology, but not by international trade
- **c.** neither technology nor international trade
- **d.** both technology and international trade
- **e.** international trade, provided there is protection for competing domestic industries

15. International trade allows a nation to increase its income by
- **a.** reaching a point beyond its production possibilities curve (PPC)
- **b.** reaching a point inside its PPC
- **c.** moving along its PPC to a point to the northwest and staying there
- **d.** moving along its PPC to a point to the southeast and staying there
- **e.** staying at the same point on its PPC

16. According to the theory of international trade,
- **a.** every Canadian citizen gains from international trade
- **b.** as a general rule, international trade in a good will benefit both producers and consumers of that good in Canada
- **c.** as a general rule, producers are damaged, but consumers gain from international trade
- **d.** as a general rule, neither consumers nor producers gain from international trade
- **e.** there is an efficiency gain to Canada from allowing international trade

17. The efficiency gain from the export of a good reflects a gain to
- **a.** consumers, plus a gain to producers
- **b.** consumers, minus damage to producers
- **c.** producers, minus a loss to consumers
- **d.** producers only
- **e.** consumers only

EXERCISES

1. Suppose that figures 31-1 and 31-2 represent the markets for shoes in England and Spain.

a. Without international trade, the price in England would be ____________, and the quantity produced in England would be ____________; the price in Spain would be ____________, and the quantity produced in Spain would be ____________. With trade, price will [rise, fall] in England and [rise, fall] in Spain.

b. With international trade the single price at which the total demand—that is, the English demand plus Spanish demand—equals the total supply is ____________. At that price English demand equals ____________, and English supply equals ____________; Spanish demand equals ____________, and Spanish supply equals ____________. In this situation [Spain, England] will export ____________ units of shoes. England has a comparative [advantage, disadvantage] in shoes, as reflected by the [lower, higher] price and cost of shoes in England before trade.

2a. This exercise is designed to help you understand comparative advantage. In Table 31-1, suppose that for country A, each acre of land will produce 100 bushels of wheat or 30 bushels of corn, whereas for country B, each acre of land will produce 40 bushels of wheat or 20 bushels of corn. Suppose that each country has 4,000 acres. Fill in Table 31-1, giving the production possibilities for A and B.

2b. Plot the PPC for the two countries in Figure 31-3.

2c. Country ____________ has an absolute advantage in producing corn; country ____________ has an absolute advantage in producing wheat; country ____________ has a comparative advantage in producing corn; and country ____________ has a comparative advantage in producing wheat. Suppose that, before trade, each country devotes half its land to each product. Then country B will produce and consume ____________ bushels of wheat and ____________ bushels of corn. Mark this on Figure 31-1. Also mark the production and consumption point for country A.

2d. Suppose that A and B were then to trade with each other at the price of 10 bushels of wheat for every 4 bushels of corn. (Note that this ratio of 10:4 is between A's pre-trade domestic exchange ratio of 100:30 = 10:3 cited at the

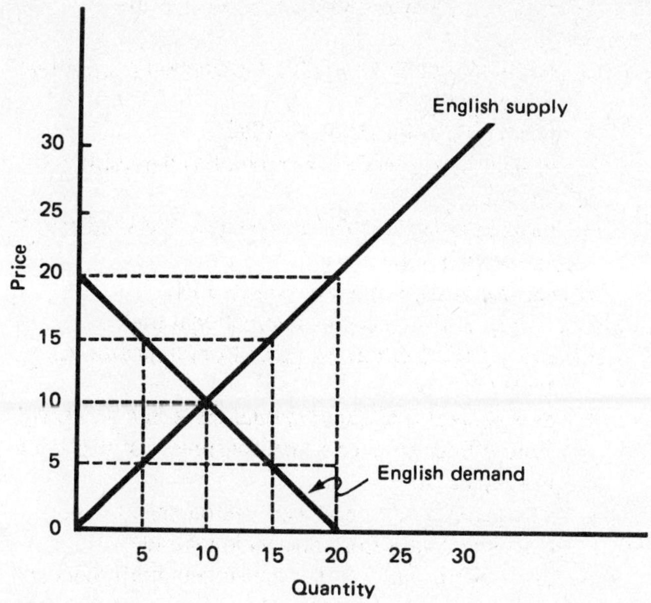

FIGURE 31-1

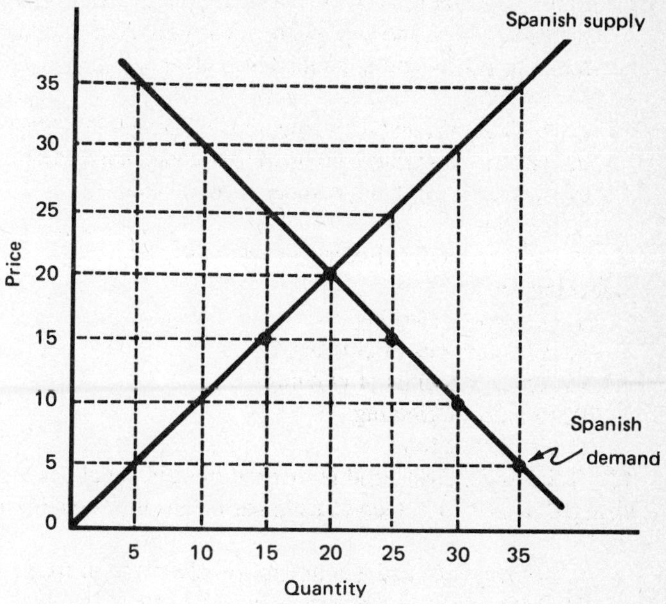

FIGURE 31-2

beginning of this question, and B's ratio of 40:20 = 10:5. Therefore, it is a rate of exchange that will make trade beneficial for both countries.) Let's see now precisely why it's in B's interest to specialize in corn and purchase its wheat from A. If it does so, and devotes all its 4,000 acres to corn, B will produce __________ bushels of corn and __________ bushels of wheat. B then keeps the original 40,000 bushels of corn for its own consumption, and takes the additional 40,000 it has produced and sells this for __________ bushels of wheat. It is now able to consume the same 40,000 bushels of corn as before, and 20,000 [more, fewer] bushels of wheat. This 20,000 bushels of wheat represents its [gain, loss] from specialization and trade. Graph B's specialization and trade with arrows in Figure 31-3, clearly indicating B's gains from trade.

Now plot similar arrows for A in Figure 31-3 to show how this exchange also benefits A. (Hint: A moves to the northwest along its PPC in order to produce the 100,000 more bushels of wheat it needs to exchange with B. When it gives up this wheat to B, it acquires 40,000 bushels of corn for it; this trade moves it back to the southeast. The question is, Does A go back to its original point or to a point superior to it and thus also acquire a gain from trade?)

Note how the trade arrows from the two countries have the same length and slope. They must; each trade arrow describes the exchange of 100,000 bushels of wheat for 40,000 bushels of corn. The only difference in the two arrows is the direction in which they are pointing. (They must point in opposite directions because an export for one country is an import for the other.) Note also that gains from trade arise because the two PPCs have different slopes, and it's therefore possible to have a mutually beneficial trade arrow with a slope in between. If the two PPCs had the same slope, then opportunity costs would be the same in both countries. Consequently, neither country would have a __________ advantage, and mutually beneficial trade would [be possible, not be possible]. We emphasize that we're concentrating here just on comparative advantage. Economies of scale also provide opportunities for mutually beneficial trade—but that's another story.

3. In Figure 31-4, *D* is the Canadian domestic demand curve for a perfectly competitive good.

a. Suppose initially that there is no international trade. Then the amount __________ will be produced, and the market price will equal __________. Suppose now that international trade is introduced,

Table 31-1

A's production possibilities		B's production possibilities	
Thousands of bushels of wheat	Thousands of bushels of corn	Thousands of bushels of wheat	Thousands of bushels of corn
0		0	
100		40	
200		80	
300		120	
400		160	

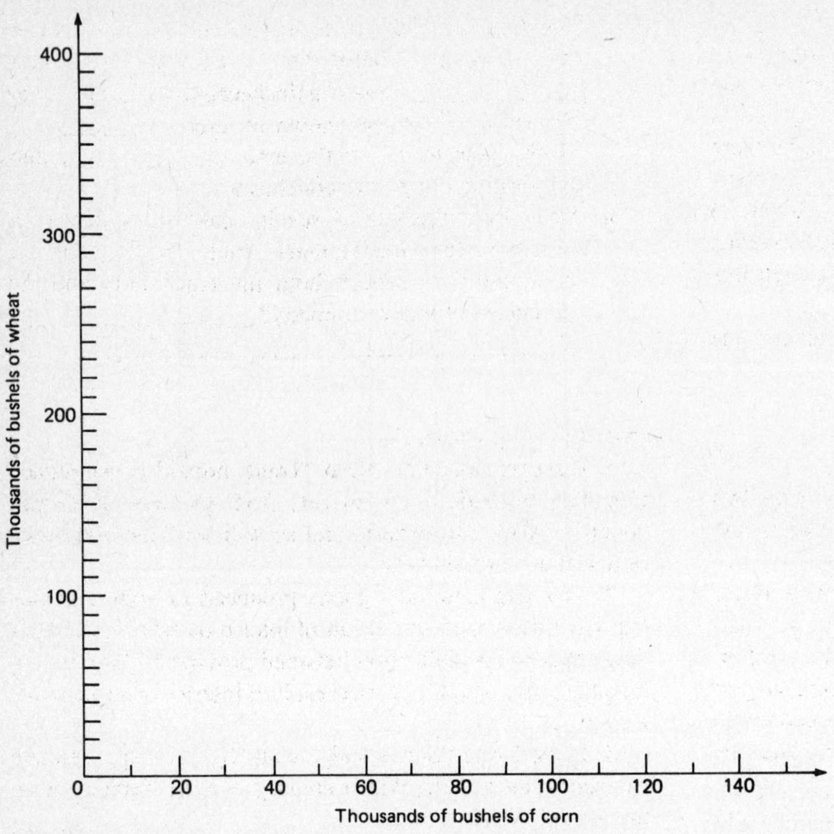

FIGURE 31-3

and that it results in a price equal to P_2. Then consumption of the good in Canada will be ___________, production of the good in Canada will be ___________, and the difference between these amounts will be ___________, which will be the amount of the good that Canada [exports, imports].

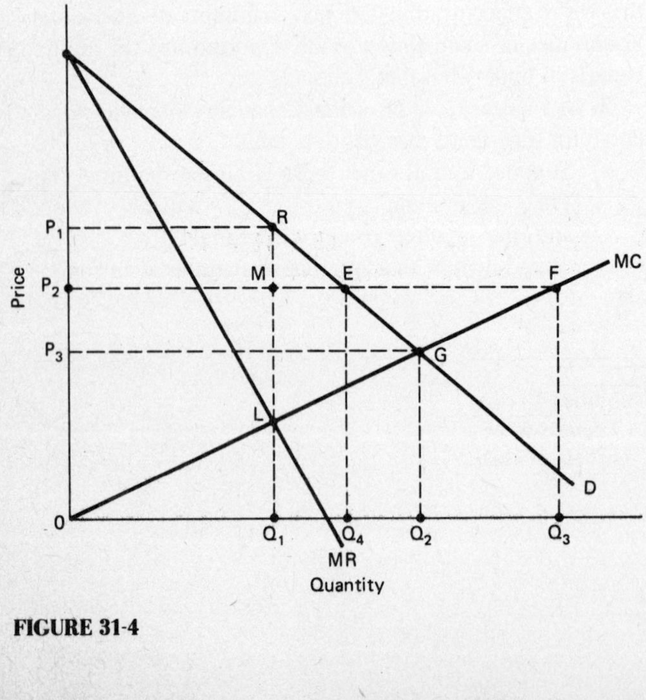

FIGURE 31-4

b. As a result of allowing international trade in this good, Canadian producers are [better, worse] off by the amount ___________, and Canadian consumers [gain, lose] the amount ___________. Therefore, the net efficiency [gain, loss] to Canada equals ___________.

c. Suppose next that there is no international trade in the good and that the market in Canada is an unregulated monopoly. Its marginal revenue will be the line ___________. The monopolist will produce the amount ___________ and will charge price ___________. The efficiency [gain, loss] from monopoly will be ___________.

Suppose now that international trade is introducednd that as a result the firm that used to have a monopoly in Canada is forced to behave as a perfect competitor. Suppose as before that with international trade the market price is P_2. Then consumption of the good in Canada will equal ___________, production of the good in Canada will equal ___________, and the difference between these two amounts equals ___________, which will be the amount of the good that Canada [exports, imports].

d. As a result of allowing international trade in this good, the total revenue received by the producer in Canada has gone from ___________ to ___________, so the net gain in total revenue equals the rectangle ___________, minus the rectangle ____________.

e. But the producer's cost has increased by the four-sided figure ____________l; thus, the net gain to the producer equals the triangle ____________, minus the rectangle ____________. At the same time, there is a consumer [gain, loss] of ____________; thus, the net gain to the country (the net gain to consumers plus the net gain to the producer) equals the area of the figure ____________. Shade in this area.

f. In this case trade brings two efficiency gains: the standard gain from trade that results even in a world of perfect competition, shown by area ____________, plus a gain because trade also ends monopoly abuse, as shown by area ____________. Both gains make up the area ____________, thus confirming our earlier conclusion.

g. Does this illustrate a special case in which it is possible for international trade in a specific commodity to benefit both the consumers and the producers of that commodity? ____________
____

ESSAY QUESTIONS

1. Who gains and who loses from a tariff that prohibits the import of a certain good? Do the gains outweigh the losses, or vice versa? Explain.

2. Looking ahead to the next chapter, can you think of any goods that a country would not want to export, no matter how great the economic benefits might be? (Hint: Canada and the United States now trade military aircraft and equipment with each other, and this trade provides economic benefits to both countries. Would you recommend that the Americans do the same with the Soviet Union?)

3. "One of the gains from international trade is that it induces firms to reduce or eliminate technical inefficiency." Is this true? Why? Did we miss this point, or was it covered under one of our three broad sources of gains from trade?

4. Why do you think the leaders of the Canadian Auto Workers are likely to favour government restrictions on the number of Japanese cars imported into Canada? If you were one of these leaders, what would be your attitude toward a similar restriction on Canadian imports of steel? Why?

5. Why might trade between Ontario and Quebec benefit both provinces? In your answer, you may want to define the concept of an "export to another province" and an "import from another province."

6. A recent slogan has been "Trade, not aid. If we reduce Canadian restrictions on imports from the less developed countries, they will benefit, and so will we." Do you agree or disagree? Explain why.

7. Can you name any goods produced in your province that have developed as a result of inter-provincial specialization—that is, specialization between provinces? Any industries that have developed as a result of international specialization?

8. If the United States and Canada have an approximate balance in their trade, which country is more dependent on that trade? Why?

9. "There is no trade in cement between Canada and Australia. The reason is that transport costs on so bulky and heavy an item more than cancel out the gains from trade." Explain this statement. Do you agree with it? Does that mean that transport costs influence trade patterns? Explain how high transport costs in a good may explain "cross-hauling"—for example, exports of potatoes from Prince Edward Island to eastern United States at the same time as potatoes are being imported into Western Canada *from* the United States.

ANSWERS

Important Terms: **1** d **2** a **3** e **4** c **5** b
True-False: **1** T **2** F **3** F **4** F **5** F **6** T **7** T **8** F **9** T **10** F
Multiple Choice: **1** d **2** c **3** a **4** e **5** b **6** d **7** c **8** a **9** b **10** a **11** e **12** d **13** c **14** d **15** a **16** e **17** c
Exercises: **1a.** $10, 10, $20, 20, rise, fall. **1b.** $15, 5, 15, 25, 15, England, 10, advantage, lower.
2a. Table 31-1 completed:

Table 31-1 completed

A		B	
Wheat	Corn	Wheat	Corn
0	120	0	80
100	90	40	60
200	60	80	40
300	30	120	20
400	0	160	0

2b. Figure 31-3 completed:

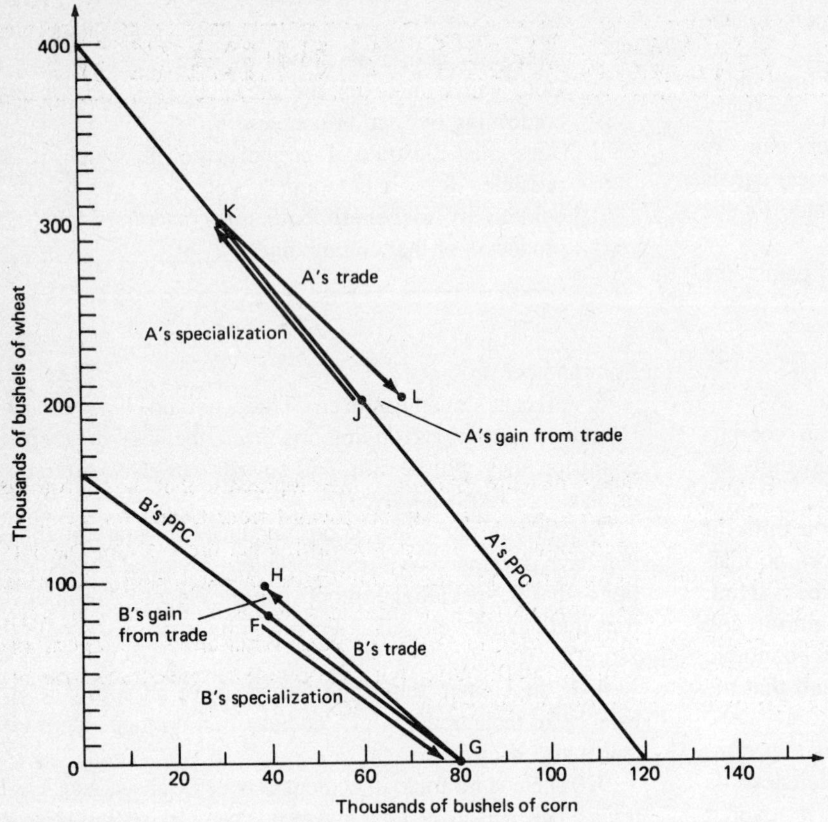

2c. A, A, B, A, 80,000, 40,000. **2d.** 80,000, zero, 100,000, more, gain, comparative, not be possible. **3a.** Q_2, P_3, Q_4, Q_3, Q_4Q_3, exports. **3b.** better, P_2FGP_3, lose, P_2EGP_3, gain, EGF. **3c.** MR, Q_1, P_1, loss, RGL, Q_4, Q_3, Q_4Q_3, exports. **3d.** P_1RQ_10, P_2FQ_30, MFQ_3Q_1, P_1RMP_2. **3e.** LFQ_3Q_1, MFL, P_1RMP_2, gain, P_1REP_2, $RLFE$. **3f.** EGF, RLG, $RLFE$. **3g.** yes.

Chapter 32

INTERNATIONAL TRADE: POLICY DEBATES

MAJOR PURPOSE

Even though the gains from trade have been evident since the days of Adam Smith, and even though tariffs have been coming down dramatically over the last 50 years, many trade barriers still remain. We are still a long way from free trade. The primary objective of this chapter is to answer the question, How is it possible for these barriers to still exist? Can they, or can they not, be justified? We will also address a number of other important and closely related questions: What are the historical developments that have moved Canada and other nations toward freer trade? As we have been moving two steps forward, what are the new barriers to trade that have been moving us one step back? An issue of particular significance to Canada is that of our trade relations with the United States. What are the potential advantages and disadvantages to Canada of a free-trade arrangement with the United States?

LEARNING OBJECTIVES

After you have studied this chapter in the textbook and the study guide, you should be able to

- Explain the military and political reasons why trade barriers still exist
- State three fallacious economic arguments for protection, explaining why they are fallacious
- State five economic arguments for protection that contain some element of truth, and the difficulties with each of these arguments
- Describe the multilateral liberalization of our trade over the last 50 years, with special reference to the major events of 1947, 1967, and 1979
- Evaluate the European Economic Community (EEC) in terms of its benefits and costs to the Europeans, and the problems it raises for U.S. exporters
- Describe the growth of non-tariff barriers, and explain why they are particularly difficult to deal with
- Explain the concept of tariff escalation and its significance to Canada
- Explain the main arguments for and against a Canadian free-trade arrangement with the United States
- Describe the U.S.–Canadian Auto Pact and how it has affected the North American automobile industry and the Canadian economy as a whole

HIGHLIGHTS OF THE CHAPTER

The trade barriers that remain—and the new ones that have been introduced—have been defended by their supporters as "in the national interest." Do the arguments they use make sense?

Arguments for Protection

Much of the defence of trade barriers has little to do with economics. It is instead an appeal to political considerations. The loss that results from allowing a good to be freely imported is felt very heavily by the few people who specialize in producing that good; in many cases, their jobs are threatened by the competition of imports. These people will often vote for a politician who promises to restrict such imports. As we saw in the last chapter, the damage to these losers from free trade will be more than offset by the benefits to the winners—all the people who are able to enjoy a wide variety of inexpensive imported goods. But these winners' benefits are widely dispersed over the public as a whole, with the benefit received by each individual being relatively small. Thus, winners usually vote for other issues on which they feel more deeply, and the politician who proposes to restrict an import is often elected. As a result, trade restrictions that make no economic sense are still introduced for political reasons.

In some countries, especially the United States, tariffs and other trade restrictions have also been justified by considerations of national security. The argument here is that some industries produce goods that are virtually important to a country's national defence. If there were no trade restrictions protecting domestic producers from import competition, some of these industries might not survive. But this would leave the country in a vulnerable position in times of war. However, in small countries that belong to military alliances (such as NATO), this national-security argument loses much of its validity if the country's military needs can be supplied from other countries within the alliance.

Now let's turn to the *economic* arguments that have been used to try to justify protection. Some are fallacious, but some contain an element of truth:

1. "Buy Canadian because it keeps our money at home. When we buy Korean goods we lose our money to Korea." This argument is fallacious. When we buy Korean goods our money eventually comes back when the Koreans buy *our* goods.

2. "We can't compete with cheap foreign labour." This argument is also fallacious. Labour in many foreign countries is less expensive because it is less productive. Our higher productivity means that, on average, we can compete with cheap foreign labour. We do particularly well in goods in which we have a comparative advantage (where our productivity advantage more than offsets our higher wage rate). We can't compete where we don't have a comparative advantage, where our productivity advantage does *not* offset our higher wage rate.

3. "Tariffs should be tailored to equalize costs at home and abroad." This, too, is a fallacious argument. According to the theory of comparative advantage, we gain from international trade because there are differences in costs between countries. Tailoring tariffs to eliminate these differences would eliminate trade, and all the gains it provides.

4. "If we buy steel from Hamilton, Ontario, rather then Japan, employment will rise in Hamilton, rather than Japan." There is a grain of truth in this argument. Restricting imports of steel from Japan may stimulate employment in Hamilton, at least in the short run. However, there are two problems. First, Japan may retaliate with its own restrictions against our exports, and this will reduce Canadian employment. Thus, we don't get employment gains after all. In short, we are following a "beggar-my-neighbour" policy that doesn't provide employment benefits, but results in shrinking trade and a loss of the gains from trade. Second, blocking out Japanese competition makes it more difficult to control costs and prices in Canadian industries. If Canadian workers don't feel that they have to compete with the Japanese, they will be less restrained in their wage demands. We saw in Chapter 31 that one of the gains from trade is that it makes our economy more competitive. We lose this gain whenever we protect our industries.

5. "Restricting trade will diversify a nation's economy." This may be true for some countries. Trade may lead a country to specialize in producing just a few goods. If world prices drop for these few goods, the country will suffer from having "put all its eggs in one basket." On the other hand, such heavy specialization will put it in a particularly favourable position if those prices rise; a prime example is the group of OPEC countries who export almost nothing but oil. But even though Canada does have very large exports of primary products such as wheat or natural gas, it also exports a whole range of other primary and manufactured products as well. Thus, a lack of diversification in international trade is not a serious enough problem in Canada to justify increased tariff protection.

6. "We need to protect our infant industries." This argument is sometimes valid. Without the protection of trade restrictions, some industries may never reach the size where they can realize the economies of scale necessary to compete in world markets. However, there are three difficulties with this argument: (a) Infant industries never seem to grow up. They typically continue to demand protection, and no government wants to lose votes by cutting the apron strings; (b) even if an industry were to grow up, it might still not be able to compete effectively; and (c) if the infant industry really does have a promising future, then why aren't private lenders willing to lend it enough money to survive until maturity?

7. "Restricting imports may reduce the price we have to pay for them." This might make sense if Canada demands so much of a good that by cutting back its demand it can significantly reduce the world price of that good. However, the Canadian demand for most goods represents only a very small fraction of the world demand for those goods. Hence, Canada's ability to influence the world price for the goods it imports is very limited.

8. "Restricting imports may increase our economic independence by reducing our vulnerability to a cut-off in foreign supplies." Cutbacks in oil supplies from OPEC countries in the 1970s made clear the force of this argument. But oil is special; for most other commodities, the risk of having our supply cut off is minimal: if one country stops selling to us, we can turn to other sources of supply.

History of Canadian Trade Policy

Perhaps the most important period in Canadian trade policy was the 1880s, when the Conservative government under Sir John A. Macdonald introduced very high tariffs as part of its National Policy—aimed at stimulating Canada's manufacturing industry and promoting interprovincial trade. Since that time, Canada's tariffs have generally been falling (except during the early 1930s when Canada and many other countries raised tariffs as a way of stimulating domestic aggregate demand and reducing unemployment). Since the Second World War, the trend toward lower Canadian tariffs can be partly explained by Canada's participation in the programs of multilateral tariff reductions negotiated by most of the world's industrialized countries under the General Agreement on Tariffs and Trade (GATT). Especially important—international tariff reductions came as a result of the "Kennedy round" of tariff negotiations in the late 1970s. (The "Tokyo round" of negotiations dealt not only with tariffs, but also with "non-tariff" barriers (NTBs), such as import quotas, special customs procedures which make import trade more costly, and discrimination in government purchasing against imported goods.)

From the viewpoint of Canada and the United States, the process of multilateral tariff reductions has been especially important since the formation of the European Economic Community (EEC) in the late 1950s. Since the countries that are members of the EEC have abolished tariffs on trade with each other, Canadian and U.S. exporters (who still face a tariff on their sales to an EEC importer) are at a disadvantage relative to suppliers in any EEC country. (For Canada, this problem became especially important in 1973 when the United Kingdom, one of Canada's important trading partners, joined the EEC.) However, this disadvantage has become less severe since the EEC has participated in all multilateral agreements to reduce tariffs on *all* imports.

One of the most controversial issues in all of Canadian trade policy concerns our policy toward the United States. Specifically, proponents of free trade have long argued that it would be in Canada's interest to enter into bilateral negotiations with the United States, with the aim of ultimately abolishing all tariffs on Canada–U.S. trade. Advocates of such an arrangement have argued that the resulting gains from industrial specialization and from an increased ability for Canadian firms to exploit economies of scale could lead to a large increase in Canada's GNP. Recent studies have suggested that this increase could be as much as 8% to 9% of GNP. Furthermore, they argue, a free-trade arrangement would be protecting Canada against the effects of future protectionist moves by the United States, in the form of increased tariffs or NTBs. Following the recommendations of the MacDonald Commission in 1985, Canada formally requested that the United States enter into negotiations about an agreement. The United States accepted, and by 1986, negotiations were underway. However, there is still considerable opposition to a Canada–U.S. free-trade agreement.

Critics argue that an elimination of our tariffs on imports from the United States would make it impossible for most of our manufacturing firms to stand up against the increased competition from U.S. firms. Hence, Canada's manufacturing sector would shrink substantially, with considerable job losses, and we would be pushed further in the direction of producing mostly primary products (being "hewers of wood and drawers of water"). Further, a free-trade arrangement would greatly increase our political dependence on the United States, in the critics' view.

In one particular industry, Canada has already entered into a limited free-trade agreement. The 1965 bilateral agreement with the United States under which car manufacturers were allowed to import and export cars and car parts between the Canadian and U.S. markets free of duty (The Auto Pact). While the Auto Pact has at times been the subject of some controversy, earlier studies indicated that the pact had a substantial positive effect on Canadian GNP, by making the auto industry more efficient.

A problem that continues to be important for Canadian international trade is the problem of tariff escalation. Because importing countries often have higher tariffs on processed goods than on raw materials, there is a tendency for the processing of many Canadian raw materials to be done in the importing country rather than in Canada. In order to promote more processing in Canada, Canadian trade negotiators have been trying hard to get our trading partners to reduce the escalation in their tariff schedules.

IMPORTANT TERMS: MATCH THE COLUMNS

Match each term in the first column with the corresponding phrase in the second column. But before you do so, write your own definition of each term in the first column.

_____ **1.** tariff
_____ **2.** non-tariff barrier (NTB)
_____ **3.** quota
_____ **4.** trade restriction
_____ **5.** protection
_____ **6.** "beggar-my-neighbour" policy
_____ **7.** infant industry
_____ **8.** terms of trade
_____ **9.** bilateral negotiations
_____ **10.** the General Agreement on Tariffs and Trade (GATT)
_____ **11.** the European Economic Community (EEC)
_____ **12.** Kennedy round
_____ **13.** Tokyo round
_____ **14.** Auto Pact
_____ **15.** multilateral negotiations
_____ **16.** U.S.–Canadian free trade agreement

a. the common market in Europe formed in the late 1950s by Germany, France, Italy, the Netherlands, Belgium, and Luxembourg, and later including other countries such as the United Kingdom and Denmark
b. the policy of imposing barriers to trade in order to shield domestic industries from foreign competition
c. negotiations between only two countries
d. a tax imposed on imported goods as they enter a country
e. the series of multilateral GATT negotiations ending with the 1979 agreement to cut tariffs by about a third, and limit NTBs
f. an industry that has not yet reached the size at which it can capture sufficient economies of scale to compete in world markets
g. any government regulation—other than a tariff—that restricts trade
h. U.S.–Canadian agreement to allow free trade in cars and car parts at the level of the manufacturer
i. a treaty signed in 1947 by Canada and 22 other countries calling for multilateral negotiations to reduce trade restrictions
j. bilateral negotiations about this proposal started in 1986
k. a limit on the number of units of a good that can be imported into a country
l. negotiations between many countries
m. the series of multilateral negotiations between GATT countries in the 1960s that was concluded by the signing of a 1967 agreement to reduce tariffs by about a third
n. the price we receive for our exports, compared to the price we pay for our imports
o. any tariff or non-tariff barrier that impedes international trade
p. the use of trade restrictions to reduce imports, increase domestic production, and therefore reduce unemployment (Such a policy transfers an unemployment problem to another country.)

TRUE-FALSE

T F **1.** When international trade is opened up in a good, Canada as a whole gains only if we end up exporting that good.
T F **2.** The promotion of economic diversity is one argument for protection.
T F **3.** If Canada were to increase restrictions on imported steel, this would tend to increase employment in Hamilton in the short run.
T F **4.** After an infant industry has been supported by the government for a year or two, political pressure to remove the protection becomes almost irresistible.
T F **5.** Because wages in Canada are high, it follows that costs of production are also high—and this justifies protecting our goods from cheap foreign products.

T F 6. By restricting its imports, a country may be able to improve its terms of trade. In practice, this argument has more relevance for a large country than for a relatively small country like Canada.

T F 7. The major purpose of the GATT is to provide for bilateral negotiations in which countries will agree to lowering their tariffs.

T F 8. Stiff safety standards that must be met by imported goods constitute a non-tariff barrier.

T F 9. Under the U.S.–Canadian Auto Pact, North American car manufacturers have agreed that all North American cars sold in Canada will be produced in Canada.

T F 10. Canadian processing of raw materials before they are exported to foreign countries is discouraged because many of the countries with which we trade have lower tariffs on unprocessed raw materials than on processed goods.

MULTIPLE CHOICE

1. A policy of protecting essential defence industries
- **a.** has been opposed by economists since the days of Adam Smith
- **b.** is sometimes abused by industries that contribute very little to national security but still try to use the defence argument to get protection
- **c.** is based on the expectation that such protection would increase real GNP
- **d.** is justified as a method of creating employment, but can't be justified in any other way
- **e.** all of the above

2. The strongest political pressure for a change in trade policy usually comes from
- **a.** producers lobbying for import restrictions
- **b.** producers lobbying for export restrictions
- **c.** consumers lobbying for import restrictions
- **d.** consumers lobbying for export restrictions
- **e.** consumers lobbying for a reduction in trade restrictions

3. With free trade between the United States and Canada, it is likely that Canada would
- **a.** give up the production of industrial goods in order to concentrate on agricultural goods
- **b.** give up the production of agricultural goods in order to concentrate on industrial goods
- **c.** give up one industry (say, electrical machinery) in order to specialize in another (say, chemicals
- **d.** give up the production of some items of electrical machinery in order to specialize in other items of electrical machinery and do the same in chemicals
- **e.** in both electrical equipment and chemicals, produce an even wider range of items than at present

4. A "beggar-my-neighbour" policy involves
- **a.** encouraging the purchase of essential materials from abroad
- **b.** export controls to prevent the sale of our natural resources to foreign countries
- **c.** import restrictions designed to capture employment from foreign countries
- **d.** subsidies to encourage imports of foreign natural resources
- **e.** subsidies to encourage imports of foreign luxury goods

5. The infant-industry argument for protection makes sense if the infant industry
- **a.** is able to compete against foreign firms now, but not in the future
- **b.** is not able to compete against foreign firms now, but will be able to in the future
- **c.** won't be able to compete now or in the future
- **d.** will be able to compete now and in the future
- **e.** won't be able to compete now; the future is irrelevant

6. "If I buy a radio from the United States, I get the radio and the United States gets the dollars. But if I buy a Canadian-built radio, I get the radio and the dollars stay here." This argument is
- **a.** misleading because the Americans don't keep the Canadian dollars they earn from us in trade; they eventually spend them on our goods
- **b.** misleading because the dollars I spend buying a Canadian-built radio also leave this country
- **c.** correct; this is why we should stop trading
- **d.** correct; we should trade only for political reasons
- **e.** true for radios, but not for most goods we import

7. Trade restrictions on a good are most likely to improve a country's terms of trade if
- **a.** the country's demand for the good is a significant part of world demand
- **b.** the country's demand for the good is an insignificant part of world demand
- **c.** the domestic industry producing the good is a natural monopoly
- **d.** the lower prices that result drive some of the country's producers out of business
- **e.** the country is already self-sufficient in this good

8. The National Policy introduced by Sir John A. Macdonald
- **a.** was a policy intended to nationalize the Canadian oil and gas industry
- **b.** proposed the establishment of a free-trade arrangement with the United States as a means of raising Canada's national income
- **c.** was an early version of the CBC program *The National*
- **d.** introduced high tariffs on imported goods as a

means of promoting trade between Canada's provinces
e. provided a large subsidy for VIA Rail passenger service

9. Canadian tariffs today are
a. higher than in the 1930s
b. slightly lower than in the 1930s
c. much lower than in the 1930s
d. about the same as in the 1930s
e. higher in most goods than in the 1930s, but lower in some

10. The formation of the European Economic Community
a. was one of the reasons for the severe scarcity of agricultural goods in the early 1980s
b. has made it easier for Canadian firms to compete against the French in the German market
c. has made it more difficult for Canadian firms to compete against the French in the German market
d. has made it more difficult for Canadian firms to compete against the Japanese in the German market
e. has had no effect on Canadian firms competing in the German market

11. The European Common Agricultural Program has
a. raised the price of North American farm exports
b. not affected the price of North American farm exports
c. increased the quantity of North American farm exports
d. led to conflicts within North America, but has reduced conflicts within Europe
e. led to conflicts within Europe

12. In the early 1980s
a. a high value of the U.S. dollar made it difficult for U.S. firms to compete and increased the pressure for protection
b. a high value of the U.S. dollar made it relatively easy for U.S. firms to compete and reduced the pressure for protection
c. a low value of the U.S. dollar made it relatively easy for U.S. firms to compete and reduced the pressure for protection
d. a low value of the U.S. dollar made it difficult for U.S. firms to compete and increased the pressure for protection
e. a low value of the U.S. dollar made it relatively easy for U.S. firms to compete. This increased U.S. political support for a free-trade agreement with Canada.

13. In the Kennedy round, participating countries cut their tariffs by about a third. In the Tokyo round that followed
a. almost no further progress was made
b. no further progress was made
c. participating countries cut their remaining tariffs by about 10%
d. participating countries cut their remaining tariffs by roughly another one-third
e. participating countries cut their remaining tariffs by roughly two-thirds

14. Non-tariff barriers are
a. designed solely to restrict trade
b. designed solely to improve health standards
c. designed solely for other non-trade reasons
d. sometimes designed to restrict trade and sometimes designed to improve health standards; but in either case, they restrict trade
e. justified so long as they provide a benefit, regardless of their cost

15. The concept of "tariff escalation" refers to
a. the policy of charging higher tariffs on more expensive goods
b. the tendency for countries to raise their tariffs in order to reduce unemployment during the Great Depression
c. the policy of countries importing raw materials to charge higher tariffs on raw materials in order to drive down the price of such imports
d. the policy of some countries to charge low tariffs on imports of unprocessed raw materials than on imports of other goods
e. the policy of charging higher tariffs on goods imported from low-wage countries

16. According to estimates by Harris and Cox, a Canada–U.S. free trade agreement would lead to
a. an increase of 0.5–1% in Canadian GNP and relocation of 4% of the labour force
b. an increase of 4–5% in Canadian GNP and relocation of 7% of the labour force
c. an increase of 8–9% in Canadian GNP and relocation of 7% of the labour force
d. an increase of 14–15% in Canadian GNP and relocation of 9% of the labour force
e. a small decrease in Canadian GNP

EXERCISE

Parts of this exercise cover the same ground as the appendix to chapter 32 in the textbook. You will probably be able to do the exercise and find it helpful, even if you are not being asked to study the appendix. However, if you encounter problems, you can refer to the appendix for help. In any case, first try to do the exercise on your own.

Figure 32-1 shows the domestic supply and demand for a good that is traded internationally.

a. Without international trade the price would be ____________, and the quantity produced would be ____________. If international trade results in a price of P_2, then domestic production will be ____________, domestic consumption will be ____________, and the country will [import, export]

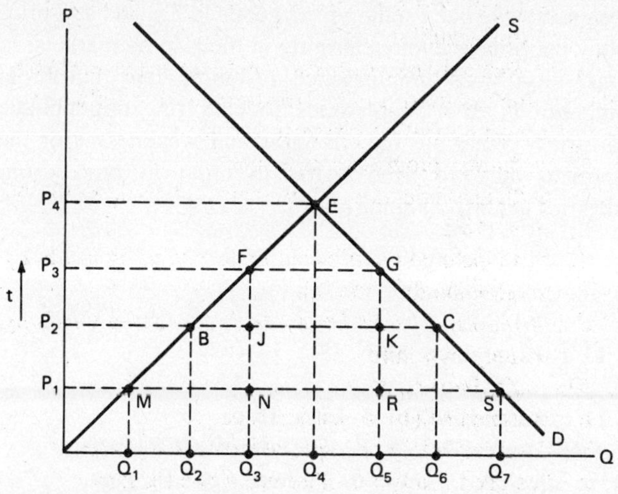

FIGURE 32-1

the amount ___________. As a result of this international trade, the [gain, loss] to consumers is area ___________, while producers are [better, worse] off by the area ___________. If we consider both producers and consumers, the effect of international trade on the nation, on balance, is an efficiency [gain, loss] of area ___________.

b. Suppose that the government imposes a tariff on this good, shown by arrow t. Suppose that this has no effect on the world price of the good. Because of the tariff, the domestic price will rise to ___________. (Importers who are willing to bring this good in for a price P_2 will need this higher price to compensate them for the tariff t that they now have to pay the government.) The quantity of imports will be ___________. As a result of the tariff, consumers [gain, lose] area ___________, while producers are [better, worse] off by area ___________. Moreover, the government is now collecting a tariff t on quantity ___________ of imports, ___________, for a total revenue of area ___________. Therefore, there is a net [gain, loss] to the nation from this tariff of areas ___________.

c. Now suppose that, instead of this tariff t, the government imposes an import quota that restricts imports to the quantity FG. With imports of FG, P_2 [is, is not] an equilibrium price, because the demand for this good at price P_2 is [more than, less than] the domestic plus imported supply. Thus, price will be [above, below] P_2. P_3 [is, is not] an equilibrium price because, with imports FG, the demand for this good at P_3 is [more than, less than, equal to] the domestic plus imported supply. Thus, this quota of FG is the quota equivalent of tariff ___________, because both raise U.S. price by ___________, and reduce imports to ___________.

d. Because of the quota, the price in the domestic market will rise to ___________, consumers will [gain, lose] area ___________, and producers will [gain, lose] area ___________. Suppose that the quota rights are held by foreigners exporting to Canada, with any of the benefits that a quota may provide going to them. The revenue the Canadian government gets from the imposition of this quota is ___________. Therefore, the net effect on the nation of this quota is its effect on producers and consumers, which is a [gain, loss] of area ___________.

e. When the Canadian government imposes an import quota and gives away these quota rights to foreigners, then a quota will result in a [larger, smaller] amount of [gain, loss] to Canada than will an equivalent tariff. The additional [gain, loss] from the quota results because duty revenue is collected by the Canadian government if there is a [tariff, quota], but is not collected if there is this type of [tariff, quota].

ESSAY QUESTIONS

1. The text argued that a country may improve its terms of trade by restricting imports. In 1973 the oil-producing countries of OPEC managed to improve their terms of trade by restricting their exports. Explain carefully what are the similarities and differences between the "terms of trade" argument for restricting imports and the "terms of trade" argument for restricting exports.

2. When a country is in a severe recession, the demand to reduce imports becomes stronger. Why? Critically evaluate such a proposal.

3. It is sometimes argued that trade restrictions protect our high standard of living from being eroded by competition from low-income countries. Evaluate this. Do trade restrictions maintain our standard of living or reduce it for the nation as a whole? For the industry that's being protected?

4. Explain carefully how a tariff tends to reduce the benefits of international specialization.

5. Consider a tariff high enough not just to reduce, but to completely prevent, imports. How would it affect consumers? producers? the nation as a whole? Would the government collect any duty revenue from such a tariff? From a tariff that only *reduces* imports?

6. Even though the complete elimination of tariffs in all countries would be likely to promote economic efficiency both in Canada and throughout the world, Canadian policymakers of course have no control over tariffs in foreign countries, and we cannot expect to be able to persuade all other countries to remove their tariffs on imports from Canada. On the other hand, it would be possible for Canada to eliminate unilaterally all tariffs on imports into Canada even if other countries do not reduce their tariffs on imports from us. Discuss arguments for and against such a unilateral tariff elimination.

7. Sometimes Canadian industries demand protection from foreign competition because foreigners have been "dumping" their goods on the Canadian market. That is, foreigners have been selling their goods in Canada at a price below the price they are charging in their home markets. In what sense does this practice resemble the "cut-throat competition" that sometimes occurs in oligopolistic industries? What are the strengths and weaknesses of the argument that we need tariffs in order to protect our industries against dumping?

ANSWERS

Important Terms: **1** d **2** g **3** k **4** o **5** b **6** p **7** f **8** n **9** c **10** i **11** a **12** m **13** e **14** h **15** l **16** j
True-False: **1** F **2** T **3** T **4** F **5** F **6** T **7** F **8** T **9** F **10** T
Multiple Choice: **1** b **2** a **3** d **4** c **5** b **6** a **7** a **8** d **9** c **10** c **11** e **12** a **13** d **14** d **15** d **16** c
Exercises: **a.** P_4, Q_4, Q_2, Q_6, import, *BC*, gain, P_4ECP_2, worse, P_4EBP_2, gain, *EBC*. **b.** P_3, *FG*, lose, P_3GCP_2, better, P_3FBP_2, *FG*, *FGKJ*, loss, *FJB* and *GKC*. **c.** is not, more than, above, is, equal to, *t*, *t*, *FG*. **d.** P_3, lose, P_3GCP_2, gain, P_3FBP_2, zero, loss, *FGCB*. **e.** larger, loss, loss, tariff, quota.

Part Seven

MICROECONOMICS: HOW INCOME IS DISTRIBUTED

Chapter 33

WAGES IN A PERFECTLY COMPETITIVE ECONOMY

MAJOR PURPOSE

In this chapter, the objective is to use the familiar tools of supply and demand developed in earlier chapters to analyse how wages are determined in perfectly competitive labour markets. The labour market for a specific industry will be perfectly competitive if (1) workers are mobile and can move in and out of this industry, (2) there are so many buyers and sellers of labour service that none can affect the wage rate, and (3) labour is standardized, with all workers being equally productive. If these assumptions hold, and there is also perfect competition in the markets for products, then the labour demand by an industry reflects the marginal product of labour in that industry, and labour supply reflects the marginal product of labour in other industries. The conclusion that follows is that perfect competition yields an efficient outcome in a labour market, just as it did in a product market. Finally, a number of real-world complications in labour markets are recognized. For example, what happens when the government intervenes to set a minimum wage? What happens when the assumption of labour mobility—assumption (1) above—does not hold? Specifically, what happens when discrimination prevents women from entering jobs traditionally held by men? These questions are addressed in this chapter. In the next chapter, assumption (2) above is realized in order to show the effects when workers form a union to raise wages—or employers form an association to lower wages. Finally in Chapter 35, assumption (3) is relaxed in order to analyse what happens when workers are not equally productive.

LEARNING OBJECTIVES

After you have studied this chapter in the textbook and the study guide, you should be able to

- Explain why, under perfect competition, the curve showing an industry's demand for labour is the same as the curve showing the marginal revenue product of labour
- State two reasons why the labour demand curve might shift to the right
- Illustrate how the labour demand curve can be used to show the total income of labour in an industry and the total income of other factors of production
- Explain why the height of the labour supply curve for an industry reflects the opportunity cost of labour—that is, labour's wage and marginal product in other industries
- Explain why perfect competition in the labour market typically results in an efficient wage and employment level
- Measure diagrammatically the efficiency loss that results when a labour market is not perfectly competitive
- Explain why one cannot necessarily jump from the conclusion that a perfectly competitive labour market is efficient, to the much stronger conclusion that a free, unregulated labour market is "best"
- Explain the effects of a minimum wage in an otherwise perfectly competitive labour market, and its more favourable effects in a labour market that is not competitive
- Discuss the effects of discrimination in a labour market
- Describe and evaluate the concept of work of equal value (comparable worth)

HIGHLIGHTS OF THE CHAPTER

As a first approximation, a wage can be viewed just like the price of any other good or service that is traded in the market. In this case, the service is labour, the demanders are employers, and the suppliers are workers.

The Demand for Labour

In defining its demand for labour, a firm begins with its *marginal physical product* (MPP). This schedule, shown in column 3 of Table 33-1 in the textbook, shows how the firm's output increases—in physical units—as it hires more labour. If markets for goods are perfectly competitive, we can multiply this increase in physical output by its price to calculate the additional *revenue* the firm receives as it hires more labour. This is called its *marginal revenue product* (MRP), and is shown in column 5 of Table 33-1. In a perfectly competitive economy, MRP will also be VMP, the value of the marginal product (or marginal product, for short). However, if there is not perfect competition in goods' markets, MRP will be less than VMP (as illustrated in problem 33-1, 33-2, and 33-3). It is very important that you are able to distinguish MPP, MRP, and VMP. If necessary, work through tables 33-1, 33-2 and 33-3 in the exercise below, in addition to Table 33-1 in the text.

The profit-maximizing firm will demand labour up to the point where the MRP is just equal to the wage rate W. The reason is that, if MRP were greater than W, the firm could increase its profits by hiring more workers; and if MRP were less than W, the firm could increase its profits by hiring fewer workers. Thus, the MRP curve shows how much the firm will hire at each possible wage. In other words, the MRP curve is the firm's labour demand curve. (The argument here is essentially the same as the one used in Chapter 21 to show that the marginal benefit curve and the demand curve for an individual are the same.)

A firm's demand for labour schedule slopes down because of diminishing returns (recall this concept from Chapter 22). As a firm hires more and more labour (with other factors fixed), it eventually finds that the marginal physical product of labour—and therefore MRP—decreases. In other words, its demand for labour slopes downward.

There are several reasons why a firm's demand curve for labour might shift: (1) If the price of the firm's output falls, this will cause a downward shift in its MRP, and therefore in its labour demand; and (2) if the firm's marginal physical product of labour shifts up, its MRP and labour demand curve will also shift up. Such an upward shift might occur, for example, if the firm increases the amount of capital it employs; this would make labour physically more productive by providing it with more machinery to work with. Another example might be a technological improvement that allows a firm to get more physical output from its workers. (Often, increased capital equipment and technological change come together, but it is possible for one to occur without the other.)

The market demand curve for labour is just the horizontal sum of the demand curves of all the individual hiring firms. Again, this is similar to the summation of the individual demand curves for a good discussed at the beginning of Chapter 21.

Before turning to the supply curve for labour, we pause briefly to consider a further important interpretation of labour demand.

How the Labour Demand Curve Shows the Distribution of Income

The total revenue of an industry is the sum of the MRPs of all workers employed in that industry. That is, in Figure 33–4 in the textbook, it is the sum of all the MRPs—such as bars *a* and *b* on the left—of all *N* workers in this industry. In total, this is equal to areas 1 and 2 under the labour demand curve. Of this area representing total industry revenue, rectangular area 2 is income, since it is the quantity of employment (the base of this rectangle) times the wage (the height of this rectangle). The rest—that is, area 1—goes to other factors of production, in the form of rent, interest, and profit.

The Supply of Labour

The labour supply curve for an industry is derived in much the same way as the supply curve for a commodity in Chapter 22. The height of the labour supply curve indicates how much must be paid to attract one more worker into the industry. This is (roughly) the wage and marginal product of this worker in another industry. In other words, the height of the labour supply curve is the opportunity cost of an additional worker.

Is a Perfectly Competitive Labour Market Efficient?

Efficiency requires that labour be hired in an industry up to the point where its marginal benefit is just equal to its marginal costs. (If there are no externalities—as assumed here—then there is no difference between social and private benefits, and no difference between social and private costs.) The marginal benefit of labour is its marginal product in this industry, as given by the labour demand curve. The marginal cost of labour is its opportunity cost—that is, its marginal product elsewhere; this is given by its supply curve. Since supply and demand for labour are equated in a perfectly competitive labour market, the marginal cost of labour is equal to the marginal benefit of labour, and this market is therefore efficient.

When a labour market has been shifted away from a perfectly competitive equilibrium, there is an efficiency loss that can be measured by the triangle between the demand curve, the supply curve, and the vertical line at the actual quantity of employment. An example is provided in panel (*b*) of Figure 33-6 in the textbook. It should be emphasized again that this measure is valid only under the twin assumptions of (1) perfect competition, and (2) no externalities. If such triangular efficiency losses are not clear, you may wish to review the similar analysis that was used in Figure 24-3 to show efficiency losses in product markets.

Although a perfectly competitive labour market is efficient, it does not necessarily follow that a free, unregulated labour market is "best" for the following four reasons:

1. In an unregulated market, employers may discriminate against women or ethnic minorities, and thus violate the mobility assumption of perfect competition; labour is *not* free to move into such an industry. (This point will be considered in more detail in a moment.)

2. In an unregulated market, employers may have market power, thus violating another assumption of perfect competition.

3. There may be externalities.

4. Even if none of these problems arise—and an unregulated labour market is efficient—it may not be best because of the way it distributes income.

The Effect of a Minimum Wage

There are four effects when a minimum wage (above the existing equilibrium wage) is introduced into a perfectly competitive labour market:

1. Employment is reduced.

2. Reduced employment leads to an efficiency loss, similar to the red triangle in panel (*c*) of Figure 33-6. (The efficiency loss is even more than this if the minimum wage is imposed across all labour markets.)

3. Although the wage received by workers who are still employed in this industry rises, the wage of those who no longer have a job here falls (or disappears altogether). Therefore, on balance, the overall effect on total labour income is uncertain.

4. The amount of income going to other factors of production will definitely decrease, because the higher wage that might be paid to labour will put a squeeze on these other incomes.

While these four effects can be predicted from our theory, there is another effect that experience has taught us: The unemployment created by minimum wage legislation falls most heavily on teenagers and minorities.

The important qualifications to this analysis include:

1. Even if the minimum wage raises total labour income, workers may not feel that they benefit overall from the change. Even though jobs pay better, they are harder to find; and employers paying a higher wage may no longer feel that they can afford the cost of on-the-job training that is so beneficial to workers.

2. The more industries covered by minimum wage legislation, the greater the unemployment it will create (the harder it is for an unemployed person to find a job elsewhere, because there are fewer and fewer of these "other jobs" available).

The Effects of Discrimination in the Labour Market

Figure 33-8 in the text shows the economic effects when employers discriminate by hiring women only for jobs with a low marginal product; the offensive moral and social dimensions are also recognized, even though they cannot be dealt with in this analysis.

When women are forced into jobs where they produce less, there is an efficiency loss roughly equal to the reduction in their output. Moreover, because they work in jobs where they are less productive, women receive a lower wage. Thus the entire efficiency loss is essentially borne by women. It is true that male workers benefit from a higher wage, due to the artificial scarcity of labour created in their part of the market because women are no longer able to work there. However, other factors of production lose because their interest, rent, and profit income is squeezed by the higher wage for men. Since most other factors of production are owned by families with a male wage earner, it is not clear that such families benefit overall or lose: They gain because of the higher wage for the male earner, but lose because of the reduced income of their other factors of production; if there is a working woman in the family, the reduction in her wage constitutes part of the loss. The one clear message is that there is an efficiency loss, and this loss will be borne primarily by single women and families without a male wage earner.

Work of Equal Value

With equal pay for men and women in the *same* job now a widely accepted principle, the focus has shifted to the question, What should be done when men and women are in *different* but equally demanding jobs, and women are paid less? Should nurses be paid less than truck drivers? Proponents of the principle of "equal pay for work of equal value" say no. If these jobs are judged comparable, in terms of the education, responsibility, skills, etc., that they require, then pay should be equalized. Moreover, certain federal and provincial labour laws now reflect this principle. However, critics are concerned because this policy requires that specific jobs be compared; and these comparisons will be based on subjective and arbitrary judgments by bureaucrats or judges who will be second-guessing labour markets. They will be imposing a detailed and complex system of wage controls that will leave many labour markets in a chronic condition of excess demand or supply.

To this argument, the proponents of equal pay for work of equal value reply: Relying on the market would allow discrimination to continue, and this is not acceptable.

IMPORTANT TERMS: MATCH THE COLUMNS

Match each term in the first column with the corresponding phrase in the second column. But before you do so, write you own definition of each term in the first column.

_____ **1.** marginal physical product (MPP) of labour
_____ **2.** marginal revenue product (MRP) of labour
_____ **3.** opportunity cost of labour
_____ **4.** value of the marginal product (VMP) of labour
_____ **5.** transfer price of labour

a. the additional revenue that a firm can earn by hiring one more worker
b. the wage necessary to induce a worker to change jobs
c. the additional number of units of output that a firm can produce by hiring one more worker
d. the marginal product of labour in another industry
e. marginal physical product of labour times the price of the employer's product

TRUE-FALSE

T F **1.** A profit-maximizing firm that is operating in perfectly competitive labour and product markets will hire labour to the point where the value of the marginal product equals the wage rate.

T F **2.** The demand for labour schedule shifts to the right whenever the marginal revenue product of labour schedule shifts to the right.

T F **3.** If the marginal revenue product of labour is less than the wage, a perfectly competitive firm can increase its profits by hiring more labour.

T F **4.** A minimum wage increases the income of some workers while decreasing the income of some others.

T F **5.** Even if there is an external cost of employing labour, a perfectly competitive labour market will still be efficient.

T F **6.** The marginal revenue product of labour is the amount the firm's revenue increases when it hires one more worker.

T F **7.** The value of the marginal product of labour is the same as the marginal revenue product of labour, if the hiring firm is a monopolist in its product market.

T F **8.** If the wage rate rises elsewhere in the economy, the wage and employment in a perfectly competitive industry will tend to rise.

T F **9.** There is a greater efficiency loss if the minimum wage is applied to just one industry, rather than to all industries.

MULTIPLE CHOICE

1. The marginal physical product of labour
- **a.** is based on the assumption that the use of all other factors is held constant as the employment of labour increases
- **b.** is based on the assumption that the use of all other factors increases by the same proportion as labour employment
- **c.** shows the additional revenue a firm can earn because it hires one more worker
- **d.** is set equal to the wage rate by an employer in equilibrium
- **e.** is the same as the value of the marginal product

2. A firm' s demand curve for labour is the curve showing its
- **a.** total physical product of labour
- **b.** average revenue product of labour
- **c.** marginal physical product of labour
- **d.** average physical product of labour
- **e.** marginal revenue product of labour

3. The demand for labour by a firm producing bolts shifts up in response to
- **a.** a rise in the price of bolts
- **b.** a fall in the marginal product of labour in the bolt-making industry
- **c.** a downward shift in the demand for bolts
- **d.** a decrease in the stock of machinery in the industry
- **e.** a decrease in the stock of other investment equipment in the industry

4. A leftward shift in the labour supply schedule may be the result of

a. a rightward shift in the marginal revenue product of labour schedule
b. a leftward shift in the marginal revenue product of labour schedule
c. higher available wages in other industries
d. a reduction in the marginal product of labour in other industries
e. a falling opportunity cost of labour

5. If there is a perfectly competitive market for farm labour, and there is a fall in the price of grain and other farm outputs, then there will be

a. a shift to the left in the labour supply curve
b. a shift to the left in the labour demand curve
c. a higher wage and more employment
d. a higher wage and less employment
e. a lower wage and more employment

6. The value of the marginal product of labour is equal to the marginal revenue product of labour

a. always
b. never
c. only if the hiring firm is a monopolist in its product market
d. only if the hiring firm is a perfect competitor in its product market
e. only if the hiring firm is an oligopolist in its product market

7. The total area under an industry's demand for labour schedule to the left of the existing quantity of employment equals

a. the income received by other factors in the industry
b. the total income of labour in the industry
c. the total income of labour and all other factors in the industry
d. total profits in the industry
e. the marginal revenue received by the industry

8. In perfect competition, the division of income in an industry is measured from the equilibrium point on its labour demand curve in the following way

a. Labour receives the triangular area to the southeast of this point, while the triangular area to the northwest goes to other factors of production.
b. Labour receives the rectangular area to the southwest of this point, while the triangular area to the northwest goes to other factors of production.
c. Other factors of production receive the rectangular area to the southwest of this point, while the triangular area to the northwest goes to labour.
d. Both the areas mentioned above go to labour; the income of other factors is shown on another diagram.
e. Both the areas mentioned above go to capital; the income of labour is shown on another diagram.

9. An increase in the price of houses (caused by an increase in the demand for houses) will result in

a. a shift to the right in the labour supply curve
b. a lower wage, and increased employment
c. a lower wage, and reduced employment
d. a higher wage, and reduced employment
e. a higher wage, and increased employment

10. In a perfectly competitive labour market for an industry, an increase in wages elsewhere in the economy will result in

a. a shift to the right in the labour supply curve
b. an increase in wages and employment in this industry
c. a decrease in wages and employment in this industry
d. a decrease in wages and an increase in employment in this industry
e. an increase in wages and a decrease in employment in this industry

11. In a perfectly competitive labour market for an industry, there will be an efficiency loss unless labour is hired to the point where

a. the marginal product of labour in this industry exceeds its marginal product elsewhere
b. the marginal product of labour in this industry is less than its marginal product elsewhere
c. the marginal product of labour in this industry is equal to its marginal product elsewhere
d. the opportunity cost of labour exceeds its marginal product in this industry
e. the opportunity cost of labour is less than its marginal product in this industry

12. If the government imposes a minimum wage above the prevailing wage in a perfectly competitive labour market

a. there will be an efficiency gain
b. some but not all workers will benefit
c. all workers taken together will benefit
d. employment will increase
e. employment won't change

13. In Canada, the minimum wage

a. is set by the federal government for the whole country
b. is higher for teenagers than for older workers in most jurisdictions
c. covers every industry in those provinces where minimum-wage legislation exists
d. is generally higher for women than for men in federal jobs
e. none of the above

14. The most likely result of discrimination against men in a perfectly competitive market for nurses' labour is

a. an increase in the income of male nurses
b. an increase in the income of female nurses
c. a decrease in the wages of female nurses
d. an increase in the income of other factors
e. a reduced supply of female nurses

15. The efficiency loss from sex discrimination in a perfectly competitive labour market

a. is borne to a large extent by single women, whose income is reduced

b. occurs because women are employed in more productive activities, while men are in less

c. occurs because income is transferred from male workers to other factors of production

d. occurs because income is transferred from female workers to non-labour factors of production

e. occurs because the other factors of production are owned by outsiders

EXERCISES

Table 33-1

Number of workers	Total physical output	Marginal physical product of labour	Marginal revenue product when price of output is $10 per unit	Marginal revenue product (MRP) when price of output is $15 per unit
0	0			
1	12			
2	19			
3	24			
4	28			
5	30			

1a. Fill in the missing data in Table 33-1 above for a hypothetical firm with a given stock of capital, which sells its output in a competitive market at a constant price.

If the wage rate is $55 per worker per day, then the firm will want to hire ___________ workers if the price of its output is $10, and ___________ workers when this price is $15.

1b. Fill in the missing data in Table 33-2 for another hypothetical firm, assuming that the wage it faces is $40 per worker per day and the price of its output is $5.

Table 33-2

Number of workers	Total physical output	Marginal physical product	Marginal revenue product
0	0	—	—
1		10	
2		9	
3		8	
4		7	
5		6	

The firm will be willing to hire no more than _________ workers. With this amount of employment, the firm's total revenue will be $___________, its total wage payment will be $___________, and the income of other factors will be $___________.

Plot the labour demand schedule of this firm in Figure 33-1. Draw a horizontal line at the wage rate of $40 per worker per day. Label as 1 the area representing labour income. Label as 2 the area representing the income going to other factors.

2. Consider the firm in Table 33-3 which is *not* selling its output in a perfectly competitive market; it is not facing a given price for its product. (In column 4, the price of its product falls as it sells more and more.)

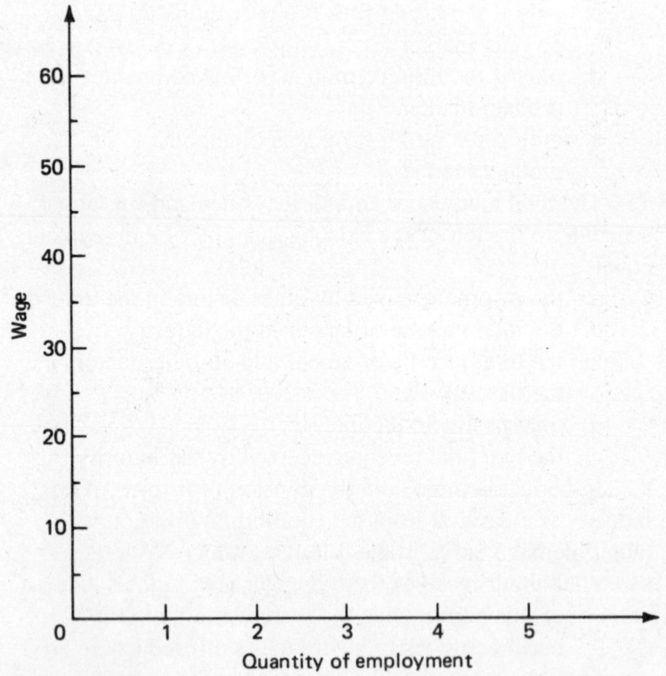

FIGURE 33-1

Fill in the missing items. Are the VMP and MRP the same? Why or why not?

3. Figure 33-2 depicts a perfectly competitive labour market with no externalities. The equilibrium wage rate is ___________, and the equilibrium quantity of employment is ___________. Suppose that a minimum wage of *U* is imposed. Then employment will be ___________. Next, suppose that the minimum wage is *H*, Then employment will be ___________, and the difference between demand and supply will be ___________. Fill in Table 33-4.

Table 33-3

(1) Number of workers	(2) Total physical product	(3) Marginal physical product	(4) Price of product	(5) Total revenue (col. 2 x col. 4)	(6) Marginal revenue product (MRP) (change in col. 5)	(7) Value of marginal product (VMP) (col. 3 x col. 4)
0						
1	16	16	$12	$192	$192	$192
2	31		11			
3	45		10			
4	58		9			
5	70		8			

Table 33-4

	Efficiency loss is area:	Total labour income is area:	Income of other factors is area:
No minimum wage			
Minimum wage at U			
Minimum wage at H			

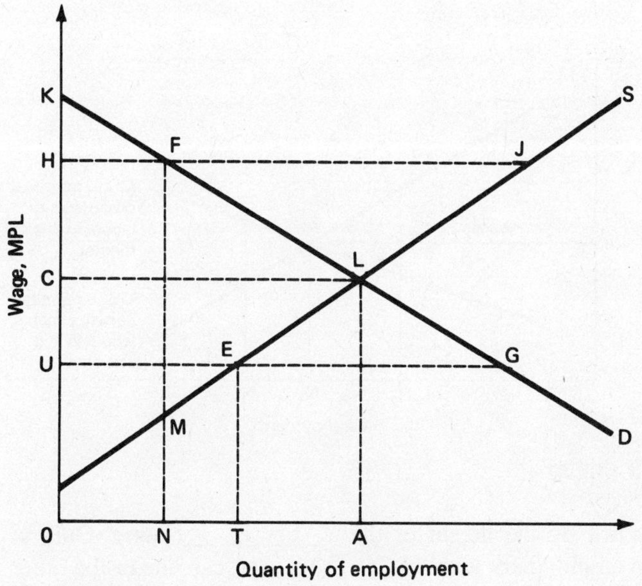

FIGURE 33-2

4a. Panel (*a*) in Figure 33-3 shows a perfectly competitive labour market in which there is no discrimination against women. The equilibrium wage rate is ___________, and employment is ___________; this is made up of N_M men and ___________ women. The income of men is area ___________, while women earn ___________. The income of other factors of production is ___________.

4b. Suppose now that there is discrimination against women and that N_F women are forced into the relatively unproductive market in panel (*b*). Equilibrium in the main labour market in panel (*a*) now moves to point ___________. In this labour market, men earn an income of ___________, while the earnings of other non–labour factors of production change from original area ___________ to ___________, for an [increase, decrease] of ___________.

4c. In the secondary, relatively unproductive labour market in panel (*b*), equilibrium is at point ___________, with ___________ females employed at a wage of ___________. Income of females is area ___________,while the income of other factors in this market is ___________.

4d. When we take *both* markets into account, we conclude that female labour income [increases, decreases] by ___________ as a result of discrimination; male labour income [increases, decreases] by ___________; and non-labour income [increases, decreases] by ___________. There is a transfer [from, to] male workers [from, to] other factors of area ___________. There is a loss overall—that is, an efficiency loss—of ___________. Since this efficiency loss is the same as the [loss, gain] to [women, men], we can therefore say that it is borne by [women, men].

5. (To answer this question, you need to study the text *and* Box 33-1 in the textbook.) A labour market in a perfectly competitive economy is shown in Figure 33-4.

a. The marginal product of labour (VMP) in this industry is shown by the ___________ curve, while the marginal product of labour elsewhere is shown by the ___________ curve. The equilibrium is at ___________, with wage ___________ and employment of ___________ workers. At this equilibrium, employers have [maximized, minimized] their profit by hiring labour up to the point where its marginal benefit—that is, the marginal product of labour in this industry as shown by the

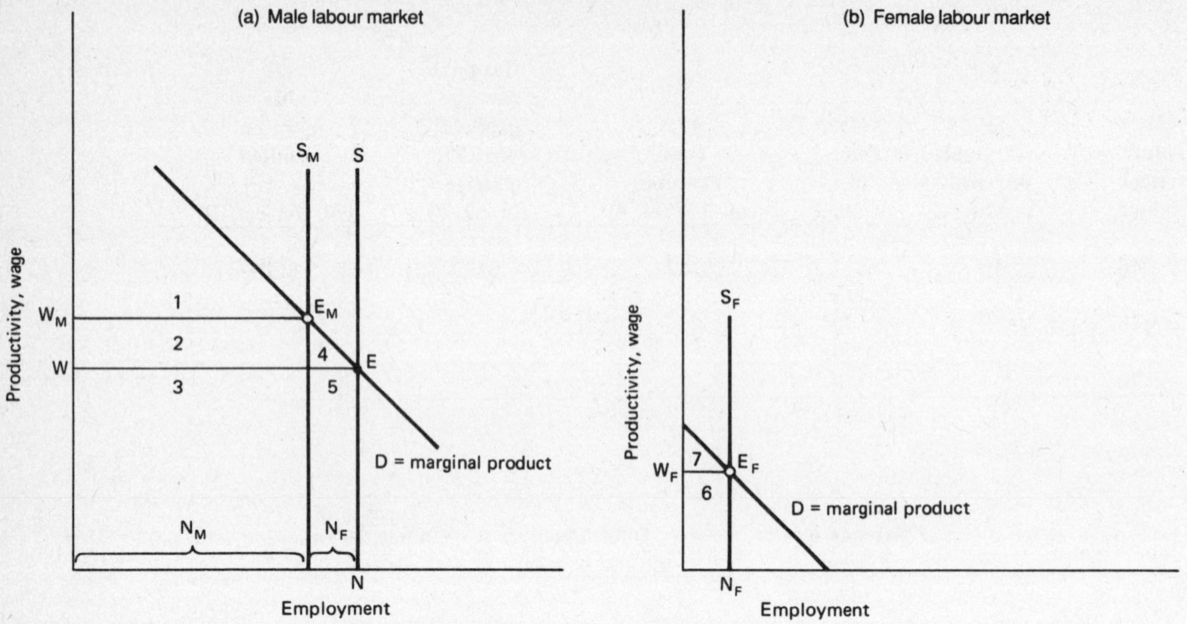

FIGURE 33-3

__________ curve—is equal to the marginal cost the *employers* face, as shown by __________. At the same time, employees have [minimized, maximized] their own benefit by offering their labour up to the point where their marginal benefit, as shown by __________, is equal to their marginal cost. This marginal cost to employees is called a [subsidy, opportunity] cost, because it represents their potential earnings in their [least, most] attractive alternative job.

b. If employment is at N_2, there is an efficiency [gain, loss] of area __________ because the N_2N_1 extra workers employed would have a [higher, lower] marginal product elsewhere—as shown by the __________ curve—than in this industry, where their marginal product is shown by the __________ curve. On the other hand, if employment in this industry is at N_3, then there is an efficiency [gain, loss] because N_3N_1 workers should be employed in this industry, but are not. These workers would have marginal product here shown by the __________ curve compared to their [lower, higher] marginal product elsewhere, as shown by the height of the __________ curve. Only at an employment level of __________ can one or the other of these efficiency losses be avoided.

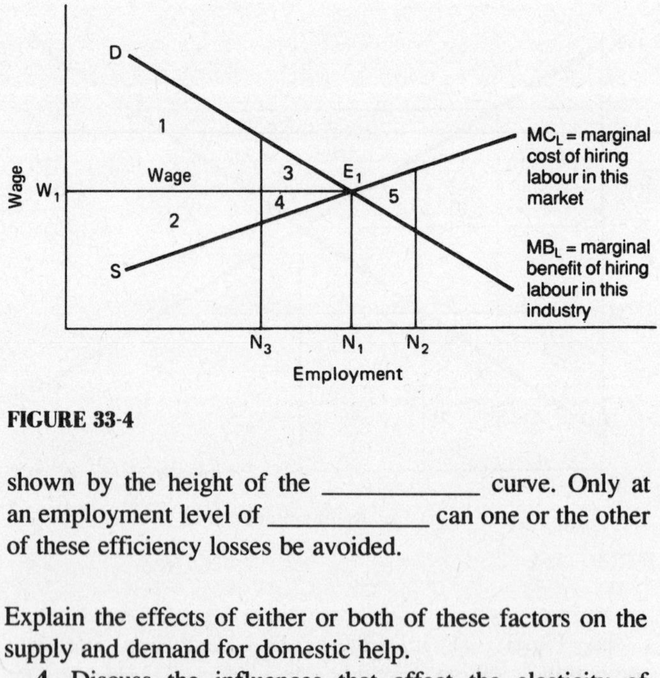

FIGURE 33-4

ESSAY QUESTIONS

1. "The labour demand schedule slopes down for the same reason that the demand curve for a consumer good slopes down." Explain to what extent this is or is not true.

2. List and explain some influences that could shift the labour supply curve for an industry. In each case, indicate in which direction the shift would occur.

3. Over the past 50 years, the number of domestic servants in the United States has fallen dramatically. Do you think this is because of the price and availability of labour-saving household appliances? Or is it due to rising wages in other occupations? Or do both factors play a role? Explain the effects of either or both of these factors on the supply and demand for domestic help.

4. Discuss the influences that affect the elasticity of demand for labour, by first reviewing the influences affecting the elasticity of demand for a consumer good discussed in Chapter 21 in the text.

5. How would the elasticity of the supply of labour in a particular market be affected by a decrease in the cost of moving from one city to another?

6. Would you expect labour market discrimination to be a greater problem in a perfectly competitive industry or in a monopolistic industry?

ANSWERS

Important Terms: **1** c **2** a **3** d **4** e **5** b
True-False: **1** T **2** T **3** F **4** T **5** F **6** T **7** F **8** F **9** F
Multiple Choice: **1** a **2** e **3** a **4** c **5** b **6** d **7** c **8** b **9** e **10** e **11** c **12** b **13** e **14** b **15** a
Exercises:
1a.

Table 33-1 completed

W	O	MPP	MRP if $P = \$10$	MRP if $P = \$15$
0	0	—	—	—
1	12	12	120	180
2	19	7	70	105
3	24	5	50	75
4	28	4	40	60
5	30	2	20	30

2,4
1b.

Table 33-2 completed

Number of workers	Total physical output	MRP
0	0	—
1	10	$50
2	19	45
3	27	40
4	34	35
5	40	30

3, $135, $120, $15
Figure 33-1 completed:

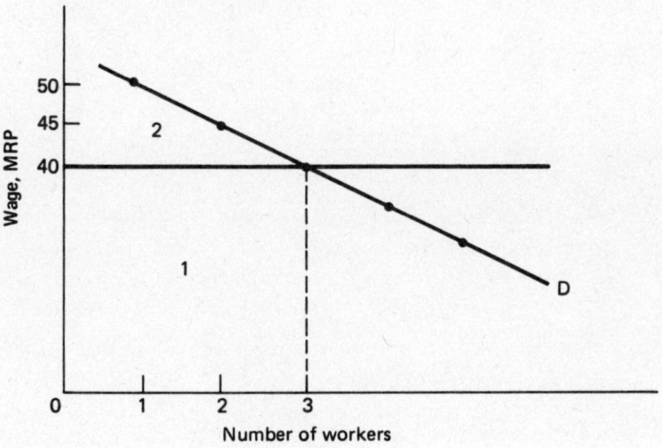

2.

Table 33-3 completed

(1) Number of workers	(2) Total physical product	(3) Marginal physical product	(4) Price of product	(5) Total revenue (col. 2 x col. 4)	(6) Marginal revenue product (MRP) (change in col. 5)	(7) Value of marginal product (VMP) (col. 3 x col. 4)
0						
1	16	16	$12	$192	$192	$192
2	31	15	11	341	149	165
3	45	14	10	450	109	140
4	58	13	9	522	72	117
5	70	12	8	560	38	96

Not the same. In column 7, the VMP of the second worker is $165—that worker's marginal physical product (MPP) of 15, times the $11 price at which the firm sells its output. In column 6, the marginal revenue product (MRP) is less than this—namely, $149, because MRP takes into account something else that happens when the second worker is hired: To sell its larger output, the firm has to reduce its price by $1, from $12 to $11. Therefore, hiring the *second* worker means that the firm gets a $1 lower price for the 16 units of output of the *first* worker. For this reason, its revenue is $16 less. Note indeed that this $16 is the difference between the $165 VMP and the $149 MRP.

3. *C, A, A, N, FJ.*

Table 33-4 completed:

Zero	OCLA	KLC
Zero	OCLA	KLC
FLM	OHFN	KFH

4a. *W, N,* N_F, 3, 5, 1 + 2 + 4. **4b.** E_M, 2 + 3, 1 + 2 + 4, 1, decrease, 2 + 4. **4c.** E_F, N_F, W_F, 6, 7. **4d.** decreases, 5 – 6, increases, 2, decreases, 2 + 4 – 7, to, from, 2, (4 + 5) – (6 + 7), loss, women, women. **5a.** *D, S,* E_1, W_1, N_1, maximized, *D,* W_1, E_1, maximized, W_1E_1, *S,* opportunity, most. **5b.** loss, 5, higher, *S, D,* loss, *D,* lower, *S,* N_1.

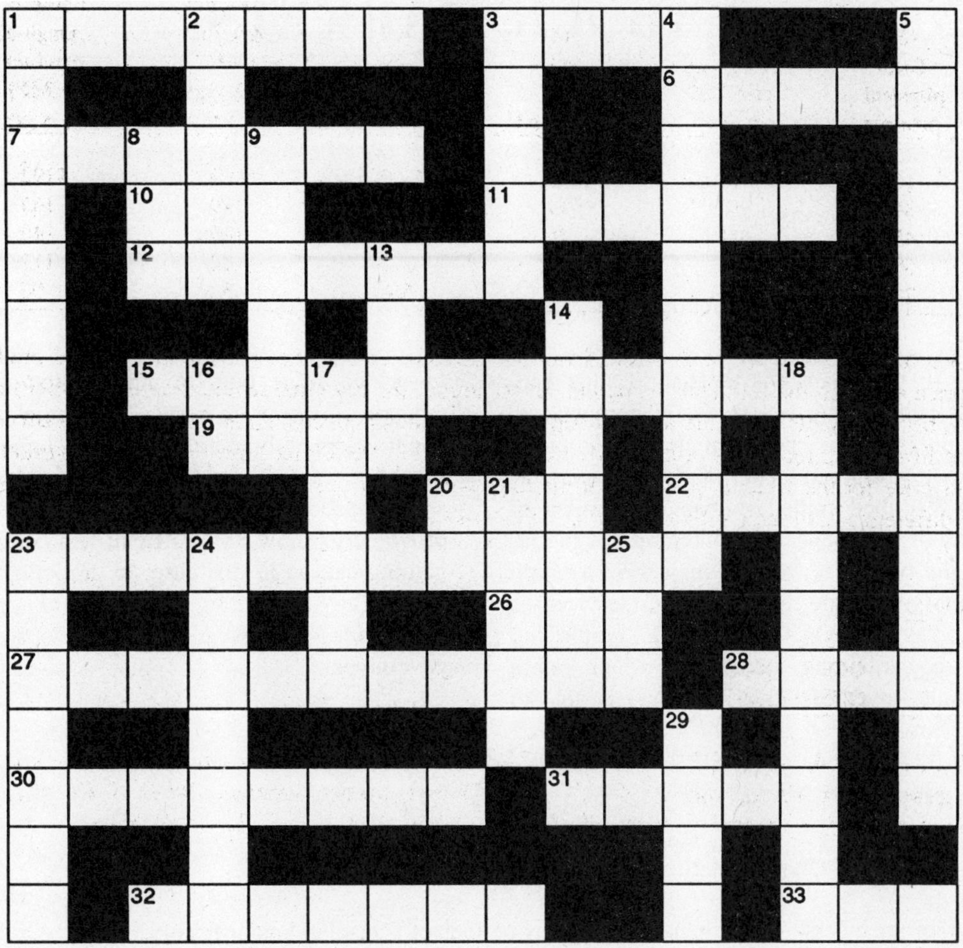

Across

1, 3. Proponents say this raises the incomes of the poor; critics say it causes unemployment.
6. gas commonly used as a refrigerant
7. He explained the idea of comparative advantage.
10. historical period
11. a barrier to international trade
12. one of the arguments for the protection of domestic industry from foreign competition
15. Bastiat suggested that these people might object to the unfair competition from the sun.
19. new (German, fem.)
20. a flying mammal
22. wept
23. the key to rising living standards
26. tool for propelling a boat
27, 28. Where this is low, a country has a comparative advantage.
30. form an association of workers
31. large mammal
32. a third type of efficiency (in addition to allocative and technological efficiency)
33. He is associated with idea that, in aggregate, supply creates its own demand.

Down

1, 23. In a perfectly competitive economy, the wage is equal to the value of this.
2. picture
3. In an efficient economy, this is avoided.
4. the goal of getting the most out of our productive efforts
5. one of the major arguments for tariffs (2 words)
8. ungentlemanly chap
9. Do this to oil to produce gasoline.
13. African river
14. He suggested that tariffs were equivalent to a "negative railway."
16. indefinite article preceding vowel
17. sweet, melodious
18. externalities
20. prefix meaning "two"
21. A good lawyer can often help clients to ____________ taxes.
24. industry with only two sellers
25. attempt (verb)
29. organization for negotiating over tariffs and other trade barriers (abbrev.)

Chapter 34

WAGES IN IMPERFECTLY COMPETITIVE LABOUR MARKETS

MAJOR PURPOSE

The key objective in this chapter is to analyse what happens when labour markets are not perfectly competitive. Typically, the result is inefficiency, and this is compared with the efficient outcome when labour markets are perfectly competitive, as described in the last chapter. Elements of imperfect competition may appear on either side of the labour market. On the one side, workers may form a union which, as a monopoly (a single seller of labour services) is able to raise the wage rate. On the other side, employing firms may form a bargaining association which, as a monopsony (a single buyer of labour services) is able to *lower* the wage rate. In either case, an inefficiently low amount of labour is hired. The interesting, and quite frequent, case of bilateral monopoly arises when there is a monopoly (a union) on the workers' side of the market, and a monopsony on the employer's side. Illustrations are provided to show how difficult and complicated wage bargaining can be in this case. In particular, special problems arise in any bargaining between a monopoly union of public service workers and their monopsony employer—the government.

LEARNING OBJECTIVES

After you have studied this chapter in the textbook and the study guide, you should be able to

- Describe how union membership has changed in various periods of Canadian labour history
- Describe the changing relationship between Canadian and American union movements
- Explain the differences between Canadian and U.S. labour legislation on the question of compulsory union membership
- Show in a diagram the inefficiency that results when a union succeeds in raising wages in an otherwise perfectly competitive labour market
- Explain the inefficiency that results when a union negotiates a featherbedding contract
- Describe, on the other hand, the special ways that a union may improve efficiency
- Show, in particular, how efficiency may be increased if a union is formed in a labour market that has previously been monopsonized
- Analyse bilateral monopoly, where market power is held by a union on one side of the market, and by a single employer (or an employers' association) on the other
- Explain why a strike may occur even though all parties lose from it
- Show why there may be large internal *and* external costs if labour negotiations break down and a strike occurs
- Identify three ways of averting an imminent strike
- Explain the possible imbalance of bargaining power when a public service union negotiates with a government
- State four reasons why workers get different wages

HIGHLIGHTS OF THE CHAPTER

The major topics covered in this chapter include (1) the history of the labour union movement in Canada, and its relationship with the U.S. labour movement; (2) the effects of introducing a union into an otherwise perfectly competitive labour market; (3) the effects of introducing a monopsony (a single buyer) into an otherwise perfectly competitive labour market; (4) a description of bilateral monopoly, where a monopoly union bargains with a monopsony employer; (5) the reasons why public service employees form a union, but the special problems that then arise; and (6) the reasons why wages aren't the same for all workers.

History

As Figure 34-1 shows, there have been four distinct periods in the modern history of the Canadian labour movement.

1. During the 1920s and 1930s, union membership in Canada did not grow by very much. The most important labour organization, the Trades and Labour Congress of Canada (TLC), was essentially a federation of *craft* unions (like its U.S. counterpart, the American Federation of Labour (AFL). As a result, it did not appeal to unskilled workers in mass-production industries who did not belong to a particular "craft." Furthermore, there was strong employer resistance to the growth of unions, and the labour legislation during that period made it hard for unions to overcome this resistance.

2. During the 1940s and early 1950s, union membership grew very rapidly in Canada. In part, the reason for this was the rapid rise in *industrial* unions, which brought the unskilled workers in mass-production industries into the union movement. Canada's industrial unions were organized in the Canadian Congress of Labour (CCL), the counterpart to the American Congress of Industrial Organizations (CIO). Furthermore, Canada's labour legislation changed during this period, with the right of workers to unionize becoming explicitly recognized; the 1945 *Rand formula* set a precedent by making it legal for a labour contract to compel all workers to contribute financially to the union.

3. In the decade between the early 1950s and early 1960s, union membership in Canada grew only slowly, in part reflecting the relatively slow growth of employment in industries in which unions have traditionally been important, in part reflecting continued strife between craft unions and industrial unions. However, this strife has gradually diminished, and most unions of either type are now affiliated with the Canadian Labour Congress (CLC), which was created in 1956 through a merger of the TLC and CCL. (In the United States, a similar merger created the AFL–CIO.)

4. Since the early 1960s, union membership has again been growing at a moderate rate. However, the pattern of growth has been different from that of earlier periods. Union membership in the private sector and in the traditional international unions has continued to grow slowly. Most of the growth in union membership in the 1960s and 1970s has occurred instead in *national unions*; that is, Canadian unions which are not affiliated with U.S. labour organizations. In particular, there has been rapid growth in union membership in the public service, and public sector unions are national unions.

(In the United States, growth in union membership has been much slower than in Canada during the last few decades. Part of the reason for this has been public hostility to unions in the United States, as well as the passage of legislation such as the Taft-Hartley Act, which outlaws compulsory checkoff of union dues and gives individual states the right to pass laws prohibiting union shops or closed shops. Closed shops and union shops are legal in Canada.)

The Effects of Unions

A union gives workers a voice in presenting grievances to their employer. It also negotiates with management to establish seniority rules and improve working conditions. These benefit not only the workers but also the employer, who is able to offer more attractive jobs and therefore reduce quit rates.

But the main objectives of a union are to protect the jobs and raise the wages of its members. According to recent estimates from both the United States and Canada, unionized workers get anywhere from 8% to 18% higher wages than comparable non-unionized workers. If a union is established that raises the wage in a previously competitive labour market, there are three main effects: (1) There is a reduction in employment and in the income of workers who lose their jobs; (2) there is an increase in the wages and incomes of workers who still have jobs, with this increase coming at the expense of other factors of production; and (3) there is a triangular efficiency loss that can be measured by the usual geometric technique. Study Figure 34-2 in the textbook until you can demonstrate these three effects on your own.

Finally, a union tries to protect its members' jobs in three ways:

1. It may try to negotiate a shorter work week. If there is unemployment, fewer hours per worker means more workers can get jobs.

2. It can press the government to restrict imports. In Chapter 32 we saw that this may indeed increase employment in Canada; however, on balance the net effect of such protection is unfavourable.

3. It can negotiate a featherbedding agreement. There are two main effects of introducing a featherbedding agreement into a previously competitive labour market with no externalities: (a) Employment in that market increases, and the job security of union members is maintained; and (b) there is an efficiency loss, not only because employment exceeds the efficient, perfectly competitive quantity, but also because workers are typically employed under such an agreement in useless jobs, rather than jobs with some productivity. (An example of a useless job was the employment of railroad firemen on diesel locomotives that had no fire. This was a zero-productivity task—a classic case of featherbedding.)

So far, this analysis of the efficiency losses that result from unions is overly harsh, because in some ways unions *improve* efficiency. First, by giving workers a voice, unions provide them with an alternative to quitting or being fired when a problem arises. Thus, they save unnecessary costs of labour turnover. Second, by improving working conditions, they can reduce the tension between workers and employers, and thus create a more productive atmosphere. Third, a union's bargaining power may simply offset the bargaining power of monopsonist employers; in this case, a union may increase efficiency. (Remember that our earlier discussion of the efficiency losses from a union applies only if the labour market is perfectly competitive before the union is formed.)

Monopsony

As a single employer of labour, a monopsonistic firm tries to exploit its market power by reducing wages. If it succeeds—in an otherwise perfectly competitive labour market—the three main effects will be to (1) transfer income from labour to other factors of production; (2) reduce employment; and (3) create an efficiency loss. Study Figure 34-3 in the textbook until you can demonstrate these three effects on your own.

Bilateral Monopoly

In many labour markets, there is bilateral (two-sided) monopoly, with market power being held both by a union on the one side and by a monopsonistic employer on the other. Unfortunately, this case is also the most difficult to analyse.

To illustrate, suppose a union is formed in a labour market where a monopsonist employer has been keeping the wage rate below the perfectly competitive level. In this case, the formation of the union may raise the wage back toward the perfectly competitive level. If this is the outcome, the union will simply be undoing some of the effects of the monopsony. Specifically, the union will (1) transfer income back from other factors of production to labour, (2) increase employment, and (3) reduce the efficiency loss from monopsony. Before reading further make sure you can illustrate these effects with a diagram similar to Figure 34-5 in the textbook.

However, the outcome is not this simple to predict, because there is no guarantee that a newly formed union will only raise wages *toward* the perfectly competitive level; it may raise wages beyond this. If this happens we can no longer be sure that the union will increase efficiency. This is the basic problem in analysing bilateral monopoly: We don't know where the wage will be set. All we know for sure is that the wage will be somewhere between the high wage the union seeks and the lower wage the monopsonistic employer seeks. At what point the wage will be determined within this range depends on the bargaining power of each side. This, in turn, depends partly on the ability of each to outlast the other in the event of a strike. Thus, the bargaining power of the union depends upon the size of the union's strike fund. The bargaining power of the employer depends upon its inventories of finished goods that it continues to sell during a strike.

Strikes

In a sense, everyone is damaged by a strike. The employer loses profits, and the labour force loses wages. Nevertheless, strikes do occur, because (1) each side may see a strike as a way of getting a more favourable wage rate than the other side's "final offer"; (2) each side may want to increase its future credibility and bargaining power by clearly demonstrating that it is prepared to allow a strike to take place; or (3) either side may make a bargaining mistake that prevents agreement from being reached before a strike deadline. In comparison with other countries, Canada has a record of relatively frequent and long-lasting strikes. Nevertheless, in an average year the typical Canadian worker spends less than one day on strike.

One reason why strikes pose an important issue for public policy is spillovers—that is, costs of strikes to people not involved in the bargaining. For example, a transit strike prevents people from getting to their jobs.

There are three main ways of averting a strike when the two sides don't seem to be able to reach an agreement by themselves. (a) The government (federal or provincial, depending on who has the jurisdiction over labour relations in the industry involved) may appoint an outsider to act as a mediator or conciliate between the parties. (b) Both sides may agree to voluntary arbitration, in which a third party decides upon a settlement that both sides agree in advance to accept. (c) If they don't agree to voluntary arbitration, the government may force them to accept compulsory arbitration.

Unions of Public Service Employees

Unions in the public sector raise problems because they have such a strong bargaining position, for the following reasons:

1. There are large spillover costs to the voting public when public servants such as transit workers or the police go on strike. Thus, voters may exert great pressure on the government to settle the dispute.

2. Public servants know that, in the last analysis, the government will almost certainly be able to find *some* way of raising the funds necessary to pay a higher wage. The government can tax or borrow in a way that is not available to private employers.

3. A union has much greater bargaining power over a financially weak government than it would have over a financially weak private employer. The reason is that a strike won't force a government out of business, but it might drive a private employer bankrupt.

4. Because public service employees now constitute a large block of voters, politicians are reluctant to fight hard against their wage demands.

Because public servants have such a strong bargaining position, it is often suggested that they should not be allowed to strike, or even form a union. But this would raise a problem. If these workers cannot form a union, how can they defend themselves against a monopsonistic employer (the government). If not with a union, what else?

Wage Differences

Wage differences can exist for at least five different reasons: First, there may be *dynamic wage differentials.* When new job opportunities open up in an industry, wages must rise temporarily to attract workers from other industries. Eventually, the influx of new workers will bring the wages back down. Second, *compensating wage differentials* give workers more pay for especially hazardous or unpleasant jobs. Third, monopoly or monopsony power may be greater in some labour markets than in others. Fourth, barriers to entry can keep wages artificially high in some jobs, while discrimination keeps them low in others. Fifth, those with special talents and skills earn a higher wage because they are more productive, as we shall see in the next chapter.

IMPORTANT TERMS: MATCH THE COLUMNS

Match each term in the first column with the corresponding phrase in the second column. But before you do so, write your own definition of each term in the first column.

_____ **1.** seniority rules
_____ **2.** industrial union
_____ **3.** craft union
_____ **4.** collective bargaining
_____ **5.** Trades and Labour Congress of Canada (TLC)
_____ **6.** Rand formula
_____ **7.** Canadian Congress of Labour (CCL)
_____ **8.** closed shop
_____ **9.** union shop
_____ **10.** open shop
_____ **11.** right-to-work law
_____ **12.** jurisdictional dispute
_____ **13.** checking off
_____ **14.** featherbedding
_____ **15.** monopsonist
_____ **16.** strike fund
_____ **17.** injunction
_____ **18.** mediation
_____ **19.** arbitration
_____ **20.** dynamic wage differentials
_____ **21.** compensating wage differentials
_____ **22.** national union
_____ **23.** Canadian Labour Congress (CLC)

a. a collection of industrial unions, like the American CIO
b. a union whose members all belong to the same craft or profession, although they may work in different industries (Examples are the plumbers' and carpenters' unions.)
c. formed through a merger of the TLC and the CCL
d. differences that may arise if labour views some jobs as less attractive then others (Employers have to pay a higher wage to fill the unattractive jobs.)
e. preference in sequencing of layoffs to those who have been longest on the job
f. a union whose members all work in the same industry or group of industries, although they may belong to different crafts or professions (Examples are the United Auto Workers and the United Mine Workers.)
g. employing labour in superfluous jobs
h. a statute making closed shops or union shops illegal
i. differences in wages that arise because of changing demand or supply conditions in the labour market (These differences tend to disappear over time as labour moves out of the relatively low-wage jobs and into those that pay a relatively high wage.)
j. a union not affiliated with a similar foreign union
k. a collection of craft unions, like the American AFL
l. negotiations between a union and an employer over wages, fringe benefits, hiring policies, job security, or working conditions
m. a court order compelling someone to refrain from a particular act, such as a strike
n. a firm in which an employer can hire only workers who are already union members

o. a sum of money owned by a union for the purpose of supporting its members while on strike
p. a single buyer
q. the practice of having employers collect union dues by deducting them from workers' paycheques
r. court decision legalizing a system of dues checkoffs
s. conflict between unions over whose members will do specific jobs
t. a firm in which employees do not have to join a union
u. the specification of a third party to suggest a compromise settlement in labour dispute (The decision of the third party is binding upon both labour and management.)
v. a firm in which anyone hired by an employer must join the union within some specified period
w. the specification of a third party to suggest a compromise settlement in a labour dispute (The third party cannot make any binding recommendations.)

TRUE-FALSE

T F **1.** Bilateral monopoly in the labour market means that employers are exercising monopsony power and labour is exercising monopoly power.
T F **2.** An industrial union draws its members from *any* industry, provided they have a common skill (such as plumbing).
T F **3.** The United Steel Workers is a craft union.
T F **4.** Like Samuel Gompers' American Federation of Labour, the Trades and Labour Congress of Canada was an attempt to organize labour for a political class struggle, rather than for the pursuit of improved wages and working conditions.
T F **5.** If wages are reduced below what they would be in perfect competition there will be a loss in efficiency.
T F **6.** A monopolist in the labour market will seek to raise wages, while a monopsonist will seek to lower them.
T F **7.** A union will tend to strike the financially weakest firm in the industry.
T F **8.** A company producing perishable goods is typically more vulnerable to strike threats than one producing durable goods.
T F **9.** The spillover cost of a strike must be less than the internal cost to the industry in which the strike occurs.
T F **10.** Public service unions have recently been growing less rapidly than other unions.
T F **11.** Compensating wage differentials would not exist if workers viewed all jobs as equally attractive.

MULTIPLE CHOICE

1. When a union negotiates seniority rules, workers with seniority are typically
- **a.** the first to be laid off, and the first to be rehired
- **b.** the first to be laid off, and the last to be rehired
- **c.** the last to be laid off, and the last to be rehired
- **d.** the last to be laid off, and the first to be rehired
- **e.** left unaffected in terms of being laid off or rehired

2. Craft unions draw their membership from
- **a.** workers in companies that build pleasure boats
- **b.** workers in companies that build any boats
- **c.** all workers in a specific industry regardless of their skills
- **d.** all workers in a specific industry provided they have the same skill
- **e.** all workers from any industry provided they have the same skill

3. Which of the following provides the greatest barrier to entry into a work force?
- **a.** an open shop
- **b.** a closed shop
- **c.** a union shop
- **d.** the Rand formula
- **e.** right-to-work legislation

4. If a firm can only hire workers who are already union members, it is described as
- **a.** a constrained shop
- **b.** a closed shop
- **c.** a union shop

d. an open shop
e. a restricted shop

5. Which of the following is most likely to occur if a union is introduced into a previously competitive labour market with no externalities?
a. Total income to labour will increase.
b. The income of some individual workers will increase.
c. Employment in that market will increase.
d. Incomes of non-labour factors of production will increase.
e. An efficiency gain will result.

6. Unionized workers in Canada and the United States are estimated to earn wages that are higher than comparable non-unionized workers by
a. 8–18%
b. 23–33%
c. 35–40%
d. 55–73%
e. less than 4%

7. The Rand formula
a. specifies that all workers must contribute to the union, whether or not they are union members
b. specifies that a strike cannot be held unless there has been a vote by all employees
c. specifies that illegal strikes during the time the agreement is in force will be penalized
d. was originally contained in a 1945 court decision
e. all of the above

8. Labour contracts in Canada specifying a closed shop
a. were prohibited by a federal law passed in 1967
b. are illegal for workers belonging to industrial unions
c. are generally legal in Canada
d. are the only kinds of labour contracts that are legal in Canada
e. are required under the Rand formula

9. Which of the following is the clearest example of featherbedding?
a. seniority rules
b. sexual harassment on the job
c. firemen employed on diesel trains
d. shorter work weeks
e. the firing of technologically displaced workers

10. Unions may have beneficial effects on efficiency
a. by removing labour's collective voice and thus reducing distractions in the workplace
b. by reducing communication between labour and management, and thus reducing distractions facing managers
c. by increasing quit rates
d. by reducing quit rates
e. by increasing management's market power to raise wages

11. Which of the following is most likely to increase employment in an otherwise perfectly competitive labour market?
a. the introduction of a union whose main effect is to raise wages
b. collusion by employers to act together like a monopsonist
c. an increase in the minimum wage
d. the introduction of a closed shop
e. featherbedding

12. A union's negotiating power will be increased most by
a. a large union strike fund
b. a small union strike fund
c. a right-to-work law
d. large inventory holdings by the employer
e. reduced tariff protection on the employer's output

13. In a labour market with a strong union, the creation of a monopsony bargaining association by employers tends to
a. raise wages even further
b. lower wages
c. transfer income from other factors of production to labour
d. (a) and (c)
e. none of the above

14. Baseball salaries before and after the players' escape from the reserve clause illustrate
a. how much unions can raise salaries
b. how much unions can lower salaries
c. how much monopsonists can raise salaries
d. how much monopsonists can lower salaries
e. the countervailing power of a union

15. In most labour negotiations
a. both sides start off close together, but they move farther and farther apart so that a strike results
b. both sides start off close together, but they move farther and farther apart, so that there is no strike
c. both sides start far apart, but they move closer together so that there is a strike
d. both sides start off far apart, but they move closer together so that eventually there is a settlement instead of a strike
e. one side sticks by its original offer, while the other makes all the concessions

16. Which of the following is *not* an example of a spillover cost of a strike?
a. the lost output in the industry in which the strike occurs
b. the lost output in other industries that depend on this one for supplies
c. the disruption of work when a transit strike stops people from getting to their jobs
d. the disruption in firms that do business through the mails when postal workers go on strike
e. the disruption of a nationwide sales conference of a chemical company when an airline goes on strike

EXERCISES

1a. In Figure 34-1, MC_L is supply, and MB_L is demand in a perfectly competitive labour market with no externalities. The equilibrium wage is ___________, and the equilibrium quantity of employment is ___________. In perfect competition the income of labour is area ___________, and the income of other factors is area ___________.

1b. Suppose now that a union is formed, which increases the wage to W_2. Then the quantity of employment will be ___________, the income going to labour still in this industry will be ___________, the income going to other factors will be ___________, and the efficiency [gain, loss] will be ___________.

1c. Now suppose that there is an external benefit from hiring labour in this activity. (To use the example cited in Chapter 33: Suppose that the workers being hired are musicians. They provide not only a direct benefit to their employer—the symphony orchestra— whenever they play in a concert, but also an external benefit because of their other contributions to the cultural life of the community.) Because of this external benefit, the marginal social benefit of labour is MB_S rather than just the employers' benefit MB_L. Then the efficient quantity of employment will be ___________. In perfect competition the wage will be ___________, the quantity of employment will be ___________, and the efficiency [gain, loss] will be ___________.

1d. With this externality, if a union is formed to raise wages to W_2, then the quantity of employment will equal ___________, and the efficiency [gain, loss] will equal ___________.

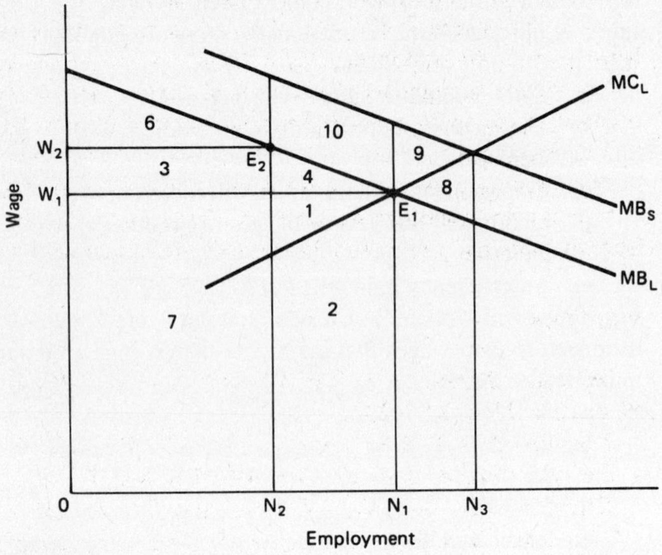

FIGURE 34-1

2. In Figure 34-2, *D* represents the demand for labour, while area 1 represents the external cost of a strike.

If a strike occurs, the cost to labour—in terms of lost wages— is area ___________, while the loss of income by other factors is area ___________. This means that the total internal cost to all factors in this industry is ___________. In addition, there is an [external, internal] cost of area ___________. Therefore, the total cost to society of a strike in this industry is ___________. The problem with a strike is that the labour and management participants in the negotiation only take into account [external, internal] costs ___________. The additional cost to other groups shown as ___________ may not be taken into account.

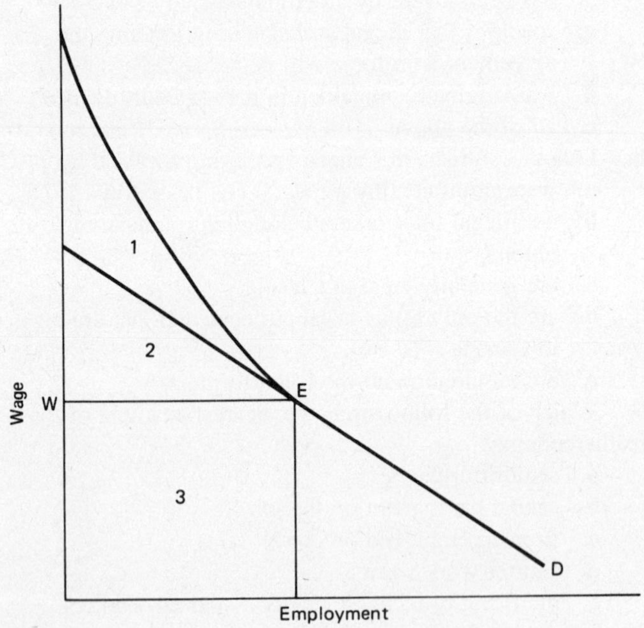

FIGURE 34-2

ESSAY QUESTIONS

1. Discuss several differences between U.S. and Canadian labour laws that give the union movement a stronger legal position in Canada than in the United States.

2. Do you think that unions help or hinder the attempt to achieve (a) stable prices and (b) an equitable distribution of income?

3. If there is no union on one side of the market to raise wages, and no collusion or association by employers on the other side of the market to lower wages, compare the bargaining position of the individual worker and the individual employer.

4. Describe the conditions under which an increase in the minimum wage may increase the amount of employment.

5. Describe the spillovers if each of the following went on strike: (a) municipal garbage workers, (b) air traffic controllers, (c) city police, and (d) steelworkers.

6. In the summer of 1980, the orchestra members of New York's Metropolitan Opera went on strike. Their union leaders thought they had a lot of bargaining power because of the opera's recent financial success. Why might this strengthen the union's bargaining power? Why might that bargaining power also have been strengthened by the knowledge that the opera would be receiving a large income from the nationally televised live performances that were to begin in the fall of 1980? After failing to reach agreement with the union, the management of the opera announced that the whole season would have to be cancelled, and offered to refund the tickets already bought. Eventually, one more round of negotiations was undertaken, agreement was reached, and management announced that the season could proceed after all, but with fewer operas than planned. Do you suppose that the announcement of cancellation of the season helped to speed up a resolution of the strike? Why or why not?

ANSWERS

Important Terms: **1** e **2** f **3** b **4** l **5** k **6** r **7** a **8** n **9** v **10** t **11** h **12** s **13** q **14** g **15** p **16** o **17** m **18** x **19** u **20** i **21** d **22** j **23** c

True-False: **1** T **2** F **3** F **4** F **5** T **6** T **7** F **8** T **9** F **10** F **11** T

Multiple Choice: **1** d **2** e **3** b **4** b **5** b **6** a **7** e **8** c **9** c **10** d **11** e **12** a **13** b **14** d **15** d **16** a

Exercises: **1a.** W_1, N_1, 7 + 1 + 2, 6 + 3 + 4. **1b.** N_2, 3 + 7, 6, loss, 1 + 4. **1c.** N_3, W_1, N_1, loss, 9. **1d.** N_2, loss, 1 + 4 + 9 + 10. **2.** 3, 2, 2 + 3, external, 1, 1 + 2 + 3, internal, 2 + 3, 1

Chapter 35

OTHER INCOMES

MAJOR PURPOSE

In the previous two chapters, we analysed labour income. The objective of this chapter is to analyse other forms of income—specifically, interest, profits, and rent. For example, in discussing interest rates, we see how they are determined by supply and demand in the market for loanable funds. This simple analysis is then extended to show the *efficiency* and *equity* effects when the government intervenes to impose a ceiling on interest rates.

Our initial emphasis in this chapter is on the income earned by physical capital, such as buildings and machinery. We analyse the role of the rate of interest in determining the amount and allocation of capital services in an economy, and how the presence of foreign capital in Canada affects the capital market and the return to capital. The focus later shifts to another important form of capital—human capital in the form of education and training. One form of human capital is a college education, and returns to such an investment are examined. Finally, this chapter analyses rent—the return to a factor of production above its opportunity cost (that is, above the income it could earn in an alternative activity). Rent is earned not only by land, but also by any other highly productive factor. Examples include the rent earned by highly skilled baseball players or business executives.

LEARNING OBJECTIVES

After you have studied this chapter in the text book and the study guide, you should be able to

- Explain the concepts of debt capital, physical capital, and human capital
- Explain how the demand for loanable funds is related to the marginal efficiency of investment schedule
- Show in a diagram how an interest-rate ceiling imposed on a perfectly competitive market for loanable funds will affect efficiency and redistribute income
- Explain why it is a fallacy to suppose that interest-rate ceilings necessarily help poor people
- State the basic reason why a substantial proportion of the capital used in Canada has been provided by foreign investors
- Describe the transfer effects that take place when foreign capital comes into Canada
- Explain why there is an efficiency gain when foreign investors are allowed to invest their funds in Canada
- Compare an investment in human capital and an investment in physical capital
- Describe the conditions under which investment in human capital could be less than the efficient amount, and the conditions under which it could be more than the efficient amount
- Explain why it is difficult to measure the rate of return on human capital
- Define rent and describe five examples
- Explain why rent can be earned not only by land, but by any factor of production
- Describe how rent is capitalized in the value of land and why this raises problems for any agricultural subsidy program that increases farm rents
- Describe the basic roles played by factor prices in a market economy

If you have studied the appendix to this chapter, you should be able to

List several reasons why multinational corporations (MNCs) exist

List several criticisms of the role of foreign capital in Canada

HIGHLIGHTS OF THE CHAPTER

About one-quarter of national income in the United States goes to factors of production other than labour. This chapter examines how these other incomes—such as interest, profit, and rent—are determined.

The Rate of Interest

The rate of interest indicates how present goods may be converted into even more future goods, through "roundabout" methods of production. The interest rate may be viewed as a price—the price that equates the demand and supply of loanable funds. The demand for loanable funds is the marginal efficiency of investment schedule, already described in Chapter 12. The supply of loanable funds measures the willingness of savers to part with present income —that is, their willingness to defer present consumption until the future when the loan is repaid. The higher the rate of interest, the greater their reward.

In practice, there is not one rate of interest but many, because of differences in risk. The greater the risk that a borrower will be unable to repay a loan, the higher the rate of interest that this particular borrower will have to pay. Interest rates are also influenced by a number of other factors, such as the expectation of inflation and the length of term of the loan. In addition, the expectation of a change in future interest rates will affect today's interest rates.

An important policy question studied in this section is, What happens if the government imposes an interest-rate ceiling? If the market for loanable funds is perfectly competitive, such a policy is likely to have four main effects:

1. The public saves less because the interest reward for savings has been reduced. Consequently, fewer loans are made and there is less investment.

2. Because of inadequate investment, there is an efficiency loss, shown by the familiar triangle in Figure 35-3 in the textbook.

3. There is an additional efficiency loss, because investment funds must be rationed, and the borrowers who do succeed in acquiring the limited funds may not be those with the most profitable investment projects.

4. Income is transferred from lenders to those borrowers who are still able to acquire loans. (They now pay a lower interest rate.)

It is a fallacy to suppose that interest-rate ceilings necessarily help poor people. The people who benefit are the borrowers who get the limited funds at a bargain price. But these borrowers may be quite rich, while those who don't get funds may be poor.

Normal profits are earned by owners of equity capital. *Normal profit* is defined as the return that could be earned in an alternative investment—in this case, the interest the owner could have earned lending these funds out instead.

Foreign-owned Capital in Canada

A large amount of the capital being used in Canada has been provided by foreign savers (today mostly from the United States, but earlier mostly from the United Kingdom). The main reason why Canada relies on a large amount of foreign saving is *not* that Canadians are less willing to save than people in other countries; instead, the reason is that Canada has a very large number of profitable investment opportunities in resource-based industries and elsewhere. Foreign capital in Canada includes both equity capital (mostly as a result of foreign direct investment) and debt capital (resulting from portfolio investment).

The presence of foreign capital in Canada has led to a much lower return to capital than would prevail if there where were no foreign capital here. As a result, *Canadian* savers earn a lower rate of return on their capital than they otherwise would (and supply less saving than they otherwise would). However, the additional capital provided by foreign savers raises the value of Canadian GNP and leads to higher incomes to other Canadian factors of production (primarily labour). As Figure 35-8 in the textbook shows, the gain to these other factors of production is larger than the loss to Canadian savers; hence, there is an efficiency gain (shown by areas 2 + 3 in the figure) from allowing foreign capital to come into Canada.

The efficiency gain shown in Figure 35-8 is computed on the assumption that the total return to foreign-owned capital (area 4 + 5 in the figure) is paid to the foreigners. In reality, however, part of the return represents a benefit to Canadians: that part which is paid to the government in taxes. (Foreign-owned firms pay corporate income tax at the same rates as Canadian-owned firms, and interest and dividends paid to foreigners are subject to Canadian withholding tax.) Thus, the efficiency gain shown in Figure 35-8 may be underestimated.

The possibility of efficiency gains provides an argument for letting foreign capital in with no restrictions. However, there are several arguments that can be used to justify *some* restrictions on the inflow of foreign capital. One argument noted in the text is that by limiting the amount of capital that we allow to come in, we may be able to attract it into Canada at a lower cost. (Other arguments against allowing unrestricted foreign-investment in Canada—such as the possible erosion of Canada's political sovereignty or cultural identity if we get too much capital—are discussed in the appendix to Chapter 35.)

Human Capital

There are two main forms of investment in human capital: (1) formal education, and (2) apprenticeship, or on-the-job training.

There are three reasons why investment in human capital could be less than the efficient amount.

1. Minimum wage laws tend to discourage employers from providing on-the-job training, because many employers cannot afford to provide an unskilled worker with both the minimum wage and such training.

2. Employers are reluctant to provide on-the-job training because trainees may quit and take their skills elsewhere.

3. There are external benefits from human capital. For example, when a highly educated scientist discovers a cure for a disease, it benefits the entire population. Because such external benefits are not taken into account by those making the decision to invest in human capital, this investment may fall short of the efficient level.

On the other hand, investment in human capital is encouraged by government subsidies to education. If these are substantial enough, then there may be *over*investment in human capital.

The concept of human capital also provides insight into the problem of discrimination. Workers will not be able to invest in human capital in the form of on-the-job training if they are discriminated against in employment that provides this training. Nor will they be able to provide their children with the best education if discrimination keeps their income low. As a consequence, minority groups may continue, over generations, to acquire inadequate human capital. Thus, they may now have low incomes, even if employers today do not discriminate.

Estimates indicate that the return graduates get from a university education fell during the 1970 and early 1980s. However, there is the prospect that, as we leave the population bulge of university graduates behind in the 1980s, the return to an education will start to increase. (Note that at recent rates of return, a university education is difficult to justify as an investment; the reason is that the returns to an education are in many cases below the returns earned on physical capital. Thus, an education must in part be justified as a consumption good.)

In practice, arriving at any sort of precise estimate of the returns to a university education are exceedingly difficult for a number of reasons. For example:

1. People with high incomes tend to have substantial education and considerable native ability. It's hard to sort out how much of their higher income is due to each.

2. Not all education is an investment; some of it is undoubtedly a consumption good.

3. Much of the return to education is in the form of a more satisfying job—and it is difficult to measure this effect.

Further complications arise if we wish to calculate the *social* return to education:

1. It is difficult to measure the external benefits of education. (How do you measure the benefits to society when a highly educated scientist discovers a new strain of wheat?)

2. It is difficult to tell whether education has increased the productivity of graduates or simply given them a "credential" that raises their income.

Rent

Perhaps the most important thing to understand about rent is that it can be earned not only by land, but also by other factors of production. It is defined as the earnings of *any* factor above its opportunity cost. The textbook gives five examples of economic rent.

1. the return to agricultural land because of differences in quality

2. the return to urban land because of differences in location

3. the income from mineral deposits of high quality

4. above-normal profits earned in an industry with barriers to entry

5. the return to an individual with a valuable talent or skill

A person's wage includes (1) a "basic wage" component, (2) a return to that individual's human capital, and (3) the rent on that person's special talents. This last item is rent as long as the opportunity cost for the individual is roughly the sum of the first two items.

The Role of Factor Prices

Factor prices do more than determine people's incomes. They also help to determine how much of each factor of production will be allocated to each task. For example, if labour becomes scarcer and capital more plentiful, wages will rise and the returns to capital will fall. This encourages firms to substitute cheap capital for expensive labour. While this may be a painful process for the workers displaced by automated capital equipment, our experience since the early days of the industrial revolution is that these people get jobs elsewhere. And this historical process of substituting capital for labour has been the source of much of our economic progress.

IMPORTANT TERMS: MATCH THE COLUMNS

Match each term in the first column with the corresponding phrase in the second column. But before you do so, write your own definition of each term in the first column.

____ 1. debt capital
____ 2. equity capital
____ 3. human capital
____ 4. physical capital
____ 5. marginal efficiency of investment
____ 6. time preference
____ 7. roundabout production
____ 8. foreign direct investment
____ 9. foreign portfolio investment
____ 10. withholding tax
____ 11. affirmative action
____ 12. economic rent
____ 13. monopoly rent

a. affects dividends and interest paid to foreign residents
b. the process of deferring the production of consumer goods in favour of producing capital goods that can be used in the future to produce even more consumer goods
c. results in more capital in foreign-controlled firms in Canada
d. funds that are lent to businesses (or others)
e. the schedule that ranks investments in terms of their percentage return
f. funds that are provided when part or complete ownership of a business is purchased
g. a program designed to correct discrimination by favouring those who have difficulty competing today because of discrimination they have suffered in the past
h. a desire to consume now rather than in the future. (This determines the supply curve for loanable funds.)
i. the return to any factor of production in excess of its opportunity cost
j. the plant, machinery, and other forms of equipment that can be used for producing goods and services
k. skills, training, and education of individuals that can be used for producing goods and services
l. includes foreign purchases of Canadian bonds
m. the above-normal profits accruing to any individual or business because of the possession of monopoly power

TRUE-FALSE

T F **1.** The return to capital (foreign-owned and Canadian-owned) is a larger share of Canadian national income than the income of all Canadian workers.
T F **2.** The greater the risk associated with a loan, the lower the interest rate will tend to be.
T F **3.** An interest-rate ceiling benefits all those who wish to borrow.
T F **4.** If a ceiling is imposed on the price of any good or service, then any necessary rationing of this good or service is likely to lead to an efficiency loss.
T F **5.** Since the Second World War, direct foreign investment in Canada has been growing steadily, but portfolio investment has been falling.
T F **6.** An inflow of foreign capital into Canada is likely to harm both Canadian labour and Canadian capital owners.
T F **7.** Factor prices act as a screening device to help allocate factors of production.
T F **8.** Human capital is like physical capital insofar as it represents an expenditure today that is expected to pay off in the future.
T F **9.** The costs of a university education include more than living, tuition, and book costs.
T F **10.** Studies indicate that the private rate of return to those acquiring a university education is the same as the social rate of return.
T F **11.** Very little of John McEnroe's tennis income is rent.

MULTIPLE CHOICE

1. What is the annual rate of return on a machine that costs $10,000 and generates enough sales over its 1-year lifetime to cover labour, materials, etc., plus $12,000?
   a. 120%
   b. 20%
   c. 12%
   d. 10%
   e. 2%
2. A company in a shaky financial position pays
   a. higher interest rate on its borrowing than it would if it were financially sound
   b. a lower interest rate on its borrowing than it would if it were financially sound
   c. the same interest rate on its borrowing as it would if it were financially sound
   d. a higher or lower rate, depending upon the rate of inflation
   e. a lower rate, because of the expectation of inflation
3. A rightward shift in the marginal efficiency of investment schedule is likely to
   a. decrease the rate of interest and decrease the amount of loanable funds
   b. decrease the rate of interest and increase the amount of loanable funds
   c. increase the rate of interest and increase the amount of loanable funds
   d. increase the rate of interest and decrease the amount of loanable funds
   e. increase the rate of interest and leave the amount of loanable funds unchanged
4. An increase in wages will induce a firm to
   a. hire more labour
   b. lower its prices
   c. use more labour-saving techniques
   d. use fewer labour-saving techniques
   e. produce more output
5. The income of a minority group is
   a. increased by current discrimination, but reduced by past discrimination
   b. reduced by current discrimination, but increased by past discrimination
   c. reduced by current discrimination, but not affected by past discrimination
   d. not affected by either current or past discrimination
   e. reduced by both current and past discrimination
6. If during the last 50 years the Canadian government had been following a policy of not allowing any foreign capital into Canada, then
   a. Canadian wage rates would have been higher than they currently are
   b. Canadian GNP would have been higher than it currently is
   c. the rate of return to capital in Canada would have been higher than it currently is
   d. the amount of Canadian-owned capital used in Canada would have been lower than it currently is
   e. none of the above
7. According to estimates from the late 1970s, the return to foreign capital represented what fraction of the total return to capital in Canada?
   a. 1/3
   b. 1/2
   c. 3/4
   d. 9/10
   e. no such estimates exist
8. The amount of net direct foreign investment (that is, direct foreign investment in Canada less direct Canadian investment in foreign countries)
   a. was lower in the 1950s than during subsequent decades
   b. was negative during the second half of the 1970s
   c. increases when a foreigner purchases bonds issued by Quebec Hydro
   d. has been larger than foreign portfolio investment since 1970
   e. increases whenever a foreigner buys shares in any Canadian corporation
9. A high school education can be viewed as
   a. a bad investment, because it yields a lower return than a university education
   b. a bad investment, even though it yields a higher return than a university education
   c. a bad investment, because it yields a lower return than physical capital
   d. a good investment, even though it yields the same return as a university education
   e. a good investment, because it yields a higher return than physical capital
10. In explaining why the private and social returns to a university education differ, we must take into account
    a. external benefits of a university education
    b. government subsidies to university education
    c. benefits—such as screening benefits—that raise graduates' incomes but may not be a benefit to society
    d. all of the above
    e. none of the above
11. The income of the typical physician includes
    a. rent on innate talents
    b. a return to human capital accumulated in medical school
    c. a return to human capital accumulated as an intern
    d. all of the above
    e. none of the above
12. For an economist, which of the following is *not* rent?
    a. an individual's potential earnings in an alternative occupation
    b. the above-normal profit of a monopolist
    c. earnings in excess of opportunity costs
    d. the income from oil land that has no other use
    e. the income from farm land that has no other use

EXERCISES

1a. Figure 35-1 shows a perfectly competitive market for loanable funds. The equilibrium rate of interest in this market is ____________, and the equilibrium quantity of loans is ____________. In a competitive equilibrium the interest income received by lenders would equal ____________.

1b. If the government imposes an interest-rate ceiling at M, then the quantity of loans will be ____________, the MEI will be ____________, the excess demand for loans will be ____________, the interest income received by lenders will be ____________, and the size of the efficiency loss will probably be [more, less] than the area ____________.

1c. If the interest ceiling is set at J, then the size of the efficiency loss will be ____________.

2a. Figure 35-2 shows a perfectly competitive market factor of production, where D is the demand curve and S_1 is the supply curve. In a competitive equilibrium, the factor price would be ____________, and the quantity of employment of the factor would be ____________. The income received by the owners of this factor would equal ____________, and the income received by the owners of all other factors would equal ____________.

2b. Now suppose that a tax is imposed on the owners of this factor, equal in amount to LE per unit of the factor that they are supplying. This would shift the supply curve up vertically by the amount LE, so that the after-tax supply curve is the one labelled S'_1. With the tax, the equilibrium price paid by the firms for the factor will equal ____________; the equilibrium price received, after tax, by the owners of the factor will equal ____________; the after-tax income accruing to the owners of the factor will be ____________; the amount of the tax collected will be ____________; the income received by other factors will be ____________; and the size of the efficiency loss will be ____________.

2c. Now suppose that there is no tax; instead, suppose that supply shifts from S_1 to S_2. S_2 is [more, less] elastic than S_1. With supply curve S_2 the equilibrium factor price will be [no different, more, less] than with S_1, and the equilibrium quantity of employment of the factor will be [no different, more, less] than with S_1.

2d. With S_2 the same tax LE will shift the supply curve up to the one labelled S'_2. With the tax, the equilibrium price paid by the firms for the factor will be ____________; the equilibrium price received, after tax, by the owners of the factor will equal ____________; the quantity of employment of the factor will equal ____________; the after-tax income accruing to the owners of the factor will equal ____________; the amount of the tax collected will equal ____________; the income received by other factors will equal ____________; and the size of the efficiency loss will equal ____________.

2e. If we consider the effects of a tax in the face of these two pre-tax supply curves S_1 and S_2, the one generating the greater tax revenue is [S_1, S_2]; the one that produces the smaller efficiency loss from the tax is [S_1, S_2]; the one generating the smaller reduction in employment is [S_1, S_2]; and the one reducing other incomes the least is [S_1, S_2].

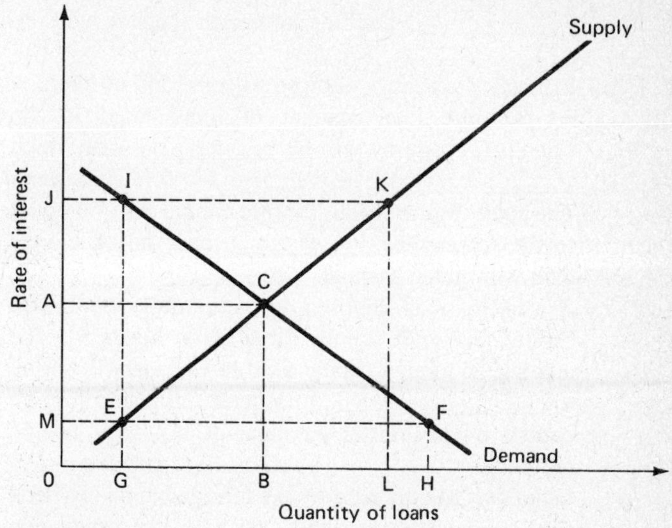

FIGURE 35-1

3. In Figure 35-3, the curve D = MEI represents the demand for capital funds in Canada, S_{Can} is the supply of funds from Canadian savers, and S_t is the total supply curve of funds, including foreign funds. The curve S_{tt} is the total supply curve of funds if a tax, given by the vertical distance T = (CG) = (AF), is imposed on the earnings of foreign capital.

a. If no foreign capital is allowed into Canada, the

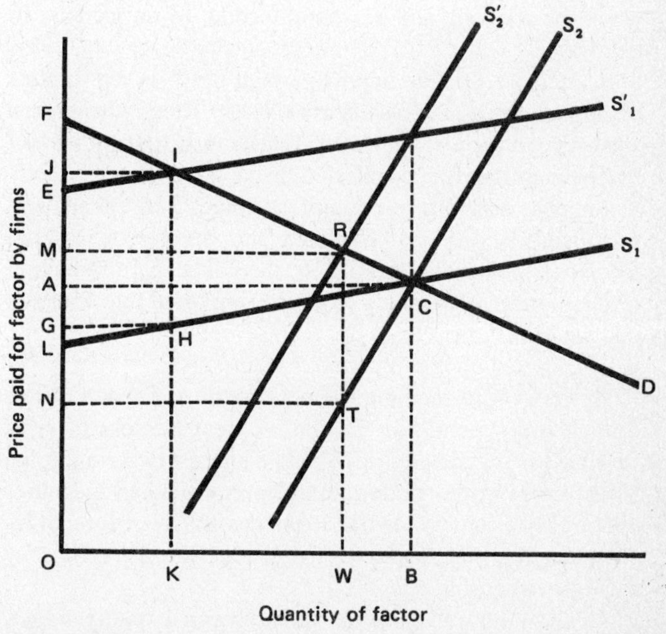

FIGURE 35-2

amount of funds used in the economy will be ____________, and the return to capital will be ____________.

b. If foreign capital *is* allowed to come in and there is no tax, the total amount of funds used in the Canadian economy will be ____________, of which ____________ will be supplied by foreign savers. The total return on the foreign capital will be equal to the rectangle ____________, and the efficiency gain will be the triangle ____________.

c. If a tax of T is imposed on the earnings of foreign capital, the total supply curve shifts up to S_{tt}. The amount of foreign capital used in Canada will shrink to ____________. The total return going to foreign capital owners (after payment of tax) will be the rectangle ____________. Canadian taxpayers will benefit by the tax paid by the foreign capital owners; the revenue from this tax is the rectangle ____________. This tax revenue, plus the triangle *ABC*, is now the total net benefit to Canadians of having this amount of foreign capital invested in Canada.

(The imposition of the tax will increase the gain to Canada from having foreign capital here if the tax paid by foreigners is greater than the reduction in the net gain to Canadian factors of production as the tax is imposed; that is, if the tax revenue rectangle is greater than the area *DICA*.)

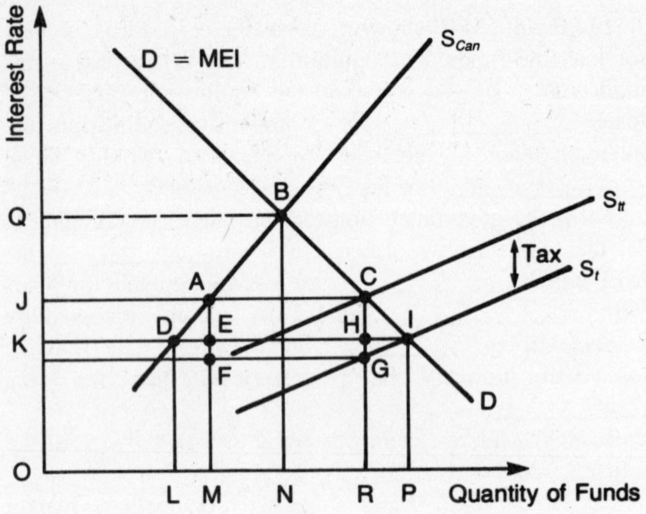

FIGURE 35-3

ESSAY QUESTIONS

1. The discoverers of insulin, Banting and Best, did not become millionaires as a result of their discovery, despite the fact that it has probably saved millions of human lives. Explain what this means if we wish to compare the private and social rates of return to human capital.

2. Name several factors that determine the position of the MEI schedule, explaining in each case how the schedule would be affected, and in what direction, by an increase in that factor.

3. Suppose Canada imposes a high tariff on the imports of a good such as washing machines. Thus, whenever a washing machine is imported, Canadian taxpayers benefit from the tariff revenue collected by the government.

Suppose now that a foreign firm comes into Canada and establishes facilities to produce a large number of washing machines in Canada; as a result, there is a sharp reduction in the number of washing machines imported into Canada, and the government loses the tariff revenue that would have been collected on the imported machines.

If we want to measure the net benefit to Canada of this foreign investment, how should we treat the loss of tariff revenue? Is it generally in Canada's interest to have foreign firms invest in production facilities in Canadian industries that are protected by tariffs? Is the possibility of foreign investment relevant when we try to measure the efficiency loss from imposing a tariff?

4. Show how the income of a surgeon is partly wages, partly return to human capital, and partly rent. Which of these components would be increased by the surgeon's efforts to develop more advanced surgical techniques? By the surgeon's honourary appointment to the Royal College of Surgeons? How would the rent component be affected if licensing requirements were relaxed to permit more people to practise surgery? Explain.

5. Most on-the-job training is job-specific. That is, the training is useful only for a particular job, such as selling insurance or operating a crane. Some on-the-job training is also firm-specific. That is, it involves "learning the ropes" of a particular firm's operations. Does the fact that workers may quit tend to discourage job-specific on-the-job training more or less than it does firm-specific on-the-job training? Explain.

6. As the interest rate rises, the price of bonds falls. (If necessary, review Box 13-1.) Bearing this in mind, show how an increase in the rate of interest affects potential lenders differently from those who have already lent money by purchasing bonds. Show also how it affects potential borrowers differently from the way it affects those who have already borrowed money by selling bonds.

7. Suppose that a factor had a totally inelastic supply. What would its opportunity cost be to society? Would it be accurate to classify all its income as rent? What can you say about the efficiency loss that would result from imposing a tax of a certain number of dollars on each firm for each unit of the factor that it uses?

8. The textbook sets out several reasons why it is difficult to measure the rate of return on investment in human capital. How many of these reasons also apply to measuring the rate of return on investment in physical capital?

ANSWERS

Important Terms: **1** d **2** f **3** k **4** j **5** e **6** h **7** b **8** c **9** l **10** a **11** g **12** i **13** m
True-False: **1** F **2** F **3** F **4** T **5** F **6** F **7** T **8** T **9** T **10** F **11** F
Multiple Choice: **1** b **2** a **3** c **4** c **5** e **6** c **7** a **8** b **9** e **10** d **11** d **12** a
Exercises: **1a.** *A*, *B*, 0*ACB*. **1b.** *G*, *J* (or *GI*), *EF* (or *GH*), 0*MEG*, more, *ICE*. **1c.** 0. **2a.** *A*, *B*, 0*ACB*, *FCA*. **2b.** *J*, *G*, 0*GHK*, *JIHG*, *FIJ*, *ICH*. **2c.** less, no different, no different. **2d.** *M*, *N*, *W*, 0*NTW*, *NMRT*, *MFR*, *RCT*. **2e.** S_2, S_2, S_2, S_2, S_2. **3a.** 0*N*, 0*Q*. **3b.** 0*P*, *LP*, *LDIP*, *DBI*. **3c.** *MR*, *MFGR*, *FACG*.

Chapter 36

INCOME INEQUALITY

MAJOR PURPOSES

In the three preceding chapters, we described how incomes are determined in our society. For example, some people have a higher income because of some innate talent or a large investment in human capital. Others may earn rent from land they own. Our first objective in this chapter is to summarize these economic reasons for differences in incomes, and complete that list with the additional reasons —such as just plain luck—that have not been dealt with in earlier chapters because they don't yield to economic analysis.

Our second objective is to examine the income distribution that results from all these influences. How much income inequality is there in Canada? This question is answered with a Lorenz curve, from which information can be extracted on how much of the nation's income is earned by low-income Canadians, and how much by high-income Canadians. The conclusion is that a great deal of inequality exists.

The next question we address is, How effective are government programs of taxation and expenditure that have been introduced to reduce inequality? The answer is that some have been more effective than others.

This, then, provides the background for tackling one of the most difficult issues in economics—the normative question. How unequal *should* incomes be? While economists cannot answer that question in a definitive way, they can throw a great deal of light on the issue.

LEARNING OBJECTIVES

After you have studied this chapter in the textbook and the study guide, you should be able to:

- Explain the reasons why some people have more income than others
- Explain how the Lorenz curve is constructed and why it provides a good picture of the nation's income distribution
- Explain why the Lorenz curve exaggerates the degree of inequality
- Identify three government policies designed to make incomes more equal, and specify which of these are most successful in achieving this objective
- Explain why the *direct* effects of policies designed to increase equality are at least partially offset by their negative *indirect* effects on incentives
- Demonstrate why it cannot be claimed that a free market leads to a fair distribution of income
- Show why complete equality of income is not necessarily fair; that is, show why equality is *not* the same as equity (fairness)
- Explain two principles for compromising between the extremes of a free market and complete equality
- Show why a conflict exists between equity and efficiency

HIGHLIGHTS OF THE CHAPTER

Four broad questions are addressed in this chapter:

1. Why is there income inequality?

2. How much income inequality exists in Canada?

3. How much of this inequality has been eliminated by government expenditures, transfers, and taxes?

4. How much inequality *should* there be?

Why Inequality?

There are at least eight reasons why some people may have more income than others: (1) their greater investment in human capital, (2) a rent earned on some innate ability, (3) greater financial wealth, either because they have inherited it or saved it, (4) greater market power due to membership in a union or possession of some other form of monopoly power, (5) a willingness to work harder or longer hours, (7) good connections and other benefits of family background, and (8) just plain luck—being at the right place at the right time. To illustrate how costly it can be if you are in the right place at the wrong time, consider the classic complaint of the failing stock-market speculator: "I got all the decisions exactly right; it was just the timing I got wrong."

While we don't have enough information to state precisely how much income inequality is due to each of these factors, there is some evidence that human capital may be the most important: In a U.S. study, it was found that as much as 60% of income differences were due to differences in human capital.

How Much Inequality Is There in Canada?

It goes without saying that the highest-income 20% of the Canadian population receives more income (before government taxes and expenditures) than the poorest 20%. But the question is, How *much* more? From the statistics, the answer seems to be: At least 20 times more. These and other similar comparisons are described, in Figure 36-1 in the text, by a Lorenz curve. This shows the percentage of the nation's income received by the poorest 20% of the population, by the poorest 40%, and so on. If everyone had exactly the same income each year, then the Lorenz curve would be the 45° "complete-equality" line shown in Figure 36-1 in the text. In this case, the poorest 20% would get 20% of the nation's income; the poorest 40% would get 40% of the nation's income; and so on. This is not true for the Canadian Lorenz curve shown in this diagram. Its large bow indicates a substantial degree of inequality.

Actually, this overstates the case. Even if there were perfect equality, with all families receiving exactly the same *lifetime* income, there would still be some bow in the Lorenz curve, since it measures incomes at a single point in time. The reason is that some families would be at the height of their earning power. They would be observed with far more income in a particular year than other, younger families, who would be just beginning their careers at a relatively low income.

How Much Do Government Expenditures and Taxes Reduce Inequality?

The Lorenz curve in Figure 36-2 in the text shows that government taxes and transfers reduce inequality by about a third. That is, the area between the complete inequality line and the Lorenz curve is reduced by a third. This reduction has been accomplished by three broad government programs:

1. *Taxation.* Taxes generally reduce inequality, because most taxes fall more heavily on the rich than on the poor.

2. *Cash transfer programs*, which include not only programs such as social assistance to needy families, but also Unemployment Insurance, Old Age Security, and family allowances.

3. *Transfers in kind*, such as education, housing, and health care services that are provided by the government.

Taken together, government transfers in cash and in kind are considerably more important than taxation in reducing inequality.

While these programs have the *direct* effect of reducing inequality, they also have an offsetting *indirect* effect. They *increase* inequality because they reduce the incentive for the poor to find and hold jobs. Furthermore, they reduce the incentive for families at all income levels to stay married. (When a family breaks up, its income is split between two families, lowering the income per family.)

What Is a "Fair" or "Equitable" Distribution of Income?

This question cannot be answered with complete certainty, because it is a normative question of "what ought to be," rather than a positive question of "what is." Nevertheless, most people would agree on two points:

1. The outcome of the free market has no special claim to being fair, because there is no way of justifying huge profits to monopolists. This is the problem of markets that are not perfectly competitive. But there are problems that go deeper than this. *Even if markets were perfectly competitive*, it would be difficult to argue that their outcome would necessarily be fair. The example in the text is of the individual who makes no effort or contribution to the nation's output, yet who receives a very high income because he owns inherited agricultural land. The only claim for perfect competition—and it's an important one—is that, in the absence of externalities, it provides an outcome that is *efficient*. But no claim can be made that this outcome is necessarily fair.

2. At the other extreme, complete equality of income

would not be fair either, because some people work harder and longer than others, and some people have more dangerous or odious jobs than others. Most would agree that such people "deserve" a higher income. After reading this section, it is essential that you be able to explain why equality and equity are not the same. Equality means "being equal," while equity means "being fair."

With these two extremes—the free market's distribution of income and a completely equal distribution of income—being judged unacceptable, what is a reasonable compromise? The text suggests two guidelines:

1. Set equality of *opportunity* as our objective, rather than equality of *reward*. View life as a race that should be fair, with all participants starting out together, although of course, not finishing that way. There should be no handicaps; for example, no one should be denied the opportunity of an education because of discrimination. But this doesn't mean that everyone should be awarded a university degree—that should depend on what people are able to do with their equal opportunity.

2. We should modify the rewards of the race. Some must finish last, but they should not be left in an impoverished state.

Perhaps the most important concept in this chapter is this: In striving for equity, it must never be forgotten that there is a *conflict between equity and efficiency*. To take the extreme care: If everyone were guaranteed an equal income, who would want to fight fires or work the long hours of the computer engineer? Equalizing the nation's income pie would reduce the size of that pie.

The ideas of Professor John Rawls discussed in Box 36-1 in the text are of considerable interest because for some time many people thought he had the solution to the problem of what the nation's income distribution should be. Rawls suggests that we imagine everyone to be in an "original position," in which no one knows what his or her particular income will be. Then ask what kind of income distribution reasonable people would choose from behind this "veil of ignorance." They would be choosing a distribution of income—that is, an "income ladder"—without knowing on which of the rungs they themselves would be located.

Rawls argues that in these circumstances, everyone would agree to his "difference principle": There should be complete equality in the distribution of income, *unless* there is an unequal distribution that leaves everyone better off. But he arrives at this conclusion by supposing that all the people who make this decision would figure that, with their luck, no matter what "income ladder" they might choose, they would end up on the lowest rung; so, they would choose an income distribution in which the lowest rung is as high as possible. In other words, they would use the *maximin principle* of choosing the distribution with the largest minimum income.

In this box, we give examples to show that Rawls' theory applies only to people who won't take a risk under *any* circumstances. Therefore, it just doesn't apply to average Canadians—let alone those who visit gambling casinos in search of risk. Thus, Rawls did not answer the question of what our income distribution should be. To this question, there may never be a clear answer.

IMPORTANT TERMS: MATCH THE COLUMNS

Match each term in the first column with the corresponding phrase in the second column. But before you do so, write your own definition of each term in the first column.

_____ **1.** Lorenz curve
_____ **2.** complete equality line
_____ **3.** cash transfers
_____ **4.** transfer-in-kind
_____ **5.** original position (Box 36-1 in the textbook)
_____ **6.** difference principle (Box 36-1 in the textbook)
_____ **7.** maximin principle (Box 36-1 in the textbook)

a. This appears in the Lorenz curve diagram and has a 45° slope. The Lorenz curve would coincide with this only if all families received exactly the same income in the year of observation.

b. the theory that income should be equally distributed unless there is some other distribution that makes everyone better off

c. This shows the percentage of national income that is received by the poorest 20% of families, by the poorest 40% of families, and so on.

d. It is in this location that Rawls would ask everyone to choose the best income distribution, without knowing what his or her position on that income scale will be.

e. payments made by the government, which receives nothing in return (These payments are not in cash, but instead are in the form of goods or services such as education or medical care.)

f. making the choice that maximizes the minimum value

g. government payments to individuals and families, such as Unemployment Insurance benefits and family allowance cheques

TRUE-FALSE

T F **1.** The category of government expenditures that shifts the Lorenz curve most is transfers-in-kind.

T F **2.** Government expenditures are more effective than taxes in reducing inequality.

T F **3.** Taxation is considerably more important than government transfers in eliminating inequality in Canada.

T F **4.** If income is defined broadly to include both money and leisure, then fairness requires that those who take a lot of their income in one form (leisure) should get less in the other form (money).

T F **5.** The only reason that complete equality is rejected as a target is that this division of the nation's income pie would shrink its overall size.

T F **6.** Equity is a normative, rather than a positive, issue.

T F **7.** Scientific evidence indicates that complete equality is the only fair way of distributing the nation's income.

T F **8.** The provable virtues of a free, perfectly competitive market have to do with its equity—not its efficiency.

T F **9.** Equity necessarily requires that everyone be paid the same income, regardless of how much and how hard he or she works.

T F **10.** It is possible to have an absolutely fair competition, but a bad system of rewards.

MULTIPLE CHOICE

1. Research indicates that, in determining differences in income
- **a.** the least important influence is wealth
- **b.** the least important influence is family background
- **c.** the most important influence is human capital
- **d.** the most important influence is luck
- **e.** the least important influence is human capital

2. The greater the degree of income inequality
- **a.** the smaller the bow in the Lorenz curve (i.e., the closer the Lorenz curve is to the 45° line)
- **b.** the larger the bow in the Lorenz curve
- **c.** the steeper the initial slope of the Lorenz curve
- **d.** the higher the point the Lorenz curve eventually reaches
- **e.** none of the above

3. What percentage of the total Canadian income (before taxes and transfers) is earned by the lowest-income 20% of Canadian families?
- **a.** less than 2%
- **b.** about 5%
- **c.** about 10%
- **d.** about 13%
- **e.** about 15%

4. Because government taxes are
- **a.** highly progressive, they are less effective than government expenditures in making incomes more equal
- **b.** highly progressive, they are less effective than government expenditures in making incomes more equal
- **c.** not highly progressive, they are less effective than government expenditures in making incomes more equal
- **d.** not highly progressive, they are more effective than government expenditures in making incomes more equal
- **e.** regressive, they are more effective than government expenditures in making incomes more equal

5. Together, taxes and government transfers in cash and in kind eliminate about what percentage of inequality in the Canadian income distribution?
- **a.** 5–6%
- **b.** 10–15%
- **c.** 20–30%
- **d.** 40–50%
- **e.** about 80%

6. Putting an end to racial discrimination is likely to
- **a.** increase the bow in the Lorenz curve
- **b.** decrease the bow in the Lorenz curve
- **c.** change the Lorenz curve so that its bow is above, rather than below, the 45° line
- **d.** make the Lorenz curve start from a different initial point
- **e.** make the Lorenz curve end at a different point

7. If some individuals acquire more and more human capital, while others do not, then this is likely to
- **a.** increase the bow in the Lorenz curve
- **b.** decrease the bow in the Lorenz curve
- **c.** change the Lorenz curve so that its bow is above, rather than below, the 45° line
- **d.** make the Lorenz curve start from a different initial point
- **e.** make the Lorenz curve end at a different point

8. Between 1951 and 1981, the total real income of the poorest 20% of Canada's population
- **a.** stayed about constant
- **b.** rose at about the same rate as the real income of the rest of the population
- **c.** increased its share of total Canadian real income by some 20%
- **d.** rose at a slower rate than the real income of the rest of the population
- **e.** declined as a share of total Canadian real income

9. Which of the following is not an example of a transfer in kind?
- **a.** subsidized housing

b. provincial health insurance
c. government job training programs
d. Old Age Security
e. free primary education

10. If we tried to pursue the goal of perfect equity, we would find that it would
a. conflict with the goal of efficiency
b. complement the goal of efficiency
c. neither conflict with nor complement the goal of efficiency
d. conflict with or complement the goal of efficiency, depending on the rate of inflation
e. expand the size of the national income pie

11. It is difficult to argue that the free market would do a completely equitable job of distributing income because
a. the free market is often not perfectly competitive; some people raise their income through the exercise of market power
b. even if the free market were perfectly competitive, it would still often provide luxuries for the wealthy, without providing adequate necessities for the poor
c. the free market is efficient
d. (a) and (b)
e. none of the above

12. The most difficult concept for economists to pin down is
a. efficiency gain
b. equity
c. equality
d. efficiency loss
e. inequality

13. A policy of trying to completely equalize incomes has been criticized because it would
a. be inefficient
b. be unfair, because it would give people who work the same reward as those who do not
c. require a change in our present system of inheritance
d. shrink the national income pie
e. all of the above

14. John Rawls argues that income should be divided equally
a. in all circumstances
b. in no circumstances
c. unless an unequal distribution benefits the majority
d. unless an unequal distribution benefits a large minority
e. unless an unequal distribution benefits everyone

EXERCISES

1. Table 36-1 below gives the income distribution of a hypothetical economy, as in panel (a) of Table 36-1 in the textbook. In Table 36-2, fill in the cumulative income distribution.

Table 36-1

	Lowest 20%	Second 20%	Third 20%	Fourth 20%	Highest 20%
Percentage of income	4	6	10	20	60

Table 36-2

	Lowest 20%	Second 20%	Third 20%	Fourth 20%	Highest 20%
Percentage of income					

Plot the Lorenz curve in Figure 36-1, and label it L_1. Suppose that the government then taxes away half the income of every family in the top 20% of the income distribution and gives it in equal amounts to every family in the lowest 60% of the distribution. Fill in the resulting income distribution in Table 36-3 and the resulting cumulative income distribution in Table 36-4.

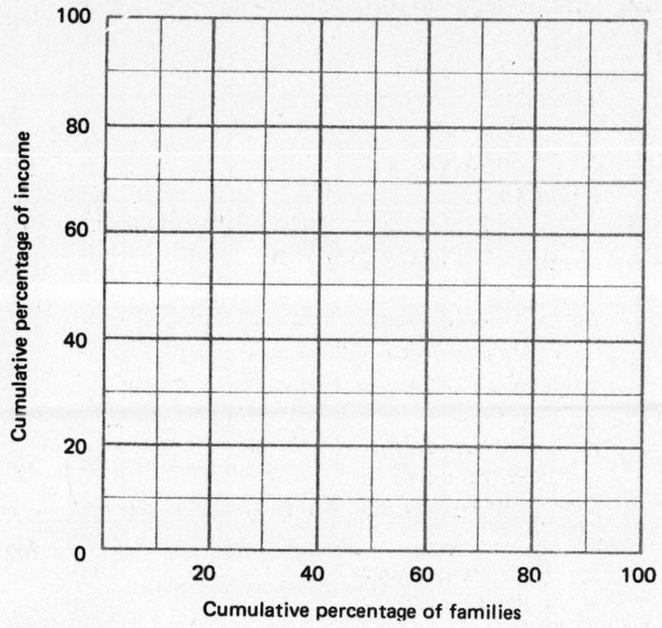

FIGURE 36-1

Table 36-3

	Lowest 20%	Second 20%	Third 20%	Fourth 20%	Highest 20%
Percentage of income					

Table 36-4

	Lowest 20%	Second 20%	Third 20%	Fourth 20%	Highest 20%
Percentage of income					

Plot the Lorenz curve for income after taxes and transfers in Figure 36-1 and label it L_2.

2. Consider the five following ways of distributing income among five families in an economy:

a. Four families receive $1,100 per year each, and the fifth family receives $600 per year.
b. Four families receive $500 per year each, and the fifth receives $3,000 per year.
c. Each family receives $500 per year.
d. Four families receive $1,100 per year each, and the fifth family receives $5,600 per year.
e. Four families receive $5,000 per year each, and the fifth receives nothing.

Fill in Table 36-5, giving the total national income according to each distribution.

Table 36-5

Total national distribution	Total national income
A	
B	
C	
D	
E	

Fill in Table 36-6 for each of the distributions, showing the cumulative percentages.

Table 36-6

		Lowest 20%	Lowest 40%	Lowest 60%	Lowest 80%	Total
Percentage of income	A					
	B					
	C					
	D					
	E					

Draw and label the Lorenz curve for each of these distributions in Figure 36-2.

Indicate in Table 36-7 the way in which these distributions would be ranked according to Rawls' maximin criterion.

Table 36-7

Rank	Distribution
Best	
Second-best	
Third-best	
Fourth-best	
Fifth-best	

According to this ranking, does the best distribution have the largest total income? ____________. Does it have the least inequality as measured by the Lorenz curve? ____________.

The reason that egalitarians (those who believe in equal incomes) were disillusioned by Rawls is illustrated in Figure 36-2, where we see that Rawls [does, does not] recommend the "complete-equality" distribution ____________. Instead, he recommends distribution ____________, which is one of the [most, least] equal of the distributions.

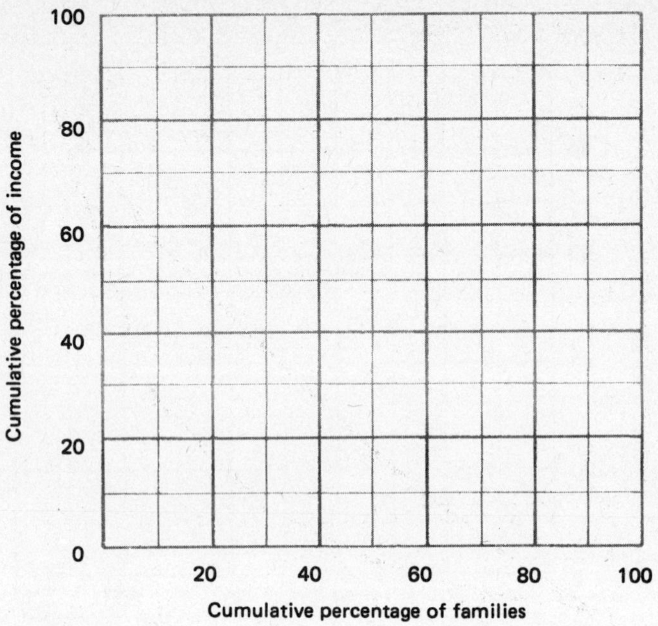

FIGURE 36-2

ESSAY QUESTIONS

1. "With a problem as perplexing as determining the best income distribution for the nation, the best approach is a simple one that strikes right to the heart of the matter: Make all incomes equal. This is philosophically and morally the fair and just solution." Do you agree? Explain your position.

2. In your view, is it possible for an unequal income distribution to be equitable? Use examples to support your position.

3. Is it fair to allow John McEnroe to earn such a high income from doing something—playing tennis—that many others in the world enjoy?

4. In what way do you think the shape of the Lorenz curve would be affected by (a) an end to racial discrimination; (b) some individuals' acquiring more and more human capital, and others not doing so; (c) unemployment insurance; (d) a highly progressive tax; (e) a special new tax on wage income; and (f) a special new tax on incomes over $100,000?

5. Marxists believe in the principle, "To each according to his needs, from each according to his abilities." Do you agree or disagree? Why or why not? Do you think that this principle would lead to a straight-line Lorenz curve? Why or why not? Do you think that a government that tried to put this principle into effect would run into problems? Would it face a conflict between equity and efficiency?

ANSWERS

Important Terms: **1** c **2** a **3** g **4** e **5** d **6** b **7** f
True-False: **1** F **2** T **3** F **4** T **5** F **6** T **7** F **8** F **9** F **10** T
Multiple Choice: **1** c **2** b **3** a **4** c **5** c **6** b **7** a **8** b **9** d **10** a **11** d **12** b **13** e **14** e
Exercises: **1.** Table 36-2: 4, 10, 20, 40, 100. Table 36-3: 14, 16, 20, 20, 30. Table 36-4: 14, 30, 50, 70, 100.

Figure 36-1 completed:

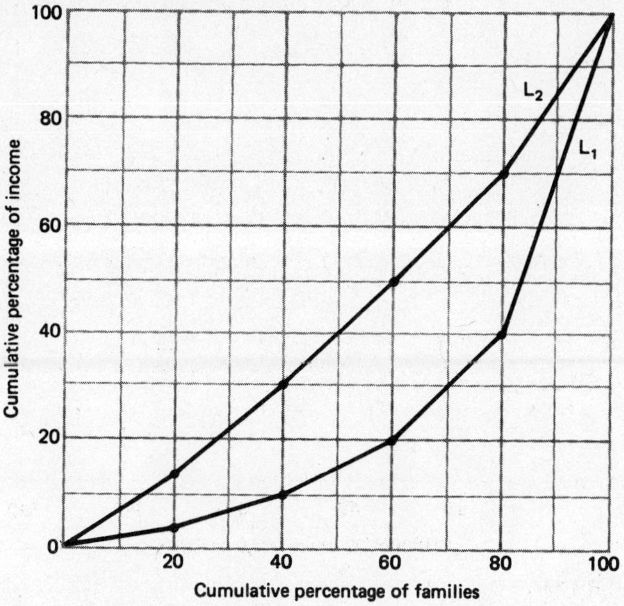

2.

Table 36-5 completed:

Total national distribution	Total national income
A	$ 4,600
B	$ 5,000
C	$ 2,500
D	$10,000
E	$20,000

Table 36-6 completed:

	Lowest 20%	Lowest 40%	Lowest 60%	Lowest 80%	Total
Percentage of income A	13	35	57	78	100
B	10	20	30	40	100
C	20	40	60	80	100
D	11	22	33	44	100
E	0	25	50	75	100

Table 36-7 completed:

Rank	Distribution
Best	D
Second-best	A
Third-best	B
Fourth-best	C
Fifth-best	E

No, no, does not; *C*, *D*, least.

Figure 36-2 completed:

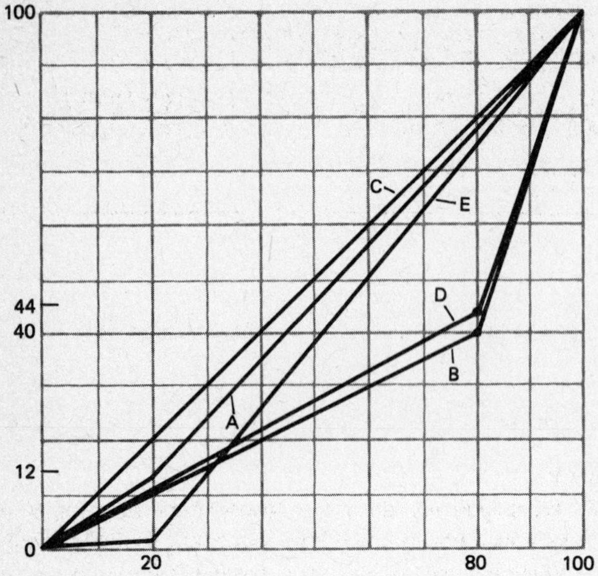

GOVERNMENT POLICIES TO REDUCE INEQUALITY: CAN WE SOLVE THE POVERTY PROBLEM?

MAJOR PURPOSE

The objective of this chapter is to evaluate what we are now doing—and what we might possibly do in the future—to alleviate the grinding effects of poverty on the poorest individuals in our population. Specifically, we will address three sets of questions:

1. How is the poverty line defined, and who are the poor below it?

2. What policies does the government now have in place to reduce poverty, and how successful have they been?

3. What income maintenance programs have been proposed to replace the present welfare system, and how likely is it that they will be successful?

LEARNING OBJECTIVES

After you have studied this chapter in the textbook and the study guide, you should be able to

- Describe how the poverty line is defined
- Explain why, over long periods of time, our definition of the poverty line tends to drift up to a higher level of real income
- State the factors that increase the likelihood of a family's being poor
- Describe the government policies that attack the causes of poverty, and the policies that reduce its symptoms
- Explain the difference between universal social insurance programs and "targeted" programs specifically designed to help the poor, giving examples of each
- Describe some problems that exist in our present welfare system
- Explain the concept of the implicit tax in a welfare program and why this is important in evaluating such programs
- Critically evaluate the guaranteed minimum income proposal
- Argue the case that income maintenance programs are the cure for poverty
- Argue the opposite case that such programs are the cause of poverty
- Describe how a negative income tax program would work
- Explain the theoretical advantages of a negative income tax program
- Explain why three objectives come into conflict when the government is trying to design a negative income tax: (1) to raise the minimum income to an acceptable level, (2) to increase the incentive to work, and (3) to keep the costs of the program from escalating
- Describe some results of experimental studies on the negative income tax
- Explain the pros and cons of a wage subsidy

HIGHLIGHTS OF THE CHAPTER

Here are the broad questions that are addressed in this chapter.

How Is the Poverty Line Defined?

The most common definition of poverty is based on poverty lines (called "low-income cut-off" lines) estimated by Statistics Canada for different groups of families or individuals. It is defined by finding the income level at which the average family or individual would have to devote as much as 58.5% of income to the basic necessities of life—namely food, clothing, and shelter. (Studies have shown that as family income increases, families spend a smaller and smaller proportion of income on these necessities.) Any family or individual below this low-income cutoff line is defined as being poor. The estimated poverty line is different for urban and rural families and for large and small families; in 1984, the poverty line for an urban family of four was $19,000 per year. The poverty line is adjusted every year to take inflation into account. It also drifts higher in real terms over long periods of time because our idea of what is barely acceptable tends to increase.

Who Are the Poor?

Table 37-1 in the text shows that the incidence of poverty in 1984 was substantially higher than the average in the Atlantic provinces and lower than the average in Ontario and the Prairie provinces. Table 37-2 shows how various characteristics of families or individuals affect the likelihood of poverty: Families (or individuals) are more likely to be poor if (1) they are old; (2) the head of the household is female; (3) the head of the household has little education; (4) the family or individual has been unable to find full-time work; (5) the family has four or more children. You should be able to explain how each of these factors is related to poverty.

What Are the Government Policies That Reduce Poverty?

Several kinds of government programs attack the *causes* (as opposed to the symptoms) of poverty: (1) subsidizing investment in human capital, such as free primary and secondary schooling and subsidized job training under the Adult Occupational Training Act; (2) laws and programs that are intended to reduce the extent of the poverty that arises from disability and illness, including laws regulating safety in the workplace and universal health insurance; (3) other policies such as provision of subsidized daycare, to make it easier for women in low-income families to earn an income outside the home.

The programs that help alleviate the symptoms of poverty include several universal social insurance programs of government transfer payments in cash or in kind: Old-Age Security, the CPP/QPP, the Family Allowance program, Unemployment Insurance, provincial health insurance programs. These programs have become very expensive and are going to become even more costly as the proportion of old people (who receive a large proportion of these payments) in Canada's population increases during the next several decades.

Other government transfer programs are *targeted*; that is, they are designed to help poor people only. These include the federal Guaranteed Income Supplement (GIS), poor people whose only source of income is Old Age Security, the federal Child Tax Credit, and provincial social assistance (or "welfare") programs.

How Successful Have Government Anti-poverty Policies Been?

The incidence of poverty in Canada has declined rapidly during the twentieth century. As Figure 37-1 in the textbook illustrates, during the last 20 years, the estimated proportion of families living in poverty has declined from about 1 in 3 families to about 1 in 7. Some people argue that most of the credit for this is due to our welfare programs. They also argue that these programs have given us the additional, "non-economic" benefit of knowing that we live in a decent society that provides for the poor.

However, critics point to a number of problems with our current welfare programs. One problem arises because the system imposes an "implicit tax" on any income the poor may earn. When a poor family earns another $1,000 of income, it may consequently have to give up, say, $800 of the welfare benefits it receives from the government. (Sometimes it's more than this, sometimes less.) This $800 is called an 80% "implicit tax, because, from the point of view of the poor, it's as though they had $800 of their additional $1,000 of income "taxed away." If they only get $200 net benefit when they go out and earn $1,000, why bother? It is critical that you understand this concept of an implicit tax, and why a high rate of this tax weakens the incentive of the poor to work. For some families in our present welfare system, this implicit tax has been very high indeed—in some instances approaching, or even exceeding, 100%. In such cases, the poor who earn another $1,000 will lose $1,000 of welfare payments from the government. Their income doesn't increase at all; they have no monetary incentive to get a job.

What Are the Proposals to Replace the Present Welfare System?

A guaranteed minimum income (GMI). Under a program like this shown in Figure 37-2 in the textbook, the government would guarantee a family a minimum income of, say, $10,000. Any shortfall in the family's earnings would be covered by a payment from the government. The problem with this policy is that it has a built-in 100% implicit tax that leaves no incentive for the poor to go to work. If they do, and earn another $1,000, their welfare payments from the government are reduced by this same amount. It doesn't matter whether they earn $5,000 or $6,000. Their income is fixed by the government at a $10,000 level. So they don't benefit at all when they earn that $1,000 more. Be sure that you fully understand this scheme shown in Figure 37-2 in the textbook before you proceed to the more complicated proposal for a negative income tax in Figure 37-4 in the text.

A negative income tax (NIT). This proposal also provides the poor with a guaranteed minimum income; but in addition it provides them with an incentive to go out and earn income on their own. Their implicit tax in this program can be set at, say, 50% (rather than the 100% implicit tax in the GMI proposal above). Thus, a family that earns another $1,000 of income has its payments from the government reduced by only $500. It therefore gets a net benefit of $500, which provides it with an incentive to work. Note that the "income-after-subsidy" line *CA* that was completely flat in Figure 37-2 in the textbook—and therefore provide no incentive to work—has now been replaced by the upward-sloping line *CQ* in Figure 37-4 in the textbook. Since some of the benefit from increased income can now be kept—it is no longer all lost—there is an incentive to go to work.

If, as its proponents recommend, the negative income tax were to replace the entire inconsistent set of present welfare policies, it would provide another benefit. It would be more equitable because all the poor would be treated alike; all would face the same minimum income and the same implicit tax. However, this policy would not be problem-free. Like any other anti-poverty program it could not simultaneously achieve the three desirable but conflicting goals of (1) providing an acceptable minimum income for everyone, (2) preserving the incentive for people to work, and (3) keeping costs down. As an example of how these goals may conflict with each other, suppose the government decides to achieve the first goal by raising the minimum income level from $10,000 to $12,000. This will shift the "income after" line *CQH* in Figure 37-4 in the textbook up by $2,000 throughout its whole length, thus increasing the gray "subsidy gap" that the government must fill. Thus, this measure may conflict with objective (3) of keeping costs down.

Unfortunately, the results of experiments in the United States suggest that, in practice, the negative income tax doesn't work as well as many economists had hoped. In fact, compared with even the present welfare system, the incentive it provides for the poor to go to work is disappointing. It also seems to cause an increase in marital breakdown. Why these adverse effects arise is not clearly understood. Perhaps it is because the subjects of these experiments had their options—such as quitting work—clearly explained to them.

The disappointment in these experimental results has led some to suggest the alternative of a wage subsidy that would provide financial assistance to the poor by increasing their wages. Because it would increase the reward for work (the wage rate), it is hoped that this scheme might provide a stronger work incentive. Its main drawback is that it would remove any guaranteed minimum income, and thus would provide no assistance to those individuals who, because of age or disability, cannot work to support themselves. Accordingly, some method would have to be devised to "tag" such people, so that they could qualify for special government support. While such a system would be necessary, it would be far from foolproof. One problem is that some of the able-bodied people who did not want to work would try fraudulently to have themselves tagged as disabled.

Concluding Remarks

So far, in analysing our present welfare system and the GMI and NIT proposals to replace it, the focus has been on the cost of a welfare system, in terms of the reduced incentive to work by the recipients of welfare. But there is another cost, as well—the cost of raising the taxes from the general public to finance the welfare expenditure. There is evidence that there is about a 25% to 35% loss when taxes are raised, because *those who are taxed* respond in such a way as to keep their taxes down, and reduce efficiency in the process. Make sure—by referring to Figure 37-3 in the text—that you can clearly distinguish between these two costs—that is, the perverse incentives imposed on the public that has to pay for welfare payments, and the disincentive to work experienced by the poor who *receive* the welfare payments.

IMPORTANT TERMS: MATCH THE COLUMNS

Match each term in the first column with the corresponding phrase in the second column. But before you do so, write your own definition of each term in the first column.

_____ **1.** poverty
_____ **2.** poverty line
_____ **3.** Adult Occupational Training Act
_____ **4.** human rights legislation
_____ **5.** Workmen's Compensation
_____ **6.** Old Age Security
_____ **7.** Canada Pension Plan/Quebec Pension Plan
_____ **8.** Family Allowances
_____ **9.** Unemployment Insurance
_____ **10.** Guaranteed Income Supplement
_____ **11.** targeted transfer program
_____ **12.** Child Tax Credit
_____ **13.** implicit tax
_____ **14.** negative income tax
_____ **15.** tagging

a. provincial programs that pay pensions to people who have been disabled through work-related injuries
b. any government transfer program in which benefits go primarily to those with low incomes
c. provincial laws prohibiting various kinds of discrimination in the labour market and elsewhere
d. that income at which a typical family would pay as much as 58.5% of its income for food, clothing, and shelter
e. targeted tax relief for low-income families with children
f. pays the same support to all Canadians over the age of 65
g. government payments to all families with children
h. a program that guarantees everyone a minimum income and provides a work incentive by allowing people to retain part of any income they earn
i. government program that pays part of the cost of retraining people who have lost their old jobs
j. government pension plan providing retirement benefits that depend on previous employer-employee contributions
k. identifies people who will get higher basic transfers than those who can work
l. government cash transfers to those who have lost their jobs
m. income inadequate to buy the necessities of life
n. supplements OAS for low-income retirees
o. when increased earnings lead to loss of government benefits

TRUE-FALSE

T F 1. By 1984, only 1 Canadian family in 20 was below the poverty line.
T F 2. Average real family income in the 1920s was well below the poverty-line income of 1984.
T F 3. The poverty-line income estimated by Statistics Canada is lower for a family in an urban area than for a comparable family in a rural area.
T F 4. Unemployment insurance benefits are an example of an in-kind transfer.
T F 5. The poverty line is not adjusted over time to take inflation into account, because inflation is not the problem
T F 6. Families in which the head of the household is a woman are more likely to be poor than are other families.
T F 7. All Canadian provinces have about the same proportion of families living in poverty.
T F 8. Transfer programs such as social assistance relieve the symptoms of poverty rather than attacking its causes.
T F 9. Under a guaranteed minimum income, all Canadians would receive the same income after taxes and subsidies.
T F 10. The implicit law in a welfare system is the sum of the benefits lost divided by the additional earned income.

MULTIPLE CHOICE

1. In 1984, Statistics Canada's estimated that the poverty-line income for a rural family of four was
   a. more than $13,000 per year
   b. higher than the poverty-line income for an urban family of four
   c. the same as the poverty line estimated for 1982
   d. about the same as for a single individual in a city
   e. less than $10,000
2. In the 1920s, a family with a real income close to today's poverty line would have been considered well off. This reflects the fact that
   a. productivity has decreased
   b. our standards of what constitutes a poverty-line income have risen
   c. government welfare programs have been reduced
   d. population has expanded
   e. food was cheaper in 1920 than it is today
3. It becomes impossible to lift all Canadians out of poverty if we define it as
   a. the bottom half of the Canadian income distribution
   b. any income less than $10,000
   c. the bottom tenth of the Canadian income distribution
   d. (a) or (c)
   e. (b) or (c)
4. Select the correct word below to put in the blank in this sentence: It is ____________ better to attack the causes of poverty than its symptoms
   a. always
   b. usually
   c. seldom
   d. almost never
   e. never
5. Which of the following kinds of government programs relieve the symptoms of poverty?
   a. those that subsidize investment in human capital
   b. social assistance payments under the cash deficit method
   c. universal health insurance
   d. policies to reduce unemployment and disability
   e. subsidized daycare
6. The percentage of all families with annual incomes below Statistics Canada's low-income cut-off
   a. was estimated to be about 1/3 of all families in the early 1960s
   b. decreased more during the period 1960–75 than during 1975–84
   c. was estimated to be less than 15% in 1984
   d. was higher in the Maritime provinces than in the rest of Canada in 1984
   e. all of the above
7. Which of the following government transfer programs is *not* specifically targeted at people with low incomes?
   a. Unemployment Insurance
   b. social assistance programs
   c. Child Tax Credit
   d. Guaranteed Income Supplement
   e. low-income housing
8. A guaranteed minimum income would result in
   a. greater equity and greater efficiency
   b. less equity and greater efficiency
   c. less equity with no change in efficiency
   d. less equity and lower efficiency
   e. greater equity and lower efficiency
9. The income–maintenance program that would provide the poor with the largest incentive to work is one in which the "income-after-subsidy" line
   a. has zero slope
   b. has a slope close to zero
   c. has a slope of 15°
   d. has a slope of 20°
   e. has a slope of 35°
10. The maximum possible implicit tax on any family facing the set of Canadian welfare programs is
    a. 50%
    b. 80%
    c. just under 100%
    d. 100%
    e. more than 100%
11. If a family living in government-subsidized housing is required to pay 25% of its income in rent, then for this reason alone it is facing an implicit tax of
    a. zero
    b. 25%
    c. 75%
    d. 100%
    e. 125%
12. A welfare program that pays you $5,000 if you earn nothing and $4,500 if you earn $2,000 has an implicit tax of
    a. zero
    b. 25%
    c. 40%
    d. 50%
    e. 105%
13. Experiments in the United States suggest that providing people with easy access to and complete information about, welfare payments
    a. reduces their incentive to work
    b. increases their incentive to work
    c. leaves their incentive to work unchanged
    d. doesn't affect the incentive to work of the poor, but raises it for middle-income families
    e. doesn't affect the incentive to work of the poor, but lowers it for middle-income families
14. Which of the following should offer the least work incentive to the very poor?

a. no taxes or subsidies
b. the present welfare system
c. a negative income tax
d. a wage-subsidy scheme
e. a guaranteed minimum income

15. With a negative income tax, an increase in the implicit tax rate will
a. increase the slope of the income-after-tax line
b. decrease the slope of that line
c. leave the slope of that line unchanged
d. raise the point where the income-after-tax line intersects the vertical axis

16. Suppose that a negative income tax is set up with the minimum income set at $8,000 and the implicit tax rate set at 50%. In this case, a subsidy would be paid by the government
a. to no one
b. only to those earning less than $4,000
c. only to those earning less than $8,000
d. only to those earning less than $12,000
e. only to those earning less than $16,000

EXERCISE

Consider the following four tax-subsidy programs:

a. Every family earning less than $5,000 receives enough subsidy to give it an income of $5,000 after taxes and subsidies. On every dollar earned over $5,000, a family must pay a 20% tax.
b. Every family receives a subsidy of $5,000, but then pays a 50% tax on every dollar earned.
c. Every family receives a subsidy of $3,000, but then pays a tax of 30% on every dollar earned.
d. Every family receives a subsidy of $3,000, but then pays a tax of 50% on every dollar earned.

In Figure 37-1 plot the line for each program showing how a family's income after taxes and subsidies is related to its income before taxes and subsidies. For each program, indicate in Table 37-1 the marginal tax rates on income earned above $5,000.

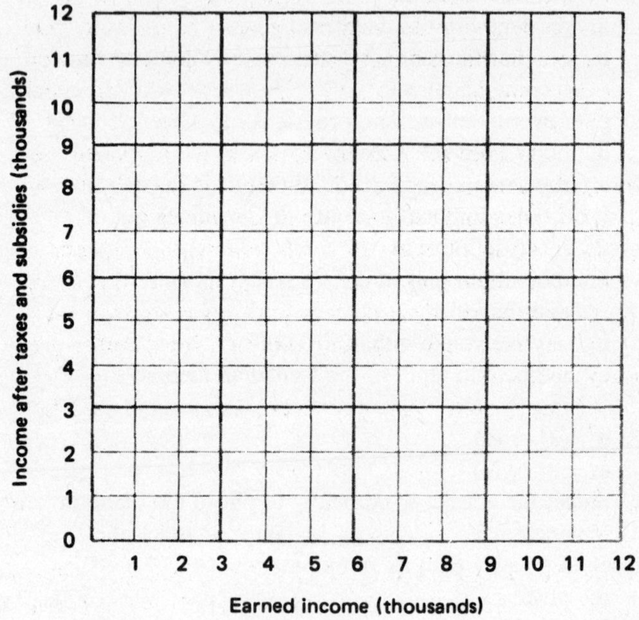

FIGURE 37-1

Table 37-1

Program	**Marginal tax rate on income earned above $5,000**
A	
B	
C	
D	

Suppose that the distribution of earned income (before taxes and subsidies) in the economy is given by Table 37-2.

Table 37-2

Annual income before taxes and transfers (thousands of dollars)	0	3	5	6	10	15	20	50
Number of families earning this income	1	2	4	4	3	2	1	1

In Table 37-3 fill in the net tax (i.e., tax minus subsidy) paid to each family under each of the programs.

Table 37-3

Income (in thousands)		**0**	**3**	**5**	**6**	**10**	**15**	**20**	**50**
Net tax of each family under program:	A								
	B								
	C								
	D								

In Table 37-4 show the total net taxes collected—that is, total taxes minus total subsidy paid. Assume that, regardless of the tax-subsidy program that is imposed, there is no change in the incentive to work and therefore the earned income of each family. In other words, the income distribution in Table 37-2 doesn't change, regardless of the tax-subsidy program.

Table 37-4

Programs	Total net taxes
A	
B	
C	
D	

ESSAY QUESTIONS

1. "Universal social insurance and welfare programs may be desirable, but they are totally unproductive. They don't add anything to the nation's capacity to produce." Do you agree with this statement or not? Explain your answer. (Use government health insurance as one of your examples.)

2. Use a numerical example to show why poverty, defined as the income of the bottom 10% of the population, is a meaningless and useless measure of hardship.

3. If the main ill effect of social assistance programs is to encourage fathers to leave home so their families can qualify for welfare, what do you think of maintaining the program but disqualifying any family whose father has abandoned them?

4. If the government gave equivalent cash transfers instead of food stamps and other types of assistance in kind, would the recipients be better off? Why? Would their children be better off? Why does the government provide assistancc in kind?

5. The textbook suggests that a real income that today barely reaches the poverty line would have been considered quite a good income during the 1920s and 1930s. In what sense is the person who receives an income equal to the poverty line in 1982 better off than a person in, say, 1928, who received a real income somewhat below 1982's poverty line? In what sense is that person worse off?

6. In the United States, the poverty line is simply defined as three times the cost of feeding a family a diet that meets certain minimal nutritional standards at the lowest possible cost. Do you think this is a better way to define the poverty line than the method used by Statistics Canada? Why or why not?

ANSWERS

Important Terms: **1** m **2** d **3** i **4** c **5** a **6** f **7** j **8** g **9** l **10** n **11** b **12** e **13** o
True-False: **1** F **2** T **3** F **4** F **5** F **6** T **7** F T **9** F **10** T
Multiple Choice: **1** a **2** b **3** d **4** b **5** b **6** e **7** a **8** e **9** e **10** e **11** b **12** b **13** a **14** e **15** b **16** e
Exercise:
Figure 37-1 completed:

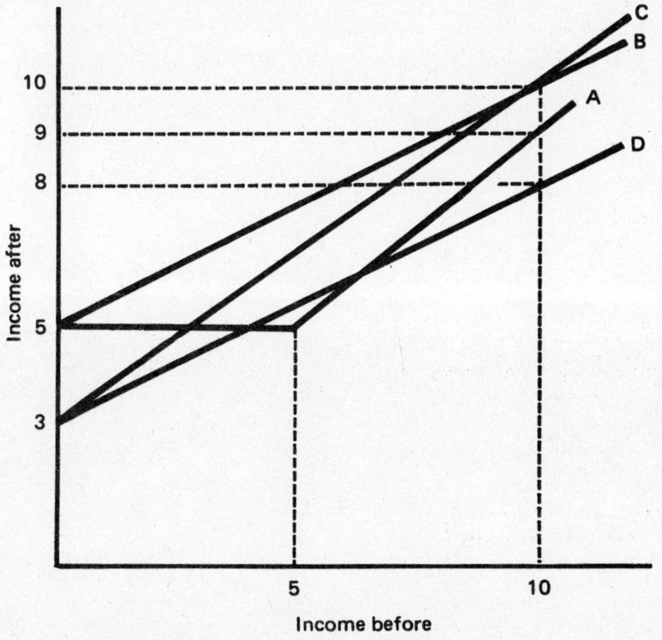

Table 37-1 completed:

20%
50%
30%
50%

Table 37-3 completed:

−5,000	−2,000	0	200	1,000	2,000	3,000	9,000
−5,000	−3,500	−2,500	−2,000	0	2,500	5,000	20,000
−3,000	−2,100	−1,500	−1,200	0	1,500	3,000	12,000
−3,000	−1,500	−500	0	2,000	4,500	7,000	22,000

Table 37-4 completed:

10,800
0
0
36,000

Across

1, 4. Education and training are examples of this.
9. consumed
10. Birds do this with their wings.
12. During a recession, there is at least a ____________ in real output.
15. illegal organization in the United Kingdom
17. popular name for provincial health insurance in Canada
20. organization fighting for the rights of blacks in South Africa (abbrev.)
21. Canada's federal and provincial programs of income support and social insurance are designed to provide more economic ____________.
24. falls when you weep
25. really like
26. tried to fight inflation in the 1970s (abbrev.)
28. not the same as equality; fairness
31. second person singular pronoun (French)
32. name used for troops from Australia and New Zealand during World War I (abbrev.)
34. charged particles
36. last two initials of Canadian institution where stocks are traded
37, 38. a diagrammatic device for illustrating inequality
41. enables plant to draw water and nourishment from the soil
42. change
45. negative
46. When you retire, you will probably get one from the government and another from your employer.
47. negative (Russian)
50. ocean fish
52. give up
53, 54. a way to discourage pollution

Down

1. based on the cash deficit method in most provinces (2 words)
3. northern deciduous tree
5. Italian river
6. a source of revenue for the government
8, 27. This illustrates the idea that something is lost when money is transferred from rich to poor.
10. Labour is a ___________ of production.
11. before noon (abbrev.)
12. one of the causes of poverty—for single women and minorities, for example
13. frozen water
14. agreement
16. health care professional (abbrev.)
18. street (French)
19. long time period
22. outlawed political organization in the United Kingdom
23. Sugar can be produced from one variety of this.
29. Imperial volume measure
30. contract whereby one party agrees to indemnify the other against loss for a fee
33. nil
35. Get plenty of this before your economics final, but not during the lectures.
39. cast a ballot
40. ski resort in the Rockies
43. machine for weaving
44. colloquial word for communists
48. positive response
49. substitute for coffee
51. nickname for future queen of England

Chapter 38

MARXISM AND MARXIST ECONOMIES

MAJOR PURPOSE

Historically, the most influential criticism of the capitalistic, free-enterprise system was that set out by Karl Marx. He charged that this system distributes income in an unfair way because it provides income to owners of capital—that is, to "capitalists." In this chapter, we examine Marx's criticism in detail and his proposed alternative: a revolution followed by a socialist state in which capital would be owned by the state on behalf of all the people. We then describe three important socialist experiments—those in the Soviet Union, Yugoslavia, and China. In the Soviet example, the focus is on the practical difficulties encountered in putting socialism into practice. In the other two examples, the focus is on what happens when a socialist state starts to introduce elements of free enterprise. In the Chinese case, this is a particularly interesting issue because there are signs that such changes are revitalizing the economy. And a rapidly growing economy of that enormous potential size could pose a serious economic challenge to the more stagnant Soviet economy.

LEARNING OBJECTIVES

After you have studied this chapter in the textbook and study guide, you should be able to

- Describe the labour theory of value, and the subsistence theory of wages
- Explain Marx's concepts of surplus value and the exploitation of the working class
- Define and clearly distinguish between socialism and communism
- State two predictions of Marx that have not been verified by history
- Criticize both the theory and practice of socialism
- Explain how capital is raised for investment purposes in a socialist state
- Describe the problems associated with central planning
- Explain why there is typically less innovation in a socialist state than in a free-enterprise economy
- Explain the problems the Soviets face in setting production targets in their 5-year plans
- Describe the "second economy" in the Soviet Union
- Describe the problems facing the consumer in an economy that is not closely oriented to the market place
- Compare the Soviet's disguised unemployment with overt unemployment in Canada
- Compare the Soviet's suppressed inflation with inflation in Canada
- Explain to what degree the Soviets have succeeded in equalizing incomes, and the problems they have encountered because of the increasing importance of human capital
- Compare the Soviet and Yugoslavian economic systems, explaining the advantages and disadvantages of the Yugoslavs' market-oriented socialism
- Describe the ways in which the government still exerts a great deal of centralized control over the Yugoslavian economy
- Describe the recent attempts to make the Chinese economy more closely oriented to the market
- Explain why there is a conflict between equity and efficiency even in a socialist economy

HIGHLIGHTS OF THE CHAPTER

This chapter can be broken down into three broad topics: (1) Marx's criticism of a free-enterprise system and the socialist-communist system he proposed, (2) the application of Marxism in the Soviet Union, and (3) the more market-oriented application of Marxism in Yugoslavia and China.

Marxism

Marxism is based on (1) the labour theory of value and (2) the subsistence theory of wages. It claims that there is a class struggle in which workers (the "proletariat") are exploited by the capitalists (the "bourgeoisie" who own the capital equipment and other means of production). Instead of enjoying all the fruits of their labour, the workers receive just enough to subsist, with the rest going in the form of "surplus value" to the capitalists. According to Marx, the only way of resolving this class struggle is a revolution in which workers forcibly seize the ownership of physical capital from their exploiters. They then set up a socialist state in which there is a dictatorship of the proletariat and capital is owned by the state. This, in turn is followed by a communist system in which the state has withered away, and capital and other forms of property are owned by the community as a whole.

One criticism of Marxist theory is that its predictions have not been borne out by history: (1) The dictatorship of the proletariat, rather than withering away, has remained powerful in Marxist states and (2) under capitalism, workers have enjoyed rising real income, rather than the increasing misery predicted by Marx.

Another criticism of Marxist theory is that if capitalists are eliminated, some other way must be found to generate physical capital for investment. The Marxist solution is to generate capital by taxation—in particular, heavy taxes on consumer goods—rather than by personal saving. However, this raises three problems: (1) Taxes (forced saving) may be more burdensome than voluntary saving; (2) when governments invest the funds they have raised, they typically lack the inventiveness of private capitalists; and (3) some substitute must be found for the profit motive as a means of allocating capital among different industries.

The concept of profit raises an important issue in the debate between capitalism and Marxism. Supporters of Marxism and capitalism alike generally agree that monopoly profits should not go unchecked. Supporters of capitalism argue that this can be done through government regulation under a basically capitalist system. Marxists argue that regulation is ineffective because big business interests are so powerful that they end up controlling their own regulators. A capitalist response to this criticism is that big business does indeed have power; and so does the government. But this is better than having all of the power in the hands of the government—as happens in a communist state.

The Soviet System

Two important features of the Soviet system are: (1) Most physical capital is owned by the state, rather than by private individuals and (2) the decisions as to how much of each good to produce and how much to invest in each industry are not made by market forces, but are instead made by a central government planning agency (Gosplan) in its 5-year plans. These plans set yearly production targets, or quotas, for each industry and—in even more detail—for each plant. There are three major problems with central planning of this sort:

1. It is difficult for the government to determine a set of consistent output quotas. For example, the right output for the steel industry depends on the output of those industries that use steel, such as machinery and autos. But at the same time, the right output for the *machinery* industry depends on the output of those industries that use machinery, such as *steel.* How do you solve for the output of either steel or machinery when each depends on the other? The answer is that it is not easy. Although there are mathematical techniques for solving such problems, it is seldom possible for a planning agency to get the quotas just right. Consequently, bottlenecks—such as a shortage of steel—are common in the Soviet Union.

2. Consumers' wants tend to be ignored in the Soviet system. When steel is in short supply, it goes to produce bridges or machinery, not refrigerators for consumers. Thus, consumer goods are in chronic short supply, and this leads to the long lineups that a feature of Soviet life. Another reason the Soviet consumer is short-changed is that each production manager tends to concentrate on satisfying a quota, rather than on producing the types of goods that consumers want. (For more on the plight of the Soviet consumer, see Box 38-1 in the textbook).

3. It is not clear that the degree of central planning that exists in the Soviet Union could be made to work without a repressive Soviet-style political dictatorship. Marxists reply that our freedom is enjoyed only by the rich and powerful. And they point to one apparent advantage of central planning: It produces very little measured unemployment. However, critics point out that if someone is working to produce unwanted goods this really constitutes "disguised" unemployment.

The 5-year plans of the Soviet Union have emphasized rapid growth. For example, during the 1960s, the real rate of Soviet growth was 6% to 10%, which exceeded the growth rates in both Canada and the United States by a substantial margin. However, the reason for this was not that the Soviet Union has a better system for generating growth. Instead, it was due primarily to the fact that investment in the Soviet Union has run at about 30% of GNP, compared to below 25% in Canada, and even less in the United States. When one looks at a country like Japan that also invests this high a percentage of its GNP, Soviet growth does not compare favourably. Moreover, despite the heavy diversion of its GNP into investment, Soviet growth has recently become particularly disappointing; it has fallen close to zero.

Market-Oriented Socialism in Yugoslavia and China

In Yugoslavia, as in the Soviet Union, the state owns most of the physical capital. But production decisions are much less centralized in Yugoslavia. Firms there are operated by workers, who elect a manager. This manager, like the manager of a capitalist enterprise attempts to maximize profits, which are then distributed to the workers.

However, the government still exerts a great deal of centralized control over the economy:

1. Although most firms are allowed to change their prices, they can do so only within fixed limits.

2. As in the Soviet Union, the government diverts about one-third of GNP into investment.

3. The allocation of this investment into different sectors of the economy is also determined by the central government.

4. The government sets out 5-year plans, as in the Soviet Union (although these plans are not strictly enforced).

There have been three special problems with the Yugoslav system:

1. Some of the "worker-enterprises" have a monopoly position. In socialist debate, it has been assumed that such an enterprise would not be able to exploit its monopoly power in a socialist system. However, that is not the case. Managers have exploited a monopoly position by restricting their output and thus raising their price.

2. There is not enough incentive to create new firms. Thus, many existing firms do not face the threat of competition.

3. Because workers share in profits, workers in profitable enterprises earn more than workers in unprofitable enterprises. The result is the sort of income inequality that Marx was trying to eliminate. Thus, the attempt to make the economy more efficient by introducing profit-sharing incentives for the labour force has also made the distribution of income less equal. Even in a socialist society, there is a conflict between efficiency and equity.

Yugoslavia is not the only market-oriented socialist economy. Some other communist countries—in particular China and Hungary—have also been moving in this direction. Incentives to increase production have worked so well in Chinese agriculture that they have been extended to industry as well. In both these sectors of the economy, the result has been substantially higher production levels. It will be interesting to watch what sort of challenge a revitalized Chinese economy may pose for the relatively stagnant Soviet economy.

IMPORTANT TERMS: MATCH THE COLUMNS

Match each term in the first column with the corresponding phrase in the second column. But before you do so, write your own definition of each term in the first column.

_____ **1.** capitalism
_____ **2.** socialism
_____ **3.** communism
_____ **4.** labour theory of value
_____ **5.** subsistence wage theory
_____ **6.** surplus value
_____ **7.** Gosplan
_____ **8.** 5-year plan
_____ **9.** proletariat
_____ **10.** bourgeoisie
_____ **11.** dictatorship of the proletariat
_____ **12.** disguised unemployment

a. the Marxist term for the working class
b. the situation that exists if people are employed, but in useless tasks
c. in Marxist theory, the ideal system, in which all means of production and other forms of property are owned by the community as a whole and the central government has "withered away"
d. an economic system in which most physical capital is privately owned
e. a plan that sets up production and investment targets for each industry
f. the theory that, in a capitalist economy, workers' wages can never rise, except temporarily, above a socially defined subsistence level
g. the transitory stage, according to Marx, that follows the workers' revolution, before the government withers away and the ideal state of communism is achieved
h. an economic system in which physical capital and other means of production, such as land, are owned by the state
i. the Marxist term for the capitalist class

j. the difference, according to Marx, between the total value of output (all of which "belongs" to labour) and the wages actually received by labour

k. the theory that the value of any good is determined solely by the amount of labour that goes into producing it, including the labour embodied in the capital used to produce the good

l. the central planning agency in the Soviet Union

TRUE-FALSE

T F **1.** According to Marx, labour receives a socially defined subsistence income barely sufficient to meet the workers' basic needs.

T F **2.** According to Marxist theory, a communist society is one in which the state has withered away.

T F **3.** A major reason why it has been difficult to control the abuse of personal power in the Soviet Union is that there are no free elections in which the public can remove the party in power and replace it with another.

T F **4.** Marx believed that the labour time spent on producing machinery and the income earned by capitalists on that machinery were both surplus value.

T F **5.** According to Marx, economic history was a story of the proletariat exploiting the bourgoisie in a class struggle.

T F **6.** Marx spent a great deal of time discussing how, in his communist society, conflicts would be resolved by groups with conflicting interests.

T F **7.** Compared to a free-enterprise system, the Soviet planning system has led to a much more efficient use of inputs.

T F **8.** The decaying czarist regime in Russia was overthrown in 1917 by Lenin and his group of communist revolutionaries.

T F **9.** Many workers in the Soviet Union (as well as in Canada) have become capitalists, in the sense that they have accumulated substantial quantities of human capital.

T F **10.** In Yugoslavia, certain workers get higher wages than others if their firm earns more profits.

T F **11.** Between 1980 and 1985, the Chinese economy was made less sensitive to market pressures.

MULTIPLE CHOICE

1. Marx's analysis was based on
- **a.** the labour theory of value
- **b.** the theory that wages tended toward their socially defined subsistence level
- **c.** the marginal productivity theory of wages
- **d.** (a) and (b)
- **e.** (a) and (c)

2. Marx's recommended system for production and income distribution was this
- **a.** From each according to his need, to each according to his ability.
- **b.** From each according to his ability; to each according to his need.
- **c.** From each according to his ability; to each according to his wants.
- **d.** From each, and to each, according to his ability.
- **e.** From each, and to each, according to his need.

3. Marx believed that once a communist society was established
- **a.** power would corrupt, and absolute power would corrupt absolutely
- **b.** power would corrupt, but absolute power would provide freedom
- **c.** the power of the state would increase, but the power of any individual would decrease
- **d.** the power of the state and all individuals would increase
- **e.** the state would wither away

4. Marx charged that capitalism was unfair because of its
- **a.** income payments to capitalists; he recommended having ownership of capital by the state
- **b.** income payments to capitalists; he recommended taxing capitalists' income more heavily
- **c.** inadequate income payments to capitalists; he recommended the transfer of some labour income to capitalists
- **d.** low income payments to highly skilled workers; he recommended paying skilled workers more
- **e.** high income payments to highly skilled workers; he recommended paying highly skilled workers less

5. Marx argued that
- **a.** surplus value goes to labour under a capitalist system

1. Marx and Engels [illegible] [illegible] [illegible] Marx's [illegible] [illegible] [illegible] violent] revolution in which the [proletariat/bourgeoisie] would seize the property of the [proletariat/bourgeoisie]. A [Communist, socialist] system would then evolve in which there would be a [illegible] and [illegible] would be owned by the [community as a whole]. Eventually, this would pave the way for a [Communist, socialist] system in which the state would [wither away/retain] political power and all property, which would be owned by the [community as a whole].

2. In the Soviet Union, investment is largely financed by [forced, voluntary] saving in the form of [illegible] substitution of [consumer, producer] goods. This investment [illegible] about [illegible] [illegible] the [illegible]

ESSAY QUESTIONS

1. A Communist society [illegible] following a socialist dictatorship of the proletariat? Explain the degree to which you agree or disagree.

2. What are the problems facing Soviet planners that do not arise in our system?

3. It was often argued in the 1960s that Soviet growth exceeded that of North America because the Soviets were playing "catch-up." Growth is easier for a less advanced economy because it is easier to copy technology than to develop it. Explain why you agree or disagree with this view.

4. The growth of the Polish union movement has severely damaged the credibility of Marxist theory in two respects. First, it has [illegible] one of Marx's predictions. Second, events in Poland in the early 1980s made it clear that a socialist government does not necessarily represent the interests of the working class. Explain why you agree or disagree.

5. Describe, in your view, the ideal organization of society. Try to ensure that the system you design would work in practice as well as in theory.

ANSWERS

Important Terms: [illegible]

True-False: [illegible]

Multiple Choice: [illegible]

Exercises: [illegible]

ANSWERS TO CROSSWORD PUZZLES

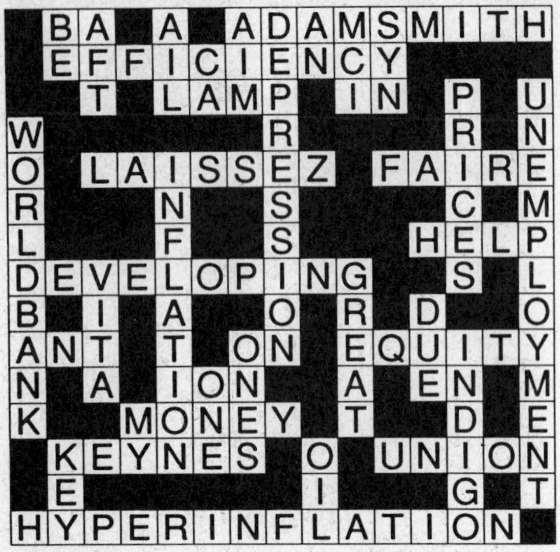

CHAPTER 1

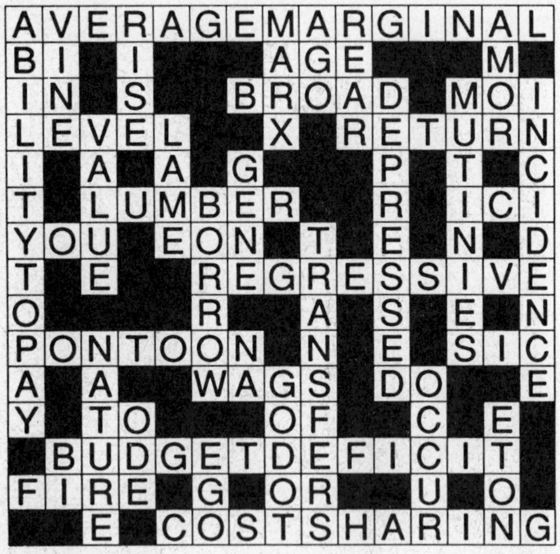

CHAPTER 5

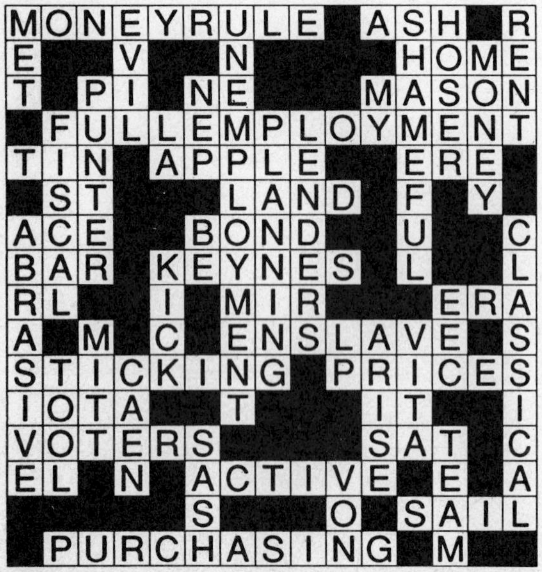

CHAPTER 9

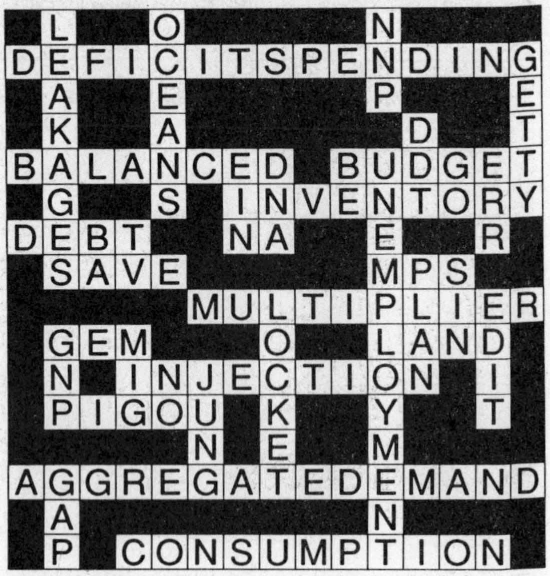

CHAPTER 11

CHAPTER 13

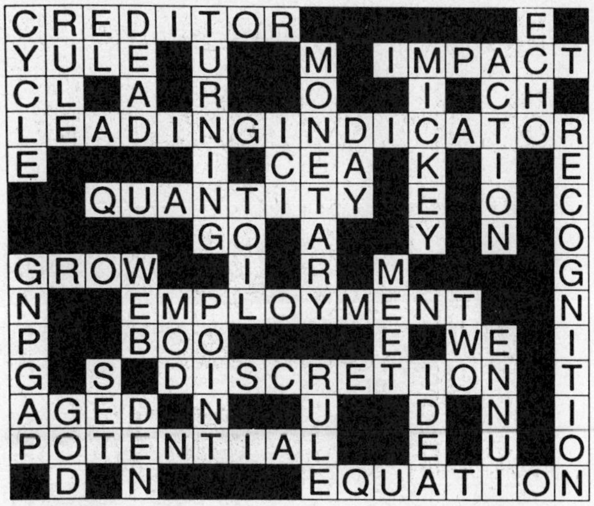

CHAPTER 16

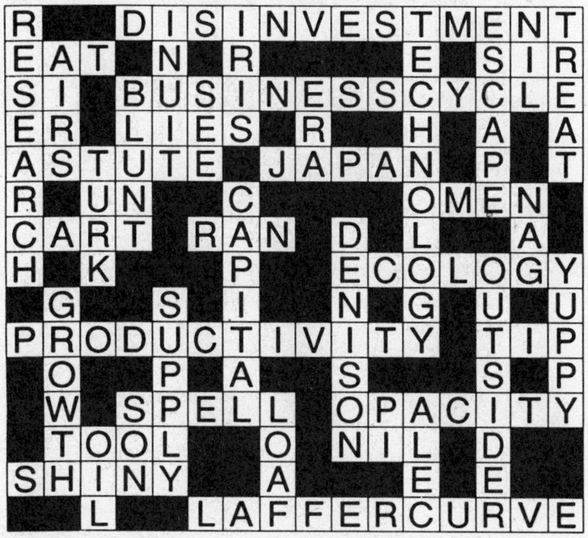

CHAPTER 19

CHAPTER 21

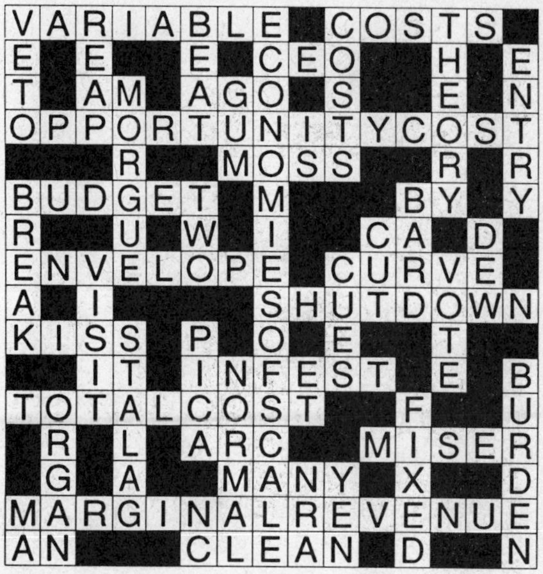

CHAPTER 23

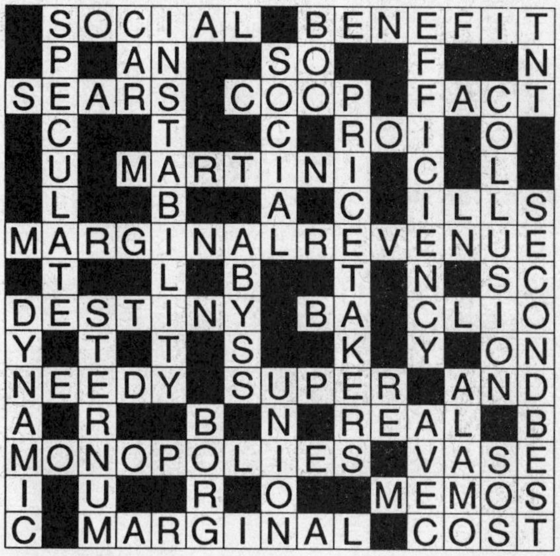

CHAPTER 25

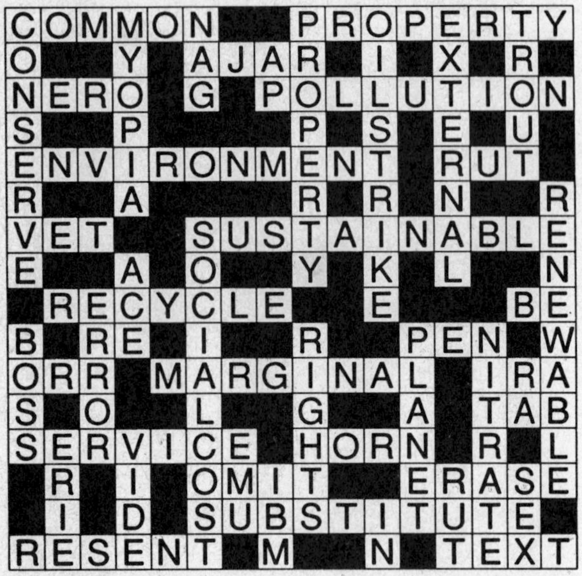

CHAPTER 29

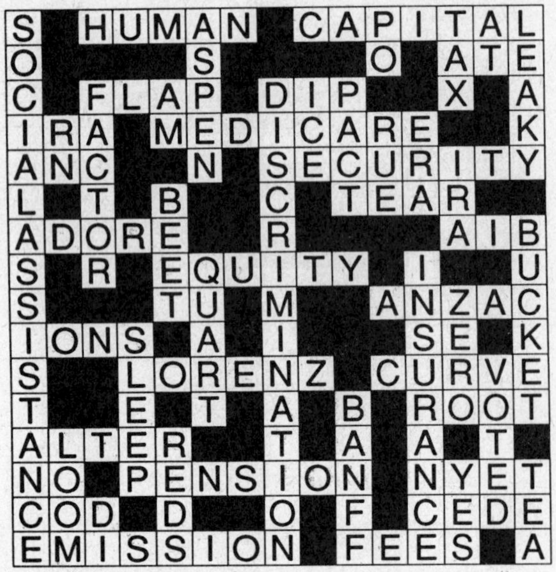

CHAPTER 37

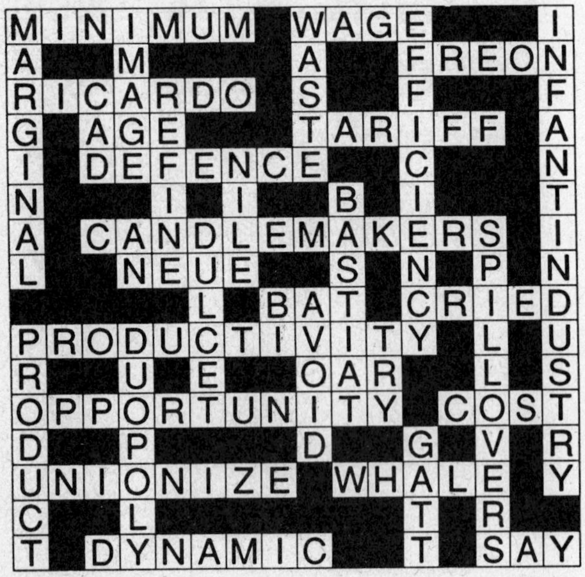

CHAPTER 33